W9-BIX-272

SELECTED NON-FICTIONS

SELECTED NON-FICTIONS

Jorge Luis Borges

EDITED BY

Eliot Weinberger

TRANSLATED BY

Esther Allen, Suzanne Jill Levine,
and Eliot Weinberger

VIKING

VIKING
Published by the Penguin Group
Penguin Putnam Inc., 375 Hudson Street,
New York, New York 10014, U.S.A.
Penguin Books Ltd, 27 Wrights Lane, London W8 5TZ, England
Penguin Books Australia Ltd, Ringwood, Victoria, Australia
Penguin Books Canada Ltd, 10 Alcorn Avenue, Toronto, Ontario, Canada M4V 3B2
Penguin Books (N.Z.) Ltd, 182–190 Wairau Road, Auckland 10, New Zealand

Penguin Books Ltd, Registered Offices:
Harmondsworth, Middlesex, England

First published in 1999 by Viking Penguin,
a member of Penguin Putnam Inc.

1   3   5   7   9   10   8   6   4   2

LIBRARY OF CONGRESS CATALOGING-IN-PUBLICATION DATA
Borges, Jorge Luis, 1899–1986.
[Essays. English. Selections]
Selected nonfictions / Jorge Luis Borges ; edited by Eliot Weinberger ;
translated by Esther Allen, Suzanne Jill Levine and Eliot Weinberger.
p.   cm.
ISBN 0-670-84947-2
1. Borges, Jorge Luis, 1899–1986—Translations into English.
I. Weinberger, Eliot. II. Title.
PQ7797.B635A22   1999
864—dc21   99-12386

This book is printed on acid-free paper.
∞

Printed in the United States of America
Set in Minion
Designed by Francesca Belanger

Contents

A Note on This Edition

Jorge Luis Borges never wrote anything long, and so it is often assumed that he never wrote much. In fact, he was a man sworn to the virtue of concision who couldn't stop writing. There are a thousand pages of Borges' stories (including the ones he wrote with Adolfo Bioy Casares), five or six hundred pages of poetry, two dozen books of translations, and—to the matter at hand—thousands of pages of non-fiction: some twelve hundred essays, prologues, book reviews, film reviews, transcribed lectures, capsule biographies, encyclopedia entries, historical surveys, and short notes on politics and culture. The accumulation of so many compact writings makes their totality seem even more immense than the collected works of a prolific author of thick books.

From this mountain—I avoid the word *labyrinth*—of non-fiction texts, much of it still uncollected in book form in Spanish, I have chosen 161: a fraction of the work. Two-thirds of these pieces have never appeared in English before, and the rest have been newly translated for this edition. (The initials of the translator follow each entry.) English-language readers who associate Borges only with certain subjects (time, dreams, *The Thousand and One Nights*, gauchos, nineteenth-century English and American literature . . .) may be amazed at the extent of his interests. Like the Aleph in his famous story—the point in a basement in Buenos Aires from which one can view everything in the world—Borges' unlimited curiosity and almost superhuman erudition becomes, in the non-fiction, a vortex for seemingly the entire universe. Where else would one find Lana Turner, David Hume, and the heresiarchs of Alexandria in a single sentence?

Those for whom Borges is the archetype of the detached and cerebral metaphysician may be surprised to find his scandalous polemics on Argentina and *machismo*, his principled stand against the Fascism and anti-Semitism of the Argentine bourgeoisie in the 1930s and 1940s, and his courageous attacks on the Perón dictatorship. Borges, the blind old man of the popular image, was for years a movie critic. Borges, the recondite scholar, was a regular contributor to the Argentine equivalent of the *Ladies' Home Journal.* He was equally at home with Schopenhauer or Ellery Queen, King Kong or the Kabbalists, Lady Murasaki or Erik the Red, Jack London, Plotinus, Orson Welles, Flaubert, the Buddha, or the Dionne Quints. More exactly, they were at home with him. Borges is both a deceptively self-effacing guide to the universe and the inventor of a universe that is a guide to Borges.

In contrast to how much he wrote, Borges published very few collections of his essays, and the publishing history and present state of these writings is indeed a labyrinth. In the 1920s, he released three books that he later disowned and refused to allow to be reprinted in his lifetime. There were another three between 1930 and 1936: two miscellanies and a thematic book on the Argentine past, *Evaristo Carriego.* His next book of essays, *Other Inquisitions,* came sixteen years later, in 1952, and includes less than forty of the hundreds of non-fiction pieces he wrote during this particularly prolific period. There were no more new books of non-fiction for another twenty-odd years. Quite late in his life, and continuing after his death in 1986, a few retrospective collections of his prologues, lectures, and reviews were gathered. (For a bibliography, see the notes.)

Borges was essentially unknown outside of Argentina, even among Spanish-language readers, until the 1950s. As his fame grew, the four unsuppressed books of essays began to go through various editions, and it was Borges' custom to include a few recent works in the reprints, while excluding or reinstating others. Thus some of the essays in a reprint of a book from 1930 could be written as much as twenty-five years later, and in a greatly changed style.

The Spanish and French standard editions take, as the basis for their texts, the contents of the last reprint of each of these books. While this may make sense in the case of an individual work revised over the years by its writer, for Borges it creates an anachronistic jumble of styles and content. Worse, no one knows what to do with the uncollected work. The five thick volumes and over three thousand pages of the Spanish *Complete Works* are arranged according to book publication, including the late or posthumous collections (such as *Prologues,* which spans over fifty years) and ignore everything that was never published in book form. (This is now being corrected by a series of volumes called *Recovered Texts.* The first to appear, recovering only the years 1919 to 1929, is over four hundred pages long.) The French Pléiade edition is based on the Spanish *Complete Works*, but adds some uncollected pieces, oddly organized according to the magazines in which they were published. Almost a third of the texts here cannot be found in the *Complete Works*.

Because the individual books of essays were (with one exception) not thematic and were essentially handy repositories for whatever Borges felt like publishing at the time of their reprinting, or were collections gathered decades after the work was written, I have decided to ignore them as an organizing principle. (The publishing history of each essay, however, may be found in the notes.) Instead, I have chosen a simple chronological arrangement, according to first publication—the date is noted at the end of each text—which allows the reader to see the evolution of Borges' style and the clusterings and revisions of his concerns, and to place each piece in its general historical moment. (I have, however, used the final version of each individual text, as some were slightly revised over the years.) I have divided the book into seven sections, and subdivided these by subgenre: essays, book reviews, film criticism, lectures, and prologues (a particularly Borgesian form: he wrote hundreds of them). Only one section and one subsection are thematic: the Dante essays and the notes he wrote on Germany and World War II; these clearly belonged together. It is hoped that this arrangement will be completely straightforward for readers, although it is unique for an edition of Borges.

Part I (Early Writings) presents eight essays from the first three books, which Borges disowned. Many feel that his self-criticism was overly severe: the essays remain interesting in themselves, and as examples both of youthfully exuberant, preliminary investigations into subjects that would become lifelong obsessions and of the early complex style he would simplify and refine over the decades.

Part II (1929–1936) begins the "canonical" Borges, and is drawn from the books of the early 1930s, as well as uncollected essays from that period and his film criticism. Part III is taken from the hundreds of articles he wrote for the women's magazine *El Hogar* [Home] every two weeks from 1936 to 1939. These include some of his one-page "Capsule Biographies" of modern writers, the very short and often hilarious book reviews and notes, and two essays. Given the special circumstances under which they were written and his intended audience, these pieces required a separate section.

Part IV (1937–1945) picks up the chronology again and opens with

Borges' short articles on Germany, anti-Semitism, and the war. It also includes essays (some of which were collected years later in *Other Inquisitions*), prologues, and further book and film reviews. Part V is the complete text of the remarkable *Nine Dantesque Essays*, written between 1945 and 1951, unpublished in their entirety in Spanish until 1982, and unknown in English. Part VI (1946–1955) returns to the chronology with more essays that would appear in *Other Inquisitions*, essays that were included in the reprints of the 1930s books or never collected, prologues, and two written lectures.

In 1955, Borges lost his sight. After that, he wrote no more essays as such, and fewer stories. He devoted himself largely to poetry, which he could compose in his head, and surveys of topics such as American, English, and medieval Germanic literature, which he wrote with collaborators. He did, however, write scores of prologues to various books and to all the volumes in the two series he edited at the end of his life, *The Library of Babel*, collections of fantastic tales, and *A Personal Library*, over seventy of his favorite books.

Before his blindness, Borges was so shy that, on the few occasions when he was asked to lecture, he sat on the stage while someone else read the text. In his last three decades, however, as his star rose and he was invited all over the world, he evolved a new form that is still misleadingly given the old label "lecture." Closer perhaps to performance art, these were spontaneous monologues on given subjects. Relaxed and conversational, necessarily less perfect than the written essays, the lectures are, like the prologues, a particularly Borgesian subgenre and delight.

To emphasize the orality of this late work, I have given the title "Dictations" to Part VII, which begins in 1956 after the loss of his sight and ends with his death in 1986. Five of the lectures are presented, and almost twenty of his prologues, including some important longer ones and some crystalline last thoughts on his readings.

"Fiction" and "non-fiction" are notoriously blurred boundaries in Borges' fiction, but not in his non-fiction. That is, his fictions may often resemble non-fiction, or include factual elements, but his non-fictions never resemble fiction, or include information that is not independently verifiable. (The word *non-fiction*, by the way, does not exist in Spanish, and Borges never used it, but *essays* seemed limiting or misleading for the types of work contained here.)

These writings have a few stylistic traits which perhaps should be signaled in advance. The first is the Borges sentence. He apparently took to heart Henry James' dictum that the true measure of civility was the proper use of the semicolon. Borges, particularly when he is compiling lists that span centuries, has a predilection for the endless sentence with semicolons as milestones along the route. Previous translators have tended to break these into short sentences that conform to the manuals of English style; the translators here have left them intact.

Second, Borges likes to quote Latin, German, Italian, and French (but surprisingly, not English) sources in the original language and almost never offers a translation, even in the Dante essays with their extensive citations. As an editor, I was torn between preserving the polyglot nature of the texts and a less utopian view of the foreign language skills of many contemporary readers. My compromise was to include both the original and a translation of all quotations and book titles that are essential for understanding the text at that moment, but to leave relatively unimportant things untranslated— for example, a book title that one can easily deduce is a German study of Buddhism. All the editorial translations are contained within square brackets [ ]; Borges' rare translations are in parentheses.

Third, and most important, are the repetitions. Readers will immediately notice that the same phrases, sentences, paragraphs and on one occasion, pages recur throughout the book. The first reaction may well be that Borges, who was earning his living by writing hundreds of articles for diverse publications, was merely cutting corners by repeating himself. This is quite clearly not the case, as I discovered when my first editorial instinct was to wonder if any could be excised. Borges nearly always uses the same sentence to make a different point, or as a bridge between points C and D that are not the points A and B that were linked the last time the sentence was used. The repetitions are part of his lifelong fascination with the way old elements can be reassembled, by chance or design, to create new variations, something entirely different, or something that is exactly the same but now somehow different. This is most clearly visible in one of his longest and most famous essays, "A New Refutation of Time," which not only cites the same paragraphs from Bishop Berkeley twice, but also reprints a prose piece from the 1920s that he had already reprinted in another "canonical" essay, "A History of Eternity." (Borges might have liked the fact that this same text is presented here in two different English versions.) Needless to say, none of these translations abridge any of the original texts.

It should also be said that this book has been edited for the English-language reader. The result is that, with a half-dozen exceptions, a large portion of Borges' writing has been neglected here: the hundreds of articles he wrote on Argentine literature and culture. Most of his subjects, unfortunately, are generally unknown outside of the country, and unlike other writers who attempt to explain the national to an international audience, Borges was writing for Argentines about Argentina. These articles would have required a rich subsoil of footnotes to produce a meager interest. But it is important to note, at least, that Borges was an active participant in his national culture and extraordinarily generous, in the form of prologues and reviews, to his contemporaries.

The English-language reader may well be misled by the practice of many of the major modern Anglo-American writers and assume that Borges' essays are merely addenda to the fiction or poetry, and now of interest mainly to fans or scholars. In Latin America, however, it is frequently said that the best Borges is the essayist: the place where nearly all the ideas that propel the short stories, and many more, are elaborated in lively, different, and more detailed ways. This is not to depreciate the stories and poems—Borges himself often complains of a criticism that finds it necessary to tear down one thing in order to promote another—but merely to indicate the high and equal regard in which the non-fiction is held.

In English, unlike many other languages, the essay has played a minor role in twentieth-century literature. In contrast to the other writing forms, there is almost no criticism on the essay, no articulated recognition of the way an essay may be written, and other than comments on its content, no consensus or dissent on how it should be read. At the present moment, it is largely represented by certain of its subgenres—memoir, travel writing, personal journalism, book review, academic criticism—and the kind of free-ranging essay that Borges wrote is almost entirely absent from periodicals, outside of small literary journals.

Abroad, essays in an unlimited variety of styles appear daily in the cultural supplements of newspapers or in large-circulation intellectual magazines. They tend to be written by poets or novelists, and it is often the case that the writers are known or respected as poets or novelists, but actually read as essayists. This is the milieu in which Borges wrote: much of the work here first appeared in newspapers. In that world, it was expected that essays be as fascinating as stories, and it is revealing that, perhaps in order for his fiction to be read, he started out by disguising his stories as essays.

ELIOT WEINBERGER

I
Early Writings
1922-1928

The Nothingness of Personality

Intention.

I want to tear down the exceptional preeminence now generally awarded to the self, and I pledge to be spurred on by concrete certainty, and not the caprice of an ideological ambush or a dazzling intellectual prank. I propose to prove that personality is a mirage maintained by conceit and custom, without metaphysical foundation or visceral reality. I want to apply to literature the consequences that issue from these premises, and erect upon them an aesthetic hostile to the psychologism inherited from the last century, sympathetic to the classics, yet encouraging to today's most unruly tendencies.

Course of action.

I have noticed that, in general, the acquiescence conceded by a man in the role of reader to a rigorous dialectical linkage is no more than a slothful inability to gauge the proofs the writer adduces and a vague trust in the latter's rectitude. But once the book has been closed and the reading has dispersed, little remains in his memory except a more or less arbitrary synthesis of the whole reading. To avoid this evident disadvantage, I will, in the following paragraphs, cast aside all strict and logical schemas, and amass a pile of examples.

There is no whole self. Any of life's present situations is seamless and sufficient. Are you, as you ponder these disquietudes, anything more than an indifference gliding over the argument I make, or an appraisal of the opinions I expound?

I, as I write this, am only a certainty that seeks out the words that are most apt to compel your attention. That proposition and a few muscular sensations, and the sight of the limpid branches that the trees place outside my window, constitute my current I.

It would be vanity to suppose that in order to enjoy absolute validity this psychic aggregate must seize on a self, that conjectural Jorge Luis Borges on whose tongue sophistries are always at the ready and in whose solitary strolls the evenings on the fringes of the city are pleasant.

There is no whole self. He who defines personal identity as the private possession of some depository of memories is mistaken. Whoever affirms such a thing is abusing the symbol that solidifies memory in the form of an enduring and tangible granary or warehouse, when memory is no more than the noun by which we imply that among the innumerable possible states of consciousness, many occur again in an imprecise way. Moreover, if I root personality in remembrance, what claim of ownership can be made on the elapsed instants that, because they were quotidian or stale, did not stamp us with a lasting mark? Heaped up over years, they lie buried, inaccessible to our avid longing. And that much-vaunted memory to whose ruling you made appeal, does it ever manifest all its past plenitude? Does it truly live? The sensualists and their ilk, who conceive of your personality as the sum of your successive states of mind, are similarly deceiving themselves. On closer scrutiny, their formula is no more than an ignominious circumlocution that undermines the very foundation it constructs, an acid that eats away at itself, a prattling fraud and a belabored contradiction.

No one will pretend that, in the glance by which we take in a limpid night, the exact number of visible stars is prefigured.

No one, on thinking about it, will accept that the self can depend on the hypothetical and never realized nor realizable sum of different states of mind. What is not carried out does not exist; the linkage of events in a temporal succession does not refer to an absolute order. They err, as well, who suppose that the negation of personality I am urging with such obstinate zealotry refutes the certainty of being the isolated, individualized, and distinct thing that each of us feels in the depths of his soul. I do not deny this consciousness of being, nor the immediate security of *here I am* that it breathes into us. What I do deny is that all our other convictions must be adjusted to the customary antithesis between the self and the non-self, and that this antithesis is constant. The sensation of cold, of spacious and pleasurable suppleness, that is in me as I open the front door and go out along the half-darkness of the street is neither a supplement to a pre-existing self nor an event that comes coupled to the other event of a continuing and rigorous self.

Moreover, even if the aforementioned reasons are misguided, I would refuse to surrender, for your conviction of being an individuality is in all ways identical to mine and to that of any human specimen, and there is no way to separate them.

There is no whole self. It suffices to walk any distance along the inexorable rigidity that the mirrors of the past open to us in order to feel like outsiders, naively flustered by our own bygone days. There is no community of intention in them, nor are they propelled by the same breeze. This has been declared by those men who have truly scrutinized the calendars from which time was discarding them. Some, extravagant as fireworks, make a boast of so muddled a confusion and say that disparity is wealth; others, far from glorifying disorder, deplore the inequality of their days and yearn for the popular uniformity. I will copy out two examples. The first bears the date 1531; it is the epigraph to *De Incertitudine et Vanitate Scientiarum*, composed by the Kabbalist and astrologer Agrippa of Nettesheim in the disillusioned latter days of his life. He says:

Among gods, all are shaken by the jeers of Momus.
Among heroes, Hercules gives chase to all the monsters.
Among demons, Pluto, the King of Hell, oppresses all the shades.
While Heraclitus weeps at everything,
Pyrrho knows naught of anything,
And Aristotle glories in knowing all.
Diogenes spurns the things of this world,
And I, Agrippa, am foreign to none of this.
I disdain, I know, I do not know, I pursue, I laugh, I tyrannize, I protest.
I am philosopher, god, hero, demon and the whole universe.

The second testimonial comes from the third part of Torres Villarroel's *Vida e historia*. This systematizer of Quevedo, learned in astrology, lord and master of all words, expert wielder of the most strident rhetorical figures, also sought to define himself and probed his fundamental incongruence. He saw that he was like everyone else: that is, that he was no one, or little more than an unintelligible cacophony, persisting in time and wearing out in space. He wrote:

I am angry, fearful, compassionate, joyous, sad, greedy, generous, enraged, meek, and all the good and bad emotions and all the praiseworthy and reprehensible actions that can be found in all men together or separately. I have tried out all the vices and all the virtues, and in a single day I feel inclined to weep and laugh, give and keep, repose and suffer, and I am always unaware of the cause and the momentum of these contrarieties. I have heard this alternative of contrary impulses called madness; if it be so, we are all mad to a greater or lesser degree for I have noticed this unforeseen and repeated alternation in everyone.

There is no whole self. Beyond all possibility of bombastic gamesmanship, I have touched this hard truth with my own emotions as I was separating from a companion. I was returning to Buenos Aires and leaving him behind in Mallorca. We both understood that, except in the perfidious or altered proximity of letters, we would not meet again. What happens at such moments happened. We knew this good-bye would jut out in our memories, and there was even a period when we tried to enhance its flavor with a vehement show of opinions for the yearnings to come. The present moment was acquiring all the prestige and indeterminacy of the past. . . .

But beyond any egotistical display, what clamored in my chest was the will to show my soul in its entirety to my friend. I would have wanted to strip myself of it and leave it there, palpitating. We went on talking and debating, on the brink of good-bye, until all at once, with an unsuspected strength of conviction, I understood that this personality, which we usually appraise at such an incompatibly exorbitant value, is nothing. The thought came over me that never would one full and absolute moment, containing all the others, justify my life, that all of my instants would be provisional phases, annihilators of the past turned to face the future, and that beyond the episodic, the present, the circumstantial, we were nobody. And I despised all mysterizing.

The last century was rootedly subjective in its aesthetic manifestations. Its writers were more inclined to show off their personalities than to establish a body of work, an aphorism that is also applicable today to the teeming and highly acclaimed mob of those who profit from the glib embers of that century's bonfires. However, my purpose is not to lash out against one or the other of these groups, but to consider the Calvary toward which idolaters of themselves are on a fatal course. We have already seen that any state of mind, however opportunistic, can entirely fill up our attention, which is much the same as saying that it can form, in its brief and absolute term, our essence. Which, translated into the language of literature, means that to try to express oneself and to want to express the whole of life are one and the same thing. A strenuous, panting dash between the prodding of time and man, who, like Achilles in the illustrious conundrum formulated by Zeno of Elea, will always see himself in last place. . . .

Whitman was the first Atlas who attempted to make this obstinacy a reality and take the world upon his shoulders. He believed he had only to enumerate the names of things in order to make their unique and surprising nature immediately palpable. Therefore, his poems, along with a great deal of fine rhetoric, string together garrulous series of words, sometimes repeated from geography or history primers, which kindle lofty signs of admiration and mimic great enthusiasms.

From Whitman on, many have been caught up in this same fallacy. They have said:

> I have not tormented the language in quest of unexpected intensities or verbal marvels. I have not spun out even a slight paradox capable of creating a stir in your conversation or sending its sparks out through your laborious silence. Nor did I invent a tale around which lengthy spans of attention would cluster, as many futile hours cluster in remembrance around one hour in which there was love. None of that did I do nor have I determined to do and yet I wish for enduring fame. My justification is as follows: I am a man astonished by the abundance of the world: I bear witness to the unicity of things. Like the most illustrious of men, my life is located in space, and the chiming of unanimous clocks punctuates my duration in time. The words I use are not redolent of far-flung readings, but signs that mark what I have felt or contemplated. If ever I made mention of the dawn, it was not merely to follow the easy current of usage. I can assure you that I know what the Dawn is: I have seen, with premeditated rejoicing, the explosion that hollows out the depths of the streets, incites the slums of the world to revolt, humiliates the stars and broadens the sky by many leagues. I also know what a jacaranda, a statue, a meadow, a cornice are. . . . I am like everyone else. This is my boast and my glory. It matters little whether I have proclaimed it in feeble verses or in rough-hewn prose.

The same is asserted, with greater skill and mastery, by painters. What is contemporary painting—that of Picasso and his pupils—but a rapt confirmation of the gorgeous unicity of a king of spades, a gatepost, or a chess board? Romantic ego-worship and loudmouthed individualism are in this way wreaking havoc on the arts. Thank God that the lengthy examination of spiritual minutiae that this demands of the artist forces him back to the eternal classic rectitude that is creation. In a book like Ramón Gómez de la Serna's *Greguerías*, the currents of both tendencies intermingle, and as we read we are unaware if what magnetizes our interest with such unique force is a copied reality or is of pure intellectual fabrication.

The self does not exist. Schopenhauer, who often appears to adhere to this opinion, at other times tacitly denies it, I know not whether deliberately or because he is compelled by the rough, homespun metaphysics—or rather ametaphysics—that lurks in the very origins of language. Nevertheless, despite this disparity, there is a passage in his work that illuminates the alternative like a sudden blast of flame. I shall transcribe it:

> An infinite time has run its course before my birth; what was I throughout all that time? Metaphysically, the answer might perhaps be: I was always I; that is, all who during that time said I, were in fact I.

Reality has no need of other realities to bolster it. There are no divinities hidden in the trees, nor any elusive thing-in-itself behind appearances, nor a mythological self that orders our actions. Life is truthful appearance. The senses do not deceive, it is the mind that deceives, said Goethe, in a maxim we could compare to this line by Macedonio Fernández:

> *La realidad trabaja en abierto misterio*
> [Reality works in overt mystery]

There is no whole self. Grimm, in an excellent presentation of Buddhism (*Die Lehre des Buddha*, Munich, 1917), describes the process of elimination whereby the Indians arrived at this certainty. Here is their millennially effective precept: "Those things of which I can perceive the beginnings and the end are not my self." This rule is correct and needs only to be exemplified in order to persuade us of its virtue. I, for example, am not the visual reality that my eyes encompass, for if I were, darkness would kill me and nothing would remain in me to desire the spectacle of the world, or even to forget it. Nor am I the audible world that I hear, for in that case silence would erase me and I would pass from sound to sound without memory of the previous one. Subsequent identical lines of argument can be directed toward the senses of smell, taste, and touch, proving not only that I am not the world of appearances—a thing generally known and undisputed—but that the apperceptions that indicate that world are not my self either. That is, I am not my own activity of seeing, hearing, smelling, tasting, touching. Nor am I my body, which is a phenomenon among others. Up to this point the argument is banal; its distinction lies in its application to spiritual matters. Are desire, thought, happiness, and distress my true self? The answer, in accordance with the precept, is clearly in the negative, since those conditions expire without annulling me with them. Consciousness—the final hideout where we might track down the self—also proves unqualified. Once the emotions, the extraneous perceptions, and even ever-shifting thought are dismissed, consciousness is a barren thing, without any appearance reflected in it to make it exist.

Grimm observes that this rambling dialectical inquiry yields a result that coincides with Schopenhauer's opinion that the self is a point whose immobility is useful for discerning, by contrast, the heavy-laden flight of time. This opinion translates the self into a mere logical imperative, without qualities of its own or distinctions from individual to individual.

[1922]   [EA]

After Images

With the ambitious gesture of a man who, contemplating the astral generosity of the spring sky, would crave yet another star and, dark in the bright night, would demand that constellations shatter their incorruptible destiny and renew their flame with signs unseen by the ancient gaze of sailors and shepherds, I sounded my throat once, imploring the incontrovertible heaven of art to sanction our gift for appending unforeseen lights and braiding into stunning crowns the perennial stars. How taciturn was Buenos Aires then! From its harsh grandeur, twice a millionaire of possible souls, no pious provider of a single true verse emerged, while the six strings of any guitar were closer to poetry than those fictive counterfeits of Rubén Darío or Luis Carlos López that infested the journals.

Youth was scattered in the penumbra, and each alone judged himself. We were like the lover who claims his heart to be the only to flaunt love, like the glowing branch heavy with spring which ignores the festive poplar groves. We proudly believed in our fictitious solitude of gods or blooming islands, unique in the sterile sea, and we felt rising to the beaches of our hearts the urgent beauty of the world, entreating us unremittingly to anchor it in verse. New moons, fences, the soft color of the outlying districts, the bright faces of little girls, were for us obligatory beauty, calling for daring inventions. We came upon the metaphor, that resonant conduit our paths will never forget and whose waters have left their mark in our writing, perhaps comparable to the red mark that revealed the chosen to the Angel or the blue mark on houses condemned by Rosas' police, promising perdition. We came upon the metaphor, the invocation by which we disordered the rigid universe. For the believer, things are the fulfillment of God's word—in the beginning Light was named, and then it illuminated the world; for the positivist they are the fated accidents of interlocking events. Metaphor, linking distant things, fractures that double rigidity. At length we exhausted it, in sleepless, assiduous nights at the shuttle of its loom, string-ing colored threads from horizon to horizon. Today metaphor is facile in any style, and its glitter—star of interior epiphanies, our gaze—multiplies in mirrors. But I do not want us to rest on our laurels; I hope our art can forget, and plunge into untouched seas, as adventurous night leaps from the beaches of day. I wish this zeal to weigh like a halo over all our heads; I shall reveal it in words.

The image is witchcraft. Turning a fire into a tempest, as did Milton, is the work of a wizard. Changing the moon into a fish, a bubble, a comet—as Rossetti did, falling into error even before Lugones—is a lesser trick. There is someone superior to the trickster or the wizard. I am speaking of a demigod, an angel, whose works alter the world. To add provinces to Being, to envision cities and spaces of a hallucinatory reality, is a heroic adventure. Buenos Aires has not yet attained its poetic immortality. On the pampas, a gaucho once improvised songs to spite a devil; nothing has happened yet in Buenos Aires, whose grandeur has not been validated by a symbol, a sur-prising fable, or even an individual destiny comparable to Martín Fierro's. I do not know if a divine will is at work in the world, but if such exists, It con-ceived the pink-walled general store, this opulent spring, that shiny red gas meter. (What a perfect drumroll for Judgment Day the latter is!) I would like to commemorate two attempts to concoct city fables: one is the total poem woven by the tangos—a vulgar, precarious distortion of the people into parodies, whose sole character is the nostalgic hoodlum, and whose only circumstance is prostitution; the other is the brilliant, oblique humor of *Papeles de Recienvenido* by Macedonio Fernández.

A final example. It is not enough to say, in the manner of all poets, that mirrors are like water. Nor is it enough to take this hypothesis as an absolute and presume, like some Huidobro, that cool breezes blow from mirrors or that thirsty birds drink from them, leaving their frames empty. We must make manifest the whim transformed into reality that is the mind. We must reveal an individual reflected in the glass who persists in his illusory country (where there are figures and colors, but they are ruled by immutable silence) and who feels the shame of being only a simulacrum obliterated by the night, existing only in glimpses.

[1924]   *[SJL]*

Joyce's *Ulysses*

I am the first traveler from the Hispanic world to set foot upon the shores of *Ulysses*, a lush wilderness already traversed by Valéry Larbaud, who traced its dense texture with the impeccable precision of a mapmaker (*Nouvelle Revue Française* XVIII), but which I too will describe, even though my visit within its borders has been inattentive and transient. I will speak of it with the license my admiration lends me and with the murky intensity of those ancient explorers who described lands new to their nomadic amazement, and whose stories about the Amazons and the City of the Caesars combined truth and fantasy.

I confess that I have not cleared a path through all seven hundred pages, I confess to having examined only bits and pieces, and yet I know what it is, with that bold and legitimate certainty with which we assert our knowledge of a city, without ever having been rewarded with the intimacy of all the many streets it includes.

James Joyce is Irish. The Irish have always been famous for being the iconoclasts of the British Isles. Less sensitive to verbal decorum than their detested lords, less inclined to pour their eyes upon the smooth moon or to decipher the impermanence of rivers in long free-verse laments, they made deep incursions into the territory of English letters, pruning all rhetorical exuberance with frank impiety. Jonathan Swift acted like a corrosive acid on the elation of human hope, and Voltaire's *Micromegas* and *Candide* are no more than cheaper versions of his severe nihilism. Laurence Sterne unraveled the novel by making merry with the reader's expectations, and those oblique digressions are now the source of his multitudinous fame; Bernard Shaw is today's most pleasing realist; but of Joyce I will say that he exercises with dignity his Irish audacity.

His life, measured in space and time, will take up a mere few lines, which my ignorance will abbreviate further. He was born in Dublin in 1882, into an eminent and piously Catholic family. He was educated by the Jesuits. We know that he possesses a classical culture, that he is not unfamiliar with scholasticism, that there are no errors of diction in his Latin phrases, that he has wandered the various countries of Europe, and that his children were born in Italy. He has composed lyrics, short stories, and a novel of cathedral-like grandeur, the motivation of this review.

Ulysses is variously distinguished. Its life seems situated on a single plane, without those steps that take us mentally from each subjective world to an objective stage, from the whimsical daydream of one man's unconscious to the frequently trafficked dreams of the collective mind. Conjecture, suspicion, fleeting thought, memories, lazy thinking, and the carefully conceived enjoy equal privilege in this book; a single point of view is noticeably absent. This amalgamation of dreams and the real might well have provoked the consent of Kant and Schopenhauer. The former did not deal with any distinction between dreams and reality other than that legitimated by the causal nexus constant in everyday life, and which from dream to dream does not exist. According to the latter, no criteria exist to distinguish dreams and reality, other than the merely empirical data provided by waking life; he added with meticulous elucidations that real life and the dream world are pages of the same book, and that custom calls real life the orderly reading, and dreams what we leaf through with lazy negligence. I wish, therefore, to remember the problem articulated by Gustav Spiller in *The Mind of Man* on the relative reality of a room seen objectively, then in the imagination, and lastly, duplicated in a mirror; he resolves that all three are real, and visually each takes up an equal amount of space.

As one can see, Minerva's olive tree casts a gentler shadow than the laurel upon the worthy *Ulysses*. I cannot find any literary ancestors, except perhaps Dostoevsky in his later years after *Crime and Punishment*, and even then, who knows. So let us admire the provisional miracle.

In Joyce's unrelenting examination of the tiniest details that constitute consciousness, he stops the flow of time and defers its movement with a pacifying gesture contrary to the impatient goading of the English drama, which encloses the life of its heroes in the narrow, thrusting rush of a few crowded hours. If Shakespeare—to use his own metaphor—invested in the turning of the hourglass the exploits of many years, Joyce inverts the procedure and unfolds his hero's single day into many days upon the reader. (I haven't said many naps.)

A total reality teems vociferously in the pages of *Ulysses*, and not the

mediocre reality of those who notice in the world only the abstract operations of the mind and its ambitious fear of not being able to overcome
death, nor that other reality that enters only our senses, juxtaposing our
flesh and the streets, the moon and the well. The duality of existence dwells
within this book, an ontological anxiety that is amazed not merely at being,
but at being in this particular world where there are entranceways and
words and playing cards and electric writing upon the translucence of the
night. In no other book (except perhaps those written by Gómez de la
Serna) do we witness the actual presence of things with such convincing
firmness. All things are latent, and the diction of any voice is capable of
making them emerge and of leading the reader down their avenue. De
Quincey recounts that it was enough to name the Roman consul in his
dreams to set off fiery visions of flying banners and military splendor. In the
fifteenth chapter of his work, Joyce sketches a delirious brothel scene, and
the chance conjuring of any loose phrase or idea ushers in hundreds—the
sum is not an exaggeration but exact—of absurd speakers and impossible
events.

Joyce portrays a day in modern life and accumulates a variety of
episodes in its course which equal in spirit those events that inform the
Odyssey.

He is a millionaire of words and styles. Aside from the prodigious funds
of voices that constitute the English language, his commerce spreads wherever the Irish clover grows, from Castilian doubloons and Judas' shekels to
Roman denarii and other ancient coinage. His prolific pen exercises all the
rhetorical figures. Each episode exalts yet another poetic strategy, another
private lexicon. One is written in syllogisms, another in questions and
answers, another in narrative sequence. In two of them there is a silent
soliloquy—a heretofore unpublished form (derived from the Frenchman
Edouard Dujardin, as Joyce told Larbaud) through which we hear his characters think at length. Beside the new humor of his incongruities and amid
his bawdyhouse banter in macaronic prose and verse, he raises rigid structures of Latin rigor like the Egyptian's speech to Moses. Joyce is as bold as
the prow of a ship, and as universal as a mariner's compass. Ten years from
now—his book having been explicated by more pious and persistent re-
viewers than myself—we will still enjoy him. Meanwhile, since I have not
the ambition to take *Ulysses* to Neuquen and study it in quiet repose, I wish
to make mine Lope de Vega's respectful words regarding Góngora:

Be what it may, I will always esteem and adore the divine genius of this Gentleman, taking from him what I understand with humility and admiring with veneration what I am unable to understand.

[1925]   *[SJL]*

A History of Angels

The angels are two days and two nights older than we: the Lord created them on the fourth day, and from their high balcony between the recently invented sun and the first moon they scanned the infant earth, barely more than a few wheatfields and some orchards beside the waters. These primitive angels were stars. For the Hebrews, the concepts of angel and star merged effortlessly: I will select, from among many, the passage of the Book of Job (38:7) in which the Lord spoke out of the whirlwind and recalled the beginning of the world, "When the morning stars sang together, and all the sons of God shouted for joy." Quite apparently, these sons of God and singing stars are the same as angels. Isaiah, too (14:12), calls the fallen angel "the morning star," a phrase Quevedo did not forget when he called him *"lucero inobediente, ángel amotinado"* [defiant star, rebel angel]. This equivalency between stars and angels (those populators of nighttime solitudes) strikes me as beautiful; it is among the distinctions of the Hebrews that they vitalized the astral bodies with souls, exalting their brilliance into life.

From beginning to end, the Old Testament throngs with angels. There are ambiguous angels who come along the straight paths of the plain and whose superhuman nature cannot immediately be divined; there are angels brawny as farmhands, like the one who fought with Jacob a whole night until the breaking of the day; there are regimental angels, like the captain of the Lord's host who appeared to Joshua; there are angels who threaten cities and others who are like expert guides through solitude; the angels in God's engines of war number two thousand times a thousand. The best-equipped angelary, or arsenal of angels, is the Revelation of St. John: there are the strong angels, who cast out the dragon; those who stand at the four corners of the earth so that it does not blow away; those who change a third part of the sea to blood; those who gather up the clusters of the vine of the earth and cast them into the great winepress of the wrath of God; those who are implements of wrath; those who are bound in the great river Euphrates and let loose like tempests; those who are a mixture of eagle and man.

Islam, too, knows of angels. The Muslims of Cairo live blotted out by angels, the real world virtually deluged by the angelic, for according to Edward William Lane, each follower of the Prophet is assigned two guardian angels, or five, or sixty, or one hundred sixty.

The Celestial Hierarchy, erroneously attributed to the Greek convert Dionysius and composed around the fifth century of our era, is a highly documented ranking of angelic order that distinguishes, for example, between the cherubim and the seraphim, allocating to the first the full, perfect, and overflowing vision of God and to the second an eternal ascension toward Him in a gesture both ecstatic and trembling, like a sudden blaze rushing upward. Twelve hundred years later, Alexander Pope, archetype of the learned poet, would recall this distinction when he penned his famous line: "As the rapt seraph, that adores and burns . . ."

Theologians, admirable in their intellectualism, did not shrink from angels and tried to penetrate this world of wings and mirages with their reasoning minds. This was no uncomplicated matter, for angels had to be defined as beings superior to man but necessarily inferior to divinity. The German speculative theologian Rothe records numerous examples of the push and pull of this dialectic. His list of angelic attributes merits consideration: those attributes include intellectual force; free will; immateriality (capable, however, of accidentally uniting itself with matter); aspatiality (neither taking up any space nor being enclosed by it); lasting duration, with a beginning but without end; invisibility, and even immutability, an attribute that harbors them in the eternal. As for the faculties they exercise, they are granted the utmost suppleness, the power of conversing among themselves instantaneously without words or signs, and that of working wonders, but not miracles. They cannot create from nothing or raise the dead. The angelic zone that lies halfway between God and man is, it would seem, highly regulated.

The Kabbalists also made use of angels. Dr. Erich Bischoff, in his German book entitled *The Elements of the Kabbalah*, published in Berlin in 1920, enumerates the ten *sefiroth*, or eternal emanations of divinity, and makes each correspond to one of the regions of the sky, one of the names of God, one of the Ten Commandments, one part of the human body, and one class of angels. Stehelin, in his *Rabbinical Literature*, links the first ten letters of the *aleph-beth*, or alphabet of the Hebrews, to these ten lofty worlds. Thus the letter *aleph* corresponds to the brain, the First Commandment, the sky of fire, the divine name "I Am That I Am," and the seraphim known as the Sacred Beasts. Those who accuse the Kabbalists of imprecision are clearly mistaken. They were, instead, fanatics of reason, and they delineated a world of deification by installments that was nevertheless as rigorous and causal as the one we feel now. . . .

Such a swarm of angels cannot have avoided meddling in literature. The examples are inexhaustible. In the sonnet by Juan de Jáuregui to St. Ignatius Loyola, the angel retains his biblical strength, his combative seriousness:

> *Ved sobre el mar, porque su golfo encienda*
> *El ángel fuerte, de pureza armado.*

[Look to the sea, for its gulf is set aflame/by the strong angel, armed with purity.]

For Luis de Góngora, the angel is a valuable decorative trinket, good for gratifying ladies and children:

> *¿Cuándo será aquel día que por yerro*
> *oh, Serafín, desates, bien nacido,*
> *Con manos de Cristal nudos de Hierro?*

[When will the day be that in error/oh, Seraph, you unloose, well-born,/ Knots of Iron with your Crystalline hands?]

In a sonnet by Lope de Vega, I ran across the agreeable and very twentieth-century metaphor:

> *Cuelgan racimos de ángeles*

[Clusters of angels dangle]

And these angels, with a whiff of the countryside about them, are from Juan Ramón Jiménez:

> *Vagos ángeles malvas*
> *apagaban las verdes estrellas*

[Vague angels, mauve as mallows, / were putting out the green stars]

Here we arrive at the near miracle that is the true motive for this writing: what we might call the survival of the angel. The human imagination has pictured a horde of monsters (tritons, hippogriffs, chimeras, sea serpents, unicorns, devils, dragons, werewolves, cyclopes, fauns, basilisks, demigods, leviathans, and a legion of others) and all have disappeared, except angels. Today, what line of poetry would dare allude to the phoenix or make itself the promenade of a centaur? None; but no poetry, however modern, is unhappy to be a nest of angels and to shine brightly with them. I always imagine them at nightfall, in the dusk of a slum or a vacant lot, in that long, quiet moment when things are gradually left alone, with their backs to the sunset, and when colors are like memories or premonitions of other colors. We must not be too prodigal with our angels; they are the last divinities we harbor, and they might fly away.

[1926]   *[EA]*

Verbiage for Poems

The Royal Spanish Academy with florid vagueness states: "All three [grammar, prosody, and rhetoric] merge their generous efforts so that our rich language may conserve its envied treasury of felicitous, picturesque and expressive words, its palette of bewitching bright and vivid rainbow colors, and its melodious, harmonious rhythm, which has earned its name and fame in the world as the beautiful tongue of Cervantes."

This paragraph abounds in shortcomings, from the moral poverty of presuming that the excellence of Spanish should motivate envy and not joy—and the celebration of that envy—to the intellectual deficiency of referring to expressive words out of context. To admire the expressivity of words (except for certain derivations and onomatopeias) is like admiring the fact that Arenales Street is a street called Arenales. Let us not get mired in this trivia, however, but rather concentrate on the substance of the academy's lengthy locution, on its insistent statement about the riches of Spanish. Are there such riches in the language?

Arturo Costa Alvarez (*Our Language*, 293) relates the simplistic process used (or abused) by the Count of Casa Valencia to compare French with Spanish. This gentleman resorted to mathematics and discovered that almost 60,000 words are registered in the dictionary of the Royal Academy, and in the corresponding French dictionary only 31,000. Does this census mean that a Spanish speaker has 29,000 more ideas than a Frenchman? Such an induction is a bit excessive. Nonetheless, if the numerical superiority of a language is not interchangeable with mental or representational superiority, why should it be so encouraging? On the other hand, if numerical criteria are worthwhile, all thoughts are impoverished unless they are thought in German or English, each of whose dictionaries have amassed over 100,000 words.

I personally believe Spanish is a rich language, but I do not think we should allow it to languish in inertia, but rather multiply its legions. Any lexicon can be perfected, which I propose to demonstrate.

The world of appearances is a jumble of shifting perceptions. The vision of a rustic sky, that persistent aroma sweeping the fields, the bitter taste of tobacco burning one's throat, the long wind lashing the road, the submissive rectitude of the cane around which we wrap our fingers, all fit together in our consciousness, almost all at once. Language is an efficient ordering of the world's enigmatic abundance. Or, in other words, we invent nouns to fit reality. We touch a sphere, see a small heap of dawn-colored light, our mouths enjoy a tingling sensation, and we lie to ourselves that those three disparate things are only one thing called an orange. The moon itself is a fiction. Outside of astronomical conventions which should not concern us here, there is no similarity whatsoever between the yellow sphere now rising clearly over the wall of the Recoleta cemetery and the pink slice I saw in the sky above the Plaza de Mayo many nights ago. All nouns are abbreviations. Instead of saying cold, sharp, burning, unbreakable, shining, pointy, we utter "dagger"; for the receding of the sun and oncoming darkness, we say "twilight."

(The prefixes in modern Chinese seem to grope for a form somewhere between nouns and adjectives. They are like name-searchers that precede nouns with sketchy outlines. Hence, the particle *pa* is used invariably for manual objects, intercalated between demonstrative adjectives or numbers and the name of the thing. For example, they usually do not say *"yi tao"* [a knife] but rather *"yi pa tao"* [a grasped knife, a handy knife], just as the prefix *ch'un* serves an encompassing function, apropos of courtyards, fences, houses. The prefix *chang* is used for flat things and precedes words like *threshold, bench, mat, plank.* As for the rest, the parts of the sentence are not plainly delineated in Chinese, and the analogical category of a word depends on its placement in the sentence. My references for this lapse into Chinese are F. Graebner [*The World of Primitive Man*, chapter IV] and Douglas, in the *Encyclopedia Britannica*.)

I am insisting on the inventive character of any language, and I do so intentionally. Languages construct realities. The various disciplines of the intelligence have engendered worlds of their own and possess an exclusive vocabulary to describe them. The mathematical sciences wield their particular language made of digits and signs, no less subtle than any other. Metaphysics, the natural sciences, the arts, have all considerably increased our general store of words. The verbal acquisitions of theology (*attrition, cleanliness, eternity*) are extremely important. Only poetry—a conspicuously verbal art, the art of engaging the imagination in a game of words, as defined by Arthur Schopenhauer—begs and borrows language from everywhere. It works with other people's tools. Preceptors speak of a poetic language, but if we try to be poetic, we end up with a few vanities like *steed, zephyr, amethystine,* and *wherefore* instead of *where*. Where is poetry's persuasion in sounds like these? What is poetic about them? The fact is that they are unbearable in prose, Samuel Taylor Coleridge would reply. I do not deny the occasional elation of some poetic locutions, and am pleased to remember that we owe to Esteban Manuel de Villegas the verb *diluviar* [to deluge], and to Juan de Mena *congloriar* [to crown with glory] and *confluir* [to converge]:

> *Tanto vos quiso la magnificencia*
> *Dotar de virtudes y congloriar*
> *Que muchos procuran de vos imitar*
> *En vida y en toda virtud y prudencia.*

[So did magnificence strive/ to crown your virtue with glory/that many seek to copy/your wise and virtuous life.]

A deliberately poetic vocabulary, a record of ideas incompatible with common speech, would be a different matter, however. The world of appearances is complicated, and language has only verbalized a minuscule part of its potential, indefatigable combinations. Why not create a word, only one, for the converging perception of the cowbells announcing day's end and the sunset in the distance? Why not invent another for the dilapidated and threatening face of the streets at dawn? And another for the well-meaning, though pitifully ineffectual, first streetlamp to go on at dusk while it is still light out? And another for our lack of trust in ourselves after we have done wrong?

I know there is something utopic in my ideas, and a distance between intellectual possibilities and real ones, but I trust in the extent of the future and that it will be no less generous than my hope.

[1926]   *[SJL]*

A Profession of Literary Faith

I am a man who ventured to write and even publish some verses that recall the memory of two neighborhoods of this city that are deeply entrenched in his life, for in one of them he spent his childhood and in the other he delighted and suffered in a love that perhaps was great. Moreover, I committed a few compositions commemorating the Rosas era, which, as a consequence of my readings and a fierce family tradition, is the old country of my emotions. I was immediately set upon by two or three critics, who hurled sophistries and maledictions at me that were astonishing in their dimness. One branded me a reactionary; the other, with false pity, pointed out neighborhoods more picturesque than those I had the fortune to know, and recommended that I take the No. 56 trolley to Patricios instead of the No. 96 to Urquiza; some attacked me in the name of the skyscrapers; others in defense of the tin shacks. Such efforts of miscomprehension (which I have toned down in my description, so that they will not appear preposterous) account for this profession of literary faith. I can affirm my literary credo as a religious man may his; it is mine insofar as I believe in it, but it is not my invention. Strictly speaking, I believe that the act of postulating it, even among those who try to deny it, is universal.

My postulate is that all literature, in the end, is autobiographical. Everything is poetic that confesses, that gives us a glimpse of a destiny. In lyric poetry, this destiny usually remains immutable, alert but always sketched by symbols that are congenial to its idiosyncracy and allow us to follow its trace. There is no other meaning in Góngora's tresses of hair, sapphires, and shattered glass, or Almafuerte's marshes and packs of dogs. The same is true for novels. The character who matters in the didactic novel *El criticón* is neither Critilo nor Adrenio nor the allegorical chorus that encircles them: it is Friar Gracián with his Lilliputian genius, his solemn puns, his bows to archbishops and grandees, his religion of distrust, his sense of excess erudition, his honeyed veneer and deep-rooted bile. Similarly, we politely suspend our disbelief of Shakespeare's age-old stories, infused with his magnificent verbiage: the one in whom we truly believe is not Lear's daughter but the dramatist himself. Let it be clear that I do not pretend to invalidate the vitality of the theater and novels; I am asserting what Macedonio Fernández has already said, that our craving for souls, destinies, idiosyncracies, knows full well what it covets; that if fantasy lives do not suffice, the author delves amorously into his own.

The same applies to metaphors. Any metaphor, as beguiling as it may be, is a possible experience, and the difficulty lies not in its invention (a simple thing, attained by the mere shuffling of fancy words) but in achieving it in a way that astonishes its reader. I will illustrate this with a few examples. Herrera y Reissig writes (*Los peregrinos de piedra*, p. 49 of the Paris edition):

> *Tirita entre algodones húmedos la arboleda;*
> *La cumbre está en un blanco éxtasis idealista . . .*

[The grove shivers amid damp cotton balls;/The peak is in a white idealist ecstasy . . .]

Two strange things occur here: instead of mist there are damp cotton balls among which the trees feel cold, and even more, the top of a mountain is in ecstasy, in pensive contemplation. These prodigious duplications do not surprise Herrera, who forges ahead. The poet himself has not realized what he writes; how are we to realize it?

Here are a few lines which I consider perfectly wrought, by Fernán Silva Valdés, another Uruguayan (so that the Montevideans will not feel neglected), about a worker who repairs the roads. They are a metaphor firmly enmeshed in reality, shaped into the moment of a destiny that truly believes in it, that delights in its miracle and even wishes to share it with others. They read:

> *Qué lindo,*
> *vengan a ver qué lindo:*
> *en medio de la calle ha caído una estrella;*
> *y un hombre enmascarado*
> *por ver qué tiene adentro se está quemando en ella . . .*

Vengan a ver qué lindo:
en medio de la calle ha caído una estrella
y la gente, asombrada,
le ha formado una rueda
para verla morir entre sus deslumbrantes
boqueadas celestes.

Estoy frente a un prodigio
—a ver quien me lo niega—
en medio de la calle
ha caído una estrella.

[How lovely,/come see how lovely:/in the street a star has fallen:/and a masked man/to see what inside her is burning . . .//Come see how lovely:/in the street a star has fallen,/and the people, astonished,/have formed a circle/to watch her die amid dazzling//celestial gasps.//I am before a miracle/—who dares deny it—/in the middle of the street/a star has fallen.]

Sometimes the autobiographical, personal substance, like a heart beating deep, disappears behind the accidents that incarnate it. There are occasional compositions or lines that are inexplicably pleasing: their images barely approximate, are never to the point; the story they tell appears to be a botched job by a lazy imagination, in stilted diction, and yet that composition or isolated verse pleases us, and does not fall easily from memory. Those divergences of aesthetic judgment and emotion are usually engendered by this incompetence; studied carefully, the verses we like despite ourselves always depict a soul, an idiosyncracy, a destiny. What's more, there are things that are poetic by merely implying a destiny: for example, the map of a city, a rosary, the names of two sisters.

Some lines earlier I insisted upon the urgency of the subjective or objective truth that images require; now I will establish that rhyme, brashly artificial, can infuse the most truthful compositions with a false aura and that, in general, its effect is counterpoetic. All poetry is a confession, and the premises of any confession are one's confidence in the listener and the candor of the speaker. Rhyme's original sin is its air of deceit. Although this deceit is only an annoyance, never plainly exposed, the mere suspicion of it serves to discourage full-blown fervor. Some will say that frills are the foibles of feeble versemakers; I believe that this is an affliction of rhymed verse itself. Some hide it well and others poorly, but it is always there. Here is an example of shameful frills, committed by a famous poet:

Mirándote en lectura sugerente
Llegué al epílogo de mis quimeras;
Tus ojos de palomas mensajeras
Volvían de los astros, dulcemente.

[Reading you with suggestive gaze/I found the epilogue of my notions;/
Your carrier pigeon eyes/Returned from the stars, sweetly.]

It is obvious that those four lines come down to two, and that the first
two have no *raison d'être* other than enabling the last two. These versifying
tricks are the same in this example of brash frills from a classic *milonga*:

Pejerrey con papas,
butifarra frita;
la china que tengo
nadie me la quita . . .

[Fish and potatoes fried/blood sausage fried/the honey I have/no one
else can have . . .]

I have already declared that all poetry is the confession of an I, a personality, a human adventure. The destiny thus revealed can be make-believe,
archetypal (novelizations like the *Quixote* or *Martín Fierro*, the protagonists
of Browning's soliloquies, the various versions of Faust), or personal: the
auto-novelizations of Montaigne, Thomas De Quincey, Walt Whitman, of
any real poet. I seek to achieve the latter.

How can we manage to illuminate the pathos of our lives? How can we
interject in the hearts of others our humiliating truth? The tools we use are
also hindrances: verse is a sing-song thing that clouds the meaning of
words; rhymes are puns, a kind of solemn wordplay; metaphor is a revoca-
tion of emphasis, a tradition of lies, a dumb thing no one takes seriously.
(And yet we cannot do without it: the "plain style" prescribed to us by
Manuel Gálvez is doubly metaphoric, because "style" means, etymologi-
cally, a pointed instrument, and "plain" is akin to a flat plain, smooth, without cracks. A plain style, a pointed instrument similar to the pampas. Who
can understand that?)

The variety of words is another error. All the academicians recommend
it, I think, mistakenly. I believe words must be conquered, lived, and that the
apparent publicity they receive from the dictionary is a falsehood. Nobody
should dare to write "outskirts" without having spent hours pacing their
high sidewalks; without having desired and suffered as if they were a lover;

without having felt their walls, their lots, their moons just around the corner from a general store, like a cornucopia. . . . I have now conquered my
poverty, recognizing among thousands the nine or ten words that get along
with my soul; I have already written more than one book in order to write,
perhaps, one page. The page that justifies me, that summarizes my destiny,
the one that perhaps only the attending angels will hear when Judgment
Day arrives.

Simply: the page that, at dusk, upon the resolved truth of day's end, at
sunset, with its dark and fresh breeze and girls glowing against the street, I
would dare to read to a friend.

[1926]   [SJL]

Literary Pleasure

I suspect that the detective novels of Eduardo Gutiérrez and a volume of Greek mythology and *The Student of Salamanca* and the reasonable and not at all fanciful fantasies of Jules Verne and Stevenson's grandiose romances and the first serial novel ever written, *The Thousand and One Nights*, are the greatest literary joys I have experienced. The list is diverse and cannot claim any unity other than the early age at which I read them. I was a hospitable reader in those days, a polite explorer of the lives of others, and I accepted everything with providential and enthusiastic resignation. I believed everything, even errata and poor illustrations. Each story was an adventure, and I sought worthy and prestigious places to live it: the highest step of a staircase, an attic, the roof of the house.

Then I discovered words: I discovered their receptive and even memorable readability, and harbored many printed in prose and verse. Some—still—accompany my solitude; the pleasure they inspired has become a second nature to me. Others have fallen mercifully from my memory, like *Don Juan Tenorio*, which I once knew by heart, and which the years and my indifference have uprooted. Gradually, through ineffable leaps of taste, I became familiar with literature. I am unable to remember the first time I read Quevedo, who is now the writer I most frequent. On the other hand, my first encounter with *Sartor Resartus* by the maniacal Thomas Carlyle was passionate—a book now huddled in some corner, which has been reading itself for years in my library. Later, I became worthy of writerly friendships that still honor me: Schopenhauer, Unamuno, Dickens, De Quincey, again Quevedo.

And today? I have turned into a writer, a critic, and I must confess (not without remorse and conscious of my deficiency) that I reread with the pleasure of remembering and that new readings do not enthrall me. Now I tend to dispute their novelty, to translate them into schools, influences, composites. I suspect that if they were sincere, all the critics in the world (and even some in Buenos Aires) would say the same. It is only normal: intelligence is economical and orderly, and a miracle strikes it as a bad habit. By admitting this I already disqualify myself.

Menéndez y Pelayo writes: "If poetry was not read with the eyes of history, so few poems would survive!" (*Historia de la poesía americana* II, 103). What seems a warning is a confession. Those often resurrected eyes of history, are they not but a network of sympathies, generosities, or simply courtesies? You may reply that without them, we would confuse the plagiarist with the inventor, the shadow with the body. Certainly, but one thing is the equitable distribution of glories, and another, pure aesthetic pleasure. I have observed with regret that any man, by merely perusing many volumes in order to judge them (and the critic's task is nothing else) can become a genealogist of styles and detective of influences. He inhabits this terrifying and almost inexpressible truth: Beauty in literature is accidental, depending on the harmony or discord of the words manipulated by the writer, and is not tied to eternity. Epigones, those who frequent already lyricized themes, usually achieve it; innovators, almost never.

Our indolence speaks of classical books, eternal books. If only some eternal book existed, primed for our enjoyment and whims, no less inventive in the populous morning as in the secluded night, oriented toward all hours of the world. Your favorite books, reader, are like the rough drafts of that book without a final reading.

If the attainments of the verbal beauty that art can provide us were infallible, non-chronological anthologies would exist, or even ones that would not mention the names of authors or of literary schools. The single evidence of each composition's beauty would be enough to justify it. Of course this behavior would be bizarre and even dangerous for those anthologies in use. How can we admire the sonnets of Juan Boscán if we do not know that they are the first to be borne by our language? How can we endure so-and-so's verse if we do not know that he has perpetrated many others that are even more flawed and that, moreover, he is a friend of the anthologist?

I fear you will not understood my point here, and so, at the risk of oversimplifying the matter, I will find an example. Let our illustration be this unfamiliar metaphor: "The fire, with ferocious jaws, devours the countryside." Is this phrase censurable or legitimate? That depends, I insist, solely on the one who forged it, and this is not a paradox. Let us suppose that in a café on the Calle Corrientes or on the Avenida 9 de Julio, a man of letters presents it to me as his own. I will think: Making metaphors is now a vulgar pastime; to substitute *swallow* for *burn* is not an auspicious exchange; the matter of jaws may amaze some people, but it is weak of the poet to allow himself to be carried away by the mechanical phrase "devouring fire"; in brief, nil. . . . Let us now suppose that it is presented to me as originating from a Chinese or Siamese poet. I will think: The Chinese turn everything into a dragon, and it will represent to me a clear fire like a celebration, slithering, which I will like. Let us suppose that the witness to a fire uses it, or even better, someone whose life was threatened by the flames. I will think: This concept of a fire with jaws is really a nightmarish horror, and adds a ghastly human evil to an unconscious event; the phrase is very strong, almost mythological. Let us suppose I am told that the father of this figure of speech is Aeschylus, and that it was uttered by Prometheus (which is true), and that the shackled titan, tied to a precipice of rocks by Force and Violence, those harsh ministers, declaimed it to the Ocean, an old gentleman who came to visit his misfortune on a winged chariot. Then the sentence would seem good, even perfect, given the extravagant nature of the speakers and its (already poetic) remote origin. I shall do as the reader, who has doubtlessly suspended his judgment, does, until confirming whose phrase it was.

I speak without intending any irony. Distance and antiquity (the emphases of space and time) pull on our hearts. Novalis has already uttered this truth, and Spengler was its grandiose advocate in his famous book. I want to discuss its relevance to literature, which is a paltry thing. If we are already sobered by the thought that men lived two thousand five hundred years ago, how could we not be moved to know that they made verses, were spectators of the world, that they sheltered in light, lasting words something of their ponderous, fleeting life, words that fulfill a long destiny?

Time, such a respected subversive, so famous for its demolitions and Italic ruins, also constructs. Upon Cervantes' lofty verse:

> *¡Vive Dios, que me espanta esta grandeza!*
> [By God, this greatness terrifies me!]

we see time refashioned and even notably widened. When the inventor and storyteller of *Don Quixote* wrote it, *"vive Dios"* was as ordinary an exclamation as "my goodness!" and "terrify" meant "astonish." I suspect that his contemporaries would have felt it to mean: "How this device astonishes me!" or something similar. It is firm and tidy in our eyes. Time—Cervantes' friend—has sagely revised his drafts.

Immortals have, generally, another destiny. The details of their feelings or thoughts tend to vanish or lie invisibly in their work, irretrievable and unsuspected. In contrast, their individuality (that simplified Platonic idea which they never purely possessed) fastens upon souls like a root: they become as impoverished and perfect as a cipher; they become abstractions. They are barely a bit of shadow, but they are so eternally. They fit too neatly into this phrase: Echoes remained, in the void of their majesty, not a whole voice, but merely the lingering absence of a word (Quevedo, *La hora de todos y la fortuna con seso*, episode XXXV). But there are many different immortalities.

A tender and sure immortality (attained sometimes by men who are ordinary but have an honest dedication and a lifelong fervor) is that of the poet whose name is linked to a place in the world. Such is the case of Burns, over the grazing lands of Scotland and unhurried rivers and little lambs; such is our Carriego's, prevailing in the shameful, furtive, almost buried outskirts of Palermo on the Southside, where an extravagant archeological effort can reconstruct the vacant lot whose current ruin is the house and the beverage store which has become an Emporium. Some are also immortalized in eternal things. The moon, springtime, the nightingales, all manifest the glory of Heinrich Heine; the sea that suffers grey skies, Swinburne; the long railway platforms and docks, Walt Whitman. But the best immortalities—those in the domain of passion—are still vacant. There is no poet who is the total voice of love, hate, or despair. That is, the great verses of humanity have still not been written. This imperfection should raise our hopes.

[1927]   *[SJL]*

An Investigation of the Word

I

I would like to proclaim one of the things of which I am ignorant, to publish a crucial indecision in my thinking, in order to see if some other doubter may help me to doubt, and the half-light we share turn into light. The subject is almost grammatical, which I announce as a warning to those readers who have condemned (in the name of friendship) my grammarianisms and requested a *human* work. I could answer that there is nothing more human (that is, less mineral, vegetal, animal, and even angelical) than grammar; but I understand and beg their indulgence this once. My joys and sufferings will be left for other pages, if anyone wishes to read them.

The crux of my meditation is this: What is the psychological process whereby we understand a sentence?

To examine this question (I dare not think to resolve it), let us analyze an ordinary sentence, not according to the (artificial) classifications recorded by diverse grammars, but rather in search of the content its words yield to its reader. Let this be a familiar, well-known sentence, whose meaning is absolutely clear: *"En un lugar de la Mancha, de cuyo nombre no quiero recordar"* [In a place in La Mancha, whose name I do not wish to recall] and the rest.

I shall proceed with the analysis:

En [in]. This is not a whole word, but the promise of others to come. It indicates that what immediately follows is not the main point in this context, but rather the location of the main point, be it in time or in space.

Un [a]. Properly speaking, this word declares the unity of the word it modifies. Here it does not. Here it announces a real existence, but one not particularly individuated or demarcated.

Lugar [place]. This is the word of location, promised by the particle *in.*

Its task is merely syntactical, not adding any representation to the one suggested by the two previous words. To represent oneself "in" and to represent oneself "in a place" is the same, as any "in" is in a place and implies this. You will reply that *place* is a noun, a thing, and that Cervantes did not write it to signify a portion of space but rather to mean "hamlet," " town," or "village." To the first, I will respond that it is risky to allude to *things in themselves*, after Mach, Hume, and Berkeley, and that, for a sincere reader, there is only a difference of emphasis between the preposition *in* and the noun *place;* in response to the second, the distinction is true, but only discernible later.

De [of]. This word is usually dependent, indicating possession. Here it is synonymous (somewhat unexpectedly) with *in.* Here it means that the scene of the still mysterious central statement of this clause is situated in turn somewhere else, which will be immediately revealed to us.

La [the]. This quasi-word (they tell us) is a derivation of *illa,* which meant "that" in Latin. That is, it was first a word of orientation, justified and almost animated by some gesture; now it is a ghost of *illa,* with no further task than to indicate a grammatical gender, an extremely asexual classification which ascribes virility to pins *("los" alfileres)* and not to lances *("las" lanzas).* (By the way, it is fitting to recall what Graebner wrote about grammatical gender: Nowadays the opinion prevails that, originally, the grammatical genders represented a scale of values, and that the feminine gender represents, in many languages—among them the Semitic—a value inferior to the masculine.)

Mancha. This name is variously representable. Cervantes wrote it so that its known reality would lend weight to the unheard-of reality of his Don Quixote. The ingenious nobleman has paid back the debt with interest: if the nations of the world have heard of La Mancha, it is his doing.

Does this mean that La Mancha was nominated because it already was a landscape for the novelist's contemporaries? I dare to assert the contrary: its reality was not visual, but sentimental; it was, irrevocably, irreconcilably, a dull provincial reality. They did not need to visualize it to understand: to say "La Mancha" was like saying "Pigüé" for us Argentines. The Castilian landscape at that time was one of Goethe's manifest mysteries *("offenbare Geheimnisse").* Cervantes did not see this: one need only consider the Italian-style countrysides he designated to make his novel more congenial. Quevedo was more erudite about Manchegan landscapes than he: read (in a letter addressed to Don Alonso Messía de Leiva) his harsh description that begins: "In La Mancha, in winter, where clouds and streams, which in other places produce poplar groves, create swamps and mudslides . . ." He ends, many lines later, with: "Dawn broke: how vile, it seems to me, for sunrise to remember such a place."

The detailed continuation of this analysis is useless. I will only note that the ending of the phrase in question is marked by a comma. This little curlicue indicates that the following locution ("whose name") must refer, not to La Mancha (whose name the author did wish to remember) but rather to the place. That is, this curlicue or orthographic sign or brief pause to summarize or atom of silence, does not differ substantively from a word. Commas are as intentional as words are tenuous.

Let us now examine the general matter.

The doctrine of every grammar I have consulted (even the extremely intelligent one by Andrés Bello) maintains that each individual word is a sign and denotes an autonomous idea. This doctrine is upheld by common consensus and fortified by the dictionaries. How can we deny that each word is a unit of thought if the dictionary (in alphabetical disorder) records, isolates, and without further consultation, defines them? Though an arduous undertaking, our inquiry is imposed by the previous analysis. It is impossible to believe that the single concept, *"En un lugar de la Mancha, de cuyo nombre no quiero acordarme,"* is composed of twelve ideas. Conversation would be the task of angels and not of men, if such were the case. It is not the case, and the proof is that the same concept fits in a larger or smaller number of words. *"En un pueblo manchego cuyo nombre no quiero recordar"* [In a Manchegan village whose name I don't want to recall] is the same, and there are nine signs instead of twelve. That is, words are not the reality of language: words—by themselves—do not exist.

This is the Crocian doctrine. To support it, Croce denies the parts of the sentence, ascertaining that they are an intrusion of logic, an insolence. The sentence (he argues) is indivisible, and the grammatical categories that disarm it are abstractions added onto reality. One thing is a spoken expression, and the other its posthumous elaboration into nouns or adjectives or verbs.

Manuel de Montolíu, in his discussion (and occasional refutation) of Croceism, elucidates and summarizes this thesis as follows, with an excess of mystery: "The only linguistic reality is the sentence. This concept of sentence has to be understood not in its grammatical sense, but in the sense of an organism expressive of a perfect meaning, whether in a simple exclamation or in a vast poem" (*El lenguaje como fenómeno estético*, Buenos Aires, 1926).

Psychologically, this Montolíu-Croce conclusion is unsustainable. Its concrete version would be: We do not understand first the preposition *in* and then the article *a* and then the noun *place* and then the preposition *in;* we prefer to take in, in a single act of cognition, the whole chapter and even the whole book.

It will be said that I am joking and that the intent of that doctrine is aesthetic, not psychological. To which I would respond that a psychological error cannot also be an aesthetic solution. Moreover, did not Schopenhauer already tell us that the shape of our intelligence is time, a thin line that only presents things to us one by one? The terrifying aspect of that narrowness is that the poems to which Montolíu-Croce allude reverently acquire unity in the frailty of our memory, but not in the successive task of the one who wrote them or the one who reads them. (I said terrifying, because that successive heterogeneity tears to bits not only those diffuse compositions, but all writing.) A close approach to that possible truth was the one argued by Poe in his essay on poetic principle, where he states that there are no long poems and that *Paradise Lost* is (effectively) a series of short compositions. I voice his opinion in my own words: If to maintain the unity of Milton's work, its effect or impression as a whole, we read it (as would be necessary) in one sitting, the result is only a continuous oscillation of excitement and discouragement. . . . From this it follows that the final, collective, or absolute effect of the best epic under the sun will forcibly be nothing, and that is the truth.

What opinion may we assume? The grammarians imply that we must spell out, word for word, comprehension; the followers of Croce, that we take it in with a single magical glance. I do not believe in either possibility. Spiller, in his beautiful Psychology (note that I use the epithet deliberately) formulates a third response. I will summarize it, though I know well that summaries add a false categorical and definitive air to whatever they condense.

Spiller observes the structure of sentences and dissociates them into small syntactical groups that correspond to units of representation. Thus, in the exemplary phrase we have taken apart, it is evident that the two words "La Mancha" are only one. It is obviously a proper noun, as indivisible in our consciousness as Castile or the Cinco Esquinas [Five Corners] or Buenos Aires. However, here the unit of representation is larger: it is the locution "in La Mancha," synonymous, we have already noted, with "Manchegan." (In Latin, the two formulas of possession coexisted and to say the valor of Caesar, there was *"virtus Caesarea"* and *"virtus Caesaris";* in Russian, any substantive noun is variable as an adjectival noun.) Another unit for comprehension is the locution *"no quiero acordarme"* [I do not wish to recall] to which we will add perhaps the word *de,* since the active verb *recordar* [to recall or remember] and the reflexive verb compounded by a preposition, *acordarse de* [to recall or remember] are only grammatically different. (A good proof of the arbitrariness of our writing is that we make *acordarme* [I remember] into a single word, and *me acuerdo* [I remember] into two.) Continuing the analysis, we will redistribute the sentence into four units: "In a place/in La Mancha/whose name/I do not wish to recall;" or "In a place in/ La Mancha /(whose name) I do not wish to recall."

I have applied (perhaps with excessive freedom) Spiller's introspective method. The other, the one which assures us that each word is significative, I have already reduced to its (careful, honest, involuntary) absurdity in the first half of this argument. I do not know if Spiller is right; it is enough for me to demonstrate the fine applicability of his thesis.

Let us move on to the much-discussed problem of whether the noun should follow the adjective (as in the Germanic languages) or the adjective follow the noun, as in Spanish. In England they are obliged to say a "brown horse"; we in Spanish are equally obliged to put the noun before the adjective. Herbert Spencer maintains that English syntax is more serviceable, and justifies it in this manner: It is enough to hear the word *caballo* [horse] in order to imagine it, and if afterward we are told it is brown, this addition does not always coincide with the image we already prefigured and tended to anticipate. That is, we will have to correct an image: a task that vanishes when the adjective is positioned in front. "Brown" is an abstract notion and merely prepares the consciousness.

Opponents may argue that the notions of "horse" and "brown" are equally concrete or equally abstract to the mind. The truth is, however, that the controversy is absurd: the amalgamated symbols *"caballo-colorado"* and "brown-horse" are already a unit of thought.

How many units of thought does language include? It is not possible to answer this question. For the chess player, the locutions "queen's gambit," "pawn to king's four," "knight to king's three check," are unities; for the beginner, they are phrases he gradually comprehends.

An inventory of all the representative units is impossible, as is their ordering or classification. To prove the latter is my immediate task.

II

The definition I shall give of the word is—like others—verbal, that is to say, also made of words, that is to say, wordy. We agree that a word's determining factor is its function as representative unit and how variable and contingent that function is. Thus *immanence* is a word for those who are trained in metaphysics, but it is a genuine locution for whoever hears it without knowing the word and must then break it into *in* and *manere:* "inside remain." ("*Innebleibendes Werk*," within-remained action, Master Eckhart translated with magnificent long-windedness.) Inversely, almost all sentences for single grammatical analysis, and true words—that is, representative units—are comprehensible for anyone who hears them often. To say, "In a place in La Mancha," is almost to say "village" or "hamlet"; to say

> *La codicia en las manos de la suerte*
> *se arroja al mar*
> [Greed in the hands of luck/plunges into the sea]

is to invite a single representation: distinct, of course, according to the listeners, but ultimately only one.

There are sentences that function like radicals, and from which others may always be deduced, with or without the intention to innovate, but of such a clearly derivative nature that they do not mislead anyone. Take the common locution "silver moon." It would be useless to try to make it new by changing the prefix, useless to write "golden moon" or "amber/stone/marble/earthen/sand/water/sulfur/desert/sugarcane/tobacco/iron moon." The reader—who, moreover, is already literate—will always suspect that we are playing at variations and feel—at the most!—an antithesis between the disillusioning prefixation of "earthen moon" or the possibly magical "water moon," and the well-known cliché. I will mention another case. It is a sentence by Joubert, cited favorably by Matthew Arnold (*Critical Essays* VII). It deals with Bossuet and is as follows: "More than a single man, he is human nature, with the moderation of a saint, the justice of a bishop, the prudence of a doctor, and the power of a great soul." Here Joubert played on variations with a certain insolence; he wrote (and perhaps thought) "the moderation of a saint," and immediately afterward the inevitability that there is in language took control of him and linked three more clauses, all filled with symmetry and an air of negligence. It is as if he stated, "With the moderation of a saint, the this of another, the whatever of a who knows what and the anything of a great soul." The original is no less vague than this framework; the intoned clauses of both correspond no longer to words but to emphatic simulations of words. If prose, with its minimal presence of rhythm, carries such servile baggage, what will verse not bring along? Poetry is always looking out for more to add simplemindedly and recklessly to that which has not gone bad.

Concerning definitions of the word: it is so imprecise that the heterodoxical concept defended here (word = representation) can fit into the sanctioned formula: "A word is a syllable or conjunction of syllables that exists independently and expresses an idea." That is the case, of course, as long as those conjunctions are not determined by the blank spaces in writing between pseudo-words. It is out of that orthographic hallucination that one surmises that, although *manchego* is one word, *de la Mancha* is three.

I spoke about language's fatality. A man, in a confidential outpouring of memories, tells of the fiancée he had, and praises her thus: "She was so pretty that . . ." and that conjunction, that insignificant particle, is already forcing him to hyperbolize, to lie, to invent a case. The writer says of a girl's eyes: "Eyes like . . ." and he finds it necessary to choose a special term of comparison. He forgets that poetry is realized through that "like," forgets that the single act of comparing (that is, of supposing difficult qualities that only through mediation allow themselves to be thought) is already poetry. He resigns himself to writing "eyes like suns." Linguistics disorders that phrase into two categories: semanthemes, words of representation (eyes, suns) and morphemes, the mere meshing of syntax. "Like" seems to be a morpheme even though the entire emotional climate of the phrase is determined by it. "Eyes like suns" seems to be an operation of his understanding, a problematic judgment which relates the concept of eyes with that of the sun. Anyone knows intuitively that this is wrong. He knows that he does not have to imagine the sun, and that the intention is to denote "eyes I wish had looked at me always," or rather "eyes with whose mistress I want to be." It is a phrase that drifts away from analysis.

A summary may be helpful. I have postulated two propositions, negatives of one another. One is the non-existence of the grammatical categories or parts of the sentence and the replacement of them with representative units, which can be a common word or many. (Representation does not have syntax. Perhaps someone will teach me not to confuse the flight of a bird with a bird that flies.) The other is the power of syntactical continuity over discourse. That power is shameful, as we know that syntax is nothing. The antimony is profound. Not to discover—not to be able to discover—the so-

lution, is the general tragedy of all writing. I accept that tragedy, that treacherous deviation of which we speak, that not thinking at all about anything.

Two attempts—both condemned to death—were made to save us. One was Llull's desperate endeavor to seek paradoxical refuge in the very heart of contingency; the other was Spinoza's. Llull—inspired by Jesus, they say—invented the so-called thinking machine, a kind of glorified lottery, though with a different mechanism; Spinoza did not postulate more than eight definitions and seven axioms to level the universe for us. As we can see, neither the latter with his geometric metaphysics nor the former with his alphabet translatable into words, and these into sentences, managed to elude language. Both systems were nourished by it. The only ones who can pass over it are the angels, who converse by intelligible species: that is, by means of direct representation and without any verbal efforts.

And those of us, never angels, who are verbal, who "on this low, relative ground" write, those of us who lowly imagine that ascending into print is the maximum reality of experiences? May resignation—the virtue to which we must resign ourselves—be with us. It will be our destiny to mold ourselves to syntax, to its treacherous chain of events, to the imprecision, the maybes, the too many emphases, the buts, the hemisphere of lies and of darkness in our speech. And to confess (not without some ironic deception) that the least impossible classification of our language is the mechanics of phrases, whether they be active, passive, gerund, impersonal, or other.

The difference among the styles is that of syntactical custom. It is obvious that upon the framework of a sentence many can be built. I already noted how "sand moon" came out of "silver moon"; the latter—through the possible collaboration of usage—could ascend from mere variation to autonomous representation. Language is nourished not by original intuitions—there are few—but by variations, happenstance, mischief. Language: to humbly speak thought.

One must not think of organizing according to kindred ideas. There are too many possible arrangements for any one of them to be unique. All ideas are akin or can be. Logical opposites can be synonymous words for art: their climate, their emotional temperature, are frequently shared. Out of this non-possibility of a psychological classification, I will not say more: the alphabetical organization (disorganization) of dictionaries clearly displays this deception. Fritz Mauthner (*Wörterbuch der Philosophie* I, 379–401) proves this with splendid sarcasm.

[1927]   [SJL/EW]

II

1929-1936

The Perpetual Race of Achilles and the Tortoise

The implications of the word *jewel*—precious little thing, delicate though not necessarily fragile, easy to transport, translucency that can also be impenetrable, ageless flower—make it pertinent here. I know of no better qualification for Achilles' paradox, so indifferent to the definitive refutations which have been nullifying it for over twenty-three centuries that we can already declare it immortal. The repeated tours of the mystery proposed by such endurance, the fine ignorance it has visited upon humanity, are gifts we have no choice but to accept gratefully. Let us revive it once more, if only to convince ourselves of perplexity and arcane intimations. I intend to devote a few pages—a few moments—to its presentation and most noteworthy revisions. Its inventor, as is well known, was Zeno of Elea, disciple of Parmenides, who denied that anything could happen in the universe.

The library has provided me with two versions of this glorious paradox. The first, from a very Spanish Spanish-American dictionary, can be reduced to this cautious observation: *Motion does not exist: Achilles could not catch up with the lazy tortoise.* I shall waive such restraint and seek out the less hurried exposition by G. H. Lewes, whose *Biographical History of Philosophy* was the first speculative reading to which vanity or curiosity (I'm not sure which) led me. I shall transcribe his exposition: Achilles, symbol of speed, has to catch up with the tortoise, symbol of slowness. Achilles runs ten times faster than the tortoise and so gives him a ten-meter advantage. Achilles runs those ten meters, the tortoise runs one; Achilles runs that meter, the tortoise runs a decimeter; Achilles runs that decimeter, the tortoise runs a centimeter; Achilles runs that centimeter, the tortoise runs a millimeter; Achilles the millimeter, the tortoise a tenth of the millimeter, and *ad infinitum,* so that Achilles can run forever without catching up. Hence the immortal paradox.

And now for the so-called refutations. The oldest—Aristotle's and Hobbes'—are implicit in the one formulated by John Stuart Mill. The problem, for him, is a mere example of the fallacy of confusion. He considers it nullified by the following argument:

At the conclusion of the sophism, *forever* means any imaginable lapse of time; under this premise, any number of subdivisions of time. It means that we can divide ten units by ten, and the quotient again by ten, as many times as we want, and that the subdivisions of the sequence have no end, nor consequently do those of the time in which it all occurs. But an unlimited number of subdivisions can occur within what is limited. The only infinity of duration the argument proves is contained in five minutes. As long as the five minutes are not over, whatever is left can be divided by ten, and again by ten, as many times as we like, which is compatible with the fact that the total duration is five minutes. This proves, in short, that crossing that finite space requires an infinitely divisible, but not infinite, time (Mill, *System of Logic* V, chap. 7).

I cannot predict the reader's opinion, but my feeling is that Mill's projected refutation is nothing more than an exposition of the paradox. Achilles' speed need only be set at a second per meter to determine the time needed:

$$10 + 1 + 1/10 + 1/100 + 1/1000 + 1/10000 \ldots$$

The limit of the sum of this infinite geometric progression is twelve (plus, exactly eleven and one-fifth; plus, exactly eleven times three twenty-fifths), but it is never reached. That is, the hero's course will be infinite and he will run forever, but he will give up before twelve meters, and his eternity will not see the end of twelve seconds. That methodical dissolution, that boundless descent into more and more minute precipices, is not really hostile to the problem; imagining it is the problem. Let us not forget, either, to visualize the runners diminishing, not only because of perspective but also because of the singular reduction required by their occupation of microscopic places. Let us also realize that those linked precipices corrupt space and, even more vertiginously, living time, in their desperate persecution of both immobility and ecstasy.

Another resolute refutation was divulged in 1910 by Henri Bergson, in his noteworthy *Essay on the Immediate Facts of Consciousness*, a title that begins by begging the question. Here is his page:

On the one hand, we attribute to motion the very divisibility of the space it traverses, forgetting that while an object can be divided, an action cannot. On the other hand, we are accustomed to projecting this very action upon space, applying it to the line traversed by the moving object, to giving it, in brief, solid form. Out of this confusion between motion and the space traversed are born, in our opinion, the sophisms of the Eleatic School: because the interval separating two points is infinitely divisible, and if motion were composed of parts as the interval is, the interval would never be traversed. But the truth is that each of Achilles' steps is a simple indivisible action, and that after a given number of these actions, Achilles would have gotten ahead of the tortoise. The Eleatic illusion came from identifying this series of individual actions *sui generis* with the homogeneous space that served as their stage. As such a space can be divided and reconstituted according to any law, they assumed the authority to redo Achilles' total movement, no longer with Achilles' steps but with tortoise steps. They replaced Achilles in pursuit of a tortoise with two tortoises at regular intervals from one another, two tortoises agreeing to make the same kind of steps or simultaneous actions so as never to catch up with each other. Why does Achilles get ahead of the tortoise? Because each of Achilles' steps and each of the tortoise's steps are indivisible as movements, and different magnitudes in space: so that it will not take long for the sum of space traversed by Achilles to be a superior length to the sum of space traversed by the tortoise and of the advantage the latter had over him. Which is what Zeno does not have in mind when reconstructing Achilles' motion according to the same law as the tortoise's motion, forgetting that only space lends itself to a mode of arbitrary construction and deconstruction, confusing it thus with motion. (*Immediate Facts*, Barnes' Spanish version, pp. 89–90. I've corrected, by the way, some obvious lapses by the translator.)

Bergson's argument is a compromise. He admits that space is infinitely divisible, but denies that time is. He displays two tortoises instead of one to distract the reader. He links a time and a space that are incompatible: the abrupt discontinuous time of William James, with its "perfect effervescence of newness," and the infinitely divisible space in common credence.

Here I reach, by elimination, the only refutation I know, the only inspiration worthy of the original, a virtue indispensable for the aesthetics of intelligence: the one formulated by Bertrand Russell. I found it in the noble work of William James (*Some Problems of Philosophy*) and the total conception it postulates can be studied in the previous books of its inventor—*Introduction to Mathematical Philosophy*, 1919; *Our Knowledge of the External World*, 1926—unsatisfactory, intense books, inhumanly lucid. For Russell, the operation of counting is (intrinsically) that of equating two series. For example, if the first-born sons of all the houses of Egypt were killed by the Angel, except those who lived in a house that had a red mark on the door, it is clear that as many sons were saved as there were red marks, and an enumeration of precisely how many of these there were does not matter. Here the quantity is indefinite; there are other operations in which it is infinite as well. The natural series of numbers is infinite, but we can demonstrate that, within it, there are as many odd numbers as even ones.

1	corresponds to	2
3	to	4
5	to	6, etc.

The proof is as irreproachable as it is banal, but does not differ from the following, in which there are as many multiples of 3018 as there are numbers.

1	corresponds to	3018
2	to	6036
3	to	9054
4	to	12072, etc.

The same can be asserted about its exponential powers, however rarified they become as we progress.

1	corresponds to	3018
2	to	3018^2 (9,108,324)
3	to	etc.

A jocose acceptance of these facts has inspired the formula that an infinite collection—that is, the series of natural numbers—is a collection whose members can in turn be broken down into infinite series. The part, in these elevated latitudes of numeration, is no less copious than the whole: the precise quantity of points in the universe is the same as in a meter in the universe, or in a decimeter, or in the deepest trajectory of a star. Achilles' problem fits within this heroic response. Each place occupied by the tortoise is in proportion to another occupied by Achilles, and the meticulous correspondence of both symmetrical series, point by point, serves to proclaim their equality. There does not remain one single periodic remnant of the initial advantage given to the tortoise. The final point in his course, the last in Achilles' course and the last in the time of the race, are terms which coincide mathematically: this is Russell's solution. James, without negating the technical superiority of *his* opponent, chooses to disagree. Russell's statements (he writes) elude the real difficulty concerning the *growing*, not the *stable*, category of infinity, the only one he takes into consideration when presuming that the race has been run and that the problem is to equilibrate the courses. On the other hand, two are not needed: the course of each runner or the mere lapse of empty time implies the difficulty of reaching a goal when a previous interval continues presenting itself at every turn, obstructing the way (*Some Problems of Philosophy* [1911], 181).

I have reached the end of my article, but not of our speculation. The paradox of Zeno of Elea, as James indicated, is an attempt upon not only the reality of space but the more invulnerable and sheer reality of time. I might add that existence in a physical body, immobile permanence, the flow of an afternoon in life, are challenged by such an adventure. Such a deconstruction, by means of only one word, *infinite*, a worrisome word (and then a concept) we have engendered fearlessly, once it besets our thinking, explodes and annihilates it. (There are other ancient punishments against commerce with such a treacherous word: there is the Chinese legend of the scepter of the kings of Liang, reduced to half its size by each new king. The scepter, mutilated by dynasties, still prevails.) My opinion, after the supremely qualified ones I have presented, runs the double risk of appearing impertinent and trivial. I will nonetheless formulate it: Zeno is incontestable, unless we admit the ideality of space and time. If we accept idealism, if we accept the concrete growth of the perceived, then we shall elude the *mise en abîme* of the paradox.

Would this bit of Greek obscurity affect our concept of the universe?—my reader will ask.

[*1929*]   [*SJL*]

The Duration of Hell

Hell has become, over the years, a wearisome speculation. Even its prosely-tizers have neglected it, abandoning the poor, but serviceable, human allu-sion which the ecclesiastic fires of the Holy Office once had in this world: a temporal torment, of course, but one that was not unworthy, within its ter-restrial limitations, of being a metaphor for the immortal, for the perfect pain without destruction that the objects of divine wrath will forever en-dure. Whether or not this hypothesis is satisfactory, an increasing lassitude in the propaganda of the institution is indisputable. (Do not be alarmed; I use *propaganda* here not in its commercial but rather its Catholic gene-alogy: a congregation of cardinals.) In the second century A.D., the Cartha-gian Tertullian could imagine Hell and its proceedings with these words:

> You who are fond of spectacles, expect the greatest of all spectacles, the last and eternal judgment of the universe. How shall I admire, how laugh, how rejoice, how exult, when I behold so many proud monarchs, and fancied gods, groaning in the lowest abyss of darkness; so many magistrates who persecuted the name of the Lord, liquefying in fiercer fires than they ever kindled against the Christians; so many sage philosophers blushing in red hot flames with their deluded scholars; so many celebrated poets trembling before the tribunal, not of Minos, but of Christ; so many tragedians, more tuneful in the expression of their own sufferings; so many dancers . . . (*De spectaculis*, 30; Gibbon's version.)

Dante himself, in his great effort to foresee, in an anecdotal way, some of the decisions of Divine Justice regarding northern Italy, did not know such enthusiasm. Later, the literary infernos of Quevedo—a mere opportunity for gossipy anachronisms—and of Torres Villarroel—a mere opportunity for metaphors—would only prove the increasing usury of dogma. The decline of Hell is in their works, as it is in Baudelaire, who was so skeptical about the perpetual torments that he pretended to adore them. (In a significant etymology, the innocuous French verb *gêner* [to bother] derives from that powerful Scriptural word, *Gehenna*.)

Let us consider Hell. The careless article on the subject in the *Hispano-American Encyclopedic Dictionary* is useful reading, not for its sparse information or terrified sacristan's theology but rather for the bewilderment it discloses. It begins by observing that the notion of Hell is not particular to the Catholic Church, a precaution whose intrinsic meaning is, *Don't let the Masons say the Church introduced these atrocities;* but this is immediately followed by the statement that Hell is dogma, and it quickly adds: "The unwithering glory of Christianity is that it brings to itself all the truths to be found scattered among the false religions." Whether Hell is a fact of natural religion, or only of revealed religion, I find no other theological assumption as fascinating or as powerful. I am not referring to the simplistic mythology of manure, roasting spits, fires, and tongs, which have gone on proliferating in the depths, and which all writers have repeated, to the dishonor of their imaginations and their decency.[1] I am speaking of the strict notion—*a place of eternal punishment for the wicked*—constituted by the dogma with no other obligation than placing it *in loco real*, in a precise spot, and *a beatorum sede distincto*, different from the place of the chosen. To imagine anything else would be sinister. In the fiftieth chapter of his *History*, Gibbon tries to diminish Hell's wonders and writes that the two populist ingredients of fire and darkness are enough to create a sensation of pain, which can then be infinitely aggravated by the idea of endless duration. This disgruntled objection proves perhaps that it is easy to design hell, but it does not mitigate the admirable terror of its invention. The attribute of eternity is what is horrible. The continuity—the fact that divine persecution knows no pause, that there is no sleep in Hell—is unimaginable. The eternity of that pain, however, is debatable.

There are two important and beautiful arguments that invalidate that eternity. The oldest is that of conditional immortality or annihilation.

---

[1]Nevertheless, the *amateur* of hells would do well not to ignore these honorable infractions: the Sabian hell, whose four superimposed halls admit threads of dirty water on the floor, but whose principal room is vast, dusty, and deserted; Swedenborg's hell, whose gloom is not perceived by the damned who have rejected heaven; Bernard Shaw's hell, in *Man and Superman,* which attempts to distract its inhabitants from eternity with the artifices of luxury, art, eroticism, and fame.

Immortality, according to its comprehensive logic, is not an attribute of fallen human nature, but of God's gift in Christ. It therefore cannot be used against the same individual upon whom it has been bestowed. It is not a curse but a gift. Whoever merits it, merits heaven; whoever proves unworthy of receiving it, "dies in death," as Bunyan wrote, dies without remains. Hell, according to this pious theory, is the blasphemous human name for the denial of God. One of its propounders was Whately, the author of that oft-remembered booklet *Historic Doubts Relative to Napoleon Bonaparte.*

A more curious speculation was presented by the evangelical theologian Rothe, in 1869. His argument—also ennobled by the secret mercy of denying infinite punishment for the damned—states that to eternalize punishment is to eternalize Evil. God, he asserts, does not want *that* eternity for His universe. He insists that it is scandalous to imagine that the sinful man and the Devil would forever mock God's benevolent intentions. (For theology, the creation of the world is an act of love. It uses the term *predestination* to mean "predestined to glory"; condemnation is merely the opposite, a non-choice translated into infernal torment that does not constitute a special act of divine goodness.) He advocates, finally, a declining, dwindling life for sinners. He foresees them roaming the banks of Creation, or the voids of infinite space, barely sustaining themselves with the leftovers of life. He concludes: As the devils are unconditionally distant from God and are unconditionally His enemies, their activity is against the kingdom of God, and they have organized themselves into a diabolical kingdom, which naturally must choose a leader. The head of that demoniacal government—the Devil—must be imagined as changing. The individuals who assume the throne of that kingdom eventually succumb to the ghostliness of their being, but they are succeeded by their diabolical descendants (*Dogmatik* I, 248).

I now reach the most incredible part of my task, the reasons contrived by humanity in favor of an eternal Hell. I will review them in ascending order of significance. The first is of a disciplinary nature: it postulates that the fearfulness of punishment lies precisely in its eternity, and that to place this in doubt undermines the efficacy of the dogma and plays into the Devil's hands. This argument pertains to the police and does not deserve to be refuted. The second argument is written thus: *Suffering should be infinite because so is the sin of offending the majesty of the Lord, an infinite Being.* It has been observed that this evidence proves so much that we can infer that it proves nothing: it proves that there are no venial sins and that all sins are unpardonable. I would like to add that this is a perfect case of Scholastic frivolity and that its trick is the plurality of meanings of the word *infinite,* which applied to the Lord means "unconditional," and to suffering means "perpetual," and to guilt means nothing that I can understand. Moreover, arguing that an error against God is infinite because He is infinite is like arguing that it is holy because God is, or like thinking that the injuries attributed to a tiger must be striped.

Now the third argument looms over me. It may, perhaps, be written thus: *Heaven and Hell are eternal because the dignity of free will requires them to be so; either our deeds transcend time, or the "I" is a delusion.* The virtue of this argument is not logic, it is much more: it is entirely dramatic. It imposes a terrible game on us: we are given the terrifying right to perdition, to persist in evil, to reject all access to grace, to fuel the eternal flames, to make God fail in our destiny, to be forever a shadow, *detestabile cum cacodaemonibus consortium* [in the detestable company of the devil]. Your destiny is real, it tells us; eternal damnation and eternal salvation are in your hands: this responsibility is your honor. A sentiment similar to Bunyan's: "God did not play in convincing me; the Devil did not play in tempting me; neither did I play when I sunk as into the bottomless pit, when the pangs of hell caught hold upon me; neither do I play in relating of them" (*Grace Abounding to the Chief of Sinners*, preface).

I believe that in our unthinkable destiny, ruled by such infamies as bodily pain, every bizarre thing is possible, even the perpetuity of a Hell, but that it is sacrilegious to believe in it.

Postscript. On this page filled with mere information, I can also report a dream. I dreamed I was awakening from another dream—an uproar of chaos and cataclysms—into an unrecognizable room. Day was dawning: light suffused the room, outlining the foot of the wrought-iron bed, the upright chair, the closed door and windows, the bare table. I thought fearfully, "Where am I?" and I realized I didn't know. I thought, "Who am I?" and I couldn't recognize myself. My fear grew. I thought: This desolate awakening is in Hell, this eternal vigil will be my destiny. Then I really woke up, trembling.

[1929] *[SJL/EW]*

The Superstitious Ethics of the Reader

The impoverished condition of our literature, its incapacity to attract readers, has produced a superstition about style, an inattentive reading that favors certain affectations. Those who condone this superstition reckon that style is not the effectiveness or ineffectiveness of a certain page but rather the writer's apparent skills: his analogies, acoustics, the rhythm of his syntax or punctuation. They are indifferent to their own convictions or feelings, and seek techniques (to quote Miguel de Unamuno) that will inform them whether or not this reading matter has the right to please them. They have heard that adjectives should not be trivial and think that a page is badly written if it does not provide startling liaisons between adjectives and nouns, even if it succeeds in fulfilling its intent. They have heard that brevity is a virtue and consider concise the use of ten short sentences rather than the command of one long locution. (Typical examples of this succinct charlatanism, or sententious frenzy, may be found in the speeches of Polonius, the famous Danish statesman in *Hamlet*, or even our native Polonius, Baltasar Gracián.) They have heard that the close repetition of syllables is cacophonic, and will pretend that in prose it hurts their ears, though it affords them a certain—I think also fake—pleasure in verse. In brief, their focus is on the effectiveness of the mechanism, not the disposition of its parts. They subordinate feelings to ethics, or rather to an irrefutable etiquette. This inhibition has become so widespread that, strictly speaking, there are no more readers left, only potential literary critics.

This superstition is so established that no one dares admit to an absence of style in compelling works, especially in the classics. There is no good book without its own style, which no one can deny—except its writer. Let us take the example of *Don Quixote*. Confronted with the proven excellence of this novel, Spanish literary critics have suppressed the thought that

Checked out ... summary

GARZON MARIA N

11-07-_ 12 11:40AM

BARCODE: R01_ _ _ 502
LOCATION: h.
TITLE: Bru_ _ : words fro_ _ _ _ _
DUE DATE: 1_ _ 2012

BARCODE: 33477476310_ _ _
LOCATION: hmntw
TITLE: _ _ _ _ movie _ _ / Roger Eber_
DUE _ _ _ _ _ _ _ _ _ _

BARCODE: 33477462151921
LOCATION: hmntw
TITLE: Nueva gramatica basica de la leng
DUE DATE: 12-19-2012 * RENEWED

BARCODE: R0111774285
LOCATION: hmntw
TITLE: Selected nonfictions / Jorge Luis
DUE DATE: 12-19-2012 * RENEWED

its greatest (and perhaps only irrefutable) worth may be its psychological acumen, and they ascribe to it a stylistic brilliance which many readers find mysterious. One need only review a few paragraphs of the *Quixote* to realize that Cervantes was not a stylist (at least in the current acoustical or decorative sense of the word) and that he was too interested in the destinies of Don Quixote and Sancho to allow himself to be distracted by his own voice. In his *Wit and the Art of Genius*, Baltasar Gracián—who lavished so much praise on other narrative prose, such as the chivalresque novel *Guzmán de Alfarache*—does not even mention *Don Quixote*. Quevedo farcically versified his death and then forgot all about him. One might object that these two examples are negative; in our own era, Leopoldo Lugones has criticized Cervantes explicitly: "Style is his weakness, and the damage caused by his influence has been severe. Colorless prose, redundancies, flimsy narrative structure, panting paragraphs unwinding in endless convolutions that never get to the point, and a complete lack of proportion comprise the legacy received by those who consider its style to be the immortal work's ultimate achievement; they have only scratched the surface whose rough edges hide its true strengths and flavor" (*El imperio jesuitico*, 59). Our own Groussac has declared: "If things are to be described as they are, we must admit that at least half of Cervantes' work has a weak, disheveled shape, which completely justifies his rivals' claim about his 'humble language.' I am referring not only to his verbal improprieties, intolerable repetitions and wordplays, to those overbearing moments of heavy-handed grandiloquence, but mostly to the generally bland texture of his post-prandial prose" (*Crítica literaria*, 41). Post-prandial prose, Cervantes' prose, spoken and not declaimed, was precisely what he needed. The same observation would be just, I believe, in the case of Dostoevsky, Montaigne, or Samuel Butler.

This vanity about style is couched in an even more pathetic conceit: perfection. There is not a single poet who, as minor as he may be, hasn't sculpted (the verb tends to figure in his conversation) the perfect sonnet, a minuscule monument that safeguards his possible immortality, and which the novelties and effacements of time will be obligated to respect. It is usually a sonnet without curlicues, though the whole thing is a curlicue, that is, a shred of futility. This everlasting fallacy (see Sir Thomas Browne's *Urn Burial*) has been formulated and recommended by Flaubert in the following sentence: "Correction (in the highest sense of the word) does to thinking what the waters of the Styx did with Achilles' body, that is, makes it invulnerable and indestructible" (*Correspondence* II, 199). His judgment is conclusive, but I personally have not experienced any confirmation. (I suppress the tonic virtues of the Styx, an infernal reference used for emphasis, not argument.) The perfect page, the page in which no word can be altered without harm, is the most precarious of all. Changes in language erase shades of meaning, and the "perfect" page is precisely the one that consists of those delicate fringes that are so easily worn away. On the contrary, the page that becomes immortal can traverse the fire of typographical errors, approximate translations, and inattentive or erroneous readings without losing its soul in the process. One cannot with impunity alter any line fabricated by Góngora (according to those who restore his texts), but *Don Quixote* wins posthumous battles against his translators and survives each and every careless version. Heine, who never heard it read in Spanish, acclaimed it for eternity. The German, Scandinavian, or Hindu ghost of the *Quixote* is more alive than the stylist's anxious verbal artifices.

I would not wish that the moral of this assertion be understood as desperation or nihilism. Nor do I wish to foment negligence, nor do I believe in a mystical virtue of the awkward locution and the shoddy epithet. I am stating that the voluntary emission of those two or three minor pleasures—the ocular distraction of metaphor, the auditory distraction of rhythm, and the surprises of an interjection or a hyperbaton—usually proves that the writer's overriding passion is his subject, and that is all. Genuine literature is as indifferent to a rough-hewn phrase as it is to a smooth sentence. Lean prosody is no less a stranger to art than is calligraphy, spelling, or punctuation, a fact which the judicial origins of rhetoric and the musical roots of song have always hidden. The most common literary mistake today is emphasis. Definitive words, words that postulate prophetic or angelic wisdom, or superhuman resolutions—*unique, never, always, all, perfection, finished*—are the habitual barter of *all* writers. They do not understand that overstating something is as inept as not saying it at all, and that readers sense the impoverishment caused by careless generalizations and amplifications. Such imprudence depletes the language. This has occurred in French, where the phrase "*Je suis navré*" really means "I won't be able to join you for tea," and where the verb for love, *aimer,* has been reduced to "like." The French tendency to exaggerate is also present in its written language; the heroically lucid and methodical Paul Valéry transcribes some forgettable and forgotten lines by La Fontaine and declares (to spite some opponent) that they are "the most beautiful verses in the world" (*Varieté*, 84).

I would now like to recall the future and not the past. Reading is now practiced in silence, a fortunate symptom. And there are mute readers of verse. From that discrete capacity to a purely ideographic writing—direct communication of experiences, not of sounds—there is an inexhaustible distance, though not as great as that of the future.

I reread these negative remarks and realize that I do not know whether music can despair of music or marble of marble. I do know that literature is an art that can foresee the time when it will be silenced, an art that can become inflamed with its own virtue, fall in love with its own decline, and court its own demise.

[1931]   *[SJL]*

Our Inabilities

This fractional note on the most apparently grievous characteristics of the Argentine requires a prior limitation. Its subject is the Argentine of the cities, the mysterious, everyday specimen who venerates the lofty splendor of the meat-packing and cattle-auctioning professions; who travels by bus, which he considers a lethal weapon; who despises the United States and celebrates the fact that Buenos Aires stands shoulder to shoulder with Chicago, homicidally speaking; who rejects the possibility of a Russian who is uncircumcised or hairless; who intuits a secret relationship between perverse or nonexistent virility and blond tobacco; who lovingly exercises the digital pantomime of the pseudo-serious; who on certain celebratory evenings engorges portions of digestive or evacuative or genetic apparatuses in traditional restaurants of recent apparition, called "grills"; who simultaneously prides himself on our "Latin idealism" and our "Buenos Aires shrewdness"; who naively believes only in shrewdness. I will not concern myself with the *criollo:* a maté-driven conversationalist and storyteller who is without racial obligations. The present-day *criollo*—the one from the province of Buenos Aires, at least—is a linguistic variation, a set of behaviors that is exercised at times to discomfort, at other times to please. An example is the aging gaucho, whose irony and pride represent a subtle form of servility, for they confirm his popular image. . . . The *criollo,* I think, needs to be studied in those regions where a foreign audience has not stylized or falsified him—for example, in Uruguay's northern provinces. I return, then, to our everyday Argentine. I will not inquire into his complete definition, but rather his most apparent traits.

The first is the poverty of his imagination. For the typical Argentine, anything irregular is monstrous—and therefore ridiculous. The dissident who lets his beard grow in an age of the clean-shaven, or is crowned by a top hat in a neighborhood of homburgs, is a wonder and an impossibility and a scandal for those who see him. In the music halls, the familiar types of the Spaniard from Galicia and the Italian immigrant are mere parodical opposites of the *criollo*. They are not evil—which would give them a kind of dignity—they are momentary objects of laughter, mere nobodies. They uselessly gesticulate: even the fundamental seriousness of death is denied them. The fantasy corresponds with crude precision to our false securities. *This,* for us, is the foreigner: an unforgivable, always mistaken, largely unreal creature. The ineptitude of our actors helps. Lately, after Buenos Aires' eleven good lads were mistreated by Montevideo's eleven bad lads, the worst foreigner of all has become the Uruguayan. When one lies to oneself and insists on irreconcilable differences with faceless outsiders, what becomes of the real people? It is impossible to admit them as responsible members of the world. The failure of that intense film *Hallelujah* to reach the audiences of this country—or rather, the failure of the audiences of this country to reach *Hallelujah*—was the inevitable combination of that incapacity (exacerbated in this case because the subjects were black) with another, no less deplorable or symptomatic: the incapacity to accept true fervor without mockery. This mortal and comfortable negligence of everything in the world that is not Argentine is a pompous self-valorization of the place our country occupies among the other nations. A few months ago, after the logical outcome of a gubernatorial election, people began talking about "Russian gold" as if the internal politics of a province of this faded republic would be even perceptible in Moscow, let alone of importance. A strong megalomaniacal will permits these legends. Our complete lack of curiosity is effusively displayed in all our graphic magazines, which are as ignorant of the five continents and the seven seas as they are solicitous toward the wealthy summer vacationers in Mar del Plata, the objects of their vile ardor, their veneration, and their vigilance. Not only is the general vision impoverished here, but also the domestic one. The native's map of Buenos Aires is well known: the Center, the Barrio Norte (aseptically omitting its tenements), the Boca del Riachuelo, and Belgrano. The rest is an inconvenient Cimmeria, a useless conjectural stop for the bus on its return trip to the outskirts.

The other trait I shall attempt to demonstrate is the unrestrainable delight in failure. In the movie houses of this city, crushed hopes are applauded in the merry balconies as if they were comic. The same occurs when there is a fight scene: the loser's humiliation is far more interesting than the winner's happiness. In one of von Sternberg's heroic films, the tall gangster Bull Weed staggers over the fallen streamers at the ruinous end of a party to kill his drunken rival, who, seeing the awkward but steadfast approach of Weed, runs for his life. The outbursts of laughter celebrating his terror remind us what hemisphere we are in. At the poorer movie houses, any hint of aggression is enough to excite the public. This ever-ready resentment had its joyous articulation in the imperative "*¡sufra!*" [suffer!], which has lately been retired from our lips, but not from our hearts. The interjection "*¡toma!*" [take it!] is also significant; it is used by Argentine women to crown any enumeration of splendors—for example, the opulent stages of a summer holiday—as if delights were measured by the envious irritation they produce. (We note, in passing, that the most sincere compliment in Spanish is "enviable.") Another illustration of the Buenos Airean's facility for hate is the considerable number of anonymous messages, among which we must now include the new auditory anonymity: the offensive telephone call, an invulnerable broadcast of insults. I do not know if this impersonal and modest literary genre is an Argentine invention, but it is practiced here often and enthusiastically. There are virtuosos in this capital who season the indecency of their vocatives with the studious untimeliness of the hour. Nor do our fellow citizens often forget that great speed may be a form of good breeding and that the insults shouted at pedestrians from a whizzing car maintain a general impunity. It is true that the recipient is equally anonymous and the brief spectacle of his rage grows smaller until it vanishes, but it is always a relief to insult. I will add another curious example: sodomy. In all the countries of the world, an indivisible reprobation falls back upon the two parties of that unimaginable contact. "Both of them have committed an abomination . . . their blood shall be upon them," says Leviticus. Not among the tough guys of Buenos Aires, who proclaim a kind of veneration for the active partner—because he took advantage of his companion. I submit this fecal dialectic to the apologists for "shrewdness," the wisecrack, and the backbite, which cover over so much hell.

A poverty of imagination and resentment define our place in death. The former is vouched for by a generalizing article by Unamuno on "The Imagination in Cochabamba"; the latter by the incomparable spectacle of a conservative government that is forcing the entire republic into socialism, merely to annoy and depress a centrist party.

I have been an Argentine for many generations and express these complaints with no joy.

[1931]   [EW]

The Postulation of Reality

Hume noted once and for all that Berkeley's arguments do not admit of the slightest reply and do not produce the slightest conviction; I would like to possess a no less cultured and lethal maxim with which to demolish the arguments of Croce. Hume's does not serve my purpose, for Croce's diaphanous doctrine does have the faculty of persuading, even if that is its only faculty. Its effect is to be unmanageable; it is good for cutting off a discussion, not for resolving one.

Its formula—my reader will recall—is the identical nature of the aesthetic and the expressive. I do not reject it, but I wish to observe that writers of a classical disposition tend rather to shun the expressive. The fact has not been given any consideration until now; I shall explain myself.

The romantic, generally with ill fortune, wishes incessantly to express; the classical writer rarely dispenses with a *petitio principii*—that is, some fundamental premise which is taken entirely for granted. I am diverting the words *classical* and *romantic* from all historical connotations; I use them to mean two archetypes of the writer (two procedures). The classical writer does not distrust language, but believes in the ample virtue of each of its signs. He writes, for example:

> After the departure of the Goths, and the separation of the allied army, Attila was surprised at the vast silence that reigned over the plains of Chalons: the suspicion of some hostile stratagem detained him several days within the circle of his wagons, and his retreat beyond the Rhine confessed the last victory which was achieved in the name of the Western empire. Meroveus and his Franks, observing a prudent distance, and magnifying the opinion of their strength by the numerous fires which they kindled every night, continued to follow the rear of the Huns till they reached the confines of Thuringia. The Thuringians

served in the army of Attila: they traversed, both in their march and in their return, the territories of the Franks; and it was perhaps in this war that they exercised the cruelties, which, about fourscore years afterwards, were revenged by the son of Clovis. They massacred their hostages, as well as their captives: two hundred young maidens were tortured with exquisite and unrelenting rage; their bodies were torn asunder by wild horses, or their bones were crushed under the weight of rolling wagons; and their unburied limbs were abandoned on the public roads, a prey to dogs and vultures. (Gibbon, *Decline and Fall of the Roman Empire* XXXV)

The clause "After the departure of the Goths" suffices to reveal the mediate character of this writing, generalized and abstract to the point of invisibility. The author presents us with a play of symbols, no doubt rigorously organized, but whose eventual animation is up to us. He is not really expressive; he does no more than record a reality, he does not represent one. The sumptuous events to whose posthumous allusion he summons us involved dense experiences, perceptions, reactions; these may be inferred from his narrative but are not present in it. To put it more precisely, he does not write reality's initial contacts, but its final elaboration in concepts. This is the classic method, the one perpetually followed by Voltaire, by Swift, by Cervantes. I shall copy down a second paragraph, at this point almost superfluous, from the last of these writers:

And thinking there was a necessity for shortening the siege, while this opportunity of Anselmo's absence lasted, Lothario assaulted Camilla's pride with the praises of her beauty; for nothing sooner succeeds in overthrowing the embattled towers of female vanity, than vanity itself, employed by the tongue of adulation: in short, he so assiduously undermined the fortress of her virtue, and plied it with such irresistible engines, that tho' she had been made of brass, she must have surrendered at mercy: he wept, entreated, promised, flattered, feigned and importuned, with such earnest expressions of love, as conquered all her reserve; at last, he obtained a complete triumph, which, tho' what he least expected, was what of all things, he most ardently desired. (*Don Quixote* I, chap. 34)

Passages like this one make up much the greater part of world literature, and the least worthless part, even now. To repudiate them so as not to inconvenience a formula would be impractical and ruinous. Within their obvious ineffectiveness, they are effective; this contradiction needs resolving.

I would recommend this hypothesis: imprecision is tolerable or plausible in literature because we almost always tend toward it in reality. The conceptual simplification of complex states is often an instantaneous operation. The very fact of perceiving, of paying attention, is selective; all attention, all focusing of our consciousness, involves a deliberate omission of what is not interesting. We see and hear through memories, fears, expectations. In bodily terms, unconsciousness is a necessary condition of physical acts. Our body knows how to articulate this difficult paragraph, how to contend with stairways, knots, overpasses, cities, fast-running rivers, dogs, how to cross the street without being run down by traffic, how to procreate, how to breathe, how to sleep, and perhaps how to kill: our body, not our intellect. For us, living is a series of adaptations, which is to say, an education in oblivion. It is admirable that the first news of Utopia Thomas More gives us is his puzzled ignorance of the "true" length of one of its bridges. . . .

I reread, in my investigation of the classic, the above paragraph by Gibbon, and I find an almost imperceptible and certainly harmless metaphor: the reign of silence. It is an initial gesture of expression—whether it falls short or is felicitous, I do not know—that appears not to conform to the strict legal execution of the rest of the prose. Of course, it is justified by its invisibility, its already conventional nature. Its use allows us to define another of the hallmarks of the classical: the belief that once an image has been brought into existence, it is public property. To the classical mind, the plurality of men and of eras is incidental; literature is always one and the same. The surprising defenders of Góngora exonerated him of the charge of innovation—by documenting the fine erudite lineage of his metaphors. They had not the slightest premonition of the romantic discovery of the personality. Now all of us are so absorbed in it that the fact of denying or neglecting it is only one of many clever ways of "being personal." With respect to the thesis that poetic language must be a single thing, we may note its evanescent resurrection by Arnold; he proposed to reduce the vocabulary of Homer's translators to that of the Authorized Version of the Scriptures, alleviated only by the eventual interpolation of certain liberties taken from Shakespeare. His argument was based on the power and dissemination of the biblical words. . . .

The reality offered up by classical writers is a question of confidence, just as paternity is for a certain character in the *Lehrjahre*. The reality the romantics seek to deplete is of a more overbearing nature; their continual method is emphasis, the partial lie. I shall not go looking for illustrations: every page of prose or verse that is professionally current can be examined with success in this respect.

The classic postulation of reality can take three forms, which are quite diversely accessible. The easiest consists of a general notification of the important facts. (Except for a few inconvenient allegories, the aforecited text by Cervantes is not a bad example of this first and spontaneous mode of the classical procedure.) The second consists of imagining a more complex reality than the one declared to the reader and describing its derivations and results. I know of no better illustration than the opening of Tennyson's heroic fragment *Morte d'Arthur*, which I reproduce here for the interest of its technique.

> So all day long the noise of battle roll'd
> Among the mountains by the winter sea;
> Until King Arthur's table, man by man,
> Had fallen in Lyonnesse about their Lord,
> King Arthur; then, because his wound was deep,
> The bold Sir Bedivere uplifted him,
> Sir Bedivere the last of all his knights,
> And bore him to a chapel nigh the field,
> A broken chancel with a broken cross,
> That stood on a dark strait of barren land.
> On one side lay the Ocean, and on one
> Lay a great water, and the moon was full.

Three times this narration has postulated a more complex reality: first, by the grammatical artifice of the adverb *so*; second (and better), by the incidental manner of transmitting a fact: "because his wound was deep"; third, by the unexpected addition of "and the moon was full." Another effective illustration of this method is supplied by Morris, who, after relating the mythical abduction of one of Jason's oarsmen by fleet-footed river divinities, closes the story in the following way:

> . . . the gurgling river hid
> The flushed nymphs and the heedless sleeping man.
> But ere the water covered them, one ran
> Across the mead and caught up from the ground
> The brass-bound spear, and buckler bossed and round,

The ivory-hilted sword, and coat of mail,
Then took the stream; so what might tell the tale,
Unless the wind should tell it, or the bird
Who from the reed these things had seen and heard?

This final testimony by beings previously unmentioned is, for us, the important part.

The third method, the most difficult and effective of them all, makes use of the invention of circumstances. A certain very memorable detail in Enrique Larreta's *La gloria de Don Ramiro* can serve as an example: the appetizing "bacon broth, served in a tureen with a padlock to protect it from the voracity of the pages," so suggestive of genteel poverty, the line of servants, the big old house full of stairways and turns and varying light. I have given a brief and linear example, but I know of extensive works—Wells' rigorous imaginative novels[1] and those of Daniel Defoe, exasperatingly plausible—which make frequent use of no other procedure than an unfolding or series of those laconic details with broad implications. I shall say the same of the cinematographic novels of Josef von Sternberg, which are also made up of significant moments. This is an admirable and difficult method, but its general applicability makes it less strictly literary than the two previous ones, particularly the second, which often functions by pure syntax, pure verbal dexterity. As is proven by these lines from Moore:

---

[1] *The Invisible Man*, for example. This character—a solitary chemistry student in the desperate London winter—must finally acknowledge that the privileges of invisibility do not make up for the inconveniences. He must go naked and barefoot, so as not to panic the city with the sight of a scurrying overcoat and a pair of autonomous boots. A revolver in his transparent hand is impossible to conceal. So are the foods he swallows, before they are digested. From sunrise on, his so-called eyelids do not block out the light, and he must get used to sleeping as if with his eyes open. It is just as useless to throw his phantasmal arm over his eyes. In the street, traffic accidents fix upon him and he is always in fear of being run over and killed. He must flee London. He must take refuge in wigs, in pince-nez made with smoked glass, in carnivalesque noses, suspicious beards, and gloves . . . *so that no one will see that he is invisible.* Once found out, he begins a miserable Reign of Terror in a wretched little village far from the sea. In order to make others respect him, he wounds a man. Then the police commissioner has him hunted down by dogs; he is cornered near the train station, and killed.

Another highly skilled example of such circumstantial phantasmagoria is Kipling's tale, "The Finest Story in the World," in the 1893 collection *Many Inventions.*

Je suis ton amant, et la blonde
Gorge tremble sous mon baiser
[I am your lover, and the blond/Throat trembles beneath my kiss]

whose virtue resides in the transition from the possessive pronoun to the direct article, the surprising use of *la*. Their symmetrical opposite is found in the following line from Kipling:

Little they trust to sparrow—dust that stop the seal in his sea!

Naturally, the antecedent of "his" is "seal": "dust that stop the seal in *his* sea."

[*1931*]   [*EA*]

A Defense of Basilides the False

In about 1905, I knew that the omniscient pages (*A* to *All*) of the first volume of Montaner and Simón's *Hispano-American Encyclopedic Dictionary* contained a small and alarming drawing of a sort of king, with the profiled head of a rooster, a virile torso with open arms brandishing a shield and a whip, and the rest merely a coiled tail, which served as a throne. In about 1916, I read an obscure passage in Quevedo: "There was the accursed Basilides the heresiarch. There was Nicholas of Antioch, Carpocrates and Cerinthus and the infamous Ebion. Later came Valentinus, he who believed sea and silence to be the beginning of everything." In about 1923, in Geneva, I came across some heresiological book in German, and I realized that the fateful drawing represented a certain miscellaneous god that was horribly worshiped by the very same Basilides. I also learned what desperate and admirable men the Gnostics were, and I began to study their passionate speculations. Later I was able to investigate the scholarly books of Mead (in the German version: *Fragmente eines verschollenen Glaubens*, 1902) and Wolfgang Schultz (*Dokumente der Gnosis*, 1910), and the articles by Wilhelm Bousset in the *Encyclopedia Britannica*. Today I would like to summarize and illustrate one of their cosmogonies: precisely that of Basilides the heresiarch. I follow entirely the account given by Irenaeus. I realize that many doubt its accuracy, but I suspect that this disorganized revision of musty dreams may in itself be a dream that never inhabited any dreamer. Moreover, the Basilidean heresy is quite simple in form. He was born in Alexandria, they say a hundred years after the Cross, they say among the Syrians and the Greeks. Theology, then, was a popular passion.

In the beginning of Basilides' cosmogony there is a God. This divinity majestically lacks a name, as well as an origin; thus his approximate name, *pater innatus*. His medium is the *pleroma* or plenitude, the inconceivable museum of Platonic archetypes, intelligible essences, and universals. He is an immutable God, but from his repose emanated seven subordinate divinities who, condescending to action, created and presided over a first heaven. From this first demiurgic crown came a second, also with angels, powers, and thrones, and these formed another, lower heaven, which was the symmetrical duplicate of the first. This second conclave saw itself reproduced in a third, and that in another below, and so on down to 365. The lord of the lowest heaven is the God of the Scriptures, and his fraction of divinity is nearly zero. He and his angels founded this visible sky, amassed the immaterial earth on which we are walking, and later apportioned it. Rational oblivion has erased the precise fables this cosmogony attributes to the origin of mankind, but the example of other contemporary imaginations allows us to salvage something, in however vague and speculative a form. In the fragment published by Hilgenfeld, darkness and light had always coexisted, unaware of each other, and when they finally saw each other, light looked and turned away, but darkness, enamored, seized its reflection or memory, and that was the beginning of mankind. In the similar system of Satornilus, heaven grants the worker-angels a momentary vision, and man is fabricated in its likeness, but he drags himself along the ground like a viper until the Lord, in pity, sends him a spark of his power. What is important is what is common to these narratives: our rash or guilty improvisation out of unproductive matter by a deficient divinity. I return to Basilides' history. Cast down by the troublesome angels of the Hebrew God, low humanity deserved the pity of the timeless God, who sent it a redeemer. He was to assume an illusory body, for the flesh degrades. His impassive phantasm hung publicly on the cross, but the essence of Christ passed through the superimposed heavens and was restored to the *pleroma*. He passed through them unharmed, for he knew the secret names of their divinities. "And those who know the truth of this history," concludes the profession of faith translated by Irenaeus, "will know themselves free of the power of the princes who built this world. Each heaven has its own name and likewise each angel and lord and each power of the heaven. He who knows their incomparable names will pass through them invisibly and safely, as the redeemer did. And as the Son was not recognized by anyone, neither shall the Gnostic be. And these mysteries shall not be pronounced, but kept in silence. Know them all, that no one shall know thee."

The numeric cosmogony of the beginning degenerates toward the end into numeric magic: 365 levels of heaven, at 7 powers per heaven, require the improbable retention of 2,555 oral amulets: a language that the years reduced to the precious name of the redeemer, which is Caulacau, and to that of the immobile God, which is Abraxas. Salvation, for this disillusioned heresy, involves a mnemotechnical effort by the dead, much as the torment of the Savior is an optical illusion—two simulacra which mysteriously harmonize with the precarious reality of their world.

To scoff at the fruitless multiplication of nominal angels and reflected symmetrical heavens in that cosmogony is not terribly difficult. Occam's restrictive principle, "*Entia non sunt multiplicanda praeter necessitatem*" [What can be done with fewer is done in vain with more], could be applied—to demolish it. For my part, I believe such rigor to be anachronistic or worthless. The proper conversion of those heavy, wavering symbols is what matters. I see two intentions in them: the first is a commonplace of criticism; the second—which I do not presume to claim as my discovery—has not, until now, been emphasized. I shall begin with the more obvious. It is a quiet resolution of the problem of evil by means of a hypothetical insertion of a gradual series of divinities between the no less hypothetical God and reality. In the system under examination, these derivations of God dwindle and weaken the further they are removed from God, finally reaching the bottom with the abominable powers who scratched out mankind from base matter. In the account of Valentinus—who did *not* claim the sea and silence to be the beginning of everything—a fallen goddess (Achamoth) has, by a shadow, two sons who are the founder of the world and the devil. An intensification of the story is attributed to Simon Magus: that of having rescued Helen of Troy, formerly first-born daughter of God and later condemned by the angels to painful transmigrations, from a sailors' brothel in Tyre.[1] The thirty-three human years of Jesus Christ and his slow extinguishing on the cross were not sufficient expiation for the harsh Gnostics.

There remains to consider the other meaning of those obscure inventions. The dizzying tower of heavens in the Basilidean heresy, the proliferation of its angels, the planetary shadow of the demiurges disrupting earth, the machinations of the inferior circles against the *pleroma*, the dense population, whether inconceivable or nominal, of that vast mythology, also point to the diminution of this world. Not our evil, but our central insignificance,

---

[1] Helen, dolorous daughter of God. That divine filiation does not exhaust the connections of her legend to that of Christ. To the latter the followers of Basilides assigned an insubstantial body; of the tragic queen it was claimed that only her *eidolon* or simulacrum was carried away to Troy. A beautiful specter redeemed us; another led to battles and Homer. See, for this Helenaic Docetism, Plato's *Phaedrus*, and Andrew Lang, *Adventures among Books*, 237–248.

is predicated in them. Like the grandiose sunsets on the plains, the sky is passionate and monumental and the earth is poor. That is the justification for Valentinus' melodramatic cosmogony, which spins an infinite plot of two supernatural brothers who discover each other, a fallen woman, a powerful mock intrigue among the bad angels, and a final marriage. In this melodrama or serial, the creation of the world is a mere aside. An admirable idea: the world imagined as an essentially futile process, like a sideways, lost glimpse of ancient celestial episodes. Creation as a chance act.

The project was heroic; orthodox religious sentiment and theology violently repudiated that possibility. The first creation, for them, was a free and necessary act of God. The universe, as St. Augustine would have it understood, did not begin in time, but rather simultaneously with it—a judgment which denies all priority to the Creator. Strauss claims as illusory the hypothesis of an initial moment, for that would contaminate with temporality not only the succeeding moments but also the "precedent" of eternity.

In the first centuries of our era, the Gnostics disputed with the Christians. They were annihilated, but we can imagine their possible victory. Had Alexandria triumphed and not Rome, the bizarre and confused stories that I have summarized would be coherent, majestic, and ordinary. Lines such as Novalis' "Life is a sickness of the spirit,"[2] or Rimbaud's despairing "True life is absent; we are not in the world," would fulminate from the canonical books. Speculations, such as Richter's discarded theory about the stellar origin of life and its chance dissemination on this planet, would know the unconditional approval of pious laboratories. In any case, what better gift can we hope for than to be insignificant? What greater glory for a God than to be absolved of the world?

[1932]   [EW]

---

[2]That dictum—*"Leben ist eine Krankheit des Geistes, ein leidenschaftliches Tun"*— owes its diffusion to Carlyle, who emphasized it in his famous article in the *Foreign Review*, 1829. Not merely a momentary coincidence, but rather an essential rediscovery of the agonies and enlightenments of Gnosticism, is the *Prophetic Books* of William Blake.

The Homeric Versions

No problem is as consubstantial to literature and its modest mystery as the one posed by translation. The forgetfulness induced by vanity, the fear of confessing mental processes that may be divined as dangerously commonplace, the endeavor to maintain, central and intact, an incalculable reserve of obscurity: all watch over the various forms of direct writing. Translation, in contrast, seems destined to illustrate aesthetic debate. The model to be imitated is a visible text, not an immeasurable labyrinth of former projects or a submission to the momentary temptation of fluency. Bertrand Russell defines an external object as a circular system radiating possible impressions; the same may be said of a text, given the incalculable repercussions of words. Translations are a partial and precious documentation of the changes the text suffers. Are not the many versions of the *Iliad*—from Chapman to Magnien—merely different perspectives on a mutable fact, a long experimental game of chance played with omissions and emphases? (There is no essential necessity to change languages; this intentional game of attention is possible within a single literature.) To assume that every recombination of elements is necessarily inferior to its original form is to assume that draft nine is necessarily inferior to draft H—for there can only be drafts. The concept of the "definitive text" corresponds only to religion or exhaustion.

The superstition about the inferiority of translations—coined by the well-known Italian adage—is the result of absentmindedness. There is no good text that does not seem invariable and definitive if we have turned to it a sufficient number of times. Hume identified the habitual idea of causality with that of temporal succession. Thus a good film, seen a second time, seems even better; we tend to take as necessity that which is no more than repetition. With famous books, the first time is actually the second, for we begin them already knowing them. The prudent common phrase "rereading the classics" is the result of an unwitting truth. I do not know if the statement "In a place in La Mancha, whose name I don't wish to recall, there lived not long ago a nobleman who kept a lance and shield, a greyhound and a skinny old nag" would be considered good by an impartial divinity; I only know that any modification would be sacrilegious and that I cannot conceive of any other beginning for the *Quixote*. Cervantes, I think, ignored this slight superstition and perhaps never noted that particular paragraph. I, in contrast, can only reject any divergence. The *Quixote*, due to my congenital practice of Spanish, is a uniform monument, with no other variations except those provided by the publisher, the bookbinder, and the typesetter; the *Odyssey*, thanks to my opportune ignorance of Greek, is an international bookstore of works in prose and verse, from Chapman's couplets to Andrew Lang's "Authorized Version" or Bérard's classic French drama or Morris' vigorous *saga* or Butler's ironic bourgeois novel. I abound in the mention of English names because English literature has always been amicable toward this epic of the sea, and the series of its versions of the *Odyssey* would be enough to illustrate the course of its centuries. That heterogenous and even contradictory richness is not attributable solely to the evolution of the English language, or to the mere length of the original, or to the deviations or diverse capacities of the translators, but rather to a circumstance that is particular to Homer: the difficult category of knowing what pertains to the poet and what pertains to the language. To that fortunate difficulty we owe the possibility of so many versions, all of them sincere, genuine, and divergent.

I know of no better example than that of the Homeric adjectives. The divine Patroclus, the nourishing earth, the wine-dark sea, the solid-hoofed horses, the damp waves, the black ship, the black blood, the beloved knees, are recurrent expressions, inopportunely moving. In one place, he speaks of the "rich noblemen who drink of the black waters of the Aesopos"; in another, of a tragic king who, "wretched in delightful Thebes, governed the Cadmeans by the gods' fatal decree." Alexander Pope (whose lavish translation we shall scrutinize later) believed that these irremovable epithets were liturgical in character. Rémy de Gourmont, in his long essay on style, writes that at one time they must have been incantatory, although they no longer are so. I have preferred to suspect that these faithful epithets were what prepositions still are: modest and obligatory sounds that usage adds to certain words and upon which no originality may be exercised. We know that it is correct to go "on foot" and not "with foot." The rhapsodist knew that the correct adjective for Patroclus was "divine." Neither case is an aesthetic proposition. I offer these speculations without enthusiasm; the only certainty is the impossibility of separating what pertains to the author from what pertains to the language. When we read, in Agustín Moreto (if we must read Agustín Moreto):

> *Pues en casa tan compuestas*
> *¿Qué hacen todo el santo día?*
> [At home so elegant/What do they do the whole blessed day?]

we know that the holiness of the day is an instance of the Spanish language, and not of the writer. With Homer, in contrast, we remain infinitely ignorant of the emphases.

For a lyric or elegiac poet, our uncertainty about his intentions could be devastating, but not for a reliable expositor of vast plots. The events of the *Iliad* and the *Odyssey* amply survive, even though Achilles and Odysseus, what Homer meant by naming them, and what he actually thought of them have all disappeared. The present state of his works is like a complex equation that represents the precise relations of unknown quantities. There is no possible greater richness for the translator. Browning's most famous book consists of ten detailed accounts of a single crime by each of those implicated in it. All of the contrast derives from the characters, not from the events, and it is almost as intense and unfathomable as that of ten legitimate versions of Homer.

The beautiful Newman-Arnold debate (1861–62), more important than either of its participants, extensively argued the two basic methods of translation. Newman defended the literal mode, the retention of all verbal singularities; Arnold, the strict elimination of details that distract or detain the reader, the subordination of the Homer who is irregular in every line to the essential or conventional Homer, one composed of a syntactical simplicity, a simplicity of ideas, a flowing rapidity, and loftiness. The latter method provides the pleasures of uniformity and nobility; the former, of continuous and small surprises.

I would like to consider the various fates of a single passage from Homer. These are the events recounted by Odysseus to the ghost of Achilles in the city of the Cimmerians, on the night without end, and they concern Achilles' son Neoptolemus (*Odyssey* XI). Here is Buckley's literal version:

> But when we had sacked the lofty city of Priam, having his share and excellent reward, he embarked unhurt on a ship, neither stricken with the

sharp brass, nor wounded in fighting hand to hand, as oftentimes happens in war; for Mars confusedly raves.

That of the equally literal but archaicizing Butcher and Lang:

But after we had sacked the steep city of Priam, he embarked unscathed with his share of the spoil, and with a noble prize; he was not smitten with the sharp spear, and got no wound in close fight: and many such chances there be in war, for Ares rageth confusedly.

Cowper in 1791:

At length when we had sack'd the lofty town
Of Priam, laden with abundant spoils
He safe embark'd, neither by spear of shaft
Aught hurt, or in close fight by faulchion's edge
As oft in war befalls, where wounds are dealt
Promiscuous, at the will of fiery Mars.

Pope's 1725 version:

And when the Gods our arms with conquest crown'd
When Troy's proud bulwarks smok'd upon the ground,
Greece to reward her soldier's gallant toils
Heap'd high his navy with unnumber'd spoils.
Thus great in glory from the din of war
Safe he return'd, without one hostile scar;
Tho' spears in the iron tempests rain'd around,
Yet innocent they play'd and guiltless of a wound.

George Chapman in 1614:

. . . In the event,
High Troy depopulate, he made ascent
To his fair ship, with prise and treasure store
Safe; and no touch away with him he bore
Of far-off-hurl'd lance, or of close-fought sword,
Whose wounds for favours and war doth oft afford,
Which he (though sought) miss'd in war's closest wage.
In close fights Mars doth never fight, but rage.

And Butler in 1900:

> Yet when we had sacked the city of Priam he got his handsome share of the prize money and went on board (such is the fortune of war) without a wound upon him, neither from a thrown spear nor in close combat, for the rage of Mars is a matter of great chance.

The first two versions—the literal ones—may be moving for a variety of reasons: the reverential mention of the sacking of the city, the ingenuous statement that one is often injured in war, the sudden juncture of the infinite disorders of battle in a single god, the fact of madness in a god. Other, lesser pleasures are also at work: in one of the texts I've copied, the excellent pleonasm of "embarked on a ship"; in another, the use of a copulative conjunction for the causal in "and many such chances there be in war."[1] The

---

[1]Another of Homer's habits is the fine abuse of adversative conjunctions. Here are some examples:

"Die, but I shall receive my own destiny wherever Zeus and the other immortal gods desire" (*Iliad* XXII).

"Astyokhe, daughter of Aktor: a modest virgin when she ascended to the upper rooms of her father's dwelling, but secretly the god Ares lay beside her" (*Iliad* II).

"[The Myrmidons] were like wolves carnivorous and fierce and tireless, who rend a great stag on a mountainside and feed on him, but their jaws are reddened with blood" (*Iliad* XVI).

"Zeus of Dodona, god of Pelasgians, O god whose home lies far! Ruler of wintry harsh Dodona! But your ministers, the Selloi, live with feet unwashed, and sleep on the hard ground" (*Iliad* XVI).

"Be happy, lady, in this love, and when the year passes you will bear glorious children, for the couplings of the immortals are not without issue. But you must look after them, and raise them. Go home now and hold your peace and tell nobody my name, but I tell it to you; I am the Earthshaker Poseidon" (*Odyssey* XI).

"After him I was aware of powerful Herakles; his image, that is, but he himself among the immortal gods enjoys their festivals, married to sweet-stepping Hebe, child of great Zeus and Hera of the golden sandals" (*Odyssey* XI).

I shall add the flamboyant translation that George Chapman did of this last passage:

> Down with these was thrust
> The idol of the force of Hercules,
> But his firm self did no such fate oppress.
> He feasting lives amongst th'immortal States
> White-ankled Hebe and himself made mates
> In heav'nly nuptials. Hebe, Jove's dear race
> And Juno's whom the golden sandals grace.

third version, Cowper's, is the most innocuous of all: it is as literal as the requirements of Miltonic stresses permit. Pope's is extraordinary. His luxuriant language (like that of Góngora) may be defined by its unconsidered and mechanical use of superlatives. For example: the hero's single black ship is multiplied into a fleet. Always subject to this law of amplification, all of his lines fall into two large classes: the purely oratorical ("And when the Gods our arms with conquest crown'd") or the visual ("When Troy's proud bulwarks smok'd upon the ground"). Speeches and spectacles: that is Pope. The passionate Chapman is also spectacular, but his mode is the lyric, not oratory. Butler, in contrast, demonstrates his determination to avoid all visual opportunities and to turn Homer's text into a series of sedate news items.

Which of these many translations is faithful? my reader will want to know. I repeat: none or all of them. If fidelity refers to Homer's imaginations and the irrecoverable men and days that he portrayed, none of them are faithful for us, but all of them would be for a tenth-century Greek. If it refers to his intentions, then any one of the many I have transcribed would suffice, except for the literal versions, whose virtue lies entirely in their contrast to contemporary practices. It is not impossible that Butler's unruffled version is the most faithful.

[1932]   [EW]

Narrative Art and Magic

The techniques of the novel have not, I believe, been analyzed exhaustively. A historical reason for this continued neglect may be the greater antiquity of other genres, but a more fundamental reason is that the novel's many complexities are not easily disentangled from the techniques of plot. Analysis of a short story or an elegy is served by a specialized vocabulary and facilitated by the pertinent quotation of brief passages; the study of the novel, however, lacks such established terms, and the critic is hard put to find examples that immediately illustrate his arguments. I therefore beg indulgence for the documentation that follows.

I shall first consider the narrative features we find in William Morris' *The Life and Death of Jason* (1867). My aim is literary, not historical; I deliberately exclude any study of the poem's Hellenic affiliation. I shall observe, however, that the ancients—including Apollonius of Rhodes—had long since set the Argonauts' deeds to verse; there is an intermediate version dating from 1474, *Les Faits et prouesses du noble et vaillant chevalier Jason*, not to be found in Buenos Aires, of course, but which scholars may readily consult in English.

Morris' difficult task was the realistic narration of the fabulous adventures of Jason, king of Iolchos. Line-by-line virtuosity, common in lyrical poetry, was impossible in a narrative of over ten thousand lines. The fable required, above all, a strong appearance of factual truth, in order to achieve that willing suspension of disbelief which, for Coleridge, is the essence of poetic faith. Morris succeeded, and I would like to determine how.

Take this example from Book I: Aeson, the old king of Iolchos, gives his son over to the charge of Chiron the centaur. The problem lies in making the centaur believable, and Morris solves it almost unwittingly: mentioning this mythical race, at the outset, among the names of other strange wild beasts, he states flatly, "Where bears and wolves the centaurs' arrows find."

This first incident is followed some thirty lines later by another reference that precedes any actual description. The old king orders a slave to take the child to the forest at the foot of the mountains, and to blow on an ivory horn to call forth the centaur—who will be, he says, "grave of face and large of limb"—and to fall upon his knees before him. He continues issuing commands until we come to a third and somewhat negative mention of the centaur, whom the king bids the slave not to fear. Then, troubled by the fate of the son he is about to lose, Aeson tries to imagine the boy's future life in the forests among the "quick-eyed centaurs"—an epithet that brings them to life and is justified by their widespread fame as archers.[1] The slave rides off with the son, and comes to the edge of a forest at dawn. He dismounts, carrying the child, and makes his way on foot among the oaks. There he blows the horn and waits. A blackbird is singing that morning, but the man can already make out the sound of approaching hoofs; the fear in his heart distracts him from the child, who has been trying to grab hold of the glittering horn. Chiron appears. We are told that he was a mighty horse, once roan but now almost white, with long grey locks on his head and a wreath of oak leaves where man was joined to beast. The slave falls to his knees. We note, in passing, that Morris need not impart to the reader his image of the centaur, nor even invite us to have our own. What is required is that we believe in his words, as we do the real world.

We find the same persuasive method employed in the episode of the sirens, in Book XIV, though in a more gradual fashion. A series of sweet images precedes the actual appearance of these divinities: a gentle sea, an orange-scented breeze, the insidious music first recognized by the sorceress Medea and reflected in the sailors' happy faces before any of them becomes fully conscious of what they hear, the true-to-life detail of their barely perceiving the words, expressed indirectly:

> And by their faces could the queen behold
> How sweet it was, although no tale it told,
> To those worn toilers o'er the bitter sea.

The sirens, finally glimpsed by the oarsmen, still keep their distance, as these lines imply:

---

[1] Cf. *Inferno* IV, 123: "*Cesare armato con gli occhi grifagni*" [Caesar armed with the eyes of a hawk].

> . . . for they were near enow
> To see the gusty wind of evening blow
> Long locks of hair across those bodies white,
> With golden spray hiding some dear delight.

This last detail, the "golden spray"—from their wild locks of hair, the waves, either or both—"hiding some dear delight" serves another intent as well: signifying the sirens' erotic allure. This twofold meaning returns a few lines later, when their bodies are hidden by the tears of longing that cloud the men's eyes. (Both artifices belong to the same order as the wreath of leaves in the depiction of the centaur.) Driven to raging despair, Jason calls the sirens "sea-witches" and prompts sweet-voiced Orpheus to sing.[2] A contest of song ensues, and with striking honesty Morris forewarns us that the songs he attributes to the unkissed mouths of the sirens and to Orpheus are no more than a transfigured memory of those remote melodies. The very precision of Morris' colors—the yellow rims of the shore, the golden spray, the grey cliffs—moves us, for they seem salvaged intact from that ancient evening. The sirens sing seductively of a bliss as vague as the waves: "Such bodies garlanded with gold,/So faint, so fair, shall ye behold . . ." Orpheus counters, singing the joys of *terra firma*. The sirens promise a languid undersea heaven, "roofed over by the changeful sea," as (2,500 years later, or only 50?) Paul Valéry would reiterate. They sing on, and Orpheus' corrective song is faintly contaminated by their deadly sweetness. At last the Argonauts slip out of danger, the contest is over, and a long wake lies behind the ship; but one tall Athenian dashes back between the rows of oarsmen to the poop and dives into the waters.

---

[2]Throughout time, the sirens have changed form. Their first chronicler, the bard of the twelfth book of the *Odyssey*, does not tell us how they were; for Ovid they are reddish-plumed birds with virginal faces; for Apollonius of Rhodes, women from the waist up, the rest, a bird; for the playwright Tirso de Molina (and for heraldry), "half women, half-fish." No less disputable is their species; the classical dictionary of Lemprière considers them nymphs, in Quicherat's they are monsters and in Grimal's they are demons. They dwell on an island in the west, near Circe's isle, but the corpse of one of them, Parthenope, was found in Campania, and her name given to the famous city now called Naples; the geographer Strabo saw her tomb and witnessed the gymnastic games and the race with torches, periodically celebrated to honor her memory.

The *Odyssey* tells that the sirens attracted and led sailors astray and that Ulysses, to hear their song and not perish, plugged with wax the ears of his oarsmen and ordered that they tie him to the mast. To tempt him, the sirens promised him knowledge of all things in the world:

Now to another work of fiction: Poe's *Narrative of Arthur Gordon Pym* (1838). This novel's secret theme is the terror and vilification of whiteness. Poe invents tribes who live near the Antarctic Circle, neighbors of an inexhaustible white continent who, for generations, have been exposed to the terrible visitations of men and driving white storms. White is anathema to these natives, and I must admit that by the last lines of the last chapter it is also anathema to the appreciative reader. This novel has two plots: the high-seas adventure is more immediate, while the other, inexorable and secretive, expands until revealed at the very end. "Naming an object," Mallarmé is said to have said, "is to suppress three-fourths of the joy of reading a poem, which resides in the pleasure of anticipation, as a dream lies in its suggestion." I refuse to believe that such a scrupulous writer would have composed the numerical frivolity of "three-fourths," but the general idea suits Mallarmé, as he illustrated in his two-line ellipse on a sunset:

Till now none sail'd this way, but stopt to hear
Our honied accents warble in his ear:
But felt his soul with pleasing raptures thrill'd:
But found his mind with stores of knowledge fill'd.
We know whate'er the kings of mighty name
Achiev'd at Ilion in the field of Fame;
Whate'er beneath the sun's bright journey lies.
O stay and learn new wisdom from the wise!
(*Odyssey* XII, tr. Pope).

A tradition gathered by the mythologist Apollodorus, in his *Bibliotheke*, tells that Orpheus, from the ship of the Argonauts, sang more sweetly than the sirens, who then threw themselves into the sea and turned into rocks, because their law was to die when no one felt bewitched by them. The Sphinx, too, leaped from on high when her riddle was answered.

In the sixth century, a siren was captured and baptized in northern Wales, and became a saint in certain ancient almanacs, under the name of Murgan. Another, in 1403, passed through an opening in a dike and lived in Haarlem until the day of her death. Nobody understood her, but they taught her to weave and she worshiped, as if by instinct, the cross. A sixteenth-century chronicler argued that she was not a fish because she knew how to weave, and that she was not a woman because she could live in the water.

In English, the classical siren is different than those with fish tails (mermaids). The formation of the latter kind had been influenced by the analogous Tritons, divinities of the court of Poseidon.

In the tenth book of Plato's *Republic*, eight sirens preside over the rotation of the eight concentric heavens.

"Siren: supposed sea beast," we read in a blunt dictionary.

Victorieusement fut le suicide beau
Tison de gloire, sang par écume, or, tempête!
[Victorious was the beautiful suicide/Firebrand of glory, blood-orange foam, gold, tempest!]

It was inspired, no doubt, by the *Narrative of Arthur Gordon Pym.* The impersonal color white itself—is it not utterly Mallarmé? (I feel that Poe chose this color intuitively, or for the same reasons later given by Melville in the chapter "The Whiteness of the Whale" of his equally brilliant and hallucinatory *Moby-Dick.*) It is impossible to illustrate or analyze here Poe's whole novel; let me merely cite a single feature (subordinate, like all its details, to the covert theme), related to the dark tribesmen mentioned above and the streams found on their island. To have specified that these waters were red or blue would have been to deny too openly any image of whiteness. With his resolution of the problem, Poe enriches us:

On account of the singular character of the water, we refused to taste it, supposing it to be polluted. . . . I am at loss to give a distinct idea of the nature of this liquid, and cannot do so without many words. Although it flowed with rapidity in all declivities where common water would do so, yet never, except when falling in a cascade, had it the customary appearance of limpidity. It was, nevertheless, in point of fact, as perfectly limpid as any limestone water in existence, the difference being only in appearance. At first sight, and especially in cases where little declivity was found, it bore resemblance, as regards consistency, to a thick infusion of gum-arabic in common water. But this was only the least remarkable of its extraordinary qualities. It was not colorless, nor was it of any one uniform color—presenting to the eye, as it flowed, every possible shade of purple, like the hues of a changeable silk. . . . Upon collecting a basinful, and allowing it to settle thoroughly, we perceived that the whole mass of liquid was made up of a number of distinct veins, each of a distinct hue; that these veins did not commingle; and that their cohesion was perfect in regard to their own particles among themselves, and imperfect in regard to neighboring veins. Upon passing the blade of a knife athwart the veins, the water closed over it immediately, as with us, and also, in withdrawing it, all traces of the passage of the knife were instantly obliterated. If, however, the blade was passed down accurately between the two veins, a perfect separation was effected, which the power of cohesion did not immediately rectify.

From the foregoing examples it can be inferred that the main problem of the novel is causality. One kind of novel, the ponderous psychological variety, attempts to frame an intricate chain of motives similar to those of real life. This type, however, is not the most common. In the adventure novel, such cumbersome motivation is inappropriate; the same may be said for the short story and for those endless spectacles composed by Hollywood with silvery images of Joan Crawford, and read and reread in cities everywhere. They are governed by a very different order, both lucid and primitive: the primeval clarity of magic.

This ancient procedure, or ambition, has been reduced by Frazer to a convenient general law, the law of sympathy, which assumes that "things act on each other at a distance" through a secret sympathy, either because their form is similar (imitative or homeopathic magic) or because of a previous physical contact (contagious magic). An example of the second is Kenelm Digby's ointment, which was applied not to the bandaged wound but to the offending weapon that inflicted it, leaving the wound, free of harsh and barbarous treatments, to heal itself. Of the first kind of magic there are numerous instances. The Indians of Nebraska donned creaking buffalo robes, horns, and manes, and day and night beat out a thunderous dance in order to round up buffalo. Medicine men in central Australia inflict a wound on their forearms to shed blood so that the imitative or consistent sky will shed rain. The Malayans often torment or insult a wax image so that the enemy it resembles will die. Barren women in Sumatra adorn and cuddle a wooden doll in their laps so that their wombs will bear fruit. For the same reasons of semblance, among the ancient Hindus the yellow root of the curcuma plant was used to cure jaundice, and locally in Argentina, a tea made of nettles was used to cure hives. A complete list of these atrocious, or ridiculous, examples is impossible; I think, however, that I have cited enough of them to show that magic is the crown or nightmare of the law of cause and effect, not its contradiction. Miracles are no less strange in this universe than in that of astronomers. It is ruled by all of the laws of nature as well as those of imagination. To the superstitious, there is a necessary link not only between a gunshot and a corpse but between a corpse and a tortured wax image or the prophetic smashing of a mirror or spilled salt or thirteen ominous people around a table.

That dangerous harmony—a frenzied, clear-cut causality—also holds sway over the novel. Saracen historians, whose works are the source of José Antonio Conde's *Historia de la dominación de los árabes en España*, do not write that a king or caliph died, but that "he was delivered unto his final reward or prize" or that "he passed into the mercy of the All-Powerful," or that "he awaited his fate so many years, so many moons, and so many days." This fear that a terrible event may be brought on by its mere mention is out of place or pointless in the overwhelming disorder of the real world, but not in a novel, which should be a rigorous scheme of attentions, echoes, and affinities. Every episode in a careful narrative is a premonition. Thus, in one of Chesterton's phantasmagorias, a man suddenly pushes a stranger off the road to save him from an oncoming truck; this necessary but alarming violence foreshadows the later act of a declaration of insanity so that he may not be hanged for a murder. In another Chesterton story, a vast and dangerous conspiracy consisting of a single man (aided by false beards, masks, and aliases) is darkly heralded by the couplet:

> As all stars shrivel in the single sun,
> The words are many, but The Word is one.

which is unraveled at the end through a shift of capital letters:

> The words are many, but the word is One.

In a third story, the initial pattern—the passing mention of an Indian who throws his knife at another man and kills him—is the complete reverse of the plot: a man stabbed to death by his friend with an arrow beside the open window of a tower. A flying knife, a plunged arrow: these words have a long repercussion. Elsewhere, I have pointed out that the single preliminary mention of stage sets taints with a disquieting unreality the depictions of dawn, the pampas, and nightfall which Estanislao del Campo has worked into his *Fausto*. Such a teleology of words and episodes is also omnipresent in good films. At the beginning of *The Showdown*, a pair of adventurers plays a game of cards to win a prostitute, or a turn at her; at the end, one of them has gambled away the possession of the woman he really loves. The opening dialogue of *Underworld* concerns stool pigeons; the opening scene, a gunfight on an avenue: these details prefigure the whole plot. In *Dishonored*, there are recurring motifs: the sword, the kiss, the cat, betrayal, grapes, the piano. But the most perfect illustration of an autonomous orb of omens, confirmations, and monuments is Joyce's preordained *Ulysses*. One need only examine Stuart Gilbert's study or, in its absence, the vertiginous novel itself.

I shall try to summarize the foregoing. I have described two causal procedures: the natural or incessant result of endless, uncontrollable causes and effects; and magic, in which every lucid and determined detail is a prophecy. In the novel, I think that the only possible integrity lies in the latter. Let the former be left to psychological simulations.

[1932]   *[SJL]*

A Defense of the Kabbalah

Neither the first time it has been attempted, nor the last time it will fail, this defense is distinguished by two facts. One is my almost complete ignorance of the Hebrew language; the other, my desire to defend not the doctrine but rather the hermeneutical or cryptographic procedures that lead to it. These procedures, as is well known, include the vertical reading of sacred texts, the reading referred to as *boustrophedon* (one line from left to right, the following line from right to left), the methodical substitution of certain letters of the alphabet for others, the sum of the numerical value of the letters, etc. To ridicule such operations is simple; I prefer to attempt to understand them.

It is obvious that their distant origin is the concept of the mechanical inspiration of the Bible. That concept, which turns the evangelists and prophets into God's impersonal secretaries, taking dictation, is found with imprudent energy in the *Formula consensus helvetica,* which claims authority for the consonants in the Scriptures and even for the diacritical marks—which did not appear in the earliest versions. (This fulfillment, in man, of God's literary intentions is *inspiration* or *enthusiasm:* words whose true meaning is "to be possessed by a god.") The Muslims can boast of exceeding this hyperbole, as they have decided that the original Koran—the Mother of the Books—is one of God's attributes, like His pity or His wrath, and they consider it to be older than speech, older than Creation. Similarly, there are Lutheran theologians who dare not include the Scriptures among created things, and define them as an incarnation of the Spirit.

Of the Spirit: here we touch on a mystery. Not the divinity in general, but rather the third hypostasis of the divinity was the One who dictated the Bible. This is the common belief. Bacon, in 1625, wrote: "The pen of the Holy Spirit hath laboured more over Job's affliction than over Solomon's good fortune."[1] And his contemporary John Donne: "The Holy Spirit is an eloquent writer, a vehement and copious writer, but not verbose, as removed from an impoverished style as from a superfluous one."

It is impossible to both name the Spirit and silence the horrendous threefold society of which it is part. Lay Catholics consider it a collegial body that is infinitely correct but also infinitely boring; the liberals, a useless theological Cerberus, a superstition which the numerous advances of the century will soon abolish. The Trinity, of course, surpasses these formulas. Imagined all at once, its concept of a father, a son, and a ghost, joined in a single organism, seems like a case of intellectual teratology, a monster which only the horror of a nightmare could spawn. This is what I believe, although I try to bear in mind that every object whose end is unknown to us is provisionally monstrous. This general observation is obstructed, however, by the professional mystery of the object.

Disentangled from the concept of redemption, the distinction of three persons in one must seem arbitrary. Considered as a necessity of faith, its fundamental mystery is not lessened, but its intention and uses are blunted. We understand that to renounce the Trinity—or at least the Duality—is to turn Jesus into the accidental delegate of the Lord, a historical incident, not the imperishable, constant receiver of our devotion. If the Son is not also the Father, then redemption is not a direct divine act; if He is not eternal, then neither will be the sacrifice of having come down to man and died on the cross. "Nothing less than infinite excellence could atone for a soul lost for infinite ages," insisted Jeremy Taylor. Thus one may justify the dogma, even if the concepts of the Son generated by the Father, and the Spirit proceeding from the two, heretically imply a priority, not to mention their guilty condition as mere metaphors. Theology, determined to differentiate the two, resolves that there is no reason for confusion because one results in the Son, and the other in the Spirit. An eternal generation of the Son, an eternal issue of the Spirit, is Irenaeus' grim conclusion: the invention of an act outside of time, a mutilated *zeitloses Zeitwort* that we can reject or worship, but not discuss. Hell is merely physical violence, but the three inextricable persons import an intellectual horror, a strangled, specious infinity like facing mirrors. Dante depicted them as a reverberation of diaphanous multicolored circles; Donne, as entangled serpents, thick and inseparable.

---

[1] In the Latin version: *"diffusius tractavit Jobi afflictiones."* In English, he had written with greater success, "hath laboured more."

"*Toto coruscat trinitas mysterio,*" wrote St. Paulinus; the Trinity shines in full mystery.

If the Son is God's reconciliation with the world, the Spirit—the beginning of sanctification, according to Athanasius; an angel among the others, for Macedonius—may best be defined as God's intimacy with us, His immanence in our breast. (For the Socinians—I fear with good reason—it was no more than a personified expression, a metaphor for divine action, that was later dizzyingly elaborated.) Whether or not a mere syntactical formality, what is certain is that the third blind person of the entangled Trinity is the recognized author of the Scriptures. Gibbon, in the chapter of his work that deals with Islam, includes a general census of the publications of the Holy Spirit, modestly calculated at a hundred and some; but the one which interests me now is Genesis: the subject matter of the Kabbalah.

The Kabbalists believed, as many Christians now do, in the divinity of that story, in its deliberate writing by an infinite intelligence. The consequences of such an assumption are many. The careless dispatch of an ordinary text—for example, journalism's ephemeral statements—allows for a considerable amount of chance. It communicates—postulates—a fact: it reports that yesterday's always unusual assault took place on such-and-such a street, at such-and-such a corner, at such-and-such an hour of the morning; a formula which represents no one, which limits itself to indicating such-and-such a place about which news was supplied. In such indications, the length and sound of the paragraphs are necessarily accidental. The contrary occurs in poetry, whose usual law is the subjection of meaning to euphonic needs (or superstitions). What is accidental in them is not the sound, but the meaning. It is thus in the early Tennyson, in Verlaine, in Swinburne's later works: dedicated only to the expression of general states by means of the rich adventures of their prosody. Let us consider a third writer: the intellectual. In his handling of prose (Valéry, De Quincey) or of verse, he has certainly not eliminated chance, but he has denied it as much as possible, and restricted its incalculable compliance. He remotely approximates the Lord, for Whom the vague concept of chance holds no meaning. The Lord, the perfected God of the theologians, Who sees all at once *(uno intelligendi actu),* not only all the events of this replete world but also those that would take place if even the most evanescent—or impossible—of them should change.

Let us imagine now this astral intelligence, dedicated to manifesting itself not in dynasties or annihilations or birds, but in written words. Let us also imagine, according to the pre-Augustinian theory of verbal inspiration, that God dictates, word by word, what he proposes to say.[2] This premise (which was the one postulated by the Kabbalists) turns the Scriptures into an absolute text, where the collaboration of chance is calculated at zero. The conception alone of such a document is a greater wonder than those recorded in its pages. A book impervious to contingencies, a mechanism of infinite purposes, of infallible variations, of revelations lying in wait, of superimpositions of light. . . . How could one not study it to absurdity, to numerical excess, as did the Kabbalah?

[1932]   *[EW]*

---

[2]Origen attributed three meanings to the words of the Scriptures: the historical, the moral, and the mystical, corresponding to the body, the soul, and the spirit which make up man; John Scotus Erigena, an infinite number of meanings, like the iridescence of a peacock's feathers.

The Art of Verbal Abuse

A conscientious study of other literary genres has led me to believe in the greater value of insult and mockery. The aggressor, I tell myself, knows that the tables will be turned, and that "anything you say may be used against you," as the honest constables of Scotland Yard warn us. That fear is bound to produce special anxieties, which we tend to disregard on more comfortable occasions. The critic would like to be invulnerable, and sometimes he is. After comparing the healthy indignations of Paul Groussac with his ambiguous eulogies (not to mention the similar cases of Swift, Voltaire, and Johnson), I nourished or inspired in myself that hope of invulnerability. It vanished as soon as I left off reading those pleasant mockeries in order to examine Groussac's method.

I immediately noticed one thing: the fundamental injustice and delicate error of my conjecture. The practical joker proceeds carefully, like a gambler admitting the fiction of a pack of cards, a corruptible paradise of two-headed people. The three kings of poker are meaningless in *truco*. The polemicist is also a creature of convention. For most people, the street formulas of insult offer a model of what polemics can become. The man in the street guesses that all people's mothers have the same profession, or he suggests that they move immediately to a general place that has several names, or he imitates a rude sound. A senseless convention has determined that the offended one is not himself but rather the silent and attentive listener. Language is not even needed. For example, Sampson's "I will take the wall of any man or maid of Montague's" or Abram's "Do you bite your thumb at us, sir?" were the legal tender of the troublemaker, around 1592, in Shakespeare's fraudulent Verona and in the beer halls, brothels, and bear-baiting pits of London. In Argentine schools, the middle finger and a show of tongue serve that purpose.

"Dog" is another very general term of insult. During the 146th night of

The Thousand and One Nights, the discreet reader learns that the son of Adam, after locking the son of the lion in a sealed chest, scolded him thus: "Oh dog of the desert . . . Fate hath upset thee, nor shall caution set thee up."

A conventional alphabet of scorn also defines polemicists. The title "sir," unwisely and irregularly omitted in spoken intercourse, is scathing in print. "Doctor" is another annihilation. To refer to the sonnets "perpetrated by Doctor Lugones" is equivalent to branding them as eternally unspeakable, and refuting each and every one of their metaphors. At the first mention of "Doctor," the demigod vanishes and is replaced by a vain Argentine gentleman who wears paper collars, gets a shave every other day, and is in danger of dying at any moment of a respiratory ailment. What remains is the central and incurable futility of everything human. But the sonnets also remain, their music awaiting a reader. An Italian, in order to rid himself of Goethe, concocted a brief article where he persisted in calling him *"il signore Wolfgang."* This was almost flattery, since it meant that he didn't know there were solid arguments against Goethe.

Perpetrating a sonnet, concocting an article. Language is a repertory of these convenient snubs which are the ordinary currency of controversy. To say that a literary man has let loose a book, or cooked it up, or ground it out, is an easy temptation. The verbs of bureaucrats or storekeepers are much more effective: dispatch, circulate, expend. Combine these dry words with more effusive ones, and the enemy is doomed to eternal shame. To a question about an auctioneer who also used to recite poetry, someone quickly responded that he was energetically raffling off the *Divine Comedy*. The witticism is not overwhelmingly ingenious, but its mechanism is typical. As with all witticisms, it involves a mere confusion. The verb *raffling* (supported by the adverb *energetically*) leaves one to understand that the incriminated gentleman is an irreparable and sordid auctioneer, and that his Dantesque diligence is an outrage. The listener readily accepts the argument because it is not presented as an argument. Were it correctly formulated, he would have to refute its validity. First of all, declaiming and auctioneering are related activities. Secondly, the old vocation of declaiming, an exercise in public speaking, could help the auctioneer at his task.

One of the satirical traditions (not despised by Macedonio Fernández, Quevedo, or George Bernard Shaw) is the unconditional inversion of terms. According to this famous prescription, doctors are inevitably accused of promoting contagion and death, notaries of theft, executioners of encouraging longevity, tellers of adventure stories of numbing or putting the reader to sleep, wandering Jews of paralysis, tailors of nudism, tigers and cannibals of preferring a diet of rhubarb. A variety of that tradition is the innocent phrase that pretends at times to condone what it is destroying. For example: "The famous camp bed under which the general won the battle." Or: "The last film of the talented director René Clair was utterly charming. When we woke up . . ."

Another handy method is the abrupt change. For instance: "A young priest of Beauty, a mind illuminated by Hellenic light, an exquisite man with the taste (of a mouse)." Similarly, these Andalusian lyrics, which quickly pass from inquiry to assault:

> *Veinticinco palillos*
> *Tiene una silla.*
> *¿Quieres que te la rompa*
> *En las costillas?*

[Twenty-five sticks/Makes a chair./Would you like me to break it/Over your ribs?]

Let me insist on the formal aspects of this game, its persistent and illicit use of confusing arguments. Seriously defending a cause and disseminating burlesque exaggerations, false generosity, tricky concessions, and patient contempt are not incompatible, but are so diverse that no one, until now, has managed to put them all together. Here are some illustrious examples: Set to demolish Ricardo Rojas' history of Argentine literature, what does Paul Groussac do? The following, which all Argentine men of letters have relished: "After resignedly hearing the two or three fragments in cumbersome prose of a certain tome publicly applauded by those who had barely opened it, I now consider myself authorized not to continue any further, contenting myself, for now, with the summaries or indexes of that bountiful history of what never organically existed. I refer particularly to the first and most indigestible part of the mass (which occupies three of the four volumes): the mumblings of natives or half-breeds . . ." Groussac, with that good ill-humor, fulfills the most eager ritual of satiric games. He pretends to be pained by the errors of the adversary ("after resignedly hearing"); allows one to glimpse the spectacle of abrupt scorn (first the word "tome," then "mass"); uses terms of praise in order to assault ("that bountiful history"); and then, at last, he reveals his hand. He does not commit sins of syntax, which is effective, but does commit sins in his arguments. Criticizing a book for its size, insinuating that no one wants to deal with that enormous brick, and finally professing indifference toward the idiocy of some gauchos or mulattoes appear to be the reactions of a hoodlum, not of a man of letters.

Here is another of his famous diatribes: "It is regrettable that the publication of Dr. Piñero's legal brief may prove to be a serious obstacle to its circulation, and that this ripened fruit of a year and a half of diplomatic leisure may cause no other 'impression' than that of its printing. This shall not be the case, God willing, and insofar as it lies within our means, so melancholy a fate will be avoided . . ." Again the appearance of compassion, again the devilish syntax. Again, too, the marvelous banality of reproof: making fun of those few who could be interested in a particular document and its leisurely production.

An elegant defense of these shortcomings may conjure up the dark root of satire. Satire, according to recent beliefs, stems from the magic curse of wrath, not from reason. It is the relic of an unlikely state in which the wounds inflicted upon the name fall upon the possessor. The particle *ël* was trimmed off the angel Satanaël, God's rebellious first-born who was adored by the Bogomiles. Without it, he lost his crown, splendor, and prophetic powers. His current dwelling is fire, and his host is the wrath of the Powerful. Inversely, the Kabbalists say that the seed of the remote Abram was sterile until the letter *he* was interpolated into his name and made him capable of begetting.

Swift, a man of radical bitterness, proposed in his chronicle of Captain Lemuel Gulliver's travels to defame humankind. The first voyages, to the tiny republic of Lilliput and to the elephantine land of Brobdingnag, are, as Leslie Stephen suggests, an anthropometric dream which in no way touches the complexities of our being, its passion, and its rigor. The third and funniest voyage mocks experimental science through the well-known technique of inversion: Swift's shabby laboratories want to propagate sheep without wool, use ice for the production of gunpowder, soften marble for pillows, beat fire into fine sheets, and make good use of the nutritious parts of fecal matter. (This book also includes a strong passage on the hardships of senility.) The fourth and last voyage shows clearly that beasts are more worthy than men. It presents a virtuous republic of talking, monogamous—that is, human—horses, with a proletariat of four-legged men who live in herds, dig for food, latch onto the udders of cows to steal milk, discharge their waste upon each other, devour rotten meat, and stink. The fable is self-defeating, as one can see. The rest is literature, syntax. In conclusion, it says: "I am not in the least provoked at the sight of a lawyer, a pickpocket, a colonel, a fool, a lord, a gamester, a politician, a whore-master . . ." Certain words, in that good enumeration, are contaminated by their neighbors.

Two final examples. One is the celebrated parody of insult which we are told was improvised by Dr. Johnson: "Your wife, sir, under pretense of keeping a bawdy-house, is a receiver of stolen goods." The other is the most splendid verbal abuse I know, an insult so much more extraordinary if we consider that it represents its author's only brush with literature: "The gods did not allow Santos Chocano to dishonor the gallows by dying there. He is still alive, having exhausted infamy." Dishonoring the gallows, exhausting infamy. Vargas Vila's discharge of these illustrious abstractions refuses to treat its patient and leaves him untouched, unbelievable, quite unimportant, and possibly immortal. The most fleeting mention of Chocano is enough to remind anyone of the famous insult, obscuring with malign splendor all reference to him—even the details and symptoms of that infamy.

I will attempt to summarize the above. Satire is no less conventional than a dialogue between lovers or the natural flower of a sonnet by José María Monner Sans. Its method is the assertion of sophisms, its only law, the simultaneous invention of pranks. I almost forgot: satire also has the obligation of being memorable.

Let me add a certain virile reply recorded by De Quincey (*Writings* XI, 226). Someone flung a glass of wine in the face of a gentleman during a theological or literary debate. The victim did not show any emotion and said to the offender: "This, sir, is a digression: now, if you please, for the argument." (The author of that reply, a certain Dr. Henderson, died in Oxford around 1787, without leaving us any memory other than those just words: a sufficient and beautiful immortality.)

A popular tale, which I picked up in Geneva during the last years of World War I, tells of Miguel Servet's reply to the inquisitors who had condemned him to the stake: "I will burn, but this is a mere event. We shall continue our discussion in eternity."

[1933]   *[SJL]*

The Translators of *The Thousand and One Nights*

1. Captain Burton

At Trieste, in 1872, in a palace with damp statues and deficient hygienic facilities, a gentleman on whose face an African scar told its tale—Captain Richard Francis Burton, the English consul—embarked on a famous translation of the *Quitab alif laila ua laila*, which the *roumis* know by the title *The Thousand and One Nights*. One of the secret aims of his work was the annihilation of another gentleman (also weatherbeaten, and with a dark and Moorish beard) who was compiling a vast dictionary in England and who died long before he was annihilated by Burton. That gentleman was Edward Lane, the Orientalist, author of a highly scrupulous version of *The Thousand and One Nights* that had supplanted a version by Galland. Lane translated against Galland, Burton against Lane; to understand Burton we must understand this hostile dynasty.

I shall begin with the founder. As is known, Jean Antoine Galland was a French Arabist who came back from Istanbul with a diligent collection of coins, a monograph on the spread of coffee, a copy of the *Nights* in Arabic, and a supplementary Maronite whose memory was no less inspired than Scheherazade's. To this obscure consultant—whose name I do not wish to forget: it was Hanna, they say—we owe certain fundamental tales unknown to the original: the stories of Aladdin; the Forty Thieves; Prince Ahmad and the Fairy Peri-Banu; Abu al-Hassan, the Sleeper and the Waker; the night adventure of Caliph Harun al-Rashid; the two sisters who envied their younger sister. The mere mention of these names amply demonstrates that Galland established the canon, incorporating stories that time would render indispensable and that the translators to come—his enemies—would not dare omit.

Another fact is also undeniable. The most famous and eloquent encomiums of *The Thousand and One Nights*—by Coleridge, Thomas De

Quincey, Stendhal, Tennyson, Edgar Allan Poe, Newman—are from readers of Galland's translation. Two hundred years and ten better translations have passed, but the man in Europe or the Americas who thinks of *The Thousand and One Nights* thinks, invariably, of this first translation. The Spanish adjective *milyunanochesco* [thousand-and-one-nights-esque]—*milyunanochero* is too Argentine, *milyunanocturno* overly variant—has nothing to do with the erudite obscenities of Burton or Mardrus, and everything to do with Antoine Galland's bijoux and sorceries.

Word for word, Galland's version is the most poorly written of them all, the least faithful, and the weakest, but it was the most widely read. Those who grew intimate with it experienced happiness and astonishment. Its Orientalism, which seems frugal to us now, was bedazzling to men who took snuff and composed tragedies in five acts. Twelve exquisite volumes appeared from 1707 to 1717, twelve volumes that were innumerably read and that passed into various languages, including Hindi and Arabic. We, their mere anachronistic readers of the twentieth century, perceive only the cloying flavor of the eighteenth century in them and not the evaporated aroma of the Orient which two hundred years ago was their novelty and their glory. No one is to blame for this disjunction, Galland least of all. At times, shifts in the language work against him. In the preface to a German translation of *The Thousand and One Nights*, Dr. Weil recorded that the merchants of the inexcusable Galland equip themselves with a "valise full of dates" each time the tale obliges them to cross the desert. It could be argued that in 1710 the mention of dates alone sufficed to erase the image of a valise, but that is unnecessary: *valise*, then, was a subspecies of saddlebag.

There have been other attacks. In a befuddled panegyric that survives in his 1921 *Morceaux choisis*, André Gide vituperates the licenses of Antoine Galland, all the better to erase (with a candor that entirely surpasses his reputation) the notion of the literalness of Madrus, who is as *fin de siècle* as Galland is eighteenth-century, and much more unfaithful.

Galland's discretions are urbane, inspired by decorum, not morality. I copy down a few lines from the third page of his *Nights:* "*Il alla droit a l'appartement de cette princesse, qui, ne s'attendant pas à le revoir, avait reçu dans son lit un des derniers officiers de sa maison*" [He went directly to the chamber of that princess, who, not expecting to see him again, had received in her bed one of the lowliest servants of his household]. Burton concretizes this nebulous *officier:* "a black cook of loathsome aspect and foul with kitchen grease and grime." Each, in his way, distorts: the original is less ceremonious than Galland and less greasy than Burton. (Effects of decorum: in

Galland's measured prose, "*recevoir dans son lit*" has a brutal ring.)

Ninety years after Antoine Galland's death, an alternate translator of the *Nights* is born: Edward Lane. His biographers never fail to repeat that he is the son of Dr. Theophilus Lane, a Hereford prebendary. This generative datum (and the terrible Form of holy cow that it evokes) may be all we need. The Arabized Lane lived five studious years in Cairo, "almost exclusively among Muslims, speaking and listening to their language, conforming to their customs with the greatest care, and received by all of them as an equal." Yet neither the high Egyptian nights nor the black and opulent coffee with cardamom seed nor the frequent literary discussions with the Doctors of the Law nor the venerable muslin turban nor the meals eaten with his fingers made him forget his British reticence, the delicate central solitude of the masters of the earth. Consequently, his exceedingly erudite version of the *Nights* is (or seems to be) a mere encyclopedia of evasion. The original is not professionally obscene; Galland corrects occasional indelicacies because he believes them to be in bad taste. Lane seeks them out and persecutes them like an inquisitor. His probity makes no pact with silence: he prefers an alarmed chorus of notes in a cramped supplementary volume, which murmur things like: *I shall overlook an episode of the most reprehensible sort; I suppress a repugnant explanation; Here, a line far too coarse for translation; I must of necessity suppress the other anecdote; Hereafter, a series of omissions; Here, the story of the slave Bujait, wholly inappropriate for translation.* Mutilation does not exclude death: some tales are rejected in their entirety "because they cannot be purified without destruction." This responsible and total repudiation does not strike me as illogical: what I condemn is the Puritan subterfuge. Lane is a virtuoso of the subterfuge, an undoubted precursor of the still more bizarre reticences of Hollywood. My notes furnish me with a pair of examples. In night 391, a fisherman offers a fish to the king of kings, who wishes to know if it is male or female and is told it is a hermaphrodite. Lane succeeds in taming this inadmissable colloquy by translating that the king asks what species the fish in question belongs to, and the astute fisherman replies that it is of a mixed species. The tale of night 217 speaks of a king with two wives, who lay one night with the first and the following night with the second, and so they all were happy. Lane accounts for the good fortune of this monarch by saying that he treated his wives "with impartiality." . . . One reason for this was that he destined his work for "the parlor table," a center for placid reading and chaste conversation.

The most oblique and fleeting reference to carnal matters is enough to make Lane forget his honor in a profusion of convolutions and occultations. There is no other fault in him. When free of the peculiar contact of this temptation, Lane is of an admirable veracity. He has no objective, which is a positive advantage. He does not seek to bring out the barbaric color of the *Nights* like Captain Burton, or to forget it and attenuate it like Galland, who domesticated his Arabs so they would not be irreparably out of place in Paris. Lane is at great pains to be an authentic descendant of Hagar. Galland was completely ignorant of all literal precision; Lane justifies his interpretation of each problematic word. Galland invoked an invisible manuscript and a dead Maronite; Lane furnishes editions and page numbers. Galland did not bother about notes; Lane accumulates a chaos of clarifications which, in organized form, make up a separate volume. To be different: this is the rule the precursor imposes. Lane will follow the rule: he needs only to abstain from abridging the original.

The beautiful Newman-Arnold exchange (1861–62)—more memorable than its two interlocutors—extensively argued the two general ways of translating. Newman championed the literal mode, the retention of all verbal singularities: Arnold, the severe elimination of details that distract or detain. The latter procedure may provide the charms of uniformity and seriousness; the former, continuous small surprises. Both are less important than the translator and his literary habits. To translate the spirit is so enormous and phantasmal an intent that it may well be innocuous; to translate the letter, a requirement so extravagant that there is no risk of its ever being attempted. More serious than these infinite aspirations is the retention or suppression of certain particularities; more serious than these preferences and oversights is the movement of the syntax. Lane's syntax is delightful, as befits the refined parlor table. His vocabulary is often excessively festooned with Latin words, unaided by any artifice of brevity. He is careless; on the opening page of his translation he places the adjective *romantic* in the bearded mouth of a twelfth-century Muslim, which is a kind of futurism. At times this lack of sensitivity serves him well, for it allows him to include very commonplace words in a noble paragraph, with involuntary good results. The most rewarding example of such a cooperation of heterogenous words must be: "And in this palace is the last information respecting lords collected in the dust." The following invocation may be another: "By the Living One who does not die or have to die, in the name of He to whom glory and permanence belong." In Burton—the occasional precursor of the always fantastical Mardrus—I would be suspicious of so satisfyingly Oriental a formula; in Lane, such passages are so scarce that I must suppose them to be involuntary, in other words, genuine.

The scandalous decorum of the versions by Galland and Lane has given rise to a whole genre of witticisms that are traditionally repeated. I myself have not failed to respect this tradition. It is common knowledge that the two translators did not fulfill their obligation to the unfortunate man who witnessed the Night of Power, to the imprecations of a thirteenth-century garbage collector cheated by a dervish, and to the customs of Sodom. It is common knowledge that they disinfected the Nights.

Their detractors argue that this process destroys or wounds the good-hearted naiveté of the original. They are in error; *The Book of the Thousand Nights and a Night* is not (morally) ingenuous; it is an adaptation of ancient stories to the lowbrow or ribald tastes of the Cairo middle classes. Except in the exemplary tales of the *Sindibad-namah,* the indecencies of *The Thousand and One Nights* have nothing to do with the freedom of the paradisiacal state. They are speculations on the part of the editor: their aim is a round of guffaws, their heroes are never more than porters, beggars, or eunuchs. The ancient love stories of the repertory, those which relate cases from the desert or the cities of Arabia, are not obscene, and neither is any production of pre-Islamic literature. They are impassioned and sad, and one of their favorite themes is death for love, the death that an opinion rendered by the *ulamas* declared no less holy than that of a martyr who bears witness to the faith. . . . If we approve of this argument, we may see the timidities of Galland and Lane as the restoration of a primal text.

I know of another defense, a better one. An evasion of the original's erotic opportunities is not an unpardonable sin in the sight of the Lord when the primary aim is to emphasize the atmosphere of magic. To offer mankind a new *Decameron* is a commercial enterprise like so many others; to offer an "Ancient Mariner," now, or a *"Bateau ivre,"* is a thing that warrants entry into a higher celestial sphere. Littmann observes that *The Thousand and One Nights* is, above all, a repertory of marvels. The universal imposition of this assumption on every Western mind is Galland's work; let there be no doubt on that score. Less fortunate than we, the Arabs claim to think little of the original; they are already well acquainted with the men, mores, talismans, deserts, and demons that the tales reveal to us.

In a passage somewhere in his work, Rafael Cansinos Asséns swears he can salute the stars in fourteen classical and modern languages. Burton dreamed in seventeen languages and claimed to have mastered thirty-five: Semitic, Dravidian, Indo-European, Ethiopic . . . This vast wealth does not complete his definition: it is merely a trait that tallies with the others, all equally excessive. No one was less vulnerable to the frequent gibes in *Hudibras* against learned men who are capable of saying absolutely nothing in several languages. Burton was a man who had a considerable amount to say, and the seventy-two volumes of his complete works say it still. I will note a few titles at random: *Goa and the Blue Mountains* (1851); *A Complete System of Bayonet Exercise* (1853); *Personal Narrative of a Pilgrimage to El-Medinah and Meccah* (1855); *The Lake Regions of Central Equatorial Africa* (1860); *The City of the Saints* (1861); *The Highlands of the Brazil* (1869); *On an Hermaphrodite from the Cape de Verde Islands* (1866); *Letters from the Battlefields of Paraguay* (1870); *Ultima Thule* (1875); *To the Gold Coast for Gold* (1883); *The Book of the Sword* (first volume, 1884); *The Perfumed Garden of Cheikh Nefzaoui*—a posthumous work consigned to the flames by Lady Burton, along with the *Priapeia, or the Sporting Epigrams of Divers Poets on Priapus*. The writer can be deduced from this catalogue: the English captain with his passion for geography and for the innumerable ways of being a man that are known to mankind. I will not defame his memory by comparing him to Morand, that sedentary, bilingual gentleman who infinitely ascends and descends in the elevators of identical international hotels, and who pays homage to the sight of a trunk. . . . Burton, disguised as an Afghani, made the pilgrimage to the holy cities of Arabia; his voice begged the Lord to deny his bones and skin, his dolorous flesh and blood, to the Flames of Wrath and Justice; his mouth, dried out by the *samun,* left a kiss on the aerolith that is worshiped in the Kaaba. The adventure is famous: the slightest rumor that an uncircumcised man, a *nasráni,* was profaning the sanctuary would have meant certain death. Before that, in the guise of a dervish, he practiced medicine in Cairo—alternating it with prestidigitation and magic so as to gain the trust of the sick. In 1858, he commanded an expedition to the secret sources of the Nile, a mission that led him to discover Lake Tanganyika. During that undertaking he was attacked by a high fever; in 1855, the Somalis thrust a javelin through his jaws (Burton was coming from Harar, a city in the interior of Abyssinia that was forbidden to Europeans). Nine years later, he essayed the terrible hospitality of the ceremonious cannibals of Dahomey; on his return there was no scarcity of rumors (possibly spread and certainly encouraged by Burton himself) that, like Shakespeare's omnivorous proconsul,[1] he had "eaten strange flesh." The Jews, democracy, the

---

[1] I allude to Mark Anthony, invoked by Caesar's apostrophe: "On the Alps/It is reported, thou didst eat strange flesh/Which some did die to look on . . ." In these lines, I think I glimpse some inverted reflection of the zoological myth of the basilisk, a ser-

British Foreign Office, and Christianity were his preferred objects of loathing;
Lord Byron and Islam, his venerations. Of the writer's solitary trade he made
something valiant and plural: he plunged into his work at dawn, in a vast
chamber multiplied by eleven tables, with the materials for a book on each
one—and, on a few, a bright spray of jasmine in a vase of water. He inspired illustrious friendships and loves: among the former I will name only that of
Swinburne, who dedicated the second series of *Poems and Ballads* to him—"in
recognition of a friendship which I must always count among the highest hon-
ours of my life"—and who mourned his death in many stanzas. A man of
words and deeds, Burton could well take up the boast of al-Mutanabbi's *Diwan:*

> The horse, the desert, the night know me,
> Guest and sword, paper and pen.

It will be observed that, from his amateur cannibal to his dreaming
polyglot, I have not rejected those of Richard Burton's personae that, without diminishment of fervor, we could call legendary. My reason is clear: the
Burton of the Burton legend is the translator of the *Nights.* I have sometimes suspected that the radical distinction between poetry and prose lies in
the very different expectations of readers: poetry presupposes an intensity
that is not tolerated in prose. Something similar happens with Burton's
work: it has a preordained prestige with which no other Arabist has ever
been able to compete. The attractions of the forbidden are rightfully his.
There was a single edition, limited to one thousand copies for the thousand
subscribers of the Burton Club, with a legally binding commitment never to
reprint. (The Leonard C. Smithers re-edition "omits given passages in
dreadful taste, whose elimination will be mourned by no one"; Bennett
Cerf's representative selection—which purports to be unabridged—
proceeds from this purified text.) I will venture a hyperbole: to peruse *The
Thousand and One Nights* in Sir Richard's translation is no less incredible

---

pent whose gaze is fatal. Pliny (*Natural History* VIII, par. 33) tells us nothing of the
posthumous aptitudes of this ophidian, but the conjunction of the two ideas of seeing
(*mirar*) and dying (*morir*)—"*vedi Napoli e poi mori*" [see Naples and die]—must have
influenced Shakespeare.
    The gaze of the basilisk was poisonous; the Divinity, however, can kill with pure
splendor—or pure radiation of *manna.* The direct sight of God is intolerable. Moses
covers his face on Mount Horeb, "for he was afraid to look on God"; Hakim, the
prophet of Khorasan, used a four-fold veil of white silk in order not to blind men's
eyes. Cf. also Isaiah 6:5, and 1 Kings 19:13.

than to read it in "a plain and literal translation with explanatory notes" by Sinbad the Sailor.

The problems Burton resolved are innumerable, but a convenient fiction can reduce them to three: to justify and expand his reputation as an Arabist; to differ from Lane as ostensibly as possible; and to interest nineteenth-century British gentlemen in the written version of thirteenth-century oral Muslim tales. The first of these aims was perhaps incompatible with the third; the second led him into a serious lapse, which I must now disclose. Hundreds of couplets and songs occur in the *Nights;* Lane (incapable of falsehood except with respect to the flesh) translated them precisely into a comfortable prose. Burton was a poet: in 1880 he had privately published *The Kasidah of Haji Abdu*, an evolutionist rhapsody that Lady Burton always deemed far superior to FitzGerald's *Rubáiyát.* His rival's "prosaic" solution did not fail to arouse Burton's indignation, and he opted for a rendering into English verse—a procedure that was unfortunate from the start, since it contradicted his own rule of total literalness. His ear was as greatly offended against as his sense of logic, for it is not impossible that this quatrain is among the best he came up with:

> A night whose stars refused to run their course,
> A night of those which never seem outworn:
> Like Resurrection-day, of longsome length
> To him that watched and waited for the morn.[2]

And it is entirely possible that this one is not the worst:

> A sun on wand in knoll of sand she showed,
> Clad in her cramoisy-hued chemisette:
> Of her lips honey-dew she gave me drink,
> And with her rosy cheeks quencht fire she set.

I have alluded to the fundamental difference between the original audience of the tales and Burton's club of subscribers. The former were roguish, prone to exaggeration, illiterate, infinitely suspicious of the present, and

---

[2]Also memorable is this variation on the themes of Abulmeca de Ronda and Jorge Manrique: "Where is the wight who peopled in the past/Hind-land and Sind; and there the tyrant played?"

credulous of remote marvels; the latter were the respectable men of the West End, well equipped for disdain and erudition but not for belly laughs or terror. The first audience appreciated the fact that the whale died when it heard the man's cry; the second, that there had ever been men who lent credence to any fatal capacity of such a cry. The text's marvels—undoubtedly adequate in Kordofan or Bûlâq, where they were offered up as true—ran the risk of seeming rather threadbare in England. (No one requires that the truth be plausible or instantly ingenious: few readers of the *Life and Correspondence of Karl Marx* will indignantly demand the symmetry of Toulet's *Contrerimes* or the severe precision of an acrostic.) To keep his subscribers with him, Burton abounded in explanatory notes on "the manners and customs of Muslim men," a territory previously occupied by Lane. Clothing, everyday customs, religious practices, architecture, references to history or to the Koran, games, arts, mythology—all had already been elucidated in the inconvenient precursor's three volumes. Predictably, what was missing was the erotic. Burton (whose first stylistic effort was a highly personal account of the brothels of Bengal) was rampantly capable of filling this gap. Among the delinquent delectations over which he lingered, a good example is a certain random note in the seventh volume, which the index wittily entitles "*capotes mélancoliques*" [melancholy French letters]. The *Edinburgh Review* accused him of writing for the sewer; the *Encyclopedia Britannica* declared that an unabridged translation was unacceptable and that Edward Lane's version "remained unsurpassed for any truly serious use." Let us not wax too indignant over this obscure theory of the scientific and documentary superiority of expurgation: Burton was courting these animosities. Furthermore, the slightly varying variations of physical love did not entirely consume the attention of his commentary, which is encyclopedic and seditious and of an interest that increases in inverse proportion to its necessity. Thus volume 6 (which I have before me) includes some three hundred notes, among which are the following: a condemnation of jails and a defense of corporal punishment and fines; some examples of the Islamic respect for bread; a legend about the hairiness of Queen Belkis' legs; an enumeration of the four colors that are emblematic of death; a theory and practice of Oriental ingratitude; the information that angels prefer a piebald mount, while Djinns favor horses with a bright bay coat; a synopsis of the mythology surrounding the secret Night of Power or Night of Nights; a denunciation of the superficiality of Andrew Lang; a diatribe against rule by democracy; a census of the names of Mohammed, on Earth, in the Fire, and in the Garden; a mention of the Amalekite people, of long years and large stature; a note on the private parts of the Muslim, which for the man extend from the navel to his knees, and for the woman from the top of the head to the tips of her toes; a consideration of the *asa'o* [roasted beef] of the Argentine gaucho; a warning about the discomforts of "equitation" when the steed is human; an allusion to a grandiose plan for cross-breeding baboons with women and thus deriving a sub-race of good proletarians. At fifty, a man has accumulated affections, ironies, obscenities, and copious anecdotes; Burton unburdened himself of them in his notes.

The basic problem remains: how to entertain nineteenth-century gentlemen with the pulp fictions of the thirteenth century? The stylistic poverty of the *Nights* is well known. Burton speaks somewhere of the "dry and business-like tone" of the Arab prosifiers, in contrast to the rhetorical luxuriance of the Persians. Littmann, the ninth translator, accuses himself of having interpolated words such as *asked, begged, answered,* in five thousand pages that know of no other formula than an invariable *said.* Burton lovingly abounds in this type of substitution. His vocabulary is as unparalleled as his notes. Archaic words coexist with slang, the lingo of prisoners or sailors with technical terms. He does not shy away from the glorious hybridization of English: neither Morris' Scandinavian repertory nor Johnson's Latin has his blessing, but rather the contact and reverberation of the two. Neologisms and foreignisms are in plentiful supply: *castrato, inconséquence, hauteur, in gloria, bagnio, langue fourrée, pundonor, vendetta, Wazir.* Each of these is indubitably the *mot juste,* but their interspersion amounts to a kind of skewing of the original. A good skewing, since such verbal—and syntactical—pranks beguile the occasionally exhausting course of the *Nights.* Burton administers them carefully: first he translates gravely, "Sulayman, Son of David (on the twain be peace!)"; then—once this majesty is familiar to us—he reduces it to "Solomon Davidson." A king who, for the other translators, is "King of Samarcand in Persia," is, for Burton, "King of Samarcand in Barbarian-land"; a merchant who, for the others, is "ill-tempered," is "a man of wrath." That is not all: Burton rewrites in its entirety—with the addition of circumstantial details and physiological traits—the initial and final story. He thus, in 1885, inaugurates a procedure whose perfection (or whose *reductio ad absurdum*) we will now consider in Mardrus. An Englishman is always more timeless than a Frenchman: Burton's heterogenous style is less antiquated than Mardrus', which is noticeably dated.

2. Doctor Mardrus

Mardrus' destiny is a paradoxical one. To him has been ascribed the *moral* virtue of being the most truthful translator of *The Thousand and One Nights*, a book of admirable lascivity, whose purchasers were previously hoodwinked by Galland's good manners and Lane's Puritan qualms. His prodigious literalness, thoroughly demonstrated by the inarguable subtitle "Literal and complete translation of the Arabic text," is revered, along with the inspired idea of writing *The Book of the Thousand Nights and One Night*. The history of this title is instructive; we should review it before proceeding with our investigation of Mardrus.

Masudi's *Meadows of Gold and Mines of Precious Stones* describes an anthology titled *Hazar afsana*, Persian words whose true meaning is "a thousand adventures," but which people renamed "a thousand nights." Another tenth-century document, the *Fihrist*, narrates the opening tale of the series; the king's heartbroken oath that every night he will wed a virgin whom he will have beheaded at dawn, and the resolution of Scheherazade, who diverts him with marvelous stories until a thousand nights have revolved over the two of them and she shows him his son. This invention—far superior to the future and analogous devices of Chaucer's pious cavalcade or Giovanni Boccaccio's epidemic—is said to be posterior to the title, and was devised in the aim of justifying it. . . . Be that as it may, the early figure of 1000 quickly increased to 1001. How did this additional and now indispensable night emerge, this prototype of Pico della Mirandola's *Book of All Things and Also Many Others*, so derided by Quevedo and later Voltaire? Littmann suggests a contamination of the Turkish phrase *"bin bir,"* literally "a thousand and one," but commonly used to mean "many." In early 1840, Lane advanced a more beautiful reason: the magical dread of even numbers. The title's adventures certainly did not end there. Antoine Galland, in 1704, eliminated the original's repetition and translated *The Thousand and One Nights*, a name now familiar in all the nations of Europe except England, which prefers *The Arabian Nights*. In 1839, the editor of the Calcutta edition, W. H. Macnaghten, had the singular scruple of translating *Quitab alif laila ua laila* as *Book of the Thousand Nights and One Night*. This renovation through spelling did not go unremarked. John Payne, in 1882, began publishing his *Book of the Thousand Nights and One Night*; Captain Burton, in 1885, his *Book of the Thousand Nights and a Night*; J. C. Mardrus, in 1899, his *Livre des mille nuits et une nuit*.

I turn to the passage that made me definitively doubt this last translator's veracity. It belongs to the doctrinal story of the City of Brass, which in all other versions extends from the end of night 566 through part of night 578, but which Dr. Mardrus has transposed (for what cause, his Guardian Angel alone knows) to nights 338–346. I shall not insist on this point; we must not waste our consternation on this inconceivable reform of an ideal calendar. Scheherazade-Mardrus relates:

> The water ran through four channels worked in the chamber's floor with charming meanderings, and each channel had a bed of a special color; the first channel had a bed of pink porphyry; the second of topaz, the third of emerald, and the fourth of turquoise; so that the water was tinted the color of the bed, and bathed by the attenuated light filtered in through the silks above, it projected onto the surrounding objects and the marble walls all the sweetness of a seascape.

As an attempt at visual prose in the manner of *The Portrait of Dorian Gray*, I accept (and even salute) this description; as a "literal and complete" version of a passage composed in the thirteenth century, I repeat that it alarms me unendingly. The reasons are multiple. A Scheherazade without Mardrus describes by enumerating parts, not by mutual reaction; does not attest to circumstantial details like that of water that takes on the color of its bed; does not define the quality of light filtered by silk; and does not allude to the Salon des Aquarellistes in the final image. Another small flaw: "charming meanderings" is not Arabic, it is very distinctly French. I do not know if the foregoing reasons are sufficient; they were not enough for me, and I had the indolent pleasure of comparing the three German versions by Weil, Henning, and Littmann, and the two English versions by Lane and Sir Richard Burton. In them I confirmed that the original of Mardrus' ten lines was this: "The four drains ran into a fountain, which was of marble in various colors."

Mardrus' interpolations are not uniform. At times they are brazenly anachronistic—as if suddenly Marchand's withdrawal were being discussed. For example:

> They were overlooking a dream city. . . . As far as the gaze fixed on horizons drowned by the night could reach, the vale of bronze was terraced with the cupolas of palaces, the balconies of houses, and serene gardens;

canals illuminated by the moon ran in a thousand clear circuits in the
shadow of the peaks, while away in the distance, a sea of metal contained the sky's reflected fires in its cold bosom.

Or this passage, whose Gallicism is no less public:

> A magnificent carpet of glorious colors and dexterous wool opened its
> odorless flowers in a meadow without sap, and lived all the artificial life
> of its verdant groves full of birds and animals, surprised in their exact
> natural beauty and their precise lines.

(Here the Arabic editions state: "To the sides were carpets, with a variety of
birds and beasts embroidered in red gold and white silver, but with eyes of
pearls and rubies. Whoever saw them could not cease to wonder at them.")

Mardrus cannot cease to wonder at the poverty of the "Oriental color"
of *The Thousand and One Nights.* With a stamina worthy of Cecil B. de
Mille, he heaps on the viziers, the kisses, the palm trees, and the moons. He
happens to read, in night 570:

> They arrived at a column of black stone, in which a man was buried up
> to his armpits. He had two enormous wings and four arms; two of
> which were like the arms of the sons of Adam, and two like a lion's
> forepaws, with iron claws. The hair on his head was like a horse's tail,
> and his eyes were like embers, and he had in his forehead a third eye
> which was like the eye of a lynx.

He translates luxuriantly:

> One evening the caravan came to a column of black stone, to which was
> chained a strange being, only half of whose body could be seen, for the
> other half was buried in the ground. The bust that emerged from the
> earth seemed to be some monstrous spawn riveted there by the force of
> the infernal powers. It was black and as large as the trunk of an old, rot-
> ting palm tree, stripped of its fronds. It had two enormous black wings
> and four hands, of which two were like the clawed paws of a lion. A tuft
> of coarse bristles like a wild ass's tail whipped wildly over its frightful
> skull. Beneath its orbital arches flamed two red pupils, while its double-
> horned forehead was pierced by a single eye, which opened, immobile
> and fixed, shooting out green sparks like the gaze of a tiger or a panther.

Somewhat later he writes:

> The bronze of the walls, the fiery gemstones of the cupolas, the ivory terraces, the canals and all the sea, as well as the shadows projected towards the West, merged harmoniously beneath the nocturnal breeze and the magical moon.

"Magical," for a man of the thirteenth century, must have been a very precise classification, and not the gallant doctor's mere urbane adjective. . . . I suspect that the Arabic language is incapable of a "literal and complete" version of Mardrus' paragraph, and neither is Latin or the Spanish of Miguel de Cervantes.

The Book of the Thousand and One Nights abounds in two procedures: one (purely formal), rhymed prose; the other, moral predications. The first, retained by Burton and by Littmann, coincides with the narrator's moments of animation: people of comely aspect, palaces, gardens, magical operations, mentions of the Divinity, sunsets, battles, dawns, the beginnings and endings of tales. Mardrus, perhaps mercifully, omits it. The second requires two faculties: that of majestically combining abstract words and that of offering up stock comments without embarrassment. Mardrus lacks both. From the line memorably translated by Lane as "And in this palace is the last information respecting lords collected in the dust," the good Doctor barely extracts: "They passed on, all of them! They had barely the time to repose in the shadow of my towers." The angel's confession—"I am imprisoned by Power, confined by Splendor, and punished for as long as the Eternal commands it, to whom Force and Glory belong"—is, for Mardrus' reader, "I am chained here by the Invisible Force until the extinction of the centuries."

Nor does sorcery have in Mardrus a co-conspirator of good will. He is incapable of mentioning the supernatural without smirking. He feigns to translate, for example:

> One day when Caliph Abdelmelik, hearing tell of certain vessels of antique copper whose contents were a strange black smoke-cloud of diabolical form, marveled greatly and seemed to place in doubt the reality of facts so commonly known, the traveller Talib ben-Sahl had to intervene.

In this paragraph (like the others I have cited, it belongs to the Story of the City of Brass, which, in Mardrus, is made of imposing Bronze), the deliberate candor of "so commonly known" and the rather implausible doubts of Caliph Abdelmelik are two personal contributions by the translator.

Mardrus continually strives to complete the work neglected by those languid, anonymous Arabs. He adds Art Nouveau passages, fine obscenities, brief comical interludes, circumstantial details, symmetries, vast quantities of visual Orientalism. An example among so many: in night 573, the Emir Musa bin Nusayr orders his blacksmiths and carpenters to construct a strong ladder of wood and iron. Mardrus (in his night 344) reforms this dull episode, adding that the men of the camp went in search of dry branches, peeled them with knives and scimitars, and bound them together with turbans, belts, camel ropes, leather cinches, and tack, until they had built a tall ladder that they propped against the wall, supporting it with stones on both sides. . . . In general, it can be said that Mardrus does not translate the book's words but its scenes: a freedom denied to translators, but tolerated in illustrators, who are allowed to add these kinds of details. . . . I do not know if these smiling diversions are what infuse the work with such a happy air, the air of a far-fetched personal yarn rather than of a laborious hefting of dictionaries. But to me the Mardrus "translation" is the most readable of them all—after Burton's incomparable version, which is not truthful either. (In Burton, the falsification is of another order. It resides in the gigantic employ of a gaudy English, crammed with archaic and barbaric words.)

I would greatly deplore it (not for Mardrus, for myself) if any constabulary intent were read into the foregoing scrutiny. Mardrus is the only Arabist whose glory was promoted by men of letters, with such unbridled success that even the Arabists still know who he is. André Gide was among the first to praise him, in August 1889; I do not think Cancela and Capdevila will be the last. My aim is not to demolish this admiration but to substantiate it. To celebrate Mardrus' fidelity is to leave out the soul of Mardrus, to ignore Mardrus entirely. It is his infidelity, his happy and creative infidelity, that must matter to us.

3. Enno Littmann

Fatherland to a famous Arabic edition of *The Thousand and One Nights*, Germany can take (vain) glory in four versions: by the "librarian though Israelite" Gustav Weil—the adversative is from the Catalan pages of a certain encyclopedia—; by Max Henning, translator of the Koran; by the man of letters Félix Paul Greve; and by Enno Littmann, decipherer of the Ethiopic inscriptions in the fortress of Axum. The first of these versions, in four volumes (1839–42), is the most pleasurable, as its author—exiled from Africa and Asia by dysentery—strives to maintain or substitute for the Oriental style. His interpolations earn my deepest respect. He has some intruders at a gathering say, "We do not wish to be like the morning, which disperses all revelries." Of a generous king, he assures us, "The fire that burns for his guests brings to mind the Inferno and the dew of his benign hand is like the Deluge"; of another he tells us that his hands "were liberal as the sea." These fine apocrypha are not unworthy of Burton or Mardrus, and the translator assigned them to the parts in verse, where this graceful animation can be an *ersatz* or replacement for the original rhymes. Where the prose is concerned, I see that he translated it as is, with certain justified omissions, equidistant from hypocrisy and immodesty. Burton praised his work—"as faithful as a translation of a popular nature can be." Not in vain was Dr. Weil Jewish, "though librarian"; in his language I think I perceive something of the flavor of Scripture.

The second version (1895–97) dispenses with the enchantments of accuracy, but also with those of style. I am speaking of the one provided by Henning, a Leipzig Arabist, to Philippe Reclam's *Universalbibliothek*. This is an expurgated version, though the publisher claims otherwise. The style is dogged and flat. Its most indisputable virtue must be its length. The editions of Bûlâq and Breslau are represented, along with the Zotenberg manuscripts and Burton's *Supplemental Nights*. Henning, translator of Sir Richard, is, word for word, superior to Henning, translator of Arabic, which is merely a confirmation of Sir Richard's primacy over the Arabs. In the book's preface and conclusion, praises of Burton abound—almost deprived of their authority by the information that Burton wielded "the language of Chaucer, equivalent to medieval Arabic." A mention of Chaucer as *one* of the sources of Burton's vocabulary would have been more reasonable. (Another is Sir Thomas Urquhart's Rabelais.)

The third version, Greve's, derives from Burton's English and repeats it, excluding only the encyclopedic notes. Insel-Verlag published it before the war.

The fourth (1923–28) comes to supplant the previous one and, like it, runs to six volumes. It is signed by Enno Littmann, decipherer of the monuments of Axum, cataloguer of the 283 Ethiopic manuscripts found in Jerusalem, contributor to the *Zeitschrift für Assyriologie*. Though it does not engage in Burton's indulgent loitering, Littmann's translation is entirely frank. The most ineffable obscenities do not give him pause; he renders them into his placid German, only rarely into Latin. He omits not a single word, not even those that register—1000 times—the passage from one night to the next. He neglects or refuses all local color: express instructions from the publisher were necessary to make him retain the name of Allah and not substitute it with God. Like Burton and John Payne, he translates Arabic verse into Western verse. He notes ingenuously that if the ritual announcement "So-and-so pronounced these verses" were followed by a paragraph of German prose, his readers would be disconcerted. He provides whatever notes are necessary for a basic understanding of the text: twenty or so per volume, all of them laconic. He is always lucid, readable, mediocre. He follows (he tells us) the very breath of the Arabic. If the *Encyclopedia Britannica* contains no errors, his translation is the best of all those in circulation. I hear that the Arabists agree; it matters not at all that a mere man of letters—and he of the merely Argentine Republic—prefers to dissent.

My reason is this: the versions by Burton and Mardrus, and even by Galland, can only be conceived of *in the wake of a literature*. Whatever their blemishes or merits, these characteristic works presuppose a rich (prior) process. In some way, the almost inexhaustible process of English is adumbrated in Burton—John Donne's hard obscenity, the gigantic vocabularies of Shakespeare and Cyril Tourneur, Swinburne's affinity for the archaic, the crass erudition of the authors of 17th-century chapbooks, the energy and imprecision, the love of tempests and magic. In Mardrus' laughing paragraphs, *Salammbô* and La Fontaine, the *Mannequin d'osier* and the *ballets russes* all coexist. In Littmann, who like Washington cannot tell a lie, there is nothing but the probity of Germany. This is so little, so very little. The commerce between Germany and the *Nights* should have produced something more.

Whether in philosophy or in the novel, Germany possesses a literature of the fantastic—rather, it possesses *only* a literature of the fantastic. There are marvels in the *Nights* that I would like to see rethought in German. As I formulate this desire, I think of the repertory's deliberate wonders—the all-powerful slaves of a lamp or a ring; Queen Lab, who transforms Muslims into birds; the copper boatman with talismans and formulae on his chest—and of those more general ones that proceed from its collective nature, from the need to complete one thousand and one episodes. Once they had run out of magic, the copyists had to fall back on historical or pious notices whose inclusion seems to attest to the good faith of the rest. The ruby that ascends into the sky and the earliest description of Sumatra, details of the court of the Abbasids and silver angels whose food is the justification of the Lord, all dwell together in a single volume. It is, finally, a poetic mixture; and I would say the same of certain repetitions. Is it not portentous that on night 602 King Schahriah hears his own story from the queen's lips? Like the general framework, a given tale often contains within itself other tales of equal length: stages within the stage as in the tragedy of *Hamlet,* raised to the power of a dream. A clear and difficult line from Tennyson seems to define them:

> Laborious orient ivory, sphere in sphere.

To further heighten the astonishment, these adventitious Hydra's heads can be more concrete than the body: Schahriah, the fantastical king "of the Islands of China and Hindustan," receives news of Tarik ibn Ziyad, governor of Tangiers and victor in the battle of Guadalete. . . . The threshold is confused with the mirror, the mask lies beneath the face, no one knows any longer which is the true man and which are his idols. And none of it matters; the disorder is as acceptable and trivial as the inventions of a daydream.

Chance has played at symmetries, contrasts, digressions. What might a man—a Kafka—do if he organized and intensified this play, remade it in line with the Germanic distortion, the *unheimlichkeit* of Germany?

[1934–1936]   *[EA]*

Among the volumes consulted, I must enumerate:
Les Mille et une Nuits, contes arabes traduits par Galland. Paris, s.d.
The Thousand and One Nights, commonly called The Arabian Nights' Entertainments. A new translation from the Arabic by E.W. Lane. London, 1839.
The Book of the Thousand Nights and a Night. A plain and literal translation by Richard F. Burton. London (?) n.d. Vols. VI, VII, VIII.
The Arabian Nights. A complete [sic] *and unabridged selection from the famous literal translation of R. F. Burton.* New York, 1932.
Le Livre des mille nuits et une nuit. Traduction littérale et complète du texte arabe par le Dr. J. C. Mardrus. Paris, 1906.
Tausend und eine Nacht. Aus dem Arabischen übertragen von Max Henning. Leipzig, 1897.
Die Erzählungen aus den Tausendundein Nächten. Nach dem arabischen Urtext der Calcuttaer Ausgabe vom Jahre 1839 übertragen von Enno Littmann. Leipzig, 1928.

I, a Jew

Like the Druzes, like the moon, like death, like next week, the distant past is one of those things that can enrich ignorance. It is infinitely malleable and agreeable, far more obliging than the future and far less demanding of our efforts. It is the famous season favored by all mythologies.

Who has not, at one time or another, played with thoughts of his ancestors, with the prehistory of his flesh and blood? I have done so many times, and many times it has not displeased me to think of myself as Jewish. It is an idle hypothesis, a frugal and sedentary adventure that harms no one, not even the name of Israel, as my Judaism is wordless, like the songs of Mendelssohn. The magazine *Crisol* [Crucible], in its issue of January 30, has decided to gratify this retrospective hope; it speaks of my "Jewish ancestry, maliciously hidden" (the participle and the adverb amaze and delight me).

Borges Acevedo is my name. Ramos Mejía, in a note to the fifth chapter of *Rosas and His Times*, lists the family names in Buenos Aires at that time in order to demonstrate that all, or almost all, "came from Judeo-Portuguese stock." "Acevedo" is included in the list: the only supporting evidence for my Jewish pretensions until this confirmation in *Crisol.* Nevertheless, Captain Honorio Acevedo undertook a detailed investigation that I cannot ignore. His study notes that the first Acevedo to disembark on this land was the Catalan Don Pedro de Azevedo in 1728: landholder, settler of "Pago de Los Arroyos," father and grandfather of cattle ranchers in that province, a notable who figures in the annals of the parish of Santa Fe and in the documents of the history of the Viceroyalty—an ancestor, in short, irreparably Spanish.

Two hundred years and I can't find the Israelite; two hundred years and my ancestor still eludes me.

I am grateful for the stimulus provided by *Crisol*, but hope is dimming that I will ever be able to discover my link to the Table of the Breads and the

Sea of Bronze; to Heine, Gleizer, and the ten *Sefiroth*; to Ecclesiastes and Chaplin.

Statistically, the Hebrews were few. What would we think of someone in the year 4000 who uncovers people from San Juan Province everywhere? Our inquisitors seek out Hebrews, but never Phoenicians, Garamantes, Scythians, Babylonians, Persians, Egyptians, Huns, Vandals, Ostrogoths, Ethiopians, Illyrians, Paphlagonians, Sarmatians, Medes, Ottomans, Berbers, Britons, Libyans, Cyclopes, or Lapiths. The nights of Alexandria, of Babylon, of Carthage, of Memphis, never succeeded in engendering a single grandfather; it was only to the tribes of the bituminous Dead Sea that this gift was granted.

[1934]   [EW]

The Labyrinths of the Detective Story
and Chesterton

The English live with the turmoil of two incompatible passions: a strange appetite for adventure and a strange appetite for legality. I write "strange" because, for a *criollo*, they are both precisely that. Martín Fierro, the sainted army deserter, and his pal Cruz, the sainted police deserter, would be astonished, swearing and laughing at the British (and American) doctrine that the law is infallibly right; yet they would never dare to imagine that their miserable fate as cutthroats was interesting or desirable. For a *criollo*, to kill is to "disgrace oneself." It is one of man's misfortunes, and in itself neither grants nor diminishes virtue. Nothing could be more opposite to "Murder Considered as One of the Fine Arts" by the "morbidly virtuous" De Quincey or to the "Theory of the Moderate Murder" by the sedentary Chesterton.

Both passions—for physical adventure and for rancorous legality—find satisfaction in the current detective narrative. Its prototypes are the old serials and current dime novels about the nominally famous Nick Carter, smiling and hygienic athlete, that were engendered by the journalist John Coryell on an insomniac typewriter that dispatched 70,000 words a month. The genuine detective story—need I say it?—rejects with equal disdain both physical risk and distributive justice. It serenely disregards jails, secret stairways, remorse, gymnastics, fake beards, fencing, Charles Baudelaire's bats, and even the element of chance. In the earliest examples of the genre ("The Mystery of Marie Rogêt," by Edgar Allan Poe, 1842) and in one of the most recent ones (*Unravelled Knots*, by the Baroness Orczy), the story is limited to the discussion and abstract resolution of a crime, often far from the event or many years after it. The everyday methods of police investigation—fingerprints, torture, accusation—would seem like solecisms there. One might object to the conventionality of this rejection, but the convention here is irreproachable: it does not attempt to avoid difficulties, but rather to impose them. It is not a convenience for the writer, like the confused confidants in Jean Racine or theatrical asides. The detective novel to some degree borders on the psychological novel (*The Moonstone* by Wilkie Collins, 1868; *Mr. Digweed and Mr. Lumb* by Eden Phillpotts, 1934). The short story is of a strict, problematic nature; its code could be the following:

A.) *A discretional limit of six characters.* The reckless infraction of this law is responsible for the confusion and tedium of all detective movies. In every one we are presented with fifteen strangers, and it is finally revealed that the evil one is not Alpha, who was looking through the keyhole, nor Beta, who hid the money, nor the disturbing Gamma, who would sob in the corners of the hallway, but rather that surly young Upsilon, whom we'd been confusing with Phi, who bears such a striking resemblance to Tau, the substitute elevator operator. The astonishment this fact tends to produce is somewhat moderate.

B.) *The declaration of all the terms of the problem.* If my memory (or lack of it) serves me, the varied infraction of this second law is the favorite defect of Conan Doyle. It involves, at times, a few particles of ashes, gathered behind the reader's back by the privileged Holmes, and only derivable from a cigar made in Burma, which is sold in only one store, which is patronized by only one customer. At other times, the cheating is more serious. It involves a guilty party, horribly unmasked at the last moment, who turns out to be a stranger, an insipid and torpid interpolation. In honest stories, the criminal is one of the characters present from the beginning.

C.) *An avaricious economy of means.* The final discovery that two characters in the plot are the same person may be appealing—as long as the instrument of change turns out to be not a false beard or an Italian accent, but different names and circumstances. The less delightful version—two individuals who imitate a third and thus provide him with ubiquity—runs the certain risk of heavy weather.

D.) *The priority of how over who.* The amateurs I excoriated in section A are partial to the story of a jewel placed within the reach of fifteen men— that is, of fifteen names, because we know nothing about their characters— which then disappears into the heavy fist of one of them. They imagine that the act of ascertaining to which name the fist belongs is of considerable interest.

E.) *A reticence concerning death.* Homer could relate that a sword severed the hand of Hypsenor and that the bloody hand rolled over the ground and that blood-red death and cruel fate seized his eyes; such displays are in-appropriate in the detective story, whose glacial muses are hygiene, fallacy, and order.

F.) *A solution that is both necessary and marvelous.* The former estab-lishes that the problem is a "determined" one, with only one solution. The latter requires that the solution be something that the reader marvels over—without, of course, resorting to the supernatural, whose use in this genre of fiction is slothful and felonious. Also prohibited are hypnotism, telepathic hallucinations, portents, elixirs with unknown effects, ingenious pseudoscientific tricks, and lucky charms. Chesterton always performs a *tour de force* by proposing a supernatural explanation and then replacing it, losing nothing, with one from this world.

The Scandal of Father Brown, Chesterton's most recent book (London, 1935), has suggested the aforementioned rules. Of the five series of chroni-cles of the little clergyman, this book is probably the least felicitous. It con-tains, however, two stories that I would not want excluded from a Brownian anthology or canon: the third, "The Blast of the Book," and the eighth, "The Insoluble Problem." The premise of the former is exciting: it deals with a tattered supernatural book that causes the instantaneous disappearance of those who foolishly open it. Somebody announces over the telephone that he has the book in front of him and that he is about to open it; the fright-ened listener "hears a kind of silent explosion." Another exploded character leaves a small hole in a pane of glass; another, a rip in a canvas; another, his abandoned wooden leg. The *dénouement* is good, but I am positive that the most devout readers correctly guessed it in the middle of page 73. There is an abundance of the characteristics typical of G. K.: for example, that gloomy masked man with the black gloves who turns out to be an aristocrat and a fierce opponent of nudism.

The settings for the crimes are remarkable, as in all of Chesterton's books, and carefully and sensationally false. Has anyone ever noted the similarities between the fantastic London of Stevenson and that of Chester-ton, between the mourning gentlemen and nocturnal gardens of *The Sui-cide Club* and those of the now five-part saga of Father Brown?

[1935]   [EW]

The Doctrine of Cycles

I

This doctrine (whose most recent inventor called it the doctrine of the Eternal Return) may be formulated in the following manner:

The number of all the atoms that compose the world is immense but finite, and as such only capable of a finite (though also immense) number of permutations. In an infinite stretch of time, the number of possible permutations must be run through, and the universe has to repeat itself. Once again you will be born from a belly, once again your skeleton will grow, once again this same page will reach your identical hands, once again you will follow the course of all the hours of your life until that of your incredible death. Such is the customary order of this argument, from its insipid preliminaries to its enormous and threatening outcome. It is commonly attributed to Nietzsche.

Before refuting it—an undertaking of which I do not know if I am capable—it may be advisable to conceive, even from afar, of the superhuman numbers it invokes. I shall begin with the atom. The diameter of a hydrogen atom has been calculated, with some margin of error, to be one hundred millionth of a centimeter. This dizzying tininess does not mean the atom is indivisible; on the contrary, Rutherford describes it with the image of a solar system, made up of a central nucleus and a spinning electron, one hundred thousand times smaller than the whole atom. Let us leave this nucleus and this electron aside, and conceive of a frugal universe composed of ten atoms. (This is obviously only a modest experimental universe; invisible, for even microscopes do not suspect it; imponderable, for no scale can place a value on it.) Let us postulate as well—still in accordance with Nietzsche's conjecture—that the number of possible changes in this universe is the number of ways in which the ten atoms can be arranged by varying the order in which they are placed. How many different states can this world know before an eternal return? The investigation is simple: it suffices to multiply 1 x 2 x 3 x 4 x 5 x 6 x 7 x 8 x 9 x 10, a tedious operation that yields the figure of 3,628,800. If an almost infinitesimal particle of the universe is capable of such variety, we should lend little or no faith to any monotony in the cosmos. I have considered ten atoms; to obtain two grams of hydrogen, we would require more than a billion billion atoms. To make the computation of the possible changes in this couple of grams—in other words, to multiply a billion billion by each one of the whole numbers that precedes it—is already an operation that far surpasses my human patience.

I do not know if my reader is convinced; I am not. This chaste, painless squandering of enormous numbers undoubtedly yields the peculiar pleasure of all excesses, but the Recurrence remains more or less Eternal, though in the most remote terms. Nietzsche might reply: "Rutherford's spinning electrons are a novelty for me, as is the idea—scandalous to a philologist—that an atom can be divided. However, I never denied that the vicissitudes of matter were copious; I said only that they were not infinite." This plausible response from Friedrich Zarathustra obliges me to fall back on Georg Cantor and his heroic theory of sets.

Cantor destroys the foundation of Nietzsche's hypothesis. He asserts the perfect infinity of the number of points in the universe, and even in one meter of the universe, or a fraction of that meter. The operation of counting is, for him, nothing else than that of comparing two series. For example, if the first-born sons of all the houses of Egypt were killed by the Angel, except for those who lived in a house that had a red mark on the door, it is clear that as many sons were saved as there were red marks, and an enumeration of precisely how many of these there were does not matter. Here the quantity is indefinite; there are other groupings in which it is infinite. The set of natural numbers is infinite, but it is possible to demonstrate that, within it, there are as many odd numbers as even.

1	corresponds to	2
3	to	4
5	to	6, etc.

This proof is as irreproachable as it is banal, and is no different from the following proof that there are as many multiples of 3018 as there are numbers—without excluding from the latter set the number 3018 and its multiples.

1	corresponds to	3018
2	to	6036
3	to	9054
4	to	12072, etc.

The same can be affirmed of its exponential powers, however rarefied they become as we progress.

1	corresponds to	3018
2	to	3018^2 which is 9,108,324
3	to	etc.

A jocose acceptance of these facts has inspired the formula that an infinite collection—for example, the natural series of whole numbers—is a collection whose members can in turn be broken down into infinite series. (Or rather, to avoid any ambiguity: an infinite whole is a whole that can be the equivalent of one of its subsets.) The part, in these elevated numerical latitudes, is no less copious than the whole: the precise quantity of points in the universe is the same as the quantity of points in a meter, or a decimeter, or the deepest trajectory of a star. The series of natural numbers is very orderly, that is, the terms that form it are consecutive: 28 precedes 29 and follows 27. The series of points in space (or of instants in time) cannot be ordered in the same way: no number has a successor or an immediate predecessor. It is like a series of fractions arranged in order of magnitude. What number will we count after ½? Not $\frac{51}{100}$, because $\frac{101}{200}$ is closer; not $\frac{101}{200}$, because $\frac{201}{400}$ is closer; not $\frac{201}{400}$, because . . . According to Cantor, the same thing happens with points. We can always interpose more of them, in infinite number. Therefore we must try not to conceive of decreasing sizes. Each point is "already" the final degree of an infinite subdivision.

The clash between Cantor's lovely game and Zarathustra's lovely game is fatal to Zarathustra. If the universe consists of an infinite number of terms, it is rigorously capable of an infinite number of combinations—and the need for a Recurrence is done away with. There remains its mere possibility, which can be calculated as zero.

II

Nietzsche writes, in the autumn of 1883: "This slow spider dragging itself towards the light of the moon and that same moonlight, and you and I whispering at the gateway, whispering of eternal things, haven't we already coincided in the past? And won't we happen again on the long road, on this long tremulous road, won't we recur eternally? This was how I spoke, and in an ever lower voice, because my thoughts and what was beyond my thoughts made me afraid." Writes Eudemus, a paraphraser of Aristotle, three centuries or so before the Cross: "If the Pythagoreans are to be believed, the same things will return at precisely their time and you will be with me again and I will repeat this doctrine and my hand will play with this staff, and so on." In the Stoic cosmogony, "Zeus feeds on the world": the universe is cyclically consumed by the fire that engendered it, and resurges from annihilation to repeat an identical history. Once again the diverse seminal particles combine, once again they give form to stones, trees, and men—and even virtues and days, since for the Greeks a substantive number was impossible without some corporeality. Once again every sword and every hero, once again every minutious night of insomnia.

Like the other conjectures of the school of the Porch, that of a general repetition spread across time entered the Gospels (Acts of the Apostles 3:21), along with its technical name, *apokatastasis,* though with indeterminate intent. Book XII of St. Augustine's *Civitas Dei* dedicates several chapters to the refutation of so abominable a doctrine. Those chapters (which I have before me now) are far too intricate for summary, but their author's episcopal fury seems to fix upon two arguments: one, the gaudy futility of this wheel; the other, the ridiculousness of the Logos dying on the cross like an acrobat in an interminable sequence of performances. Farewells and suicides lose their dignity if repeated too often; St. Augustine must have thought the same of the Crucifixion. Hence his scandalized rejection of the viewpoint of the Stoics and Pythagoreans, who argued that God's science cannot understand infinite things and that the eternal rotation of the world's process serves to allow God to learn more and familiarize Himself with it. St. Augustine mocks their worthless revolutions and affirms that Jesus is the straight path that allows us to flee from the circular labyrinth of such deceptions.

In the chapter of his *Logic* that addresses the law of causality, John Stuart Mill maintains that a periodic repetition of history is conceivable—but not true—and cites Virgil's "Messianic eclogue":

> *Iam redit et virgo, redeunt Saturnia regna*
> [Now the Maiden returns, the reign of Saturn returns]

Can Nietzsche, the Hellenist, have been ignorant of these "precursors"? Was Nietzsche, author of the fragments on the pre-Socratics, perhaps unaware of a doctrine learned by the disciples of Pythagoras?[1] This is hard to believe—*and futile.* True, Nietzsche has indicated, in a memorable page, the precise spot on which the idea of the Eternal Return visited him: a path in the woods of Silvaplana, near a vast pyramidal block, one midday in August 1881—"six thousand feet beyond men and time." True, this instant is one of Nietzsche's great distinctions. "Immortal the instant in which I engendered the eternal recurrence. For that instant I endure the Recurrence," were the words he would leave (*Unschuld des Werdens* II, 1308). Yet, in my opinion, we need not postulate a startling ignorance, nor a human, all too human, confusion between inspiration and memory, nor a crime of vanity. My key to this mystery is grammatical, almost syntactical. Nietzsche knew that the Eternal Recourse is one of the fables, fears, diversions, that eternally recur, but he also knew that the most effective of the grammatical persons is the first. Indeed, we would be justified in saying that, for a prophet, the only grammatical person is the first. It was not possible for Zarathustra to derive his revelation from a philosophical compendium or from the *Historia philosophiae graeco-romanae* of the surrogate professors Ritter and Preller, for reasons of voice and anachronism, not to speak of typography. The prophetic style does not allow for the use of quotation marks nor the erudite attestation of books and authors. . . .

If my human flesh can assimilate the brute flesh of a sheep, who can prevent the human mind from assimilating human mental states? Because he rethought it at great length, and endured it, the eternal recurrence of things is now Nietzsche's and does not belong to some dead man who is barely more than a Greek name. I will not insist; Miguel de Unamuno already has his page on the adoption of thoughts.

Nietzsche wanted men who were capable of enduring immortality. I say this in words that appear in his personal notebooks, the *Nachlass*, where he also inscribed these others: "If you envision a long peace before you are reborn, I swear to you that you are thinking wrongly. Between the final instant of consciousness and the first gleam of a new life there is 'no time'— the lapse lasts as long as a bolt of lightning, though billions of years are insufficient to measure it. If a self is absent, infinity can be the equivalent of succession."

---

[1]This perplexity is futile. Nietzsche, in 1874, jeered at the Pythagorean thesis that history repeats itself cyclically (*Vom Nutzen und Nachteil der Historie*). (Note added in 1953.)

Before Nietzsche, personal immortality was no more than a blundering hope, a hazy plan. Nietzsche postulates it as a duty and gives it all the ghastly lucidity of insomnia. "Waking, by reason of their continual cares, fears, sorrows, dry brains," (I read in Robert Burton's antique treatise) "is a symptom that much crucifies melancholy men." We are told that Nietzsche endured this crucifixion and had to seek deliverance in the bitterness of chloral hydrate. Nietzsche wanted to be Walt Whitman; he wanted to fall minutely in love with his destiny. He adopted a heroic method: he disinterred the intolerable Greek hypothesis of eternal repetition, and he contrived to make this mental nightmare an occasion for jubilation. He sought out the most horrible idea in the universe and offered it up to mankind's delectation. The languid optimist often imagines himself to be a Nietzschean; Nietzsche confronts him with the circles of the eternal recurrence and spits him out of his mouth.

Nietzsche wrote: "Not to yearn for distant ventures and favors and blessings, but to live in such a way that we wish to come back and live again, and so on throughout eternity." Mauthner objects that to attribute the slightest moral, in other words practical, influence to the hypothesis of eternal return is to negate the hypothesis—since it is comparable to imagining that something can happen in another way. Nietzsche would answer that the formulation of the eternal return and its extensive moral (in other words, practical) influence and Mauthner's cavils and his refutation of Mauthner's cavils are naught but a few more necessary moments in the history of the world, the work of atomic agitations. He could, with reason, repeat the words he had already written: "It suffices that the doctrine of circular repetition be probable or possible. The image of a mere possibility can shatter and remake us. How much has been accomplished by the possibility of eternal damnation!" And in another passage: "The instant that this idea presents itself, all colors are different—and there is another history."

III

At one time or another, the sensation of "having lived this moment already" has left us all pensive. Partisans of the eternal recurrence swear to us that it is so and investigate a possible corroboration of their faith in these perplexed states of mind. They forget that memory would import a novelty that negates the hypothesis, and that time would gradually perfect that memory until the distant heaven in which the individual now foresees his destiny and prefers to act in another way. . . . In any case, Nietzsche never spoke of a mnemonic confirmation of the Recurrence.[2]

Nor—and this deserves to be emphasized as well—did he speak of the finiteness of atoms. Nietzsche *negates* the atom; atomic theory seemed to him nothing but a model of the world made exclusively for the eyes and the mathematical mind. . . . To ground his hypothesis, he spoke of a limited force, evolving in infinite time, but incapable of an unlimited number of variations. His procedure was not without perfidy: first he sets us on guard against the idea of an infinite force—"let us beware such orgies of thought!"— and then he generously concedes that time is infinite. Similarly, it pleases him to fall back on the Prior Eternity. For example: an equilibrium of cosmic forces is impossible, since if it were not it would already have occurred in the Prior Eternity. Or: universal history has happened an infinite number of times—in the Prior Eternity. The invocation seems valid, but it should be repeated that this Prior Eternity (or *aeternitas a parte ante*, as the theologians would call it) is nothing but our natural incapacity to conceive of a beginning to time. We suffer the same incapacity where space is concerned, so that invoking a Prior Eternity is as decisive as invoking the Infinity To My Right. In other words, if time is infinite to our intuition, so is space. This Prior Eternity has nothing to do with the real time that has elapsed; we go back to the first second and note that it requires a predecessor, and that that predecessor requires one as well, and so on infinitely. To close off this *regressus in infinitum* [regression into infinity], St. Augustine declares that the first second of time coincides with the first second of the Creation: "*non in tempore sed cum tempore incepit creatio*" [The Creation begins not in time but with time].

Nietzsche appeals to energy; the second law of thermodynamics declares that some energetic processes are irreversible. Heat and light are no

---

[2]Of this apparent confirmation, Néstor Ibarra writes: "It also happens that some new perception strikes us as a memory, and we believe we recognize objects or accidents that we are nevertheless sure of meeting for the first time. I imagine that this must have to do with a curious operation of our memory. An initial perception, any perception, takes place, but *beneath the threshold of consciousness.* An instant later, the stimulus acts, but this time we receive it *in our conscious mind.* Our memory comes into play and offers us the feeling of *déjà vu*, but situates the recollection wrongly. To justify its weakness and its disturbing quality, we imagine that a considerable amount of time has passed, or we may even send it further, into the repetition of some former life. In reality it is an immediate past, and the abyss that separates us from it is that of our own distraction."

more than forms of energy. It suffices to project a light onto a black surface to convert it into heat. Heat, however, will never return to the form of light. This inoffensive or insipid-seeming proof annuls the "circular labyrinth" of the Eternal Return.

The first law of thermodynamics declares that the energy of the universe is constant; the second, that this energy tends toward isolation and disorder, though its total quantity does not decrease. This gradual disintegration of the forces that make up the universe is entropy. Once maximum entropy is reached, once different temperatures have been equalized, once any action of one body on another has been neutralized (or compensated for), the world will be a random assemblage of atoms. In the deep center of the stars, this difficult, mortal equilibrium has been achieved. By dint of constant interchange, the whole universe will reach it, and will be warm and dead.

Light is gradually lost in the form of heat; the universe, minute by minute, is becoming invisible. It grows more inconstant, as well. At some point, it will no longer be anything but heat: an equilibrium of immobile, evenly distributed heat. Then it will have died.

A final uncertainty, this one of a metaphysical order. If Zarathustra's hypothesis is accepted, I do not fully understand how two identical processes keep from agglomerating into one. Is mere succession, verified by no one, enough? Without a special archangel to keep track, what does it mean that we are going through the thirteen thousand five hundred and fourteenth cycle and not the first in the series or number three hundred twenty-two to the two thousandth power? Nothing, in practice—which is no impairment to the thinker. Nothing, for the intellect—which is serious indeed.

[1936]   [EA]

Among the books consulted for the foregoing article, I must make mention of the
    following:
Die Unschuld des Werdens von Friedrich Nietzsche. Leipzig, 1931.
Also sprach Zaarathustra von Friedrich Nietzsche. Leipzig, 1892.
Introduction to Mathematical Philosophy by Bertrand Russell. London, 1919.
The ABC of Atoms by Bertrand Russell. London, 1927.
The Nature of the Physical World by A. S. Eddington. London, 1928.
Die Philosophie der Griechen von Dr. Paul Deussen. Leipzig, 1919.
Wörterbuch der Philosophie von Fritz Mauthner. Leipzig, 1923.
La ciudad de Dios por San Agustín. Versión de Díaz de Beyral. Madrid, 1922.

A History of Eternity

I

The passage of the *Enneads* that seeks to question and define the nature of time states that a prior acquaintance with eternity is indispensable since—as everyone knows—eternity is the model and archetype of time. This prefatory statement, all the more crucial if we take it to be sincere, appears to annihilate any hope of our reaching an understanding of the man who wrote it. For us, time is a jarring, urgent problem, perhaps the most vital problem of metaphysics, while eternity is a game or a spent hope. We read in Plato's *Timaeus* that time is a moving image of eternity, and it barely strikes a chord, distracting no one from the conviction that eternity is an image wrought in the substance of time. I propose to give a history of that image, that awkward word enriched by human discord.

Inverting Plotinus' method (the only way to make any use of it), I will begin by listing some of the obscurities inherent in time, a natural, metaphysical mystery that must precede eternity, which is a daughter of mankind. One such obscurity, neither the most challenging nor the least beautiful, keeps us from ascertaining the direction in which time moves. It is commonly held to flow from past to future, but the opposite notion, established in Spanish verse by Miguel de Unamuno, is no less logical:

> *Nocturno el río de las horas fluye*
> *desde su manatial que es el mañana*
> *eterno...*

[Nocturnal the river of hours flows/from its source, the eternal tomorrow...][1]

[1] The Scholastic concept of time as the flow of the potential into the actual is akin to this idea. Cf. Whitehead's eternal objects, which constitute "the kingdom of possibility" and participate in time.

Both directions are equally probable—and equally unverifiable. Bradley denies both possibilities and advances a personal hypothesis, which consists in ruling out the future, a mere construction of our hopes, and reducing the "actual" to the death throes of the present moment as it disintegrates into the past. This temporal regression usually corresponds to states of decline or dullness, while any kind of intensity seems to us to advance on the future. . . . While Bradley negates the future, one school of Indian philosophy negates the present as unattainable. *The orange is about to fall from the branch, or else it lies on the ground,* these curious simplifiers affirm. *No one sees it fall.*

Other difficulties are suggested by time. One, perhaps the greatest—that of synchronizing each person's individual time with the general time of mathematicians—has been greatly vociferated by the recent relativist scare, and everyone remembers it, or remembers having remembered it until very recently. (I retrieve it by distorting it in the following way: If time is a mental process, how can it be shared by thousands of men, or even two different men?) The Eleatic refutation of movement raises another problem, which can be expressed thus: *It is impossible for fourteen minutes to elapse in eight hundred years of time, because first seven minutes must pass, and before seven, three and a half, and before three and a half, one and three-quarters, and so on infinitely, so that the fourteen minutes will never be completed.* Russell rebuts this argument by affirming the reality and even the triteness of infinite numbers, which, however, by definition occur once and for all, and not as the "final" term of an endless enumerative process. Russell's non-normal numbers are a fine anticipation of eternity, which also refuses to be defined by the enumeration of its parts.

None of the several eternities men have charted—nominalism's, Irenaeus', Plato's—is a mechanical aggregate of past, present, and future. Eternity is something simpler and more magical: the simultaneity of the three tenses. This is something of which ordinary language and the stupefying dictionary *dont chaque édition fait regretter la précédente* [whose every new edition makes us long for the preceding one] appear to be unaware, but it was how the metaphysical thinkers conceived of eternity. "The objects of the Soul are successive, now Socrates and now a horse"—I read in the fifth book of the *Enneads*—"always some one thing which is conceived of and thousands that are lost; but the Divine Mind encompasses all things together. The past is present in its present, and the future as well. Nothing comes to pass in this world, but all things endure forever, steadfast in the happiness of their condition."

I will pause to consider this eternity, from which the subsequent ones derive. While it is true that Plotinus was not its founder—in an exceptional book, he speaks of the "antique and sacred philosophers" who preceded him—he amplifies and splendidly sums up all that those who went before him had imagined. Deussen compares him to the sunset: an impassioned final light. All the Greek conceptions of eternity, already rejected, already tragically elaborated upon, converge in his books. I therefore place him before Irenaeus, who ordained the second eternity: the one crowned by the three different but inextricable beings.

Plotinus says with unmistakable fervor,

> For all in the Intelligible Heaven is heaven; earth is heaven, and sea heaven; and animal, plant and man. For spectacle they have a world that has not been engendered. In beholding others they behold themselves. For all things There are translucent: nothing is dark, nothing impenetrable, for light is manifest to light. All are everywhere, and all is all, and the whole is in each as in the sum. The sun is one with all the stars and every star with the sun and all its fellows. No one walks there as upon an alien earth.

This unanimous universe, this apotheosis of assimilation and interchange, is not yet eternity; it is an adjacent heaven, still not wholly emancipated from space and number. Another passage from the fifth Ennead exhorts us to the contemplation of eternity itself, the world of universal forms:

> Whatsoever man is filled with admiration for the spectacle of this sensible universe, having regard to its greatness and loveliness and the ordinance of its everlasting movement, having regard also to the gods which are in it, divinities both visible and invisible, and daemons, and all creatures and plants; let him next lift up his thoughts to the truer Reality which is its archetype. There let him see all things in their intelligible nature, eternal not with a borrowed eternity, but in their proper consciousness and their proper life; their captain also he shall see, the uncontaminable Intelligence and the Wisdom that passes approach, and the true age of Kronos, whose name is Fullness. For in him are embraced all deathless things, every intelligence, every god, every soul, immutable forever. It is well with him: what should he seek to change? He has all things present to him: whither should he move? He did not at first lack this blessed state, then win it: all things are his in one eternity,

and the true eternity is his, which time does but mimic; for time must fetch the compass of the Soul, ever throwing a past behind it, ever in chase of a future.

The repeated affirmations of plurality in the preceding paragraphs can lead us into error. The ideal universe to which Plotinus summons us is less intent on variety than on plenitude; it is a select repertory, tolerating neither repetition nor pleonasm: the motionless and terrible museum of the Platonic archetypes. I do not know if mortal eyes ever saw it (outside of oracular vision or nightmare), or if the remote Greek who devised it ever made its acquaintance, but I sense something of the museum in it: still, monstrous, and classified. . . . But that is a bit of personal whimsy which the reader may disregard, though some general notion of these Platonic archetypes or primordial causes or ideas that populate and constitute eternity should be retained.

A protracted discussion of the Platonic system is impossible here, but certain prerequisite remarks can be offered. For us, the final, solid reality of things is matter—the spinning electrons that cross interstellar distances in their atomic solitude. But for those capable of thinking like Plato, it is the species, the form. In the third book of the *Enneads*, we read that matter is unreal, a mere hollow passivity that receives the universal forms as a mirror would; they agitate and populate it, but without altering it. Matter's plenitude is exactly that of a mirror, which simulates fullness and is empty; matter is a ghost that does not even disappear, for it lacks even the capacity to cease being. Form alone is truly fundamental. Of form, Pedro Malón de Chaide would write much later, repeating Plotinus:

> When God acts, it is as if you had an octagonal seal wrought of gold, in one part of which was wrought the shape of a lion; in another, a horse; in another, an eagle, and so for the rest; and in a bit of wax you imprinted the lion; in another, the eagle; in another, the horse; and it is certain that all that appears in the wax is in the gold, and you can print nothing but what is sculpted there. But there is a difference; in the wax it is of wax and worth little, but in the gold it is of gold and worth much. The perfections of the creatures of this world are finite and of little value; in God they are of gold, they are God Himself.

We may infer from this that matter is nothing.

We hold this to be a poor, even incomprehensible criterion, yet we apply it continually. A chapter by Schopenhauer is not the paper in the Leipzig archives, nor the act of printing, nor the contours and curlicues of the gothic letters, nor an enumeration of the sounds that comprise it, nor even the opinion we may have of it. Miriam Hopkins is made up of Miriam Hopkins, not of the nitrogenous or mineral rudiments, the carbohydrates, alkaloids, and neutral lipids that constitute the transitory substance of that slender silver specter or intelligible essence of Hollywood. These illustrations or well-intentioned sophistries may encourage us to tolerate the Platonic hypothesis which we will formulate thus: *Individuals and things exist insofar as they participate in the species that includes them, which is their permanent reality.*

I turn to the most promising example: the bird. The habit of flocking; smallness; similarity of traits; their ancient connection with the two twilights, the beginnings of days, and the endings; the fact of being more often heard than seen—all of this moves us to acknowledge the primacy of the species and the almost perfect nullity of individuals.[2] Keats, entirely a stranger to error, could believe that the nightingale enchanting him was the same one Ruth heard amid the alien corn of Bethlehem in Judah; Stevenson posits a single bird that consumes the centuries: "the nightingale that devours time." Schopenhauer—impassioned, lucid Schopenhauer—provides a reason: the pure corporeal immediacy in which animals live, oblivious to death and memory. He then adds, not without a smile:

> Whoever hears me assert that the grey cat playing just now in the yard is the same one that did jumps and tricks there five hundred years ago will think whatever he likes of me, but it is a stranger form of madness to imagine that the present-day cat is fundamentally an entirely different one.

And later:

> It is the life and fate of lions to seek lion-ness which, considered in time, is an immortal lion that maintains itself by the infinite replacement of individuals, whose engendering and death form the pulse of this undying figure.

[2]Alive, Son of Awake, the improbable metaphysical Robinson of Abubeker Abentofail's novel, resigns himself to eating only those fruits and fish that abound on his island, and always tries to ensure that no species will perish and the universe be thus impoverished by his fault.

And earlier:

> An infinite time has run its course before my birth; what was I through-
> out all that time? Metaphysically, I could perhaps answer myself: "I was
> always I", that is, all who throughout that time said "I" were none other
> than I.

I presume that my readers can find it within themselves to approve of
this eternal Lion-ness, and that they may feel a majestic satisfaction at the
thought of this single Lion, multiplied in time's mirrors. But I do not hope
for the same response to the concept of an eternal Humanity: I know that
our own "I" rejects it, preferring to jettison it recklessly onto the "I"s of others. This is an unpromising beginning, for Plato has far more laborious universal forms to propose. For example, Tableness, or the Intelligible Table
that exists in the heavens; the four-legged archetype pursued by every
cabinetmaker, all of them condemned to daydreams and frustration. (Yet I
cannot entirely negate the concept: without an ideal table, we would never
have achieved solid tables.) For example, Triangularity, an eminent three-
sided polygon that is not found in space and does not deign to adopt an
equilateral, scalene, or isosceles form. (I do not repudiate this one either: it
is the triangle of the geometry primers.) For example, Necessity, Reason,
Postponement, Connection, Consideration, Size, Order, Slowness, Position, Declaration, Disorder. With regard to these conveniences of thought,
elevated to the status of forms, I do not know what to think, except that
no man will ever be able to take cognizance of them without the assistance
of death, fever, or madness. And I have almost forgotten one more archetype that includes and exalts them all: Eternity, whose shredded copy is
time.

My readers may already be equipped with specific arguments for dis-
crediting the Platonic doctrine. In any case, I can supply them with several:
one, the incompatible cluster of generic and abstract terms coexisting *sans
gêne* in the storehouse of the archetypal world; another, their inventor's silence concerning the process by which things participate in the universal
forms; yet another, the conjecture that these antiseptic archetypes may
themselves suffer from mixture and variety. Far from being indissoluble,
they are as confused as time's own creatures, repeating the very anomalies they seek to resolve. Lion-ness, let us say: how would it dispense with
Pride and Tawniness, Mane-ness and Paw-ness? There is no answer to this
question, nor can there be: we do not expect from the term *lion-ness* a

virtue any greater than that of the word without the suffix.[3]

To return to Plotinus' eternity, the fifth book of the *Enneads* contains a rather vague inventory of its parts. Justice is there, as well as the Numbers (how many?) and the Virtues and Actions and Movement, but not mistakes and insults, which are diseases of a matter whose Form has been corrupted. Music is present, not as melody, but as Rhythm and Harmony. There are no archetypes from pathology or agriculture because they are not needed. Also excluded are tax collection, strategy, rhetoric, and the art of government—though, over time, they derive something from Beauty and Number. There are no individuals; there is no primordial form of Socrates, nor even of the Tall Man or the Emperor; there is, in a general way, Man. Only the primary colors are present: this eternity has no Grey or Purple or Green. In ascending order, its most ancient archetypes are these: Difference, Identity, Motion, Rest, and Being.

We have examined an eternity that is more impoverished than the world. It remains for us to see how our Church adopted it, and endowed it with a wealth far greater than the years can transport.

II

The best document of the first eternity is the fifth book of the *Enneads*; that of the second, or Christian, eternity, the eleventh book of St. Augus-

[3]I do not wish to bid farewell to Platonism (which seems icily remote) without making the following observation, in the hope that others may pursue and justify it: *The generic can be more intense than the concrete.* There is no lack of examples to illustrate this. During the boyhood summers I spent in the north of the province of Buenos Aires, I was intrigued by the rounded plain and the men who were butchering in the kitchen, but awful indeed was my delight when I learned that the circular space was the "pampa" and those men "gauchos." The same is true of the imaginative man who falls in love. The generic (the repeated name, the type, the fatherland, the tantalizing destiny invested in it) takes priority over individual features, *which are tolerated only because of their prior genre.*

The extreme example—the person who falls in love by word of mouth—is very common in the literatures of Persia and Arabia. To hear the description of a queen—her hair like nights of separation and exile, but her face like a day of delight, her breasts like marble spheres that lend their light to moons, her gait that puts antelopes to shame and is the despair of willow trees, the onerous hips that keep her from rising, her feet, narrow as spearheads—and to fall in love with her unto tranquillity and death is one of the traditional themes of *The Thousand and One Nights.* Read, for example, the story of Badrbasim, son of Shahriman, or that of Ibrahim and Yamila.

tine's *Confessions*. The first eternity is inconceivable without the Platonic hypothesis; the second, without the professional mystery of the Trinity and the attendant debates over predestination and damnation. Five hundred pages in folio would not exhaust the subject; I hope these two or three in octavo will not seem excessive.

It can be stated, with an adequate margin of error, that "our" eternity was decreed only a few years after a chronic intestinal pain killed Marcus Aurelius, and that the site of this vertiginous mandate was the hillside of Fourvière, formerly named Forum Vetus, famous now for its funicular and basilica. Despite the authority of the man who ordained it—Bishop Irenaeus—this coercive eternity was much more than a vain priestly adornment or an ecclesiastical luxury: it was a solution and a weapon. The Word is engendered by the Father, the Holy Spirit is produced by the Father and the Word. The Gnostics habitually inferred from these two undeniable operations that the Father preceded the Word, and both of them preceded the Spirit. This inference dissolved the Trinity. Irenaeus clarified that the double process—the Son engendered by the Father, the Holy Spirit issuing from the two—did not occur in time, but consumes past, present, and future once and for all. His clarification prevailed and is now dogma. Eternity—theretofore barely tolerated in the shadows of one or another unauthorized Platonic text—thus came to be preached. The proper connection among, or distinction between, the three hypostases of the Lord seems an unlikely problem now, and its futility may appear to contaminate the solution, but there can be no doubt of the grandeur of the result, at least to nourish hope: "*Aeternitas est merum hodie, est immediata et lucida fruitio rerum infinitarum*" [Eternity is merely today; it is the immediate and lucid enjoyment of the things of infinity]. Nor is there doubt of the emotional and polemical importance of the Trinity.

Today, Catholic laymen consider the Trinity a kind of professional organization, infinitely correct and infinitely boring; liberals, meanwhile, view it as a useless theological Cerberus, a superstition that the Republic's great advances have already taken upon themselves to abolish. The Trinity clearly exceeds these formulae. Imagined all at once, the concept of a father, a son, and a ghost articulated in a single organism seems like a case of intellectual teratology, a distortion only the horror of a nightmare could engender. Hell is mere physical violence, but the three inextricable Persons add up to an intellectual horror, stifled and specious like the infinity of facing mirrors. Dante sought to denote them by a symbol showing three multicolored, diaphanous circles, superimposed; Donne, by complicated serpents, sumptuous and indivisible. "*Toto coruscat trinitas mysterio,*" wrote St. Paulinus, the Trinity gleams in full mystery.

Detached from the concept of redemption, the three-persons-in-one distinction seems arbitrary. Considered a necessity of faith, its fundamental mystery remains intact, but its use and intention begin to shine through. We understand that to renounce the Trinity—or, at least, the Duality—is to make of Jesus an occasional delegate of the Lord, an incident of history rather than the deathless and continual auditor of our devotion. If the Son is not also the Father, redemption is not the direct work of the divine; if He is not eternal, the sacrifice of having lowered Himself to become a man and die on the cross will not be eternal either. Nothing less than an infinite excellence could suffice for a soul lost for infinite ages, Jeremy Taylor admonished. . . . The dogma may thus be justified, though the concepts of the generation of the Son by the Father and the emanation of the Spirit from both continue to insinuate a certain priority, their guilty condition as mere metaphors notwithstanding. Theology, at pains to distinguish between them, resolves that there is no reason for confusion, since the result of one is the Son, and of the other, the Spirit. Eternal generation of the Son, eternal emanation of the Spirit, is Irenaeus' superb verdict: the invention of a timeless act, a mutilated *zeitloses Zeitwort* that we can discard or venerate, but not debate. Irenaeus set out to save the monster, and did. We know he was the philosophers' enemy; to have appropriated their weapon and turned it against them must have afforded him a bellicose pleasure.

For the Christian, the first second of time coincides with the first second of the Creation—a fact that spares us the spectacle (recently reconstructed by Valéry) of a vacant God reeling in the barren centuries of the eternity "before." Emanuel Swedenborg (*Vera Christiana Religio,* 1771) saw at the outer limit of the spiritual orb a hallucinatory statue depicting the voracious inferno into which are plunged all who "engaged in senseless and sterile deliberations on the condition of the Lord before creating the world."

As soon as Irenaeus had brought it into being, the Christian eternity began to differ from the Alexandrian. No longer a world apart, it settled into the role of one of the nineteen attributes of the mind of God. As objects of popular veneration, the archetypes ran the risk of becoming angels or divinities: consequently, while their reality—still greater than that of mere creatures—was not denied, they were reduced to eternal ideas in the creating Word. This concept of the *universalia res* [universal things] is addressed by Albertus Magnus: he considers them eternal and prior to the things of Creation, but only as forms or inspirations. He separates them very deliberately from the *universalia in rebus* [the universal in things], which are the divine concepts themselves, now variously embodied in time, and, above all, from the *universalia post res* [the universal beyond things], which are those same concepts rediscovered by inductive thought. Temporal things are distinguished from divine things by their lack of creative efficacy but in no other way; the suspicion that God's categories might not precisely coincide with those of Latin has no place in Scholastic thought. . . . But I see I am getting ahead of myself.

Theology handbooks do not linger with any special devotion on the subject of eternity. They merely note that eternity is the contemporary and total intuition of all fractions of time, and make a dogged inspection of the Hebrew scriptures in search of fraudulent confirmations in which the Holy Spirit seems to have expressed very badly what the commentator expresses so well. To that end, they like to brandish this declaration of illustrious disdain or simple longevity: "One day is with the Lord as a thousand years, and a thousand years as one day," or the grand words heard by Moses—"I Am That I Am," the name of God—or those heard by St. John the Theologian on Patmos, before and after the sea of glass and the scarlet beast and the fowls that eat the flesh of captains: "I am Alpha and Omega, the beginning and the end."[4] They also like to repeat the definition by Boethius (conceived in prison, perhaps on the eve of his execution), "*Aeternitas est interminabilis vitae tota et perfect possessio*" [Eternity is all of life interminable and perfect possession], and, more to my liking, Hans Lassen Martensen's almost voluptuous repetition: "*Aeternitas est merum hodie, est immediata et lucida fruitio rerum infinitarum*" [Eternity is merely today; it is the immediate and lucid enjoyment of the things of infinity]. However, they generally seem to disdain the obscure oath of the angel who stood upon the sea and upon the earth "and sware by him that liveth for ever and ever, who created heaven, and the things that therein are, and the earth, and the things that therein are, and the sea, and the things which are therein, that there should be time no longer" (Revelations 10:6). It is true that *time* in this verse must be synonymous with *delay*.

---

[4]The idea that the time of men is not commensurable with God's is prominent in one of the Islamic traditions of the cycle of the *miraj*. It is known that the Prophet was carried off to the seventh heaven by the resplendent mare Alburak and that he conversed with each one of the patriarchs and angels that dwell there and that he traversed Unity and felt a coldness that froze his heart when the hand of the Lord clapped his shoulder. Leaving the earth, Alburak's hoof knocked over a jug full of water; on returning, the Prophet picked up the jug and not a single drop had been spilled.

Eternity became an attribute of the unlimited mind of God, and as we know, generations of theologians have pondered this mind, in its image and likeness. No stimulus has been as sharp as the debate over predestination *ab aeterno*. Four hundred years after the Cross, the English monk Pelagius conceived of the outrageous notion that innocents who die without baptism can attain eternal glory.[5] Augustine, bishop of Hippo, refuted him with an indignation that was applauded by his editors. He noted the heresies intrinsic to this doctrine, which is abhorred by the righteous and the martyrs: its negation of the fact that in Adam all men have already sinned and died, its abominable heedlessness of the transmission of this death from father to son by carnal generation, its scorn for the bloody sweat, the supernatural agony and the cry of He Who died on the Cross, its rejection of the secret favors of the Holy Spirit, its infringement upon the freedom of the Lord. The British monk had the gall to invoke justice. The Saint—grandiloquent and forensic, as ever—concedes that in justice all men are impardonably deserving of hellfire, but maintains that God has determined to save some, *according to His inscrutable will,* or, as Calvin would say much later, and not without a certain brutality, *because He wants to (quia voluit)*. Those few are the predestined. The hypocrisy or reticence of theologians has reserved the term for those predestined for heaven. Men predestined for torment there cannot be: though it is true that those not chosen descend into eternal flame, that is merely an omission on the Lord's part, not a specific action. . . . Thus the concept of eternity was renewed.

Generations of idolatrous men had inhabited the earth without having occasion to reject or embrace the word of God; it was as insolent to imagine they could be saved without this means as to deny that some of them, renowned for their virtue, would be excluded from glory everlasting. (Zwingli in 1523 expressed his personal hope of sharing heaven with Hercules, Theseus, Socrates, Aristides, Aristotle, and Seneca.) An amplification of the Lord's ninth attribute (omniscience) effectively did away with the difficulty. This attribute, it was proclaimed, amounted to a knowledge of all things, that is to say, not only real things, but also those that are merely possible. The Scriptures were scoured for a passage that would allow for this infinite supplement, and two were found: in I Samuel, when the Lord tells

---

[5]Jesus Christ had said: "Suffer the little children to come unto me"; Pelagius was accused, naturally, of interposing himself between the little children and Jesus Christ, thus delivering them to hell. Like that of Athanasius (Sathanasius) his name was conducive to wordplay: everyone said Pelagius had to be an ocean (*pelagus*) of evils.

David that the men of Keilah will deliver him up to his enemy if he does not leave the city, and he goes; and in the Gospel According to Matthew, which includes the following curse on two cities: "Woe unto thee, Chorazin! woe unto thee, Bethsaida! for if the mighty works, which were done in you, had been done in Tyre and Sidon, they would have repented long ago in sackcloth and ashes." With this repeated support, the potential modes of the verb could extend into eternity: Hercules dwells in heaven beside Ulrich Zwingli because God knows he would have observed the ecclesiastical year, but He is also aware that the Hydra of Lerna would have rejected baptism and so has relegated the creature to outer darkness. We perceive real events and imagine those that are possible (or future); in the Lord this distinction has no place, for it belongs to time and ignorance. His eternity registers once and for all (*uno intelligendi actu*) not only every moment of this replete world but also all that would take place if the most evanescent instant were to change—as well as all that are impossible. His precise and combinatory eternity is much more copious than the universe.

Unlike the Platonic eternities, whose greatest danger is tedium, this one runs the risk of resembling the final pages of *Ulysses*, or even the preceding chapter, the enormous interrogation. A majestuous scruple on Augustine's part modified this prolixity. His doctrine, at least verbally, rejects damnation: the Lord concentrates on the elect and overlooks the reprobates. He knows all, but prefers to dwell on virtuous lives. John Scotus Erigena, the court schoolteacher of Charles the Bald, gloriously distorted this idea. He proclaimed an indeterminate God and an orb of Platonic archetypes; he spoke of a God who perceives neither sin nor the forms of evil, and also mused on deification, the final reversion of all creatures (including time and the demon) to the primal unity of God: "*Divina bonitas consummabit malitiam, aeterna vita absorbebit mortem, beatitudo miseriam*" [Divine goodness consumed evil, eternal life absorbed death, and beatitude misery]. This hybrid eternity (which, unlike the Platonic eternities, includes individual destinies, and unlike the orthodox institution, rejects all imperfection and misery) was condemned by the synods of Valencia and Langres. *De divisione naturae libri V*, the controversial work that described it, was publicly burned, an adroit maneuver that awoke the interest of bibliophiles and enabled Erigena's book to survive to the present day.

The universe requires eternity. Theologians are not unaware that if the Lord's attention were to waver for a single second from my right hand as it writes this, it would instantly lapse into nothingness as if blasted by a lightless fire. They affirm, therefore, that the conservation of the world is a perpetual creation and that the verbs *conserve* and *create,* so antagonistic here below, are synonyms in Heaven.

III

Up to this point, in chronological order, a general history of eternity. Or rather, of the eternities, for human desire dreamed two successive and mutually hostile dreams by that name: one, realist, yearns with a strange love for the still and silent archetypes of all creatures; the other, nominalist, denies the truth of the archetypes and seeks to gather up all the details of the universe in a single second. The first is based on realism, a doctrine so distant from our essential nature that I disbelieve all interpretations of it, including my own; the second, on realism's opponent, nominalism, which affirms the truth of individuals and the conventional nature of genres. Now, like the spontaneous and bewildered prose-speaker of comedy, we all do nominalism *sans le savoir,* as if it were a general premise of our thought, an acquired axiom. Useless, therefore, to comment on it.

Up to this point, in chronological order, the debated and curial development of eternity. Remote men, bearded, mitred men conceived of it, ostensibly to confound heresies and defend the distinction of the three persons in one, but secretly in order to staunch in some way the flow of hours. "To live is to lose time; we can recover or keep nothing except under the form of eternity," I read in the work of that Emersonized Spaniard, George Santayana. To which we need only juxtapose the terrible passage by Lucretius on the fallacy of coitus:

> Like the thirsty man who in sleep wishes to drink and consumes forms of water that do not satiate him and dies burning up with thirst in the middle of a river; so Venus deceives lovers with simulacra, and the sight of a body does not satisfy them, and they cannot detach or keep anything, though their indecisive and mutual hands run over the whole body. At the end, when there is a foretaste of delight in the bodies and Venus is about to sow the woman's fields, the lovers grasp each other anxiously, amorous tooth against tooth; entirely in vain, for they do not succeed in losing themselves in each other or becoming a single being.

The archetypes, eternity—these two words—hold out the promise of more solid possessions. For it is true that succession is an intolerable misery, and magnanimous appetites are greedy for all the minutes of time and all the variety of space.

Personal identity is known to reside in memory, and the annulment of that faculty is known to result in idiocy. It is possible to think the same thing of the universe. Without an eternity, without a sensitive, secret mirror of what passes through every soul, universal history is lost time, and along with it our personal history—which rather uncomfortably makes ghosts of us. The Berliner Company's gramophone records or the transparent cinema are insufficient, mere images of images, idols of other idols. Eternity is a more copious invention. True, it is inconceivable, but then so is humble successive time. To deny eternity, to suppose the vast annihilation of the years freighted with cities, rivers, and jubilations, is no less incredible than to imagine their total salvation.

How did eternity come into being? St. Augustine ignores the problem, but notes something that seems to allow for a solution: the elements of past and future that exist in every present. He cites a specific case: the recitation of a poem.

> Before beginning, the poem exists in my expectation; when I have just finished, in my memory; but as I am reciting it, it is extended in my memory, on account of what I have already said; and in my expectation, on account of what I have yet to say. What takes place with the entirety of the poem takes place also in each verse and each syllable. This also holds true of the larger action of which the poem is part, and of the individual destiny of a man, which is composed of a series of actions, and of humanity, which is a series of individual destinies.

Nevertheless, this verification of the intimate intertwining of the diverse tenses of time still includes succession, which is not commensurate with a model of unanimous eternity.

I believe nostalgia was that model. The exile who with melting heart remembers his expectations of happiness sees them *sub specie aeternitatis* [under the aspect of eternity], completely forgetting that the achievement of one of them would exclude or postpone all the others. In passion, memory inclines toward the intemporal. We gather up all the delights of a given past in a single image; the diversely red sunsets I watch every evening will in memory be a single sunset. The same is true of foresight: nothing prevents the most incompatible hopes from peacefully coexisting. To put it differently: eternity is the style of desire. (The particular enjoyment that

enumeration yields may plausibly reside in its insinuation of the eternal—
the *immediata et lucida fruitio rerum infinitarum.*)

IV

There only remains for me to disclose to the reader my personal theory of
eternity. Mine is an impoverished eternity, without a God or even a co-
proprietor, and entirely devoid of archetypes. It was formulated in my 1928
book *The Language of the Argentines.* I reprint here what I published then;
the passage is entitled "Feeling in Death."

> I wish to record an experience I had a few nights ago: a triviality too
> evanescent and ecstatic to be called an adventure, too irrational and
> sentimental for thought. It was a scene and its word: a word I had spo-
> ken but had not fully lived with all my being until then. I will recount
> its history and the accidents of time and place that revealed it to me.
>
> I remember it thus: On the afternoon before that night, I was in
> Barracas, an area I do not customarily visit, and whose distance from
> the places I later passed through had already given the day a strange sa-
> vor. The night had no objective whatsoever; the weather was clear, and
> so, after dinner, I went out to walk and remember. I did not want to es-
> tablish any particular direction for my stroll: I strove for a maximum
> latitude of possibility so as not to fatigue my expectant mind with the
> obligatory foresight of a particular path. I accomplished, to the unsatis-
> factory degree to which it is possible, what is called strolling at random,
> without other conscious resolve than to pass up the avenues and broad
> streets in favor of chance's more obscure invitations. Yet a kind of fa-
> miliar gravitation pushed me toward neighborhoods whose name I
> wish always to remember, places that fill my heart with reverence. I am
> not alluding to my own neighborhood, the precise circumference of my
> childhood, but to its still mysterious outskirts; a frontier region I have
> possessed fully in words and very little in reality, at once adjacent and
> mythical. These penultimate streets are, for me, the opposite of what is
> familiar, its other face, almost as unknown as the buried foundations of
> our house or our own invisible skeleton. The walk left me at a street
> corner. I took in the night, in perfect, serene respite from thought. The
> vision before me, not at all complex to begin with, seemed further sim-
> plified by my fatigue. Its very ordinariness made it unreal. It was a street
> of one-story houses, and though its first meaning was poverty, its

second was certainly bliss. It was the poorest and most beautiful thing. The houses faced away from the street; a fig tree merged into shadow over the blunted streetcorner, and the narrow portals—higher than the extending lines of the walls—seemed wrought of the same infinite substance as the night. The sidewalk was embanked above a street of elemental dirt, the dirt of a still unconquered America. In the distance, the road, by then a country lane, crumbled into the Maldonado River. Against the muddy, chaotic earth, a low, rose-colored wall seemed not to harbor the moonlight but to shimmer with a gleam all its own. Tenderness could have no better name than that rose color.

I stood there looking at this simplicity. I thought, undoubtedly aloud: "This is the same as it was thirty years ago." I imagined that date: recent enough in other countries, but already remote on this ever-changing side of the world. Perhaps a bird was singing and I felt for it a small, bird-sized fondness; but there was probably no other sound in the dizzying silence except for the equally timeless noise of crickets. The glib thought *I am in the year eighteen hundred and something* ceased to be a few approximate words and deepened into reality. I felt as the dead feel, I felt myself to be an abstract observer of the world: an indefinite fear imbued with knowledge that is the greatest clarity of metaphysics. No, I did not believe I had made my way upstream on the presumptive waters of Time. Rather, I suspected myself to be in possession of the reticent or absent meaning of the inconceivable word *eternity*. Only later did I succeed in defining this figment of my imagination.

I write it out now: This pure representation of homogenous facts—the serenity of the night, the translucent little wall, the small-town scent of honeysuckle, the fundamental dirt—is not merely identical to what existed on that corner many years ago; it is, without superficial resemblances or repetitions, the same. When we can feel this oneness, time is a delusion which the indifference and inseparability of a moment from its apparent yesterday and from its apparent today suffice to disintegrate.

The number of such human moments is clearly not infinite. The elemental experiences—physical suffering and physical pleasure, falling asleep, listening to a piece of music, feeling great intensity or great apathy—are even more impersonal. I derive, in advance, this conclusion: life is too impoverished not to be immortal. But we lack even the certainty of our own poverty, given that time, which is easily refutable by the senses, is not so easily refuted by the intellect, from whose essence the concept of succession appears inseparable. Let there remain, then, the glimpse of an idea in an emotional anecdote, and, in the acknowledged irresolution of this page, the true moment of ecstasy and the possible intimation of eternity which that night did not hoard from me.

[1936]   *[EA]*

In the aim of adding dramatic interest to this biography of eternity I committed certain distortions, for instance, that of condensing into five or six names a step that took centuries.

I worked with whatever was at hand in my library. Among the most useful volumes, I must mention the following:

Die Philosophie der Griechen von Dr. Paul Deussen. Leipzig, 1919.

Selected Works of Plotinus. Translated by Thomas Taylor. London, 1817.

Passages Illustrating Neoplatonism. Translated with an introduction by E. R. Dodds. London, 1932.

La Philosophie de Platon par Alfred Fouillée. Paris, 1869.

Die Welt als Wille und Vorstellung von Arthur Schopenhauer. Herausgegeben von Eduard Grisebach. Leipzig, 1892.

Die Philosophie des Mittelalters von Dr. Paul Deussen. Leipzig, 1920.

Las confesiones de San Agustín. Versión literal por el P. Angel C. Vega, Madrid, 1932.

A Monument to Saint Augustine. London, 1930.

Dogmatik von Dr. R. Rothe. Heidelberg, 1870.

Ensayos de crítica filosófica de Menéndez y Pelayo. Madrid, 1892.

FILM REVIEWS AND CRITICISM

The Cinematograph, the Biograph

A film was once called a "biograph"; now we generally say "cinematograph." The first term died, perhaps because fame required more clamor, perhaps because the implication of Boswell or Voltaire made it threateningly lofty. I would not lament that demise (similar to thousands of others in the continuing necrology of semantics) if words were indifferent symbols. I doubt that they are, for they traffic in similarities, opinions, condemnations. Every word implies an argument that may be a sophistry. Here, without entering into a discussion of which is the best, it is easy to observe that the word *cinematograph* is better than *biograph*. The latter, if my intuitive grasp of Greek does not betray me, means "life-writing"; the former refers solely to motion. The two ideas, although dialectically reducible to the same thing, imply different orientations, variations that entitle me to distinguish them and to assign one meaning to *cinematograph* and another to *biograph*. Let me assure my reader that such a distinction, limited to this article, is not of major significance.

"Cinematography" is the writing of motion, signifying in its emphasis rapidity, solemnity, turmoil. This mode of operation pertains to its origins, whose only material is speed; ridiculous in the unhappy bewilderment of those who only knew how to carry on with stages and sets, epic in the dust storm of a cowboy picture. It is also peculiar, by the malicious paradox of things, to the so-called avant-garde cinema; an institution reduced to nourishing, with more enriched means, the same old fluster. The original spectator would be amazed by a single horseman; today's equivalent needs many men or the superimposed vision of a railroad train, a column of workers, a ship. The substance of the emotion is the same: bourgeois shock at the devilish antics produced by machines, as invented with an excessive name, "magic lantern," for the toy Athanasius Kircher presented in his *Ars magna lucis et umbrae*. For the spectator, it is mere frightening technological stupidity; for the fabricator, it is lazy invention, taking advantage of the fluency of visual images. His inertia is comparable precisely to that of metrical poets, who are aided by the continuity of syntax and the linked inference from one phrase to another. The gaucho troubadours also make use of that continuity. I say this without the slightest contempt; it cannot be decisively proven that thinking—ours, Schopenhauer's, Shaw's—is more freely determined; a doubt I possess thanks to Fritz Mauthner.

Having eliminated, to our relief, the cinematograph, what follows is the biograph. How should we see it, entangled as it is with an inferior crowd? The quickest procedure is to look for the names of Charlie Chaplin, Emil Jannings, George Bancroft, or of a few afflicted Russians. An efficient way, but too contemporary, too circumstantial. We may formulate a general application (though not, like the other, predictive) as follows: The biograph reveals to us individual lives; it presents souls to the soul. The definition is brief; its proof (feeling a presence, a human rapport, or not) is an elementary act. It is the reaction we all use to judge books of imagination. A novel presents the fates of many; a poem or an essay, one single life. (The poet or essayist is a novelist of one character: Heinrich Heine's twelve volumes are only inhabited by Heinrich Heine, Unamuno's works by Unamuno. The dramatic poets—Browning, Shakespeare—and the narrative essayists— Lytton Strachey, Macaulay—are completely novelists, the only difference being their less hidden passions.) I repeat: the biograph is that which adds people. The other, the non-biograph, the cinematograph, is deserted, without any other connection to human lives except through factories, machinery, palaces, cavalry charges, and other allusions to reality or easy generalities. It is an inhospitable, oppressive zone.

To go back to Chaplin as the perfect defense of the biograph is an obligation that delights me. I cannot think of more lovely inventions. There is his tremulous epic *The Gold Rush*—a title well translated into French, *La Ruée ver l'or* [The Rush toward Gold], and badly into Spanish, *La quimera del oro* [The Chimera of Gold]. Recall a few of its moments. Chaplin, a fine little Jewish fellow, walks vertiginously along a narrow path, with the mountain wall on one side and a deep ravine on the other. A big bear emerges and follows him. Chaplin, angelically absentminded, has not noticed. They continue in this manner a few more suspenseful seconds: the beast almost sniffing at his heels, the man keeping his balance with his cane, his ill-fitting top hat, and almost with his straight black mustache. The spectator expects Chaplin to be smacked by a paw at any moment and frightfully awakened. At that moment the bear comes upon and enters his cave and the man continues on his way, without having seen anything. The situation has been resolved—or dissolved—magically. Two were absent-minded instead of just one; God, this time, has been no less delicate than Chaplin. I will describe another incident, also constructed upon absent-mindedness. Chaplin, in a frock coat, uncomfortable, returns as a million-aire from Alaska. The danger is that we will feel he is too triumphant, too identified with his dollars. He is received by a steamship whose crew ap-pears to consist exclusively of fawning photographers. On deck, Chaplin strolls between admiring rows of onlookers. Suddenly, uncouth angel that he is, he notices a twisted cigarette butt on the floor, bends over, and picks it up. Is he not absentminded to an almost saintly degree? Each scene of *The Gold Rush* is equally intense. Moreover, Chaplin's is not the only story—which distinguishes this film from others, pure monologues by their inven-tor, such as *The Kid* and *The Circus*—Jim, who discovered a mountain of gold and no longer knows where it is, tramps around the brothels with that perturbed memory and impervious oblivion; Georgina, the dancer, faithful only to her imperious beauty, light-footed on earth; Larsen, the man whose greeting is a gunshot, resigned to being the bad guy, possessed by the mortal innocence of depravity: all of these are complete stories.

Chaplin is his own narrator, that is, the poet of the biograph; Jannings is its manifold novelist. I cannot transcribe anything of his: his lively vo-cabulary of gestures and his direct facial language do not seem translatable to any other. Aside from the agonies of tragedy, Jannings knows how to ren-der the strictly everyday. He knows not only how to die (an easy task, or easy to pretend because it cannot be verified) but how to live. Made of in-cessant, minute realizations, his unpretentious style is as efficient as Cer-vantes' or Butler's. His characters—the opaque heap of sensuality in *Tartuffe*, always with a tiny breviary before his eyes like a sardonic mask; the emperor in *Quo Vadis*, repulsively effeminate and grossly vain; the proper and complacently methodical cashier Schilling; the great gentleman in *The Last Command*, no less dedicated to the fatherland than knowledgeable of his frailties and complexities—are all so disparate, all so self-contained, that we are unable to imagine them understanding each other. How ironically uninterested the general is in Schilling's menial tragedy, and what prophetic anathemas (written in Martin Luther's heroic German) he would cast at Nero!

To die one need only be alive, I heard an Argentine woman say, indisputably. I would add that this precondition is indispensable and that the German cinematograph—as disinterested in persons as it is determined to seek symmetries and symbols—tends to omit it with a fatal frivolity. The German cinema tries to move us with universal shortcomings, or with the martyrdom of multitudes whose lives we have not witnessed and which, as insignificant bas-reliefs, are even further defamiliarized. Not realizing that the crowd is less than one man, it erects a forest to hide the lack of a tree. But in art, as in the biblical deluge, the loss of humanity does not matter as long as the concrete human couple inherits the world. Defoe would divide this example by two and substitute: *as long as Robinson . . .*

[1929]   [SJL]

Films

Here is my opinion of some recent films:

Surpassing the others, *Der Morder Dimitri Karamasoff* [The Murderer Dimitri Karamazov] (Filmreich) is by far the best. Its director, Ozep, appears to have skirted effortlessly the much praised and voguish flaws of the German cinema—lugubrious symbolism, tautology or the meaningless repetition of equivalent images, obscenity, a propensity for teratology and Satanism—while also eluding the Soviet school's even more glaring pitfalls: the omission of characters, photographic anthologies, and the awkward charms of the Committee. (I will not even mention the French: thus far their one and only desire has been not to resemble the Americans, a risk, I assure them, they do not run.)

I am not familiar with the cavernous novel from which this film was extracted, a *felix culpa* allowing me to enjoy it without the constant temptation to compare the present spectacle with the remembered book in order to see if they coincide. Pristinely disregarding, therefore, its irreverent desecrations and virtuous fidelities—both unimportant—I find the present film most powerful. Purely hallucinatory, neither subordinate nor cohesive, its reality is no less torrential than Josef von Sternberg's teeming *Docks of New York*. Among the high points is a depiction of genuine, candid joy after a murder: the sequence of shots—approaching dawn, huge billiard balls awaiting collision, Smerdiakov's clerical hand taking the money—is brilliantly conceived and executed.

Here is another film. All our critics have unconditionally applauded

Charlie Chaplin's latest, mysteriously entitled *City Lights*. The truth behind this published acclaim, however, has more to do with our faultless telegraphic and postal services than with any inherent, individual judgment. Would anyone dare ignore that Charlie Chaplin is one of the established gods in the mythology of our time, a cohort of de Chirico's motionless nightmares, of Scarface Al's ardent machine guns, of the finite yet unlimited universe of Greta Garbo's lofty shoulders, of the goggled eyes of Gandhi? Could anyone afford not to know that Chaplin's most recent *comédie larmoyante* had to be astonishing? In reality—in what I believe is reality—this much-attended film from the splendid creator and hero of *The Gold Rush* is merely a weak collection of minor mishaps imposed on a sentimental story. Some episodes are new; one is not: the garbage collector's professional joy upon seeing the providential (and then false) elephant who will presumably supply him with a *raison d'être* is a carbon copy of the Trojan garbage collector and the fake Greek horse in that neglected film *The Private Life of Helen of Troy*.

Objections of a more general nature can also be leveled against *City Lights*. Its lack of reality is comparable only to its equally exasperating lack of unreality. Some movies are true to life—*For the Defense, Street of Chance, The Crowd,* even *The Broadway Melody*—and some are willfully unrealistic, such as the highly individualistic films of Frank Borzage, Harry Langdon, Buster Keaton, and Eisenstein. Chaplin's early escapades belong to the second type, undeniably based as they are on depthless photography and eerily accelerated action, as well as on the actors' fake moustaches, absurd false beards, fright wigs, and ominous overcoats. Not attaining such unreality, *City Lights* remains unconvincing. Except for the luminous blind girl, extraordinary in her beauty, and for Charlie himself—always a wraith, always disguised—all the film's characters are recklessly normal. Its ramshackle plot relies on the disjointed techniques of continuity from twenty years ago. Archaism and anachronism are literary modes too, I know, but to handle them intentionally is different than perpetrating them ineptly. I relinquish my hope—so often fulfilled—of being wrong.

In von Sternberg's *Morocco*, too, I notice a certain weariness, though to a less overwhelming and suicidal degree. The terse photography, exquisite direction, and oblique yet suitable methods of *Underworld* have been replaced here by hordes of extras and broad brushstrokes of excessive local color. To indicate Morocco, von Sternberg has thought up nothing less vulgar than an ornate forgery of a Moorish city in the Hollywood suburbs, with a cornucopia of burnooses, fountains, and tall guttural muezzins preceding the dawn and the camels in sunlight. The film's overall plot, on the other hand, is good, resolved at the end in the open desert, returned once more to the beginning, like our first *Martín Fierro* or the novel *Sanin* by the Russian Artsybashev. One may watch *Morocco* with pleasure, but not with the intellectual satisfaction derived from the first viewing (and even the second) of earlier works by von Sternberg, nor with the cogent intellectual satisfaction produced by that heroic film *The Dragnet*.

[1931]   [SJL]

Street Scene

The Russians discovered that the oblique—and consequently—distorted shot of a bottle, a bull's neck, or a column had greater visual value than Hollywood's thousand and one extras, hastily camouflaged as Assyrians and then shuffled into total confusion by Cecil B. DeMille. They also discovered that Midwestern cliches—the merits of espionage and betrayal, of everlasting wedded bliss, the untarnished purity of prostitutes, the finishing uppercut dealt by a sober young man—could be exchanged for other, no less admirable cliches. (Thus, in one of the noblest Soviet films, a battleship bombards the teeming port of Odessa at close range, with no casualties except for some marble lions. This marksmanship is harmless because it comes from a virtuous, maximum battleship.)

Such discoveries, proposed to a world saturated to the point of disgust with Hollywood productions, were honored by a world that extended its gratitude to the point of pretending that Soviet cinema had wiped out American cinema forever. (Those were the years when Alexander Blok proclaimed, in the characteristic tones of Walt Whitman, that the Russians were Scythians.) The world forgot, or tried to forget, that the Russian cinema's greatest virtue was to interrupt a steady fare from California. Also ignored was the absurdity of equating a few good, even excellent acts of violence (*Ivan the Terrible, Battleship Potemkin,* perhaps *October*) with a vast and complex literature, successfully executed in all genres, from the incomparably comedic (Charlie Chaplin, Buster Keaton, and Harry Langdon) to the purely fantastic mythologies of Krazy Kat and Bimbo. Alarm over the Russians grew. Hollywood reformed or enriched some of its photographic techniques, and did not get too worried.

King Vidor did, however. I speak of the uneven director of works as memorable as *Hallelujah* and as superfluously trivial as *Billy the Kid*, that shameful chronicle of the twenty murders (not counting Mexicans) committed by the famous gunslinger from Arizona, a film made with no distinction other than the accumulation of panoramic takes and, to denote the desert, the methodical elimination of close-ups. His most recent work, *Street Scene,* adapted from the comedy of the same name by the ex-expressionist Elmer Rice, is inspired by the simple, negative desire not to look "standard." It has an unsatisfying, minimal plot: its hero is virtuous but under the influence of a thug; it has a romantic couple, but any civil or religious union is forbidden to them. It has a gloriously exuberant, larger-than-life Italian who is obviously responsible for all the comedy in the piece, a man whose unlimited unreality also rubs off on his normal colleagues. It has characters who seem true to life and others in masquerade. Fundamentally not realist, this film is a frustrated, or repressed, romantic work.

Two great scenes elevate the film: a dawn where the splendid course of the night is epitomized in music, and a murder indirectly presented to us in the tumult and tempest of faces.

Actors and photography: excellent.

[1932]   [SJL]

King Kong

A monkey forty feet tall (some fans say forty-five) may have obvious charms, but those charms have not convinced this viewer. King Kong is no full-blooded ape but rather a rusty, desiccated machine whose movements are downright clumsy. His only virtue, his height, did not impress the cinematographer, who persisted in photographing him from above rather than from below—the wrong angle, as it neutralizes and even diminishes the ape's overpraised stature. He is actually hunchbacked and bowlegged, attributes that serve only to reduce him in the spectator's eye. To keep him from looking the least bit extraordinary, they make him do battle with far more unusual monsters and have him reside in caves of false cathedral splendor, where his infamous size again loses all proportion. But what finally demolishes both the gorilla and the film is his romantic love—or lust—for Fay Wray.

[1933]   [SJL]

The Informer

I am not familiar with the popular novel from which this film was adapted, a *felix culpa* that has allowed me to watch it without the constant temptation to compare the present spectacle with the remembered reading in order to determine coincidences. I have watched it and do consider it one of the best films offered us this past year; I also consider it too memorable not to provoke discussion and not to deserve reproach. Several reproaches, really, since it has run the beautiful risk of being entirely satisfactory and, for two or three reasons, has not succeeded.

The first is the hero's excessive motivations for his actions. I recognize that realism is the goal, but film directors (and novelists) tend to forget that many justifications, and many circumstantial details, are counterproductive. Reality is not vague, but our general perception of reality is: herein lies the danger of overly justifying actions or inventing too many details. In this particular case (a man suddenly turns Judas, denounces his friend to the police with their machine guns, condemning him to death), the erotic motive invoked seems to diminish the treachery of the deed and its heinous miracle. Infamy committed absentmindedly, or out of mere brutality, would have been more striking, artistically. I also think it would have been more believable. (L'Herbier's *Le Bonheur* is another excellent film invalidated by its excess of psychological motives.) Obviously, a plurality of motives does not seem, in essence, wrong to me: I admire the scene where the informer squanders his thirty pieces of silver because of his triple need to confuse, to bribe his threatening friends (who are perhaps his judges and will end up as his executioners), and to rid himself of those banknotes that dishonor him.

Another weakness of *The Informer* is how it begins and ends. The opening episodes do not ring true. This is partly the fault of the street we are shown—too typical, too European (in the California sense of the word). A street in Dublin is certainly not identical to a street in San Francisco, but because both are authentic, the location resembles more the latter than an obvious sham, overloaded with thick local color. More than universal similarities, local differences seem to have made a great impression on Hollywood: there is no American director, faced with the hypothetical problem of showing a railroad crossing in Spain or an open field in Austro-Hungary, who does not solve the problem by representing the site with a set, built especially for the occasion, whose only merit must be its ostentatious cost. The ending has other faults: while it is appropriate for the audience to be moved by the horrifying fate of the informer, the fact that the director of the film is moved and grants him a sentimental death amid Catholic stained-glass windows and choir music seems less admirable.

The merits of this film are less subtle than its faults and do not need emphasis. Nevertheless, I would like to note one very effective touch: the dangling man's fingernails grating on the ledge at the very end and the disappearance of his hand as he is machine-gunned and falls to the ground.

Of the three tragic unities, two have been observed: the unities of time and action. Neglect of the third—unity of place—cannot be a cause for complaint. By its very nature, film seems to reject this third norm, requiring, instead, continuous displacements. (The dangers of dogmatism: the admirable memory of *Payment Deferred* cautions me against mistaken generalizations. In that film, the fact that everything takes place in one house, almost in a single room, is a fundamental tragic virtue.)

[1935]   [SJL]

Two Films

One is called *Crime and Punishment*, by Dostoevsky/von Sternberg. The fact that the first collaborator—the deceased Russian—has not actually collaborated will alarm no one, given the practices of Hollywood; that any trace left by the second—the dreamy Viennese—is equally unnoticeable borders on the monstrous. I can understand how the "psychological" novel might not interest a man, or might not interest him any longer. I could imagine that von Sternberg, devoted to the inexorable Muse of Bric-à-Brac, might reduce all the mental (or at least feverish) complexities of Rodion Romanovich's crime to the depiction of a pawnbroker's house crammed with intolerable objects, or a police station resembling Hollywood's notion of a Cossack barracks. Indoctrinated by the populous memory of *The Scarlet Empress*, I was expecting a vast flood of false beards, miters, samovars, masks, surly faces, wrought-iron gates, vineyards, chess pieces, balalaikas, prominent cheekbones, and horses. In short, I was expecting the usual von Sternberg nightmare, the suffocation and the madness. All in vain! In this film, von Sternberg has discarded his usual caprices, which could be an excellent omen, but unfortunately, he has not replaced them with anything. Without transition or pause, he has merely passed from a hallucinatory state (*The Scarlet Empress*, *The Devil Is a Woman*) to a foolish state. Formerly he seemed mad, which at least was something; now he seems merely simple-minded. Nevertheless, there is no cause for despair: perhaps *Crime and Punishment*, a totally vacuous work, is a sign of remorse and penitence, a necessary act of purification. Perhaps *Crime and Punishment* is only a bridge between the vertiginous sound and fury of *The Scarlet Empress* and a forthcoming film that will reject not only the peculiar charms of chaos but will also resemble—once again—intelligence. (In writing "once again," I am thinking of Josef von Sternberg's early films.)

From an extraordinarily intense novel, von Sternberg has derived an empty film; from an absolutely dull adventure story—*The Thirty-nine Steps* by John Buchan—Hitchcock has made a good film. He has invented episodes, inserted wit and mischief where the original contained only hero-ism. He has thrown in delightfully unsentimental erotic relief, and also a thoroughly charming character, Mr. Memory. Infinitely removed from the other two faculties of the mind, this man reveals a grave secret simply be-cause someone asks it of him and because to answer, at that moment, is his role.

[1936]   [SJL]

The Petrified Forest

It is commonly observed that allegories are tolerable insofar as they are vague and inconsistent; this is not an apology for vagueness and inconsis-tency but rather proof, or at least a sign, that the genre of allegory is at fault. I said the "genre of allegory," not elements or the suggestion of allegory. (The best and most famous allegory, *The Pilgrim's Progress from This World to That Which Is to Come*, by the Puritan visionary John Bunyan, must be read as a novel, not as a prophecy; but if we eliminated all the symbolic jus-tifications, the book would be absurd.)

The measure of allegory in *The Petrified Forest* is perhaps exemplary: light enough so as not to obliterate the drama's reality, substantial enough so as to sanction the drama's improbabilities. There are two or three short-comings or pedantries in the dialogue, however, which continue to annoy me: a nebulous theological theory of neuroses, the (meticulously inaccu-rate) summary of a poem by T. S. Eliot, the forced allusions to Villon, Mark Twain, and Billy the Kid, contrived to make the audience feel erudite in rec-ognizing those names.

Once the allegorical motive is dismissed or relegated to a secondary level, the plot of *The Petrified Forest*—the magical influence of approaching death on a random group of men and women—strikes me as admirable. Death works in this film like hypnosis or alcohol: it brings the recesses of the soul into the light of day. These characters are extraordinarily clear-cut: the smiling, storytelling grandpa who sees everything as a performance and greets the desolation and the bullets as a happy return to the turbulent normalcy of his youth; the weary gunman Mantee, as resigned to killing (and making others kill) as the rest are to dying; the imposing and wholly vain banker with his consul's air of "a great man of our conservative party"; the young Gabrielle, given to attributing her romantic turn of mind to her French blood, and her housekeeping virtues to her Yankee origins; the poet, who advises her to reverse the terms of such an American—and such a mythical—attribution. I do not recall any other movies by Archie Mayo. This film (along with *The Passing of the Third Floor Back*) is one of the most intense that I have seen.

[1936]   [SJL]

Wells, the Visionary

The author of *The Invisible Man, The First Men in the Moon, The Time Machine,* and *The Island of Dr. Moreau* (his best novels, though not his most recent) has published in a 140-page book the detailed text of his recent film, *Things to Come.* Did he do this, perhaps, to dissociate himself from, or at least not to be held responsible for, the film as a whole? The suspicion is not unfounded. Indeed it is justified, or validated by his "Introductory Remarks," which provide instructions. Here he writes that people in the future will not be rigged up like telephone poles or as if they had just escaped from some sort of electrical operating room, nor will they wear aluminum pots or costumes of cellophane glowing under neon lights. "I want Oswald Cabal," Wells writes, "to look like a fine gentleman, not an armored gladiator or a padded lunatic . . . not nightmare stuff, not jazz. . . . Human affairs in that more organized world will not be hurried, they will not be crowded, there will be more leisure, more dignity. . . . Things, structures will be great, but not monstrous." Unfortunately, the grandiose film that we have seen— "grandiose" in the worst sense of this awful word—has very little to do with his intentions. To be sure, there are not a lot of cellophane pots, aluminum neckties, padded gladiators, or madmen in shining armor, but the overall effect (much more important than the details) is nightmare stuff. I am not referring to the first part, which is deliberately monstrous. I am referring to the last, where order should counter the bloody mess of the first part: not only is it not orderly, but it is even more gruesome than the first part. Wells starts out by showing us the terrors of the immediate future, visited by plagues and bombardments—a very effective introduction. (I recall a clear sky stained and darkened by airplanes as obscene and pestilent as locusts.) Then, in the author's words, "the film broadens out to display the grandiose spectacle of a reconstructed world." That "broadening out" is rather poignant: the heaven of Wells and Alexander Korda, like that of so many other eschatologists and set designers, is not much different than their hell, though even less charming.

Another comparison: the book's memorable lines do not correspond— cannot correspond to the film's memorable moments. On page 19, Wells speaks of "a rapid succession of flashes that evokes . . . the confused inadequate efficiency of our world." As might have been foreseen, the contrast between the words *confusion* and *efficiency* (not to mention the value judgment in the epithet *inadequate*) has not been translated into images. On page 56, Wells speaks of the masked aviator Cabal "standing out against the sky, a tall portent." The sentence is beautiful; its photographed version is not. (Even if it had been, it could never have corresponded to the sentence, since the arts of rhetoric and cinema—oh, classic ghost of Ephraim Lessing!—are absolutely incompatible.) On the other hand, there are successful sequences that owe nothing at all to the text's indications.

Tyrants offend Wells, but he likes laboratories; hence his forecast of laboratory technicians joining together to unite a world wrecked by tyrants. Reality has yet to resemble his prophecy: in 1936, the power of almost all tyrants arises from their control of technology. Wells worships pilots and chauffeurs; the tyrannical occupation of Abyssinia was the work of pilots and chauffeurs—and perhaps of the slightly mythological fear of Hitler's depraved laboratories.

I have found fault with the film's second half, but I insist on praising the first part and its wholesome effect for those people who still imagine war as a romantic cavalcade or an opportunity for glorious picnics and free tourism.

[1936]   [SJL]

III

Writings for
El Hogar (*Home*) Magazine
1936-1939

Ramón Llull's Thinking Machine

Toward the end of the thirteenth century, Ramón Llull (Raimundo Lulio or Raymond Lully) invented the thinking machine. Four hundred years later, Athanasius Kircher, his reader and commentator, invented the magic lantern. The first invention is recorded in a work entitled *Ars magna generalis;* the second, in an equally inaccessible opus called *Ars magna lucis et umbrae.* The names of both inventions are generous. In reality, in mere lucid reality, the magic lantern is not magical, nor is the mechanism devised by Ramón Llull capable of thinking a single thought, however rudimentary or fallacious. To put it another way: measured against its objective, judged by its inventor's illustrious goal, the thinking machine does not work. For us, that fact is of secondary importance. The perpetual motion machines depicted in sketches that confer their mystery upon the pages of the most effusive encyclopedias don't work either, nor do the metaphysical and theological theories that customarily declare who we are and what manner of thing the world is. Their public and well-known futility does not diminish their interest. This may (I believe) also be the case with the useless thinking machine.

The Invention of the Machine

We do not and will never know (it would be risky to await a revelation from the all-knowing machine) how it first came into being. Happily, one of the engravings in the famous Mainz edition (1721–42) affords us room for conjecture. While it is true that Salzinger, the edition's editor, considers this model to be a simplification of another, more complex one, I prefer to think of it as the modest precursor of the others. Let us examine this ancestor (fig. 1). It is a schema or diagram of the attributes of God. The letter A, at the center, signifies the Lord. Along the circumference, the letter B stands

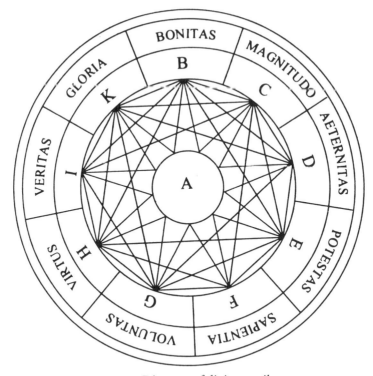

FIGURE 1: *Diagram of divine attributes*

for goodness, C for greatness, D for eternity, E for power, F for wisdom, G for volition, H for virtue, I for truth, and K for glory. The nine letters are equidistant from the center, and each is joined to all the others by chords or diagonal lines. The first of these features means that all of these attributes are inherent; the second, that they are systematically interrelated in such a way as to affirm, with impeccable orthodoxy, that glory is eternal or that eternity is glorious; that power is true, glorious, good, great, eternal, power- ful, wise, free, and virtuous, or benevolently great, greatly eternal, eternally powerful, powerfully wise, wisely free, freely virtuous, virtuously truthful, etc., etc.

I want my readers to grasp the full magnitude of this etcetera. Suffice it to say that it embraces a number of combinations far greater than this page can record. The fact that they are all entirely futile—the fact that, for us, to say that glory is eternal is as rigorously null and void as to say that eternity is glorious—is of only secondary interest. This motionless diagram, with its nine capital letters distributed among nine compartments and linked by a star and some polygons, is already a thinking machine. It was natural for its inventor—a man, we must not forget, of the thirteenth century—to feed it with a subject matter that now strikes us as unrewarding. We now know that the concepts of goodness, greatness, wisdom, power, and glory are incapable of engendering an appreciable revelation. We (who are basically no less naive than Llull) would load the machine differently, no doubt with the words *Entropy, Time, Electrons, Potential Energy, Fourth Dimension, Relativity, Protons, Einstein.* Or with *Surplus Value, Proletariat, Capitalism, Class Struggle, Dialectical Materialism, Engels.*

The Three Disks

If a mere circle subdivided into nine compartments can give rise to so many combinations, what wonders may we expect from three concentric, manually revolving disks made of wood or metal, each with fifteen or twenty compartments? This thought occurred to the remote Ramón Llull on his red and zenithal island of Mallorca, and he designed his guileless machine. The circumstances and objectives of this machine (fig. 2) no longer interest us, but its guiding principle—the methodical application of chance to the resolution of a problem—still does.

In the preamble to this article, I said that the thinking machine does not work. I have slandered it: *elle ne fonctionne que trop,* it works all too well. Let us select a problem at random: the elucidation of the "true" color of a tiger. I give each of Llull's letters the value of a color, I spin the disks, and I decipher that the capricious tiger is blue, yellow, black, white, green, purple, orange, and grey, or yellowishly blue, blackly blue, whitely blue, greenly blue, purplishly blue, bluely blue, etc. Adherents of the *Ars magna* remained undaunted in the face of this torrential ambiguity; they recommended the simultaneous deployment of many combinatory machines, which (according to them) would gradually orient and rectify themselves through "multiplications" and "eliminations." For a long while, many people believed that the certain revelation of all the world's enigmas lay in the patient manipulation of these disks.

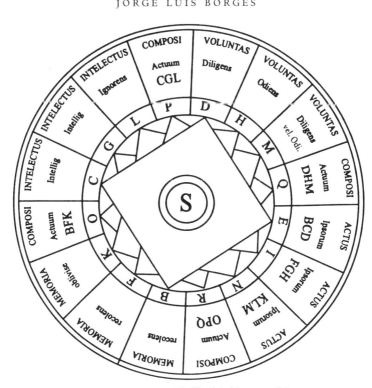

FIGURE 2: *Ramón Llull's thinking machine*

Gulliver and His Machine

My readers may perhaps recall that Swift ridicules the thinking machine in the third part of *Gulliver's Travels*. He proposes or describes another, more complex machine, in which human intervention plays a far lesser role.

This machine, Captain Gulliver relates, is a wooden frame filled with cubes the size of dice joined by slender wires. Words are written on all six sides of the cubes. Iron handles are attached around the edges of the frame. When the handles are moved, the cubes turn over; at each turn of the handle, the words and their order change. The cubes are then attentively perused, and if two or three form a sentence or part of a sentence, the students copy it out in a notebook. "The professor," Gulliver adds impassively, "shewed me several Volumes in large folio, already collected, of broken Sentences, which he intended to piece together; and out of those rich Materials to give the World a compleat Body of all Arts and Sciences. . . ."

A Final Defense

As an instrument of philosophical investigation, the thinking machine is absurd. It would not be absurd, however, as a literary and poetic device. (Discerningly, Fritz Mauthner notes—*Wörterbuch der Philosophie* I, 284— that a rhyming dictionary is a kind of thinking machine.) The poet who requires an adjective to modify "tiger" proceeds in a manner identical to the machine. He tries them out until he finds one that is sufficiently startling. "Black tiger" could be a tiger in the night; "red tiger," all tigers, for its connotation of blood.

[1937]   [EA]

When Fiction Lives in Fiction

I owe my first inkling of the problem of infinity to a large biscuit tin that was a source of vertiginous mystery during my childhood. On one side of this exceptional object was a Japanese scene; I do not recall the children or warriors who configured it, but I do remember that in a corner of the image the same biscuit tin reappeared with the same picture, and in it the same picture again, and so on (at least by implication) infinitely. . . . Fourteen or fifteen years later, around 1921, I discovered in one of Russell's works an analogous invention by Josiah Royce, who postulates a map of England drawn on a portion of the territory of England: this map—since it is exact—must contain a map of the map, which must contain a map of the map of the map, and so on to infinity. . . . Earlier, in the Prado Museum, I had seen Velázquez' famous painting *Las meninas*. In the background is Velázquez himself, working on a double portrait of Philip IV and his consort, who are outside the frame but reflected in a mirror. The painter's chest is decorated with the cross of Santiago; it is rumored that the king painted it there, thus making him a knight of that order. . . . I remember that the Prado's administrators had installed a mirror in front of the painting to perpetuate these enchantments.

The pictorial technique of inserting a painting within a painting corresponds, in the world of letters, to the interpolation of a fiction within another fiction. Cervantes included a short novel in the *Quixote;* Lucius Apuleius famously inserted the fable of Cupid and Psyche into *The Golden Ass.* Parentheses of such an unequivocal nature are as banal as the occurrence, in reality, of someone reading aloud or singing. The two planes—the actual and the ideal—do not intermingle. In contrast, *The Thousand and One Nights* doubles and dizzyingly redoubles the ramifications of a central tale into digressing tales, but without ever trying to gradate its realities, and the effect (which should be one of depth) is superficial, like a Persian carpet. The story that introduces the series is well known: the king's heartbroken oath that each night he will wed a virgin who will be decapitated at dawn, and the fortitude of Scheherazade, who distracts him with wondrous tales until a thousand and one nights have revolved over their two heads and she presents him with his son. The need to complete a thousand and one segments drove the work's copyists to all sorts of digressions. None of them is as disturbing as that of night 602, a bit of magic among the nights. On that strange night, the king hears his own story from the queen's lips. He hears the beginning of the story, which includes all the others, and also—monstrously—itself. Does the reader have a clear sense of the vast possibility held out by this interpolation, its peculiar danger? Were the queen to persist, the immobile king would forever listen to the truncated story of the thousand and one nights, now infinite and circular. . . . In *The Thousand and One Nights*, Scheherazade tells many stories; one of them is, almost, the story of *The Thousand and One Nights.*

In the third act of *Hamlet*, Shakespeare erects a stage on the stage; the fact that the play enacted there—the poisoning of a king—in some way mirrors the primary play suffices to suggest the possibility of infinite involutions. (In an 1840 article, De Quincey observes that the stolid, heavy-handed style of this minor play makes the overall drama that includes it appear, by contrast, more lifelike. I would add that its essential aim is the opposite: to make reality appear unreal to us.)

Hamlet dates from 1602. Toward the end of 1635, the young writer Pierre Corneille composed the magical comedy *L'Illusion comique*. Pridamant, father of Clindor, has traveled the nations of Europe in search of his son. With more curiosity than faith, he visits the cave of the "prodigious magician" Alcandre. The latter shows him, in phantasmagorical fashion, his son's hazardous life. We see Clindor stabbing a rival, fleeing from the law, being murdered in a garden, then chatting with some friends. Alcandre clears up the mystery. Having killed his rival, Clindor becomes an actor, and the scene of the blood-drenched garden belongs not to reality (the "reality" of Corneille's fiction), but to a tragedy. We were, without knowing it, in a theater. A rather unexpected panegyric to that institution brings the work to its close:

> *Même notre grand Roi, ce foudre de la guerre,*
> *Dont le nom se fait craindre aux deux bouts de la terre,*
> *Le front ceint de lauriers, daigne bien quelquefois*
> *Prêter l'oeil et l'oreille au Théâtre Français.*

[That thunderbolt of war himself, our great King/Whose name sounds at earth's ends with fearsome ring/His forehead wreathed in laurels, sometimes deigns/To lend eye and ear to the French Theater's refrains.]

It is painful to note that Corneille puts these not very magical verses in the mouth of a magician.

Gustav Meyrink's novel *The Golem* (1915) is the story of a dream; within this dream there are dreams; and within those dreams (I believe) other dreams.

I have enumerated many verbal labyrinths, but none so complex as the recent book by Flann O'Brien, *At Swim-Two-Birds*. A student in Dublin writes a novel about the proprietor of a Dublin public house, who writes a novel about the habitués of his pub (among them, the student), who in their turn write novels in which proprietor and student figure along with other writers of novels about other novelists. The book consists of the extremely diverse manuscripts of these real or imagined persons, copiously annotated by the student. *At Swim-Two-Birds* is not only a labyrinth: it is a discussion of the many ways to conceive of the Irish novel and a repertory of exercises in prose and verse which illustrate or parody all the styles of Ireland. The magisterial influence of Joyce (also an architect of labyrinths; also a literary Proteus) is undeniable but not disproportionate in this manifold book.

Arthur Schopenhauer wrote that dreaming and wakefulness are the pages of a single book, and that to read them in order is to live, and to leaf through them at random, to dream. Paintings within paintings and books that branch into other books help us sense this oneness.

[1939]   *[EA]*

CAPSULE BIOGRAPHIES

Isaac Babel

He was born in the jumbled catacombs of the stair-stepped port of Odessa, late in 1894. Irreparably Semitic, Isaac was the son of a rag merchant from Kiev and a Moldavian Jewess. Catastrophe has been the normal climate of his life. In the uneasy intervals between pogroms he learned not only to read and write but to appreciate literature and enjoy the work of Maupassant, Flaubert, and Rabelais. In 1914, he was certified a lawyer by the Faculty of Law in Saratov; in 1916, he risked a journey to Petrograd. In that capital city "traitors, malcontents, whiners, and Jews" were banned: the category was somewhat arbitrary, but—implacably—it included Babel. He had to rely on the friendship of a waiter who took him home and hid him, on a Lithuanian accent acquired in Sebastopol, and on an apocryphal passport. His first writings date from that period: two or three satires of the Czarist bureaucracy, published in *Annals*, Gorky's famous newspaper. (What must he think, and not say, about Soviet Russia, that indecipherable labyrinth of state offices?) Those two or three satires attracted the dangerous attention of the government. He was accused of pornography and incitement of class hatred. From this catastrophe he was saved by another catastrophe: the Russian Revolution.

In early 1921, Babel joined a Cossack regiment. Those blustering and useless warriors (no one in the history of the universe has been defeated more often than the Cossacks) were, of course, anti-Semitic. The mere idea of a Jew on horseback struck them as laughable, and the fact that Babel was a good horseman only added to their disdain and spite. A couple of well-timed and flashy exploits enabled Babel to make them leave him in peace.

By reputation, though not according to the bibliographies, Isaac Babel is still a *homo unius libri*.

His unmatched book is titled *Red Cavalry*.

The music of its style contrasts with the almost ineffable brutality of certain scenes.

One of the stories—"Salt"—enjoys a glory seemingly reserved for poems, and rarely attained by prose: many people know it by heart.

[1938]   [EA]

Ernest Bramah

A German scholar, around 1731, spent many pages debating the issue of whether Adam was the best politician of his time, the best historian, and the best geographer and topographer. This charming hypothesis takes into account not only the perfection of the paradisiacal state and the total absence of competitors but also the simplicity of certain topics in those early days of the world. The history of the universe was the history of the universe's only inhabitant. The past was seven days old: how easy it was to be an archeologist!

This biography runs the risk of being no less useless and encyclopedic than a history of the world according to Adam. We know nothing about Ernest Bramah, except that his name is not Ernest Bramah. In August 1937, the editors of Penguin Books decided to include *Kai Lung Unrolls His Mat* in their collection. They consulted *Who's Who* and came upon the following entry: "Bramah, Ernest, writer," followed by a list of his works and the address of his agent. The agent sent them a photograph (undoubtedly apocryphal) and wrote that if they wished for more information, they should not hesitate to consult *Who's Who* anew. (This suggestion may indicate that there is an anagram in the list.)

Bramah's books fall into two very unequal categories. Some, fortunately the smaller part, record the adventures of the blind detective, Max Carrados. These are competent, mediocre books. The rest are parodic in nature: they pass themselves off as translations from the Chinese, and their boundless perfection achieved the unconditional praise of Hilaire Belloc in 1922. Their names: *The Wallet of Kai Lung* (1900), *Kai Lung's Golden Hours* (1922), *Kai Lung Unrolls His Mat* (1928), *The Mirror of Kong Ho* (1931), *The Moon of Much Gladness* (1936).

Here are two of his apophthegms:

"He who aspires to dine with the vampire must bring his own meat."

"A frugal dish of olives seasoned with honey is preferable to the most resplendent pie of puppy tongues presented on thousand-year-old lacquered trays and served to other people."

[1938]   *[EA]*

Benedetto Croce

Benedetto Croce, one of the few important writers in Italy today—the other is Luigi Pirandello—was born in the hamlet of Pescasseroli, in the province of Aquila, on February 25, 1866. He was still a child when his family resettled in Naples. He received a Catholic education, much attenuated by the indifference of his teachers and by his own eventual disbelief. In 1883, an earthquake that lasted ninety seconds shook the south of Italy. In that earthquake, he lost his parents and his sister; he himself was buried by rubble. Two or three hours later, he was rescued. To ward off total despair, he resolved to think about the Universe—a general procedure among the unfortunate, and sometimes a balm.

He explored the methodical labyrinths of philosophy. In 1893, he published two essays: one on literary criticism, the other on history. In 1899, he realized, with a fear which at times resembled panic and at other times happiness, that the problems of metaphysics were organizing themselves within him, and that the solution—a solution—was almost imminent. He stopped reading and dedicated his mornings and nights to the vigil, pacing across the city without seeing anything, speechless and furtively watched. He was thirty-three years old, the age, the Kabbalists say, of the first man when he was formed out of mud.

In 1902, he inaugurated his Philosophy of the Spirit with an initial volume: the *Aesthetics*. (In this sterile but brilliant book, he rejects the distinction between form and content and reduces everything to intuition.) The *Logic* appears in 1905; the *Practice* in 1908; the *Theory of Historiography* in 1916.

From 1910 to 1917, Croce was a senator of the Kingdom. When war was declared and other writers gave themselves over to the lucrative pleasures of hatred, Croce remained impartial. From June 1920 to July 1921 he occupied the post of Minister of Public Instruction.

In 1923, Oxford University granted him a doctorate *honoris causa*.

His complete work exceeds twenty volumes and includes a history of

Italy, a study of the literatures of Europe during the nineteenth century, and monographs on Hegel, Vico, Dante, Aristotle, Shakespeare, Goethe, and Corneille.

[1936]   [F.A]

Theodore Dreiser

Dreiser's head is an arduous, monumental head, geological in character, a head of the afflicted Prometheus bound to the Caucasus, and which, across the inexorable centuries, has become ingrained with the Caucasus and now has a fundamental component of rock that is pained by life. Dreiser's work is no different from his tragic face: it is as torpid as the mountains or the deserts, but like them it is important in an elemental and inarticulate way.

Theodore Dreiser was born in the state of Indiana on August 27, 1871. He is the son of Catholic parents. As a child he was on familiar terms with poverty; as a youth he plied many and diverse trades with the easy universality that is one of the defining characteristics of American destinies and that once (Sarmiento, Hernández, Ascasubi) defined those of this Republic as well. In 1887, long before Scarface Al's punctual machine guns, he roamed a Chicago where men in bustling beerhalls argued endlessly over the harsh fate of the seven anarchists the government had sentenced to the gallows. Around 1889 he developed the strange ambition of becoming a journalist. He started hanging around newspaper offices, "stubborn as a stray dog." In 1892, he was hired by the *Chicago Daily Globe;* in 1894, he went to New York, where for four years he edited a music magazine called *Ev'ry Month.* During that time he read Spencer's *First Principles* and with pain and sincerity lost the faith of his forefathers. Toward 1898, he married a girl from St. Louis, "beautiful, religious, thoughtful, addicted to books," but the marriage was not a happy one. "I couldn't stand being tied down. I asked her to give me back my freedom and she did."

Sister Carrie, Theodore Dreiser's first novel, appeared in the year 1900. Someone has observed that Dreiser always chose his enemies well. Barely had *Sister Carrie* been published when its publishers withdrew it from circulation, an event that was catastrophic at the time, but infinitely favorable to his later reputation. After ten years of silence, he published *Jennie Gerhardt;* then, in 1912, *The Financier;* in 1913, his autobiography, *A Traveler at Forty;* in 1914, *The Titan;* in 1915, *Genius* (which was banned); in 1922, another autobiographical exercise entitled *A Book About Myself.* The novel *An American Tragedy* (1925) was outlawed in several states and disseminated by the motion picture industry across the globe.

"To understand North America better," Dreiser went to Russia in 1928. In 1930, he published "a book of the mystery and wonder and terror of life" and a volume of "natural and supernatural" dramas.

Many years ago, he recommended that his country cultivate a literature of despair.

[1938]   *[EA]*

T. S. Eliot

An unlikely compatriot of the St. Louis Blues, Thomas Stearns Eliot was born in the energetic city of that name, in the month of September 1888, on the banks of the mythical Mississippi. Scion of a wealthy family with commercial and ecclesiastical interests, he was educated at Harvard and in Paris. In the autumn of 1911, he returned to North America and dedicated himself to the fervent study of psychology and metaphysics. Three years later he went to England. On that island (and not without a certain initial wariness) he found his wife, his homeland, and his renown; on that island he published his first essays—two technical articles on Leibniz—and his first poems: "Rhapsody on a Windy Night," "Mr. Apollinax," "The Love Song of J. Alfred Prufrock." The influence of Laforgue is apparent, and sometimes fatal, in these preludes. His construction is languid, but the clarity of certain images is unsurpassable. For example:

> I should have been a pair of ragged claws
> Scuttling across the floors of silent seas.

In 1920, he published *Poems*, perhaps the most disordered and uneven of his books of verse; its pages include the despairing monologue "Gerontion" and several trivial exercises—"*Le Directeur*," "*Mélange adultère de tout*," "*Lune de miel*"—perpetrated in a hapless French.

In 1922, he published *The Waste Land*; in 1925, *The Hollow Men*; in 1930, *Ash Wednesday*; in 1934, *The Rock*; in 1936, *Murder in the Cathedral*, a lovely title that sounds like Agatha Christie. The erudite obscurity of the first of these poems disconcerted (and still disconcerts) the critics, but is less important than the poem's beauty. The perception of this beauty, moreover, precedes any interpretation and does not depend on it. (Analyses of the poem abound: the most sensitive and faithful is F. O. Matthiessen's in *The Achievement of T. S. Eliot.*)

Eliot—whose poetry, like Paul Valéry's, can be gloomy and inadequate—is, like Valéry, an exemplary prose stylist. The volume *Selected Essays* (London, 1932) includes his essential prose. The previous volume, *The Use of Poetry and the Use of Criticism* (London, 1933), can be omitted without great loss.

[1937]   *[EA]*

Will James

Our Argentine Republic has a vast literature of the gaucho—*Paulino Lucero,* the *Fausto, Martín Fierro, Juan Moreira, Santos Vega, Don Segundo Sombra, Ramón Hazaña*—a body of work produced exclusively by the literati of our capital city and documented by childhood memories or a summer in the provinces.

The United States has not produced analogous works of a corresponding prestige—cowboys count for less in their country's literature than the black men of the South or the farmers of the Middle West, and to this day they have not inspired a good film—but it can boast of this almost scandalous phenomenon: books about cowboys written by an authentic cowboy. Written and illustrated.

One night in early June 1892, a covered wagon on its weary way from Texas made a stop in the wilderness of the Bitter Root Mountains, near the Canadian border. On that night, in that lost wagon, Will James was born to a Texas trooper and a woman with some Spanish blood. James was orphaned at the age of four. An old hunter, Jean Baupré, took him in. Will James grew up on horseback. A Bible and some old magazines in his adopted father's shack gradually taught him to read. (Until he was fourteen, he knew how to write only in block letters.) Driven by poverty or by his own will, he worked as a hired hand, trooper, bronco buster, foreman, cavalryman. In 1920 he married a girl from Nevada; in 1924, he published his first book: *Cowboys, North and South.*

Will James' books are rather curious. They are not sentimental; they are not savage. They do not transmit heroic anecdotes. They contain an infinite abundance of descriptions (and discussions) on the many ways to use stirrups, lasso, work in a corral or in open country, drive herds of cattle across rough terrain, break colts. These are pastoral and theoretical documents; they deserve better readers than myself. They are entitled: *The Drifting Cow-Boy* (1925), *Smoky the Cowhorse* (1926), *Cow Country* (1927), *Sand* (1929), the autobiography *Lone Cow-Boy* (1930), and the series of tales *Sun Up* (1931).

Will James is now the owner of a ranch in Montana.

[1938]   [EA]

Liam O'Flaherty

Liam O'Flaherty is a "man of Aran." He was born in 1896 to parents who were poor and desperately Catholic. He was educated in a Jesuit college. From boyhood he professed two passions: hatred of England and reverence for the Catholic Church. (The first of these passions was mitigated by his love of English literature; the second, by socialism.) In 1914, the two loyalties clashed. O'Flaherty wished for an English defeat, but was enraged by the spectacle of a small Catholic country, Belgium—so comparable to Ireland at that moment!—trampled by a strong, heretic nation, Germany—so much like England! In 1915, he solved the problem by enlisting under a false name to keep his family honor intact. He spent two years fighting the Germans. On his return he seized the opportunity provided by the Irish Revolution to fight England. As a revolutionary, he achieved such distinction that for a time he had to relinquish the Empire. We know he was a lumberjack in Canada, a stevedore in a Venezuelan port, a Turkish agent in Asia Minor, and a busboy, linotypist, and "subversive" orator in Minnesota and Wisconsin. In a tire factory in St. Paul, he scribbled out his first stories. Every night he wrote one; every morning he reread it indignantly and threw it in the trash bin.

Thy Neighbor's Wife, his first novel, was published in London in 1924. In 1925, he published *The Informer;* in 1927, *The Life of Tim Healy;* in 1928, *The Assassin;* in 1929, *A Tourist's Guide to Ireland* (with detailed indications of the tenements, barren lands, vacant lots, and swamps); in 1930, the autobiographical book, *Two Years;* in 1931, *I Went to Russia.* O'Flaherty is a generous, talkative man. He is said to look like a refined gangster. He likes unfamiliar cities, alcohol, games of chance, early mornings, nights, arguments.

[1937]   [EA]

Oswald Spengler

It may legitimately be observed (with the lightness and peculiar brutality of such observations) that the philosophers of England and France are directly interested in the universe itself, or in one or another of its features, while the Germans tend to consider it a simple motive, a mere material cause for their enormous dialectical edifices, which are always groundless but always grandiose. Their passion is for the proper symmetry of systems, not for any eventual correspondence with the impure and disorderly universe. The latest of these illustrious Germanic architects—a fitting successor to Albertus Magnus, Meister Eckhart, Leibniz, Kant, Herder, Novalis, Hegel—is Spengler.

Spengler was born on May 29, 1880, in the town of Blankenburgam-Harz, in the duchy of Brunswick. He studied in Munich and Berlin. At the beginning of this century he completed a degree in philosophy and letters; his doctoral thesis on Heraclitus (Halle, 1904) was the only thing he published before the sensational work that would make him famous. Spengler spent six years writing *The Decline of the West*. Six stubborn years in a hungry Munich tenement, in a lugubrious room that faced a destitute landscape of chimneys and grimy rooftops. During this period, Oswald Spengler owns no books. He spends his mornings at the public library, lunches in working-class cafeterias, drinks vast, scalding quantities of tea when ill. Around 1915, he finishes revising the first volume. He has no friends. Secretly, he compares himself to Germany, which is also alone.

In the summer of 1918, *The Decline of the West* appears in Vienna.

Schopenhauer wrote: "There is no general science of history. History is the insignificant tale of humanity's interminable, weighty, fragmented dream." In his book, Spengler set out to demonstrate that history could be something more than a mere gossipy enumeration of individual facts. He wanted to determine its laws, lay down the foundations of a morphology of cultures. His manly pages, composed in the period between 1912 and 1917, were never contaminated by the singular hatred of those years.

Around 1920, his glory began.

Spengler rented an apartment on the Isar River, lingered amorously over the purchase of several thousand books, collected Persian, Turkish, and Hindu weaponry, climbed high mountains, and denied himself to the persistence of photographers. Above all, he wrote. He wrote *Pessimism* (1921), *Political Duties of German Youth* (1924), *Reconstruction of the German State* (1926).

Oswald Spengler died in the middle of this year. His biological concept of history is open to debate, but not the splendor of his style.

[1936]   *[EA]*

Paul Valéry

To enumerate the facts of Valéry's life is to ignore Valéry, is not even to allude to Paul Valéry. Facts, for him, are worthwhile only as stimulants to thought; thought, for him, is worthwhile only insofar as we can observe it; the observation of that observation also interests him. . . .

Paul Valéry was born in the small town of Sète, in the year 1871. Good classic that he is, he disdains or disregards childhood memories. He does little more than make us aware that one morning, facing the mobile sea, he experienced the natural ambition to be a sailor.

In the year 1888, at the University of Montpellier, Valéry chatted with Pierre Loüys, who a year later founded the magazine *La Conque*. Valéry's first poems, duly mythological and sonorous, appeared in those pages.

Around 1891, Valéry went to Paris. To him, that urgent city signified two passions: Stéphane Mallarmé's conversation and the infinite study of geometry and algebra. In Valéry's typographical habits there remains some trace of this juvenile commerce with the Symbolists: a certain charlatanry of ellipses, italics, capital letters.

He published his first volume in 1895: *Introduction to the Method of Leonardo da Vinci*. In this book, which is of a divinatory or symbolic nature, Leonardo is an eminent pretext for the exemplifying description of a type of creator. Leonardo is the rough draft for "Edmond Teste," the limit or demigod on which Paul Valéry verges. This personage—the calm, half-glimpsed hero of the short *La Soirée avec Monsieur Teste*—is perhaps the most extraordinary invention of contemporary letters.

In 1921, the writers of France, questioned by the magazine *La Connaissance*, declared that the foremost contemporary poet was Paul Valéry. In 1925, he was admitted to the Academy.

It is not impossible that *La Soirée avec Monsieur Teste* and the ten volumes of *Variété* constitute Valéry's lasting work. His poetry—perhaps—is not as organized for immortality as his prose. In the *Cimetière marin* itself—his poetic masterpiece—there is no organic melding of the speculative and visual passages, there is merely rotation. Spanish versions of this poem abound; to my mind, the most dexterous of them appeared in Buenos Aires in 1931.

[1937]   *[EA]*

S. S. Van Dine

Willard Huntington Wright was born in 1888, in Virginia; S. S. Van Dine (whose name blazes from all the multicolored kiosks in the world) was born in 1926, in a California sanitarium. Willard Huntington Wright was born as all men are born; S. S. Van Dine (his close-fitting and lightweight pseudonym) was born in the happy penumbra of a convalescence.

Here is the story of both. The first, educated at Pomona College and Harvard, had plied, remuneratively and without glory, the trades of drama critic and music critic. He had tried his hand at the autobiographical novel (*The Man of Promise*), aesthetic theory (*Philology and the Writer, The Creative Will, Modern Literature, Modern Painting*), the exposition and discussion of doctrines (*What Nietzsche Taught*), and even a bit of casual Egyptology and prophecy: *The Future of Painting*. The universe had examined these works with more resignation than enthusiasm. To judge by the dazed fragments that survive encrusted in his novels, the universe was correct. . . .

Around 1925, Wright was recovering from an illness that had been serious. Convalescence and criminological fantasies go well together: Wright, by then relaxed and happy in his sickbed, turned away from the laborious resolution of one of Mr. Edgar Wallace's incompetent labyrinths, preferring to construct a problem of his own. He wrote *The Benson Murder Case*, and signed it with a name that had been his for four generations: that of a maternal great-grandfather, Silas S. Van Dine.

The novel's success was considerable. The following year he published *The Canary Murder Case*, perhaps his best book, though the central idea (a phonograph record used as alibi) is taken from Conan Doyle. An astute morning newspaper compared the novel's style to certain pages of *Philology and the Writer* and discovered "that the omnipresent Van Dine was the distinguished philosopher, Mr. Willard Huntington Wright." An astute evening newspaper compared the style of this revelation with the two works in question and discovered that *its* author "was also the distinguished philosopher, Mr. Willard Huntington Wright."

Van Dine published *The Bishop Murder Case* in 1929; in 1930, the ingenious *Scarab Murder Case;* in 1936, *The Dragon Murder Case.* This last book presents us with the baleful spectacle of an amphibious millionaire, equipped with trident and diving suit, who installs himself at the bottom of a swimming pool and gracefully skewers his guests.

Van Dine has also compiled a couple of anthologies.

[*1937*]   [*EA*]

Virginia Woolf

Virginia Woolf has been called "England's leading novelist." The precise hierarchy is unimportant—literature not being a contest—but hers is indisputably among the most sensitive of the minds and imaginations now felicitously experimenting with the English novel.

Adelina Virginia Stephen was born in London in 1882. (Her first name vanished without a trace.) She is the daughter of Mr. Leslie Stephen, a compiler of biographies of Swift, Johnson, and Hobbes—books whose value lies in the fine clarity of the prose and factual precision, and which attempt little analysis and no invention.

Adelina Virginia was the third of four children. The illustrator Rothenstein remembers her as "absorbed and quiet, all in black, with white lace collar and cuffs." From infancy, she was raised not to speak if she had nothing to say. She was never sent to school, but her domestic training included the study of Greek. Sundays at the house were crowded: Meredith, Ruskin, Stevenson, John Morley, Gosse, and Hardy were all frequently in attendance.

She spent the summers in Cornwall, at the seaside, in a small house lost on an enormous, untended estate, with terraces, a garden, and a greenhouse. The estate reappears in a 1927 novel. . . .

In 1912, Virginia Stephen marries Mr. Leonard Woolf in London, and the two acquire a printing press. Typography, that sometimes treacherous accomplice of literature, appeals to them, and they compose and print their own books. They undoubtedly have in mind the glorious precedent of William Morris, printer and poet.

Three years later Virginia Woolf publishes her first novel: *The Voyage Out.* In 1919, *Night and Day* appears, and in 1922, *Jacob's Room.* This book is already fully characteristic. There is no plot, in the narrative sense of the word; the subject is a man's character, studied not in the man himself, but indirectly in the objects and people around him.

Mrs. Dalloway (1925) narrates a day in a woman's life; it is a reflection—though not at all excessive—of Joyce's *Ulysses*. *To the Lighthouse* (1927) employs the same technique. it depicts a few hours in several peoples' lives, so that in those hours we see their past and future. The preoccupation with time is present, as well, in *Orlando* (1928). The hero of this extremely original novel—undoubtedly Virginia Woolf's most intense and one of the most singular and maddening of our era—lives for three hundred years and is, at times, a symbol of England and of its poetry in particular. Magic, bitterness, and happiness collude in this book. It is also a musical work, not only in the euphonious virtues of its prose but in the structure of its composition, which consists of a limited number of themes that return and combine. We also hear a kind of music in *A Room of One's Own* (1930), in which dream and reality alternate and reach an equilibrium.

In 1931, Virginia Woolf published another novel: *The Waves*. The waves that give their name to the book take in, across time and its many vicissitudes, the characters' inner soliloquies. Each phase of their lives corresponds to a different hour of the day, from morning to night. There is no plot, no conversation, no action. Yet the book is moving. Like the rest of Virginia Woolf's work, it is weighted with delicate, physical facts.

[1936]   *[EA]*

BOOK REVIEWS AND NOTES

Gustav Meyrink, *Der Engel vom Westlichen Fenster*

This more or less theosophical novel—*The Angel of the Western Window*—is not as beautiful as its title. Its author, Gustav Meyrink, was made famous by his fantasy novel, *The Golem*, an extraordinarily visual book that enchantingly combined mythology, eroticism, tourism, the "local color" of Prague, prophetic dreams, dreams of past or future lives, and even reality. That wonderful book was followed by others that were less delightful. In them one could see the influence, no longer of Hoffmann or Poe, but of the various theosophical sects that swarmed (and swarm) in Germany. They revealed that Meyrink had been "enlightened" by Oriental wisdom, with the baneful results that are customary to such visitations. He gradually became identified with the most naive of his readers. His books became acts of faith, and then of propaganda.

The Angel of the Western Window is a chronicle of confused miracles, barely salvaged, from time to time, by its poetic ambience.

[1936]   [EW]

Alan Pryce-Jones, *Private Opinion*

Unquestionably, though there are many Englishmen who speak very little, there are far more who do not speak at all. Hence (perhaps) the no less unquestionable excellence of the "oral style" of English prose writers. In this regard, the book under review is exemplary.

The author's opinions, unfortunately, are less irreproachable than his syntax. In one passage he speaks of Stuart Merrill as "perhaps the greatest

American lyric poet since Edgar Allan Poe." Such a promotion is absurd: compared with his own colleagues in Symbolism, Stuart Merrill is largely insignificant; compared with Frost, Sandburg, Eliot, Masters, Lindsay, and twenty others (not to mention Sidney Lanier), he is decidedly invisible.

Elsewhere the author states: "At times I have played with the idea of an essay on the subject that modern poetry owes half of its forms and contexture to the city of Montevideo." The thesis (qualified and weakened by numerous preliminary vacillations) is appealing, but frankly, we find it difficult to believe that the infancy of Jules Laforgue and the boyhood years of the insufferable Comte de Lautréamont are enough to justify it.

Moreover, Mr. Pryce-Jones claims that Montevideo has no charm. Quietly, but with complete conviction, I would beg to disagree, in the name of the pink patios of the Old City and the damp and affecting mansions of the Paso del Molino.

[1936]   [EW]

Louis Golding, *The Pursuer*

It has been said (and often repeated) that the protagonist of a true novel or of a serious play cannot be insane. Limiting ourselves to Macbeth, his colleague the analytical murderer Raskolnikov, Don Quixote, King Lear, Hamlet, and the almost monomaniacal Lord Jim, we might say (and repeat) that the protagonist of a novel or a play must be insane.

It will be argued that no one can sympathize with a madman, and that the mere suspicion of madness is enough to estrange a man infinitely from all others. We would respond that madness is one of the terrible possibilities for any soul, and that the narrative or scenic problem of showing the origin and growth of that terrifying flower is certainly not illegitimate. (Cervantes, by the way, did not attempt it; he merely says that his fifty-year-old knight "from little sleep and much reading, dried up his brain to the point where he lost his judgment." We do not witness the transition from the ordinary to the hallucinatory, the gradual disfiguration of the common order by the world of phantoms.)

These general observations were provoked by the reading of this intense novel by Louis Golding, *The Pursuer*. The book has two heroes, and both go mad: one from fear, the other from a horrible, rancorous love. Of course, neither the word nor the concept of "madness" appears in the book:

we share the mental processes of the characters, we see them become troubled, we see them act, and the abstract diagnosis that they are insane is rather less compelling than their troubles and acts. (Acts that sometimes involve a crime, which becomes a kind of relief, however momentary, from the tension of panic and evil. It is such that when the crime has been committed, the reader fears for many pages that it is a hallucination of fear.)

Horror is gradual in this novel, as in nightmares. The style is transparent, calm. As for its interest . . . I can only say that I began it after lunch, with the intention of skimming it, and that I did not put it down until page 285 (the last) at two in the morning.

There are certain typographical conventions derived from William Faulkner: for example, the narrative is sometimes interrupted by the thoughts of the characters, which are presented in the first person and in italics.

[1936]   [EW]

Lord Halifax's Ghost Book

Ever since a certain Byzantine historian of the sixth century noted that the island of England consists of two parts—one with rivers and cities and bridges, the other inhabited by snakes and ghosts—relations between England and the Other World have been celebrated and cordial. In 1666, Joseph Glanvill published his *Philosophical Considerations of Sorcery and Sorcerers*, a book that was inspired by an invisible drum that was heard every night in a well in Wiltshire. Around 1705, Daniel Defoe wrote his *True Relation of the Apparition of One Mrs. Veal*. At the end of the nineteenth century, statistical rigor was applied to these nebulous problems, and they were verified with two censuses of hypnotic and telepathic hallucinations. (The later census involved 16,000 adults.) Now, in London, they have just published this book—*Lord Halifax's Ghost Book*—which gathers and exhausts the charms of superstition and of snobbism. It deals with select ghosts, "apparitions who have troubled the rest of the greatest names of England, and whose comings and goings have invariably been noted by an august hand." Lady Goring, Lord Desborough, Lord Lytton, the Marquis of Hartingdom, and the Duke of Devonshire are among the names whose rest has been troubled and who have furnished their august hands. The Honorable Reginald Fortescue became a firm believer in the existence of "an alarming spectre." As for myself, I don't know what to think: for the moment, I refuse to believe in the alarming Reginald Fortescue until an honorable spectre becomes a firm believer in his existence.

The preface contains this beautiful anecdote: Two ladies are sharing a railway compartment. "I don't believe in ghosts," says one to the other. "Oh really?" the other replies, and vanishes.

[1936]   *[EW]*

William Faulkner, *Absalom! Absalom!*

I know of two kinds of writers: those whose central preoccupation is verbal technique, and those for whom it is human acts and passions. The former tend to be dismissed as "Byzantine" or praised as "pure artists." The latter, more fortunately, receive the laudatory epithets "profound," "human," or "profoundly human," and the flattering vituperation "savage." The former is Swinburne or Mallarmé; the latter, Céline or Theodore Dreiser. Certain exceptional cases display the virtues and joys of both categories. Victor Hugo remarked that Shakespeare contained Góngora; we might also observe that he contained Dostoevsky. . . . Among the great novelists, Joseph Conrad was perhaps the last who was interested both in the techniques of the novel and in the fates and personalities of his characters. The last, that is, until the tremendous appearance of Faulkner.

Faulkner likes to expound the novel through his characters. This method is not entirely original—Robert Browning's *The Ring and the Book* (1868) details the same crime ten times, through ten voices and ten souls— but Faulkner infuses it with an intensity that is almost intolerable. There is an infinite decomposition, an infinite and black carnality, in this book. The theater is the state of Mississippi: the heroes, men disintegrating from envy, alcohol, loneliness, and the erosions of hate.

Absalom, Absalom! is comparable to *The Sound and the Fury.* I know no higher praise.

[1937]   *[EW]*

Gustaf Janson, *Gubben Kommer*

I have frequented with true moderation the literature of Sweden. Three or four theological-hallucinatory volumes of Swedenborg, fifteen or twenty of Strindberg (who was, for a time, my god, alongside Nietzsche), a novel by Selma Lagerlöf, and a book of Heidenstam's stories strain the limits of my Hyperborean education. Now I have just read *Gubben Kommer* by the very new writer Gustaf Janson, in an admirable English translation by Claude Napier, published in London under the title *The Old Man's Coming Out.*

Measured against the author's exalted intentions—the revelation of a semi-divine man, slandered and loathed by the others, who appears in the last chapters and decrees his omniscient Final Judgment on the characters in the novel—the work itself is a disaster. A most forgivable disaster. Milton insisted that the poet himself be a poem. A demand that is interminably capable of reductions to the absurd (to require, for example, that the sculptor himself be a Roman chariot, the architect himself a foundation, the playwright himself an intermission) and yet it raises a fundamental problem: Can writers create characters who are superior to themselves? Intellectually, one must say no. Sherlock Holmes seems more intelligent than Conan Doyle, but we are all in on the secret: the one is only communicating the solutions that the other has devised. Zarathustra—oh, the dangerous consequences of the prophetic style!—is less intelligent than Nietzsche. As for Charles-Henri de Grévy, the semi-divine hero of this novel, his triviality is no less obvious than his loquacity. Janson, moreover, is hardly astute. The four hundred pages in octavo that precede the return of the hero do not include a single line that would feed or flatter our unease and allow us to speculate, even in passing, that his detractors may have their reasons. In the end, the object of vilification reappears, and we confirm that he is indeed a saint. Our surprise, of course, is null.

I have criticized the mechanism, or rather the conduct, of this novel. The only praise I have is for the characters. Putting aside the symbolic or supernatural hero (who mercifully delays his ominous appearance until page 414), the others are all convincing, and some—like Bengt—remarkable.

[1937]   [EW]

Aldous Huxley, *Stories, Essays and Poems*

To be inducted into the Everyman's Library, rubbing shoulders with the Venerable Bede and Shakespeare, with *The Thousand and One Nights* and *Peer Gynt*, was, until recently, a sort of beatification. Lately, however, this narrow gate has widened, admitting Pierre Loti and Oscar Wilde. And now Aldous Huxley has entered. There are 160,000 of his words in this volume, divided into four unequal parts: stories, travel accounts, articles, and poems. The articles and travel accounts demonstrate Huxley's just pessimism and almost intolerable lucidity; the stories and poems his incurable poverty of invention. What is one to think of these melancholy exercises? They are not unskillful, they are not stupid, they are not extraordinarily boring: they are, simply, worthless. They engender (at least in me) an infinite bewilderment. Occasionally a single isolated line saves him. This, for example, that refers to the flowing of time:

> The wound is mortal and is mine.

The poem "Theater of Varieties" wants to be like Browning; "The Gioconda Smile" wants to be a detective story. That at least is something, or is quite a lot, as it demonstrates the intention. I know what they want to be, even if they are nothing, and for that I am grateful. But as for the other stories and poems in this book, I cannot even imagine why they were written. As it is my job to understand, I make this public declaration in complete humility.

Aldous Huxley's fame has always struck me as excessive. I realize that his literature is of a type that is produced naturally in France and more artificially in England. There are readers of Huxley who do not feel this discomfort: I feel it continually, and can only derive an impure pleasure from his work. It seems to me that Huxley always speaks with a borrowed voice.

[1937]   [EW]

Rabindranath Tagore, *Collected Poems and Plays*

Thirteen years ago, I had the slightly terrifying honor of talking with the venerated and mellifluous Rabindranath Tagore. We were speaking of the poetry of Baudelaire. Someone recited "*La Mort des amants*," that sonnet so appointed with beds, couches, flowers, chimneys, mantelpieces, mirrors, and angels. Tagore listened intently, but at the end he exclaimed, "I don't like your furniture poet!" I deeply agreed. Now, rereading his writings, I suspect that he was moved less by a horror of Romantic bric-à-brac than by an unconquerable love of vagueness.

Tagore is incorrigibly imprecise. In his thousand and one lines there is no lyric tension and not the least verbal economy. In the prologue he states that one "has submerged oneself in the depths of the ocean of forms." The image is typical of Tagore; it is typically fluid and formless. Here is a translation of one of the poems. [...]

[*1937*]   [*EW*]

Ellery Queen, *The Door Between*

There is a problem of enduring interest: the corpse in the locked room "which no one has entered and no one has left." Edgar Allan Poe invented it, and proposed a good solution, although perhaps not the best. (I speak of the one concocted for the story "The Murders in the Rue Morgue": a solution that requires a high window and an anthropomorphic ape.) Poe's story is from 1841; in 1892 the English writer Israel Zangwill published a short novel, *The Big Bow Mystery*, that took up the problem once again. Zangwill's solution was ingenious: two people enter the room of the crime at the same time; one of them screams that the landlord's throat has been slit and, taking advantage of the other's stupefaction, murders the landlord. Another excellent solution was offered by Gaston Leroux in his *The Mystery of the Yellow Room;* another, less remarkable, was that of Eden Phillpotts in *Jigsaw*. (In the latter, a man is stabbed in a tower; in the end it turns out that the knife was fired from a rifle.) In the story "The Oracle of the Dog," Chesterton returns to the problem; a sword and the crevices in an arbor form the solution.

The present volume by Ellery Queen formulates, for the sixth time, this classic problem. I will not commit the blunder of revealing the key. In any event, it is an unsatisfactory one, overly dependent on chance. *The Door Between* is interesting, but the plot is quite inferior to Queen's best novels: *Chinese Orange*, *Siamese Twin*, and *The Egyptian Cross*.

[*1937*]   [*EW*]

Sir William Barrett, *Personality Survives Death*

This book is truly posthumous. The late Sir William Barrett (ex-president and founder of the Society for Psychic Research) has dictated it from the Other World to his widow. (The transmissions were through the medium Mrs. Osborne Leonard.) In life, Sir William was not a spiritualist, and nothing delighted him more than to prove the falsehood of some "psychic" phenomenon. In death, surrounded by ghosts and angels, he remains unpersuaded. He believes in the other world, of course, "because I know that I am dead and because I do not wish to believe that I am mad." Nevertheless, he denies that the dead can assist the living, and he emphasizes that the most important thing is to believe in Jesus. He states:

"I have seen Him, I have talked with Him, and I will see Him again this coming Easter, in those days when you will think of Him and of me."

The other world described by Sir William Barrett is no less material than that of Swedenborg or Sir Oliver Lodge. The first of those explorers— *De coelo et inferno*, 1758—reported that things in heaven are brighter, more solid, and more numerous than those on earth, and that there are streets and avenues. Sir William Barrett corroborates these facts, and speaks of hexagonal houses made of brick and stone. (Hexagonal . . . is there an affinity between the dead and bees?)

Another curious feature: Sir William says that each country on earth has its double in heaven, exactly above it. There is a celestial England, a celestial Afghanistan, a celestial Belgian Congo. (The Arabs believed that a rose falling from Paradise would land precisely on the Temple in Jerusalem.)

[1938]   [EW]

Wolfram Eberhard, translator, *Chinese Fairy Tales and Folk Tales*

Few literary genres are as tedious as the fairy tale, except, of course, the fable. (The innocence and irresponsibility of animals is the source of their charm; to reduce them to instruments of morality, as Aesop and La Fontaine did, seems to me an aberration.) I have confessed that fairy tales bore me; now I must confess that I have read the first half of this book with great interest. The same occurred, ten years ago, with Wilhelm's *Chinesische Volksmaerchen*. How to resolve this contradiction?

The problem is simple. The European fairy tale, and the Arab, are all conventional. A ternary law rules them: there are two jealous sisters and a good younger sister, there are the king's three sons, there are three crows, there is a riddle that is guessed by the third one who tries. The Western tale is a sort of symmetrical artifact, divided into compartments. It is one of perfect symmetry. Is there anything less like beauty than perfect symmetry? (I am not making an apology for chaos, but I know that in the arts nothing is as pleasing as imperfect symmetries. . . .) The Chinese fairy tale, however, is irregular. The reader begins by finding them incoherent. He thinks that there are too many loose ends, things that don't come together. Later— perhaps suddenly—he discovers why these gaps exist. He realizes that these vagaries and anacoluthons imply that the narrator totally believes in the reality of the wonders that he tells. Reality is neither symmetrical nor schematic.

Of the stories that comprise this volume, the most delightful are "Brother Ghost," "The Empress of Heaven," "The Tale of the Silver Men," "The Son of the Turtle Spirit," "Tung Po-hua Sells Thunder," and "The Strange Picture." This last is the story of a painter with immortal hands who painted a moon that waxed and waned just like the moon in the sky.

I note, in the index, some titles that are worthy of Chesteron: "The Gratitude of the Snake," "The King of the Ashes," "The Actor and the Ghost."

[1938]   *[EW]*

The Literary Life: Marinetti

F. T. Marinetti is perhaps the most celebrated example of the kind of writer who lives by his wits and to whom something witty rarely occurs. Here, according to a telegram from Rome, is his latest pretense: "To the red of their lips and fingernails, the women of Italy must add light touches of the green of the Lombard plains and the white of the Alpine snows. Attractive tricolor lips will perfect the words of love and kindle the longing for a kiss in the rustic soldiers returning undefeated from the wars."

This bit of labial heraldry, suitable for kindling chastity and moderating or annihilating the "longing for a kiss," has not exhausted Marinetti's ingenuity. He has also proposed that Italians replace *chic* with *elettrizzante* [electrifying] (five syllables instead of one) and *bar* with *qui si beve* [here one drinks]—four syllables for one, and the unresolved enigma of how the plural will be formed. "Our Italian language must not be despoiled by foreignisms!" declares Filippo Tommaso with a Puritanism not unworthy of the aseptic Cejador or the forty stalls of the Spanish Royal Academy. Foreignisms! The old impresario of Futurism cannot abide such mischief.

[1938]   [EW]

Richard Hull, *Excellent Intentions*

One of the projects that keeps me company, that will in some way justify me before God, and that I do not think I will accomplish (for the pleasure is in foreseeing it, not in bringing it to term) is a detective novel that would be somewhat heterodox. (This last is important, for the detective genre, like all genres, lives on the continual and delicate infraction of its rules.)

I conceived it one night, one wasted night in 1935 or 1934, upon leaving a café in the Barrio Once. These meager circumstantial facts will have to suffice for the reader; I have forgotten the others, forgotten them to the point where I don't know whether I invented some of them. Here was my plan: to plot a detective novel of the current sort, with an indecipherable murder in the first pages, a long discussion in the middle, and a solution at the end. Then, almost in the last line, to add an ambiguous phrase—for example: "and everyone thought the meeting of the man and woman had been by chance"—that would indicate, or raise the suspicion, that the solution was false. The perplexed reader would go through the pertinent chapters again, and devise his own solution, the correct one. The reader of this imaginary book would be sharper than the detective. . . .

Richard Hull has written an extremely pleasant book. His prose is able, his characters convincing, his irony civilized. His solution, however, is so unsurprising that I cannot free myself from the suspicion that this quite real book, published in London, is the one I imagined in Balvanera, three or four years ago. In which case, *Excellent Intentions* hides a secret plot. Ah me, or ah Richard Hull! I can't find that secret plot anywhere.

[1938]   [EW]

Meadows Taylor, *The Confessions of a Thug*

This unusual book—published in April 1839 in three austere volumes, and republished exactly ninety-nine years later by Major Yeats-Brown—arouses a curiosity that is left unsatisfied. The subject is the "thugs," a sect or corporation of hereditary stranglers who for eight centuries brought horror (with bare feet and fatal scarves) to the streets and shadows of India. Hired assassination was, for them, a religious duty. They were devotees of Bhawani, the goddess whose idol is black, and who is worshiped under the names Durga, Parvati, and Kali Ma, and they would offer for her blessing the executionary scarf, the piece of sacred sugar the proselytes had to eat, and the hoe that dug the graves. Not everyone, however, was worthy of the scarf and the hoe: devotees were forbidden to murder "launderers, poets, fakirs, Sikhs, musicians, dancers, oil-pressers, carpenters, blacksmiths, and sweepers, as well as cripples and lepers."

The adepts swore to be valiant, submissive, and secretive, and they roamed the vast countryside in bands of fifteen to two hundred men. They had a language, Ramasee, that is now lost, and a sign language that could be understood anywhere in India, from Amritsar to Ceylon. Their fraternity consisted of four orders: the Seducers, who lured travelers with songs and fantastic tales; the Executioners, who strangled them; the Hospitalers, who dug the graves; and the Purifiers, whose mission was to strip the corpses. The dark goddess allowed them treachery and treason: it is well known that thugs were sometimes hired as escorts to protect against other thugs. They would travel for leagues and leagues to the precise and remote spot indicated by auspicious signs, and there the massacre would occur. There was a famous strangler—Buhram of Allahabad—who in forty years on the job killed more than nine hundred people.

This book was based on authentic court documents, and in its time was praised by Thomas De Quincey and Bulwer-Lytton. The present editor, Yeats-Brown, has added gaudy titles—"The Jeweler and His Astrologer," "The Lady Who Knew Too Much," "The Episode of the Obese Banker"— that are unsuited to the simplicity of the style.

I have said that this book arouses a curiosity that is left unsatisfied, and that no doubt cannot be satisfied. For example, I would have liked to know if the thugs were bandits who sanctified their work with the cult of the goddess Bhawani, or if the cult of Bhawani made them bandits.

[1938]   [EW]

William Faulkner, *The Unvanquished*

It is a general rule that novelists do not present a reality, but rather the memory of one. They may write about true or believable events, but these have been revised and arranged by recollection. (This process, needless to say, has nothing to do with the verb tenses they employ.) Faulkner, however, at times wants to recreate the pure present, neither simplified by time nor polished by attention. The "pure present" is no more than a psychological ideal—and thus some of Faulkner's decompositions are more confused— and richer—than the original events.

In earlier works, Faulkner has played powerfully with time, deliberately shuffling chronological order, deliberately complicating the labyrinths and ambiguities. He did it to such an extent that there were those who insisted that his virtues as a novelist were entirely derived from those involutions. This novel—direct, irresistible, straightforward—will destroy that suspicion. Faulkner does not try to explain his characters: he shows us what they feel and what they do. The events are extraordinary, but his narration is so vivid that we cannot imagine them any other way. "*Le vrai peut quelquefois n'être pas vraisemblable,*" said Boileau. (What is true may sometimes not be plausible.) Faulkner heaps his implausibilities in order to seem truthful, and he succeeds. Or more exactly: the world he imagines is so real that it also encompasses the implausible.

William Faulkner has been compared to Dostoevsky. This is not unjust, but the world of Faulkner is so physical, so carnal, that next to Colonel Bayard Sartoris or Temple Drake, the explicative murderer Raskolnikov is as slight as a prince in Racine. . . . Rivers of brown water, crumbling mansions, black slaves, battles on horseback, idle and cruel: the strange world of *The Unvanquished* is a blood relation of this America, here, and its history; it, too, is *criollo*.

There are books that touch us physically, like the closeness of the sea or of the morning. This—for me—is one of them.

        [1938]   *[EW]*

Lady Murasaki, *The Tale of Genji*

The publishers of the Orientalist Arthur Waley have gathered into a single serviceable volume his now-famous translation of Murasaki's *Tale of Genji,* which previously was barely available (or unavailable) in six onerous volumes. This version may be characterized as a classic: it is written with an almost miraculous naturalness, and what interests us is not the exoticism—that horrible word—but rather the human passions of the novel. Such interest is just: Murasaki's work is what one would quite precisely call a psychological novel. It was written a thousand years ago by a noble lady in the court of the second Empress of Japan; in Europe it would have been inconceivable before the nineteenth century. This is not to say that Murasaki is more intense or more memorable or "better" than Fielding or Cervantes; rather that she is more complex, and the civilization to which she belonged was more refined. To put it another way: I don't claim that Murasaki Shikibu had the talent of Cervantes, but rather that she was heard by a public that was far more subtle. In the *Quixote*, Cervantes limits himself to distinguishing day from night; Murasaki (*The Bridge of Dreams*, chapter X) notes in a window "the blurred stars behind the falling snow." In the previous paragraph, she mentions a long bridge, damp in the mist, "that seems much farther away." Perhaps the first detail is implausible; the two together are strangely effective.

I have mentioned two visual details; now I would like to note a psychological one. A woman, behind a curtain, sees a man enter. Murasaki writes: "Instinctively, although she knew quite well that he couldn't see her, she smoothed her hair with her hand."

It is obvious that two or three fragmentary lines cannot take the measure of a novel of fifty-four chapters. I dare to recommend this book to those who read me. The English translation that has inspired this brief insufficient note is called *The Tale of Genji*; it was also translated into German last year (*Die Geschichte vom Prinzen Genji*). In French, there is a complete translation of the first nine chapters (*Le roman de Genji*, 1928) and a few pages in Michel Revon's *Anthologie de la littérature japonaise*.

[1938]   [EW]

Lord Dunsany, *Patches of Sunlight*

This book, adorned with hunting and military figures, is the autobiography of Lord Dunsany: an autobiography that deliberately avoids confessions. This avoidance is not a mistake: there are autobiographies that relentlessly inflict intimacies upon us, but whose intimacy eludes us; there are others, perhaps involuntarily so, that cannot recall a sunset or mention a tiger without revealing in some way the singular style of the soul who wrote it. Of the former, Frank Harris is an example; of the latter, George Moore . . . Lord Dunsany, too, prefers the indirect manner; unfortunately that manner, in his hands, is not always effective.

It is enough to recall some of the *Dreamer's Tales* (for example, the one about the man buried forever in the mud of the Thames by a secret society, or the one about the sandstorm, or the one about the field haunted by the dead of a future battle) to admit that imagination is not a virtue that Lord Dunsany lacks. Nevertheless, I suspect that he has made a mistake in asserting that he has invented "skies and earths, and kings and peoples and customs." I suspect that this vast invention is limited to a series of proper names, propping up a vague Oriental ambience. Those names are no less incompetent than those that bring horror to the cosmogonies of William Blake (Ololon, Fuzon, Golgonooza), but it is difficult to share the jubilation of the baptizer of Glorm, Mlo, Belzund, Perdondaris, Golnuz, and Kyph, or his repentence at having written *Babbulkund, City of Wonders*, instead of *Babdarun, City of Wonders*.

Here is a paragraph from chapter XXX, which describes the Sahara:

I shall always remember how, as we left the station, I lifted my left hand to see the time by my wrist-watch, and rode into the desert. Time was of enormous importance on the railway; and so was one's luggage, and there were speed and noise there, among other worries; but in the desert there were only sunrise and sunset to notice, and noon, when all animals slept and the gazelles were not to be found.

In this disheveled and comfortable book, Lord Dunsany talks of watches and gazelles, swords and moons, angels and millionaires. In the whole universe there is only one thing of which he doesn't speak, and that is writers. There are two explanations for this staggering omission. The first (and the most petty) is that writers do not speak of him. The second (the more plausible) is that the writers of England may be as avoidable as those that adorn our city.

[1938]   [EW]

Two Fantasy Novels

Jacques Spitz (who, in *Sever the Earth*, imagined that the Americas slipped off the earth and formed their own planet) plays with dwarves and giants in his latest book, *L'Homme élastique* [Elastic Man]. The fact that Wells, Voltaire, and Jonathan Swift have previously played this curious anthropometrical game is as obvious and indisputable as it is insignificant. Spitz's novelty is in the variations he provides. He has imagined a biologist—Dr. Flohr—who discovers a way to reduce or enlarge atoms, a discovery that allows him to alter the dimensions of living organisms, particularly humans. The doctor begins by correcting a dwarf. Later, an opportune European war allows him to expand his experiments. The War Ministry sends him seven thousand men. Instead of turning them into ostentatious and vulnerable giants, Flohr makes them four centimeters tall. These abbreviated warriors secure a victory for France. Humanity, later on, opts for a variable stature. There are people of only a few millimeters, and others who cast enormous threatening shadows. Spitz quite humorously investigates the psychology, ethics, and politics of this uneven humanity.

Still stranger is the plot of *Man with Four Lives*, by the American writer William Joyce Cowen. An English captain, in the 1918 war, kills four times the same German captain, with the same manly features, the same name, the same heavy gold ring with the same seal of a tower and the head of a unicorn. Toward the end, the author posits an explanation that is quite beautiful: the German is an imprisoned soldier who, through meditation, projects a kind of corporeal phantom that fights and dies again and again for his country. On the last page, however, the author absurdly decides that a magical explanation is inferior to an unbelievable explanation, and he offers us four facsimilar brothers, with identical manly features, names, and unicorns. This profusion of twins, this implausible and cowardly tautology, left me in a stupor. I can only repeat the words of Adolfo Bécquer:

> *Cuando me lo contaron, sentí el frío*
> *de una hoja de acero en las entrañas*
> [When they told me, I felt the cold/of a steel blade in my entrails]

More stoic than I am, Hugh Walpole writes: "I am not quite sure of the veracity of the solution offered by Mr. Cowen."

[1938] *[EW]*

The Literary Life: Oliver Gogarty

Toward the end of the civil war in Ireland, the poet Oliver Gogarty was im-prisoned by some Ulster men in a huge house on the banks of the Barrow, in County Kildare. He knew that at dawn he would be shot. Under some pretext, he went into the garden and threw himself into the glacial waters. The night grew large with gunshots. Swimming under the black water ex-ploding with bullets, he promised the river that he would give it two swans if it allowed him to reach the other bank. The god of the river heard him and saved him, and the poet later fulfilled his pledge.

[1938]   *[EW]*

An English Version of the Oldest Songs in the World

Around 1916, I decided to devote myself to the study of the Oriental litera-tures. Working with enthusiasm and credulity through the English version of a certain Chinese philosopher, I came across this memorable passage: "A man condemned to death doesn't care that he is standing at the edge of a precipice, for he has already renounced life." Here the translator attached an asterisk, and his note informed me that this interpretation was preferable to that of a rival Sinologist, who had translated the passage thus: "The servants destroy the works of art, so that they will not have to judge their beauties and defects." Then, like Paolo and Francesca, I read no more. A mysterious skepticism had slipped into my soul.

Each time fate brings me before a "literal version" of some masterpiece of Chinese or Arabian literature, I remember that sorry incident. Now I re-call it again, reading the translations that Arthur Waley has just published of the *Shih Ching,* or *The Book of Songs.* These songs are of a popular na-ture, and it is believed they were composed by Chinese soldiers or peasants in the seventh or eighth century B.C. Here are some translations of a few of them. [. . .]

[1938]   *[EW]*

Alan Griffiths, *Of Course, Vitelli!*

The plot of this novel is not entirely original (it was anticipated by Jules Romains and more than once by reality), but it is extremely entertaining. The protagonist, Roger Diss, invents an anecdote. He tells it to a few friends, who don't believe him. To persuade them, he claims that the event took place around 1850 in the south of England, and he attributes the story to the "famous cellist Vitelli." Everyone, of course, recognizes this invented name. Encouraged by his success, Diss publishes an article on Vitelli in a local magazine. Various strangers miraculously appear who point out mistakes in the article, and a polemic ensues. Diss, victorious, publishes a full-length biography of Vitelli, "with portraits, sketches, and manuscripts."

A movie company acquires the rights to the book and makes a technicolor film. The critics declare that the film has distorted the facts of Vitelli's life. . . . Diss becomes embroiled in another polemic, and they demolish him. Furious, he decides to reveal the hoax. No one believes him, and people hint that he has gone mad. The collective myth is stronger than he is. A Mr. Clutterbuck Vitelli defends the affronted memory of his late uncle. A spiritualist center in Tunbridge Wells receives direct messages from the deceased. If this were a book by Pirandello, Diss would end up believing in Vitelli.

"Every book contains its counter-book," Novalis said. The counter of this book would be cruel and far stranger. It would be the story of a group of conspirators who plot that a certain person does not exist or has never existed.

[1938]   *[EW]*

A Grandiose Manifesto from Breton

Twenty years ago there were swarms of manifestos. Those authoritarian documents rehabilitated art, abolished punctuation, avoided spelling, and often achieved solecism. If issued by writers, they delighted in slandering rhyme and exculpating metaphor; if by painters, they defended (or attacked) pure color; if by composers, they worshiped cacophony; if by architects, they preferred the humble gas meter to the cathedral of Milan. Each, nevertheless, had its moment. Those garrulous sheets (of which I had a collection that I donated to the fireplace) have now been surpassed by the pamphlet that André Breton and Diego Rivera have just emitted.

The pamphlet is adamantly titled, *For an Independent Revolutionary Art: Manifesto by Diego Rivera and André Breton for the Definitive Liberation of Art.* The text is even more stuttering and effusive. It consists of some three thousand words that say exactly two (incompatible) things. The first is that art should be free and that it is not free in Russia. Rivera-Breton remark:

> Under the influence of the totalitarian regime of the USSR, a deep twilight has extended over the entire world, hostile to the emergence of any kind of spiritual value. A twilight of mud and blood in which, disguised as intellectuals and artists, men who have made servility a recourse, the denial of their principles a perverse game, false venal testimony a habit, and the apology for crime a pleasure, practice their deceptions. The official art of the Stalinist era reflects their risible attempts to deceive and to disguise their true mercenary role. . . . To those who urge us, be it today or tomorrow, to admit that art can be subordinated to a discipline which we consider to be radically incompatible with its nature, we offer in opposition a nameless negative, and our deliberate decision to ally ourselves to the formula "All license in art."

What conclusions may we draw from this? I believe, and only believe, that Marxism (like Lutheranism, like the moon, like a horse, like a line from Shakespeare) may be a stimulus for art, but it is absurd to decree that it is the only one. It is absurd for art to be a department of politics. That, however, is precisely what this incredible manifesto claims. Having barely stamped the formula "All license in art," Breton repents his daring and dedicates two fleeting pages to the denial of that reckless statement. He rejects "political indifference," denounces pure art, "which generally serves the most impure aims of reaction," and proclaims that "the supreme task of contemporary art is to participate consciously and actively in the preparation of revolution." He then proposes "the organization of modest local and international congresses." Eager to exhaust the delights of rhymed prose, he announces that "in the next stage, a world congress will meet for the official dedication of the foundation of the International Federation of Independent Revolutionary Art (IFIRA)."

A poor independent art they are imagining, subordinate to the pedantries of committees and five capital letters!

[1938] *[EW]*

H. G. Wells' Latest Novel

Except for the always astonishing *Book of the Thousand Nights and One Night* (which the English, equally beautifully, called *The Arabian Nights*) I believe that it is safe to say that the most celebrated works of world literature have the worst titles. For example, it is difficult to conceive of a more opaque and visionless title than *The Ingenious Knight Don Quixote of La Mancha*, although one must grant that *The Sorrows of Young Werther* or *Crime and Punishment* are almost as dreadful. . . . (In poetry, I need only mention one unforgivable name: *Flowers of Evil.*) I raise these illustrious examples so that my readers will not tell me that a book with the absurd title *Apropos of Dolores* must necessarily be unreadable.

Apropos of Dolores is superficially identical to the psychological detective novels of Francis Iles. Its pages detail the initial love and growing unbearable hatred between a man and a woman. In order for there to be a suitably tragic outcome, it would have been convenient if we gradually sensed that the narrator would end up killing the woman. But of course Wells is not interested in tragic presentiments. He does not believe in the solemnity of either death or murder itself. No one is less disposed toward funerals, no one less likely to believe that the final day is more important than those previous. It is not unjust to say that Wells is interested in everything, except perhaps the story he is telling at that moment. Of the human beings who comprise this talkative book, he is interested in only one: Dolores Wilbeck. The others must hopelessly compete with biology, ethnography, and politics. Among the perpetual digressions in which the author takes pleasure, there is this invective against the Greeks:

"Hellenic culture! Have you asked yourself what it was? Omnipresent Corinthian capitals, buildings painted red, pink statues, bosses in the atriums, the incessant resounding Homer and his hysterical heroes, pure tears and rhetoric."

[1938] *[EW]*

E. S. Pankhurst, *Delphos, or the Future of International Language*

This entertaining book pretends to be a general defense of artificial languages and a particular defense of "Interlingua," Peano's simplified Latin. It appears to have been written with enthusiasm, but the strange circumstance of the author having based her documentation exclusively on the articles contributed to the *Encyclopedia Britannica* by Dr. Henry Sweet leads us to suppose that her enthusiasm is rather moderate or fictitious.

The author (and Dr. Henry Sweet) divide artificial languages into *a priori* and *a posteriori;* that is, original and derived languages. The former are ambitious and impractical. Their superhuman goal is to classify, in a permanent fashion, all human ideas. They do not consider a definitive classification of reality to be impossible, and they plot dizzying inventories of the universe. The most illustrious of these rationalizing catalogs is undoubtedly that of John Wilkins, in 1668. Wilkins distributed the universe into forty categories, indicated by two-letter monosyllabic names. Those categories were subdivided into genuses (indicated by a consonant), and the genuses into species (indicated by a vowel). Thus *de* meant element, *deb* was fire, and *deba* a flame.

Two hundred years later, Letellier invented a similar process. *A*, in the international language he proposed, stood for animal, *ab* for mammal, *abo* for carnivore, *aboj* for feline, *aboje* for cat, *abod* for canine, *abode* for dog, *abi* for herbivore, *abiv* for equine, *abive* for horse, *abivu* for donkey.

The languages composed *a posteriori* are less interesting. Of all of them, the most complex is Volapük. It was invented in 1879 by a German priest, Johann Martin Schleyer, in order to promote peace among nations. In 1880, he added the finishing touches and dedicated it to God. His vocabulary is absurd, but his ability to encompass many nuances in a single word merits some respect. Volapük is interminably abundant with inflections: a verb may have 505,440 different forms. (*Peglidalöd*, for example, means "You ought to be greeted.")

Volapük was displaced by Esperanto, Esperanto by Neutral Idiom, Neutral Idiom by Interlingua. The latter two—"equitable, simple, and economical," according to Lugones—are immediately comprehensible to those who know a Romance language. Here is a sentence written in Neutral Idiom:

Idiom Neutral es usabl no sole pra skribasion, ma et pro perlasion; sikause in kongres internasional de medisinisti mi av intension sar ist idiom pro mie raport di maladrit "lupus," e mi esper esar komprended per omni medisinisti present.

[1939]   [EW]

Joyce's Latest Novel

Work in Progress has appeared at last, now titled *Finnegans Wake,* and is, they tell us, the ripened and lucid fruit of sixteen energetic years of literary labor. I have examined it with some bewilderment, have unenthusiastically deciphered nine or ten *calembours,* and have read the terror-stricken praise in the *N.R.F.* and the *T.L.S.* The trenchant authors of those accolades claim that they have discovered the rules of this complex verbal labyrinth, but they abstain from applying or formulating them; nor do they attempt the analysis of a single line or paragraph. . . . I suspect that they share my essential bewilderment and my useless and partial glances at the text. I suspect that they secretly hope (as I publicly do) for an exegetical treatise from Stuart Gilbert, the official interpreter of James Joyce.

It is unquestionable that Joyce is one of the best writers of our time. Verbally, he is perhaps the best. In *Ulysses* there are sentences, there are paragraphs, that are not inferior to Shakespeare or Sir Thomas Browne. In *Finnegans Wake* itself there are some memorable phrases. (This one, for example, which I will not attempt to translate: "Beside the rivering waters of, hither and thithering waters of, night.") In this enormous book, however, efficacy is an exception.

Finnegans Wake is a concatenation of puns committed in a dreamlike English that is difficult not to categorize as frustrated and incompetent. I don't think that I am exaggerating. *Ameise,* in German, means "ant." Joyce, in *Work in Progress,* combines it with the English *amazing* to coin the adjective *ameising,* meaning the wonder inspired by an ant. Here is another example, perhaps less lugubrious. Joyce fuses the English words *banister* and *star* into a single word, *banistar,* that combines both images.

Jules Laforgue and Lewis Carroll have played this game with better luck.

[1939]   [EW]

The Literary Life: The Dionne Quints

One of the disconcerting features of our time is the enthusiasm generated across the entire planet by the Dionne sisters, for numerical and biological reasons. Dr. William Blatz has devoted a large volume to them, predictably illustrated with charming photographs. In the third chapter, he states: "Yvonne is easily recognizable for being the eldest, Marie for being the youngest, Annette because everyone mistakes her for Yvonne, and Cecile because she is completely identical to Emilie."

[1939]   [EW]

IV

1937-1945

NOTES ON
GERMANY & THE WAR

A Pedagogy of Hatred

Displays of hatred are even more obscene and denigrating than exhibition-ism. I defy pornographers to show me a picture more vile than any of the twenty-two illustrations that comprise the children's book *Trau keinem Fuchs auf gruener Heid und keinem Jud bei seinem Eid* [Don't Trust Any Fox from a Heath or Any Jew on his Oath] whose fourth edition now infests Bavaria. It was first published a year ago, in 1936, and has already sold 51,000 copies. Its goal is to instill in the children of the Third Reich a distrust and animosity toward Jews. Verse (we know the mnemonic virtues of rhyme) and color engravings (we know how effective images are) collaborate in this veritable textbook of hatred.

Take any page: for example, page 5. Here I find, not without justifiable bewilderment, this didactic poem—"The German is a proud man who knows how to work and struggle. Jews detest him because he is so hand-some and enterprising"—followed by an equally informative and explicit quatrain: "Here's the Jew, recognizable to all, the biggest scoundrel in the whole kingdom. He thinks he's wonderful, and he's horrible." The engrav-ings are more astute: the German is a Scandinavian, eighteen-year-old ath-lete, plainly portrayed as a worker; the Jew is a dark Turk, obese and middle-aged. Another sophistic feature is that the German is clean-shaven and the Jew, while bald, is very hairy. (It is well known that German Jews are *Ashkenazim*, copper-haired Slavs. In this book they are presented as dark half-breeds so that they'll appear to be the exact opposite of the blond beasts. Their attributes also include the permanent use of a fez, a rolled cigar, and ruby rings.)

Another engraving shows a lecherous dwarf trying to seduce a young German lady with a necklace. In another, the father reprimands his daughter for accepting the gifts and promises of Solly Rosenfeld, who certainly will not make her his wife. Another depicts the foul body odor and shoddy negligence of Jewish butchers. (How could this be, with all the precautions they take to make meat kosher?) Another, the disadvantages of being swindled by a lawyer, who solicits from his clients a constant flow of flour, fresh eggs, and veal cutlets. After a year of this, the clients have lost their case but the Jewish lawyer "weighs two hundred and forty pounds." Yet another depicts the opportune expulsion of Jewish professors as a relief for the children: "We want a German teacher," shout the enthusiastic pupils, "a joyful teacher who knows how to play with us and maintain order and discipline. We want a German teacher who will teach us common sense." It is difficult not to share such aspirations.

What can one say about such a book? Personally I am outraged, less for Israel's sake than for Germany's, less for the offended community than for the offensive nation. I don't know if the world can do without German civilization, but I do know that its corruption by the teachings of hatred is a crime.

[1937]   [SJL]

A Disturbing Exposition

Doctor Johannes Rohr (of Berlin) has revised, rewritten, and Germanized the very Germanic *Geschichte der deutschen National-Literatur* [History of German Literature] by A. F. C. Vilmar. In editions previous to the Third Reich, Vilmar's work was decidedly mediocre; now it is alarming. This perverse catalog includes about seven hundred authors but, incredibly, silences the name of Heine.

> *Nennt man die besten Namen*
> *So wird auch der meine genannt*
> [When the best men were named/my name was among them]

wrote Heine around 1823, not foreseeing that the racial pedantry of 1938 would contradict him. Also obliterated are Franz Werfel, Alfred Döblin, Johannes Becher, Wilhelm Klemm, Gustav Meyrink, Max Brod, Franz Kafka, Gottfried Benn, Martin Buber, Albert Ehrenstein, Fritz von Unruh, Kasimir Edschmid, Lion Feuchtwanger, Arnold Zweig, Stefan Zweig, Erich Maria

Remarque, and Bertholt Brecht. . . . I do not want to list names; I need only recall that three of them—Becher, Döblin, Franz Kafka—belong to extraordinary writers and that, among the others, there is not one that in all honesty should be excluded from a history of German literature. The (unreasonable) reasons for this manifold silence are evident: most of those eliminated are Jewish, none is a National Socialist. As for the rest of the book, let us examine one of the last pages, number 435. Written on that severe page is: "Rivers of fire of a verbal potency previously unheard on German soil inundated the people: the great speeches of the Führer, swelling with lofty thoughts, yet opened wide to the understanding of the simple man, thoughts braced by remote, almost invisible hope, and yet instantly revered." Next we are regaled with a eulogy of the literary labors of Joseph Goebbels, the unexpected author of a vast symbolic novel "which because of the exemplary, vital, revolutionary conduct of the hero, its manly but chaste idealism and fiery language, is the book of the new youth and youths everywhere." The book *The Myth of the Twentieth Century* by Alfred Rosenberg provokes yet another enthusiastic critique. (How immeasurable is Rohr's anti-Semitism! It prohibits any mention of Heine in a history of German literature, but allows him to extol Rosenberg.)

As if that were not enough, Goethe, Lessing, and Nietzsche have been distorted and mutilated. Fichte and Hegel appear, but there is not even a mention of Schopenhauer. Of Stefan George we are informed only of a lively preamble which advantageously prefigures Adolf Hitler . . .

Things are worse in Russia, I hear people say. I infinitely agree, but Russia does not interest us as much as Germany. Germany—along with France, England, the United States—is one of the essential nations of the western world. Hence we feel devastated by its chaotic descent into darkness, hence the symptomatic seriousness of such books as this.

I find it normal for the Germans to reject the treaty of Versailles. (There is no *good European* who does not detest that ruthless contrivance.) I find it normal to detest the Republic, an opportunistic (and servile) scheme to appease Wilson. I find it normal to support with fervor a man who promises to defend their honor. I find it insane to sacrifice to that honor their culture, their past, and their honesty, and to perfect the criminal arts of barbarians.

[1938]   *[SJL]*

An Essay on Neutrality

It is easy to prove that an immediate (and even instantaneous) effect of this much-desired war has been the extinction or abolishment of all intellectual processes. I am not speaking of Europe, where George Bernard Shaw luckily endures; I am thinking of the charlatans and apologists that indefatigable fate obliges me to encounter on the streets and in the houses of Buenos Aires. Exclamations have taken over the function of reasoning; it is true that the scatterbrains who carelessly utter them give their slogans a discursive air, and that this tenuous syntactical simulacrum satisfies and persuades whoever happens to be listening. He who swears that the war is a kind of liberal *jihad* against dictatorships yearns, in the next minute, for Mussolini to fight Hitler, an act that would annihilate his thesis. He who swore forty days ago that Warsaw was impregnable, now wonders (sincerely) how it held out so long. He who denounces the English for being pirates is the same one who ardently declares that Adolf Hitler is acting in the spirit of Zarathustra, beyond good and evil. He who proclaims that Nazism is a regime that frees us from parliamentary charlatans and hands the government of nations over to a group of "strong silent men," listens in awe to the effusions of the incessant Hitler or—an even more secret pleasure—Göring. He who praises the current inaction of the French troops will applaud tonight the first signs of an offensive. He who disapproves of Hitler's greed, greets Stalin's with veneration. The bitter promise of the immediate disintegration of the unjust British Empire also shows that Germany has the right to possess colonies. (We should note, in passing, that the juxtaposition of the terms *colonies* and *right* is what some dead science—logic—denominates as a *contradictio in adjecto.*) He who rejects with superstitious fear the mere insinuation that the Reich can be defeated, pretends that the slightest success of its weapons is an incomprehensible miracle. I shall not continue: I do not want this page to be infinite.

I must take care, then, not to add an exclamation to the already innumerable ones that are overwhelming us. (I do not understand, for example, how someone could prefer a German victory to an English one: it would be easy for me to attach a figure of logic to such a conviction, but I cannot defend a *raison de coeur.*)

Those who hate Hitler usually hate Germany. I have always admired Germany. My blood and love of literature make me a natural ally of England; the years and books draw me to France; but to Germany, pure inclination. (That inclination moved me, around 1917, to undertake the study of German, without any guide other than Heine's *Lyrisches Intermezzo* and a laconic, sporadically dependable German-English glossary.) I am certainly not one of those fake Germanists who praise the eternal Germany in order to deny it any participation in the present. I am not sure that having produced Leibniz and Schopenhauer cripples Germany's capacity for political action. Nobody asks England to choose between its Empire and Shakespeare, nor insists in France that Descartes and Condé are incompatible. I naively believe that a powerful Germany would not have saddened Novalis or been repudiated by Hölderlin. I detest Hitler precisely because he does not share my faith in the German people; he has decided that to undo 1918, the only possible lesson is barbarism; the best incentive, concentration camps. Bernard Shaw, on this point, coincides with the melancholy Führer and thinks that only an incessant regime of marches, countermarches, and salutes to the flag can turn the placid Germans into passable warriors. . . .

If I had the tragic honor of being German, I would not resign myself to sacrificing to mere military efficiency the intelligence and integrity of my fatherland; if I were English or French, I would be grateful for the perfect coincidence of my country's particular cause with the universal cause of humanity.

It is possible that a German defeat might be the ruin of Germany; it is indisputable that its victory would debase and destroy the world. I am not referring to the imaginary danger of a South American colonial adventure; I am thinking of those native imitators, those homespun *Übermenschen* that inexorable chance would bring down upon us.

I hope the years will bring us the auspicious annihilation of Adolf Hitler, this atrocious offspring of Versailles.

[1939] *[SJL]*

Definition of a Germanophile

The implacable detractors of etymology argue that the origins of words do not instruct us in what they now mean; its defenders could reply that origins always instruct us in what words no longer mean. They demonstrate, for example, that pontiffs are not builders of bridges; that miniatures are not painted with minium; that crystal is not composed of ice; that the leopard is not a cross between a panther and a lion; that a candidate need not be robed in white; that sarcophagi are not the opposite of vegetarians; that alligators are not lizards; that rubrics are not red; that the discoverer of America was not Amerigo Vespucci; and that Germanophiles are not devotees of Germany.

This last is neither incorrect, nor even an exaggeration. I have been naive enough to talk with many Argentine Germanophiles; I have tried to speak of Germany and the German things that are imperishable; I have mentioned Hölderlin, Luther, Schopenhauer, and Leibniz; I have discovered that my "Germanophile" interlocutor could barely identify those names and preferred to discuss a more or less Antarctic archipelago that the English discovered in 1592 and whose relation to Germany I have yet to perceive.

Total ignorance of things Germanic does not, however, exhaust the definition of our Germanophiles. There are other unique characteristics that are, perhaps, equally essential. Among them: the Germanophile is greatly distressed that the railroad companies of a certain South American republic have English stockholders. He is also troubled by the hardships of the South African war of 1902. He is also anti-Semitic, and wishes to expel from our country a Slavo-Germanic community in which names of German origin predominate (Rosenblatt, Gruenberg, Nierenstein, Lilienthal) and which speaks a German dialect: Yiddish.

One might infer from this that the Germanophile is actually an Anglophobe. He is perfectly ignorant of Germany, and reserves his enthusiasm for any country at war with England. We shall see that such is the truth, but not the whole truth, nor even its most significant part. To demonstrate this I will reconstruct, reducing it to its essentials, a conversation I have had with many Germanophiles—something in which I swear never to involve myself again, for the time granted to mortals is not infinite and the fruit of these discussions is vain.

Invariably, my interlocutor begins by condemning the Treaty of Versailles, imposed by sheer force on Germany in 1919. Invariably, I illustrate the inculpatory judgment with a text from Wells or Bernard Shaw, who, in the hour of victory, denounced that implacable document. The Germanophile never rejects this text. He proclaims that a victorious country must abjure oppression and vengeance. He proclaims it natural that Germany wanted to annul that outrage. I share his opinion. Afterward, immediately afterward, the inexplicable occurs. My prodigious interlocutor argues that the old injustice suffered by Germany authorizes it, in 1940, to destroy not only England and France (why not Italy?), but also Denmark, Holland, and Norway, who are all completely free of blame for that injustice. In 1919, Germany was badly treated by its enemies: that all-powerful reason now allows it to burn, raze, and conquer all the nations of Europe and perhaps the globe. . . . The reasoning is monstrous, as can be seen.

I timidly point out this monstrousness to my interlocutor. He laughs at my antiquated scruples and raises Jesuitical or Nietzschean arguments: the end justifies the means, necessity knows no law, there is no law other than the will of the strongest, the Reich is strong, the air forces of the Reich have destroyed Coventry, etc. I mumble that I am resigned to passing from the morality of Jesus to that of Zarathustra or the Black Ant but that our rapid conversion then prohibits us from pitying Germany for the injustice it suffered in 1919. On that date which he does not want to forget, England and France were strong; there is no law other than the will of the strongest; therefore, those calumnied nations acted correctly in wanting to ruin Germany, and one cannot condemn them for anything other than having been indecisive (and even culpably merciful) in the execution of that plan. Disdaining these dry abstractions, my interlocutor begins or outlines a panegyric to Hitler: that providential man whose indefatigable discourses preach the extinction of all charlatans and demagogues, and whose incendiary bombs, unmitigated by verbose declarations of war, announce from the firmament the ruin of rapacious imperialism. Afterward, immediately afterward, a second wonder occurs. It is of a moral nature and almost unbelievable.

I always discover that my interlocutor idolizes Hitler, not in spite of the high-altitude bombs and the rumbling invasions, the machine guns, the accusations and lies, but because of those acts and instruments. He is delighted by evil and atrocity. The triumph of Germany does not matter to him; he wants the humiliation of England and a satisfying burning of London. He admires Hitler as he once admired his precursors in the criminal underworld of Chicago. The discussion becomes impossible because the offenses I ascribe to Hitler are, for him, wonders and virtues. The apologists of Amigas, Ramírez, Quiroga, Rosas, or Urquiza pardon or gloss over their crimes; the defender of Hitler derives a special pleasure from them. The Hitlerist is always a spiteful man, and a secret and sometimes public worshiper of criminal "vivacity" and cruelty. He is, thanks to a poverty of imagination, a man who believes that the future cannot be different from the present, and that Germany, till now victorious, cannot lose. He is the cunning man who longs to be on the winning side.

It is not entirely impossible that there could be some justification for Adolf Hitler; I know there is none for the Germanophile.

[1940]   [EW]

1941

The notion of an atrocious conspiracy by Germany to conquer and oppress all the countries of the atlas is (I rush to admit) irrevocably banal. It seems an invention of Maurice Leblanc, of Mr. Phillips Oppenheim, or of Baldur von Schirach. Notoriously anachronistic, it has the unmistakable flavor of 1914. Symptomatic of a poor imagination, grandiosity, and crass make-believe, this deplorable German fable counts on the complicity of the oblique Japanese and the docile, untrustworthy Italians, a circumstance that makes it even more ridiculous . . . Unfortunately, reality lacks literary scruples. All liberties are permitted, even a coincidence with Maurice Leblanc. As versatile as it is monotonous, reality lacks nothing, not even the purest indigence. Two centuries after the published ironies of Voltaire and Swift, our astonished eyes have seen the Eucharist Congress; men fulminated against by Juvenal rule the destinies of the world. That we are readers of Russell, Proust, and Henry James matters not; we are in the rudimentary world of the slave Aesop and cacophonic Marinetti. Ours is a paradoxical destiny.

Le vrai peut quelque fois n'être pas vraisemblable: the unbelievable, indisputable truth is that the directors of the Third Reich are procuring a universal empire, the conquest of the world. I will not enumerate the countries they have already attacked and plundered, not wishing this page to be infinite. Yesterday the Germanophiles swore that the maligned Hitler did not even dream of attacking this continent; now they justify and praise his latest hostility. They have applauded the invasion of Norway and Greece, the Soviet Republics and Holland; who knows what celebrations they will unleash the day our cities and shores are razed. It is childish to be impatient; Hitler's charity is ecumenical; in short (if the traitors and Jews don't disrupt him) we will enjoy all the benefits of torture, sodomy, rape, and mass executions. Do not our plains abound in *Lebensraum,* unlimited and precious matter? Someone, to frustrate our hopes, observes that we are very far away. My answer to him is that colonies are always far from the metropolis; the Belgian Congo is not on the borders of Belgium.

[1941]   [SJL]

Two Books

Wells' latest book—*Guide to the New World: A Handbook of Constructive World Revolution*—runs the risk of seeming, at first glance, like a mere encyclopedia of insults. His extremely readable pages denounce the Führer, who squeals "like a gripped rabbit"; Göring, who " 'destroys' towns overnight and they resume work and sweep up their broken glass in the morning"; Eden, who, "having wedded himself to the poor dead League of Nations, still cannot believe it dead"; Joseph Stalin, who, in an unreal dialect, continues to defend the dictatorship of the proletariat, although "nobody knows really what and where this 'proletariat' is, still less do they know how and where it dictates"; "the absurd Ironside"; the generals of the French army, "beaten by a sudden realization of their own unpreparedness and incompetence, by tanks that had been made in Czechoslovakia, by radio voices around them, and behind them, messenger boys on motor bicycles who told them to surrender"; the "positive will for defeat" of the British aristocracy; the "spite slum," southern Ireland; the British Foreign Office, which, although "the Germans have already lost it, seem to be doing their utmost to throw it back to them"; Sir Samuel Hoare, "not only silly mentally but morally silly"; the Americans and English who "betrayed the liberal cause in Spain"; those who believe that this war is "a war of ideologies" and not a criminal formula "of the current disorder"; the naifs who imagine that merely exorcising or destroying the demons Göring and Hitler will make the world a paradise.

I have gathered some of Wells' invectives: they are literarily memorable; some strike me as unjust, but they demonstrate the impartiality of his hatred or his indignation. They also demonstrate the freedom enjoyed by writers in England, even in the crucial hours of the battle. More important than his epigrammatic ill-humor (the few examples I have given could easily be tripled or quadrupled) is the doctrine of this revolutionary manual. That doctrine may be summarized as a specific alternative: either Britain identifies her cause with that of a general revolution (with that of a federated world), or victory is unattainable and worthless. Chapter XII (pp. 48–54) establishes the basic principles of the new world. The three final chapters discuss some lesser problems.

Wells, incredibly, is not a Nazi. Incredibly, because nearly all my contemporaries are, although they either deny it or don't know it. Since 1925, no writer has failed to claim that the inevitable and trivial fact of having been

born in a certain country and of belonging to a certain race (or certain mixture of races) is a singular privilege and an effective talisman. Defenders of
democracy, who believe themselves to be quite different from Goebbels,
urge their readers, in the same language as the enemy, to listen to the beating of a heart that answers the call of the blood and the land. I remember,
during the Spanish Civil War, certain impenetrable discussions. Some declared themselves Republicans; others, Nationalists; others, Marxists; yet all,
in a lexicon of a *Gauleiter,* spoke of the Race and of the People. Even the
men of the hammer and the sickle turned out to be racists. . . . I also remember with some amazement a certain assembly that was convoked to
condemn anti-Semitism. For various reasons, I am not an anti-Semite; the
principal one is that I find the difference between Jews and non-Jews generally insignificant, and sometimes illusory or imperceptible. No one, that
day, wanted to share my opinion; they all swore that a German Jew was
vastly different from a German. In vain I reminded them that Adolf Hitler
said the same thing; in vain I suggested that an assembly against racism
should not tolerate the doctrine of a Chosen People; in vain I quoted the
wise words of Mark Twain: "I have no race prejudices. . . . All that I care to
know is that a man is a human being—that is enough for me; he can't be
any worse." (*The Man that Corrupted Hadleyburg,* 204).

　　In this book, as in others—*The Fate of Homo Sapiens* (1939), *The Common Sense of War and Peace* (1940)—Wells exhorts us to remember our essential humanity and to suppress our miserable differential traits, no matter
how poignant or picturesque. In fact, that suppression is not exorbitant: it
merely demands of states, for a better coexistence, what an elementary
courtesy demands of individuals. "No one in his right mind," says Wells,
"thinks the British are a chosen people, a more noble species of Nazis, who
are disputing the hegemony of the world with the Germans. They are the
battle front of humanity. If they are not that front, they are nothing. That
duty is a privilege."

　　Let the People Think is the title of a selection of essays by Bertrand Russell. Wells, in the book I outlined above, urges us to rethink the history of
the world without geographical, economic, or ethnic preferences; Russell
also advises universality. In the third article, "Free Thought and Official
Propaganda," he proposes that elementary schools teach the art of reading
the newspaper with incredulity. I believe that this Socratic discipline would
not be useless. Of the people I know, very few practice it at all. They let
themselves be deceived by typographical or syntactical devices; they think
that an event has occurred because it is printed in large black letters; they

don't want to know that the statement "All the aggressor's attempts to advance beyond B have failed miserably" is merely a euphemism for admitting the loss of B. Even worse: they practice a kind of magic, and think that to express any fear is to collaborate with the enemy. . . . Russell proposes that the State attempt to immunize people against such deceptions and sophistries. For example, he suggests that students should study Napoleon's final defeats through the ostensibly triumphant bulletins in *Moniteur*. A typical assignment would be to read the history of the wars with France in English textbooks, and then to rewrite that history from the French point of view. Our own "nationalists" have already adopted that paradoxical method: they teach Argentine history from a Spanish viewpoint, if not Quechua or Querandí.

Of the other articles, among the most accurate is the one entitled "Genealogy of Fascism." The author begins by observing that political events derive from much older theories, and that often a great deal of time may elapse between the formulation of a doctrine and its application. This is so: the "burning reality," which exasperates or exalts us and frequently annihilates us, is nothing but an imperfect reverberation of former discussions. Hitler, so horrendous with his public armies and secret spies, is a pleonasm of Carlyle (1795–1881) and even of J. G. Fichte (1762–1814); Lenin, a transcription of Karl Marx. That is why the true intellectual refuses to take part in contemporary debates: reality is always anachronous.

Russell ascribes the theory of fascism to Fichte and to Carlyle. The former, in the fourth and fifth of the famous *Reden an die deutsche Nation*, attributes the superiority of the Germans to their uninterrupted possession of a pure language. Such reasoning is almost inexhaustibly fallacious; we can hypothesize that there is no pure language on earth (even if the words were, the representations would not be; although Spanish-language purists say *deporte*, they write *sport*); we can recall that German is less "pure" than Basque or Hottentot; we can ask why an unmixed language should be preferable. . . . Carlyle's contribution is more complex and more eloquent. In 1843, he wrote that democracy was the despair of not finding heroes to lead us. In 1870, he hailed the victory of "noble, patient, deep, pious and solid Germany" over "vapouring, vainglorious, gesticulatory, quarrelsome, restless and oversensitive France" (*Miscellanies* VII, 251). He praised the Middle Ages, condemned the windbags of Parliament, defended the memory of the god Thor, William the Bastard, Knox, Cromwell, Frederick II, the taciturn Dr. Francia, and Napoleon; longed for a world that was not "chaos equipped with ballot urns"; deplored the abolition of slavery; proposed that statues, "horrible bronze solecisms," be converted into bronze bathtubs; praised the death penalty; rejoiced that every town had a barracks; adulated and invented the Teutonic Race. Those who yearn for further imprecations or apotheoses may consult *Past and Present* (1843) and the *Latter-Day Pamphlets* (1850).

Bertrand Russell concludes: "In a certain sense, it is legitimate to state that the atmosphere at the beginning of the eighteenth century was rational, and that of our time is antirational." I would omit the timid adverbial phrase with which the sentence begins.

[1941]   [EW]

A Comment on August 23, 1944

That crowded day gave me three distinct surprises: the physical degree of joy I felt when they told me that Paris had been liberated; the discovery that a collective emotion can be noble; the puzzling and flagrant enthusiasm of many who were supporters of Hitler. I know that if I question that enthusiasm, I may easily resemble those futile hydrographers who asked why a single ruby was enough to arrest the course of a river; many will accuse me of trying to explain a fantastic event. Still, it happened, and thousands of persons in Buenos Aires can bear witness.

I realized immediately that it was useless to ask those people themselves. They are fickle, and by behaving incoherently they are no longer aware that incoherence need be justified. They adore the German race, but they abhor "Saxon" America; they condemn the articles of Versailles, but they applaud the wonders of the *Blitzkrieg;* they are anti-Semitic, but they profess a religion of Hebrew origin; they celebrate submarine warfare, but they vigorously condemn British acts of piracy; they denounce imperialism, but they defend and proclaim the theory of *Lebensraum;* they idolize San Martín, but they regard the independence of America as a mistake; they apply the canon of Jesus to the actions of England, but the canon of Zarathustra to those of Germany.

I also reflected that any other uncertainty was preferable to the uncertainty of a dialogue with these siblings of chaos, exonerated from honor and piety by the infinite repetition of the interesting formula *I am Argentine.* Furthermore, did Freud not argue and Walt Whitman not foresee that men have very little knowledge of the real motives for their conduct? Perhaps, I said to myself, the magic of the symbols *Paris* and *liberation* is so powerful that Hitler's partisans have forgotten that the defeat of his forces is the meaning of those symbols. Wearily, I chose to imagine that the probable explanation for this conundrum was their fear, their inconstancy, and their mere adherence to reality.

Several nights later, I was enlightened by a book and a memory. The book was Shaw's *Man and Superman;* the passage in question was John Tanner's metaphysical dream, where he affirms that the horror of Hell is its unreality. This conviction can be compared with the doctrine of another Irishman, John Scotus Erigena, who denied the substantive existence of sin and evil, and declared that all creatures, including the Devil, will return to God. The memory was the day that had been the exact and hateful opposite of August 23, 1944: June 14, 1940. A certain Germanophile, whose name I do not wish to remember, came to my house that day. Standing in the doorway, he announced the dreadful news: the Nazi armies had occupied Paris. I felt a confusion of sadness, disgust, malaise. Then it occurred to me that his insolent joy did not explain the stentorian voice or the abrupt proclamation. He added that the German troops would soon be in London. Any opposition was useless, nothing could prevent their victory. That was when I knew that he, too, was terrified.

I do not know whether the facts I have related require clarification. I believe I can interpret them like this: for Europeans and Americans, one order and only one is possible; it used to be called Rome, and now it is called Western Culture. To be a Nazi (to play the energetic barbarian, Viking, Tartar, sixteenth-century conquistador, gaucho, or Indian) is, after all, mentally and morally impossible. Nazism suffers from unreality, like Erigena's hell. It is uninhabitable; men can only die for it, lie for it, wound and kill for it. No one, in the intimate depths of his being, can wish it to triumph. I shall risk this conjecture: *Hitler wants to be defeated.* Hitler is blindly collaborating with the inevitable armies that will annihilate him, as the metal vultures and the dragon (which must have known that they were monsters) collaborated, mysteriously, with Hercules.

[1944]   *[SJL]*

A Note on the Peace

A worthy heir of the English nominalists, H. G. Wells repeats that to speak of the desires of Iraq or the perspicacity of Holland is to fall into foolish mythologies. France, he likes to remind us, consists of children, women, and men; it is not a tempestuous woman with a liberty cap. To this admonition, we may respond, with the nominalist Hume, that every person is equally plural and consists of a series of perceptions; or with Plutarch, "Nobody is what he was, nor will be what he is now"; or with Heraclitus, "No one steps into the same river twice." To speak is to make metaphors, to falsify; to speak is to resign oneself to being Góngora. We know (or think we know) that history is a perplexing, incessant web of causes and effects; that web, in its natural complexity, is inconceivable; we cannot think about it without resorting to the names of nations. Moreover, such names are ideas that operate within history, that rule and transform history.

Having said this, I would like to state that, for me, one single fact justifies this tragic moment; that joyous fact, which no one can ignore and few can evaluate, is England's victory. To say that England has triumphed is to say that Western civilization has triumphed, that Rome has triumphed;[1] it is also the triumph of that secret portion of divinity that exists in the soul of every person, even that of the executioner destroyed by this victory. I am not fabricating a paradox; the psychology of the Germanophile is that of the defender of gangsters, of Evil; we all know that during the war the historical triumphs of Germany interested him less than the notion of a secret army or of the satisfying burning of London.

The military strength of the three nations that have thwarted the German *complot* is more equally admirable than the cultures they represent. The United States has not fulfilled the great promise of its nineteenth century; Russia naturally combines the stigmas of the rudimentary, the scholarly, the pedantic, and the tyrannical. Of England, of the complex and almost infinite England, of that torn and lateral island that rules continents and seas, I will not risk a definition; it is enough to recall that it is perhaps

---

[1] In Macaulay's *Lays of Ancient Rome* (so vilified by Arnold), Rome is almost a metaphor for England; the feeling of an identity between the two is the basic theme of Kipling's *Puck of Pook's Hill*. To identify Imperial Rome with the momentary and pompous *Impero* that Mussolini botched in the shadow of the Third Reich is almost a play on words.

the only country that is not fascinated with itself, that does not believe itself to be Paradise or Utopia. I think of England as one thinks of a loved one, as something unique and irreplaceable. It is capable of reproachable indecision, of terrible slowness (it tolerates Franco, it tolerates the subsidiaries of Franco), but it is also capable of rectification and contrition, of returning to wage once more, when the shadow of a sword falls across the world, the cyclical battle of Waterloo.

[1945]   *[EW]*

The Total Library

The fancy or the imagination or the utopia of the Total Library has certain characteristics that are easily confused with virtues. In the first place, it's a wonder how long it took mankind to think of the idea. Certain examples that Aristotle attributes to Democritus and Leucippus clearly prefigure it, but its belated inventor is Gustav Theodor Fechner, and its first exponent, Kurd Lasswitz. (Between Democritus of Abdera and Fechner of Leipzig flow—heavily laden—almost twenty-four centuries of European history.) Its correspondences are well known and varied: it is related to atomism and combinatory analysis, to typography and to chance. In his book *The Race with the Tortoise* (Berlin, 1919), Dr. Theodor Wolff suggests that it is a derivation from, or a parody of, Ramón Llull's thinking machine; I would add that it is a typographical avatar of that doctrine of the Eternal Return which, adopted by the Stoics or Blanqui, by the Pythagoreans or Nietzsche, eternally returns.

The oldest glimpse of it is in the first book of Aristotle's *Metaphysics*. I speak of the passage that expounds the cosmogony of Leucippus: the formation of the world by the fortuitous conjunction of atoms. The writer observes that the atoms required by this hypothesis are homogeneous and that their differences derive from position, order, or form. To illustrate these distinctions, he adds: "A is different from N in form; AN from NA in order; Z from N in position." In the treatise *De generatione et corruptione*, he attempts to bring the variety of visible things into accord with the simplicity of the atoms, and he argues that a tragedy consists of the same elements as a comedy—that is, the twenty-four letters of the alphabet.

Three hundred years pass, and Marcus Tullius Cicero composes an inconclusive, skeptical dialogue and ironically entitles it *De natura deorum* [On the Nature of the Gods]. In the second book, one of the speakers argues: "I do not marvel that there should be anyone who can persuade himself that certain solid and individual bodies are pulled along by the force of gravity, and that the fortuitous collision of those particles produces this beautiful world that we see. He who considers this possible will also be able to believe that if innumerable characters of gold, each representing one of the twenty-one letters of the alphabet, were thrown together onto the ground, they might produce the *Annals* of Ennius. I doubt whether chance could possibly create even a single verse to read."[1]

Cicero's typographical image had a long life. Toward the middle of the seventeenth century, it appears in an academic discourse by Pascal; Swift, at the beginning of the eighteenth, emphasizes it in the preamble to his indignant "Trivial Essay on the Faculties of the Soul," which is a museum of commonplaces, similar to Flaubert's later *Dictionnaire des idées reçues*.

A century and a half later, three men support Democritus and refute Cicero. After such an enormous space of time, the vocabulary and the metaphors of the polemic have changed. Huxley (who is one of these men) does not say that the "golden characters" would finally compose a Latin verse if they were thrown a sufficient number of times; he says that a half-dozen monkeys provided with typewriters would, in a few eternities, produce all the books in the British Museum.[2] Lewis Carroll (one of the other refuters) observes in the second part of his extraordinary dream novel *Sylvie and Bruno*—in the year 1893—that as the number of words in any language is limited, so too is the number of their possible combinations or of their books. "Soon," he says, "literary men will not ask themselves, 'What book shall I write?' but 'Which book?' " Lasswitz, stimulated by Fechner, imagines the Total Library. He publishes his invention in a volume of fantastic tales, *Traumkristalle*.

Lasswitz's basic idea is the same as Carroll's, but the elements of his game are the universal orthographic symbols, not the words of a language. The number of such elements—letters, spaces, brackets, suspension marks, numbers—is reduced and can be reduced even further. The alphabet could relinquish the *q* (which is completely superfluous), the *x* (which is an abbreviation), and all the capital letters. It could eliminate the algorithms in the decimal system of enumeration or reduce them to two, as in Leibniz's

---

[1]As I do not have the original text, I have copied this passage from Menéndez y Pelayo's Spanish version (*Obras completas de Marco Tulio Cicerón* III, 88). Deussen and Mauthner speak of a sack of letters but do not say they are made of gold; it is not impossible that the "illustrious bibliophage" has contributed the gold and removed the sack.

[2]Strictly speaking, one immortal monkey would be sufficient.

binary notation. It could limit punctuation to the comma and the period. There would be no accents, as in Latin. By means of similar simplifications, Lasswitz arrives at twenty-five symbols (twenty-two letters, the space, the period, the comma), whose recombinations and repetitions encompass everything possible to express in all languages. The totality of such variations would form a Total Library of astronomical size. Lasswitz urges mankind to construct that inhuman library, which chance would organize and which would eliminate intelligence. (Wolff's *The Race with the Tortoise* expounds the execution and the dimensions of that impossible enterprise.)

Everything would be in its blind volumes. Everything: the detailed history of the future, Aeschylus' *The Egyptians*, the exact number of times that the waters of the Ganges have reflected the flight of a falcon, the secret and true name of Rome, the encyclopedia Novalis would have constructed, my dreams and half-dreams at dawn on August 14, 1934, the proof of Pierre Fermat's theorem, the unwritten chapters of *Edwin Drood*, those same chapters translated into the language spoken by the Garamantes, the paradoxes Berkeley invented concerning Time but didn't publish, Urizen's books of iron, the premature epiphanies of Stephen Dedalus, which would be meaningless before a cycle of a thousand years, the Gnostic Gospel of Basilides, the song the sirens sang, the complete catalog of the Library, the proof of the inaccuracy of that catalog. Everything: but for every sensible line or accurate fact there would be millions of meaningless cacophonies, verbal farragoes, and babblings. Everything: but all the generations of mankind could pass before the dizzying shelves—shelves that obliterate the day and on which chaos lies—ever reward them with a tolerable page.

One of the habits of the mind is the invention of horrible imaginings. The mind has invented Hell, it has invented predestination to Hell, it has imagined the Platonic ideas, the chimera, the sphinx, abnormal transfinite numbers (whose parts are no smaller than the whole), masks, mirrors, operas, the teratological Trinity: the Father, the Son, and the unresolvable Ghost, articulated into a single organism. . . . I have tried to rescue from oblivion a subaltern horror: the vast, contradictory Library, whose vertical wildernesses of books run the incessant risk of changing into others that affirm, deny, and confuse everything like a delirious god.

[1939]   *[EW]*

Time and J. W. Dunne

In number 63 of *Sur* (December 1939) I published a prehistory, a first basic history, of infinite regression. Not all my omissions were involuntary: I deliberately did not mention J. W. Dunne, who has derived from the endless *regressus* a rather surprising doctrine on time and its observer. The discussion (the mere outline) of his thesis would have exceeded the limitations of an article. Its complexity requires a separate essay, which I shall now attempt. My study is inspired by Dunne's latest book, *Nothing Dies* (1940), which reiterates or retraces the plots of his earlier works.

Or rather, the plot. Nothing in his argument is new, but the author's conclusions are most unusual, almost shocking. Before discussing them, I shall mention some earlier manifestations of the premises.

The seventh of India's many philosophical systems recorded by Paul Deussen (*Nachvedische Philosophie der Inder*, 318) denies the self as an immediate object of knowledge, "because if our soul were knowable, a second soul would be required to know the first and a third to know the second." The Hindus have no sense of history (they stubbornly prefer to examine ideas rather than the names and dates of philosophers), but we know that this radical negation of introspection is about eight centuries old. Schopenhauer rediscovered it around 1843. "The subject who knows," he repeated, "cannot be known precisely as such, otherwise he would be known by another subject" (*Welt als Wille und Vorstellung* II, 19). Herbart played similar ontological multiplication games: before he was twenty he had reasoned that the self must be infinite, because knowing oneself postulates another self that knows itself, a self that in turn postulates another self (Deussen, *Die neuere Philosophie* [1920], 367). Dunne reworks this plot, embellished with anecdotes, parables, strokes of irony, and diagrams.

Dunne (*An Experiment with Time*, chap. 22) argues that a conscious subject is conscious not only of what it observes, but of a subject A that also observes and, therefore, of another subject B that is conscious of A and, therefore, of another subject C conscious of B. He adds, somewhat mysteriously, that these innumerable intimate observers do not fit into the three dimensions of space, but they do in the no less numerous dimensions of time. Before clarifying such a clarification, I invite my readers to join me in thinking about the meaning of this paragraph again.

Huxley, heir to the British nominalists, claims there is only a verbal difference between the act of perceiving a pain and the act of knowing that one perceives it; he derides the pure metaphysicians who distinguish in every sensation a sensible subject, a sensation-producing object, and that imperious personage, the Ego (*Essays* VI, 87). Gustav Spiller (*The Mind of Man*, 1902) admits that awareness of pain and pain itself are two different things, but he considers them to be as comprehensible as the simultaneous perception of a voice and a face. I believe his opinion is valid. Regarding the consciousness of consciousness invoked by Dunne to establish in each individual a bewildering and nebulous hierarchy of subjects, or observers, I prefer to assume that they are successive (or imaginary) states of the initial subject. Leibnitz has said, "If the spirit had to reflect on each thought, the mere perception of a sensation would cause it to think of the sensation and then to think of the thought and then of the thought of the thought, and so to infinity" (*Nouveaux essais sur l'entendement humain* II, chap. 1).

Dunne's method to attain an infinite number of times simultaneously is less convincing and more ingenious. Like Juan de Mena in *El laberinto de Fortuna*,[1] like Ouspensky in *Tertium Organum*, he states that the future, with its details and vicissitudes, already exists. Toward the pre-existent future (or from the pre-existent future, as Bradley prefers) flows the absolute river of cosmic time, or the mortal rivers of our lives. Like all movement, that motion or flow requires a definite length of time—a second time for the movement of the first, a third for the movement of the second, and so on to infinity.[2] Such is the system proposed by Dunne. These hypothetical or illusory times provide endless room for the imperceptible subjects multiplied by the other *regressus*.

---

[1]In this fifteenth-century poem there is a vision of "three great wheels": the first, motionless, is the past; the second, in motion, is the present; the third, motionless, is the future.

[2]A half century before Dunne proposed it, "the absurd conjecture of a second time, in which the first flows rapidly or slowly," was discovered and rejected by Schopenhauer, in a handwritten note added to his *Welt als Wille und Vorstellung* which is recorded on p. 829 of vol. II of the historico-critical edition by Otto Weiss.

I wonder what my reader thinks. I do not pretend to know what sort of thing time is—or even if it is a "thing"—but I feel that the passage of time and time itself are a single mystery and not two. Dunne, I suspect, makes an error like the one made by those absentminded poets who speak, say, of the moon revealing its red disk, thus substituting a subject, verb, and object for an undivided visual image. The object is merely the subject itself, flimsily disguised. Dunne is an illustrious victim of that bad intellectual habit—denounced by Bergson—of conceiving of time as a fourth dimension of space. He postulates that the future toward which we must move already exists, but this postulate merely converts it into space and requires a second time (also conceived in spatial form, in the form of a line or a river) and then a third and a millionth. Not one of Dunne's four books fails to propose the infinite dimensions of time, but those dimensions are spatial.[3] For Dunne, real time is the unattainable final boundary of an infinite series.

What reasons are there for assuming that the future already exists? Dunne gives two: one, premonitory dreams; another, the relative simplicity this hypothesis lends to the complicated diagrams typical of his style. He also wishes to elude the problems of a continuous creation. . . .

Theologians define eternity as the lucid and simultaneous possession of all instants of time, and declare it a divine attribute. Dunne, surprisingly, presumes that eternity already belongs to us, as corroborated by the dreams we have each night. In them, according to him, the immediate past and the immediate future intermingle. Awake, we pass through successive time at a uniform speed; in dreams we may span a vast zone. To dream is to orchestrate the objects we viewed while awake and to weave from them a story, or a series of stories. We see the image of a sphinx and the image of a drugstore, and then we invent a drugstore that turns into a sphinx. We put the mouth of a face that looked at us the night before last on the man we shall meet tomorrow. (Schopenhauer wrote that life and dreams were pages from the same book, and that to read them in their proper order was to live, but to leaf through them was to dream.)

Dunne assures us that in death we shall finally learn how to handle eternity. We shall recover all the moments of our lives and combine them as we please. God and our friends and Shakespeare will collaborate with us.

So splendid a thesis, makes any fallacy committed by the author insignificant.

[1940]   [SJL]

---

[3]The phrase is revealing. In chapter 21 of *An Experiment with Time* he speaks of a time that is perpendicular to another.

A Fragment on Joyce

Among the works I have not written and will not write (but which in some way, however mysterious and rudimentary, justify me) is a story eight or ten pages long whose profuse first draft is titled "Funes the Memorious," and which in other, more chastened, versions is called "Ireneo Funes." The protagonist of this doubly chimerical fiction is a typically wretched *compadrito* living in Fray Bentos or Junín around 1884. His mother irons clothes for a living; the problematic father is said to have been a tracker. Certainly the boy has the blood and the silence of an Indian. In childhood, he was expelled from primary school for having slavishly copied out two chapters, along with their illustrations, maps, vignettes, block letters, and even a corrigendum. . . . He dies before the age of twenty. He is incredibly idle: he spends virtually his entire life on a cot, his eyes fixed on the fig tree in the backyard, or on a spiderweb. At his wake, the neighbors remember the humble facts of his history: a visit to the cattleyards, another to a brothel, another to so-and-so's ranch. . . . Someone provides the explanation. The deceased was perhaps the only lucid man on earth. His perceptions and memory were infallible. We, at first glance, perceive three glasses on a table; Funes, every leaf and grape on a vine. He knew the shapes of the southernmost clouds in the sunrise of April 30, 1882, and he could compare them in his memory to the veins in the stiff marbled binding of a book he once held in his hands during his childhood. He could reconstruct every dream, every reverie. He died of pneumonia, and his incommunicable life was the richest in the universe.

My story's magical *compadrito* may be called a precursor of the coming race of supermen, a partial Zarathustra of the outskirts of Buenos Aires; indisputably, he is a monster. I have evoked him because a consecutive, straightforward reading of the four hundred thousand words of *Ulysses* would require similar monsters. (I will not venture to speak of what

Finnegans Wake would demand; for me, its readers are no less inconceivable than C. H. Hinton's fourth dimension or the trinity of Nicaea.) Everyone knows that Joyce's book is indecipherably chaotic to the unprepared reader. Everyone knows that Stuart Gilbert, its official interpreter, has revealed that each of the novel's eighteen chapters corresponds to an hour of the day, a bodily organ, an art, a symbol, a color, a literary technique, and one of the adventures of Ulysses, son of Laertes, of the seed of Zeus. These imperceptible and laborious correspondences had only to be announced for the world to honor the work's severe construction and classic discipline. Among these voluntary tics, the most widely praised has been the most meaningless: James Joyce's contacts with Homer, or (simply) with the Senator from the *département du Jura,* M. Victor Bérard.

Far more admirable, without a doubt, is the multitudinous diversity of styles. Like Shakespeare, like Quevedo, like Goethe, like no other writer, Joyce is less a man of letters than a literature. And, incredibly, he is a literature within the compass of a single volume. His writing is intense, as Goethe's never was; it is delicate, a virtue whose existence Quevedo did not suspect. I (like the rest of the universe) have not read *Ulysses,* but I read and happily reread certain scenes: the dialogue on Shakespeare, the *Walpurgisnacht* in the whorehouse, the questions and answers of the catechism: "They drank in jocoserious silence Epp's massproduct, the creature cocoa." And, on another page: "A dark horse riderless, bolts like a phantom past the winningpost, his name moon-foaming, his eyeballs stars." And on another: "Bridebed, childbed, bed of death, ghostcandled."[1]

Plenitude and indigence coexist in Joyce. Lacking the capacity to construct (which his gods did not bestow on him, and which he was forced to make up for with arduous symmetries and labyrinths), he enjoyed a gift for words, a felicitous verbal omnipotence that can without exaggeration or imprecision be likened to *Hamlet* or the *Urn Burial.* . . . *Ulysses* (as everyone knows) is the story of a single day, within the perimeter of a single city. In this voluntary limitation, it is legitimate to perceive something more than an Aristotelian elegance: it can legitimately be inferred that for Joyce every day was in some secret way the irreparable Day of Judgment; every place, Hell or Purgatory.

[1941]   *[EA]*

---

[1]The French version is rather unfortunate: *"Lit nuptial, lit de parturition, lit de mort aux spectrales bougies."* The fault, of course, lies with the language, which is incapable of compound words.

The Creation and P. H. Gosse

"The man without a Navel yet lives in me," Sir Thomas Browne curiously writes (*Religio Medici*, 1642), meaning that, as a descendant of Adam, he was conceived in sin. In the first chapter of *Ulysses*, Joyce similarly evokes the immaculate and smooth belly of the woman without a mother: "Heva, naked Eve. She had no navel." The subject (I know) runs the risk of seeming grotesque and trivial, but the zoologist Philip Henry Gosse connected it to the central problem of metaphysics: the problem of time. That was in 1857; eighty years of oblivion equal, perhaps, something new.

In two places in the Scriptures (Romans 5; I Corinthians 15), the first Adam, in whom all die, is compared to the last Adam, who is Jesus.[1] This comparison, in order not to become mere blasphemy, must presuppose a certain enigmatic parity, which is translated into myths and symmetry. The *Legenda Aurea* states that the wood of the Cross comes from the forbidden Tree that is in Paradise; the theologians, that Adam was created by the Father and the Son at the exact age at which the Son died: thirty-three. This senseless precision must have influenced Gosse's cosmogony.

He revealed it in the book *Omphalos* (London, 1857), which is subtitled *An Attempt to Untie the Geological Knot*. I have searched the libraries for this book in vain; to write this note, I will use the summaries made by Edmund Gosse (*Father and Son*, 1907) and H. G. Wells (*All Aboard for Ararat*, 1940). I

---

[1]This conjunction is common in religious poetry. Perhaps the most intense example is in the penultimate stanza of the "Hymn to God, my God, in my sickness," March 23, 1630, composed by John Donne:

> We think that Paradise and Calvary,
> Christ's Cross, and Adam's tree, stood in one place,
> Look Lord, and find both Adams met in me;
> As the first Adam's sweat surrounds my face,
> May the last Adam's blood my soul embrace.

will introduce some illustrations that do not appear on those brief pages, but I believe they are compatible with Gosse's thought.

In the chapter of *Logic* that deals with the law of causality, John Stuart Mill argues that the state of the universe at any given moment is a consequence of its state at the previous moment, and that, for an infinite intelligence, the perfect knowledge of a *single moment* would be enough to know the history of the universe, past and future. (He also argues—oh Louis Auguste Blanqui, oh Nietzsche, oh Pythagoras!—that the repetition of any one state of the universe would entail the repetition of all the others and would turn universal history into a cyclical series.) In that moderate version of one of Laplace's fantasies—he had imagined that the present state of the universe is, in theory, reducible to a formula, from which Someone could deduce the entire future and the entire past—Mill does not exclude the possibility that a future exterior intervention may break the series. He asserts that state *q* will inevitably produce state *r;* state *r, s;* state *s, t,* but he concedes that before *t* a divine catastrophe—the *consummatio mundi,* let us say—may have annihilated the planet. The future is inevitable and exact, but it may not happen. God lies in wait in the intervals.

In 1857, people were disturbed by a contradiction. Genesis assigned six days—six unequivocal Hebrew days, from sunset to sunset—to the divine creation of the world, but the paleontologists impiously insisted on enormous accumulations of time. (De Quincey unavailingly repeated that the Scriptures have an obligation *not* to instruct mankind in any science, for the sciences constitute a vast mechanism to develop and train the human intellect.) How could one reconcile God with the fossils, Sir Charles Lyell with Moses? Gosse, fortified by prayer, proposed an astonishing answer.

Mill imagines a causal, infinite time that may be interrupted by a future act of God; Gosse, a rigorously causal, infinite time that has been interrupted by a past act: the Creation. State *n* will inevitably produce state *v,* but before *v* the Universal Judgment may occur; state *n* presupposes state *c,* but state *c* has not occurred, because the world was created in *f* or in *b.* The first moment of time coincides with the moment of the Creation, as St. Augustine says, but that first instant involves not only an infinite future, but an infinite past. A past that is hypothetical, to be sure, but also detailed and inevitable. Adam appears, and his teeth and his skeleton are thirty-three years old; Adam appears (Edmund Gosse writes) and he has a navel, although no umbilical cord attached him to a mother. The principle of reason requires that no effect be without a cause; those causes require other causes, which are multiplied regressively;[2] there are concrete vestiges of them all, but only those that are posterior to the Creation have really existed. There are skeletons of glyptodonts in the gorge of Luján, but there have never been glyptodonts. Such is the ingenious (and, above all, unbelievable) thesis that Philip Henry Gosse proposed to religion and to science.

Both rejected it. The newspapers reduced it to the doctrine that God had hidden fossils under the earth to test the faith of the geologists; Charles Kingsley denied that the Lord had carved a "superfluous and vast lie" into the rocks. In vain, Gosse explained the metaphysical foundation of his thesis: that one moment of time was inconceivable without the moment before it and the one after it, and so on to infinity. I wonder if he knew the ancient sentence that is quoted at the beginning of Rafael Cansinos Asséns' Talmudic anthology: "It was only the first night, but a number of centuries had already preceded it."

There are two virtues I would claim for Gosse's forgotten thesis. First: its somewhat monstrous elegance. Second: its involuntary reduction to absurdity of a *creatio ex nihilo*, its indirect demonstration that the universe is eternal, as the Vedanta and Heraclitus, Spinoza and the atomists all thought. Bertrand Russell has brought this up to date. In the ninth chapter of his book, *The Analysis of Mind* (London, 1921), he imagines that the planet was created only a few minutes ago, with a humanity that "remembers" an illusory past.

Postscript: In 1802, Chateaubriand (*Génie du christianisme* I, 4, 5), for aesthetic reasons, formulated a thesis identical to that of Gosse. He denounced as banal and ridiculous a first day of the Creation, populated by baby pigeons, larvae, puppies, and seeds. "Without this original antiquity, there would have been neither beauty nor magnificence in the work of the Almighty; and, what could not possibly be the case, nature, in a state of innocence, would have been less charming than she is in her present degenerate condition," he wrote.

[1941]   [EW]

2Cf. Spencer, *Facts and Comments* [1902], 148–151.

Circular Time

I tend to return eternally to the Eternal Return. In the following lines I will attempt (with the aid of a few historical illustrations) to define its three fundamental modes.

The first has been attributed to Plato, who, in the thirty-ninth paragraph of the *Timaeus*, claims that once their diverse velocities have achieved an equilibrium, the seven planets will return to their initial point of departure in a cycle that constitutes the perfect year. Cicero (*On the Nature of the Gods* II) acknowledges that this vast celestial period is not easy to compute, but holds that it is certainly not an unlimited span of time; in one of his lost works, he sets it at twelve thousand nine hundred and fifty four "of what we call years" (Tacitus, *Dialogue of the Orators*, 16). Once Plato was dead, astrology became increasingly popular in Athens. This science, as no one can pretend not to know, maintains that the destiny of men is ruled by the position of the stars. An unknown astrologer, who had not read the *Timaeus* in vain, formulated this irreproachable argument: if the planetary periods are cyclical, so must be the history of the universe; at the end of each Platonic year, the same individuals will be born again and will live out the same destinies. Posterity would attribute this conjecture to Plato himself. In 1616, Lucilio Vanini wrote, "Again will Achilles go to Troy, rites and religions be reborn, human history repeat itself. Nothing exists today that did not exist long ago; what has been, shall be; but all of that in general, and not (as Plato establishes) in particular" (*De admirandis naturae arcanis*, dialogue 52). In 1643, Thomas Browne defined "Plato's year" in a note to the first book of the *Religio Medici:* "A revolution of certain thousand years when all things should return unto their former estate and he be teaching again in his school as when he delivered this opinion." In this initial conception of the eternal return, the argument is astrological.

The second is linked to the glory of Nietzsche, the most touching of its inventors or promoters. It is justified by an algebraic principle: the observation that a quantity n of objects—atoms in Le Bon's hypothesis, forces in Nietzsche's, elements in the *communard* Blanqui's—is incapable of an infinite number of variations. Of the three doctrines I have listed, the most well-reasoned and complex is that of Blanqui, who, like Democritus (Cicero, *Academic Questions* II, 40), packs not only time but interminable space as well with facsimile worlds and dissimilar worlds. His book is beautifully entitled *L'Eternité par les astres;* it dates from 1872. A laconic but sufficient passage from David Hume dates from long before that; it appears in the *Dialogues Concerning Natural Religion* (1779), which Schopenhauer proposed to translate. As far as I know, no one has pointed it out until now. "Instead of supposing matter infinite, as Epicurus did; let us suppose it finite. A finite number of particles is only susceptible of finite transpositions: And it must happen, in an eternal duration, that every possible order or position must be tried an infinite number of times. This world, therefore, with all its events, even the most minute, has before been produced and destroyed, and will again be produced and destroyed, without any bounds and limitations" (*Dialogues* VIII).

Of this perpetual series of identical universal histories, Bertrand Russell observes:

> Many writers have imagined that history is cyclic, that the present state of the world, exactly as it is now, will sooner or later recur. How shall we state this hypothesis in our view? We shall have to say that the later state is numerically identical with the earlier state; and we cannot say that this state occurs twice, since that would imply a system of dating which the hypothesis makes impossible. The situation would be analogous to that of a man who travels round the world: he does not say that his starting-point and his point of arrival are two different but precisely similar places, he says they are the same place. The hypothesis that history is cyclic can be expressed as follows: form the group of all qualities contemporaneous with a given quality: in certain cases the whole of this group precedes itself. (*An Inquiry into Meaning and Truth* [1940], 102)

I now arrive at the final mode of interpreting eternal repetitions, the least melodramatic and terrifying of the three, but the only one that is conceivable. I mean the concept of similar but not identical cycles. The infinite catalogue of authorities would be impossible to complete: I think of the days and nights of Brahma; the epochs whose unmoving clock is a pyramid slowly worn down by a bird's wing that brushes against it every thousand and one years; I think of Hesiod's men, who degenerate from gold to iron; the world of Heraclitus, which is engendered by fire and cyclically devoured by fire, and the world of Seneca and Chrysippus, annihilated by fire and renewed by water; I think of Virgil's fourth *Eclogue* and Shelley's splendid echo; Ecclesiastes, the theosophists, Condorcet's decimal history; I think of Francis Bacon and Ouspensky; Gerald Heard and Spengler; Vico, Schopenhauer, and Emerson; Spencer's *First Principles* and Poe's *Eureka.* . . . Out of this profusion of testimony I will cite only one passage, from Marcus Aurelius:

> Though the years of your life numbered three thousand, or ten times three thousand, remember that none can lose another life than that he lives now, nor live another than that he loses. The lengthiest and briefest periods are equal. The present belongs to all; to die is to lose the present, which is the briefest of lapses. No one loses the past or the future, because no man can be deprived of what he does not have. Remember that all things turn and turn again in the same orbits, and for the spectator it is the same to watch for a century or for two or infinitely. (*Reflections* II, 14)

If we read the preceding lines with any degree of seriousness (*id est*, if we decide not to consider them a mere exhortation or moral object lesson), we will see that they proclaim, or presuppose, two curious ideas. The first is a negation of the reality of the past and the future, enunciated in the following passage from Schopenhauer:

> The form of the phenomenon of the will is really only the *present*, not the future or the past. Future and past are only in the concept, exist only in the connection and continuity of knowledge in so far as this follows the principle of sufficient reason. No man has lived in the past, and none will ever live in the future; the *present* alone is the form of all life. (*The World as Will and Representation* I, 54)

The second is a negation of all novelty, following the author of Ecclesiastes. This conjecture—that all of mankind's experiences are (in some way) analogous—may at first seem a mere impoverishment of the world.

If Edgar Allan Poe, the Vikings, Judas Iscariot, and my reader all secretly share the same destiny—the only possible destiny—then universal history is the history of a single man. Marcus Aurelius does not, strictly speaking, force this enigmatic simplification upon us. (A while ago I imagined a fantastic tale in the manner of León Bloy: a theologian dedicates his entire life to refuting a heresiarch; he bests him in intricate polemics, denounces him, has him burned at the stake. In Heaven he discovers that in God's eyes he and the heresiarch form a single person.) Marcus Aurelius affirms the analogous, but not identical, nature of multifarious human destinies. He affirms that any time span—a century, a year, a single night, perhaps the ungraspable present—contains the entirety of history. In its extreme form, this conjecture is easily refuted: one taste is different from another, ten minutes of physical pain are not the same as ten minutes of algebra. Applied to lengthier periods, to the seventy years of age that the Book of Psalms allots us, the conjecture is plausible and tolerable. It becomes no more than an affirmation that the number of human perceptions, emotions, thoughts, and vicissitudes is limited, and that before dying we will exhaust them all. Marcus Aurelius repeats: "To see the things of the present moment is to see all that is now, all that has been since time began, and all that shall be unto the world's end; for all things are of one kind and one form" (*Reflections* VI, 37).

In times of ascendancy, the conjecture that man's existence is a constant, unvarying quantity can sadden or irritate us; in times of decline (such as the present), it holds out the assurance that no ignominy, no calamity, no dictator, can impoverish us.

[1941]   [EA]

John Wilkins' Analytical Language

I see that the fourteenth edition of the *Encyclopedia Britannica* has omitted the article on John Wilkins. The omission is justifiable if we recall its triviality (twenty lines of mere biographical data: Wilkins was born in 1614; Wilkins died in 1672; Wilkins was the chaplain of the Prince Palatine, Charles Louis; Wilkins was appointed rector of one of the colleges of Oxford; Wilkins was the first secretary of the Royal Society of London; etc.) but inexcusable if we consider Wilkins' speculative work. He was full of happy curiosity: interested in theology, cryptography, music, the manufacture of transparent beehives, the course of an invisible planet, the possibility of a trip to the moon, the possibility and the principles of a world language. He devoted a book to this last problem: *An Essay Towards a Real Character and a Philosophical Language* (600 pages in quarto, 1668). Our National Library does not have a copy; to write this note I have consulted *The Life and Times of John Wilkins* by P. A. Wright Henderson (1910); the *Wörterbuch der Philosophie* by Fritz Mauthner (1924); *Delphos* by E. Sylvia Pankhurst (1935); and *Dangerous Thoughts* by Lancelot Hogben (1939).

All of us, at one time or another, have suffered through those unappealable debates in which a lady, with copious interjections and anacolutha, asserts that the word *luna* is more (or less) expressive than the word *moon*. Apart from the obvious comment that the monosyllable *moon* may be more appropriate as a representation of a simple object than the disyllabic *luna,* nothing can be contributed to such discussions; except for compound words and derivatives, all the languages in the world (not excluding Johann Martin Schleyer's Volapük and Peano's romantic Interlingua) are equally inexpressive. There is no edition of the Royal Spanish Academy Grammar that does not ponder "the envied treasure of picturesque, felicitous, and expressive words in the riches of the Spanish language," but that is mere boasting, with no corroboration. Meanwhile, that same Royal Academy

produces a dictionary every few years in order to define those words. . . .
In the universal language conceived by Wilkins in the middle of the
seventeenth century, each word defines itself. Descartes, in a letter dated
November 1619, had already noted that, by using the decimal system of numeration, we could learn in a single day to name all quantities to infinity,
and to write them in a new language, the language of numbers;[1] he also proposed the creation of a similar, general language that would organize and
contain all human thought. Around 1664, John Wilkins undertook that
task.

He divided the universe into forty categories or classes, which were
then subdivided into differences, and subdivided in turn into species. To
each class he assigned a monosyllable of two letters; to each difference, a
consonant; to each species, a vowel. For example, *de* means element; *deb,*
the first of the elements, fire; *deba,* a portion of the element of fire, a flame.
In a similar language invented by Letellier (1850), *a* means animal; *ab,* mam-
malian; *abo,* carnivorous; *aboj,* feline; *aboje,* cat; *abi,* herbivorous; *abiv,*
equine; etc. In that of Bonifacio Sotos Ochando (1845), *imaba* means building; *imaca,* brothel; *imafe,* hospital; *imafo,* pesthouse; *imarri,* house; *imaru,*
country estate; *imedo,* post; *imede,* pillar; *imego,* floor; *imela,* ceiling; *imogo,*
window; *bire,* bookbinder; *birer,* to bind books. (I found this last census in a
book published in Buenos Aires in 1886: the *Curso de lengua universal*
[Course in Universal Language] by Dr. Pedro Mata.)

The words of John Wilkins' analytical language are not dumb and arbitrary symbols; every letter is meaningful, as those of the Holy Scriptures
were for the Kabbalists. Mauthner observes that children could learn this
language without knowing that it was artificial; later, in school, they would
discover that it was also a universal key and a secret encyclopedia.

Having defined Wilkins' procedure, we must examine a problem that is
impossible or difficult to postpone: the merit of the forty-part table on
which the language is based. Let us consider the eighth category: stones.
Wilkins divides them into common (flint, gravel, slate); moderate (marble,
amber, coral); precious (pearl, opal); transparent (amethyst, sapphire); and
insoluble (coal, fuller's earth, and arsenic). The ninth category is almost as

---

[1]Theoretically, the number of systems of numeration is unlimited. The most
complex (for use by divinities and angels) would record an infinite number of symbols, one for each whole number; the simplest requires only two. Zero is written *0,* one
1, two *10,* three *11,* four *100,* five *101,* six *110,* seven *111,* eight *1000.* . . . It is the invention
of Leibniz, who was inspired (it seems) by the enigmatic hexagrams of the *I Ching.*

alarming as the eighth. It reveals that metals can be imperfect (vermilion, quicksilver); artificial (bronze, brass); recremental (filings, rust); and natural (gold, tin, copper). The whale appears in the sixteenth category: it is a viviparous, oblong fish. These ambiguities, redundancies, and deficiencies recall those attributed by Dr. Franz Kuhn to a certain Chinese encyclopedia called the *Heavenly Emporium of Benevolent Knowledge.* In its distant pages it is written that animals are divided into (a) those that belong to the emperor; (b) embalmed ones; (c) those that are trained; (d) suckling pigs; (e) mermaids; (f) fabulous ones; (g) stray dogs; (h) those that are included in this classification; (i) those that tremble as if they were mad; (j) innumerable ones; (k) those drawn with a very fine camel's-hair brush; (l) etcetera; (m) those that have just broken the flower vase; (n) those that at a distance resemble flies. The Bibliographical Institute of Brussels also exercises chaos: it has parceled the universe into 1,000 subdivisions, of which number 262 corresponds to the Pope, number 282 to the Roman Catholic Church, number 263 to the Lord's Day, number 268 to Sunday schools, number 298 to Mormonism, and number 294 to Brahmanism, Buddhism, Shintoism, and Taoism. Nor does it disdain the employment of heterogeneous subdivisions, for example, number 179: "Cruelty to animals. Protection of animals. Dueling and suicide from a moral point of view. Various vices and defects. Various virtues and qualities."

I have noted the arbitrariness of Wilkins, the unknown (or apocryphal) Chinese encyclopedist, and the Bibliographical Institute of Brussels; obviously there is no classification of the universe that is not arbitrary and speculative. The reason is quite simple: we do not know what the universe is. "This world," wrote David Hume, "was only the first rude essay of some infant deity who afterwards abandoned it, ashamed of his lame performance; it is the work only of some dependent, inferior deity, and is the object of derision to his superiors; it is the production of old age and dotage in some superannuated deity, and ever since his death has run on . . ." (*Dialogues Concerning Natural Religion* V [1779]). We must go even further, and suspect that there is no universe in the organic, unifying sense of that ambitious word. If there is, then we must speculate on its purpose; we must speculate on the words, definitions, etymologies, and synonymies of God's secret dictionary.

The impossibility of penetrating the divine scheme of the universe cannot, however, dissuade us from planning human schemes, even though it is clear that they are provisional. Wilkins' analytical language is not the least remarkable of those schemes. The classes and species that comprise it are contradictory and vague; the artifice of using the letters of the words to indicate divisions and subdivisions is undoubtedly ingenious. The word *salmon* tells us nothing; *zana*, the corresponding word, defines (for the person versed in the forty categories and the classes of those categories) a scaly river fish with reddish flesh. (Theoretically, a language in which the name of each being would indicate all the details of its fate, past and future, is not inconceivable.)

Hopes and utopias aside, perhaps the most lucid words written about language are these by Chesterton: "Man knows that there are in the soul tints more bewildering, more numberless, and more nameless than the colors of an autumn forest. . . . Yet he seriously believes that these things can every one of them, in all their tones and semi-tones, in all their blends and unions, be accurately represented by an arbitrary system of grunts and squeals. He believes that an ordinary civilized stockbroker can really produce out of his own inside noises which denote all the mysteries of memory and all the agonies of desire" (*G. F. Watts* [1904], 88).

[1942]   [EW]

On Literary Description

Lessing, De Quincey, Ruskin, Rémy de Gourmont, Unamuno, have all pondered and elucidated the problem I am about to discuss. I do not propose to refute or to corroborate what they have said, but rather to indicate, with an abundance of illustrative examples, the frequent flaws of the genre. The first is of a metaphysical nature; in the disparate examples that follow, the curious reader will easily recognize it:

> The towers of the churches and the chimneys of the factories raise their pointed pyramids and their rigid stalks (Groussac)

> > The moon led
> > its white vessel along the serene orbit (Oyuela)

> Oh moon driving like a clever *sportswoman*, through zodiacs and eclipses, your lovely cabriolet (Lugones)

> If we vary ever so slightly the direction of our gaze we see the pond inhabited by an entire landscape. The orchard bathes in it: apples swim reflected in the liquid and the first quarter moon sheds light on its depths with its inspector's face. (Ortega y Gasset)

> The old bridge extends its arch over the river, joining the villas with the tranquil field. (Guiraldes)

If I am not mistaken, the illustrious fragments I have gathered suffer a slight inconvenience. They substitute a subject, verb, and direct object for an undivided image. To further complicate matters, the direct object is the same as the subject, slightly disguised. The "vessel" led by the moon is the moon itself; the chimneys and towers erect pointed pyramids and stiff stalks that are the same towers and chimneys; the first quarter moon sheds its inspector's face over the depths of the pool, which is no different than the first quarter moon. Guiraldes very superfluously distinguishes the arch over the river and the old bridge and allows two active verbs—*extend* and *join*—to stir up a single immobile image. In the jocular apostrophe by Lugones, the moon is a "sportswoman" who drives through "zodiacs and eclipses a lovely cabriolet"—which is the moon itself. The defenders of this verbal doubling may argue that the act of perceiving something—the much-frequented moon, shall we say—is no less complicated than its metaphors, because memory and suggestion intervene; I would retort with Occam's restrictive principle: We should not multiply entities uselessly.

Another censurable method is the enumeration and definition of the parts of a whole. I will limit myself to a single example:

She offered her feet in sandals of purple suede, fastened with a frosting of precious stones. . . . her naked arms and throat, without a glimmer of jewels; her firm, raised breasts; her sunken flat belly, fleeing the opulence sprouting from her waist; her cheeks, golden; her eyes, of a sunken splendor, enlarged by antimony; her mouth, lit with the juicy sparkle of certain flowers; her forehead, interrupted by a path of amethysts that lost its way amid her shining steel tresses, spread over her shoulders in braids of an intimate undulation. (Miró)

Thirteen or fourteen terms form the chaotic series; the author invites us to conjure up those *disjecta membra* and coordinate them in a single coherent image. That mental operation is impractical: no one would think of imagining type X's feet and then adding them to type Y's throat and type Z's cheeks. . . . Herbert Spencer (*The Philosophy of Style*, 1852) has already discussed this problem.

The above does not intend to prohibit all enumerations. The lists in the Psalms, in Whitman and Blake, have exclamatory value; others exist verbally, even though they are unrepresentable. For example:

Suddenly out of a shuffling deck of cops and crooks sprang an old devil, broken and doddering, legs akimbo, gap-toothed, cavern-cheeked, with scratching tools long as a beetle's. He appeared pulled by the reins of a defunct dromedary with a day's worth of body so heavy, sluggish, and stubborn, that leading her to the theater almost burst the aged demon. (Torres Villarroel)

I have condemned here the usual errors of the genre. In other pages I have discussed the procedure that seems valid to me: the indirect, which William Shakespeare handles splendidly in the first scene of Act V of *The Merchant of Venice.*

[1942]   [SJL]

On William Beckford's *Vathek*

Wilde attributes this joke to Carlyle: a biography of Michelangelo that would make no mention of the works of Michelangelo. So complex is reality, and so fragmentary and simplified is history, that an omniscient observer could write an indefinite, almost infinite, number of biographies of a man, each emphasizing different facts; we would have to read many of them before we realized that the protagonist was the same. Let us greatly simplify, and imagine that a life consists of 13,000 facts. One of the hypothetical biographies would record the series 11, 22, 33 . . . ; another, the series 9, 13, 17, 21 . . . ; another, the series 3, 12, 21, 30, 39. . . . A history of a man's dreams is not inconceivable; another, of the organs of his body; another, of the mistakes he made; another, of all the moments when he thought about the Pyramids; another, of his dealings with the night and with the dawn. The above may seem merely fanciful, but unfortunately it is not. No one today resigns himself to writing the literary biography of an author or the military biography of a soldier; everyone prefers the genealogical biography, the economic biography, the psychiatric biography, the surgical biography, the typographical biography. One life of Poe consists of seven hundred octavo pages; the author, fascinated by changes of residence, barely manages one parenthesis for the Maelstrom or the cosmogony of "Eureka." Another example: this curious revelation in the prologue to a biography of Bolivar: "As in the author's book on Napoleon, the battles are scarcely discussed." Carlyle's joke predicted our contemporary literature: in 1943, the paradox would be a biography of Michelangelo that allowed for some mention of the works of Michelangelo.

The examination of a recent biography of William Beckford (1760–1844) has provoked the above observations. William Beckford of Fonthill was the embodiment of a rather trivial type of millionaire: distinguished gentleman, traveler, bibliophile, builder of palaces, and libertine. Chapman, his biographer, unravels (or tries to unravel) his labyrinthine life, but omits an analysis of *Vathek*, the novel whose final ten pages have brought William Beckford his fame.

I have compared various critical works on *Vathek*. The prologue that Mallarmé wrote for the 1876 edition abounds in felicitous observations (for example: he points out that the novel begins atop a tower from which the heavens may be read in order to end in an enchanted subterranean vault), but it is written in an etymological dialect of French that is difficult or impossible to read. Belloc (*A Conversation with an Angel*, 1928), opines on Beckford without condescending to explanations; he compares the prose to that of Voltaire and judges him to be "one of the vilest men of his time." Perhaps the most lucid evaluation is that of Saintsbury in the eleventh volume of the *Cambridge History of English Literature*.

In essence, the fable of *Vathek* is not complex. Vathek (Haroun Benalmotasim Vatiq Bila, the ninth Abbasid caliph) erects a Babylonian tower in order to decipher the planets. They foretell a succession of wonders to be brought about by a man unlike any other who will come from an unknown land. A merchant arrives at the capital of the empire; his face is so atrocious that the guards who bring him before the caliph advance with eyes closed. The merchant sells a scimitar to the caliph, then disappears. Engraved on the blade are some mysterious changing characters which pique Vathek's curiosity. A man (who then also disappears) deciphers them; one day they mean, "I am the least of the marvels in a place where everything is marvelous and worthy of the greatest Prince of the earth"; another day, "Woe to the rash mortal who aspires to know that which he is not supposed to know." The caliph surrenders to the magic arts; from the shadows, the voice of the merchant urges him to renounce the Muslim faith and worship the powers of darkness. If he will do that, the Palace of Subterranean Fire will be opened to him. Within its vaults he will be able to contemplate the treasures that the stars have promised him, the talismans that subdue the world, the diadems of the pre-Adamite sultans and of Suleiman Ben Daoud. The greedy caliph agrees; the merchant demands forty human sacrifices. Many bloody years pass; Vathek, his soul black from abominations, arrives at a deserted mountain. The earth opens; in terror and hope, Vathek descends to the bottom of the world. A pale and silent crowd of people who do not look at one another wanders through the magnificent galleries of an infinite palace. The merchant did not lie: the Palace of Subterranean Fire abounds in splendors and talismans, but it is also Hell. (In the congeneric story of Doctor Faustus, and in the many medieval legends that prefigured it, Hell is the punishment for the sinner who makes a pact with the gods of Evil; here, it is both the punishment and the temptation.)

Saintsbury and Andrew Lang claim or suggest that the invention of the Palace of Subterranean Fire is Beckford's greatest achievement. I would maintain that it is the first truly atrocious Hell in literature.[1] I will venture this paradox: the most famous literary Avernus, the *dolente regno* of the *Divine Comedy*, is not an atrocious place; it is a place where atrocious things happen. The distinction is valid.

Stevenson ("A Chapter on Dreams") tells of being pursued in the dreams of his childhood by a certain abominable "hue" of the color brown; Chesterton *(The Man Who Was Thursday)* imagines that at the western borders of the world there is perhaps a tree that is more or less than a tree; and that at the eastern borders, there is something, perhaps a tower, whose very shape is wicked. Poe, in his "MS Found in a Bottle," speaks of a southern sea where the ship itself will grow in bulk like the living body of the seaman; Melville devotes many pages of *Moby-Dick* to an elucidation of the horror of the unbearable whiteness of the whale. . . . I have given several examples, but perhaps it is enough to observe that Dante's Hell magnifies the notion of a jail; Beckford's, the tunnels of a nightmare. The *Divine Comedy* is the most justifiable and solid book in all literature, *Vathek* is a mere curiosity, "the perfume and suppliance of a minute"; yet I believe that *Vathek* foretells, in however rudimentary a way, the satanic splendors of Thomas De Quincey and Poe, of Charles Baudelaire and Huysmans. There is an untranslatable English epithet, "uncanny," to denote supernatural horror; that epithet (*unheimlich* in German) is applicable to certain pages of *Vathek*, but not, as far as I recall, to any other book before it.

Chapman notes some of the books that influenced Beckford: the *Bibliothéque orientale* of Barthélemy d'Herbelot; Hamilton's *Quatre Facardins;* Voltaire's *La Princesse de Babylone;* the always reviled and admirable *Mille et une nuits* of Galland. To that list I would add Piranesi's *Carceri d'invenzione:* etchings, praised by Beckford, that depict mighty palaces which are also impenetrable labyrinths. Beckford, in the first chapter of *Vathek*, enumerates five palaces dedicated to the five senses; Marino, in the *Adone*, had already described five similar gardens.

William Beckford needed only three days and two nights in the winter of 1782 to write the tragic history of his caliph. He wrote it in French;

---

[1] In literature, that is, not in mysticism: the elective Hell of Swedenborg—*De coelo et inferno*, 545, 554—is of an earlier date.

Henley translated it into English in 1785. The original is unfaithful to the translation; Saintsbury observes that eighteenth-century French is less suitable than English for communicating the "undefined horrors" (the phrase is Beckford's) of this unusual story.

Henley's English version is volume 856 of the Everyman's Library; Perrin, in Paris, has published the original text, revised and prologued by Mallarmé. It is strange that Chapman's laborious bibliography does not mention that revision and that prologue.

[1943]   *[EW]*

Coleridge's Flower

Around 1938, Paul Valéry wrote: "The history of literature should not be the history of authors and the course of their careers or of the career of their works, but rather the history of the Spirit as the producer or consumer of literature; such a history could be written without mentioning a single writer." It was not the first time the Spirit had made this observation; in 1844, one of its amanuenses in Concord had noted: "I am very much struck in literature by the appearance that one person wrote all the books . . . there is such equality and identity both of judgment and point of view in the narrative that it is plainly the work of one all-seeing, all-hearing gentleman" (Emerson, *Essays: Second Series*, "Nominalist and Realist," 1844). Twenty years earlier, Shelley expressed the opinion that all the poems of the past, present, and future were episodes or fragments of a single infinite poem, written by all the poets on earth.

These considerations (implied, of course, in pantheism) could give rise to an endless debate; I invoke them now to carry out a modest plan: a history of the evolution of an idea through the diverse texts of three authors. The first, by Coleridge—I am not sure if he wrote it at the end of the eighteenth or beginning of the nineteenth century—says: "If a man could pass through Paradise in a dream, and have a flower presented to him as a pledge that his soul had really been there, and if he found that flower in his hand when he awoke—Ay!—and what then?"

I wonder what my reader thinks of such a fancy; to me it is perfect. To use it as the basis for other inventions seems quite impossible, for it has the wholeness and unity of a *terminus ad quem*, a final goal. Of course, it is just that: in literature as in other spheres, every act crowns an infinite series of causes and causes an infinite series of effects. Behind Coleridge's idea is the general and age-old idea of generations of lovers who craved the gift of a flower.

The second text I shall quote is a novel Wells drafted in 1887 and rewrote seven years later, in the summer of 1894. The first version was called *The Chronic Argonauts* (*chronic* in this rejected title is the etymological equivalent of *temporal*); the final version, *The Time Machine*. In this novel, Wells continued and renewed an ancient literary tradition: that of foreseeing future events. Isaiah sees the destruction of Babylon and the restoration of Israel; Aeneas, the military destiny of his descendants, the Romans; the prophetess of the *Edda Saemundi*, the return of the gods who, after the cyclical battle in which our world will be destroyed, will discover, lying on the grass of a new meadow, the same chess pieces they played with before. . . . Wells' protagonist, unlike those prophetic spectators, travels physically to the future. He returns tired, dusty, shaken; he returns from a remote humanity that has split into species who hate each other (the idle Eloi, who live in dilapidated palaces and ruined gardens; and the subterranean and nyctalopic Morlocks, who feed on the Eloi). He returns with his hair grown grey and brings from the future a wilted flower. This is the second version of Coleridge's image. More incredible than a celestial flower or a dream flower is a future flower, the contradictory flower whose atoms, not yet assembled, now occupy other spaces.

The third version I shall mention, the most improbable of all, is by a writer much more complex than Wells, though less gifted with those pleasant virtues we usually call classical. I refer to the author of "The Abasement of the Northmores," the sad, labyrinthine Henry James. When he died, he left an unfinished novel, *The Sense of the Past*, a fantastic invention that was a variation or elaboration on *The Time Machine*.[1] Wells' protagonist travels to the future in an outlandish vehicle that advances or regresses in time as other vehicles do in space; James' protagonist returns to the past, to the eighteenth century, by identifying himself with that period. (Both techniques are impossible, but James' is less arbitrary.) In *The Sense of the Past* the nexus between the real and the imaginary (between present and past) is not a flower, as in the previous stories, but an eighteenth-century portrait that mysteriously represents the protagonist. Fascinated by this canvas, he succeeds in going back to the day when it was painted. Among the persons he meets, he finds, of course, the artist, who paints him with fear and aver-

---

[1] I have not read *The Sense of the Past*, but I am acquainted with the competent analysis of it by Stephen Spender in his book *The Destructive Element* (pp. 105–110). James was a friend of Wells; to learn more about their relationship, consult the latter's vast *Experiment in Autobiography*.

sion, having sensed something unusual and anomalous in those future features. James thus creates an incomparable *regressus in infinitum* when his
hero Ralph Pendrel returns to the eighteenth century because he is fascinated by an old portrait, but Pendrel needs to have returned to the eighteenth century for that portrait to exist. The cause follows the effect, or the
reason for the journey is a consequence of the journey.

Wells was probably not acquainted with Coleridge's text; Henry James
knew and admired Wells' text. If the doctrine that all authors are one is
valid, such facts are, of course, insignificant.[2] Strictly speaking, it is not necessary to go that far; the pantheist who declares the plurality of authors to
be illusory finds unexpected support in the classicist, to whom such a plurality barely matters. For the classical mind, literature is the essential thing,
not individuals. George Moore and James Joyce incorporated in their works
the pages and sentences of others; Oscar Wilde used to give plots away for
others to develop; both procedures, though apparently contradictory, may
reveal an identical sense of art, an ecumenical, impersonal perception. Another witness of the Word's profound unity, another who defied the limitations of the individual, was the renowned Ben Jonson, who, upon writing
his literary testament and the favorable or adverse opinions he held of his
contemporaries, simply combined fragments from Seneca, Quintilian, Jus-
tus Lipsius, Vives, Erasmus, Machiavelli, Bacon, and the two Scaligers.

One last observation. Those who carefully copy a writer do so impersonally, because they equate that writer with literature, because they suspect
that to depart from him in the slightest is to deviate from reason and orthodoxy. For many years I thought that the almost infinite world of literature
was in one man. That man was Carlyle, he was Johannes Becher, he was
Whitman, he was Rafael Cansinos Asséns, he was De Quincey.

[1945]   [SJL]

---

[2]Around the middle of the seventeenth century the epigrammist of pantheism,
Angelus Silesius, said that all the blessed are one (*Cherubinscher Wandersmann* V, 7)
and that every Christian must be Christ (*ibid.,* V, 9).

PROLOGUES

Adolfo Bioy Casares, *The Invention of Morel*

Around 1882, Stevenson observed that the adventure story was regarded as an object of scorn by the British reading public, who believed that the ability to write a novel without a plot, or with an infinitesimal, atrophied plot, was a mark of skill. In *The Dehumanization of Art* (1925), José Ortega y Gasset, seeking the reason for that scorn, said, "I doubt very much whether an adventure that will interest our superior sensibility can be invented today" (p. 96), and added that such an invention was "practically impossible" (p. 97). On other pages, on almost all the other pages, he upheld the cause of the "psychological" novel and asserted that the pleasure to be derived from adventure stories was nonexistent or puerile. That was undoubtedly the prevailing opinion of 1882, 1925, and even 1940. Some writers (among whom I am happy to include Adolfo Bioy Casares) believe they have a right to disagree. The following, briefly, are the reasons why.

The first of these (I shall neither emphasize nor attenuate the fact that it is a paradox) has to do with the intrinsic form of the adventure story. The typical psychological novel is formless. The Russians and their disciples have demonstrated, tediously, that no one is impossible: happy suicides, benevolent murderers, lovers who adore each other to the point of separation, informers who act out of fervor or humility. . . . In the end such complete freedom is tantamount to chaos. But the psychological novel would also be a "realistic" novel, and have us forget that it is a verbal artifice, for it uses each vain precision (or each languid obscurity) as a new proof of verisimilitude. There are pages, there are chapters in Marcel Proust that are unacceptable as inventions, and we unwittingly resign ourselves to them as we resign ourselves to the insipidity and the emptiness of each day. The adventure story, on the other hand, does not propose to be a transcription of reality: it is an artificial object, no part of which lacks justification. It must have a rigid plot if it is not to succumb to the mere sequential variety of *The Golden Ass*, the seven voyages of Sinbad, or the *Quixote*.

I have given one reason of an intellectual sort; there are others of an empirical nature. We hear sad murmurs that our century lacks the ability to devise interesting plots; no one attempts to prove that if this century has any ascendancy over the preceding ones it lies in the quality of its plots. Stevenson is more passionate, more diverse, more lucid, perhaps more deserving of our unqualified friendship than is Chesterton, but his plots are inferior. De Quincey plunged deep into labyrinths on his nights of meticulously detailed horror, but he did not coin his impression of "unutterable and self-repeating infinities" in fables comparable to Kafka's. Ortega y Gasset was right when he said that Balzac's "psychology" does not satisfy us; the same thing could be said of his plots. Shakespeare and Cervantes were both delighted by the antinomian idea of a girl who, without losing her beauty, could be taken for a man; but we find that idea unconvincing now. I believe I am free from every superstition of modernity, of any illusion that yesterday differs intimately from today or will differ from tomorrow; but I maintain that during no other era have there been novels with such admirable plots as *The Turn of the Screw*, *The Trial*, *Le Voyageur sur la terre*, and the one you are about to read, which was written in Buenos Aires by Adolfo Bioy Casares.

Detective stories—another popular genre in this century that cannot invent plots—tell of mysterious events that are later explained and justified by reasonable facts. In this book, Adolfo Bioy Casares easily solves a problem that is perhaps more difficult. The odyssey of marvels he unfolds seems to have no possible explanation other than hallucination or symbolism, and he uses a single fantastic, but not supernatural, postulate to decipher it. My fear of making premature or partial revelations restrains me from examining the plot and the wealth of delicate wisdom in its execution. Let me say only that Bioy renews in literature a concept that was refuted by St. Augustine and Origen, studied by Louis Auguste Blanqui, and expressed in memorable cadences by Dante Gabriel Rossetti:

> I have been here before,
> But when or how I cannot tell:
> I know the grass beyond the door,
> The sweet keen smell,
> The sighing sound, the lights around the shore . . .

. In Spanish, works of reasoned imagination are infrequent and even very rare. The classicists employed allegory, the exaggerations of satire, and sometimes simple verbal incoherence. The only recent works of this type I remember are a story in *Las fuerzas extrañas* and one by Santiago Dabove: now unjustly forgotten. *The Invention of Morel* (the title alludes filially to another island inventor, Moreau) brings a new genre to our land and our language.

I have discussed with the author the details of his plot; I have reread it; it seems to me neither imprecise nor hyperbolic to classify it as perfect.

[1940]   *[SJL]*

Herman Melville, *Bartleby the Scrivener*

In the winter of 1851, Melville published *Moby-Dick*, the infinite novel that brought about his fame. Page by page, the story grows until it takes on the dimensions of the cosmos: at the beginning the reader might consider the subject to be the miserable life of whale harpooners; then, that the subject is the madness of Captain Ahab, bent on pursuing and destroying the white whale; finally, that the whale and Ahab and the pursuit which exhausts the oceans of the planet are symbols and mirrors of the universe. To insinuate that the book is symbolic, Melville declares emphatically that it is not and that no one should "scout at Moby-Dick as a monstrous fable or, still worse and more detestable, a hideous and intolerable allegory" (chap. 45). The usual connotation of the word *allegory* seems to have confused the critics; they all prefer to limit themselves to a moral interpretation of the work. Thus, E. M. Forster (*Aspects of the Novel*, chap. 7) summarizes the spiritual theme as, more or less, the following: "a battle against evil conducted too long or in the wrong way."

I agree, but the symbol of the whale is less apt to suggest that the cosmos is evil than to suggest its vast inhumanity, its beastly or enigmatic stupidity. In some of his stories, Chesterton compares the atheists' universe to a centerless labyrinth. Such is the universe of *Moby-Dick*: a cosmos (a chaos) not only perceptibly malignant as the Gnostics had intuited, but also irrational, like the cosmos in the hexameters of Lucretius.

Moby-Dick is written in a romantic dialect of English, a vehement dialect that alternates or conjugates the techniques of Shakespeare, Thomas De Quincey, Browne, and Carlyle; "Bartleby," in a calm and evenly jocular language deliberately applied to an atrocious subject, seems to foreshadow Kafka. There is, however, a secret and central affinity between both fictions. Ahab's monomania troubles and finally destroys all the men on board; Bartleby's candid nihilism contaminates his companions and even the stolid gentleman who tells his tale and endorses his imaginary tasks. It is as if Melville had written, "It's enough for one man to be irrational for others and the universe itself to be so as well." Universal history prolifically confirms that terror.

"Bartleby" belongs to the volume entitled *The Piazza Tales* (New York and London, 1896). About another story in the book, John Freeman observed that it would not be fully understood until Joseph Conrad published certain analogous pieces almost a half-century later; I would observe that Kafka's work casts a curious ulterior light on "Bartleby." Melville's story defines a genre which, around 1919, Franz Kafka would reinvent and further explore: the fantasies of behavior and feelings or, as they are now wrongly called, psychological tales. As it is, the first pages of "Bartleby" are not anticipations of Kafka but rather allude to or repeat Dickens. . . . In 1849, Melville published *Mardi*, an impenetrable and almost unreadable novel, but one with an essential plot that prefigures the obsessions and the mechanism of *The Castle, The Trial,* and *Amerika:* the subject is an infinite chase on an infinite sea.

I have stated Melville's affinities with other writers. But this is not to demean his achievements: I am following one of the laws of description or definition, that of relating the unknown to the known. Melville's greatness is unquestionable, but his glory is recent. Melville died in 1891; twenty years after his death the eleventh edition of the *Encyclopedia Britannica* considers him a mere chronicler of sea life; Lang and George Saintsbury, in 1922 and 1914, entirely ignore him in their histories of English literature. Later, he was defended by Lawrence of Arabia and D. H. Lawrence, Waldo Frank, and Lewis Mumford. In 1921, Raymond Weaver published the first American monograph, *Herman Melville, Mariner and Mystic;* John Freeman, in 1926, the critical biography *Herman Melville.*

Vast populations, towering cities, erroneous and clamorous publicity, have conspired to make unknown great men one of America's traditions. Edgar Allan Poe was one of these; so was Melville.

[1944]   [SJL]

Henry James, *The Abasement of the Northmores*

Son of the Swedenborgian convert of the same name and brother of the famous psychiatrist who founded pragmatism, Henry James was born in New
York on April 15, 1843. The father wanted his sons to be cosmopolitan—
citizens of the world in the Stoic sense of the word—and he provided for
their education in England, France, Geneva, and Rome. In 1860, Henry returned to America, where he undertook and abandoned a vague study of
law. In 1864, he dedicated himself to literature, with growing self-denial, lucidity, and happiness. Beginning in 1869, he lived in London and in Sussex.
His later trips to America were occasional and never went beyond New England. In July 1915, he adopted British citizenship because he understood
that the moral duty of his country was to declare war on Germany. He died
February 28, 1916. "Now, at last, that distinguished thing, death," he said in
his dying hour.

The definitive edition of his works covers thirty-five volumes edited
meticulously by himself. The principal part of that scrupulous accumulation consists of stories and novels. It also includes a biography of
Hawthorne, whom he always admired, and critical studies of Turgenev and
Flaubert, close friends of his. He had little regard for Zola and, for complex
reasons, Ibsen. He protected Wells, who corresponded ungratefully. He was
the best man at Kipling's wedding. The complete works comprise studies of
a most diverse nature: the art of narrative, the discovery of as yet unex-
plored themes, literary life as a subject, indirect narrative techniques, evil
and the dead, the risks and virtues of improvisation, the supernatural, the
course of time, the need to be interesting, the limits that the illustrator must
impose upon himself so as not to compete with the text, the unacceptability
of dialect, point of view, the first-person narration, reading aloud, the representation of unspecified evil, the American exiled in Europe, man exiled
in the universe. . . . These analyses, duly organized in a volume, would form
an enlightening rhetoric.

He presented several comedies on the London stage, which were
greeted with hisses and Bernard Shaw's respectful disapproval. He was
never popular; the English critics offered him a careless and frigid glory that
usually excluded the effort of reading him.

"The biographies of James," Ludwig Lewisohn wrote, "are more significant for what they omit than for what they contain."

I have visited some literatures of the East and West; I have compiled an encyclopedic anthology of fantastic literature; I have translated Kafka, Melville, and Bloy; I know of no stranger work than that of Henry James. The writers I have enumerated are, from the first line, amazing; the universe postulated by their pages is almost professionally unreal; James, before revealing what he is, a resigned and ironic inhabitant of Hell, runs the risk of appearing to be no more than a mundane novelist, less colorful than others. As we begin to read him, we are annoyed by some ambiguities, some superficial features; after a few pages we realize that those deliberate faults enrich the book. Of course, we are not dealing here with that pure vagueness of the Symbolists, whose imprecisions, by eluding meaning, can mean anything. We are dealing with the voluntary omission of a part of the novel, which allows us to interpret it in one way or another; both premeditated by the author, both defined. Thus we shall never know, in "The Lesson of the Master," if the advice given to the disciple is or is not treacherous; if, in "The Turn of the Screw," the children are victims or agents of the ghosts which in turn could be demons; in "The Sacred Fount," which of the ladies who pretend to investigate the mystery of Gilbert Long is the protagonist of that mystery; in "The Abasement of the Northmores," the final destiny of Mrs. Hope's project. I want to point out another problem of this delicate story of revenge: the intrinsic merits or demerits of Warren Hope, whom we have met only through his wife's eyes.

James has been accused of resorting to melodrama; this is because the facts, to him, merely exaggerate or emphasize the plot. Thus, in *The American*, Madame Belleregarde's crime is incredible in itself, but acceptable as a sign of the corruption of an ancient family. Thus, in that story titled "The Death of the Lion," the demise of the hero and the senseless loss of the manuscript are merely metaphors which declare the indifference of those who pretend to admire him. Paradoxically, James is not a psychological novelist. The situations in his books do not emerge from his characters; the characters have been fabricated to justify the situations. With Meredith, the opposite occurs.

There are many critical studies of James. One may consult Rebecca West's monograph (*Henry James*, 1916); *The Craft of Fiction* (1921) by Percy Lubbock; the special issue of *Hound and Horn* corresponding to the months April–May 1934; *The Destructive Element* (1935) by Stephen Spender; and the passionate article by Graham Greene in the collective work, *The English Novelists* (1936). That article ends with these words: "Henry James, as solitary in the history of the novel as Shakespeare in the history of poetry."

[1945]   [SJL]

BOOK REVIEWS

Edward Kasner & James Newman, *Mathematics and the Imagination*

Looking over my library, I am intrigued to find that the works I have most reread and scribbled with notes are Mauthner's *Dictionary of Philosophy*, Lewes' *Biographical History of Philosophy*, Liddell Hart's *History of the War of 1914–1918*, Boswell's *Life of Samuel Johnson*, and Gustav Spiller's psychological study *The Mind of Man*, 1902. To this heterogeneous catalog (not excluding works that are mere habits, such as G. H. Lewes) I predict that the years will append this charming book.

Its four hundred pages lucidly record the immediate and accessible charms of mathematics, those which even a mere man of letters can understand, or imagine he understands: the endless map of Brouwer, the fourth dimension glimpsed by More and which Charles Howard Hinton claims to have intuited, the mildly obscene Moebius strip, the rudiments of the theory of transfinite numbers, the eight paradoxes of Zeno, the parallel lines of Desargues that intersect in infinity, the binary notation Leibniz discovered in the diagrams of the *I Ching*, the beautiful Euclidean demonstration of the stellar infinity of the prime numbers, the problem of the tower of Hanoi, the equivocal or two-pronged syllogism.

Of the latter, with which the Greeks played (Democritus swears that the Abderites are liars, but Democritus is an Abderite; then it is not true that the Abderites are liars; then Democritus is not lying; then it is true that the Abderites are liars; then Democritus lies; then ...) there are almost innumerable versions which do not vary in method, though the characters and the story change. Aulus Gellius (*Attic Nights* V, chap. 10) resorts to an orator and his student; Luis Barahona de Soto (*Angelica*, Canto XI), to two slaves; Miguel de Cervantes (*Quixote* II, chap. 51), to a river, a bridge, and a gallows; Jeremy Taylor, in some sermon, to a man who has dreamed a voice revealing to him that all dreams are meaningless; Bertrand Russell (*Introduction to Mathematical Philosophy*, 136), to the sum total of all sum totals which do not include themselves.

To these illustrious perplexities I dare add this one:

In Sumatra, someone wishes to receive a doctorate in prophecy. The master seer who administers his exam asks if he will fail or pass. The candidate replies that he will fail. . . . One can already foresee the infinite continuation.

[1940]   [SJL]

Edward Shanks, *Rudyard Kipling: A Study in Literature and Political Ideas*

Impossible to mention the name of Kipling without bringing up this pseudo-problem: should art be a political instrument or not? I use the prefix pseudo- because those who bludgeon us (or amuse themselves) with such a foolhardy inquiry seem to forget that in art nothing is more secondary than the author's intentions. Let us imagine that, around 1853, Walt Whitman had been motivated not by Emerson's ebullient doctrine but by the somber philosophy of Schopenhauer. Would his songs be much different? I think not. The biblical citations would maintain their fundamental bitterness, the enumerations would display our planet's appalling diversity, the Americanisms and barbarisms would be no less apt for complaint as they were for joy. Technically the work would be the same. I have imagined a counterproposal: in any literature there are famous books whose purpose is imperceptible or dubious. *Martín Fierro*, for Miguel de Unamuno, is the song of the Spanish fighter who, after having planted the cross in Granada, went to America to serve as advance scout for civilization and to clear the road to the wilderness; for Ricardo Rojas it is "the spirit of our native land," and also "an elemental voice of nature"; I always believed it was the story of a decent countryman who degenerates into a barroom knife-fighter. . . . Butler, who knew the *Iliad* by heart and translated it into English, considered the author a Trojan humorist; there are scholars who do not share that opinion.

Kipling's case is curious. For glory, but also as an insult, Kipling has been equated with the British Empire. The partisans of that federation have vociferated his name as well as the ethics of "If," and those pages cast in bronze which proclaim the untiring variety of the Five Nations and the glad sacrifice of the individual to imperial destiny. The enemies of the Empire (partisans of other empires) refute or ignore it. The pacifists counter his manifold work with Erich Maria Remarque's one or two novels, and forget that the most alarming news in *All Quiet on the Western Front*—the discomforts of war, signs of physical fear among the heroes, the use and abuse of military jargon—is in the *Barrack-Room Ballads* of reprobate Rudyard, whose first series dates from 1892. Naturally, that "crude realism" was condemned by Victorian critics, and now his realist successors will not forgive its sentimental features. The Italian Futurists forget that he was the first European poet to celebrate the superb and blind activity of machines. . . .[1] Whether detractors or worshipers, they all reduce him to a mere apologist for the Empire, and tend to believe that a couple of simpleminded political opinions can exhaust the analysis of the diverse aesthetics of thirty-five volumes. The error of so dim-witted a belief is exposed by merely alluding to it.

What is indisputable is that Kipling's prose and poetic works are infinitely more complex than the theses they elucidate. Compared with "Dayspring Mishandled," "The Gardener," and "The Church That Was at Antioch," the best of Maupassant's stories—"*Le lit 29,*" we could say, or "*Boule de Suif*"—is like a child's drawing. The related circumstance that Kipling was the author of children's stories and that his writing always obeyed a certain verbal restraint has obscured this truth. Like all men, Rudyard Kipling was many men (English gentleman, Eurasian journalist, bibliophile, spokesman for soldiers and mountains), but none with more conviction than the artificer. The experimental artificer, secret, anxious, like James Joyce or Mallarmé. In his teeming life there was no passion like the passion for technique.

Edward Shanks (the author of forgettable poems and a mediocre study of Poe) declares in this book that Kipling ended up hating war and predicting that mankind would eliminate or reduce the State.

[*1941*]   [*SJL*]

---

[1] In this case, as in others, the precursor is infinitely more valuable than the successors.

Arthur Waley, *Monkey*

Arthur Waley, whose delicate versions of Murasaki are classic works of English literature, has now translated Wu Ch'eng-en's *Tale of Journeys to the Western Lands*. This is an allegory from the sixteenth century; before commenting on it, I would like to examine the problem or pseudo-problem that the genre of allegory poses.

We all tend to believe that interpretation exhausts the meaning of a symbol. There is nothing more false. I will take a simple example: the prophecy. Everyone knows that Oedipus was asked by the Theban sphinx: What is the animal that has four legs in the morning, two at noon, and three in the evening? Everyone also knows that Oedipus responded that it was a man. But who among us does not immediately perceive that the bare concept of *man* is as inferior to the magical animal that is glimpsed in the question as an ordinary man is to that changeable monster, seventy years to one day, and an old man's staff to a third foot? Symbols, beyond their representative worth, have an intrinsic worth; in riddles (which may consist of only twenty words) it is natural that every characteristic is justifiable; in allegories (which often surpass twenty thousand words) such rigor is impossible. It is also undesirable, for the investigation of continual minute correspondences would numb any reader. De Quincey (*Writings* XI, 199) states that we may attribute any speech or act to an allegorical character as long as it does not contradict the idea he personifies. "Allegorical characters," he says, "occupy an intermediate place between the absolute truths of human life and the pure abstractions of logical understanding." The lean and hungry wolf of the first canto of the *Divine Comedy* is not an emblem or a figure of avarice: it is a wolf and it is also avarice, as in dreams. That plural nature is the property of all symbols. For example, the vivid heroes of *Pilgrim's Progress*—Christian, Apollyon, Master Great-Heart, Master Valiant-for-Truth—maintain a double intuition; they are not figures who may be exchanged for abstract nouns. (An insoluble problem would be the creation of a short and secret allegory in which everything one of the characters says or does would be an insult; another character, a favor; another, a lie; etc.)

I am familiar with an earlier version by Timothy Richard of the novel translated by Waley, curiously entitled *A Mission to Heaven* (Shanghai, 1940). I have also looked at the excerpts Giles includes in his *History of Chinese Literature* (1901) and Sung-Nien Hsu in the *Anthologie de la littérature chinoise* (1933).

Perhaps the most obvious characteristic of Wu Ch'eng-en's dizzying allegory is its panoramic vastness. Everything seems to take place in a detailed infinite world, with intelligible zones of light and some of darkness. There are rivers, caves, mountains, seas, and armies; there are fish and drums and clouds; there is a mountain of swords and a punitive lake of blood. Time is no less marvelous than space. Before crossing the universe, the protagonist—an insolent stone monkey, produced by a stone egg—idles away centuries in a cave. In his journeys he sees a root that matures every 3,000 years; those who find it live 370 years; those who eat it, 47,000 years. In the Western Paradise, the Buddha tells him about a god whose name is the Jade Emperor; every 1,750 *kalpas* this Emperor perfects himself, and each *kalpa* consists of 129,000 years. *Kalpa* is a Sanskrit term; the love of cycles of enormous time and of unlimited spaces is typical of the nations of India, as it is of contemporary astronomy and the Atomists of Abdera. (Oswald Spengler, as I recall, stated that the intuition of an infinite time and space was particular to the culture he called Faustian, but the most unequivocal monument to that intuition of the world is not Goethe's wandering and miscellaneous drama but rather the ancient cosmological poem *De rerum natura.*)

A unique characteristic of this book: the notion that human time is not commensurate with that of God. The monkey enters the Jade Emperor's palace and returns at dawn; on earth a year has passed. The Muslim traditions offer something similar. They say that the Prophet was carried off on the resplendent mare Alburak through the seven heavens, and that in each one of them he talked with the patriarchs and angels who inhabited it, and that he crossed the Oneness and felt a chill that froze his heart when the hand of the Lord clapped him on his shoulder. On leaving the planet, the supernatural hoof of Alburak had smashed a water jar; the Prophet returned before a single drop of water had spilled. . . . In the Muslim story, the time of God is richer than that of man; in the Chinese story it is poorer and protracted.

An exuberant monkey, a lazy pig, a dragon of the western seas turned into a horse, and a confused and passive evildoer whose name is Sand embark on the difficult adventure of immortality, and in order to obtain it practice fraud, violence, and the magic arts; such is the general plot of this allegorical composition. It should also be added that this task purifies all of the characters who, in the final chapter, ascend to the Buddhas and return to the world with the precise cargo of 5,048 sacred books. J. M. Robertson, in his *Short History of Christianity*, suggests that the Gnostics based their divine hierarchies on the earthly bureaucracy; the Chinese also employed this method. Wu Ch'eng-en satirizes the angelical bureaucracy and consequently the one of this world. The genre of allegory tends toward sadness and tedium; in this exceptional book, we find an unrestrained happiness. Reading it does not remind us of *El Criticón* or the mystery plays, but rather the last book of *Pantagruel* or *The Thousand and One Nights*.

Wonders abound in this journey. The hero, imprisoned by demons in a metal sphere, magically grows larger, but the sphere grows too. The prisoner shrinks to the point of invisibility, and so does his prison. In another chapter there is a battle between a magician and a demon. The magician, wounded, turns into four thousand magicians. The demon, horribly, tells him: "To multiply yourself is a trifle; what is difficult is putting yourself back together."

There are also humorous moments. A monk, invited by some fairies to an atrocious banquet of human flesh, pleads that he is a vegetarian and leaves.

One of the last chapters includes an episode that combines the symbolic and the poignant. A real human, Hsian Tsang, guides the fantastic pilgrims. After many adventures, they arrive at a swollen and dark river tossed with high waves. A boatman offers to carry them across. They accept, but the man notices with horror that the boat has no bottom. The boatman declares that since the beginning of time he has peacefully carried thousands of generations of humans. In the middle of the river they see a corpse being pulled along by the current. Again the man feels the chill of fear. The others tell him to look at it more carefully: it is his own corpse. They all congratulate and embrace him.

Arthur Waley's version, although literarily far superior to Richard's, is perhaps less felicitous in its selection of adventures. It is called *Monkey* and was published in London this year. It is the work of one of the very few Sinologists who is also a man of letters.

[1942]   [EW]

Leslie Weatherhead, *After Death*

I have recently compiled an anthology of fantastic literature. While I admit that such a work is among the few a second Noah should rescue from a second deluge, I must confess my guilty omission of the unsuspected major masters of the genre: Parmenides, Plato, John Scotus Erigena, Albertus Magnus, Spinoza, Leibniz, Kant, Francis Bradley. What, in fact, are the wonders of Wells or Edgar Allan Poe—a flower that visits us from the future, a dead man under hypnosis—in comparison to the invention of God, the labored theory of a being who in some way is three and who endures alone *outside of time*? What is the bezoar stone to pre-established harmony, what is the unicorn to the Trinity, who is Lucius Apuleius to the multipliers of Buddhas of the Greater Vehicle, what are all the nights of Scheherazade next to an argument by Berkeley? I have worshiped the gradual invention of God; Heaven and Hell (an immortal punishment, an immortal reward) are also admirable and curious designs of man's imagination.

The theologians define Heaven as a place of everlasting glory and good fortune and advise us that such a place is not devoted to infernal torments. The fourth chapter of *After Death* denies such a division between Heaven and Hell, which, it argues, are not topographical locations but rather extreme states of the soul. This concurs fully with André Gide (*Journal*, 677), who speaks of an immanent Hell—already confirmed by Milton's verse: "Which way I fly is Hell; myself am Hell"—and partially with Swedenborg, whose unredeemable lost souls prefer caverns and swamps to the unbearable splendor of Heaven. Weatherhead proposes the thesis of a single heterogeneous world beyond, alternating between hell and paradise according to the souls' capacity.

For almost all men, the concepts of Heaven and happiness are inseparable. Nonetheless, in the final decade of the nineteenth century, Butler conceived of a Heaven in which everything was slightly frustrating (since no one can tolerate total contentment) and a comparable Hell lacking all unpleasant stimuli except those which prevent sleep. Around 1902, Bernard Shaw installed in Hell the illusions of eros, self-denial, glory, and pure undying love; in Heaven, the comprehension of reality (*Man and Superman*, act 3). Weatherhead is a mediocre and almost nonexistent writer, stimulated by pious readings, but he intuits that the direct pursuit of a pure and perpetual happiness is no less laughable on the other side of death than on this side. He writes: "The highest form of joy that we have conceived as Heaven is the experience of serving, that is, a fulfilling and voluntary participation in the work of Christ. This can occur among other spirits, perhaps in other worlds; perhaps we can help save our own." In another chapter he asserts: "Heaven's pain is intense, but the more we have evolved in this world, the more we can share in the other the life of God. The life of God is painful. In his heart are all the sins and suffering of the world. As long as there remains a single sinner in the universe, there will be no happiness in Heaven." (Origen, predicating a final reconciliation of the Creator with all creatures, including the devil, had already dreamed that dream.)

I do not know what the reader will think of such semi-theosophical conjectures. Catholics (read: Argentine Catholics) believe in an ultraterrestrial world, but I have noticed that they are not interested in it. With me the opposite occurs: I am interested but I do not believe.

[1943]   [SJL]

FILM REVIEWS AND CRITICISM

Two Films

I have seen two films on two consecutive nights. The first (in both senses), according to the director himself, was "inspired by Joseph Conrad's novel *The Secret Agent.*" Even without his statement, however, I must admit that I would have stumbled upon the connection he reveals, but never that respiratory and divine verb *inspire*. Skillful photography, clumsy filmmaking—these are my indifferent opinions "inspired" by Hitchcock's latest film. As for Joseph Conrad ... There is no doubt, aside from certain distortions, that the story line of *Sabotage* (1936) coincides with the plot of *The Secret Agent* (1907); there also is no doubt that the actions narrated by Conrad have a psychological value—only a psychological value. Conrad unfolds for us the destiny and character of Mr. Verloc, a lazy, fat, and sentimental man who comes to "crime" as a result of confusion and fear. Hitchcock prefers to translate him into an inscrutable Slavo-Germanic Satan. An almost prophetic passage in *The Secret Agent* invalidates and refutes this translation:

> But there was also about Mr. Verloc [. . .] the air common to men who live on the vices, the follies, or the baser fears of mankind; the air of moral nihilism common to keepers of gambling halls and disorderly houses; to private detectives and inquiry agents; to drink sellers and, I should say, to the sellers of invigorating electric belts and to the inventors of patent medicines. But of that last I am not sure, not having carried my investigations so far into the depths. For all I know, the expression of these last may be perfectly diabolic. I shouldn't be surprised. What I want to affirm is that Mr. Verloc's expression was by no means diabolic.

Hitchcock has chosen to disregard this indication. I do not regret his strange infidelity; I do regret the petty task he has assigned himself. Conrad enables us to understand completely a man who causes the death of a child; Hitchcock devotes his art (and the slanting, sorrowful eyes of Sylvia Sidney) to making that death reduce us to tears. Conrad's undertaking was intellectual; the other's merely sentimental. That is not all: the film—oh complementary, insipid horror—adds a love interest whose characters, as chaste as they are enamored, are the martyred Mrs. Verloc and a dapper, good-looking detective, disguised as a greengrocer.

The other film is informatively titled *Los muchachos de antes no usaban gomina* [*The Boys of Yesteryear Didn't Slick Their Hair*]. (Some informative titles are beautiful: *The General Died at Dawn.*) This film—*The Boys of Yesteryear*, etc.—is unquestionably one of the best Argentine films I have seen, that is, one of the worst films in the world. The dialogue is totally unbelievable. The characters—gangland bosses and hoodlums in 1906—speak and live solely as a function of their difference from people in 1937. They have no existence outside of local and historical color. There is one fistfight and another fight with knives. The actors do not know how to thrust and parry nor how to box, which dims these spectacles.

The film's theme, "moral nihilism" or the progressive decline of Buenos Aires, is certainly appealing, but is wasted by the film's director. The hero, who ought to be emblematic of the old virtues—and the old skepticism—is a citizen of Buenos Aires who has already been Italianized, a *porteño* cloyingly susceptible to the shameful seduction of apocryphal patriotism and sentimental tangos.

[1937]   [SJL]

An Overwhelming Film

Citizen Kane (called *The Citizen* in Argentina) has at least two plots. The first, pointlessly banal, attempts to milk applause from dimwits: a vain millionaire collects statues, gardens, palaces, swimming pools, diamonds, cars, libraries, men and women. Like an earlier collector (whose observations are usually ascribed to the Holy Ghost), he discovers that this cornucopia of miscellany is a vanity of vanities: all is vanity. At the point of death, he yearns for one single thing in the universe, the humble sled he played with as a child!

The second plot is far superior. It links the Koheleth to the memory of another nihilist, Franz Kafka. A kind of metaphysical detective story, its subject (both psychological and allegorical) is the investigation of a man's inner self, through the works he has wrought, the words he has spoken, the many lives he has ruined. The same technique was used by Joseph Conrad in *Chance* (1914) and in that beautiful film *The Power and the Glory*: a rhapsody of miscellaneous scenes without chronological order. Overwhelmingly, endlessly, Orson Welles shows fragments of the life of the man, Charles Foster Kane, and invites us to combine them and to reconstruct him. Forms of multiplicity and incongruity abound in the film: the first scenes record the treasures amassed by Kane; in one of the last, a poor woman, luxuriant and suffering, plays with an enormous jigsaw puzzle on the floor of a palace that is also a museum. At the end we realize that the fragments are not governed by any secret unity: the detested Charles Foster Kane is a simulacrum, a chaos of appearances. (A possible corollary, foreseen by David Hume, Ernst Mach, and our own Macedonio Fernández: no man knows who he is, no man is anyone.) In a story by Chesterton—"The Head of Caesar," I think—the hero observes that nothing is so frightening as a labyrinth with no center. This film is precisely that labyrinth.

We all know that a party, a palace, a great undertaking, a lunch for writers and journalists, an atmosphere of cordial and spontaneous camaraderie, are essentially horrendous. *Citizen Kane* is the first film to show such things with an awareness of this truth.

The production is, in general, worthy of its vast subject. The cinematography has a striking depth, and there are shots whose farthest planes (like Pre-Raphaelite paintings) are as precise and detailed as the close-ups.

I venture to guess, nonetheless, that *Citizen Kane* will endure as certain Griffith or Pudovkin films have "endured"—films whose historical value is undeniable but which no one cares to see again. It is too gigantic, pedantic, tedious. It is not intelligent, though it is the work of genius—in the most nocturnal and Germanic sense of that bad word.

[1941]   *[SJL]*

Dr. Jekyll and Mr. Hyde, Transformed

Hollywood has defamed, for the third time, Robert Louis Stevenson. In Argentina the title of this defamation is *El hombre y la bestia* [The Man and the Beast] and it has been perpetrated by Victor Fleming, who repeats with ill-fated fidelity the aesthetic and moral errors of Mamoulian's version—or perversion. I shall begin with the moral errors.

In the 1886 novel, Dr. Jekyll is morally duplicitous in the way all men are double, while his hypostasis—Edward Hyde—is relentlessly, unredeemably fiendish. In the 1941 film, Dr. Jekyll is a young pathologist who practices chastity while his hypostasis—Hyde—is a sadistic and acrobatic profligate. For the sages of Hollywood, Good is the courtship of the chaste and wealthy Miss Lana Turner, and Evil (which similarly concerned David Hume and the heresiarchs of Alexandria) is illicit cohabitation with *Fröken* Ingrid Bergman or Miriam Hopkins. It would be futile to observe that Stevenson is completely innocent of such limitations or distortions of the problem. In the book's last chapter, he asserts that Jekyll's vices are sensuality and hypocrisy; in one of his *Ethical Studies*—in 1888—he tried to list "all the displays of the truly diabolic" and proposed the following: "envy, malice, the mean lie, the mean silence, the calumnious truth, the backbiter, the petty tyrant, the peevish poisoner of family life." (I would add that ethics do not include sexual matters so long as they are not contaminated by betrayal, greed, or vanity.)

The structure of the film is even more rudimentary than its theology. In the book, the identity of Jekyll and Hyde is a surprise: the author saves it for the end of the ninth chapter. The allegorical tale pretends to be a detective story; no reader guesses that Hyde and Jekyll are the same person. The very title of the book makes us assume they are two. There is nothing easier than shifting this device to the screen. Let us imagine any detective mystery: two well-known actors figure in the plot (let us say George Raft and Spencer Tracy); they may use analogous words or refer to events that presuppose a common past. When the mystery seems inexplicable, one of them swallows the magic drug and changes into the other. (Of course the successful execution of this plan would require two or three phonetic adjustments, such as changing the protagonists' names.) More civilized than I, Victor Fleming avoids all surprise and mystery: in the early scenes of the film, Spencer Tracy fearlessly drinks the versatile potion and transforms himself into Spencer Tracy, with a different wig and Negroid features.

Beyond Stevenson's dualist parable and closer to the *Conference of the Birds,* which Farid al-Din Attar composed in the twelfth century (of the Christian era), we may imagine a pantheist film, whose numerous characters finally become One, who is everlasting.

[1941]   [SJL]

Two Films

The doctrine of the transmigration of souls and circular time, or the Eternal Return, was suggested (it is said) by paramnesia, by the sudden, disturbing impression of having already lived the present moment. No matter how forgetful, there is not a single moviegoer in Buenos Aires—at 6:30 and 10:45 P.M.—who has not experienced this impression. Hollywood, like the Greek tragedians, has stuck for many years to ten or twelve basic plots: the aviator who dies in a convenient catastrophe in order to save the friend whom his wife loves; the deceitful typist who does not refuse the gifts of furs, apartments, cars, and tiaras, but who slaps or kills the giver when he "goes too far"; the unspeakable and acclaimed reporter who seeks the friendship of a gangster with the sole motive of betraying him and making him die on the gallows. . . .

The latest victim of this disconcerting asceticism is Miss Bette Davis. They have made her portray the following romance: a woman, weighed down by a pair of eyeglasses and a domineering mother, considers herself ugly and insipid; a psychiatrist (Claude Rains) persuades her to vacation among palm trees, to play tennis, to visit Brazil, to take off her glasses, to change dressmakers. The five-part treatment works: the captain of the ship who brings her home repeats the obvious truth that not one of the other women aboard has had Miss Davis' success. In the face of this endorsement, a niece, previously intimidating in her sarcasm, now sobs for forgiveness. Across the screens of the most remote movie houses, the film spreads its bold thesis: *A disfigured Miss Davis is less beautiful.*

The distorted drama I have summarized is called *Now Voyager.* It was directed by a certain Irving Rapper, who might not be stupid, but who has now unfortunately degraded the tragic heroine of *The Little Foxes, The Letter,* and *Of Human Bondage.*

Nightmare is less ambitious and more tolerable. It begins as a detective film but wastes no time in lapsing into an erratic adventure film. It suffers from all the defects of both genres, with the sole virtue of not belonging to the genre of the boring. Its plot is the kind that has surprised every spectator hundreds of times: a pretty girl and an average man battle against an all-powerful, malicious society, which before the war was China and now is the Gestapo or the international spies of the Third Reich. The hapless directors of such films are motivated by two intentions, first, to show that Orientals (or Prussians) combine perfect evil with perfect intelligence and treachery, and secondly, to show that there is always a well-intentioned man who will succeed in outwitting them. Inevitably, these cross-purposes cancel each other out. Various impending dangers threaten the heroine and hero, which turn out to be imaginary and ineffectual since the spectators know very well that the film must last an hour—a well-known fact that guarantees the characters a longevity or immortality of sixty minutes. Another convention that spoils pictures of this sort is the protagonists' superhuman courage: they are told they are going to die, and they smile. The audience smiles too.

[1943]   [SJL]

On Dubbing

The art of combination is not infinite in its possibilities, though those possibilities are apt to be frightening. The Greeks engendered the chimera, a monster with the head of a lion, the head of a dragon, and the head of a goat; the second-century theologians, the Trinity, in which the Father, the Son, and the Holy Ghost are inextricably linked; the Chinese zoologists, the *ti-yiang*, a bright red, supernatural bird equipped with six feet and six wings but with neither face nor eyes; nineteenth-century geometrists, the hypercube, a four-dimensional figure enclosing an infinite number of cubes and bounded by eight cubes and twenty-four squares. Hollywood has just enriched this frivolous museum of teratology: by means of a perverse artifice they call dubbing, they devise monsters that combine the famous face of Greta Garbo with the voice of Aldonza Lorenzo. How can we fail to proclaim our admiration for this bleak magic, for these ingenious audio-visual deformations?

Those who defend dubbing might argue (perhaps) that objections to it can also be raised against any kind of translation. This argument ignores, or avoids, the principal defect: the arbitrary implant of another voice and another language. The voice of Hepburn or Garbo is not accidental but, for the world, one of their defining features. Similarly, it is worth remembering that gestures are different in English and Spanish.[1]

I have heard that dubbing is appreciated in the provinces. This is a simple authoritarian argument, and as long as they do not publish the syllo-

[1]More than one spectator will ask himself: Since they are usurping voices, why not also faces? When will the system be perfect? When will we see Juana González playing the role of Greta Garbo playing the role of Queen Christina of Sweden?

gisms of those rustic connoisseurs from Chilecito and Chivilcoy, I, for one, shall not let myself be intimidated. I also hear that people who do not know English find dubbing delightful, or tolerable. My understanding of English is less perfect than my ignorance of Russian, but I would never resign myself to seeing *Alexander Nevsky* again in any language other than the original, and I would see it eagerly, nine or ten times, if they showed it in the original or in a version I believed to be the original. The latter is important: worse than dubbing or the substitution that dubbing implies, is one's general awareness of a substitution, of a fake.

There is no advocate of dubbing who does not invoke determinism and predestination, swearing that this expedient is the result of an inevitable evolution and that soon we will have to choose between dubbed films or no films whatsoever. Given the global decline of motion pictures—scarcely corrected by a single exception such as *The Mask of Dimitrios*—the second alternative is not painful. Recent bad films—I am thinking of Moscow's *The Diary of a Nazi* and Hollywood's *The Story of Dr. Wassell*—prompt us to regard the movies as a kind of negative paradise. "Sightseeing is the art of disappointment," Stevenson noted. The definition applies to films and, with sad frequency, to that continuous and unavoidable exercise called life.

[*1945*]   [*SJL*]

V

Nine Dantesque Essays
1945-1951

Prologue

Imagine, in an Oriental library, a panel painted many centuries ago. It may be Arabic, and we are told that all the legends of *The Thousand and One Nights* are represented on its surface; it may be Chinese, and we learn that it illustrates a novel that has hundreds or thousands of characters. In the tumult of its forms, one shape—a tree like an inverted cone; a group of mosques, vermilion in color, against an iron wall—catches our attention, and from there we move on to others. The day declines, the light is wearing thin, and as we go deeper into the carved surface we understand that there is nothing on earth that is not there. What was, is, and shall be, the history of past and future, the things I have had and those I will have, all of it awaits us somewhere in this serene labyrinth. . . . I have fantasized a magical work, a panel that is also a microcosm: Dante's poem is that panel whose edges enclose the universe. Yet I believe that if we were able to read it in innocence (but that happiness is barred to us), its universality would not be the first thing we would notice, and still less its grandiose sublimity. We would, I believe, notice other, less overwhelming and far more delightful characteristics much sooner, perhaps first of all the one singled out by the British Danteans: the varied and felicitous invention of precise traits. In describing a man intertwined with a serpent, it is not enough for Dante to say that the man is being transformed into a serpent and the serpent into a man; he compares this mutual metamorphosis to a flame devouring a page, preceded by a reddish strip where whiteness dies but that is not yet black (*Inferno* XXV, 64). It is not enough for him to say that in the darkness of the seventh circle the damned must squint to see him; he compares them to men gazing at each other beneath a dim moon or to an old tailor threading a needle (*Inferno* XV, 19). It is not enough for him to say that the water in the depths of the universe has frozen; he adds that it looks like glass, not water (*Inferno* XXXII, 24). . . . Such comparisons were in Macaulay's mind when he declared, in opposition to Cary, that Milton's "vague sublimity" and "magnificent generalities" moved him less than Dante's specifics. Later, Ruskin (*Modern Painters* IV, XIV) also condemned Milton's fog and uncertainty and approved of the strictly accurate topography by which Dante engineered his infernal plane. It is common knowledge that poets proceed by hyperbole: for Petrarch or for Góngora, every woman's hair is gold and all water is crystal. This crude, mechanical alphabet of symbols corrupts the rigor of words and appears to arise from the indifference of an imperfect observation. Dante forbids himself this error; not one word in his book is unjustified.

The precision I have just noted is not a rhetorical artifice but an affirmation of the integrity, the plenitude, with which each incident of the poem has been imagined. The same may be said of the psychological traits which are at once so admirable and so modest. The poem is interwoven with such traits, of which I will cite a few. The souls destined for hell weep and blaspheme against God; then, when they step onto Charon's bark, their fear changes to desire and an intolerable eagerness (*Inferno* III, 124). Dante hears from Virgil's own lips that Virgil will never enter heaven; immediately he calls him "master" and "sir," perhaps to show that this confession does not lessen his affection, perhaps because, knowing Virgil to be lost, he loves him all the more (*Inferno* IV, 39). In the black hurricane of the second circle, Dante wishes to learn the root of Paolo and Francesca's love; Francesca tells him that the two loved each other without knowing it, *"soli eravamo e sanza alcun sospetto"* [we were alone, suspecting nothing], and that their love was revealed to them by a casual reading. Virgil rails against proud spirits who aspire to encompass infinite divinity with mere reason; suddenly he bows his head and is silent, because one of those unfortunates is he (*Purgatorio* III, 34). On the rugged slope of Purgatory, the shade of Sordello the Mantuan inquires of Virgil's shade as to its homeland; Virgil says Mantua; Sordello interrupts and embraces him (*Purgatorio* VI, 58). The novels of our own day follow mental processes with extravagant verbosity; Dante allows them to glimmer in an intention or a gesture.

Paul Claudel has observed that the sights that await us after dying will not, in all likelihood, include the nine circles of Hell, the terraces of Purgatory, or the concentric heavens. Dante would undoubtedly have agreed; he devised his topography of death as an artifice demanded by Scholasticism and by the form of his poem.

Dante's universe is described by Ptolemaic astronomy and Christian theology. Earth is a motionless sphere; in the center of the Boreal hemisphere—the one permitted to mankind—is the Mount of Zion; ninety degrees to the east of that mountain, a river, the Ganges, dies; ninety degrees to the west, a river, the Ebro, is born. The Austral hemisphere consists of water, not land, and is barred to mankind; in the center is a mountain that is the antipode of Zion, the Mount of Purgatory. The two rivers and the two mountains, all equidistant, inscribe a cross on the terrestrial orb. Beneath the Mount of Zion, but considerably wider, an inverted cone—Hell—tapers toward the center of the earth, divided into diminishing circles like the rows of an amphitheater. The circles are nine in number, and their topography is appalling and ruinous; the first five form the Upper Inferno, the last four, the Lower Inferno, a city with red mosques surrounded by walls of iron. Within it are crypts, pits, precipices, swamps, and dunes; at the cone's apex is Lucifer, "the worm that gnaws the world." A crack opened in the rock by the waters of Lethe connects Hell's lowest depths to the base of the Mount of Purgatory, which is an island and has a door. Its slopes are stepped with terraces that signify the mortal sins; at its peak, the Garden of Eden blossoms. Nine concentric spheres spin around the earth; the first seven are the planetary heavens (those of the Moon, Mercury, Venus, the Sun, Mars, Jupiter, and Saturn); the eighth is the Heaven of the Fixed Stars; the ninth, the Crystalline Heaven, also called the Primum Mobile. This is surrounded by the empyrean, where the Rose of the Just opens, immeasurable, around a point, which is God. Predictably, the choirs that make up the Rose are nine in number. . . . Such are the broad outlines of the general configuration of Dante's world, which is subordinate, as the reader will have observed, to the preeminence of the numbers 1 and 3 and of the circle. The Demiurge or Craftsman of the *Timaeus,* a book mentioned by Dante (*Convivio* III, 5; *Paradiso* IV, 49) considered rotation the most perfect form of movement, and the sphere the most perfect body; this dogma, which Plato's Demiurge shared with Xenophanes and Parmenides, governs the geography of the three worlds traversed by Dante.

The nine revolving circles and the southern hemisphere made of water with a mountain at its center plainly correspond to an antiquated cosmology; there are those who feel that the same adjective is applicable to the supernatural economy of the poem. The nine circles of Hell (they argue) are no less outdated and indefensible than the nine heavens of Ptolemy, and Purgatory is as unreal as the mountain where Dante places it. A variety of considerations can serve to counter this objection: first, that Dante did not propose to establish the true or realistic topography of the other world. He stated this himself: in his famous epistle to Can Grande, written in Latin, he wrote that the subject of his *Commedia* is, literally, the state of souls after death and, allegorically, man, whose merits and faults make him deserving of divine punishment or reward. Iacopo di Dante, the poet's son, developed this idea further. In the prologue to his commentary, we read that the *Commedia* seeks to paint humanity's three modes of being in allegorical colors, so that in the first part the author considers vice, calling it Hell; in the second, the passage from vice to virtue, calling it Purgatory; in the third, the condition of perfect men, calling it Paradise, "to demonstrate the loftiness of their virtues and their happiness, both of which are necessary to man in order for him to discern the highest good." Other time-honored commentators understood it in the same way; Iacopo della Lana, for example, explains that "the poet, considering human life to be of three conditions, which are the life of the sinful, the life of the penitent and the life of the good, divided his book into three parts, which are Hell, Purgatory and Paradise."

Another trustworthy testimony is that of Francesco da Buti, who annotated the *Commedia* toward the end of the fourteenth century. He makes the words of Dante's letter his own: "The subject of this poem is, literally, the state of souls once separated from their bodies and, morally, the rewards or pains that man attains by the exercise of his free will."

In *Ce que dit la bouche d'ombre*, Hugo writes that in Hell, the shade that appears to Cain in the form of Abel is the same shade Nero recognizes as Agrippina.

Much more serious than the accusation of obsolescence is that of cruelty. Nietzsche, in the *Twilight of the Idols* (1888), gave currency to this notion in the befuddled epigram that defines Dante as "the hyena that *poetizes on graves*"—a definition that is clearly more emphatic than ingenious. It owes its fame, its excessive fame, to the fact that it formulates, with thoughtless violence, a commonplace opinion. The best way to refute that opinion is to investigate the reason for it.

There is a technical explanation for the hardheartedness and cruelty of which Dante has been accused. The pantheistic idea of a God who is also the universe, a god who is every one of his creatures and the destiny of those creatures, may be a heresy and an error if we apply it to reality, but it is indisputable when applied to the poet and his work. The poet is each one of the men in his fictive world, he is every breath and every detail. One of his tasks, and not the easiest of them, is to hide or disguise this omnipresence. The problem was particularly burdensome in Dante's case, for he was forced by the nature of his poem to mete out glory or damnation, but in such a way as to keep his readers from noticing that the Justice handing down these sentences was, in the final analysis, he himself. To achieve this, he included himself as a character in the *Commedia,* and made his own re-actions contrast or only rarely coincide—in the case of Filippo Argenti, or in that of Judas—with the divine decisions.

[1945–51/1982]   *[EA]*

The Noble Castle of the Fourth Canto

Toward the beginning of the nineteenth century, or the end of the eighteenth, certain adjectives of Saxon or Scottish origin *(eerie, uncanny, weird)* came into circulation in the English language, serving to define those places or things that vaguely inspire horror. Such adjectives correspond to a romantic concept of landscape. In German, they are perfectly translated by the word *unheimlich;* in Spanish, the best word may be *siniestro.* With this peculiar quality of *uncanniness* in mind, I once wrote, "The Palace of Subterranean Fire that we find in the final pages of William Beckford's *Vathek* (1782) is the first truly atrocious hell in literature. The most famous literary Avernus, the *dolente regno* of the *Commedia,* is not an atrocious place; it is a place where atrocious things happen. The distinction is valid."

Stevenson ("A Chapter on Dreams") relates that in the dreams of his childhood he was pursued by an abominable hue of brown; Chesterton (*The Man Who Was Thursday*) imagines that at the western limits of the world there exists, perhaps, a tree that is more and less than a tree, and at the eastern limits, something else, perhaps a tower, whose very shape is wicked. Poe, in the "MS Found in a Bottle," speaks of a southern sea where the ship itself will grow in bulk like the living body of the seaman; Melville spends many pages of *Moby-Dick* dilucidating the horror of the whale's unendurable whiteness. . . . I have been lavish with examples; perhaps it would have sufficed to observe that Dante's hell magnifies the idea of a jail;[1] Beckford's, the tunnels of a nightmare.

Several nights ago, on a platform at the Constitución railway station, I suddenly recalled a perfect case of *uncanniness,* of calm, silent horror, at the very entrance to the *Commedia.* An examination of the text confirmed the

---

[1] *"Carcere cieco,"* blind prison, says Virgil of Hell (*Purgatorio* XXII, 103; *Inferno* X, 58–59).

correctness of this delayed recollection. I am speaking of Canto IV of the *Inferno,* one of the most celebrated.

To one who has reached the final pages of the *Paradiso,* the *Commedia* can be many things, perhaps all things; at the beginning, it is obviously a dream dreamt by Dante, who for his part is no more than the subject of the dream. He tells us he does not know how he found himself in the dark wood, *"tant' era pien di sonno a quel punto"* [I was so full of sleep at the moment]; the *sonno* is a metaphor for the bewilderment of the sinning soul, but it suggests the indefinite onset of the act of dreaming. He then writes that the she-wolf who blocks his path has caused many to live in sorrow; Guido Vitali observes that this information could not have emanated from the mere sight of the beast; Dante knows it as we know things in dreams. A stranger appears in the wood; Dante has only just seen him, but knows that he has long been silent—another bit of oneiric knowledge, justified, Momigliano notes, for poetic, not logical reasons. They embark on their fantastic journey. Entering the first circle of the abyss, Virgil pales; Dante attributes his pallor to fear. Virgil avers that it is pity which moves him, and that he is one of the damned: *"e di questi cotai son io medesmo"* [and I myself am one of these]. To disguise the horror of this affirmation or to express his pity, Dante lavishes him with reverential titles: *"Dimmi, maestro mio, dimmi segnore"* [Tell me, master, tell me, sir]. Sighs, sighs of sadness without torment, make the air shudder; Virgil explains that they are in the hell of those who died before the Faith was established. Four looming shades greet him, neither sorrow nor joy in their faces; they are Homer, Horace, Ovid, and Lucan; in Homer's right hand is a sword, symbol of his sovereignty in the epic. These illustrious phantoms honor Dante as their equal and lead him to their eternal dwelling place, which is a castle encircled seven times by lofty walls (the seven liberal arts or the three intellectual and four moral virtues), and by a stream (earthly goods or eloquence) which they pass over as if it were solid ground. The residents of the castle are persons of great authority; they speak seldom and with gentle voices; their gaze is slow and grave. Within the castle's courtyard is a meadow, mysteriously green; Dante, from on high, sees classical and biblical figures and the occasional Muslim: *"Averois, che'l gran comento feo"* [Averroës, who made the great commentary]. At times, one of them is marked by a trait that makes him memorable— *"Cesare armato, con gli occhi grifagni"* [armed Caesar, with falcon eyes]—or by a solitude that enlarges him: *"e solo, in parte, vidi'l Saladino"* [and by himself apart I saw Saladin]. An arid catalogue of proper names, less stimulating than informative, brings the canto to a close.

A Limbo of the Fathers, also called the Bosom of Abraham (Luke 16: 22), and a Limbo for the souls of infants who die without baptism are theological commonplaces; the idea of housing virtuous pagans in this place or places was, according to Francesco Torraca, Dante's own invention. To allay the horror of an adverse era, the poet sought refuge in the great memory of Rome. He wished to honor it in his book, but could not help understanding—the observation is Guido Vitali's—that too great an insistence on the classical world did not accord well with his doctrinal aims. Dante, who could not go against the Faith to save his heroes, envisioned them in a negative Hell, denied the sight and possession of God in heaven, and took pity on their mysterious fate. Years later, imagining the Heaven of Jupiter, he would return to the same problem. Boccaccio says that a long interruption, caused by exile, came between the writing of Canto VII and Canto VIII of the *Inferno*; that fact—suggested or corroborated by the verse "*Io dico, seguitando ch'assai prima*" [I say, continuing, that long before]— may be true, but far more profound is the difference between the canto of the castle and those that follow. In Canto V, Dante made Francesca da Rimini speak immortal words; in the preceding canto, what words might he have given to Aristotle, Heraclitus, or Orpheus if the artifice had occurred to him then? Deliberate or not, his silence deepens the horror and is appropriate to the setting. Benedetto Croce notes: "In the noble castle, among the great and the wise, dry information usurps the place of measured poetry. Feelings of admiration, reverence, and melancholy are stated, not represented" (*La poesia di Dante,* 1920). Commentators have deplored the contrast between the medieval construction of the castle and its classical guests; this fusion or confusion is characteristic of the painting of that era and undoubtedly heightens the oneiric tone of the scene.

In the invention and execution of Canto IV, Dante plotted out a series of circumstances, some of them theological in nature. A devout reader of the *Aeneid,* he imagined the dead in the Elyseum or in a medieval variant of those glad fields; the line "*in loco aperto, luinoso e alto*" [an open place that was luminous and high] recalls the burial mound from which Aeneas saw his Romans, and of the "*largior hic campos aether.*" For pressing reasons of dogma, Dante had to situate his noble castle in Hell. Mario Rossi discovers in this conflict between formal and poetic concerns, between heavenly intuition and frightful damnation, the canto's innermost discord and the root of certain contradictions. In one place it is said that the eternal air shudders with sighs; in another, that there is neither sorrow nor joy in the faces. The poet's visionary faculty had not yet reached its plenitude. To this relative clumsiness we owe the rigidity that gives rise to the singular horror of the castle and its inhabitants, or prisoners. There is something of the oppressive wax museum about this still enclosure: Caesar, armed and idle; Lavinia, eternally seated next to her father. The certainty that tomorrow will be like today, which was like yesterday, which was like every day. A much later passage of the *Purgatorio* adds that the shades of the poets, who are barred from writing, since they are in the *Inferno,* seek to distract their eternity with literary discussions.[2]

The technical reasons—that is, the reasons of a verbal order that make the castle fearsome—can thus be established; but the intimate reasons remain to be determined. A theologian of God would say that the absence of God is sufficient to make the castle terrible. Such a theologian might acknowledge an affinity with the tercet that proclaims the vanity of earthly glories:

> *Non è il mondan romore altro ch'un fiato*
> *di vento, ch'or vien quinci e or vien quindi,*
> *e muta nome perché muta lato.*

[Earthly fame is naught but a breath/of wind which now comes hence and now comes thence,/changing its name because it changes quarter.]

I would propose another reason, one of a personal nature. At this point in the *Commedia,* Homer, Horace, Ovid, and Lucan are projections or figurations of Dante, who knew he was not inferior to these great ones, in deed or potential. They are examples of the type that Dante already was for himself and would foreseeably be for others: the famous poet. They are great, venerated shades who receive Dante into their conclave:

> *ch'e si mi fecer della loro schiera*
> *si ch'io fui sesto tra cotanto senno.*

[for they made me one of their company/so that I was sixth amid so much wisdom.]

---

[2]In the early cantos of the *Commedia,* Dante was what Gioberti considered him to be throughout the poem, "a little more than a mere witness to the plot he himself invented" (*Primato morale e civile degli italiani,* 1840).

They are forms of Dante's incipient dream, barely detached from the dreamer. They speak interminably about literary matters (what else can they do?). They have read the *Iliad* or the *Pharsalia* or they are writing the *Commedia*; they are magisterial in the exercise of their art, yet they are in Hell because Beatrice forgets them.

[1951]   [EA]

The False Problem of Ugolino

I have not read all the commentaries on Dante (no one has), but I suspect that in the case of the famous seventy-fifth line of the *Inferno*'s penultimate canto they have created a problem that arises from a confusion of art with reality. In that line, Ugolino of Pisa, after recounting the death of his children in the Gaol of Hunger, says that fasting did more than grief had done (*"Poscia, piú che'l dolor, potè il digiuno"*). I must exempt the earliest commentators—for whom the verse is not problematic—from my reproach; they all take the line to mean that grief could not kill Ugolino, but fasting did. This is also how Geoffrey Chaucer understands it, in the rough outline of the episode he inserted into the Canterbury cycle.

Let us reconsider the scene. At the glacial nadir of the ninth circle, Ugolino infinitely gnaws the nape of Ruggieri degli Ubaldini's neck and wipes his bloodthirsty mouth on that same sinner's hair. He raises his mouth, not his face, from the ferocious repast, and tells how Ruggieri betrayed him and imprisoned him with his children. He saw many moons wax and wane through the cell's narrow window, until he dreamed that Ruggieri, with slavering mastiffs, was hunting a wolf and its cubs on a mountainside. At dawn he heard the pounding of the hammer that was sealing up the entrance to the tower. A day and a night went by, in silence. Ugolino, in his sorrow, bites his hands; his children think he does so out of hunger and offer him their flesh, the flesh he engendered. Between the fifth and sixth day he sees them die, one by one. He loses his sight, and speaks to his dead, and weeps, and gropes for them in the darkness; then fasting did more than grief.

I have said what meaning the first commentators attributed to this final event. Thus, in the fourteenth century, Rimbaldi de Imola: "It amounts to saying that hunger overcame one whom great sorrow could not vanquish and kill." Among the moderns, Francesco Torraca, Guido Vitali, and Tommaso Casini profess the same opinion. Torraca sees stupor and remorse in Ugolino's words; Casini adds, "Modern interpreters have fantasized that Ugolino ended by feeding on the flesh of his children, a conjecture that goes against nature and history," and considers the controversy futile. Benedetto Croce is of the same view, and maintains that of the two interpretations, the most plausible and congruent is the traditional one. Bianchi very reasonably glosses: "Others understand Ugolino to have eaten the flesh of his children, an improbable interpretation, but one that cannot legitimately be discarded." Luigi Pietrobono (to whose point of view I will return) says the verse is deliberately mysterious.

Before taking my own turn in the *inutile controversia*, I wish to dwell for a moment on the children's unanimous offer. They beg their father to take back the flesh he engendered:

> *. . . tu ne vestisti*
> *queste misere carni, e tu le spoglia.*
>
> [. . . you did clothe us/with this wretched flesh, and do you strip us of it.]

I suspect that this utterance must cause a growing discomfort in its admirers. De Sanctis (*Storia della letteratura italiana* IX) ponders the unexpected conjunction of heterogenous images; D'Ovidio concedes that "this gallant and epigrammatic expression of a filial impulse is almost beyond criticism." For my part, I take this to be one of the very few false notes in the *Commedia*. I consider it less worthy of Dante than of Malvezzi's pen or Gracián's veneration. Dante, I tell myself, could not have helped but feel its falseness, which is certainly aggravated by the almost choral way in which all four children simultaneously tender the famished feast. Someone might suggest that what we are faced with here is a lie, made up after the fact by Ugolino to justify (or insinuate) his crime.

The historical question of whether Ugolino della Gherardesca engaged in cannibalism in the early days of February in the year 1289 is obviously insoluble. The aesthetic or literary problem is of a very different order. It may be stated thus: Did Dante want us to believe that Ugolino (the Ugolino of his *Inferno*, not history's Ugolino) ate his children's flesh? I would hazard this response: Dante did not want us to believe it, but he wanted us to suspect it.[1] Uncertainty is part of his design. Ugolino gnaws the base of the

---

[1]Luigi Pietrobono observes "that the *digiuno* does not affirm Ugolino's guilt, but allows it to be inferred, without damage to art or to historical rigor. It is enough that we judge it *possible*" (*Inferno*, 47).

archbishop's skull; Ugolino dreams of sharp-fanged dogs ripping the wolves' flanks *("e con l'agute scane/mi parea lor veder fender li fianchi")*. Driven by grief, Ugolino bites his hands; Ugolino hears his children implausibly offering him their flesh; Ugolino, having delivered the ambiguous line, turns back to gnaw the archbishop's skull. Such acts suggest or symbolize the ghastly deed. They play a dual role: we believe them to be part of the tale, and they are prophecies.

Robert Louis Stevenson ("Some Gentlemen in Fiction") observes that a book's characters are only strings of words; blasphemous as this may sound to us, Achilles and Peer Gynt, Robinson Crusoe and Don Quixote, may be reduced to it. The powerful men who ruled the earth, as well: Alexander is one string of words, Attila another. We should say of Ugolino that he is a verbal texture consisting of about thirty tercets. Should we include the idea of cannibalism in this texture? I repeat that we should suspect it, with uncertainty and dread. To affirm or deny Ugolino's monstrous crime is less tremendous than to have some glimpse of it.

The pronouncement "A book is the words that comprise it" risks seeming an insipid axiom. Nevertheless, we are all inclined to believe that there is a form separable from the content and that ten minutes of conversation with Henry James would reveal to us the "true" plot of *The Turn of the Screw*. I think that the truth is not like that; I think that Dante did not know any more about Ugolino than his tercets relate. Schopenhauer declared that the first volume of his major work consists of a single thought, and that he could find no more concise way of conveying it. Dante, on the contrary, would say that whatever he imagined about Ugolino is present in the debated tercets.

In real time, in history, whenever a man is confronted with several alternatives, he chooses one and eliminates and loses the others. Such is not the case in the ambiguous time of art, which is similar to that of hope and oblivion. In that time, Hamlet is sane and is mad.[2] In the darkness of his Tower of Hunger, Ugolino devours and does not devour the beloved corpses, and this undulating imprecision, this uncertainty, is the strange matter of which he is made. Thus, with two possible deaths, did Dante dream him, and thus will the generations dream him.

[1948]   *[EA]*

---

[2] Two famous ambiguities may aptly be recalled here, as curiosities. The first, Quevedo's *"sangrienta luna,"* the bloody moon that is at once the moon over the battlefields and the moon of the Ottoman flag; the other, the "mortal moon" of Shakespeare's Sonnet 107, which is the moon in the heavens and the Virgin Queen.

The Last Voyage of Ulysses

My aim is to reconsider, in the light of other passages of the *Commedia,* the enigmatic tale that Dante places in the mouth of Ulysses (*Inferno* XXVI, 90–142). In the calamitous depths of the circle where deceivers are punished, Ulysses and Diomedes endlessly burn in a single two-pronged flame. Pressed by Virgil to describe how he met his death, Ulysses relates that after having left Circe, who kept him in Gaeta for more than a year, neither the sweetness of his son, nor the reverence Laertes inspired in him, nor the love of Penelope could conquer the ardor in his breast to know the world and the defects and virtues of men. With his last ship and the few loyal men left to him, he ventured upon the open seas; they arrived, old men by then, at the narrows where Hercules set his columns. At that outer limit marked by a god to ambition or audacity, he urged his comrades on, to see, since so little life was left to them, the unpeopled world, the untraveled seas of the antipodes. He reminded them of their origin, he reminded them that they were not born to live like brutes, but to seek virtue and knowledge. They sailed toward the sunset, and then to the south, and saw all the stars that the southern hemisphere alone encompasses. For five months their prow cleaved the ocean, and one day they caught sight of a dark mountain on the horizon. It seemed to them higher than any other, and their souls rejoiced. This joy soon turned to grief, for a tempest arose that spun the ship around three times and sank it on the fourth, as pleased Another, and the sea closed over them.

Such is Ulysses' tale. Many commentators, from the anonymous Florentine to Raffaele Andreoli, consider it a digression on the author's part. In their estimation, Ulysses and Diomedes, deceivers, suffer in the pit of the deceivers—*"e dentro dalla lor fiamma si geme/l'agguato del caval"* [and in their flame they groan for the ambush of the horse]—and the journey is no more than an incidental embellishment. Tommaseo, however, cites a passage of the *Civitas Dei*, and could have cited another from Clement of Alexandria, denying that men can reach the lower part of the earth; later, Casini and Pietrobono object to the journey as a sacrilege. Indeed, the mountain glimpsed by the Greek before the abyss entombs him is the holy mountain of Purgatory, forbidden to mortals (*Purgatorio* I, 130–32). Hugo Friedrich acutely observes: "The journey ends in a catastrophe which is not mere human destiny but the word of God" (*Odysseus in der Hölle*, Berlin, 1942).

As he recounts his exploit, Ulysses characterizes it as senseless ("*folle*"); Canto XXVII of the *Paradiso* refers to the *"varco folle d'Ulisse,"* to Ulysses' rash or senseless route. The same adjective is applied by Dante in the dark wood to Virgil's tremendous invitation (*"temo che la venuta non sia folle"* [I fear that the coming may be folly]); the repetition is deliberate. When Dante sets foot on the beach Ulysses glimpsed before dying, he says that no one has navigated those waters and been able to return; then he says that Virgil girded him with a bulrush, *"com' Altrui piacque"* [as pleased Another]—the same words spoken by Ulysses as he declared his tragic end. Carlo Steiner writes: "Was Dante thinking of Ulysses, shipwrecked within sight of this beach? Of course. But Ulysses wished to reach it by relying on his own strength and defying the decreed limits of what mankind can do. Dante, a new Ulysses, will set foot there as a victor, girded with humility and guided not by pride but by reason, illuminated by grace." August Rüegg restates this opinion (*Jenseitsvorstellungen vor Dante* II, 114): "Dante is an adventurer who, like Ulysses, walks along virgin paths, travels across worlds no man has ever glimpsed and aspires to the most difficult and remote goals. But the comparison ends there. Ulysses sets forth on his own account and risks forbidden adventures; Dante allows himself to be guided by higher powers."

Two famous passages justify this distinction. One is where Dante deems himself unworthy to visit the three otherworlds—*"Io non Enëa, io non Paulo sono"* [I am not Aeneas, I am not Paul]—and Virgil announces the mission Beatrice has entrusted to him; the other, where Cacciaguida recommends that the poem be published (*Paradiso* XVII, 100–142). Given this testimony, it would be preposterous to place Dante's peregrination, which leads to the beatific vision and the best book mankind has ever written, on the same level as Ulysses' sacrilegious adventure, which culminates in Hell. The former action seems the reverse of the latter.

This argument, however, contains an error. Ulysses' act is undoubtedly Ulysses' journey, because Ulysses is nothing other than the subject to whom that act is attributed; Dante's act or undertaking is not Dante's journey, but the composition of his book. The fact is obvious, but tends to be forgotten because the *Commedia* is written in the first person, and the man who died has been overshadowed by the immortal protagonist. Dante was a theologian; the writing of the *Commedia* must often have seemed no less laborious and perhaps no less audacious and fatal than the final voyage of Ulysses. He had dared to conjure up arcana that the pen of the Holy Spirit barely indicates; the intention may well have entailed a sin. He had dared to place Beatrice Portinari on the same level as the Virgin and Jesus.[1] He had dared to anticipate the pronouncements of the inscrutable Last Judgment that the blessed do not know; he had judged and condemned the souls of simoniac Popes and had saved that of the Averroëist Siger, who lectured on circular time.[2] So much laborious effort for glory, which is an ephemeral thing!

> *Non è il mondan romore altro ch'un fiato*
> *di vento, ch'or vien quinci e or vien quindi,*
> *e muta nome perchè muta lato.*

[Earthly fame is naught but a breath/of wind which now comes hence and now comes thence,/changing its name because it changes quarter.]

Plausible traces of this discord survive in the text. Carlo Steiner recognized one in the dialogue in which Virgil overcomes Dante's fears and persuades him to undertake his unprecedented journey. Steiner writes, "The debate which by a fiction occurs with Virgil, in reality occurred in Dante's mind, when he had not yet decided on the composition of the poem. It corresponds to the other debate in Canto XVII of the *Paradiso*, which envisages the poem's publication. Having written the work, can he publish it and defy the wrath of his enemies? In both cases, the consciousness of its worth and the high end he had set for himself won out" (*Commedia*, 15). In such passages, then, Dante would have symbolized a mental conflict. I suggest that he also symbolized it, perhaps without wanting to or suspecting he had done so, in the tragic legend of Ulysses, and that its tremendous power is due to that emotional charge. Dante was Ulysses, and in some way he could fear Ulysses' punishment.

A final observation. Devoted to the sea and to Dante, the two literatures written in English have felt the influence of the Dantesque Ulysses. Eliot

---

[1]Cf. Giovanni Papini, *Dante vivo* III, 34.
[2]Cf. Maurice de Wulf, *Histoire de la philosophie médiévale.*

(and before him Andrew Lang and before him Longfellow) has implied that Tennyson's admirable *Ulysses* proceeds from this glorious archetype. As far as I know, a deeper affinity has not previously been noted: that of the infernal Ulysses with another unfortunate captain: Ahab of *Moby-Dick*. Like his predecessor, he accomplishes his own perdition by means of vigilance and courage; the general story is the same, the grand finale is identical, the last words almost repeat each other. Schopenhauer has written that nothing in our lives is involuntary; both fictions, in the light of this prodigious maxim, describe the process of a secret and intricate suicide.

[1948]   *[EA]*

Postscript, 1981: It has been said that Dante's Ulysses prefigures the famous explorers who, centuries later, arrived on the coasts of America and India. Centuries before the *Commedia* was written, that human type had already come into being. Erik the Red discovered Greenland around the year 985; his son Leif disembarked in Canada at the beginning of the eleventh century. Dante could not have known this. The things of Scandinavia tend to be secret, as if they were a dream.

The Pitying Torturer

Dante (as everyone knows) consigns Francesca to the Inferno, and listens with infinite compassion to the tale of her sin. How can this contradiction be lessened, how can it be justified? I see four possible conjectures.

The first is technical. Dante, having determined the general shape of his book, feared that unless it were enlivened by the confessions of lost souls it could degenerate into a worthless catalog of proper names or topographical descriptions. The thought made him place an interesting and not too alien sinner in each of the circles of his Hell. (Lamartine, worn out by these guests, said the *Commedia* was a "*gazette florentine.*") Naturally it was preferable that the confessions be poignant, and they could be poignant without risk, for the author, having imprisoned the narrators in Hell, was safely beyond any suspicion of complicity. This conjecture is perhaps the most plausible (its notion of a poetical orb imposed on an arid theological novel was argued by Croce), but it has a nasty pettiness about it that does not seem to harmonize with our concept of Dante. Moreover, interpretations of a book as infinite as the *Commedia* cannot be so simple.

The second conjecture, following the doctrine of Jung,[1] equates literary and oneiric inventions. Dante, who has become our dream, dreamed Francesca's pain and dreamed his own compassion. Schopenhauer observes

---

[1] Jung's doctrine is somehow prefigured by the classic metaphor of the dream as a theatrical event. Thus Góngora, in the sonnet "*Varia imaginación*" ("*El sueno, autor de representaciones./En su teatro sobre el viento armado/sombras suele vestir de bulto bello*" [Sleep, author of representations./Within its theater mounted on the wind/ bedecks shadows in lovely forms]); thus Quevedo, in the "*Sueño de la muerte*" ("Once unburdened, the soul became idle, without the labor of the external senses, and in this way the following comedy struck me; and my powers recited it in darkness, with myself as the audience and theater of my fantasies"); thus Joseph Addison, in number 487 of the *Spectator* ("She [the dreaming soul] is herself the theater, the actors, and the

that what we see and hear in dreams can astonish us, though ultimately it has its roots in us; Dante, likewise, could feel pity for things he himself dreamed or invented. It could also be said that Francesca is a mere projection of the poet, as, for that matter, is Dante himself, in his role as a traveller through Hell. I suspect, however, that this conjecture is fallacious, for it is one thing to attribute a common origin to books and dreams, and another to tolerate, in books, the disjunction and irresponsibility of dreams.

The third, like the first, is of a technical nature. Over the course of the *Commedia*, Dante had to anticipate the inscrutable decisions of God. By no other light than that of his fallible mind, he attempted to predict certain pronouncements of the Last Judgment. He damned—even if only as a literary fiction—Celestin V and saved Siger de Brabant, who defended the astrological hypothesis of the Eternal Return.

To conceal this operation, he made justice the defining characteristic of God in Hell—*"Giustizia mosse il mio alto fattore"* [Justice moved my high maker]—and reserved the attributes of understanding and pity for himself. He placed Francesca among the lost souls, and he felt sorry for Francesca. Benedetto Croce declares, "Dante, as a theologian, as a believer, as an ethical man, condemns sinners; but in sentiment he neither condemns nor absolves" (*La poesia di Dante*, 78).[2]

The fourth conjecture is less precise. A prefatory discussion is required to make it intelligible. Consider these two propositions. One: murderers deserve the death penalty; the other: Rodion Raskolnikov deserves the death penalty. The fact that the propositions are not synonymous is inarguable. Paradoxically, this is not because murderers are concrete and Raskolnikov is abstract or illusory. On the contrary, the concept of murderers betokens a mere generalization; Raskolnikov, for anyone who has read his story, is a real being. In reality there are, strictly speaking, no murderers; there are individuals whom the torpor of our languages includes in that indeterminate ensemble. (Such, in the final analysis, is the nominalist hypothesis of Roscelin and William of Occam.) In other words, anyone who has read

---

beholder"). Centuries before, the pantheist Omar Khayyam composed a strophe translated as follows in McCarthy's literal version: "Now Thou art hidden from all things, now Thou art displayed in all things. It is for Thy own delight that Thou workest these wonders, being at once the sport and the spectator."

[2]Andrew Lang writes that Dumas wept when he killed off Porthos. Likewise, we feel Cervantes' emotion at the death of Alonso Quijano, "who, amidst the tears and lamentations of all present, gave up the ghost, or in other words, departed this life."

Dostoevsky's novel has in some way been Raskolnikov and knows that his "crime" is not free because an inevitable network of circumstances predetermined and dictated it. The man who killed is not a murderer, the man who lied is not an impostor; and this is known (or, rather, felt) by the damned; there is, consequently, no punishment without injustice. The judicial fiction of "the murderer" may well deserve the death penalty, but not the luckless wretch who killed, driven by his own prior history and perhaps—oh Marquis de Laplace!—by the history of the universe. Madame de Staël has compressed these ratiocinations into a famous sentence: *"Tout comprendre c'est tout pardonner"* [To understand all is to forgive all].

Dante tells the story of Francesca's sin with such delicate compassion that all of us feel its inevitability. That is how the poet must have felt it, in defiance of the theologian who argued in the *Purgatorio* (XVI, 70) that if actions depended on the influences of the stars, our free will would be annulled, and to reward good while punishing evil would be an injustice.[3]

Dante understands and does not forgive; this is the insoluble paradox. For my part, I take it that he found a solution beyond logic. He felt (but did not understand) that the acts of men are necessary and that an eternity of heavenly bliss or hellish perdition incurred by those acts is similarly necessary. The Spinozists and the Stoics also promulgated moral laws. Here there is no need to bring up Calvin, whose *decretum Dei absolutum* predestines some for hell and others for heaven. I read in the introductory pages of Sale's *Koran* that one of the Islamic sects also upholds this view.

The fourth conjecture, as is evident, does not disentangle the problem but simply raises it in a vigorous manner. The other conjectures were logical; this last one, which is not, seems to me to be true.

[1948]   [EA]

---

[3]Cf. *De monarchia* I, 14; *Purgatorio* XVIII, 73; *Paradiso* V, 19. More eloquent still are the great words of Canto XXXI: *"Tu m'hai di servo tratto a libertate"* [It is you who have drawn me from bondage into liberty] (*Paradiso*, 85).

Dante and the Anglo-Saxon Visionaries

In Canto X of the *Paradiso*, Dante recounts that he ascended to the sphere of the sun and saw around that planet—in the Dantesque economy the sun is a planet—a flaming crown of twelve spirits, even more luminous than the light against which they stood out. The first of them, Thomas Aquinas, announces the names of the others: the seventh is *Beda*, or Bede. Dante's commentators explain that this is the Venerable Bede, deacon of the monastery of Jarrow and author of the *Historia Ecclesiastica Gentis Anglorum*.

Despite the adjective, this, the first history of England, composed in the eighth century, transcends the strictly ecclesiastical. It is the touching, personal work of a man of letters and a scrupulous researcher. Bede had mastered Latin and knew Greek; a line from Virgil could spring spontaneously from his pen. Everything interested him: universal history, the exegesis of Holy Scripture, music, rhetorical figures,[1] spelling, numerical systems, the natural sciences, theology, Latin poetry, and poetry in the vernacular. There is one point, however, on which he deliberately remains silent. In his chronicle of the tenacious missions that finally succeeded in imposing the faith of Jesus on the Germanic kingdoms of England, Bede could have done for Saxon paganism what Snorri Sturluson, five hundred years or so later, would do for Scandinavian paganism. Without betraying his work's pious intent, he could have elucidated or sketched out the mythology of his elders. Predictably, he did not. The reason is obvious: the religion, or mythology, of the Germans was still very near. Bede wanted to forget it; he wanted his England to forget it. We will never know if a twilight awaits the gods

---

[1]Bede sought the examples he gives of rhetorical figures in the Scriptures. Thus, for synecdoche, where the part stands for the whole, he cited verse 14 of the first chapter of the Gospel According to John, "And the Word was made flesh. . . ." Strictly speaking, the Word was made not only flesh, but also bone, cartilage, water, and blood.

who were adored by Hengist, or if, on that tremendous day when the sun and the moon are devoured by wolves, a ship made of the fingernails of the dead will depart from the realms of ice. We will never know if these lost divinities formed a pantheon, or if they were, as Gibbon suspected, the vague superstitions of barbarians. Except for the ritual phrase *"cujus pater Voden"* which figures in all his genealogies of royal lineages—and the case of the cautious king who had one altar for Jesus and another, smaller one for the demons—Bede did little to satisfy the future curiosity of Germanists. He did, however, stray far enough from the straight and narrow path of chronology to record certain otherworldly visions that prefigure the work of Dante.

Let us recall one of them. Fursa, Bede tells us, was an Irish ascetic who had converted many Saxons. In the course of an illness, he was carried off in spirit by angels and rose up to heaven. During his ascension, he saw four fires, not far distant from each other, reddening the black air. The angels explained that these fires would consume the world and that their names were Falsehood, Covetousness, Discord, and Iniquity. The fires extended until they met one another and drew near him; Fursa was afraid, but the angels told him: "The fire which you did not kindle shall not burn you." Indeed, the angels parted the flames and Fursa reached Paradise, where he saw many admirable things. On his way back to earth, he was threatened a second time by a fire, out of which a demon hurled the incandescent soul of a sinner, which burned his right shoulder and chin. An angel told him: "Now the fire you kindled burns you. For as you accepted the garment of him who was a sinner, so you must partake of his punishment." Fursa bore the stigma of this vision to the day of his death.

Another of these visions is that of a man of Northumbria named Dryhthelm. After an illness that lasted for several days, he died at nightfall, and suddenly came back to life at the break of dawn. His wife was keeping vigil for him; Dryhthelm told her he had indeed been reborn from among the dead and that he now intended to live in a very different way. After praying, he divided his estate into three parts, and gave the first to his wife, the second to his sons, and the third to the poor. He bade them all farewell and retired to a monastery, where his rigorous life was testimony to the many dreadful and desirable things that were revealed to him during the night he was dead, which he spoke of thus:

> He that led me had a shining countenance and a bright garment, and we went on silently, as I thought, towards the north-east. We came to a

vale of great breadth and depth, but of infinite length; on the left it appeared full of dreadful flames, the other side was no less horrid for violent hail and cold snow flying in all directions; both places were full of men's souls, which seemed by turns to be tossed from one side to the other, as it were by a violent storm; for when the wretches could no longer endure the excess of heat, they leaped into the cutting cold, and so on infinitely. I began to think that this region of intolerable torments perhaps might be hell. But my guide who went before me answered my thoughts: "You are not yet in Hell."

When he had led me further on, the darkness grew so thick that I could see nothing else but the garment of him that led me. Innumerable globes of black flames rose out of a great pit and fell back again into the same. My leader suddenly vanished and left me alone in the midst of the globes of fire that were full of human souls. An insufferable stench came forth from the pit.

When I had stood there in much dread for a time that seemed endless, I heard a most hideous and wretched lamentation, and at the same time a loud laughing, as of a rude multitude insulting captured enemies. A gang of evil spirits was dragging five howling and lamenting souls of men into the darkness, whilst they themselves laughed and rejoiced. One of these men was shorn like a clergyman; another was a woman. As they went down into the burning pit, I could no longer distinguish between the lamentation of the men and the laughing of the devils, yet I still had a confused sound in my ears. Dark spirits ascended from that flaming abyss beset me on all sides and tormented me with the noisome flame that issued from their mouths and nostrils, yet they durst not touch me. Being thus on all sides enclosed with enemies and darkness, I could not seem to defend myself. Then there appeared behind me, on the way that I came, the brightness of a star shining amidst the darkness; which increased by degrees and came rapidly toward me. All those evil spirits dispersed and fled and I saw that the star was he who had led me before; he turned towards the right and began to lead me towards the south-east, and having soon brought me out of the darkness, conducted me into an atmosphere of clear light. I saw a vast wall before us, the length and height of which, in every direction seemed to be altogether boundless. I began to wonder why we went up to the wall, seeing no door, window, or path through it. Presently, I know not by what means, we were on the top of it, and within it was a vast and delightful field, so full of fragrant flowers that the odor of its delightful sweetness immediately dispelled the stink of the dark furnace. In this field were innumerable assemblies of men in white. As my guide led me through these happy inhabitants, I began to think that this might be the kingdom of heaven, of which I had heard so much, but he answered to my thought, saying "You are not yet in heaven."

Further on I discovered before me a much more beautiful light and therein heard sweet voices of persons singing, and so wonderful a fragrancy proceeded from the place that the other which I had before thought most delicious then seemed to me but very indifferent. When I began to hope we should enter that delightful place, my guide on a sudden stood still; and then turning back, led me back by the way we came.

He then told me that that vale I saw so dreadful for consuming flames and cutting cold is purgatory; the fiery noisome pit is the very mouth of hell; this flowery place is where the souls are received of the just who await the Last Judgment, and the place where I heard the sound of sweet singing, with the fragrant odor and bright light is the kingdom of heaven. "As for you" he added, "who are now to return to your body and live among men again, if you will endeavor to direct your behavior in righteousness, you shall, after death, have a place or residence among these joyful troops of blessed souls; for when I left you for a while, it was to know what your future would be." I much abhorred returning to my body, however I durst not say a word and, on a sudden, I found myself alive among men.

In the story I have just transcribed, my readers will have noted passages that recall—or prefigure—passages in Dante's work. The monk is not burned by the fire he did not light; Beatrice, similarly, is invulnerable to the flames of the Inferno: "*nè fiamma d'esto 'ncendio non m'assale*" [and no flame of this burning assails me].

To the right of the valley that seems without end, torrents of sleet and ice punish the damned; the Epicureans of the third circle endure the same affliction. The man of Northumbria is plunged into despair by the angel's momentary abandonment, as Dante is by Virgil's: "*Virgilio a cui per mia salute die'mi*" [Virgil, to whom I gave myself for my salvation]. Dryhthelm does not know how he was able to rise to the top of the wall; Dante, how he was able to cross the sad Acheron.

Of greater interest than these correspondences, of which there are undoubtedly many more than I have mentioned, are the circumstantial details that Bede weaves into his narrative and that lend a singular verisimilitude to the otherworldly visions. I need only recall the permanence of the burns, the fact that the angel reads the man's silent thought, the fusion of moaning and laughter, the visionary's perplexity before the high wall. It may be that an oral tradition carried these details to the historian's pen; certainly they already contain the union of the personal and the marvelous that is typical of Dante, and that has nothing to do with the customs of allegorical literature.

Did Dante ever read the *Historia Ecclesiastica*? It is highly probable that he did not. In strict logic, the inclusion of the name *Beda* (conveniently disyllabic for the line) in an inventory of theologians proves little. In the Middle Ages, people trusted other people; it was not compulsory to have read the learned Anglo-Saxon's volumes in order to acknowledge his authority, as it was not compulsory to have read the Homeric poems, closed off in an almost secret language, to know that Homer ("*Mira colui con quella spada in mano*" [Note him there with sword in hand]) could well be chief among Ovid, Lucan, and Horace. Another observation may be made, as well. For us, Bede is a historian of England; to his medieval readers he was a commentator on Scripture, a rhetorician, and a chronologist. There was no reason for a history of the then rather vague entity called England to have had any particular attraction for Dante.

Whether or not Dante knew of the visions recorded by Bede is less important than the fact that Bede considered them worthy of remembrance and included them in his book. A great book like the *Divina commedia* is not the isolated or random caprice of an individual; many men and many generations built toward it. To investigate its precursors is not to subject oneself to a miserable drudgery of legal or detective work; it is to examine the movements, probings, adventures, glimmers, and premonitions of the human spirit.

[1945–51/1957]   *[EA]*

Purgatorio I, 13

Like all abstract words, the word *metaphor* is a metaphor; in Greek it means "transfer." Metaphors generally consist of two terms, one of which is briefly transformed into the other. Thus, the Saxons called the sea the "whale's path" or the "swan's path." In the first example, the whale's hugeness corresponds to the hugeness of the sea; in the second, the swan's smallness contrasts with the vastness of the sea. We will never know if the inventors of these metaphors were aware of these connotations. Line 60 of Canto I of the *Inferno* reads: "*mi ripigneva là dove'l sol tace*" [she pushed me back to where the sun is silent].

"Where the sun is silent": the auditory verb expresses a visual image, as in the famous hexameter of the *Aeneid:* "*a Tenedo, tacitae per amica silentia lunae*" [from Tenedos, silently in the quiet friendship of the moon].

Beyond discussing the fusion of two terms, my present purpose is to examine three curious lines.

The first is line 13 of Canto I of the *Purgatorio*: "*Dolce color d'oriental zaffiro*" [Sweet hue of oriental sapphire].

Buti explains that the sapphire is a precious stone, of a color between sky blue and azure, most delightful to the eyes, and that the oriental sapphire is a variety found in Media.

In the aforementioned line, Dante suggests the color of the East, the Orient, by a sapphire that includes the Orient in its name. He thus implies a reciprocal play that may well be infinite.[1]

---

[1] We read in the initial strophe of Góngora's *Soledades*:

> *Era del año la estación florida*
> *en que el mantido robador de Europa,*
> *media luna las armas de su frente*
> *y el Sol todos los rayos de su pelo*

In Byron's *Hebrew Melodies* (1815), I have discovered a similar artifice: "She walks in beauty, like the night."

To accept this line, the reader must imagine a tall, dark woman who walks like the Night, which, in turn, is a tall, dark woman, and so on to infinity. 2

The third example is from Robert Browning. He includes it in the dedication to his vast dramatic poem, *The Ring and the Book* (1868): "O lyric Love, half angel and half bird . . ."

The poet says that Elizabeth Barrett, who has died, is half angel and half bird, but an angel is already half bird, and thus a subdivision is proposed that may be interminable.

I do not know whether to include in this casual anthology Milton's controversial line (*Paradise Lost* IV, 323): "the fairest of her daughters, Eve."

To the intellect, the line is absurd, but not, perhaps, to the imagination.

[1945–51/1982]   *[EA]*

> *luciente honor del cielo,*
> *en campos de zafiros pasce estrellas.*

[It was in the year's flowery season/that Europa's cloaked abductor/his arms a half-moon on his brow/and all the rays of his hair the Sun/glittering honor of the sky/ in fields of sapphires grazes on stars.]

The line from the *Purgatorio* is delicate; that of the *Soledades*, deliberately clamorous.

2Baudelaire writes, in *"Recueillement"*: *"Entends, ma chère, entends, la douce Nuit qui marche"* [Hear, my darling, hear, the sweet Night who walks]. The silent walking of the night should not be heard.

The Simurgh and the Eagle

Literarily speaking, what might be derived from the notion of a being composed of other beings, a bird, say, made up of birds?[1] Thus formulated, the problem appears to allow for merely trivial, if not actively unpleasant, solutions. One might suppose its possibilities to have been exhausted by the multiply feathered, eyed, tongued, and eared *"monstrum horrendum ingens"* [vast, horrible monster] that personifies Fame (or Scandal or Rumor) in Book IV of the *Aeneid*, or that strange king made of men who occupies the frontispiece of the *Leviathan*, armed with sword and staff. Francis Bacon (*Essays*, 1625) praised the first of these images; Chaucer and Shakespeare imitated it; no one, today, considers it any better than the "beast Acheron" who, according to the fifty-odd manuscripts of the *Visio Tundali*, stores sinners in the roundness of its belly, where they are tormented by dogs, bears, lions, wolves, and vipers.

In the abstract, the concept of a being composed of other beings does not appear promising: yet, in incredible fashion, one of the most memorable figures of Western literature, and another of Eastern literature, correspond to it. The purpose of this brief note is to describe these marvelous fictions, one conceived in Italy, the other in Nishapur.

The first is in Canto XVIII of the *Paradiso*. In his journey through the concentric heavens, Dante observes a greater happiness in Beatrice's eyes and greater power in her beauty, and realizes that they have ascended from the ruddy heaven of Mars to the heaven of Jupiter. In the broader arc of this sphere, where the light is white, celestial creatures sing and fly, successively forming the letters of the phrase DILIGITE IUSTITIAM and the shape of an eagle's head, not copied from earthly eagles, of course, but directly manu-

[1]Similarly, in Leibniz' *Monadology* (1714), we read that the universe consists of inferior universes, which in turn contain the universe, and so on *ad infinitum*.

factured by the Spirit. Then the whole of the eagle shines forth: it is composed of thousands of just kings. An unmistakable symbol of Empire, it speaks with a single voice, and says "I" rather than "we" (*Paradiso* XIX, 11). An ancient problem vexed Dante's conscience: Is it not unjust of God to damn, for lack of faith, a man of exemplary life who was born on the bank of the Indus and could know nothing of Jesus? The Eagle answers with the obscurity appropriate to a divine revelation: it censures such foolhardy questioning, repeats that faith in the Redeemer is indispensable, and suggests that God may have instilled this faith in certain virtuous pagans. It avers that among the blessed are the Emperor Trajan and Ripheus the Trojan, the former having lived just after and the latter before the Cross.[2] (Though resplendent in the fourteenth century, the Eagle's appearance is less effective in the twentieth, which generally reserves glowing eagles and tall, fiery letters for commercial propaganda. Cf. Chesterton, *What I Saw in America*, 1922.)

That anyone has ever been able to surpass one of the great figures of the *Commedia* seems incredible, and rightly so: nevertheless, the feat has occurred. A century after Dante imagined the emblem of the Eagle, Farid al-Din Attar, a Persian of the Sufi sect, conceived of the strange Simurgh (Thirty Birds), which implicitly encompasses and improves upon it. Farid al-Din Attar was born in Nishapur,[3] land of turquoises and swords. In Persian, Attar means "he who traffics in drugs." In the *Lives of the Poets*, we read that such indeed was his trade. One afternoon, a dervish entered the apothecary's shop, looked over its many jars and pillboxes, and began to weep. Attar, astonished and disturbed, begged him to leave. The dervish answered: "It costs me nothing to go, since I carry nothing with me. As for you, it will cost you greatly to say good-bye to the treasures I see here." Attar's heart went as cold as camphor. The dervish left, but the next morning, Attar abandoned his shop and the labors of this world.

A pilgrim to Mecca, he crossed Egypt, Syria, Turkestan, and the north of India; on his return, he gave himself over to literary composition and the fervent contemplation of God. It is a fact of some renown that he left

---

[2]Pompeo Venturi disapproves of the election of Ripheus, a personage who until this apotheosis had existed only in a few lines of the *Aeneid* (II, 339, 426). Virgil declares him the most just of the Trojans and adds to the report of his end the resigned ellipsis: "*Dies aliter visum*" [The gods ruled otherwise]. There is not another trace of him in all of literature. Perhaps Dante chose him as a symbol by virtue of his vagueness. Cf. the commentaries of Casini (1921) and Guido Vitali (1943).

[3]Katibi, author of the *Confluence of the Two Seas*, declared: "I am of the garden of Nishapur, like Attar, but I am the thorn of Nishapur and he was the rose."

behind twenty thousand distichs: his works are entitled *The Book of the Nightingale, The Book of Adversity, The Book of Instruction, The Book of Mysteries, The Book of Divine Knowledge, The Lives of the Saints, The King and the Rose, A Declaration of Wonders,* and the extraordinary *Conference of the Birds (Mantıq al-Tayr).* In the last years of his life, which is said to have reached a span of one hundred and ten years, he renounced all worldly pleasures, including those of versification. He was put to death by the soldiers of Tule, son of Genghis Khan. The vast image I have alluded to is the basis of the *Mantiq al-Tayr,* the plot of which is as follows:

The faraway king of all the birds, the Simurgh, lets fall a magnificent feather in the center of China: tired of their age-old anarchy, the birds resolve to go in search of him. They know that their king's name means thirty birds; they know his palace is located on the Kaf, the circular mountain that surrounds the earth.

They embark upon the nearly infinite adventure. They pass through seven valleys or seas; the name of the penultimate is Vertigo; the last, Annihilation. Many pilgrims give up; others perish. Thirty, purified by their efforts, set foot on the mountain of the Simurgh. At last they gaze upon it: they perceive that they are the Simurgh and that the Simurgh is each one of them and all of them. In the Simurgh are the thirty birds and in each bird is the Simurgh.[4] (Plotinus, too—*The Enneads* V, 8.4—asserts a paradisiacal extension of the principle of identity: "Everywhere in the intelligible heaven is all, and all is all and each all. The sun, there, is all the stars; and every star, again, is all the stars and sun.")

The disparity between the Eagle and the Simurgh is no less obvious than their resemblance. The Eagle is merely implausible; the Simurgh, impossible. The individuals who make up the Eagle are not lost in it (David serves as the pupil of one eye; Trajan, Ezekiel, and Constantine as brows); the birds that gaze upon the Simurgh are at the same time the Simurgh. The Eagle is a transitory symbol, as were the letters before it; those who form its shape with their bodies do not cease to be who they are: the ubiquitous

---

[4]Silvina Ocampo (*Espacios métricos,* 12) has put this episode into verse:

> *Era Dios ese pájaro como un enorme espejo:*
> *los contenía a todos; no era un mero reflejo.*
> *En sus plumas hallaron cada uno sus plumas*
> *en los ojos, los ojos con memorias de plumas.*

[Like an enormous mirror this bird was God:/containing them all, and not a mere reflection./In his feathers each one found his own feathers/in his eyes, their eyes with memories of feathers.]

Simurgh is inextricable. Behind the Eagle is the personal God of Israel and Rome; behind the magical Simurgh is pantheism.

A final observation. The imaginative power of the legend of the Simurgh is apparent to all; less pronounced, but no less real, is its rigor and economy. The pilgrims go forth in search of an unknown goal; this goal, which will be revealed only at the end, must arouse wonder and not be or appear to be merely added on. The author finds his way out of this difficulty with classical elegance; adroitly, the searchers are what they seek. In identical fashion, David is the secret protagonist of the story told him by Nathan (II Samuel 12); in identical fashion, De Quincey has proposed that the individual man Oedipus, and not man in general, is the profound solution to the riddle of the Theban Sphinx.

[*1948*]   [*EA*]

The Meeting in a Dream

Having traversed the circles of Hell and the arduous terraces of Purgatory, Dante, now in the earthly Paradise, sees Beatrice at last. Ozanam speculates that this scene (certainly one of the most astonishing that literature has achieved) is the primal nucleus of the *Commedia*. My purpose here is to narrate the scene, summarize the comments of the scholiasts, and make an observation—perhaps a new one—of a psychological nature.

On the morning of the thirteenth day of April of the year 1300, the penultimate day of his journey, Dante, his labors complete, enters the earthly Paradise that crowns the summit of Purgatory. He has seen the temporal fire and the eternal, he has crossed through a wall of flame, his will is free and upright. Virgil has crowned and mitred him over himself (*"per ch'io te sovra te corono e mitrio"*). Along the paths of the ancient garden he reaches a river purer than any other, though the trees allow neither sun nor moon to shine on it. A melody runs through the air, and on the other bank a mysterious procession advances. Twenty-four elders, dressed in white garments, and four animals, each plumed with six wings that are studded with open eyes, go before a triumphal chariot drawn by a griffin; on the right are three women, dancing, one of them so red that in a fire she would barely be visible to us; to the left are four more women, dressed in purple, one of them with three eyes. The coach stops, and a veiled woman appears; her dress is the color of living flame. Not by sight, but by the bewilderment of his spirit and the fear in his blood, Dante understands that she is Beatrice. On the threshold of Glory, he feels the love that so often had pierced him in Florence. Like an abashed child, he seeks Virgil's protection, but Virgil is no longer next to him.

Ma Virgilia n'avea lasciati scemi
di sè, Virgilio dolcissimo patre,

Virgilio a cui per mia salute die'mi.
[But Virgil had left us bereft/of himself, Virgil sweetest father,/Virgil to whom I gave myself for my salvation.]

Beatrice calls out his name imperiously. She tells him he should not be weeping for Virgil's disappearance but for his own sins. She asks him ironically how he has condescended to set foot in a place where man is happy. The air has become populated with angels; Beatrice, implacable, enumerates the errors of Dante's ways to them. She says she searched for him in dreams, but in vain, for he had fallen so low that there was no other means for his salvation except to show him the eternally damned. Dante lowers his eyes, mortified; he stammers and weeps. As the fabulous beings listen, Beatrice forces him to make a public confession. . . . Such, in my bad prose, is the aching scene of the first meeting with Beatrice in Paradise. It is curious, as Theophil Spoerri observes (*Einführung in die Göttliche Komödie*, Zurich, 1946): "Undoubtedly Dante himself had envisioned this meeting differently. Nothing in the preceding pages indicates that the greatest humiliation of his life awaits him there."

The commentators decipher the scene figure by figure. The four and twenty preliminary elders of Revelations 4:4 are the twenty-four books of the Old Testament, according to St. Jerome's *Prologus Galeatus.* The animals with six wings are the apostles (Tommaseo) or the Gospels (Lombardi). The six wings are the six laws (Pietro di Dante) or the dispersion of holy doctrine in the six directions of space (Francesco da Buti). The chariot is the universal Church; its two wheels are the two Testaments (Buti) or the active and the contemplative life (Benvenuto da Imola) or St. Dominic and St. Francis (*Paradiso* XII, 106–11) or Justice and Pity (Luigi Pietrobono). The griffin—lion and eagle—is Christ, because of the hypostatic union of the Word with human nature; Didron maintains that it is the Pope "who as pontiff or eagle rises to the throne of God to receive his orders and like a lion or king walks the earth with strength and vigor." The women who dance on the right are the theological virtues; those who dance on the left are the cardinal virtues. The woman with three eyes is Prudence, who sees past, present, and future. Beatrice emerges and Virgil disappears because Virgil is reason and Beatrice faith. Also, according to Vitali, because classical culture was replaced by Christian culture.

The interpretations I have mentioned are undoubtedly worthy of consideration. In logical (not poetic) terms they provide an amply rigorous justification of the text's ambiguous features. Carlo Steiner, after supporting certain of them, writes: "A woman with three eyes is a monster, but the Poet does not submit here to the restraints of art, because it matters much more to him to express the moralities he holds dear. Unmistakable proof that in the soul of this greatest of artists, it was not art that occupied the first place, but love of the Good." Less effusively, Vitali corroborates this view: "His zeal for allegorizing drives Dante to inventions of dubious beauty."

Two facts seem to me to be indisputable. Dante wanted the procession to be beautiful (*"Non che Roma di carro così bello, rallegrasse Affricano"* [Not only did Rome with a chariot so splendid never gladden an Africanus]) and the procession is of a convoluted ugliness. A griffin tied to a chariot, animals with wings that are spotted with open eyes, a green woman, another who is crimson, another with three eyes, a man walking in his sleep: such things seem better suited to the circles of the Inferno than to the realms of Glory. Their horror is undiminished even by the fact that some of these figures proceed from the books of the prophets (*"ma leggi Ezechiel che li dipigne"* [but read Ezekiel who depicts them]) and others from the Revelation of St. John. My reproach is not an anachronism; the other paradisiacal scenes exclude any element of the monstrous.[1]

All the commentators have emphasized Beatrice's severity; some, the ugliness of certain emblems. For me, both anomalies derive from a common origin. This is obviously no more than a conjecture, which I will sketch out in a few words.

To fall in love is to create a religion with a fallible god. That Dante professed an idolatrous adoration for Beatrice is a truth that cannot be contradicted; that she once mocked and on another occasion snubbed him are facts registered in the *Vita nuova*. Some would maintain that these facts are the images of others; if so, this would further reinforce our certainty of an unhappy and superstitious love. With Beatrice dead, Beatrice lost forever, Dante, to assuage his sorrow, played with the fiction of meeting her again. It is my belief that he constructed the triple architecture of his poem in order to insert this encounter into it. What then happened is what often happens in dreams: they are stained by sad obstructions. Such was Dante's case. Forever denied Beatrice, he dreamed of Beatrice, but dreamed her as terribly severe, dreamed her as inaccessible, dreamed her in a chariot pulled by a

---

[1]Having written this, I read in the glosses of Francesco Torraca that in a certain Italian bestiary the griffin is a symbol of the devil (*"Per lo Grifone intendo lo nemico"*). I don't know if it is permissible to add that in the Exeter Codex, the panther, a beast with a melodious voice and delicate breath, is a symbol of the Redeemer.

lion that was a bird and that was all bird or all lion while Beatrice's eyes were awaiting him (*Purgatorio* XXXI, 121). Such images can prefigure a nightmare; and it is a nightmare that begins here and will expand in the next canto. Beatrice disappears; an eagle, a she-fox, and a dragon attack the chariot, and its wheels and body grow feathers: the chariot then sprouts seven heads ("*Trasformato così 'l dificio santo/mise fuor teste*" [Thus transformed, the holy structure put forth heads upon its parts]); a giant and a harlot usurp Beatrice's place.[2]

Beatrice existed infinitely for Dante. Dante very little, perhaps not at all, for Beatrice. All of us tend to forget, out of pity, out of veneration, this grievous discord which for Dante was unforgettable. Reading and rereading the vicissitudes of his illusory meeting, I think of the two lovers that Alighieri dreamed in the hurricane of the second circle and who, whether or not he understood or wanted them to be, were obscure emblems of the joy he did not attain. I think of Paolo and Francesca, forever united in their Inferno: "*questi, che mai da me non fia diviso*" [this one, who never shall be parted from me]. With appalling love, with anxiety, with admiration, with envy.

[1948]   [EA]

---

[2]It could be objected that such ugliness is the reverse of a preceding "Beauty." Of course, but it is significant. . . . Allegorically, the eagle's aggression represents the first persecutions; the she-fox, heresy; the dragon, Satan or Mohammed or the Antichrist; the heads, the deadly sins (Benvenuto da Imola) or the sacraments (Buti); the giant, Philippe IV, known as Philippe le Beau, king of France.

Beatrice's Last Smile

My intention is to comment on the most moving lines literature has achieved. They form part of Canto XXXI of the *Paradiso*, and although they are well known, no one seems to have discerned the weight of sorrow that is in them; no one has fully heard them. True, the tragic substance they contain belongs less to the work than to the author of the work, less to Dante the protagonist than to Dante the author or inventor.

Here is the situation. On the summit of the mountain of Purgatory, Dante loses Virgil. Guided by Beatrice, whose beauty increases with each new circle they reach, he journeys from sphere to concentric sphere until he emerges into the one that encircles all the others, the Primum Mobile. At his feet are the fixed stars; beyond them is the empyrean, no longer the corporeal heaven, but now the eternal heaven, made only of light. They ascend to the empyrean; in this infinite region (as on the canvases of the pre-Raphaelites) distant forms are as sharply distinct as those close by. Dante sees a high river of light, sees bands of angels, sees the manifold rose of paradise formed by the souls of the just, arranged in the shape of an amphitheater. He is suddenly aware that Beatrice has left him. He sees her on high, in one of the circles of the Rose. Like a man who raises his eyes to the thundering heavens from the depths of the sea, he worships and implores her. He gives thanks to her for her beneficent pity and commends his soul to her. The text then says:

> *Così orai; e quella, sì lontana*
> *come parea, sorrise e riguardommi;*
> *poi si tornò all'etterna fontana.*

[So did I pray; and she, so distant/as she seemed, smiled and looked on me, / then turned again to the eternal fountain.]

How to interpret this? The allegorists tell us: reason (Virgil) is an instrument for attaining faith; faith (Beatrice), an instrument for attaining divinity; both are lost once their end is achieved. This explanation, as the reader will have observed, is as irreproachable as it is frigid; never could these lines have emerged from so paltry a schema.

The commentaries I have examined see in Beatrice's smile no more than a symbol of acquiescence. "Final gaze, final smile, but certain promise," Francesco Torraca notes. "She smiles to tell Dante his prayer has been granted; she looks at him to bear witness to him once again of the love she has for him," Luigi Pietrobono confirms. This assertion (shared by Casini) strikes me as apt, but obviously it only grazes the surface of the scene.

Ozanam (*Dante et la philosophie catholique*, 1895) believes that Beatrice's apotheosis was the primal subject of the *Commedia*; Guido Vitali wonders if Dante, in creating his Paradise, was moved, above all, by the prospect of founding a kingdom for his lady. A famous passage of the *Vita nuova* ("I hope to say of her what has never been said of any woman") justifies or allows for this conjecture. I would go further. I suspect that Dante constructed the best book literature has achieved in order to interpolate into it a few encounters with the irrecuperable Beatrice. More exactly, the circles of damnation and the austral Purgatory and the nine concentric circles and the siren and the griffin and Bertrand de Born are the interpolations; a smile and a voice—that he knows to be lost—are what is fundamental. At the beginning of the *Vita nuova* we read that once, in a letter, he listed sixty women's names in order to slip in among them, in secret, the name of Beatrice. I think he repeats this melancholy game in the *Commedia*.

There is nothing unusual about a wretch who imagines joy; all of us, every day, do the same. Dante does as we do, but something always allows us to catch sight of the horror concealed by these glad fictions. A poem by Chesterton speaks of "nightmares of delight"; this oxymoron more or less defines the tercet of the *Paradiso* I have cited. But in Chesterton's phrase the emphasis is on the word *delight;* in the tercet, on *nightmare.*

Let us reconsider the scene. Dante, with Beatrice at his side, is in the empyrean. Above them, immeasurable, arches the Rose of the just. The Rose is distant, but the forms that people it are sharply defined. This contradiction, though justified by the poet (*Paradiso* XXX, 118), is perhaps the first indication of an inner discord. All at once Beatrice is no longer beside him. An elder has taken her place: *"credea ver Beatrice, e vidi un sene"* [I thought to see Beatrice, and I saw an elder]. Dante is barely able to ask where Beatrice is: *"Ov'è ella?"* he cries. The old man shows him one of the circles of the lofty Rose. There, in an aureole of reflected glory, is Beatrice; Beatrice, whose gaze used to suffuse him with intolerable beatitude; Beatrice, who used to dress in red; Beatrice, whom he thought of so constantly that he was astonished by the idea that some pilgrims he saw one morning in Florence had never heard speak of her; Beatrice, who once refused to greet him; Beatrice, who died at the age of twenty-four; Beatrice de Folco Portinari, who married Bardi. Dante gazes at her on high; the azure firmament is no farther from the lowest depths of the sea than she is from him. Dante prays, as if to God, but also as if to a longed-for woman:

> *O donna in cui la mia speranza vige,*
> *e che soffristi per la mia salute*
> *in inferno lasciar le tue vestige*

[O lady, in whom my hope is strong,/and who for my salvation did endure/to leave in Hell your footprints]

Beatrice looks at him a moment and smiles, then turns away toward the eternal fountain of light.

Francesco De Sanctis (*Storia della letteratura italiana* VII) understands the passage thus: "When Beatrice withdraws, Dante does not utter a single lament: all earthly residue in him has been consumed and destroyed." This is true if we think of the poet's intention; erroneous, if we think of his emotion.

We must keep one incontrovertible fact in mind, a single, humble fact: the scene was *imagined* by Dante. For us, it is very real; for him, it was less so. (The reality, for him, was that first life and then death had taken Beatrice from him.) Forever absent from Beatrice, alone and perhaps humiliated, he imagined the scene in order to imagine he was with her. Unhappily for him, happily for the centuries that would read him, his consciousness that the meeting was imaginary distorted the vision. Hence the appalling circumstances, all the more infernal for taking place in the empyrean: the disappearance of Beatrice, the elder who replaces her, her abrupt elevation to the Rose, the fleetingness of her glance and smile, the eternal turning away of the face.[1] The horror shows through in the words: *come parea* refers to *lontana* but contaminates *sorrise,* and therefore Longfellow could translate, in his 1867 version:

[1] The Blessed Damozel painted by Rossetti, who had translated the *Vita nuova*, is also unhappy in paradise.

Thus I implored; and she, so far away,
Smiled as it seemed, and looked once more at me . . .

And *eterna* seems to contaminate *si tornò*.

[1945–51/1982]   *[EA]*

VI

1946-1955

Our Poor Individualism

There is no end to the illusions of patriotism. In the first century of our era, Plutarch mocked those who declared that the Athenian moon is better than the Corinthian moon; Milton, in the seventeenth, observed that God is in the habit of revealing Himself first to His Englishmen; Fichte, at the beginning of the nineteenth, declared that to have character and to be German are obviously one and the same thing. Here in Argentina we are teeming with nationalists, driven, they claim, by the worthy or innocent resolve of promoting the best traits of the Argentine people. Yet they ignore the Argentine people; in their polemics they prefer to define them as a function of some external fact, the Spanish conquistadors, say, or an imaginary Catholic tradition, or "Saxon imperialism."

The Argentine, unlike the Americans of the North and almost all Europeans, does not identify with the State. This is attributable to the circumstance that the governments in this country tend to be awful, or to the general fact that the State is an inconceivable abstraction.[1] One thing is certain: the Argentine is an individual, not a citizen. Aphorisms such as Hegel's "The State is the reality of the moral idea" strike him as sinister jokes. Films made in Hollywood often hold up for admiration the case of a man (usually a journalist) who seeks out the friendship of a criminal in order to hand him over to the police; the Argentine, for whom friendship is a passion and the police a mafia, feels that this "hero" is an incomprehensible swine. He feels with Don Quixote that "everybody hath sins of his own to answer for" and that "it is not seemly, that honest men should be the executioners of their fellow-creatures, on account of matters with which they have no concern" (*Quixote* I, XXII). More than once, confronted with the vain symmetries of the Spanish style, I have suspected that we are irredeemably differ-

---

[1] The State is impersonal; the Argentine can only conceive of personal relations. Therefore, to him, robbing public funds is not a crime. I am noting a fact; I am not justifying or excusing it.

ent from Spain; these two lines from the *Quixote* have sufficed to convince me of my error; they seem to be the secret, tranquil symbol of our affinity. This is profoundly confirmed by a single night in Argentine literature: the desperate night when a sergeant in the rural police shouted that he was not going to consent to the crime of killing a brave man, and started fighting against his own soldiers alongside the fugitive Martín Fierro.

The world, for the European, is a cosmos in which each individual personally corresponds to the role he plays; for the Argentine, it is a chaos. The European and the North American consider that a book that has been awarded any kind of prize must be good; the Argentine allows for the possibility that the book might not be bad, despite the prize. In general, the Argentine does not believe in circumstances. He may be unaware of the fable that humanity always includes thirty-six just men—the Lamed Wufniks—who are unknown to one another, but who secretly sustain the universe; if he hears of it, it does not strike him as strange that these worthies are obscure and anonymous. . . . His popular hero is the lone man who quarrels with the group, either actually (Fierro, Moreira, the Black Ant), potentially, or in the past (Segundo Sombra). Other literatures do not record analogous events. Consider, for example, two great European writers: Kipling and Franz Kafka. At first glance, the two have nothing in common, but Kipling's subject is the defense of order, of an order (the road in *Kim*, the bridge in *The Bridge-Builders*, the Roman wall in *Puck of Pook's Hill*); Kafka's, the unbearable, tragic solitude of the individual who lacks even the lowliest place in the order of the universe.

It may be said that the traits I have pointed out are merely negative or anarchic; it may be added that they are not subject to political explanation. I shall venture to suggest the opposite. The most urgent problem of our time (already denounced with prophetic lucidity by the near-forgotten Spencer) is the gradual interference of the State in the acts of the individual; in the battle with this evil, whose names are communism and Nazism, Argentine individualism, though perhaps useless or harmful until now, will find its justification and its duties.

Without hope and with nostalgia, I think of the abstract possibility of a party that had some affinity with the Argentine people; a party that would promise (let us say) a strict minimum of government.

Nationalism seeks to captivate us with the vision of an infinitely tiresome State; this utopia, once established on earth, would have the providential virtue of making everyone yearn for, and finally build, its antithesis.

[1946]   [EA]

The Paradox of Apollinaire

With some obvious exceptions (Montaigne, Saint-Simon, Bloy), we can safely affirm that France tends to produce its literature in conformity with the history of that literature. If we compare manuals of French literature (Lanson's, for example, or Thibaudet's) with their English equivalents (Saintsbury's or Sampson's), we discover, not without surprise, that the latter consist of conceivable human beings, and the former, of schools, manifestos, generations, avant-gardes, rear guards, lefts and rights, cenacles, and allusions to the tortuous fate of Captain Dreyfus. The strangest part is that reality corresponds to those frantic abstractions: before writing a line, the Frenchman wants to understand, define, classify himself. The Englishman writes in good faith, the Frenchman in favor of *a*, against *b*, conforming to *c*, toward *d*. . . . He wonders (let us say): What kind of sonnet would be composed by a young atheist with a Catholic background, born and bred in Nivernais but of Breton stock, and affiliated with the Communist Party since 1944? Or, more technically: How should one apply the vocabulary and methods of Zola's *Les Rougon-Macquart* to the elaboration of an epic poem on the fishermen of Morbihan, combining Fénelon's ardor with Rabelais' garrulous profusion and, of course, without ignoring a psychoanalytical interpretation of the figure of Merlin? This system of premeditation, the mark of French literature, fills its pages with compositions of a classical rigor, but also with fortunate, or unfortunate, extravagances. In fact, when a French man of letters professes a doctrine, he always applies it to the end, with a kind of ferocious integrity. Racine and Mallarmé are the same writer (I hope this metaphor is acceptable), executing with the same decorum two dissimilar tasks. . . . To mock excessive forethought is not difficult; it is important to remember, however, that it has produced French literature, perhaps the finest in the world.

Of all the obligations that an author can impose upon himself, the most common and doubtless the most harmful is that of being modern. *"Il faut être absolument moderne"* [One must be absolutely modern], Rimbaud decided, a temporal limitation corresponding to the triviality of the nationalist who brags of being hermetically Danish or inextricably Argentine. Schopenhauer (*Welt als Wille und Vorstellung* II, 15) concludes that the greatest imperfection of the human intellect is its successive, linear character, its tie to the present; to venerate that imperfection is an unfortunate whim. Guillaume Apollinaire embraced, justified, and preached it to his contemporaries. What is more, he devoted himself to that imperfection. He did so—remember the poem *"La Jolie Rousse"*—with an admirable and clear conscience of the sad dangers of his adventure.

Those dangers were real; today, like yesterday, the general value of Apollinaire's work is more documentary than aesthetic. We visit it to recover the flavor of the "modern" poetry of the first decades of our century. Not a single line allows us to forget the date on which it was written—an error not incurred, for example, in the contemporary works of Valéry, Rilke, Yeats, Joyce. . . . (Perhaps, for the future, the only achievement of "modern" literature will be the unfathomable *Ulysses*, which in some way justifies, includes, and goes beyond the other texts.)

To place Apollinaire's name next to Rilke's might seem anachronistic, so close is the latter to us, so distant (already) is the former. However, *Das Buch der Bilder* [The Book of Pictures], which includes the inexhaustible *"Herbsttag"* [Autumn Day], is from 1902; *Calligrammes*, from 1918. Apollinaire, adorning his compositions with trolleys, airplanes, and other vehicles, did not identify with his times, which are our times.

For the writers of 1918, the war was what Tiberius Claudius Nero was for a professor of rhetoric: "mud kneaded with blood." They all perceived it thus, Unruh as well as Barbusse, Wilfred Owen as well as Sassoon, the solitary Klemm as well as the frequented Remarque. (Paradoxically, one of the first poets to emphasize the monotony, tedium, desperation, and physical humiliations of contemporary war was Rudyard Kipling, in his *Barrack-Room Ballads* of 1903.) For Artillery Lieutenant Guillaume Apollinaire, war was, above all, a beautiful spectacle. His poems and his letters express this. Guillermo de Torre, the most devoted and lucid of his critics, observes: "In the long nights of the trenches, the soldier-poet could contemplate the sky starred with mortar fire, and imagine new constellations." Thus Apollinaire fancied himself attending a dazzling spectacle in *"La Nuit d'avril 1915"*:

> *Le ciel est étoilé par les obus des Boches*
> *La forêt merveilleuse où je vis donne un bal*

[The sky is starry with Boche shells/The marvelous forest where I live is giving a ball]

A letter dated July 2 confirms this: "War is decidedly a beautiful thing and, despite all the risks I run, the exhaustion, the total lack of water, of everything, I am not unhappy to be here. . . . The place is very desolate, neither water, nor trees, nor villages are here, only the super-metallic, arch-thundering war."

The meaning of a sentence, like that of an isolated word, depends on the context, which sometimes can be the entire life of its author. Thus the phrase "war is a beautiful thing" allows for many interpretations. Uttered by a South American dictator, it could express his hope of throwing incendiary bombs on the capital of a neighboring country. Coming from a journalist, it could signify his firm intention to adulate that dictator in order to obtain a good position in his administration. A sedentary man of letters could be suggesting his nostalgia for a life of adventure. For Guillaume Apollinaire, on the battlefields of France, it signifies, I believe, a frame of mind that ignores horror effortlessly, an acceptance of destiny, a kind of fundamental innocence. It is not unlike that Norwegian who conquered six feet of English earth and, what is more, nicknamed the battle Viking Feast; not unlike the immortal and unknown author of the *Chanson de Roland*, singing to the brilliance of a sword:

> *E Durendal, cum ies clere et blanche*
> *Cuntre soleil si reluis et refeambes*
[And Durendal, how you are bright and white/Against the sun you glitter and shine]

Apollinaire's line, "The marvelous forest where I live is giving a ball," is not a rigorous description of the artillery exchanges of 1915, but it is an accurate portrait of Apollinaire. Although he lived his days among the *baladins* of Cubism and Futurism, he was not a modern man. He was somewhat less complex and more happy, more ancient, and stronger. (He was so unmodern that modernity seemed picturesque, and perhaps even moving, to him.) He was the "winged and sacred thing" of Platonic dialogue; he was a man of elemental and, therefore, eternal feelings; he was, when the fundaments of earth and sky shook, the poet of ancient courage and ancient honor. His legacy is these pages that move us like the nearness of the sea: "*La Chanson du mal-aimé*," "*Désir*," "*Merveilles de la guerre*," "*Tristesse d'une étoile*," "*La Jolie Rousse*."

[1946]   [SJL]

On Oscar Wilde

To speak Wilde's name is to speak of a dandy who was also a poet; it is to evoke the image of a gentleman dedicated to the meager proposition of shocking by means of cravats and metaphors. It is also to evoke the notion of art as an elite or occult game—as in the tapestries of Hugh Vereker or of Stefan George—and the poet as a laborious *"monstrorum artifex"* [maker of monsters] (Pliny, XXVIII). It is to evoke the tired crepuscule of the nineteenth century, with its oppressive pomp of hothouse and masked ball. None of these evocations is false, but all of them, I maintain, correspond to partial truths, and contradict or disregard well-known facts.

Let us consider, for example, the idea that Wilde was a kind of symbolist. A nebula of circumstances supports it: in 1881, Wilde was the leader of the aesthetes, and ten years later of the decadents; Rebecca West perfidiously accuses him (*Henry James*, III) of giving the second of these two sects "the middle-class touch"; the vocabulary of the poem "The Sphinx" is studiously magnificent; Wilde was a friend to Schwob and to Mallarmé. The notion is refuted, however, by an essential fact: in verse or in prose, Wilde's syntax is always very simple. Of the many British writers, none is so accessible to foreigners. Readers who are incapable of deciphering a single paragraph by Kipling or a stanza of William Morris begin reading *Lady Windermere's Fan* and finish it that same afternoon. Wilde's meter is spontaneous, or seeks to appear spontaneous; his complete work does not include a single experimental line such as this hard and wise Alexandrine by Lionel Johnson: "Alone with Christ, desolate else, left by mankind."

Wilde's *technical* insignificance may be an argument in favor of his intrinsic greatness. If Wilde's work corresponded to the nature of his fame, it would consist merely of artifices, after the fashion of *Les Palais nomades* or *Los crepúsculos del jardín*. In Wilde's work such artifices are numerous—we can mention the eleventh chapter of *Dorian Gray* or "The Harlot's House" or "Symphony in Yellow"—but their adjectival nature is obvious. Wilde can do without these "purple patches," a phrase Ricketts and Hesketh Pearson credit him with coining, but which is already inscribed in the preamble to Cicero's *In Pisonem*. This misattribution is proof of the custom of linking the notion of decorative passages to Wilde's name.

Reading and rereading Wilde over the years, I note a fact that his panegyrists seem not even to have suspected: the elementary and demonstrable fact that Wilde is nearly always right. "The Soul of Man under Socialism" is not only eloquent; it is correct. The miscellaneous notes he so copiously contributed to the *Pall Mall Gazette* and the *Speaker* abound in limpid observations that exceed the very best abilities of Leslie Stephen or Saintsbury. Wilde has been accused of practicing a kind of *ars combinatoria,* in the manner of Ramón Llull; this may be applicable to certain of his jokes ("One of those British faces which, once seen, are always forgotten") but not to the pronouncement that music reveals to us an unknown and perhaps real past ("The Critic as Artist"), or that all men kill the thing they love (*The Ballad of Reading Gaol*), or that to repent of an action is to modify the past (*De Profundis*), or that—and the statement is not unworthy of León Bloy or Swedenborg[1]—there is no man who is not, at each moment, all that he has been and will be (*De Profundis*). I do not transcribe these lines so that the reader may revere them; I produce them as signs of a mentality that differs greatly from the one generally attributed to Wilde. If I am not mistaken, he was much more than a sort of Irish Moréas; he was a man of the eighteenth century who occasionally condescended to the games of symbolism. Like Gibbon, like Johnson, like Voltaire, he was a wit; a wit who was also right. He existed "in order, at last, to speak fateful words, in short, a classic."[2] He gave the century what the century demanded—*comédies larmoyantes* for the majority and verbal arabesques for the few—and he accomplished these dissimilar things with a kind of negligent felicity. Perfection has injured him; his work is so harmonious that it can seem inevitable and even banal. It takes an effort for us to imagine the universe without Wilde's epigrams; that difficulty does not make them any less plausible.

A passing observation. The name of Oscar Wilde is linked to the cities

---

[1] Cf. the curious hypothesis of Leibniz, which so scandalized Arnauld: "The concept of each individual encloses *a priori* all the events that will happen to him." According to this dialectical fatalism, the fact that Alexander the Great would die in Babylon is one of the qualities of that king, like pride.

[2] The phrase is from Reyes, who applies it to the Mexican man (*Reloj de sol,* 158).

of the plain; his glory, to condemnation and jail. Yet (and Hesketh Pearson has sensed this well), the fundamental flavor of his work is happiness. By contrast, the estimable work of Chesterton, that prototype of physical and moral health, is always on the point of becoming a nightmare. Horrors and things diabolical lurk within it; the most innocuous page can take on the forms of terror. Chesterton is a man who wishes to recover childhood; Wilde, a man who retains, despite the habits of wickedness and misfortune, an invulnerable innocence.

Like Chesterton, like Lang, like Boswell, Wilde is one of the fortunates who can forego the approval of critics and even, at times, of the reader, because the delight we derive from his company is constant and irresistible.

[1946]   *[EA]*

A New Refutation of Time

Vor mir keine Zeit, nach mir wird keine seyn.
Mit mir gebiert sie sich, mit mir geht sie auch ein.
[Before me there was no time, after me there will be none./With me it is
born, with me it will also die.]
     —Daniel von Czepko, *Sexcenta Monidisticha Sapientum* III, II (1655)

Preliminary Note

Had this refutation (or its title) been published in the middle of the eighteenth century, it would be included in a bibliography by Hume, or at least
mentioned by Huxley or Kemp Smith. But published in 1947 (after Bergson) it is the anachronistic *reductio ad absurdum* of an obsolete system, or
even worse, the feeble artifice of an Argentine adrift on a sea of metaphysics. Both conjectures are plausible and perhaps even true, but I cannot
promise some startling new conclusion on the basis of my rudimentary dialectics. The thesis I shall expound is as old as Zeno's arrow or the chariot of
the Greek king in the *Milinda Pañha*; its novelty, if any, consists in applying
to my ends the classic instrument of Berkeley. Both he and his successor
David Hume abound in paragraphs that contradict or exclude my thesis;
nonetheless, I believe I have deduced the inevitable consequence of their
doctrine.

The first article (A) was written in 1944 and appeared in number 115 of
Sur; the second, from 1946, is a revision of the first. I have deliberately refrained from making the two into one, deciding that two similar texts could
enhance the reader's comprehension of such an unwieldy subject.

A word on the title: I am not unaware that it is an example of that monster called a *contradictio in adjecto* by logicians, for to say that a refutation of

time is new (or old, for that matter) is to recognize a temporal predicate that restores the very notion the subject intends to destroy. But I shall let this fleeting joke stand to prove, at least, that I do not exaggerate the importance of wordplay. In any case, language is so saturated and animated by time that, quite possibly, not a single line in all these pages fails to require or invoke it.

I dedicate these exercises to my ancestor Juan Crisótomo Lafinur (1797–1824), who left a memorable poem or two to Argentine letters and who strove to reform the teaching of philosophy by refining out traces of theology and by explaining the theories of Locke and Condillac in his courses. He died in exile: as with all men, it was his lot to live in bad times.[1]

Buenos Aires, December 23, 1946

A

I

In the course of a life dedicated to belles-lettres and, occasionally, to the perplexities of metaphysics, I have glimpsed or foreseen a refutation of time, one in which I myself do not believe, but which tends to visit me at night and in the hours of weary twilight with the illusory force of a truism. This refutation is to be found, in one form or another, in all of my books. It is prefigured in the poems "Inscription on Any Tomb" and "Truco" in my *Fervor of Buenos Aires* (1923); it is openly stated on a certain page of *Evaristo Carriego;* and in the story "Feeling in Death," which I transcribe below. None of these texts satisfies me, not even the last on the list, which is less logical and explanatory than sentimental and divinatory. I will attempt, in this present writing, to establish a basis for them all.

Two arguments led me to this refutation of time: Berkeley's idealism and Leibniz's principle of indiscernibles.

---

[1]All expositions of Buddhism mention the *Milinda Pañha*, an Apology from the second century; this work recounts a debate between the king of the Bactrians, Menander, and the monk Nagasena. The latter argues that just as the king's chariot is not the wheels nor the chassis nor the axle nor the shaft nor the yoke, neither is man matter nor form nor impressions nor ideas nor instincts nor consciousness. He is not the combination of those parts, nor does he exist outside them. . . . After this discussion, which lasts several days, Menander (Milinda) converts to the faith of the Buddha. The *Milinda Pañha* has been rendered into English by Rhys Davids (Oxford, 1890–94).

Berkeley (*The Principles of Human Knowledge*, par. 3) observed:

That neither our thoughts, nor passions, nor ideas formed by the imagination, exist without the mind is what everybody will allow. And to me it is no less evident that the various *Sensations* or *ideas imprinted on the sense,* however blended or combined together (that is, whatever *objects* they compose), cannot exist otherwise than in a mind perceiving them. . . . The table I write on, I say exists, that is, I see and feel it; and if I were out of my study I should say it existed—meaning thereby that if I was in my study I might perceive it, or that some other spirit actually does perceive it. . . . For as to what is said of the absolute existence of unthinking things without any relation to their being perceived, that is to me perfectly unintelligible. Their *esse* is *percipi,* nor is it possible they should have any existence out of the minds or thinking things which perceive them.

In paragraph 23 he added, foreseeing objections:

But, say you, surely there is nothing easier than for me to imagine trees, for instance, in a park, or books existing in a closet, and nobody by to perceive them. I answer, you may so, there is no difficulty in it; but what is all this, I beseech you, more than framing in *your* mind certain ideas which you call books and trees, and at the same time omitting to frame the idea of anyone that may perceive them? But do not you yourself perceive or think of them all the while? This therefore is nothing to the purpose; it only shews you have the power of imagining or forming ideas in your mind: but it doth not shew that you can conceive it possible that the objects of your thought may exist without the mind.

In another paragraph, number 6, he had already declared:

Some truths there are so near and obvious to the mind that a man need only open his eyes to see them. Such I take this important one to be, viz., that all the choir of heaven and furniture of the earth, in a word all those bodies which compose the mighty frame of the world have not any subsistence without a mind—that their *being* is *to be perceived or known;* that consequently so long as they are not actually perceived by me, or do not exist in my mind or that of any other created spirit, they must either have no existence at all, or else subsist in the mind of some Eternal Spirit.

Such is, in the words of its inventor, the idealist doctrine. To understand it is easy; the difficulty lies in thinking within its limitations. Schopenhauer himself, in expounding it, is guilty of some negligence. In the first lines of his book *Die Welt als Wille und Vorstellung*—from the year 1819—he formulates the following declaration, which makes him a creditor as regards the sum total of imperishable human perplexity: "The world is my representation. The man who confesses this truth clearly understands that he does not know a sun nor an earth, but only some eyes which see a sun and a hand which feels an earth." That is, for the idealist Schopenhauer, a man's eyes and hands are less illusory or unreal than the earth or the sun. In 1844 he publishes a supplementary volume. In the first chapter he rediscovers and aggravates the previous error: he defines the universe as a cerebral phenomenon, and he distinguishes between the "world in the head" and the "world outside the head." Berkeley, nevertheless, will have made his Philonous say, in 1713: "The brain therefore you speak of, being a sensible thing, exists only in the mind. Now, I would fain know whether you think it reasonable to suppose, that one idea or thing existing in the mind, occasions all other ideas. And if you think so, pray how do you account for the origin of that primary idea or brain itself?" To Schopenhauer's dualism, or cerebralism, Spiller's monism may legitimately be counterposed. Spiller (*The Mind of Man* [1902], chap. 8) argues that the retina, and the cutaneous surface invoked to explain visual and tactile phenomena, are in turn two tactile and visual systems, and that the room we see (the "objective" one) is no greater than the imagined ("cerebral") one, and that the former does not contain the latter, since two independent visual systems are involved. Berkeley (*The Principles of Human Knowledge*, 10 and 116) likewise denied primary qualities—the solidity and extension of things—or the existence of absolute space.

Berkeley affirmed the continuous existence of objects, inasmuch as when no individual perceives them, God does. Hume, with greater logic, denied this existence (*A Treatise of Human Nature* I, 4, 2). Berkeley affirmed personal identity, "for I myself am not my ideas, but somewhat else, a thinking, active principle that perceives" (*Dialogues*, 3). Hume, the skeptic, refuted this belief, and made each man "a bundle or collection of different perceptions, which succeed each other with an inconceivable rapidity" (I, 4, 6). Both men affirmed the existence of time: for Berkeley it is "the succession of ideas in my mind, flowing uniformly, and participated in by all beings" (*The Principles of Human Knowledge*, 98). For Hume, it is "a succession of indivisible moments" (I, 2, 2).

I have accumulated quotations from the apologists of idealism, I have provided their canonical passages, I have reiterated and explained, I have censured Schopenhauer (not without ingratitude), to help my reader penetrate this unstable world of the mind. A world of evanescent impressions; a world without matter or spirit, neither objective nor subjective; a world without the ideal architecture of space; a world made of time, of the absolute uniform time of the *Principia;* an inexhaustible labyrinth, a chaos, a dream—the almost complete disintegration that David Hume reached.

Once the idealist argument is accepted, I believe that it is possible—perhaps inevitable—to go further. For Hume, it is not justifiable to speak of the form of the moon or its color: its form and color are the moon. Neither can one speak of the mind's perceptions, inasmuch as the mind is nothing but a series of perceptions. The Cartesian "I think, therefore I am" is thus invalid: to say I think is to postulate the I, a *petitio principii.* In the eighteenth century, Lichtenberg proposed that instead of "I think," we should say impersonally "It thinks," as we say "It thunders" or "There is lightning." I repeat: there is not, behind the face, a secret self governing our acts or receiving our impressions; we are only the series of those imaginary acts and those errant impressions. The series? If we deny matter and spirit, which are continuities, and if we also deny space, I do not know what right we have to the continuity that is time. Let us imagine a present moment, any one at all. A night on the Mississippi. Huckleberry Finn wakes up. The raft, lost in the shadows of twilight, continues downstream. It may be a bit cold. Huckleberry Finn recognizes the soft, ceaseless sound of the water. Negligently he opens his eyes: he sees an indefinite number of stars, a nebulous line of trees. Then he sinks into a sleep without memories, as into dark waters.[2] Metaphysical idealism declares that to add to these perceptions a material substance (the object) and a spiritual substance (the subject) is precarious and vain. I maintain that it is no less illogical to think that they are terms in a series whose beginning is as inconceivable as its end. To add to the river and the riverbank perceived by Huck the notion of yet another substantive river with another riverbank, to add yet another perception to that immediate network of perceptions, is altogether unjustifiable in the eyes of idealism. In my eyes, it is no less unjustifiable to add a chronological precision: for instance, the fact that the above-mentioned event should have

---

[2]For the reader's convenience I have chosen a moment between two intervals of sleep, a literary, not a historical, instant. If anyone suspects a fallacy, he can insert another example, if he wants, one from his own life.

taken place on the night of June 7, 1849, between 4:10 and 4:11. In other words, I deny, using the arguments of idealism, the vast temporal series that idealism permits. Hume denied the existence of an absolute space, in which each thing has its place; I deny the existence of one single time, in which all events are linked. To deny coexistence is no less difficult than to deny succession.

I deny, in a large number of instances, the existence of succession. I deny, in a large number of instances, simultaneity as well. The lover who thinks, "While I was so happy, thinking about the faithfulness of my beloved, she was busy deceiving me," is deceiving himself. If every state in which we live is absolute, that happiness was not concurrent with that betrayal. The discovery of that betrayal is merely one more state, incapable of modifying "previous" states, though not incapable of modifying their recollection. Today's misfortune is no more real than yesterday's good fortune. I will look for a more concrete example: At the beginning of August 1824, Captain Isidoro Suárez, at the head of a squadron of Peruvian hussars, assured the Victory of Junín; at the beginning of August 1824, De Quincey issued a diatribe against *Wilhelm Meisters Lehrjahre;* these deeds were not contemporaneous (they are now), inasmuch as the two men died—the one in the city of Montevideo, the other in Edinburgh—knowing nothing of each other. . . . Every instant is autonomous. Not vengeance nor pardon nor jails nor even oblivion can modify the invulnerable past. No less vain to my mind are hope and fear, for they always refer to future events, that is, to events which will not happen to us, who are the diminutive present. They tell me that the present, the "specious present" of the psychologists, lasts between several seconds and the smallest fraction of a second, which is also how long the history of the universe lasts. Or better, there is no such thing as "the life of a man," nor even "one night in his life." Each moment we live exists, not the imaginary combination of these moments. The universe, the sum total of all events, is no less ideal than the sum of all the horses—one, many, none?—Shakespeare dreamed between 1592 and 1594. I might add that if time is a mental process, how can it be shared by countless, or even two different men?

The argument set forth in the preceding paragraphs, interrupted and encumbered by examples, may seem intricate. I shall try a more direct method. Let us consider a life in which repetitions abound: my life, for instance. I never pass the Recoleta cemetery without remembering that my father, my grandparents, and my great-grandparents are buried there, as I shall be; then I remember that I have remembered the same thing many times before; I cannot stroll around the outskirts of my neighborhood in the solitude of night without thinking that night is pleasing to us because, like memory, it erases idle details; I cannot lament the loss of a love or a friendship without reflecting how one loses only what one really never had; each time I cross one of the southside corners, I think of you, Helena; each time the air brings me the scent of eucalyptus I think of Adrogué in my childhood; each time I recall fragment 91 of Heraclitus, "You cannot step into the same river twice," I admire his dialectical skill, for the facility with which we accept the first meaning ("The river is another") covertly imposes upon us the second meaning ("I am another") and gives us the illusion of having invented it; each time I hear a Germanophile deride Yiddish, I reflect that Yiddish is, after all, a German dialect, barely tainted by the language of the Holy Ghost. These tautologies (and others I shall not disclose) are my whole life. Naturally, they recur without design; there are variations of emphasis, temperature, light, general physiological state. I suspect, nonetheless, that the number of circumstantial variants is not infinite: we can postulate, in the mind of an individual (or of two individuals who do not know each other but in whom the same process is operative), two identical moments. Once this identity is postulated, we may ask: Are not these identical moments the same moment? Is not one single repeated terminal point enough to disrupt and confound the series in time? Are the enthusiasts who devote themselves to a line of Shakespeare not literally Shakespeare?

I am still not certain of the ethics of the system I have outlined, nor do I know whether it exists. The fifth paragraph of chapter IV in the *Sanhedrin* of the Mishnah declares that, in the eyes of God, he who kills a single man destroys the world. If there is no plurality, he who annihilated all men would be no more guilty than the primitive and solitary Cain—an orthodox view—nor more global in his destruction—which may be magic, or so I understand it. Tumultuous and universal catastrophes—fires, wars, epidemics—are but a single sorrow, multiplied in many illusory mirrors. Thus Bernard Shaw surmises (*Guide to Socialism*, 86):

> What you yourself can suffer is the utmost that can be suffered on earth. If you starve to death, you experience all the starvation that ever has been or ever can be. If ten thousand other women starve to death with you, their suffering is not increased by a single pang: their share in your fate does not make you ten thousand times as hungry, nor prolong

your suffering ten thousand times. Therefore do not be oppressed by "the frightful sum of human suffering": there is no sum. . . . Poverty and pain are not cumulative.

(Cf. also C. S. Lewis, *The Problem of Pain* VII.)

Lucretius (*De rerum natura* I, 830) attributes to Anaxagoras the doctrine that gold consists of particles of gold; fire, of sparks; bone, of imperceptible little bones. Josiah Royce, perhaps influenced by St. Augustine, proposes that time is made up of time and that "every now within which something happens is therefore *also* a succession" (*The World and the Individual* II, 139). That proposition is compatible with my essay.

II

All language is of a successive nature; it does not lend itself to reasoning on eternal, intemporal matters. Those readers who are displeased with the preceding arguments may prefer this note from 1928, titled "Feeling in Death," which I mentioned earlier:

> I wish to record here an experience I had some nights ago, a trifling matter too evanescent and ecstatic to be called an adventure, too irrational and sentimental to be called a thought. I am speaking of a scene and its word, a word I had said before but had not lived with total involvement until that night. I shall describe it now, with the incidents of time and place that happened to reveal it. This is how I remember it: I had spent the afternoon in Barracas, a place I rarely visited, a place whose distance from the scene of my later wanderings lent a strange aura to that day. As I had nothing to do that night and the weather was fair, I went out after dinner to walk and remember. I had no wish to have a set destination; I followed a random course, as much as possible; I accepted, with no conscious anticipation other than avoiding the avenues or wide streets, the most obscure invitations of chance. A kind of familiar gravitation, however, drew me toward places whose name I shall always remember, for they arouse in me a certain reverence. I am not speaking of the specific surroundings of my childhood, my own neighborhood, but of its still mysterious borders, which I have possessed in words but little in reality, a zone that is familiar and mythological at the same time. The opposite of the known—its reverse

side—are those streets to me, almost as completely hidden as the buried foundation of our house or our invisible skeleton. My walk brought me to a corner. I breathed the night, in peaceful respite from thought. The vision before me, in no way complicated, in any case seemed simplified by my fatigue. It was so typical that it seemed unreal. It was a street of low houses, and although the first impression was poverty, the second was undoubtedly joyous. The street was both very poor and very lovely. No house stood out on the street; a fig tree cast a shadow over a corner wall; the street doors—higher than the lines extending along the walls—seemed made of the same infinite substance as the night. The sidewalk sloped up the street, a street of elemental clay, the clay of a still unconquered America. Farther away, the narrow street dwindled into the pampa, toward Maldonado. Over the muddy, chaotic earth a red pink wall seemed not to harbor moonglow but to shed a light of its own. There is probably no better way to name tenderness than that red pink.

I stood looking at that simple scene. I thought, no doubt aloud: "This is the same as it was thirty years ago. . . ." I guessed at the date: a recent time in other countries, but already remote in this changing part of the world. Perhaps a bird was singing and I felt for him a small, bird-size affection; but most probably the only noise in this vertiginous silence was the equally timeless sound of the crickets. The easy thought *I am somewhere in the 1800s* ceased to be a few careless words and became profoundly real. I felt dead, I felt I was an abstract perceiver of the world, struck by an undefined fear imbued with science, or the supreme clarity of metaphysics. No, I did not believe I had traversed the presumed waters of Time; rather I suspected that I possessed the reticent or absent meaning of the inconceivable word *eternity*. Only later was I able to define these imaginings.

Now I shall transcribe it thus: that pure representation of homogeneous facts—calm night, limpid wall, rural scent of honeysuckle, elemental clay—is not merely identical to the scene on that corner so many years ago; it is, without similarities or repetitions, the same. If we can intuit that sameness, time is a delusion: the impartiality and inseparability of one moment of time's apparent yesterday and another of time's apparent today are enough to make it disintegrate.

It is evident that the number of these human moments is not infinite. The basic elemental moments are even more impersonal—physical suffering and physical pleasure, the approach of sleep, listening to a single piece of music, moments of great intensity or great dejection. I have reached, in advance, the following conclusion: life is too impoverished not to be also immortal. But we do not even possess the certainty of our poverty, inasmuch as time, easily denied by the senses, is not so easily denied by the intellect, from whose essence the concept of succession seems inseparable. So then, let my glimpse of an idea remain as an emotional anecdote; let the real moment of ecstasy and the possible insinuation of eternity which that night lavished on me, remain confined to this sheet of paper, openly unresolved.

B

Of the many doctrines recorded in the history of philosophy, idealism is perhaps the most ancient and most widely divulged. The observation is Carlyle's (*Novalis*, 1829). Without hope of completing the infinite list, one could add to the philosophers he mentioned the Platonists, for whom the only realities are archetypes (Norris, Judah Abrabanel, Gemistus, Plotinus); the theologians, for whom everything that is not the divinity is provisional (Malebranche, Johannes Eckhart); the monists, who make the universe a vain adjective of the Absolute (Bradley, Hegel, Parmenides). . . . Idealism is as ancient as metaphysical angst. Its most clever apologist, George Berkeley, flourished in the eighteenth century. Contrary to what Schopenhauer declared (*Die Welt als Wille und Vorstellung* II, 1), his merit did not consist in the intuitive perception of that doctrine, but in the arguments he conceived to rationalize it. Berkeley used those arguments against the notion of matter; Hume applied them to consciousness; I propose to apply them to time. First I shall briefly summarize the various stages of this dialectic.

Berkeley denied matter. This did not mean, of course, that he denied colors, smells, tastes, sounds, and tactile sensations; what he denied was that aside from these perceptions—components of the external world—there might be something invisible, intangible, called matter. He denied that there were pains no one feels, colors no one sees, forms no one touches. He argued that to add matter to perceptions is to add to the world another inconceivable and superfluous world. He believed in the world of appearances fabricated by our senses, but he considered that the material world (Toland's, say) was an illusory duplication. He observed (*The Principles of Human Knowledge*, para. 3):

That neither our thoughts, nor passions, nor ideas formed by the imagination, exist without the mind, is what everybody will allow. And to me it is no less evident that the various *Sensations* or *ideas imprinted on the sense*, however blended or combined together (that is, whatever *objects* they compose), cannot exist otherwise than in a mind perceiving them. . . . The table I write on I say exists, that is, I see and feel it; and if I were out of my study I should say it existed—meaning thereby that if I was in my study I might perceive it, or that some other spirit actually does perceive it. . . . For as to what is said of the absolute existence of unthinking things without any relation to their being perceived, that is to me perfectly unintelligible. Their *esse* is *percipi,* nor is it possible they should have any existence out of the minds or thinking things which perceive them.

Foreseeing objections, he added in paragraph 23:

But, say you, surely there is nothing easier than for me to imagine trees, for instance, in a park, or books existing in a closet, and nobody by to perceive them. I answer, you may so, there is no difficulty in it; but what is all this, I beseech you, more than framing in *your* mind certain ideas which you call books and trees, and at the same time omitting to frame the idea of any one that may perceive them? But do not you yourself perceive or think of them all the while? This therefore is nothing to the purpose; it only shews you have the power of imagining or forming ideas in your mind: but it does not shew that you can conceive it possible the objects of your thought may exist without the mind.

In paragraph 6 he had already stated:

Some truths there are so near and obvious to the mind that a man need only open his eyes to see them. Such I take this important one to be, viz., that all the choir of heaven and furniture of the earth, in a word all those bodies which compose the mighty frame of the world, have not any subsistence without a mind—that their *being* is *to be perceived or known*; that consequently so long as they are not actually perceived by me, or do not exist in my mind or that of any other created spirit, they must either have no existence at all, or else subsist in the mind of some Eternal Spirit.

(Berkeley's God is a ubiquitous spectator whose purpose is to give coherence to the world.)

The doctrine I have just explained has been perversely interpreted. Herbert Spencer believed he had refuted it (*The Principles of Psychology* VIII, 6), arguing that if nothing exists outside consciousness, then consciousness must be infinite in time and space. The first is evident if we understand that all time is time perceived by someone, but erroneous if we infer that this time must necessarily embrace an infinite number of centuries; the second is illicit, inasmuch as Berkeley repeatedly denied an absolute space (*The Principles of Human Knowledge*, 116; *Siris*, 266). Even more indecipherable is the error Schopenhauer made (*Die Welt als Wille und Vorstellung* II, 1) when he held that for the idealists the world is a cerebral phenomenon. Berkeley, however, had written (*Dialogues between Hylas and Philonous* II): "The brain . . . being a sensible thing, exists only in the mind. Now, I would fain know whether you think it reasonable to suppose, that one idea or thing existing in the mind, occasions all other ideas. And if you think so, pray how do you account for the origin of that primary idea or brain itself?" The brain, in truth, is no less a part of the external world than the constellation Centaurus.

Berkeley denied that there was an object behind sense impressions. David Hume denied that there was a subject behind the perception of changes. Berkeley denied matter; Hume denied the spirit. Berkeley did not wish us to add the metaphysical notion of matter to the succession of impressions; Hume did not wish us to add the metaphysical notion of a self to the succession of mental states. This expansion of Berkeley's arguments is so logical that Berkeley had already foreseen it (as Alexander Campbell Fraser noted), and had even tried to dispute it by means of the Cartesian *ergo sum*. Hylas, foreshadowing Hume, had said in the third and last of the *Dialogues*: "In consequence of your own principles, it should follow that you are only a system of floating ideas, without any substance to support them. Words are not to be used without a meaning. And as there is no more meaning in spiritual substance than in material substance, the one is to be exploded as well as the other." Hume corroborates this (*A Treatise of Human Nature* I, 4, 6):

> [We] are nothing but a bundle or collection of different perceptions, which succeed each other with an inconceivable rapidity. . . . The mind is a kind of theater, where several perceptions successively make their appearance; pass, repass, glide away, and mingle in an infinite variety of

postures and situations. . . . The comparison of the theater must not mislead us. They are the successive perceptions only, that constitute the mind; nor have we the most distant notion of the place, where these scenes are represented, or of the materials of which it is composed.

Having admitted the idealist argument, I believe it is possible—perhaps inevitable—to go further. For Berkeley, time is "the succession of ideas in my mind, which flows uniformly and is participated in by all beings" (*The Principles of Human Knowledge*, 98); for Hume, it is "a succession of indivisible moments" (*A Treatise of Human Nature* I, 2, 3). However, with the continuities of matter and spirit denied, with space denied, I do not know by what right we retain that continuity which is time. Outside each perception (real or conjectural), matter does not exist; outside each mental state, spirit does not exist; neither then must time exist outside each present moment. Let us choose a moment of the utmost simplicity, for example, Chuang Tzu's dream (Herbert Allen Giles, *Chuang Tzu*, 1899). Some twenty-four centuries ago, Chuang Tzu dreamed he was a butterfly, and when he awoke he was not sure whether he was a man who had dreamed he was a butterfly or a butterfly who dreamed he was a man. Let us not consider the awakening, but the moment of the dream itself, or one of its moments. "I dreamed I was a butterfly fluttering through the air knowing nothing at all of Chuang Tzu," says the ancient text. We shall never know whether Chuang Tzu saw a garden over which he seemed to fly, or a moving yellow triangle, which was doubtlessly himself, but it is clear that the image was subjective, even though it was supplied to him by memory. The doctrine of psycho-physical parallelism will avow that this image must have resulted from a change in the dreamer's nervous system; according to Berkeley, at that moment the body of Chuang Tzu did not exist, nor did the dark bedroom in which he was dreaming, save as a perception in the mind of God. Hume simplifies what happened even more: at that moment the spirit of Chuang Tzu did not exist; all that existed were the colors of the dream and the certainty of his being a butterfly. He existed as a momentary term in the "bundle or collection of different perceptions" which constituted, some four centuries before Christ, the mind of Chuang Tzu; he existed as the term n in an infinite temporal series, between $n - 1$ and $n + 1$. There is no other reality for idealism than mental processes; to add an objective butterfly to the butterfly one perceives therefore seems a vain duplication; to add a self to the mental processes seems, therefore, no less exorbitant. Idealism holds that there was a dreaming, a perceiving, but not a dreamer nor even a dream; it holds that to speak of objects and subjects is to fall into an impure mythology. Now then, if each psychic state is self-sufficient, if to connect it to a circumstance or an ego is an illicit and idle addition, with what right do we later assign it a place in time? Chuang Tzu dreamed he was a butterfly, and during the course of that dream he was not Chuang Tzu but a butterfly. With space and self abolished, how can we link those dreaming moments to his waking moments and the feudal age of Chinese history? This does not mean that we shall never know, even if only approximately, the date of that dream; I merely mean that the chronological determination of an event, of any event in the world, is alien and exterior to the event. In China, the dream of Chuang Tzu is proverbial; let us imagine that one of its almost infinite readers dreams he is a butterfly and then that he is Chuang Tzu. Let us imagine that, by a not impossible chance, this dream repeats exactly the dream of the master. Having postulated such an identity, we may well ask: Are not those coinciding moments identical? Is not *one single repeated term* enough to disrupt and confound the history of the world, to reveal that there is no such history?

To deny time involves two negations: denying the succession of the terms in a series, and denying the synchronism of terms in two series. In fact, if each term is absolute, its relations are reduced to the consciousness that those relations exist. One state precedes another if it knows it is anterior; state G is contemporaneous with state H if it knows it is contemporaneous. Contrary to Schopenhauer's statement in his table of fundamental truths (*Die Welt als Wille und Vorstellung* II, 4), each fraction of time does not fill all space simultaneously: time is not ubiquitous.[3] (Of course, at this stage in the argument, space no longer exists.)

Meinong, in his theory of apprehension, admits the apprehension of imaginary objects: the fourth dimension, say, or Condillac's sentient statue, or Lotze's hypothetical animal, or the square root of minus one. If the reasons I have indicated are valid, then matter, the ego, the external world, universal history, our lives, also belong to that nebulous sphere.

Furthermore, the phrase "negation of time" is ambiguous. It can mean the eternity of Plato or Boethius and also the dilemmas of Sextus Empiricus. The latter (*Adversus mathematicos* XI, 197) denies the past, which already was, and the future, which is not yet, and argues that the present is either divisible or indivisible. It is not indivisible, for in that case it would

---

[3]Newton had previously asserted: "Each particle of space is eternal, each indivisible moment of duration is everywhere" (*Principia* III, 42).

have no beginning to connect it to the past nor end to connect it to the future, nor even a middle, because whatever has no beginning or end has no middle. Neither is it divisible, for in that case it would consist of a part that was and another that is not. *Ergo*, the present does not exist, and since the past and the future do not exist either, time does not exist. F. H. Bradley rediscovers and improves upon this conundrum: he observes (*Appearance and Reality* IV) that if the now can be divided into other nows, it is no less complicated than time; and that if it is indivisible, time is merely a relation between intemporal things. Such reasoning, obviously, denies the parts in order to deny the whole; I reject the whole in order to exalt each one of the parts. Via the dialectic of Berkeley and Hume, I have arrived at Schopenhauer's dictum:

> The form of the appearance of the will is only the present, not the past or the future; the latter do not exist except in the concept and by the linking of the consciousness, so far as it follows the principle of reason. No man has ever lived in the past, and none will live in the future; the present alone is the form of all life, and is a possession that no misfortune can take away. . . . We might compare time to an infinitely revolving circle: the half that is always sinking would be the past, that which is always rising would be the future; but the indivisible point at the top which the tangent touches, would be the present. Motionless like the tangent, that extensionless present marks the point of contact of the object, whose form is time, with the subject, which has no form because it does not belong to the knowable but is the precondition of all knowledge. (*Die Welt als Wille und Vorstellung* I, 54)

A fifth-century Buddhist treatise, the *Visuddhimagga*, or *The Path to Purity*, illustrates the same doctrine with the same figure: "Strictly speaking, the life of a being lasts as long as an idea. Just as a rolling carriage wheel touches earth at only one point, so life lasts as long as a single idea" (Radhakrishnan, *Indian Philosophy* I, 373). Other Buddhist texts say that the world is annihilated and resurges six billion five hundred million times a day and that every man is an illusion, vertiginously wrought by a series of solitary and momentary men. "The man of a past moment," *The Path to Purity* advises us, "has lived, but he does not live nor will he live; the man of a future moment will live, but he has not lived nor does he now live; the man of the present moment lives, but he has not lived nor will he live" (I, 407), a dictum we may compare with Plutarch's "Yesterday's man died in the man of today, today's man dies in the man of tomorrow" (*De E apud Delphos*, 18).

And yet, and yet . . . To deny temporal succession, to deny the self, to deny the astronomical universe, appear to be acts of desperation and are secret consolations. Our destiny (unlike the hell of Swedenborg and the hell of Tibetan mythology) is not terrifying because it is unreal; it is terrifying because it is irreversible and iron-bound. Time is the substance of which I am made. Time is a river that sweeps me along, but I am the river; it is a tiger that mangles me, but I am the tiger; it is a fire that consumes me, but I am the fire. The world, unfortunately, is real; I, unfortunately, am Borges.

> *Freund, es ist auch genug. Im Fall du mehr willst lesen,*
> *So geh und werde selbst die Schrift und selbst das Wesen.*

[Friend, this is enough. Should you wish to read more,/Go and yourself become the writing, yourself the essence.]

—Angelus Silesius, *Cherubinischer Wandersmann* VI, 263 (1675)

[1944–47]   [SJL]

Biathanatos

I owe to De Quincey (to whom my debt is so vast that to point out only one part of it may appear to repudiate or silence the others) my first notice of *Biathanatos*, a treatise composed at the beginning of the seventeenth century by the great poet John Donne,[1] who left the manuscript to Sir Robert Carr without other restriction than that it be given "to the Press or the Fire." Donne died in 1631; in 1642 civil war broke out; in 1644, the poet's firstborn son gave the old manuscript to the press to save it from the fire. *Biathanatos* extends to about two hundred pages; De Quincey (*Writings* VIII, 336) abridges them thus: Suicide is one of the forms of homicide; the canonists make a distinction between willful murder and justifiable homicide; by parity of reason, suicide is open to distinctions of the same kind. Just as not every homicide is a murder, not every suicide is a mortal sin. Such is the apparent thesis of *Biathanatos;* this is declared by the subtitle (*That Self-homicide is not so Naturally Sin that it may never be otherwise*), and is illustrated or overtaxed by a learned catalog of fabled or authentic examples, ranging from Homer,[2] "who had written a thousand things, which no man else understood, and is said to have hanged himself because he understood not the fishermen's riddle," to the pelican, symbol of paternal love, and the bees, which, according to St. Ambrose's *Hexameron*, put themselves to death "when they find themselves guilty of having broken any of their king's Laws." The catalog takes up three pages, and in them I note this vanity: the

[1]That he was truly a great poet may be demonstrated by these lines:

> Licence my roving hands and let them go
> Before, behind, between, above, below.
> O my America! my new-found-land. . . (*Elegies* XIX)

[2]Cf. the sepulchral epigram of Alcaeus of Messene (*Greek Anthology* VII, I).

inclusion of obscure examples ("Festus, Domitianus' minion, who killed himself only to hide the deformity of a Ringworm in his face") and the omission of others that are more forcefully persuasive—Seneca, Themistocles, Cato—but which may have seemed too obvious.

Epictetus ("Remember the essential thing: the door is open") and Schopenhauer ("Is Hamlet's soliloquy the meditation of a criminal?") have defended suicide in copious pages; the foregone certainty that these defenders are in the right makes us read them negligently. That was my case with *Biathanatos* until I perceived, or thought I perceived, an implicit or esoteric argument beneath the obvious one.

We will never know if Donne wrote *Biathanatos* with the deliberate aim of insinuating this hidden argument, or if some glimmer of it, however fleeting or crepuscular, called him to the task. The latter hypothesis strikes me as more likely: the hypothesis of a book which in order to say A says B, like a cryptogram, is artificial, but that of a work driven by an imperfect intuition is not. Hugh Fausset has suggested that Donne was thinking of crowning his defense of suicide with a suicide; that Donne may have toyed with the idea is possible or probable; that it is enough to explain *Biathanatos* is, naturally, ridiculous.

In the third part of *Biathanatos*, Donne considers the voluntary deaths that are mentioned in the Scriptures; he dedicates more pages to Samson's than to any other. He begins by establishing that this "exemplary man" is an emblem of Christ and that he seems to have served the Greeks as an archetype for Hercules. Francisco de Vitoria and the Jesuit Gregorio de Valencia did not wish to include him among suicides; Donne, to refute them, copies the last words he spoke, before carrying out his vengeance: "Let me die with the Philistines" (Judges 16:30). He likewise rejects St. Augustine's conjecture that Samson, breaking the pillars of the temple, was not guilty of the deaths of others nor of his own, but was obeying an inspiration of the Holy Spirit, "like the sword that directs its blades by disposition of he who wields it" (*The City of God* I, 20). Donne, having proven that this conjecture is unwarranted, closes the chapter with a phrase from Benito Pererio, saying that Samson, in his manner of dying, as much as in anything else, was a type of Christ.

Inverting Augustine's thesis, the quietists believed that Samson "by the demon's violence killed himself along with the Philistines" (*Heterodoxos españoles* V, I, 8); Milton (*Samson Agonistes*) defended him against the charge of suicide; Donne, I suspect, saw in this casuistical problem no more than a metaphor or simulacrum of a death. The case of Samson did not matter to him—and why should it have?—or only mattered as, shall we say, an "emblem of Christ." There is not a hero in the Old Testament who has not been promoted to this authority: for St. Paul, Adam is the figure of He who was to come; for St. Augustine, Abel represents the death of the Savior, and his brother Seth the resurrection; for Quevedo, Job was a "prodigious design" for Christ. Donne perpetrated his trivial analogy to make his readers understand: "The foregoing, said of Samson, may well be false; it is not when said of Christ."

The chapter that speaks directly of Christ is not effusive. It does no more than evoke two passages of Scripture: the phrase "I lay down my life for the sheep" (John 10:15) and the curious expression, "He gave up the ghost," that all four evangelists use to say "He died." From these passages, which are confirmed by the verse "No man taketh my life from me, but I lay it down of myself" (John 10:18), he infers that the agony on the cross did not kill Jesus Christ and that in truth Christ took his own life with a voluntary and marvelous emission of his soul. Donne wrote this conjecture in 1608: in 1631 he included it in a sermon he preached, while virtually in the throes of death, in the Whitehall Palace chapel.

The stated aim of *Biathanatos* is to mitigate suicide; the fundamental aim, to indicate that Christ committed suicide.[3] That, in demonstrating this hypothesis, Donne would find himself reduced to a verse from St. John and the repetition of the verb *to expire,* is an implausible and even incredible thing; he undoubtedly preferred not to insist on a blasphemous point. For the Christian, the life and death of Christ are the central event in the history of the world; the centuries before prepared for it, those after reflect it. Before Adam was formed from the dust of the earth, before the firmament separated the waters from the waters, the Father knew that the Son was to die on the cross and, as the theater of this future death, created the heavens and the earth. Christ died a voluntary death, Donne suggests, and this means that the elements and the terrestrial orb and the generations of mankind and Egypt and Rome and Babylon and Judah were extracted from nothingness in order to destroy him. Perhaps iron was created for the nails, and thorns for the mock crown, and blood and water for the wound. This baroque idea glimmers behind *Biathanatos.* The idea of a god who creates the universe in order to create his own gallows.

Rereading this note, I think of the tragic Philipp Batz, known to the

---

[3]Cf. De Quincey, *Writings* VIII, 398; Kant, *Religion innehalb der Grenzen der Vernunft* II, 2.

history of philosophy as Philipp Mainländer. He, like me, was an impassioned reader of Schopenhauer, under whose influence (and perhaps under that of the Gnostics) he imagined that we are fragments of a God who, at the beginning of time, destroyed himself, avid for non-being. Universal history is the shadowy death throes of those fragments. Mainländer was born in 1841; in 1876, he published his book *Philosophy of Redemption*. That same year he took his own life.

[1948]   [EA]

From Allegories to Novels

For all of us, allegory is an aesthetic mistake. (I first wrote, "is nothing but an error of aesthetics," but then I noticed that my sentence involved an allegory.) As far as I know, the genre of allegory has been analyzed by Schopenhauer (*Welt als Wille und Vorstellung* I, 50), De Quincey (*Writings* XI, 198), Francisco de Sanctis (*Storia della letteratura italiana* VII), Croce (*Estetica*, 39), and Chesterton (*G. F. Watts*, 83); in this essay I will limit myself to the last two. Croce rejects allegorical art, Chesterton defends it; to my mind, right is on Croce's side, but I would like to know how a form that seems unjustifiable to us now can once have enjoyed such favor.

Croce's words are crystalline; I need only repeat them:

If the symbol is conceived of as inseparable from artistic intuition, then it is synonymous with that intuition itself, which is always of an ideal nature. If the symbol is conceived as separable, if the symbol can be expressed on the one hand, and the thing symbolized can be expressed on the other, we fall back into the intellectualist error; the supposed symbol is the exposition of an abstract concept; it is an allegory; it is science, or an art that apes science. But we must also be fair to allegory and caution that in some cases it is innocuous. Any ethics whatsoever can be extracted from the *Gerusalemme liberata*; and from the *Adone*, by Marino, poet of all that is lascivious, the reflection that disproportionate pleasure ends in pain may be educed. Next to a statue, the sculptor may place a sign saying that the statue is Mercy or Goodness. Such allegories added to a finished work do it no harm. They are expressions extrinsic to other expressions. To the *Gerusalemme* is added a page in prose that expresses another thought by the poet; to the *Adone*, a line or stanza that expresses what the poet wished to be understood; to the statue, the word *mercy* or *goodness*.

On page 222 of *La poesía* (Bari, 1946), the tone is more hostile: "Allegory is not a direct mode of spiritual manifestation, but a kind of writing or cryptography."

Croce admits of no difference between content and form. Content is form and form is content. Allegory strikes him as monstrous because it seeks to encode two contents—the immediate or literal (Dante, guided by Virgil, reaches Beatrice), and the figurative (man finally attains faith, guided by reason)—into a single form. In his view, this way of writing entails laborious enigmas.

Chesterton, in defense of allegory, begins by denying that language fully expresses all reality.

> Man knows that there are in the soul tints more bewildering, more numberless and more nameless than the colors of an autumn forest. . . . Yet he seriously believes that these things can every one of them, in all their tones and semitones, in all their blends and unions, be accurately represented by an arbitrary system of grunts and squeals. He believes that an ordinary civilized stockbroker can really produce out of his own inside noises which denote all the mysteries of memory and all the agonies of desire.

Once our language has been declared insufficient, room is left for others; allegory can be one of them, like architecture or music. Allegory is made up of words, but it is not a language of language, a sign of other signs. For example, Beatrice is not a sign of the word *faith;* she is a sign of the valiant virtue and secret illuminations indicated by that word. A sign more precise, richer, and more felicitous, than the monosyllable *faith.*

I do not know with any certainty which of the two eminent parties to this dispute is right; I know that allegorical art seemed enchanting at one time (the labyrinthine *Roman de la Rose,* which lives on in two hundred manuscripts, consists of twenty-four thousand lines) and is now intolerable. And not only intolerable; we also feel it to be stupid and frivolous. Neither Dante, who represented the history of his passion in the *Vita nuova,* nor Boethius, the Roman, writing his *De consolatione* in the tower of Pavia under the shadow of an executioner's sword, would have understood this feeling. How can this discord be explained without recourse to the *petitio principii* that tastes change?

Coleridge observes that all men are born Aristotelians or Platonists.

The Platonists sense intuitively that ideas are realities; the Aristotelians, that they are generalizations; for the former, language is nothing but a system of arbitrary symbols; for the latter, it is the map of the universe. The Platonist knows that the universe is in some way a cosmos, an order; this order, for the Aristotelian, may be an error or fiction resulting from our partial understanding. Across latitudes and epochs, the two immortal antagonists change languages and names: one is Parmenides, Plato, Spinoza, Kant, Francis Bradley; the other, Heraclitus, Aristotle, Locke, Hume, William James. In the arduous schools of the Middle Ages, everyone invokes Aristotle, master of human reason (*Convivio* IV, 2), but the nominalists are Aristotle; the realists, Plato. George Henry Lewes has opined that the only medieval debate of some philosophical value is between nominalism and realism; the opinion is somewhat rash, but it underscores the importance of this tenacious controversy, provoked, at the beginning of the ninth century, by a sentence from Porphyry, translated and commented upon by Boethius; sustained, toward the end of the eleventh, by Anselm and Roscelin; and revived by William of Occam in the fourteenth.

As one would suppose, the intermediate positions and nuances multiplied *ad infinitum* over those many years; yet it can be stated that, for realism, universals (Plato would call them ideas, forms; we would call them abstract concepts) were the essential; for nominalism, individuals. The history of philosophy is not a useless museum of distractions and wordplay; the two hypotheses correspond, in all likelihood, to two ways of intuiting reality. Maurice de Wulf writes: "Ultra-realism garnered the first adherents. The chronicler Heriman (eleventh century) gives the name '*antiqui doctores*' to those who teach dialectics *in re;* Abelard speaks of it as an 'antique doctrine,' and until the end of the twelfth century, the name *moderni* is applied to its adversaries." A hypothesis that is now inconceivable seemed obvious in the ninth century, and lasted in some form into the fourteenth. Nominalism, once the novelty of a few, today encompasses everyone; its victory is so vast and fundamental that its name is useless. No one declares himself a nominalist because no one is anything else. Let us try to understand, nevertheless, that for the men of the Middle Ages the fundamental thing was not men but humanity, not individuals but the species, not the species but the genus, not the genera but God. From such concepts (whose clearest manifestation is perhaps the quadruple system of Erigena) allegorical literature, as I understand it, derived. Allegory is a fable of abstractions, as the novel is a fable of individuals. The abstractions are personified; there is something of the novel in every allegory. The individuals that novelists present aspire to be generic (Dupin is Reason, Don Segundo Sombra is the Gaucho); there is an element of allegory in novels.

The passage from allegory to novel, from species to individual, from realism to nominalism, required several centuries, but I shall have the temerity to suggest an ideal date: the day in 1382 when Geoffrey Chaucer, who may not have believed himself to be a nominalist, set out to translate into English a line by Boccaccio—"*E con gli occulti ferri i Tradimenti*" (And Betrayal with hidden weapons)—and repeated it as "The smyler with the knyf under the cloke." The original is in the seventh book of the *Teseide;* the English version, in "The Knightes Tale."

[1949]   *[EA]*

From Someone to Nobody

In the beginning, God is the Gods (*Elohim*), a plural that some believe implies majesty and others plenitude, and which some have thought is an echo of earlier polytheisms or a prefiguring of the doctrine, declared in Nicaea, that God is One and is Three. *Elohim* takes a singular verb; the first verse of the Law says, literally: "In the beginning the Gods [He] created the heaven and the earth." Despite the vagueness this plural suggests, *Elohim* is concrete; God is called "Jehovah" and we read that He walked in the garden in, as the English versions say, "the cool of the day." Human qualities define Him; in one part of the Scriptures we read: "And it repented Jehovah that He had made man on the earth, and it grieved Him at His heart"; and in another, "For I the Lord thy God am a jealous God"; and in another, "In the fire of My wrath have I spoken." The subject of such locutions is indisputably Someone, a corporal Someone whom the centuries will magnify and blur. His titles vary: "Strength of Jacob," "Rock of Israel," "I Am That I Am," "God of the Armies," "King of Kings." This last—which no doubt conversely inspired Gregory the Great's "Servant of the Servants of God"—is, in the original text, a superlative of "king": as Fray Luis de León writes, "It is a property of the Hebrew language to use the same word twice when one wants to emphasize something, either favorably or unfavorably. Thus, to say 'Song of Songs' is the same as our 'A Song among Songs' or 'he is a man among men,' that is, famous and eminent among all and more excellent than many others." In the first centuries of our era, theologians began to use the prefix *omni*, which previously had been reserved for adjectives pertaining to nature or Jupiter; they coined words like *omnipotent, omnipresent, omniscient*, which make of God a respectful chaos of unimaginable superlatives. That nomenclature, like the others, seems to limit the divinity: at the end of the fifth century, the unknown author of the *Corpus Dionysiacum* declares that no affirmative predicate is fitting for God. Nothing should be affirmed of Him, everything can be denied. Schopenhauer notes dryly: "That theology is the only true one, but it has no content." Written in Greek, the tracts and letters that make up the *Corpus Dionysiacum* find a reader in the ninth century who puts them into Latin: John Erigena or Scotus, that is, John the Irishman, whose name in history is Scotus Erigena, or Irish Irish. He formulates a doctrine of a pantheistic nature: particular things are theophanies (revelations or appearances of the divine) and behind them is God, who is the only reality, "but who does not know what He is, because He is not a what, and is incomprehensible to Himself and to all intelligence." He is not sapient, He is more than sapient; He is not good, He is more than good; He inscrutably exceeds and repels all attributes. John the Irishman, to define Him, used the word *nihilum,* which is nothingness; God is the primordial nothingness of the *creatio ex nihilo,* the abyss where first the archetypes and then concrete beings were engendered. He is Nothing and Nobody; those who imagined Him in this way did so in the belief that this was more than being a What or a Who. Similarly, Shankara teaches that all mankind, in a deep sleep, is the universe, is God.

The process I have illustrated is not, of course, aleatory. A magnification to nothingness occurs or tends to occur in all cults; we may observe it unmistakably in the case of Shakespeare. His contemporary, Ben Jonson, loves him "on this side of Idolatry"; Dryden declares that he is the Homer of the dramatic poets of England, but admits that he is often insipid and pompous; the discursive eighteenth century attempts to appraise his virtues and rebuke his faults; in 1774, Maurice Morgann states that King Lear and Falstaff are nothing but modifications of the mind of their inventor; at the beginning of the nineteenth century that opinion is recreated by Coleridge, for whom Shakespeare is no longer a man but a literary variation of the infinite God of Spinoza. Shakespeare as an individual person, he wrote, was a *natura naturata,* an effect, but "the universal which is potentially in each particular opened out to him . . . not as an abstraction of observation from a variety of men, but as the substance capable of endless modifications, of which his own personal existence was but one." Hazlitt corroborated or confirmed this: "He was just like any other man, but that he was unlike other men. He was nothing in himself, but he was all that others were, or that could become." Later, Hugo compared him to the ocean, which is the seedbed of all possible forms.

To be something is inexorably not to be all the other things; the confused intuition of this truth has induced mankind to imagine that being nothing is more than being something and is, in some way, to be everything. This fallacy is inherent in the words of that legendary king of India who renounces power and goes out to beg in the streets: "From this day forward I have no realm or my realm is limitless, from this day forward my body does not belong to me or all the earth belongs to me." Schopenhauer has written that history is an interminable and perplexing dream of human generations; in the dream there are recurring forms, perhaps nothing but forms; one of them is the process reported on this page.

[1950]   *[EW]*

The Wall and the Books

He, whose long wall the wand'ring Tartar bounds . . .
—*Dunciad* III, 76

I read, a few days ago, that the man who ordered the building of the almost infinite Chinese Wall was that first Emperor, Shih Huang Ti, who also decreed the burning of all the books that had been written before his time. That these two vast undertakings—the five or six hundred leagues of stone against the barbarians, and the rigorous abolition of history, that is, of the past—were the work of the same person and were, in a sense, his attributes, inexplicably satisfied and, at the same time, disturbed me. To investigate the reasons for that emotion is the purpose of this note.

Historically, there is nothing mysterious about these two measures. At the time of the wars of Hannibal, Shih Huang Ti, king of Tsin, conquered the Six Kingdoms and put an end to the feudal system; he built the wall because walls were defenses; he burned the books because his opponents invoked them to praise earlier emperors. Burning books and erecting fortifications are the usual occupations of princes; the only thing unique about Shih Huang Ti was the scale on which he worked. That, at least, is the opinion of certain Sinologists, but I believe that both acts were something more than an exaggeration or hyperbole of trivial dispositions. To enclose an orchard or a garden is common, but not an empire. Nor is it a small matter to require the most traditional of races to renounce the memory of its past, mythical or real. Chinese chronology was already three thousand years long (and included the Yellow Emperor and Chuang Tzu and Confucius and Lao Tzu) when Shih Huang Ti ordered that history would begin with him.

Shih Huang Ti had exiled his mother as a libertine; the orthodox saw this stern justice as an impiety; Shih Huang Ti, perhaps, wanted to erase the canonical books because they condemned him; Shih Huang Ti, perhaps, wanted to abolish all the past to abolish a single memory: his mother's dishonor. (Not unlike a king, in Judea, who killed all the children in order to kill one child.) This speculation is tenable, but it tells us nothing about the wall, the other side of the myth. Shih Huang Ti, according to the historians, prohibited the mention of death and searched for the elixir of immortality and cloistered himself in a figurative palace with as many rooms as the days in the year; these facts suggest that the wall in space and the bonfire in time were magic barriers intended to stop death. All things desire to persist in their being, Baruch Spinoza wrote; perhaps the Emperor and his magicians believed that immortality was intrinsic and that decay could not enter a closed sphere. Perhaps the Emperor wanted to recreate the beginning of time and called himself the First to truly be the first, and called himself Huang Ti to somehow be Huang Ti, the legendary emperor who invented writing and the compass. It was he who, according to the *Book of Rites*, gave things their true names; similarly, Shih Huang Ti boasted, on inscriptions that still exist, that all things under his reign had the names that befitted them. He dreamed of founding an immortal dynasty; he decreed that his heirs should be called Second Emperor, Third Emperor, Fourth Emperor, and so on to infinity. . . . I have spoken of a magic plan; it may also be supposed that the building of the wall and the burning of the books were not simultaneous acts. Thus (depending on the order we choose) we would have the image of a king who began by destroying and then resigned himself to conserving; or the image of a disillusioned king who destroyed what he had once defended. Both conjectures are dramatic; but they lack, as far as I know, historical foundation. Herbert Allen Giles recounts that anyone who concealed books was branded with a hot iron and condemned to work on the endless wall until the day of his death. This favors or tolerates another interpretation. Perhaps the wall was a metaphor; perhaps Shih Huang Ti condemned those who adored the past to a work as vast as the past, as stupid and as useless. Perhaps the wall was a challenge and Shih Huang Ti thought, "Men love the past and against that love there is nothing that I nor my executioners can do, but someday there will be a man who feels as I do, and he will destroy my wall, as I have destroyed the books, and he will erase my memory and will be my shadow and my mirror and will not know it." Perhaps Shih Huang Ti walled his empire because he knew that it was fragile, and destroyed the books because he knew that they were sacred books, books that teach what the whole universe teaches or the conscience of every man. Perhaps the burning of the libraries and the building of the wall are acts that in some secret way erase each other.

The unyielding wall which, at this moment and all moments, casts its system of shadows over lands I shall never see, is the shadow of a Caesar who ordered the most reverent of nations to burn its past; that idea is what moves us, quite apart from the speculations it allows. (Its virtue may be in the contrast between construction and destruction, on an enormous scale.) Generalizing, we might infer that *all* forms have virtue in themselves and not in an imagined "content." That would support the theory of Benedetto Croce; by 1877, Pater had already stated that all the arts aspire to resemble music, which is nothing but form. Music, states of happiness, mythology, faces worn by time, certain twilights and certain places, all want to tell us something, or have told us something we shouldn't have lost, or are about to tell us something; that imminence of a revelation as yet unproduced is, perhaps, the aesthetic fact.

[1950]   *[EW]*

Personality and the Buddha

In the volume that Edmund Hardy, in 1890, devoted to an exposition of Buddhism—*Der Buddhismus nach älteren Pali-Werken*—there is a chapter that Schmidt, who revised the second edition, was about to omit but whose theme is central (sometimes secretly, always inevitably) to all erroneous Western views about the Buddha. I am referring to the comparison of the Buddha's personality with that of Jesus. Such a comparison is defective, not only because of the profound differences (of culture, of nature, of purpose) that separate the two masters, but also because of the very concept of personality, which is appropriate to one culture, but not to the other. In the prologue to Karl Eugene Neumann's admired and doubtlessly admirable version, the "personal rhythm" of the Buddha's sermons is praised; Hermann Beckh (*Buddhismus* I, 89) believes he perceives in the texts of the Pali canon "the stamp of a singular personality"; both of these statements, as I understand it, can lead us into error.

It is true that there is no lack, in the legend and in the history of the Buddha, of those slight and irrational contradictions that are the signs of egocentrism—the admission of his son Rahula into the order at the age of seven, contradicting the very rules established by him; the choice of a pleasant place, "with a river of crystal-clear waters and fields and villages nearby," for his hard years of penitence; the mildness of the man who, upon preaching, does it "with the voice of a lion"; the deplored lunch of salt pork (or, according to Friedrich Zimmerman, of mushrooms) that precipitated the premature death of the great ascetic—but their number is limited. So limited that Senart, in an *Essai sur la légende du Buddha* published in 1882, proposed a "solar hypothesis" according to which the Buddha is, like Hercules, a personification of the sun; hence his life story becomes an advanced case of *symbolisme atmosphérique*. Mara is the stormy clouds, the Wheel of the Law that the Buddha turned in Benares is the disk of the sun, the

Buddha dies at sunset. . . . Even more skeptical—or more credulous—than Senart, the Dutch Indologist H. Kern saw in the first Buddhist council the allegorical figuration of a constellation. Otto Franke, in 1914, was able to write that "Buddha Gautama is the strict equivalent of Name Unknown."

We know that the Buddha, before becoming the Buddha (before being the Awakened One), was a prince named Gautama or Siddhartha. We know that at the age of twenty-nine he left his wife, his women, his son, and practiced the ascetic life, as before he had practiced the carnal life. We know that during six years he wasted his body in penitences; when the sun or the rain fell upon him, he did not move; the gods who saw him so emaciated thought that he had died. We know that in the end he understood that mortification was useless, and he bathed in the waters of a river, and his body recovered its former splendor. We know he sought the sacred fig tree that in each cycle of history emerges in the continent of the South so that in its shadow the Buddhas can attain *nirvana*. Afterward, allegory or legend blur the facts. Mara, god of love and of death, tries to overwhelm him with armies of boars, fish, horses, tigers, and monsters; Siddhartha, seated and immobile, conquers them, thinking them unreal. Infernal troops bombard him with mountains of fire; these, through the work of his love, turn into palaces of flowers. Projectiles configure aureoles or form a cupola over the hero. The daughters of Mara try to tempt him; he tells them they are empty and corruptible. Before dawn, the illusory battle ceases and Siddhartha sees his former incarnations (which now will end but which had no beginning) and those of all creatures, and the ceaseless web woven by the effects and causes of the universe. He intuits, then, the Four Noble Truths that he will preach in the Deer Park. He is no longer Prince Siddhartha; he is the Buddha. He is the Awakened One, he who no longer dreams he is someone, he who does not say: "I am; this is my father, this my mother, this my inheritance." He is also Tathagata, he who traveled his road, the weary traveler.

In the first vigil of the night, Siddhartha remembers the animals, the men, and the gods he has been, but it is a mistake to speak of transmigrations of the soul. Unlike the other philosophical systems of India, Buddhism denies that there are souls. The *Milinda Pañha*, an apologia of the second century, speaks of a debate whose discussants are the king of Bactriana, Menander, and the monk Nagasena; the latter argues that just as the king's carriage is not the wheels nor the chassis nor the axis nor the shaft nor the yoke, man too is not matter, form, impressions, ideas, instincts, or consciousness. He is not the combination of these parts, nor does he exist outside of them. The first theological *summa* of Buddhism, the *Visud-dhimagga*, or *The Path of Purity*, declares that every man is an illusion, pro-jected by a series of transitory and solitary men. "The man of a past moment," that book warns us, "has lived, but does not live nor will live; the man of a future moment will live, but has not lived nor lives; the man of the present moment lives, but has not lived nor will live," a notion comparable to Plutarch's: "Yesterday's man has died in today's, today's dies in tomor-row's." A character, not a soul, wanders in the cycles of *samsara* from one body to another; a character, not a soul, finally reaches *nirvana*, that is, ex-tinction. (For years the neophyte prepares for *nirvana* through rigorous ex-ercises of unreality. Walking around his house, chatting, eating, drinking, he must reflect that such acts are illusory and do not require an actor, a con-stant subject.)

The Path of Purity reads: "In no place am I something for someone, nor is anyone something for me"; to believe that one's self is an "I"—*attavada*—is the worst heresy for Buddhism. Nagarjuna, founder of the school of the Greater Vehicle, formulated arguments that showed that the apparent world is emptiness; drunk with reason, he later turned them (he couldn't avoid turning them) against the Noble Truths, against *nirvana,* against the Bud-dha. To be or not to be, to be and not to be, neither be nor not be: Nagar-juna refuted the possibility of those alternatives. Denying matter and attributes, he also had to deny extinction; if there is no *samsara,* then there is no extinction of *samsara* and it is wrong to say that *nirvana is.* It is no less erroneous, he observed, to say that *is* isn't, because having denied being, not being is also denied, for the latter depends (even verbally) on the former. "There are no objects, there is no knowledge, there is no ignorance, there is no destruction of ignorance, there is no pain, there is no origin of pain, there is no annihilation of pain, there is no road that leads to the annihila-tion of pain, there is no obtaining, there is no non-obtaining of *nirvana,*" one of the *sutras* of the Greater Vehicle informs us. Another fuses in a single hallucinatory plane the universe and liberation, *nirvana* and *samsara:* "Nobody is extinguished in *nirvana,* because the extinction of incommen-surable, numerous beings in *nirvana* is like the extinction of a phantas-magoria created by magic arts." Negation is not enough and one arrives at the negation of negations; the world is emptiness and emptiness is also empty. The first books of the canon had declared that the Buddha, during his sacred night, intuited the infinite chain of all effects and causes; the last books, written centuries later, argue that all knowledge is unreal and that if there had been as many Ganges as grains of sand in the present Ganges, the number of grains of sand would be less than the number of things that the Buddha does not know.

Such passages are not rhetorical exercises; they come out of a metaphysics and an ethics. We can contrast them with many from Western sources, for example, with that letter in which Caesar says that he has freed his political adversaries, risking their taking up arms again, "because I desire nothing more than to be as I am and that they be as they are." The Western cult of personality throbs in these words, which Macaulay judged the most noble that had ever been written. Even more illustrative is the catastrophe of Peer Gynt; the mysterious Smelter prepares to melt the hero; this consummation, infernal in America and in Europe, is the exact equivalent of *nirvana.*

Oldenberg has observed that India is the land of generic types, not of individuals. Their vast works are of a collective or anonymous nature; it is common to attribute to them certain schools, families, or communities of monks, when not to mythic beings, or, with splendid indifference, to Time.

Buddhism denies the permanence of the I; Buddhism preaches annulment; to imagine that the Buddha, who willed himself to cease being Prince Siddhartha, could resign himself to keeping the trivial differential features that inform the so-called personality, is to misunderstand his doctrine. It is also to transpose—anachronistically, absurdly—Western superstition to Eastern terrain. Léon Bloy or Francis Thompson would have been, for the Buddha, consummate examples of lost and fallible men, not only for believing that they deserve divine attention but for elaborating, within the common language, a small and vain dialect. It is not necessary to be Buddhist to understand this; we all feel that Bloy's style, in which each sentence seeks to shock us, is morally inferior to Gide's, which is, or pretends to be, proper to its genre.

From Chaucer to Marcel Proust, the novel's substance is the unrepeatable, the singular flavor of souls; for Buddhism there is no such flavor, or it is one of the many vanities of the cosmic simulacrum. Christ preached so that men would have life, and have it in abundance (John 10:10); the Buddha, to proclaim that this world, infinite in time and in space, is a dwindling fire. "Buddha Gautama is the exact equivalent of Name Unknown," wrote Otto Franke; it would be appropriate to add that the Buddha wanted to be Name Unknown.

[1950]   [SJL]

Pascal's Sphere

Perhaps universal history is the history of a few metaphors. To outline a chapter of that history is the purpose of this note.

Six centuries before the Christian era, the rhapsodist Xenophanes of Colophon, tired of the Homeric verses he recited from city to city, denounced the poets for giving the gods anthropomorphic traits and proposed to the Greeks a single God who was an eternal sphere. In Plato's *Timaeus* we read that the sphere is the most perfect and most uniform shape, because all points on its surface are equidistant from the center; Olof Gigon (*Ursprang der griechischen Philosophie*, 183) understands Xenophanes as speaking analogically; God is spherical, because that form is the best, or the least bad, for representing divinity. Parmenides, forty years later, repeated the image: "Being is like the mass of a well-rounded sphere, whose force is constant from the center in any direction." Calogero and Mondolfo argue that he envisioned an infinite, or infinitely growing sphere, and that those words have a dynamic meaning (Albertelli, *Gli Eleati*, 148). Parmenides taught in Italy; a few years after he died, the Sicilian Empedocles of Agrigento devised a laborious cosmogony; there is one stage in which the particles of earth, air, fire, and water form an endless sphere, "the round *Sphairos*, which rejoices in its circular solitude."

Universal history followed its course, the too-human gods that Xenophanes attacked were reduced to poetic fictions or to demons, but it was said that one of them, Hermes Trismegistus, had dictated a variable number of books (42, according to Clement of Alexandria; 20,000, according to Iamblichus; 36,525, according to the priests of Thoth, who is also Hermes) on whose pages all things were written. Fragments of that illusory library, compiled or forged since the third century, form what is called the *Corpus Hermeticum*; in one of the books, or in one part of the *Asclepius*, which was also attributed to Trismegistus, the French theologian Alain de Lille—

Alanus de Insulis—discovered, at the end of the twelfth century, this formula which the ages to come would not forget: "God is an intelligible sphere, whose center is everywhere and whose circumference is nowhere." The Pre-Socratics spoke of an endless sphere; Albertelli (like Aristotle before him) thinks that such a statement is a *contradictio in adjecto*, for the subject and predicate negate each other; this may be so, but the formula in the Hermetic books enables us, almost, to envision that sphere. In the thirteenth century, the image reappeared in the symbolic *Roman de la Rose*, which attributed it to Plato, and in the encyclopedia *Speculum Triplex*; in the sixteenth, the last chapter of the last book of *Pantagruel* referred to "that intellectual sphere, whose center is everywhere and whose circumference nowhere, which we call God." For the medieval mind, the meaning was clear: God is in each one of his creatures, but is not limited by any one of them. "Behold, the heaven and heaven of heavens cannot contain thee," said Solomon (I Kings 8:27); the geometrical metaphor of the sphere must have seemed like a gloss on those words.

Dante's poem has preserved Ptolemaic astronomy, which ruled mankind's imagination for fourteen hundred years. The earth is the center of the universe. It is an immobile sphere; around it nine concentric spheres revolve. The first seven are the planetary heavens (the heavens of the Moon, Mercury, Venus, the Sun, Mars, Jupiter, and Saturn); the eighth, the Heaven of Fixed Stars; the ninth, the Crystalline Heaven, also called the Primum Mobile. This in turn is surrounded by the empyrean, which is made of light. This whole laborious apparatus of hollow, transparent, and revolving spheres (one system required fifty-five) had come to be a mental necessity; *De hypothesibus motuum coelestium commentariolus* [Commentary on the Hypothesis of Heavenly Motions] was the timid title that Copernicus, the disputer of Aristotle, gave to the manuscript that transformed our vision of the cosmos. For one man, Giordano Bruno, the breaking of the stellar vaults was a liberation. In *La cena de le ceneri* [The Feast of the Ashes] he proclaimed that the world is the infinite effect of an infinite cause and that the divinity is near, "because it is in us even more than we are in ourselves." He searched for the words that would explain Copernican space to mankind, and on one famous page he wrote: "We can state with certainty that the universe is all center, or that the center of the universe is everywhere and the circumference nowhere" (*De la causa, principio e urco*, V).

That was written exultantly in 1584, still in the light of the Renaissance; seventy years later not even a glimmer of that fervor remained, and men felt lost in time and space. In time, because if the future and the past are infinite, there cannot really be a when; in space, because if every being is equidistant from the infinite and the infinitesimal, there cannot be a where. No one exists on a certain day, in a certain place; no one knows the size of his own face. In the Renaissance, humanity thought it had reached adulthood, and it said as much through the mouths of Bruno, Campanella, and Bacon. In the seventeenth century, humanity was discouraged by a feeling of old age; to justify itself, it exhumed the belief in a slow and fatal degeneration of all creatures because of Adam's sin. (In the fifth chapter of Genesis, we read that "all the days of Methuselah were nine hundred sixty and nine years"; in the sixth, that "there were giants in the earth in those days.") The First Anniversary of John Donne's elegy "Anatomy of the World" lamented the brief life and the small stature of contemporary men, who were like fairies and dwarfs. Milton, according to Johnson's biography, feared that the genre of the epic had become impossible on earth; Glanvill thought that Adam, "the medallion of God," enjoyed both a telescopic and microscopic vision; Robert South notably wrote: "An Aristotle was but the fragment of an Adam, and Athens, the rudiments of Paradise." In that dejected century, the absolute space that inspired the hexameters of Lucretius, the absolute space that had been a liberation for Bruno was a labyrinth and an abyss for Pascal. He hated the universe and yearned to adore God, but God was less real to him than the hated universe. He lamented that the firmament did not speak; he compared our lives to the shipwrecked on a desert island. He felt the incessant weight of the physical world; he felt confusion, fear, and solitude; and he expressed it in other words: "Nature is an infinite sphere, the center of which is everywhere, the circumference nowhere." That is the text of the Brunschvieg edition, but the critical edition of Tourneur (Paris, 1941), which reproduces the cancellations and hesitations in the manuscript, reveals that Pascal started to write the word *effroyable:* "a frightful sphere, the center of which is everywhere, and the circumference nowhere."

Perhaps universal history is the history of the various intonations of a few metaphors.

[1951]   [EW]

The Innocence of Layamon

Legouis saw the paradox of Layamon but not his pathos. The preamble to the *Brut*, written in the third person at the beginning of the thirteenth century, contains the facts of his life. Layamon writes:

> There was in the land a priest named Layamon; he was the son of Leovenath (may God have mercy on his soul!), and he lived in Emley in a noble church on the banks of the Severn, a good place to be. It came to his mind the idea of relating the exploits of Englishmen, what they were named and where they came from, the earliest owners of our England, after the Great Flood. . . . Layamon traveled throughout the land and acquired the noble books that were his models. He took the English book made by St. Bede; he took another in Latin made by St. Albin and St. Augustine, who brought us the faith; he took a third and placed it in the middle, the work of a French cleric named Wace, who knew how to write well, and gave it to the noble Leonor, queen of the great Henry. Layamon opened those three books and turned the pages; he looked at them lovingly—may God have mercy on him!—and picked up the pen and wrote on parchment and summoned the right words and made the three books into one. Now Layamon, for the love of God Omnipotent, begs those who read this book and learn the truths it teaches to pray for the soul of his father, who begot him, and for the soul of his mother, who bore him, and for his own soul, to make it better. Amen.

Thirty thousand irregular verses then recount the battles of the Britons, particularly Arthur, against the Picts, the Norse, and the Saxons.

The first impression, and perhaps the last, given by Layamon's preamble is of an infinite, almost incredible, ingenuousness. Adding to this impression is the poet's childlike trait of saying "Layamon" for "I," but behind the innocent words the emotion is complex. Layamon is moved not only by the subject matter of the songs, but also by the almost magical circumstance of seeing himself singing them; this reciprocity corresponds to the "*Illo Virgilium me tempore*" [In that time, Virgil] of the *Georgics* or to the beautiful "*Ego ille qui quondam*" [I, who one day] that someone wrote to preface the *Aeneid*.

A legend recounted by Dionysius of Halicarnassus and famously adopted by Virgil states that Rome was founded by men descended from Aeneas, the Trojan who battles Achilles in the pages of the *Iliad;* similarly a *Historia Regum Britanniae* from the beginning of the twelfth century attributes the founding of London ("Citie that some tyme cleped was New Troy") to Aeneas' great-grandson Brutus, whose name would be perpetuated in Britannia. Brutus is the first king in Layamon's secular chronicle; he is followed by others who have known rather varied fortunes in later literature: Hudibras, Lear, Gorboduc, Ferrex and Porrex, Lud, Cymbeline, Vortigern, Uther Pendragon (Uther Dragon's Head), and Arthur of the Round Table, "the king who was and shall be," according to his mysterious epitaph. Arthur is mortally wounded in his last battle, but Merlin—who in the *Brut* is not the son of the Devil but of a silent golden phantom loved by his mother in dreams—prophesies that he will return (like Barbarossa) when his people need him. Fruitlessly waging war against him are those rebellious hordes, the "pagan dogs" of Hengest, the Saxons who were scattered over the face of England, beginning in the fifth century.

It has been said that Layamon was the first English poet; it is more accurate and more poignant to think of him as the last of the Saxon poets. The latter, converted to the faith of Jesus, applied the harsh accents and the military images of the Germanic epics to the new mythology (the Twelve Apostles, in one of Cynewulf's poems, are skilled in the use of shields and fend off a sudden attack by swordsmen; in the *Exodus*, the Israelites who cross the Red Sea are Vikings); Layamon applied the same rigor to the courtly and magical fictions of the *Matière de Bretagne*. Because of his subject matter, or a large part of it, he is one of the many poets of the Breton Cycle, a distant colleague of that anonymous writer who revealed to Francesca da Rimini and Paolo the love they felt for each other without knowing it. In spirit, he is a lineal descendant of those Saxon rhapsodists who reserved their joyful words for the description of battles and who, in four centuries, did not produce a single amatory stanza. Layamon has forgotten the metaphors of his ancestors—in the *Brut*, the sea is not the "whale's path," nor are arrows "vipers of war"—but the vision of the world is the same. Like Stevenson, like Flaubert, like so many men of letters, the sedentary cleric takes pleasure in verbal violence; where Wace wrote, "On that day the Britons killed Passent and the Irish King," Layamon expands:

> And Uther the Good said these words: "Passent, here you will remain, for here comes Uther on his horse!" He hit him on his head and knocked him down and plunged his sword down his throat (giving him a food that was new to him) and the point of the sword disappeared into the ground. Then Uther said: "Now it is well with you, Irishman; all England is yours. I deliver it into your hands so that you may stay here and live with us. Look, here it is; now you will have it forever."

In every line of Anglo-Saxon verse there are certain words, two in the first half and one in the second, that begin with the same consonant or vowel. Layamon tries to observe that old metrical law, but the octosyllabic couplets of Wace's *Geste des Bretons*—one of the three "noble books"—continually distract him with the new temptation to rhyme, and so we have *brother* after *other* and *night* after *light....* The Norman Conquest took place around the middle of the eleventh century; the *Brut* comes from the beginning of the thirteenth, but the vocabulary of the poem is almost entirely Germanic; in its thirty thousand lines there are not even fifty words of French origin. Here is a passage that scarcely prefigures the English language but has evident affinities with the German:

> And seothe ich cumen wulle
> to mine kineriche
> and wumien mid Brutten
> mid muchelere wunne.

Those were Arthur's last words. Their meaning is: "And then I shall go to my kingdom, and I shall dwell among Britons with great delight."

Layamon ardently sang of the ancient battles of the Britons against the Saxon invaders as if he himself were not a Saxon, and as if the Britons and the Saxons had not been, since that day in Hastings, conquered by the Normans. This fact is extraordinary and leads to various speculations. Layamon, son of Leovenath (Liefnoth), lived not far from Wales, the bulwark of the Celts and the source (according to Gaston Paris) of the complex myth of Arthur; his mother might well have been a Briton. This theory is possible, unverifiable, and impoverished; one could also suppose that the poet was the son and grandson of Saxons, but that, at heart, the *jus soli* was stronger than the *jus sanguinis*. This is not very different from the Argentine with no Querandí blood who identifies with the Indian defenders of his land rather than with the Spaniards of Cabrera or Juan de Garay. Another possibility is that Layamon, whether knowingly or not, gave the Britons of the *Brut* the value of Saxons, and the Saxons the value of Normans. The riddles, the Bestiary, and Cynewulf's curious runes prove that such cryptographic or allegorical exercises were not alien to that ancient literature; something, however, tells me that this speculation is fantastic. If Layamon had thought that yesterday's conquerors were the conquered of today, and today's conquerors could be the conquered of tomorrow, he would, I think, have used the simile of the Wheel of Fortune, which is in the *De Consolatione,* or had recourse to the prophetic books of the Bible, not to the intricate romance of Arthur.

The subjects of the earlier epics were the exploits of a hero or the loyalty that warriors owe to their captain; the true subject of the *Brut* is England. Layamon could not foresee that two centuries after his death his alliteration would be ridiculous ("I can not geste—rum, ram, ruf—by lettre," says a character in Chaucer) and his language, a rustic jargon. He could not have suspected that his insults to the Hengests' Saxons would be the last words in the Saxon language, destined to die and be born again in the English language. According to the Germanic scholar Ker, he barely knew the literature whose tradition he inherited; he knew nothing of the wanderings of Widsith among the Persians and Hebrews or of Beowulf's battle at the bottom of the red marsh. He knew nothing of the great verses from which his own were to spring; perhaps he would not have understood them. His curious isolation, his solitude, make him, now, touching. "No one knows who he himself is," said León Bloy; of that personal ignorance there is no symbol better than this forgotten man, who abhorred his Saxon heritage with Saxon vigor, and who was the last Saxon poet and never knew it.

[1951]   [EW]

On the Cult of Books

In Book VIII of the *Odyssey*, we read that the gods weave misfortunes so that future generations will have something to sing about; Mallarmé's statement, "The world exists to end up in a book," seems to repeat, some thirty centuries later, the same concept of an aesthetic justification for evils. These two teleologies, however, do not entirely coincide; the former belongs to the era of the spoken word, and the latter to an era of the written word. One speaks of telling the story and the other of books. A book, any book, is for us a sacred object: Cervantes, who probably did not listen to everything that everyone said, read even "the torn scraps of paper in the streets." Fire, in one of Bernard Shaw's comedies, threatens the library at Alexandria; someone exclaims that the memory of mankind will burn, and Caesar replies: "A shameful memory. Let it burn." The historical Caesar, in my opinion, might have approved or condemned the command the author attributes to him, but he would not have considered it, as we do, a sacrilegious joke. The reason is clear: for the ancients the written word was nothing more than a substitute for the spoken word.

It is well known that Pythagoras did not write; Gomperz (*Griechische Denker* I, 3) maintains that it was because he had more faith in the virtues of spoken instruction. More forceful than Pythagoras' mere abstention is Plato's unequivocal testimony. In the *Timaeus* he stated: "It is an arduous task to discover the maker and father of this universe, and, having discovered him, it is impossible to tell it to all men"; and in the *Phaedrus* he recounted an Egyptian fable against writing (the practice of which causes people to neglect the exercise of memory and to depend on symbols), and said that books are like the painted figures "that seem to be alive, but do not answer a word to the questions they are asked." To alleviate or eliminate that difficulty, he created the philosophical dialogue. A teacher selects a pupil, but a book does not select its readers, who may be wicked or stupid; this Platonic mistrust persists in the words of Clement of Alexandria, a man of pagan culture: "The most prudent course is not to write but to learn and teach by word of mouth, because what is written remains" (*Stromateis*), and in the same treatise: "To write all things in a book is to put a sword in the hands of a child," which derives from the Gospels: "Give not that which is holy unto the dogs, neither cast ye your pearls before swine, lest they trample them under their feet, and turn again and rend you." That sentence is from Jesus, the greatest of the oral teachers, who only once wrote a few words on the ground, and no man read what He had written (John 8:6).

Clement of Alexandria wrote about his distrust of writing at the end of the second century; the end of the fourth century saw the beginning of the mental process that would culminate, after many generations, in the predominance of the written word over the spoken one, of the pen over the voice. A remarkable stroke of fortune determined that a writer would establish the exact instant (and I am not exaggerating) when this vast process began. St. Augustine tells it in Book VI of the *Confessions*:

> When he [Ambrose] was reading, his eyes ran over the page and his heart perceived the sense, but his voice and tongue were silent. He did not restrict access to anyone coming in, nor was it customary even for a visitor to be announced. Very often when we were there, we saw him silently reading and never otherwise. After sitting for a long time in silence (for who would dare to burden him in such intent concentration?) we used to go away. We supposed that in the hubbub of other people's troubles, he would not want to be invited to consider another problem. We wondered if he read silently perhaps to protect himself in case he had a hearer interested and intent on the matter, to whom he might have to expound the text being read if it contained difficulties, or who might wish to debate some difficult questions. If his time were used up in that way, he would get through fewer books than he wished. Besides, the need to preserve his voice, which used easily to become hoarse, could have been a very fair reason for silent reading. Whatever motive he had for his habit, this man had a good reason for what he did.

St. Augustine was a disciple of St. Ambrose, Bishop of Milan, around the year 384; thirteen years later, in Numidia, he wrote his *Confessions* and was still troubled by that extraordinary sight: a man in a room, with a book, reading without saying the words.[1]

That man passed directly from the written symbol to intuition, omitting sound; the strange art he initiated, the art of silent reading, would lead to marvelous consequences. It would lead, many years later, to the concept of the book as an end in itself, not as a means to an end. (This mystical concept, transferred to profane literature, would produce the unique destinies of Flaubert and Mallarmé, of Henry James and James Joyce.) Superimposed on the notion of a God who speaks with men in order to command them to do something or to forbid them to do something was that of the Absolute Book, of a Sacred Scripture. For Muslims, the Koran (also called "The Book," *al-Kitab*) is not merely a work of God, like men's souls or the universe; it is one of the attributes of God, like His eternity or His rage. In chapter XIII we read that the original text, the Mother of the Book, is deposited in Heaven. Muhammad al-Ghazali, the Algazel of the scholastics, declared: "The Koran is copied in a book, is pronounced with the tongue, is remembered in the heart and, even so, continues to persist in the center of God and is not altered by its passage through written pages and human understanding." George Sale observes that this uncreated Koran is nothing but its idea or Platonic archetype; it is likely that al-Ghazali used the idea of archetypes, communicated to Islam by the *Encyclopedia of the Brethren of Purity* and by Avicenna, to justify the notion of the Mother of the Book.

Even more extravagant than the Muslims were the Jews. The first chapter of the Jewish Bible contains the famous sentence: "And God said, 'Let there be light,' and there was light"; the Kabbalists argued that the virtue of that command from the Lord came from the letters of the words. The *Sepher Yetzirah* (Book of the Formation), written in Syria or Palestine around the sixth century, reveals that Jehovah of the Armies, God of Israel and God Omnipotent, created the universe by means of the cardinal numbers from one to ten and the twenty-two letters of the alphabet. That numbers may be instruments or elements of the Creation is the dogma of Pythagoras and Iamblichus; that letters also are is a clear indication of the new cult of writing. The second paragraph of the second chapter reads: "Twenty-two fundamental letters: God drew them, engraved them,

---

[1]The commentators have noted that it was customary at that time to read out loud in order to grasp the meaning better, for there were no punctuation marks, nor even a division of words, and to read in common because there was a scarcity of manuscripts. The dialogue of Lucian of Samosata, *Against an Ignorant Buyer of Books*, includes an account of that custom in the second century.

combined them, weighed them, permutated them, and with them produced everything that is and everything that will be." Then the book reveals which letter has power over air, and which over water, and which over fire, and which over wisdom, and which over peace, and which over grace, and which over sleep, and which over anger, and how (for example) the letter *kaf,* which has power over life, served to form the sun in the world, the day Wednesday in the week, and the left ear on the body.

The Christians went even further. The thought that the divinity had written a book moved them to imagine that he had written two, and that the other one was the universe. At the beginning of the seventeenth century, Francis Bacon declared in his *Advancement of Learning* that God offered us two books so that we would not fall into error: the first, the volume of the Scriptures, reveals His will; the second, the volume of the creatures, reveals His power and is the key to the former. Bacon intended much more than the making of a metaphor; he believed that the world was reducible to essential forms (temperatures, densities, weights, colors), which formed, in a limited number, an *abecedarium naturae* or series of letters with which the universal text is written.[2] Sir Thomas Browne, around 1642, confirmed that "Thus there are two Books from whence I collect my Divinity; besides that written one of God, another of His servant Nature, that universal and publick Manuscript, that lies expans'd unto the Eyes of all: those that never saw Him in the one, have discover'd Him in the other" (*Religio Medici* I, 16). In the same paragraph we read: "In brief, all things are artificial; for Nature is the Art of God." Two hundred years passed, and the Scot Carlyle, in various places in his books, particularly in the essay on Cagliostro, went beyond Bacon's hypothesis; he said that universal history was a Sacred Scripture that we decipher and write uncertainly, and in which we too are written. Later, Léon Bloy would write:

> There is no human being on earth who is capable of declaring who he is. No one knows what he has come to this world to do, to what his acts, feelings, ideas correspond, or what his real *name* is, his imperishable

---

[2]Galileo's works abound with the concept of the universe as a book. The second section of Favaro's anthology (*Galileo Galilei: Pensieri, motti e sentenze;* Florence, 1949) is entitled "*Il libro della Natura.*" I quote the following paragraph: "Philosophy is written in that very large book that is continually opened before our eyes (I mean the universe), but which is not understood unless first one studies the language and knows the characters in which it is written. The language of that book is mathematical and the characters are triangles, circles, and other geometric figures."

Name in the registry of Light. . . . History is an immense liturgical text, where the i's and the periods are not worth less than the versicles or whole chapters, but the importance of both is undeterminable and is profoundly hidden. (*L'Ame de Napoleon*, 1912)

The world, according to Mallarmé, exists for a book; according to Bloy, we are the versicles or words or letters of a magic book, and that incessant book is the only thing in the world: more exactly, it is the world.

[1951]   *[EW]*

Kafka and His Precursors

At one time I considered writing a study of Kafka's precursors. I had thought, at first, that he was as unique as the phoenix of rhetorical praise; after spending a little time with him, I felt I could recognize his voice, or his habits, in the texts of various literatures and various ages. I will note a few of them here, in chronological order.

The first is Zeno's paradox against motion. A moving body at point *A* (Aristotle states) will not be able to reach point *B,* because it must first cover half of the distance between the two, and before that, half of the half, and before that, half of the half of the half, and so on to infinity; the form of this famous problem is precisely that of *The Castle,* and the moving body and the arrow and Achilles are the first Kafkaesque characters in literature. In the second text that bibliographic chance brought my way, the affinity is not in the form but in the tone. It is a fable by Han Yu, a prose writer of the ninth century, and it is found in the admirable *Anthologie raisonée de la littérature chinoise* (1948) by Margouliès. This is the mysterious and tranquil paragraph I marked:

It is universally admitted that the unicorn is a supernatural being and one of good omen; thus it is declared in the Odes, in the Annals, in the biographies of illustrious men, and in other texts of unquestioned authority. Even the women and children of the common people know that the unicorn is a favorable portent. But this animal does not figure among the domestic animals, it is not easy to find, it does not lend itself to any classification. It is not like the horse or the bull, the wolf or the deer. Under such conditions, we could be in the presence of a unicorn and not know with certainty that it is one. We know that a given animal with a mane is a horse, and that one with horns is a bull. We do not know what a unicorn is like.[1]

The third text comes from a more predictable source: the writings of Kierkegaard. The mental affinity of both writers is known to everyone; what has not yet been emphasized, as far as I know, is that Kierkegaard, like Kafka, abounded in religious parables on contemporary and bourgeois themes. Lowrie, in his *Kierkegaard* (Oxford University Press, 1938), mentions two. One is the story of a counterfeiter who, under constant surveillance, examines Bank of England notes; in the same way, God could be suspicious of Kierkegaard and yet entrust him with a mission precisely because He knew he was accustomed to evil. Expeditions to the North Pole are the subject of the other. Danish clergymen had declared from their pulpits that to participate in such expeditions would serve the eternal health of the soul. They had to admit, however, that reaching the Pole was difficult and perhaps impossible, and that not everyone could undertake the adventure. In the end, they announced that any journey—from Denmark to London, say, in a steamship, or a Sunday outing in a hackney coach—could be seen as a veritable expedition to the North Pole. The fourth prefiguration I found in Browning's poem "Fears and Scruples," published in 1876. A man has, or thinks he has, a famous friend. He has never seen this friend, and the fact is that this friend has never been able to help him, but he knows that the friend has very noble qualities, and he shows others the letters his friend has written. Some have doubts about his nobility, and handwriting experts declare the letters to be fake. In the last line, the man asks: "What if this friend happened to be—God?"

My notes also include two short stories. One is from *Histoires désobligeantes* by Léon Bloy, and refers to the case of some people who amass globes, atlases, train schedules, and trunks, and who die without ever having left the town where they were born. The other is entitled "Carcassonne" and is by Lord Dunsany. An invincible army of warriors departs from an infinite castle, subjugates kingdoms and sees monsters and crosses deserts and mountains, but never reaches Carcassonne, although they once catch a glimpse of it. (This story is, as it is easily noticed, the exact opposite of the

---

[1]The failure to recognize the sacred animal and its shameful or casual death at the hands of the people are traditional themes in Chinese literature. See the last chapter of Jung's *Psychologie und Alchemie* (Zurich, 1944), which includes two curious illustrations.

previous one; in the first, they never leave the city; in the second, they never reach it.)

If I am not mistaken, the heterogenous pieces I have listed resemble Kafka; if I am not mistaken, not all of them resemble each other. This last fact is what is most significant. Kafka's idiosyncracy is present in each of these writings, to a greater or lesser degree, but if Kafka had not written, we would not perceive it; that is to say, it would not exist. The poem "Fears and Scruples" by Robert Browning prophesies the work of Kafka, but our reading of Kafka noticeably refines and diverts our reading of the poem. Browning did not read it as we read it now. The word "precursor" is indispensable to the vocabulary of criticism, but one must try to purify it from any connotation of polemic or rivalry. The fact is that each writer *creates* his precursors. His work modifies our conception of the past, as it will modify the future.[2] In this correlation, the identity or plurality of men doesn't matter. The first Kafka of "*Betrachtung*" is less a precursor of the Kafka of the gloomy myths and terrifying institutions than is Browning or Lord Dunsany.

[1951]   [EW]

[2]See T. S. Eliot, *Points of View* (1941), 25–26.

The Enigma of Edward FitzGerald

A man, Omar ben Ibrāhīm, is born in Persia in the eleventh century of the Christian era (that century was, for him, the fifth of the Hejira); he studies the Koran and its traditions with Hassan ben Sabbah, the future founder of the sect of the Hashishin, or Assassins, and with Nizam al-Mulk, who will become the vizier of Alp Arslan and conqueror of the Caucasus. The three friends, half in jest, swear that if fortune some day favors one of them, the luckiest will not forget the others. After a number of years, Nizam attains the position of a vizier; Omar asks only for a corner in the shade of this good fortune, where he may pray for his friend's prosperity and think about mathematics. (Hassan requests and obtains a high post and, in the end, has the vizier stabbed to death.) Omar receives an annual pension of ten thousand *dinars* from the treasury of Nishapur, and is able to devote himself to study. He does not believe in judicial astrology, but he takes up astronomy, collaborates on the reform of the calendar promoted by the Sultan, and writes a famous treatise on algebra, which gives numerical solutions for first- and second-degree equations, and geometrical ones—by means of the intersection of cones—for those of the third degree. The arcana of numbers and stars do not drain his attention; he reads, in the solitude of his library, the works of Plotinus, who in the vocabulary of Islam is the Egyptian Plato or the Greek Master, and the fifty-odd epistles of the heretical and mystical *Encyclopedia of the Brethren of Purity*, where it is argued that the universe is an emanation of the Unity, and will return to the Unity. . . . It is said at the time that he is a proselyte of Alfarabi, who believed that universal forms do not exist apart from things, and of Avicenna, who taught that the world is eternal. One account tells us that he believes, or pretends to believe, in the transmigration of the soul from human to animal body, and that he once spoke with a donkey, as Pythagoras spoke with a dog. He is an atheist, but knows how to interpret, in orthodox style, the most difficult passages of the

Koran, for every educated man is a theologian, and faith is not a requisite. In the intervals between astronomy, algebra, and apologetics, Omar ben Ibrāhīm al-Khayyāmī works on the composition of quatrains whose first, second, and last lines rhyme; the most extensive manuscript attributes five hundred to him, a paltry number that will be unfavorable for his reputation, for in Persia (as in the Spain of Lope de Vega and Calderón) the poet must be prolific. In the year 517 of the Hejira, Omar is reading a treatise titled *The One and the Many;* an uneasiness or a premonition interrupts him. He gets up, marks the page that his eyes will not see again, and reconciles himself with God, with that God who perhaps exists and whose blessing he has implored on the difficult pages of his algebra. He dies that same day, at the hour of sunset. Around that time, on an island to the north and west that is unknown to the cartographers of Islam, a Saxon king who defeated a king of Norway is defeated by a Norman duke.

Seven centuries go by with their enlightenments and agonies and transformations, and in England a man is born, FitzGerald, less intellectual than Omar, but perhaps more sensitive and sadder. FitzGerald knows that his true fate is literature, and he practices it with indolence and tenacity. He reads and rereads the *Quixote,* which seems to him almost the best of all books (but he does not wish to be unjust to Shakespeare and "dear old Virgil"), and his love extends to the dictionary in which he looks for words. He knows that every man who has some music in his soul can write poetry ten or twelve times in the natural course of his life, if the stars are propitious, but he does not propose to abuse that modest privilege. He is a friend of famous people (Tennyson, Carlyle, Dickens, Thackeray) to whom he does not feel inferior, despite his modesty and courteousness. He has published a decorously written dialogue, *Euphranor,* and mediocre versions of Calderón and the great Greek tragedians. From the study of Spanish he has moved on to Persian, and has begun a translation of the *Mantiq al-Tayr,* that mystical epic about the birds who are searching for their king, the Simurgh, and who finally reach his palace beyond the seven seas, and discover that they are the Simurgh, that the Simurgh is each one and all of them. Around 1854 he is lent a manuscript collection of Omar's compositions, arranged according to the alphabetical order of the rhymes; FitzGerald turns a few into Latin and glimpses the possibility of weaving them into a continuous and organic book that would begin with images of morning, the rose, and the nightingale, and end with those of night and the tomb. To this improbable and even unbelievable proposition, FitzGerald devotes his life, that of an indolent, solitary, maniacal man. In 1859, he publishes a first version of the

Rubáiyát, which is followed by others, rich in variations and refinements. A miracle happens: from the fortuitous conjunction of a Persian astronomer who condescended to write poetry and an eccentric Englishman who peruses Oriental and Hispanic books, perhaps without understanding them completely, emerges an extraordinary poet who resembles neither of them. Swinburne writes that FitzGerald "has given to Omar Khayyām a permanent place among the major English poets," and Chesterton, sensitive to the romantic and classical elements of this extraordinary book, observes that it has both "an elusive melody and a lasting message." Some critics believe that FitzGerald's Omar is, in fact, an English poem with Persian allusions; FitzGerald interpolated, refined, and invented, but his *Rubáiyát* seems to demand that we read it as Persian and ancient.

The case invites speculations of a metaphysical nature. Omar professed (we know) the Platonic and Pythagorean doctrine of the soul's passage through many bodies; centuries later, his own soul perhaps was reincarnated in England to fulfill, in a remote Germanic language streaked with Latin, the literary destiny that had been suppressed by mathematics in Nishapur. Isaac Luria the Lion taught that the soul of a dead man can enter an unfortunate soul to nourish or instruct it; perhaps, around 1857, Omar's soul took up residence in FitzGerald's. In the *Rubáiyát* we read that the history of the universe is a spectacle that God conceives, stages, and watches; that notion (whose technical name is pantheism) would allow us to believe that the Englishman could have recreated the Persian because both were, in essence, God or the momentary faces of God. More believable and no less marvelous than these speculations of a supernatural kind is the supposition of a benevolent coincidence. Clouds sometimes form the shapes of mountains or lions; similarly, the unhappiness of Edward FitzGerald and a manuscript of yellow paper and purple letters, forgotten on a shelf of the Bodleian at Oxford, formed, for our benefit, the poem.

All collaboration is mysterious. That of the Englishman and the Persian was even more so, for the two were quite different, and perhaps in life might not have been friends; death and vicissitudes and time led one to know the other and make them into a single poet.

[1951]   [EW]

Coleridge's Dream

The lyric fragment "Kubla Khan" (fifty-odd rhymed and irregular lines of exquisite prosody) was dreamed by the English poet Samuel Taylor Coleridge on a summer day in 1797. Coleridge writes that he had retired to a farm near Exmoor; an indisposition obliged him to take a sedative; sleep overcame him a few moments after reading a passage in Purchas that describes the construction of a palace by Kublai Khan, the emperor whose fame in the West was the work of Marco Polo. In Coleridge's dream, the text he had coincidentally read sprouted and grew; the sleeping man intuited a series of visual images and, simply, the words that expressed them. After a few hours he awoke, certain that he had composed, or received, a poem of some three hundred lines. He remembered them with particular clarity and was able to transcribe the fragment that is now part of his work. An unexpected visitor interrupted him, and it was later impossible for him to recall the rest. "To his no small surprise and mortification," Coleridge wrote, "that though he still retained some vague and dim recollection of the general purport of the vision, yet, with the exception of some eight or ten scattered lines and images, all the rest had passed away like the images on the surface of a stream into which a stone has been cast, but, alas! without the after restoration of the latter!" Swinburne felt that what he had been able to recover was the supreme example of music in the English language, and that the person capable of analyzing it would be able—the metaphor is Keats'— to unravel a rainbow. Translations or summaries of poems whose principal virtue is music are useless and may be harmful; it is best simply to bear in mind, for now, that Coleridge was given a page of undisputed splendor *in a dream.*

The case, although extraordinary, is not unique. In his psychological study, *The World of Dreams*, Havelock Ellis has compared it with that of the violinist and composer Giuseppe Tartini, who dreamed that the Devil (his slave) was playing a marvelous sonata on the violin; when he awoke, the dreamer deduced, from his imperfect memory, the "*Trillo del Diavolo.*" Another classic example of unconscious cerebration is that of Robert Louis Stevenson, to whom—as he himself described it in his "Chapter on Dreams"—one dream gave the plot of *Olalla* and another, in 1884, the plot of *Jekyll and Hyde.* Tartini, waking, wanted to imitate the music he had heard in a dream; Stevenson received outlines of stories—forms in general—in his. Closer to Coleridge's verbal inspiration is the one attributed by the Venerable Bede to Caedmon (*Historia ecclesiastica gentis Anglorum* IV, 24). The case occurred at the end of the seventh century in the missionary and warring England of the Saxon kingdoms. Caedmon was an uneducated shepherd and was no longer young; one night he slipped away from some festivity because he knew that the harp would be passed to him and he didn't know how to sing. He fell asleep in a stable, among the horses, and in a dream someone called him by his name and ordered him to sing. Caedmon replied that he did not know how, but the voice said, "Sing about the origin of created things." Then Caedmon recited verses he had never heard. He did not forget them when he awoke, and was able to repeat them to the monks at the nearby monastery of Hild. Although he couldn't read, the monks explained passages of sacred history to him and he,

> as it were, chewing the cud, converted the same into most harmonious verse; and sweetly repeating the same made his masters in their turn his hearers. He sang the creation of the world, the origin of man, and all the history of Genesis: and made many verses on the departure of the children of Israel out of Egypt, and their entering into the land of promise, with many other histories from holy writ; the incarnation, passion, resurrection of our Lord, and his ascension into heaven; the coming of the Holy Ghost, and the preaching of the apostles; also the terror of future judgment, the horror of the pains of hell, and the delights of heaven; besides many more about the Divine benefits and judgments . . .

He was the first sacred poet of the English nation. "None could ever compare with him," Bede wrote, "for he did not learn the art of poetry from men, but from God." Years later, he foretold the hour of his death and awaited it in sleep. Let us hope that he met his angel again.

At first glance, Coleridge's dream may seem less astonishing than that of his precursor. "Kubla Khan" is a remarkable composition, and the nine-line hymn dreamed by Caedmon barely displays any virtues beyond its oneiric origin; but Coleridge was already a poet while Caedmon's vocation was revealed to him. There is, however, a later event, which turns the marvel of the dream that engendered "Kubla Khan" into something nearly unfathomable. If it is true, the story of Coleridge's dream began many centuries before Coleridge and has not yet ended.

The poet's dream occurred in 1797 (some say 1798), and he published his account of the dream in 1816 as a gloss or justification of the unfinished poem. Twenty years later, in Paris, the first Western version of one of those universal histories that are so abundant in Persian literature appeared in fragmentary form: the *Compendium of Histories* by Rashid al-Din, which dates from the fourteenth century. One line reads as follows: "East of Shang-tu, Kublai Khan built a palace according to a plan that he had seen in a dream and retained in his memory." The one who wrote this was a vizier of Ghazan Mahmud, a descendant of Kublai.

A Mongolian emperor, in the thirteenth century, dreams a palace and builds it according to his vision; in the eighteenth century, an English poet, who could not have known that this construction was derived from a dream, dreams a poem about the palace. Compared with this symmetry of souls of sleeping men who span continents and centuries, the levitations, resurrections, and apparitions in the sacred books seem to me quite little, or nothing at all.

How is it to be explained? Those who automatically reject the supernatural (I try always to belong to this group) will claim that the story of the two dreams is a coincidence, a line drawn by chance, like the shapes of lions or horses that are sometimes formed by clouds. Others will argue that the poet somehow knew that the Emperor had dreamed the palace, and then claimed he had dreamed the poem in order to create a splendid fiction that would palliate or justify the truncated and rhapsodic quality of the verses.[1] This seems reasonable, but it forces us to arbitrarily postulate a text unknown to Sinologists in which Coleridge was able to read, before 1816, about Kublai's dream.[2] More appealing are the hypotheses that transcend reason: for example, that after the palace was destroyed, the soul of the Em-

---

[1]At the end of the 18th or beginning of the 19th century, judged by readers with classical taste, "Kubla Khan" was much more scandalous than it is now. In 1884, Coleridge's first biographer, Traill, could still write: "The extravagant dream poem 'Kubla Khan' is little more than a psychological curiosity."

[2]See John Livingston Lowes, *The Road to Xanadu* (1927) 358, 585.

peror penetrated Coleridge's soul in order that the poet could rebuild it in words, which are more lasting than metal and marble.

The first dream added a palace to reality; the second, which occurred five centuries later, a poem (or the beginning of a poem) suggested by the palace; the similarity of the dreams hints of a plan; the enormous length of time involved reveals a superhuman executor. To speculate on the intentions of that immortal or long-lived being would be as foolish as it is fruitless, but it is legitimate to suspect that he has not yet achieved his goal. In 1691, Father Gerbillon of the Society of Jesus confirmed that ruins were all that was left of Kublai Khan's palace; of the poem, we know that barely fifty lines were salvaged. Such facts raise the possibility that this series of dreams and works has not yet ended. The first dreamer was given the vision of the palace, and he built it; the second, who did not know of the other's dream, was given the poem about the palace. If this plan does not fail, someone, on a night centuries removed from us, will dream the same dream, and not suspect that others have dreamed it, and he will give it a form of marble or of music. Perhaps this series of dreams has no end, or perhaps the last one will be the key.

After writing this, I glimpsed or thought I glimpsed another explanation. Perhaps an archetype not yet revealed to mankind, an eternal object (to use Whitehead's term), is gradually entering the world; its first manifestation was the palace; its second, the poem. Whoever compares them will see that they are essentially the same.

[1951]   [EW]

Forms of a Legend

People find it repugnant to see an aged, ill, or dead person, and yet we all are subject to death, illnesses, and old age; the Buddha said that this reflection caused him to abandon his house and parents and to put on the yellow robe of the ascetics. This testimony is in one of the books of the canon; another book records the parable of the five secret messengers sent by the gods: a child, a stooped old man, a cripple, a criminal on the rack, and a corpse. They tell him that it is our fate to be born, grow old, become ill, suffer just punishment, and die. The Judge of the Shadows (in Indian mythology, Yama has that role because he was the first man who died) asks the sinner if he has seen the messengers; he admits that he has, but he has not deciphered their message; the guards imprison him in a house filled with fire. Perhaps the Buddha did not invent this terrifying parable; it is enough to know that he said it (*Majjhima-nikaya*, 130) and that he never, perhaps, connected it to his own life.

Reality may be too complex for oral transmission; legends recreate it in a way that is only accidentally false and which permits it to travel through the world from mouth to mouth. In both the parable and the Buddha's statement, an old man, a sick man, and a dead man appear; time made the two texts into one and, confusing them, forged a new story.

Siddhartha, the Bodhisattva, the pre-Buddha, is the son of a great king, Suddhodana, of the lineage of the sun. On the night of his conception, his mother dreams that a snow-white elephant with six tusks enters her right side.[1]

---

[1]For us, this dream is merely ugly. For Hindus it is not. The elephant, a domestic animal, is a symbol of gentleness; the multiplication of tusks could not be disturbing to the spectators of an art that, to suggest that God is everything, carves figures with multiple arms and faces; six is the usual number (six paths of transmigration; six Buddhas anterior to the Buddha; six cardinal points, counting the zenith and the nadir; six divinities, which the *Yajur-Veda* calls the six doors of Brahma).

The sages interpret this to mean that her son will reign over the world or will make the wheel of the doctrine turn,[2] and will teach men how to free themselves from life and death. The king would rather have Siddhartha attain temporal than eternal grandeur, and shuts him up in a palace divested of all the things that could show him he is corruptible. Thus twenty-nine years of illusory happiness go by, dedicated to sensual pleasures, but Siddhartha, one morning, goes out in his chariot and sees with amazement a stooped man, "whose hair is not like other men's, whose body is not like other men's," who leans on a cane to walk and whose flesh trembles. He asks who the man is; the chariot driver explains that he is an old man, and that all men on earth will be like him one day. Siddhartha, disturbed, orders his driver to return home at once, but on another outing he sees a man wasted by fever, covered with leprosy and sores; the driver explains that he is a sick man, and that no one is exempt from that danger. On another outing he sees a man being carried on a bier; that motionless man is a dead man, they tell him, and to die is the rule for everyone who is born. On another outing, the last, he sees a monk of the mendicant orders who desires neither to live nor to die. Peace is on his face; Siddhartha has found the way.

Hardy *(Der Buddhismus nach älteren Pali-Werken)* praised the coloring of that legend; a contemporary Indologist, A. Foucher—whose mocking tone is not always intelligent or urbane—writes that, given the Bodhisattva's previous ignorance, the story lacks both dramatic climax and philosophical worth. At the beginning of the fifth century of our era, the monk Fa-Hsien made a pilgrimage to the kingdoms of Hindustan in search of sacred books, and saw the ruins of the city of Kapilavastu with the four images that Ashoka erected at the north, south, east, and west of the walls to commemorate Siddhartha's encounters. At the beginning of the seventh century, a Christian monk wrote a novel called *Barlaam and Josaphat*; Josaphat (Joasaf, Bodhisattva) is the son of an Indian king; the astrologers predict that he will reign over a larger kingdom, the Kingdom of Glory; the king confines him in a palace, but Josaphat discovers the unfortunate condition of mankind in the form of a blind man, a leper, and a dying man, and he is converted, finally, to the faith by the hermit Barlaam. This Christian version of the legend was translated into many languages, including Dutch and

---

[2]This metaphor may have suggested to the Tibetans the invention of the prayer machines, wheels or cylinders that revolve around an axis, filled with strips of rolled paper on which magic words are repeated. Some of the machines are manually operated; others are like large mills and are moved by water or the wind.

Latin; at the request of Hakon Hakonarson, a *Barlaam's Saga* was written in Iceland in the middle of the thirteenth century. Cardinal Cesare Baronio included Josaphat in his revision (1585–90) of the Roman Martyrology; in 1615, in his continuation of the *Décadas*, Diego de Couto denounced the similarity of the spurious Indian fable to the true and pious history of St. Josaphat. The reader will find all this and much more in the first volume of *Origenes de la novela* by Menéndez y Pelayo.

The legend that, in the West, led to the Buddha's canonization by Rome had one defect: the encounters it postulates are powerful but unbelievable. Siddhartha's four excursions and the four didactic figures do not coincide with the operations of chance. Less attentive to the aesthetic than to the conversion of souls, the scholars tried to justify that anomaly; Koeppen (*Die Religion des Buddha* I, 82) notes that, in the final form of the legend, the leper, the dead man, and the monk are illusions produced by the gods to instruct Siddhartha. Thus, in the third book of the Sanskrit epic *Buddhacarita*, it is said that the gods created a dead man, and that no one, except the chariot driver and the prince, saw him being carried. In a legendary biography from the sixteenth century, the four apparitions are four metamorphoses of a god (Wieger, *Vies chinoises du Bouddha*, 37–41).

The *Lalitavistara* went even further. It is customary to speak of that compilation of prose and poetry, written in an impure Sanskrit, with a certain sarcasm: in its pages the history of the Redeemer is inflated to the point of oppression and vertigo. The Buddha, surrounded by twelve thousand monks and thirty-two thousand Bodhisattvas, reveals the text of the work to the gods; from the fourth heaven he determines the time, the continent, the kingdom, and the caste into which he will be reborn to die for the last time; eighty thousand kettledrums accompany the words of his speech, and his mother's body has the strength of ten thousand elephants. The Buddha, in this strange poem, directs each stage of his destiny; he causes the gods to project the four symbolic figures, and when he questions the chariot driver, he already knows who they are and what they mean. Foucher sees this as mere servility on the part of the authors, who cannot tolerate the thought that the Buddha does not know what a servant knows; the enigma, to my mind, merits another solution. The Buddha creates the images and then questions a third party about their meaning. Theologically it would perhaps be possible to answer: the book pertains to the Mahayana school, which teaches that the temporal Buddha is the emanation or reflection of an eternal Buddha; the Buddha of heaven orders events, the earthly Buddha suffers or performs them. (Our century, with another mythology or vocabulary, speaks of the unconscious.) The humanity of the Son, the second person of God, was able to cry from the Cross: "My God, my God, why hast thou forsaken me?"; similarly, the humanity of the Buddha could be capable of horror at the forms his own divinity had created. . . . To unravel the problem, such dogmatic subtleties are not indispensable; it suffices to remember that all the religions of India, and Buddhism in particular, teach that the world is illusory. "The detailed narration of the game" (of a Buddha) is what *Lalitavistara* means, according to Winternitz; a game or a dream is, for Mahayana, the life of the Buddha on this earth, which is another dream. Siddhartha chooses his nation and his parents. Siddhartha creates four forms that will overwhelm him; Siddhartha orders that another form shall declare the meaning of the first forms; all of which is reasonable if we think of it as a dream dreamt by Siddhartha. Or, more exactly, if we think of it as a dream in which Siddhartha figures (as the leper and the monk figure) and as a dream which no one dreams, for in the eyes of northern Buddhism the world and the proselytes and *nirvana* and the wheel of transmigrations and the Buddha are equally unreal. No one is extinguished in *nirvana*, we read in a famous treatise, because the extinction of innumerable beings in *nirvana* is like the disappearance of a phantasmagoria created by a sorcerer at a crossroads; elsewhere it is written that everything is mere emptiness, mere name, including the book that states it and the man who reads it. Paradoxically, the numerical excesses of the poem subtract, rather than add, reality; twelve thousand monks and thirty-two thousand Bodhisattvas are less concrete than one monk and one Bodhisattva. The vast forms and the vast numbers (chapter XII includes a series of twenty-three words that indicate the unit followed by an increasing number of zeros, from 9 to 49, 51, and 53) are vast and monstrous bubbles, emphases of Nothing. The unreal, then, forms cracks in the story; first it makes the characters fantastic, then the prince, and with the prince, all the generations and the universe itself.

At the end of the nineteenth century Oscar Wilde proposed a variation: The happy prince dies in the seclusion of the palace, without having discovered sorrow, but his posthumous effigy discerns it from atop his pedestal.

The chronology of India is unreliable; my erudition is even more so; Koeppen and Hermann Beckh are perhaps as fallible as the compiler who has attempted this note; it would not surprise me if my history of the legend was itself legendary, formed of substantial truth and accidental errors.

[1952]   [EW]

The Scandinavian Destiny

That the destiny of nations can be no less interesting and poignant than that of individuals is a thing Homer did not know, but Virgil did, and the Hebrews felt it intensely. Another problem (the Platonic problem) is that of investigating whether nations exist in a verbal or a real way, whether they are collective words or eternal entities; the fact is that we can imagine them, and Troy's misfortune can touch us more than Priam's. Lines such as this one from the *Purgatorio*:

> *Vieni a veder la tua Roma che piagne*
> [Come see your Rome that weeps]

are proof of the poignancy of the generic, and Manuel Machado has successfully lamented, in an unquestionably beautiful poem, the melancholy destiny of the Arab lineages "*que todo lo tuvieron y todo lo perdieron*" [who had everything and lost everything]. Here, we might briefly recall the differential traits of this destiny: the revelation of Divine Unity that almost fourteen centuries ago brought together the shepherds in a desert and plunged them into a battle that has not ceased and whose limits were Aquitaine and the Ganges; the cult of Aristotle, which the Arabs taught Europe, perhaps without entirely understanding it, as if they were repeating or transcribing a coded message. . . . All that aside, it is the common vicissitude of peoples to have and to lose. To be on the verge of having everything and to lose everything is the tragic destiny of Germany. Rarer and more dreamlike is the Scandinavian destiny, which I shall attempt to define.

Jordanes, towards the middle of the sixth century, said of Scandinavia that this island (the Latin cartographers and historians took it for an island) was like the workshop or seedpod of nations; Scandinavia's sudden eruptions at the most heterogenous points of the globe would seem to confirm this viewpoint, from which De Quincey inherited the phrase *officinia gentium*. In the ninth century, the Vikings invaded London, demanded from Paris a tribute of seven thousand pounds of silver, and pillaged the ports of Lisbon, Bordeaux, and Seville. Hasting, by a wily strategem, took control of Luna, in Etruria, put its defenders to the knife, and burned down the city, in the belief that he had seized Rome. Thorgils, chief of the White Foreigners (Finn Gaill), ruled the north of Ireland; after the libraries were destroyed, the clerics fled; one of the exiles was John Scotus Erigena. Rurik, a Swede, founded the kingdom of Russia, whose capital city, before it was called Novgorod, was called Holmgard. Toward the year 1000, the Scandinavians, under Leif Eriksson, reached the coast of America. No one bothered them, but one morning (as *Erik the Red's Saga* tells it) many men disembarked from canoes made of leather and stared at them in a kind of stupor. "They were dark and very ill-looking, and the hair on their heads was ugly; they had large eyes and broad cheeks." The Scandinavians gave them the name of *skraelingar*, inferior people. Neither the Scandinavians nor the Eskimos knew that the moment was historic; America and Europe looked upon each other in all innocence. A century later, disease and the inferior people had done away with the colonists. The annals of Iceland say: "In 1121, Erik, Bishop of Greenland, departed in search of Vinland." We know nothing of his fate; both the bishop and Vinland (America) were lost.

Viking epitaphs are scattered across the face of the earth on runic stones. One of them reads:

> Tola erected this stone in memory of his son Harald, brother of Ingvar. They departed in search of gold, and went far and sated the eagle in the East. They died in the South, in Arabia.

Another says:

> May God have pity on the souls of Orm and Gunnlaug, but their bodies lie in London.

This one was found on an island in the Black Sea:

> Grani built this barrow in memory of Karl, his friend.

And this one was engraved on a marble lion found in Piraeus, which was moved to Venice:

Warriors carved the runic letters . . . Men of Sweden put it on the lion.

Conversely, Greek and Arab coins and gold chains and old jewels brought from the Orient are often discovered in Norway.

Snorri Sturluson, at the beginning of the thirteenth century, wrote a series of biographies of the kings of the North; the geographic nomenclature of this work, which covers four centuries of history, is another testimony to the breadth of the Scandinavian sphere; its pages speak of Jorvik (York); of Biarmaland, which is Archangel or the Urals; of Nörvesuud (Gibraltar); of Serkland (Land of the Saracens), which borders the Islamic kingdoms; of Blaaland (Blue Land, Land of Blacks), which is Africa; of Saxland or Saxony, which is Germany; of Helluland (Land of Smooth Stones), which is Labrador; of Markland (Land of Forests), which is Newfoundland; and of Miklagard (Large Population), which is Constantinople, where, until the fall of the East, the Byzantine Emperor's guardsmen were Swedes and Anglo-Saxons. Despite the vastness of this list, the work is not the epic of a Scandinavian empire. Hernán Cortés and Francisco Pizarro conquered lands for their king: the Vikings' prolonged expeditions were individual. "They lacked political ambitions," as Douglas Jerrold explains. After a century, the Normans (men of the North) who, under Rolf, settled in the province of Normandy and gave it their name, had forgotten their language, and were speaking French. . . .

Medieval art is inherently allegorical; thus, in the *Vita nuova*, an autobiographical narrative, the chronology of events is subordinated to the number 9, and Dante speculated that Beatrice herself was a nine, "that is, a miracle, whose root is the Trinity." That happened around 1292; a hundred years earlier, the Icelanders had written the first sagas,[1] which are realism in its most perfect form, as this sober passage from *Grettir's Saga* proves:

Days before St. John's eve, Thorbjörn rode his horse to Bjarg. He had a

---

[1]The *Dictionary of the Royal Academy of Spain* (1947) reads: "Saga (from the German *sage*, legend) f. Each one of the poetic legends contained mainly in the two collections of early heroic and mythological traditions of ancient Scandinavia, called the Eddas." This entry is an almost inextricable amalgamation of errors. *Saga* is derived from the Icelandic verb *segja* (to say), not from *sage*, a word which did not mean "legend" in medieval German; the sagas are prose narratives, not poetical legends; they are not contained in *"los dos Eddas"* [the two Eddas] (and whose gender is feminine). The most ancient songs of the Edda date from the ninth century; the most ancient sagas, from the twelfth.

helmet on his head, a sword in his belt, and a lance in his hand, with a very wide blade. At daybreak it rained. Among Atli's serfs, some were reaping hay; others had gone fishing to the North, to Hornstrandir. Atli was in his house, with few other people. Thorbjörn arrived around midday. Alone, he rode to the door. It was closed and there was no one outside. Thorbjörn knocked and hid behind the house so as not to be seen from the door. The servants heard the knock and a woman went to open the door. Thorbjörn saw her but did not let himself be seen, because he had another purpose. The woman returned to the chamber. Atli asked who was outside. She said she had seen no one and as they were speaking of it, Thorbjörn pounded forcefully.

Then Atli said: "Someone is looking for me and bringing a message that must be very urgent." He opened the door and looked out: there was no one. By now it was raining very hard, so Atli did not go out; with a hand on the doorframe, he looked all around. At that moment, Thorbjörn jumped out and with both hands thrust the lance into the middle of his body.

As he took the blow, Atli said: "The blades they use now are so wide." Then he fell face down on the threshold. The women came out and found him dead. From his horse, Thorbjörn shouted that he was the killer and returned home.

The classical rigor of this prose coexisted (the fact is remarkable) with a baroque poetry; the poets did not say "raven" but "red swan" or "bloody swan"; they did not say "corpse" but "meat" or "corn" of "the bloody swan." "Sword's water" or "death's dew" were their words for blood; "pirate's moon" for a shield. . . .

The realism of the Spanish picaresque suffers from a sermonizing tone and a certain prudishness regarding sexual matters, though not with respect to excrement; French realism oscillates between erotic stimulation and what Paul Groussac termed "garbage dump photography"; the realism of the United States goes from mawkishness to cruelty; that of the sagas represents an impartial observation. With fitting exaltation, William Paton Ker wrote: "The great achievement of the older world in its final days was in the prose histories of Iceland, which had virtue enough in them to change the whole world, if they had only been known and understood" (*English Literature, Medieval*, 1912), and on another page of another book he recalled "the great Icelandic school, the school that died without an heir until all its methods were reinvented, independently, by the great novelists, after centuries of floundering and uncertainty" (*Epic and Romance*, 1896).

These facts suffice, in my understanding, to define the strange and futile destiny of the Scandinavian people. In universal history, the wars and books of Scandinavia are as if they had never existed; everything remains isolated and without a trace, as if it had come to pass in a dream or in the crystal balls where clairvoyants gaze. In the twelfth century, the Icelanders discovered the novel—the art of Flaubert, the Norman—and this discovery is as secret and sterile, for the economy of the world, as their discovery of America.

[1953]   [EA]

The Dialogues of Ascetic and King

A king is a plenitude, an ascetic is nothing or wants to be nothing, and so people enjoy imagining a dialogue between these two archetypes. Here are a few examples, from Eastern and Western sources:

Tradition has it from Diogenes Laërtius that the philosopher Heraclitus was invited by Darius to visit his court. He refused with these words: "Heraclitus the Ephesian to King Darius, Son of Hystaspes: hail! All men are estranged from the truth and seek vainglory. As for myself, I flee the vanities of palaces and will not go to Persia, contenting myself with my inconsequentiality, which is sufficient for me."

In this letter—which is surely apocryphal, as there were eight centuries between the historian and the philosopher—there is, at first glance, nothing more than Heraclitus' independence or misanthropy; the resentful pleasure of snubbing the invitation of a king and, moreover, of a king who is a foreigner. But beneath the trivial surface beats a dark opposition of symbols, and the magic in which the zero, the ascetic, may in some way equal or surpass the infinite king.

This story is told in the ninth book of Diogenes Laërtius' *Lives of the Philosophers*. The sixth book has another version, from sources unknown, whose protagonists are Alexander and Diogenes the Cynic. The former had arrived in Corinth to lead the war against the Persians, and everyone had come out to see and welcome him.

Diogenes refused to leave his house, and there Alexander found him one morning, taking the sun. "Ask me for anything you'd like," said Alexander, and Diogenes, lying on the ground, asked him to move a little, so as not to block the light. This anecdote (repeated by Plutarch) puts the two speakers in opposition; in others there is a suggestion of a secret kinship. Alexander told his courtiers that had he not been Alexander, he would have liked to have been Diogenes; and the day one died in Babylonia, the other died in Corinth.

The third version of this eternal dialogue is the most extended: it takes up two volumes of the *Sacred Books of the East* series edited by Max Müller in Oxford. It is the *Milinda Pañha* (The Questions of Milinda), a novel of doctrinal intent, composed in the north of India at the beginning of our era. The Sanskrit original has been lost, and the English translation by Rhys Davids is from the Pali. Milinda, sweetened by Oriental pronunciation, is Menander, the Greek king of Bactriana who, a hundred years after the death of Alexander of Macedonia, brought his armies to the mouth of the Indus River. According to Plutarch, he governed wisely, and at his death, his ashes were divided among the cities of his kingdom.[1] Relics of the power he exerted, numismatic cases now hold over twenty different kinds of gold and bronze coins. On some, there is the image of a youth, on others that of an old man, and we may infer that his reign lasted many years. The inscriptions say "Menander the Just King," and on the obverse of the coins one finds a Minerva, a horse, a bull's head, a dolphin, a boar, an elephant, a palm branch, a wheel. The latter three figures are perhaps Buddhist.

In the *Milinda Pañha* we read that as the deep Ganges seeks the Ocean, which is even deeper, so Milinda the king sought out Nagasena, the bearer of the torch of Truth. Five hundred Greeks protected the King, who identified Nagasena in a crowd of ascetics by his leonine serenity (*"a guisa di león quando si posa"*). The King asked him his name. Nagasena replied that names are mere conventions that do not define permanent subjects. He explained that, as the King's chariot is neither the wheels nor the chassis, neither the axle, the shaft, nor the yoke, so man is not matter, form, perceptions, ideas, instinct, or consciousness. He is neither the combination of these parts nor does he exist apart from them . . . and he compared this to the flame of a lamp that burns every night and that endlessly both is and ceases to be. He spoke of reincarnation, of faith, of *karma* and *nirvana*, and after two days of discussion, or catechism, he converted the King, who put on the yellow robe of a Buddhist monk. That is the general plot of the *Questions of Milinda*, in which Albrecht Weber has perceived a deliberate imitation of the Platonic mode, a thesis rejected by Winternitz, who observes that the device of the dialogue is traditional in Indian letters, and that there is not the least trace of Hellenic culture in the *Questions*.[2]

Dressing himself as an ascetic, the King becomes indistinguishable

---

[1] The same story is told of the Buddha, in the book of his *nirvana*.

[2] Similarly, Wells believed that the Book of Job, whose date is problematical, was influenced by Plato's dialogues.

from one, and he brings to mind another king of the Sanskrit era who left his palace to beg alms in the streets, and who said these dizzying words: "From now on I have no kingdom or my kingdom is limitless; from now on my body does not belong to me or the whole earth belongs to me."

Five hundred years went by, and mankind devised another version of the infinite dialogue, this time not in India, but in China.[3] An emperor of the Han Dynasty dreamed that a man of gold flew into his room, and his ministers explained that he could only be the Buddha, who had achieved the Tao in Western lands. An emperor of the Liang Dynasty had protected that barbarian and his faith, and had founded temples and monasteries. The brahmin Boddhidharma, twenty-eighth patriarch of Indian Buddhism, had arrived (they say after three years of wandering) at his palace in Nanking, in the south. The Emperor enumerated all the pious works he had performed. Boddhidharma listened attentively, and then told him that all those monasteries and temples and copies of the sacred books were things of the world of appearances, which is a long dream, and thus were of no consequence. Good works, he said, can lead to good retributions, but never to *nirvana*, which is the absolute extinction of the will, not the consequence of an act. There is no sacred doctrine, because nothing is sacred or fundamental in an illusory world. Events and beings are momentary, and we can neither say whether they are or are not.

The Emperor then asked who was the man who had spoken in this manner, and Boddhidharma, loyal to his nihilism, replied:

"Nor do I know who I am."

These words resonated for a long time in Chinese memory. Written in the middle of the eighteenth century, the novel *The Dream of the Red Chamber* has this curious passage:

> He had been dreaming and then he woke up. He found himself in the ruins of a temple. On one side there was a beggar dressed in the robe of a Taoist monk. He was lame and was killing fleas. Hsiang-Lien asked him who he was and what place they were in. The monk answered:
>
> "I don't know who I am, nor where we are. I only know that the road is long."
>
> Hsiang-Lien understood. He cut off his hair with his sword and followed the stranger.

[3]I follow the text in Hackmann, *Chinesische Philosophie*, 1927, pp. 257 and 269.

In the stories I have mentioned, the ascetic and the king symbolize nothing and plentitude, zero and infinity. More extreme symbols of that contrast would be a god and a dead man, and their fusion would be more economical: a god that dies. Adonis wounded by the boar of the moon goddess, Osiris thrown by Set into the waters of the Nile, Tammuz carried off to the land from which he cannot return, are all famous examples of this fusion. No less poignant is this, which tells of the modest end of a god:

In the court of Olaf Tryggvason, who had been converted in England to the faith of Christ, an old man arrived one night, dressed in a dark cape and with the brim of his hat over his eyes. The King asked him if he knew how to do anything; the stranger answered that he knew how to play the harp and tell stories. He sang some ancient airs, told of Gudrun and Gunnar, and then spoke of the birth of Odin. He said that three Fates came, that the first two pronounced great happiness, but the third, in a rage, said, "You will not live longer than that candle burning by your side." His parents put the candle out so that Odin would not die with it. Olaf Tryggvason didn't believe the story; the stranger, insisting it was true, took out a candle and lit it. As the others watched it burn, he said it was late and that he had to leave. When the candle was consumed, they searched for him. A few steps from the King's house, Odin was lying dead.

Apart from their greater or lesser virtues, these texts, scattered in time and space, suggest the possibility of a morphology (to use Goethe's word) or science of the fundamental forms of literature. I have occasionally speculated in these pages that all metaphors are variants of a small number of archetypes; perhaps this proposition is also applicable to fables.

[1953]   [EW]

A Defense of *Bouvard and Pécuchet*

The story of Bouvard and Pécuchet is deceptively simple. Two copyists (whose age, like Alonso Quijano's, verges on fifty) forge a close friendship: an inheritance allows them to leave their work and move to the country; there they try their hand at agronomy, gardening, putting up preserves, anatomy, archaeology, history, mnemonics, literature, hydrotherapy, spiritualism, gymnastics, pedagogy, veterinary medicine, philosophy, and religion, and each of these heterogeneous disciplines holds a disaster in store for them; after twenty or thirty years, disenchanted (as we shall see, the "action" takes place not in time but in eternity), they ask a carpenter to build them a double writing stand, and they set themselves to copying, as before.[1]

For six years of his life, the final years, Flaubert dedicated himself to the design and execution of this book, which ultimately remained incomplete, which Gosse, so devout an admirer of *Madame Bovary*, would deem an aberration, and which Rémy de Gourmont considered the principal work of French literature, and almost of literature itself.

Emile Faguet ("that greyish Faguet," Gerchunoff once called him) published a monograph in 1899 that has the virtue of exhausting all the arguments against *Bouvard and Pécuchet*, which is a convenience for the critical examination of the work. Flaubert, according to Faguet, dreamed of an epic of human idiocy and (moved by memories of Pangloss and Candide and perhaps of Sancho and Quixote) superfluously endowed it with *two* protagonists who do not complement or oppose one another and whose duality is no more than a verbal artifice. Having created or postulated these nonentities, Flaubert makes them read an entire library *so that they will not understand it.* Faguet denounces the puerility of this game, and the danger, since Flaubert, in order to come up with the reactions of his two imbeciles, read

---

[1]I believe I detect an ironic reference to Flaubert's own fate.

one thousand five hundred treatises on agronomy, pedagogy, medicine, physics, metaphysics, etc., in the aim of not understanding them. Faguet notes: "If one stubbornly insists on reading from the point of view of a man who reads without understanding, in a very short while one achieves the feat of understanding absolutely nothing and being obtuse oneself." The fact is that more than five years of coexistence gradually transformed Flaubert into Pécuchet and Bouvard or (more accurately) Pécuchet and Bouvard into Flaubert. The two characters are initially two idiots, scorned and abused by the author, but in the eighth chapter the famous words occur: "Then a lamentable faculty arose in their spirits, that of seeing stupidity and no longer being able to tolerate it." And: "They were saddened by insignificant things: the advertisements in the newspapers, the profile of a bourgeois, a mindless remark overheard by chance." Flaubert, at this point, reconciles himself with Bouvard and Pécuchet, God with his creatures. This may happen in every long, or simply living, work (Socrates becomes Plato; Peer Gynt, Ibsen), but here we surprise the moment in which the dreamer, to use a kindred metaphor, notes that he is dreaming and that the forms of his dream are himself.

The first edition of *Bouvard et Pécuchet* appeared in March 1881. In April, Henry Céard attempted this definition: "a kind of two-man Faust." In the Pléiade edition, Dumesnil confirms: "The first words of Faust's monologue, at the beginning of the first part, are the entire plot of *Bouvard and Pécuchet*." Those are the words in which Faust deplores having studied philosophy, jurisprudence, medicine, and alas! theology, all in vain. In any case, Faguet had already written: "*Bouvard and Pécuchet* is the story of a Faust who was also an idiot." We must keep that epigram in mind, for the whole intricate polemic may in some way be read in it.

Flaubert declared that one of his aims was to pass all modern ideas in review; his detractors argue that the fact that the review is carried out by two imbeciles suffices, in all rigor, to invalidate it. To infer the vanity of all religions, sciences, and arts from the mishaps of these two buffoons is nothing but an insolent sophistry or a crude fallacy. The failures of Pécuchet do not entail a failure by Newton.

This conclusion is customarily refuted by a denial of its premise. Digeon and Dumesnil invoke a passage from Flaubert's close friend and disciple Maupassant in which we read that Bouvard and Pécuchet are "two fairly lucid, mediocre, and simple minds." Dumesnil emphasizes the adjective *lucid*, but the testimony of Maupassant—or of Flaubert, if it could be found—will never be as convincing as the text of the work itself, which appears to impose the term "imbeciles."

The justification of *Bouvard and Pécuchet*, I would venture to suggest, is of an aesthetic order, and has little or nothing to do with the four figures and nineteen modes of the syllogism. Logical rigor is one thing and the (now) almost instinctive tradition of placing essential words in the mouths of simpletons and madmen is another. Let us not forget the reverence Islam pays to idiots, in the understanding that their souls have been snatched away from heaven; let us not forget the passages in Scripture where we read that God hath chosen the foolish things of the world to confound the wise. Or, if concrete examples are preferable, we might think of Chesterton's Manalive, who is a visible mountain of simplicity and an abyss of divine wisdom, or of John Scotus Erigena, who argued that the best name for God is *nihilum* (nothing) and that "he himself does not know what he is, because he is not a what. . . ." The emperor Montezuma said that fools teach more than wise men because they dare to speak the truth; Flaubert (who, in the final analysis, was not constructing a rigorous demonstration, a *Destructio Philosophorum*, but a satire) may well have taken the precaution of confiding his final doubts and most secret fears to two mental incompetents.

A deeper justification may also be glimpsed. Flaubert was a devotee of Spencer; in the master's *First Principles* we read that the universe is unknowable, for the clear and adequate reason that to explain a fact is to relate it to another more general fact, a process that has no end,[2] or that conducts us to a truth so general that we cannot relate it to any other, that is, explain it. Science is a finite sphere that grows in infinite space; each new expansion makes it include a larger zone of the unknown, but the unknown is inexhaustible. Flaubert writes: "We still know almost nothing and we would wish to divine the final word that will never be revealed to us. The frenzy for reaching a conclusion is the most sterile and disastrous of manias." Art, of necessity, operates by symbols; the largest sphere is a point in infinity; two absurd copyists can represent Flaubert, and also Schopenhauer and Newton.

Taine repeatedly told Flaubert that the subject of his novel demanded an eighteenth-century pen, the concision and mordancy ("*le mordant*") of a Jonathan Swift. Perhaps he spoke of Swift because in some way he felt the affinity between these two great, sad writers. Both hated human stupidity with a minutious ferocity; both documented that hatred with trivial phrases and idiotic opinions compiled across the years; both wanted to de-

---

[2]Agrippa the Skeptic argued that any proof demands a proof in its turn, and so on to infinity.

molish the ambitions of science. In the third part of *Gulliver,* Swift describes a grand and venerated academy whose individuals propose that humanity abstain from oral language so as not to wear out the lungs. Others soften marble for the fabrication of pillows and pin-cushions; others aspire to propagate a breed of naked sheep, with no wool; others think to resolve the enigmas of the universe by means of a wooden frame with iron handles that combines words at random, an invention that goes against Llull's *Ars magna....*

René Descharmes has examined, and reproached, the chronology of *Bouvard and Pécuchet.* The action requires about forty years; the protagonists devote themselves to gymnastics at the age of seventy-eight, the same year in which Pécuchet discovers love. The book is full of events, yet time stands still: outside of the attempts and failures of the two Fausts (or of the two-headed Faust), nothing happens; the common vicissitudes of life and fatality and chance are all absent. "The supernumeraries of the book's outcome are those of its preamble; no one travels, no one dies," observes Claude Digeon. On another page he concludes, "Flaubert's intellectual honesty played him a terrible turn: it led him to overburden his philosophical tale, to write it with his novelist's pen."

The negligences or disdains or liberties of the final Flaubert have disconcerted the critics; I believe I see in them a symbol. The man who, with *Madame Bovary,* forged the realist novel was also the first to shatter it. Chesterton, only yesterday, wrote: "The novel may well die with us." Flaubert instinctively sensed that death, which is indeed taking place (is not *Ulysses,* with its maps and timetables and exactitudes the magnificent death throes of a genre?), and in the fifth chapter of the work, he condemned the "statistical or ethnographic" novels of Balzac and, by extension, of Zola. That is why the time of *Bouvard and Pécuchet* tends toward eternity; that is why the protagonists do not die and will go on copying their anachronistic *Sottisier* near Caen, as unaware of 1914 as they were of 1870; that is why the work looks back to the parables of Voltaire and Swift and the Orientals, and forward to those of Kafka.

There is, perhaps, another key. To mock humanity's yearnings, Swift attributed them to pygmies or apes; Flaubert, to two grotesque individuals. Obviously, if universal history is the history of Bouvard and Pécuchet, everything it consists of is ridiculous and insignificant.

[1954]   *[EA]*

Flaubert and His Exemplary Destiny

In an article intended to abolish or discourage the cult of Flaubert in England, John Middleton Murry observes that there are two Flauberts: one, a large-boned, strapping man, lovable, rather simple, with the look and laugh of a rustic, who spent his life agonizing over the intensive husbandry of half a dozen dissimilar volumes; the other, an incorporeal giant, a symbol, a battle cry, a banner. I must say that I do not understand this opposition; the Flaubert who agonized to produce a precious and parsimonious body of work is identical to the Flaubert of legend and (if the four volumes of his correspondence do not deceive us) of history. This Flaubert is more important than the important literature he premeditated and carried out, for he was the Adam of a new species: the man of letters as priest, ascetic, and almost martyr.

Antiquity, for reasons we shall examine, could not produce this figure. In the *Ion* we read that the poet is an "ethereal, winged, and sacred thing who can compose nothing until he is inspired, which is to say, mad." Such a doctrine of the spirit that bloweth where it listeth (John 3:8) was hostile to a personal appreciation of the poet, who was reduced to a fleeting instrument of divinity. A Flaubert is inconceivable in the Greek city-states, or in Rome; perhaps the man who most closely approximated him was Pindar, the priestly poet who compared his odes to paved roads, a tide, gold and marble carvings, and buildings, and who felt and embodied the dignity of the literary profession.

To this "romantic" doctrine of inspiration professed by the classics,[1] one fact may be added: the general feeling that Homer had already exhausted the possibilities of poetry, or in any case had discovered its utmost form, the

---

[1] Its reverse is the "classic" doctrine of Poe, the romantic, who makes the poet's work an intellectual exercise.

heroic poem. Each night, Alexander of Macedonia placed his knife and his *Iliad* beneath his pillow, and Thomas De Quincey tells of an English pastor who swore from the pulpit "by the greatness of human suffering, by the greatness of human aspirations, by the immortality of human creations, by the *Iliad*, by the *Odyssey!*" The wrath of Achilles and the rigors of Ulysses' voyage home are not universal themes, and posterity based its hopes on that limitation. To superimpose the course and configuration of the *Iliad* on other plots, invocation by invocation, battle by battle, supernatural device by supernatural device, was the highest aspiration of poets for twenty centuries. It is very easy to make fun of this, but not of the *Aeneid*, which was its fortunate result. (Lemprière discreetly includes Virgil among Homer's beneficiaries.) In the fourteenth century, Petrarch, a devout follower of the glory of Rome, believed he had found in the Punic Wars the durable subject of the epic poem; in the sixteenth, Tasso chose the first crusade, to which he dedicated two works, or two versions of one work. The first—the *Gerusalemme liberata*—is famous; the other, the *Conquistata*, which attempts to stay closer to the *Iliad*, is barely even a literary curiosity. In the *Conquistata*, the emphases of the original text are muted, an operation which, when carried out on an essentially emphatic work, can amount to its destruction. Thus, in the *Liberata* (VIII, 23), we read of a valiant, wounded man who still resists death:

> *La vita no, ma la virtù sostenta quel cadavere indomito e feroce*
> [Not life, but valor sustained the fierce, indomitable corpse]

In the revised version, hyperbole and impact disappear:

> *La vita no, ma la virtù sostenta*
> *il cavaliere indomito e feroce*
> [Not life, but valor sustained the fierce, indomitable cavalier]

Milton, later, lives to construct a heroic poem. From childhood, perhaps before ever writing a single line, he knows himself to be dedicated to letters. He fears he was born too late for the epic (too distant from Homer, and from Adam) and in too cold a latitude, but he schools himself in the art of versification for many years. He studies Hebrew, Aramaic, Italian, French, Greek, and naturally, Latin. He composes Latin and Greek hexameters and Tuscan hendecasyllables. He practices self-restraint, because he feels that profligacy might waste his poetic faculty. He writes, at the age of thirty-three, that the poet ought himself to be a true poem, "that is, a composition and pattern of the best and honourablest things," and that no one unworthy of praise himself should dare to sing high praises of "heroic men or famous cities." He knows that a book mankind will not let die is to emerge from his pen, but its subject has yet to be revealed, and he seeks it in the *Matière de Bretagne* and in the two Testaments. On a casual scrap of paper (today called the Cambridge Manuscript) he notes down a hundred or so possible subjects. Finally he chooses the fall of the angels and of man—a historical subject in that century, though today we consider it symbolic and mythical.[2]

Milton, Tasso, and Virgil consecrated themselves to the composition of poems; Flaubert was the first to consecrate himself (and I use the word in its full etymological rigor) to the creation of a purely aesthetic work *in prose*. In the history of literatures, prose is later than verse; this paradox was a goad to Flaubert's ambition. "Prose was born yesterday," he wrote. "Verse is the form *par excellence* of the literatures of antiquity. The combinations of metrics have been used up; not so those of prose." And in another passage: "The novel awaits its Homer."

Milton's poem encompasses Heaven, Hell, the world, and chaos, but remains an *Iliad*, an *Iliad* the size of the universe; Flaubert did not wish to repeat or surpass a prior model. He thought that each thing can be said in only one way, and that the writer's obligation is to find that way. As classics and romantics waged thundering debates, Flaubert said that his failures might differ but his successes were the same, because beauty is always precise, always right, and a good line by Boileau is a good line by Hugo. He believed in the pre-established harmony of the euphonious and the exact, and marveled at the "inevitable relation between the right word and the musical word." This superstitious idea of language would have made another writer devise a small dialect of bad syntactical and prosodical habits, but not Flaubert, whose fundamental decency saved him from the risks of his doctrine. With sustained high-mindedness, he pursued the *mot juste*, which of

---

[2]Let us follow the variations of a Homeric trait across time. Helen of Troy, in the *Iliad*, weaves a tapestry, and what she weaves are the battles and misadventures of the Trojan War. In the *Aeneid*, the hero, a fugitive from the Trojan War, arrives in Carthage and sees, in a temple, representations of scenes from that war and, among the many images of warriors, his own image as well. In the second *Gerusalemme*, Godofredo receives the Egyptian ambassadors in a muraled pavilion whose paintings represent his own battles. Of the three versions, the last is the least felicitous.

course did not exclude the common word and which would later degenerate into the vainglorious *mot rare* of the Symbolist salons.

History has it that the famous Lao Tzu wanted to live in secret, without
a name; a similar will to be ignored and a similar celebrity mark the destiny
of Flaubert. He wished to be absent from his books, or barely, invisibly,
there, like God in his works; and it is a fact that if we did not already know
that one and the same pen wrote *Salammbô* and *Madame Bovary*, we would
not guess it. No less undeniable is the fact that to think of Flaubert's work is
to think of Flaubert, of the anxious, painstaking workman and his lengthy
deliberations and impenetrable drafts. Quixote and Sancho are more real
than the Spanish soldier who invented them, but none of Flaubert's creatures is as real as Flaubert. Those who claim that his *Correspondence* is his
masterpiece can argue that those virile volumes contain the face of his
destiny.

That destiny continues to be exemplary, as Byron's was for the romantics. To an imitation of Flaubert's technique we owe *The Old Wives' Tale* and
O primo Basilio; his destiny has been repeated, with mysterious magnifications and variations, in Mallarmé (whose epigram "Everything in the world
exists to end up in a book" voices one of Flaubert's convictions), in Moore,
in Henry James, and in the intricate and near-infinite Irishman who wove
Ulysses.

[1954]   [EA]

A History of the Tango

Vicente Rossi, Carlos Vega, and Carlos Muzzio Sáenz Pena, each a diligent historian, have all investigated the origins of the tango. I must say that I subscribe to all of their conclusions—as well as to others. There is also a history of the tango that the cinema periodically divulges; according to this sentimental version, the tango was born in the riverbank tenements of Buenos Aires (the Boca, by virtue of the area's photogenic features); the upper classes rejected it at first but, around 1910, indoctrinated by the good example of Paris, finally threw open their doors to that interesting product of the slums. This "from rags to riches" *Bildungsroman* is by now a sort of incontestable or proverbial truth; my memories (and I am over fifty) and my own informal inquiries by no means support such a version.

I have spoken to José Saborido, who wrote "*Felicia*" and "*La morocha*" [The Brunette] with Ernesto Poncio (who also wrote the tango "*Don Juan*"); to the brothers of Vicente Greco, author of "*La viruta*" [The Woodchip] and "*La tablada*" [The Wooden Board]; to Nicolás Paredes (once the political boss of Palermo), and to a few gaucho ballad singers he knew. I let them talk; I carefully avoided formulating questions that might suggest determined answers. The derivations of the tango, the topography, and even the geography they related were singularly diverse: Saborido (a Uruguayan) preferred a Montevidean cradle on the east bank; Poncio (from Retiro) opted for Buenos Aires and for his own neighborhood; those from the Southside docks invoked the Calle Chile; those from the northern part of town, the raucous Calle Temple or the Calle Junín.

In spite of the divergences I have enumerated, which could be easily multiplied by asking people from La Plata or from around Rosario, my advisers agree on one essential fact, that the tango was born in the brothels. (And also on the date of its origins, which none felt was much before 1880

or after 1890.) The primitive instrumentation of its earliest orchestras—
piano, flute, violin, and later the concertina—confirms, with its extravagance, the evidence that the tango did not arise from the riverbank slums
where, as everyone knows, the six strings of the guitar were sufficient. Other
confirmations also abound—the lascivious movements, the obvious connotations of certain titles ("*El choclo*" [The Corn-cob], "*El fierrazo*" [The
Iron Rod]), and what I observed as a boy in Palermo and, years later, in La
Chacarita and Boedo: that on the streetcorners pairs of men would dance,
since the women of the town would not want to take part in such lewd de-
bauchery. Evaristo Carriego portrayed it in his *Misas herejes* [Heathen
Masses]:

> *En la calle, la buena gente derrocha*
> *sus guarangos decires más lisonjeros,*
> *porque al compás de un tango, que es "La morocha,"*
> *lucen ágiles cortes dos orilleros.*

[The gentlefolk on the street lavish/their rude flattery,/because to the
beat of a tango about a dark-eyed girl,/two men from the slums dance
light-footed steps in a lewd embrace.]

On another page, with a wealth of poignant details, Carriego depicts a
humble wedding party; the groom's brother is in jail; two rowdy boys are
itching for a fight, and the neighborhood tough has to pacify them with
threats; there is mistrust, ill feeling, and horseplay, but

> *El tío de la novia, que se ha creído*
> *obligado a fijarse si el baile toma*
> *buen carácter, afirma, medio ofendido:*
> *que no se admiten cortes, ni aun en broma.*
> *Que, la modestia a un lado, no se la pega*
> *ninguno de esos vivos . . . seguramente.*
> *La casa será pobre, nadie lo niega:*
> *todo lo que se quiera, pero decente.*

[The bride's uncle takes it upon himself/to see that the dancing stays
proper though festive./There'll be no slithering tangos here, he says,/
nothing suggestive, not even in fun.//All modesty aside, not that these
louts would/understand, this house may be poor—no denying that—
/whatever you say, but/one thing at least, it's respectable.]

The momentary glimpse of the strict uncle, which the two stanzas cap-
ture, highlights people's first reaction to the tango—"that reptile from the
brothel," as Lugones would define it with laconic contempt (*El Payador*,
117). It took many years for the Northside to compel the tenements to adopt
the tango—by then made respectable by Paris, of course—and I am not
sure that this has been completely successful. What was once a devilish orgy
is now a way of walking.

The Fighting Tango

The sexual nature of the tango has often been noted, but not so its violence.
Certainly both are modes or manifestations of the same impulse; in all the
languages I know, the word for "man" connotes both sexual potency and
combative potential, and the word *virtus*, Latin for "courage," comes from
vir, meaning "male." Similarly, an Afghan on a page in *Kim* states flatly—as
if the two acts were essentially one—"When I was fifteen, I had shot my
man and begot my man."

To speak of the "fighting tango" is not strong enough; I would say that
the tango and the *milonga* directly express a conviction that poets have
often tried to voice with words: that a fight can be a celebration. In the famous *History of the Goths* that Jordanes wrote in the sixth century, we read
that Attila, before his defeat at Châlons, harangued his armies, telling them
that fortune had reserved for them "the joys of this battle" (*"certaminis hu-
jus gaudia"*). The *Iliad* speaks of Achaeans for whom war was sweeter than
returning home in hollowed ships to their beloved native land, and relates
how Paris, son of Priam, ran with rapid feet into battle like a stallion with
flowing mane in pursuit of mares. In *Beowulf*—the Saxon epic that
launched the Germanic literatures—the bard calls battle a *"sweorda gelac"*
or "game of swords." Scandinavian poets of the eleventh century called it
the "Vikings' feast." In the early seventeenth century, Quevedo, in one of his
ballads, called a duel a "dance of swords"—almost the same as the anonymous Anglo-Saxon's "game of swords." In his splendid evocation of the
Battle of Waterloo, Hugo said that the soldiers, realizing they were going to
die in that festivity (*"comprenant qu'ils allaient mourir dans cette fête"*),
saluted their god (the Emperor) standing amid the storm.

These examples, recorded in the course of my random readings, could
be effortlessly multiplied; in the *Chanson de Roland* or in Ariosto's vast
poem there are similar passages. Any of those mentioned here—Quevedo's

or the one about Attila, let us say—are undeniably effective. All of them, nonetheless, suffer from the original sin of literariness: they are structures of words, forms made of symbols. "Dance of swords," for example, invites us to link two dissimilar images in order for "dance" to imbue "combat" with joy, but it does not speak directly to our blood, does not recreate such joy in us. Schopenhauer (*Welt als Wille und Vorstellung* I, 52) has written that music is as near to us as the world itself; without the world, without a common stock of memories summoned by language, there would be no literature, but music does not need, could exist, without the world. Music is will and passion; the old tango, as music, immediately transmits that joy of combat which Greek and German poets, long ago, tried to express in words. Certain composers today strive for that heroic tone and sometimes conceive competent *milongas* about the Bateria slums or the Barrio Alto, but their labors—with deliberately old-fashioned lyrics and music—are exercises in nostalgia for what once was, laments for what is now lost, intrinsically sad even when their melody is joyful. They are to the rough and innocent *milongas* in Rossi's book what *Don Segundo Sombra* is to *Martín Fierro* or to *Paulino Lucero*.

We read in one of Oscar Wilde's dialogues that music reveals a personal past which, until then, each of us was unaware of, moving us to lament misfortunes we never suffered and wrongs we did not commit. For myself, I confess that I cannot hear *"El Marne"* or *"Don Juan"* without remembering in detail an apocryphal past, simultaneously stoic and orgiastic, in which I have challenged and fought, in the end to fall silently, in an obscure knife fight. Perhaps this is the tango's mission: to give Argentines the belief in a brave past, in having met the demands of honor and bravery.

A Partial Mystery

Having accepted the tango's compensatory function, we still have a small mystery to resolve. South America's independence was, to a great extent, an Argentine enterprise. Argentine men fought in battles all over the continent: in Maipù, in Ayacucho, in Junín. Then came the civil wars, the war in Brazil, the campaigns against Rosas and Urquizas, the war in Paraguay, the frontier war with the Indians. . . . Our military past is populous, but, indisputably, though Argentines consider themselves brave, they do not identify with that past (despite the bias in schools in favor of the study of history), but rather with the vast generic figures of the Gaucho and the Hoodlum. If

I am not mistaken, this instinctual paradox has an explanation: the Argentine finds his symbol in the gaucho and not the soldier because the courage ascribed to the former by oral tradition is not in the service of a cause but rather is pure. The gaucho and the hoodlum are seen as rebels; Argentines, unlike North Americans and most Europeans, do not identify with the state. This can be attributed to the fact that the state is an inconceivable abstraction.[1] The Argentine is an individual, not a citizen; to him, aphorisms such as Hegel's "The State is the reality of the moral idea" are sinister jokes. Films made in Hollywood repeatedly intend for us to admire the case of a man (usually a newspaper reporter) who befriends a criminal in order to turn him in to the police; Argentines, for whom friendship is a passion and the police a mafia, consider such a "hero" to be an incomprehensible scoundrel. Along with Don Quixote, the Argentine feels that "up there, each man will have to answer for his own sins" and that "an honest man should not be the hangmen of others, with whom he has nothing to do" (*Don Quixote* I, 22). When faced, more than once, with the empty symmetries of Spanish style, I have thought that we differ irredeemably from Spain; these lines from the *Quixote* are enough to convince me of my error. They are the secret, quiet symbol of an affinity. One night in Argentine literature confirms this affinity, that desperate night when a rural police sergeant exclaimed he would not commit the crime of killing a brave man and began to fight against his own soldiers, together with the deserter Martín Fierro.

The Lyrics

Uneven in quality, as they conspicuously proceed from hundreds and thousands of diversely inspired or merely industrious pens, the lyrics of the tango, after half a century, now constitute an almost impenetrable *corpus poeticum* which historians of Argentine literature will read or, in any case, defend. Popular culture, when the people no longer understand it, when the years have made it antiquated, gains the nostalgic veneration of scholars and validates polemics and glossaries. By 1990, the suspicion or certainty may arise that the true poetry of our time is not in Banchs' *La Urna* [The Urn] or Mastronardi's *Luz de provincia* [Provincial Light] but rather those imperfect pieces conserved in the songbook *El alma que canta* [The Singing

---

[1]The state is impersonal; the Argentine thinks only in terms of personal relationships. For him, therefore, stealing public monies is not a crime. I am stating the fact, not justifying or condoning it.

Soul]. Such a conjecture is melancholy. A culpable negligence has kept me from acquiring and studying this chaotic repertory, but I am not unacquainted with its variety and the growing compass of its themes. At the beginning the tango had no lyrics, or else they were obscene and haphazard. Some were rustic—"*Yo soy la fiel compañera/del noble gaucho porteño*" [I am the girlfriend, ever true/of the noble dockside city gaucho]—because their composers sought a popular flavor, but the low life and the slums were not poetic material, then. Others, like the related dance, the *milonga*,[2] were jolly, showy fanfare: "*En el tango soy tan taura/que cuando hago un doble corte/corre la voz por el Norte/si es que me encuentro en el Sur*" [When I tango I'm so tough/that, when I whirl a double cut/word reaches the Northside/if I'm dancing in the South]. Later, the genre chronicled, like certain French naturalist novels or certain Hogarth engravings, the local perils of the "harlot's progress": "*Luego fuiste la amiguita/de un viejo boticario/y el hijo de un comisario/todo el vento te sacó*" [Next you became the mistress/of an old pharmacist/and the police chief's son/knocked the wind out of your sails]. Still later, the deplorable gentrification of rough or rundown neighborhoods, like "*Puente Alsina,/¿dónde está ese malevaje?*" [Puente Alsina,/where are all your hooligans?] or "*¿Dónde están aquellos hombres y esas chinas,/vinchas rojas y chambergos que Requena conoció?/¿Dónde está mi Villa Crespo de otros tiempos?/Se vinieron los judios, Triunvirato se acabó*" [Where are those men and their gals/those red bandannas and slouch hats that Requena once knew?/Where's the Villa Crespo I used to know?/Then Jews moved in and the Triumvirato moved on]. From early on, the woes of secret or sentimental love had kept the pens busy: "*¿No te acordás que conmigo/te pusistes un sombrero/y aquel cinturón de cuero/que a otra mina la afané?*" [Remember when, with me/you wore that hat, and more,/around your waist that leather belt/I'd swiped from another broad?]. Tangos of guilt, tangos of hatred, tangos of sarcasm and bitterness, were written, difficult to transcribe and even to remember. All sides of city life began entering the tango; the low life and the slums were not its only subjects. In the preface to his *Satires*, Juvenal wrote memorably that everything which moved men—desire, fear, anger, carnal pleasure, intrigues, happiness—would be the subject of his book; with excusable exaggeration, we might apply his famous

---

[2] *Yo soy del barrio del Alto,/soy del barrio del Retiro./Yo soy aquel que no miro/con quién tengo que pelear,/y a quién en milonguear,/ninguno se puso a tiro.* [I'm from the Barrio del Alto,/from the Retiro, I am./I'm the man who barely notices/whomever I have to fight,/or whomever I *milonga*,/nobody fools with me.]

"*quidquid agunt homines*" to the whole of tango lyrics. We might also say that these lyrics form a vast, unconnected *comédie humaine* of Buenos Aires life. At the end of the eighteenth century, Wolf wrote that the *Iliad* was a series of songs and rhapsodies before it became an epic; this knowledge may allow for the prophecy that, in time, tango lyrics will form a long civic poem, or will suggest to some ambitious person the writing of that poem.

Andrew Fletcher's similar statement is well known: "If they let me write all a nation's ballads, I don't care who writes the laws"; the dictum suggests that common or traditional poetry can influence feelings and dictate conduct. The Argentine tango, if we apply this conjecture, might appear as a mirror of our reality and, at the same time, a mentor or model with a certain malignant influence. The first *milongas* and tangos might have been foolish, or at least slipshod, but they were heroic and happy. The later tango is resentful, deplores with sentimental excess one's miseries, and celebrates shamelessly the misfortunes of others.

Around 1926, I remember blaming the Italians (particularly the Genoese in the Boca) for the tango's decline. In that myth, or fantasy, of our "native" tango corrupted by "foreigners," I now see a clear symptom of certain nationalist heresies that later devastated the world—coming from the foreigners, of course. It was not the concertina, which I once ridiculed as contemptible, nor the hardworking composers who made the tango what it is, but the whole republic. Those old "natives" who engendered the tango, moreover, were named Bevilacqua, Greco, de Bassi. . . .

Some may object to my denigration of today's tango, arguing that the transition from boldness or swagger to sadness is not necessarily a bad thing and might even be a sign of maturity. My imagined adversary might well add that the innocent, brave Ascasubi is to the plaintive Hernández what the first tango is to the latest and that no one—save, perhaps, Jorge Luis Borges—has dared to infer from this diminished happiness that *Martín Fierro* is inferior to *Paulino Lucero*. The answer is easy: the difference is not only in its hedonistic tone but in its moral tone as well. In the everyday tango of Buenos Aires—the tango of family gatherings and respectable tearooms—there is a trivial vulgarity, a taste of infamy that the tango of the knife and the brothel never even suspected.

Musically, the tango is probably not important; its only importance is what we give it. This reflection is correct, but perhaps applies to everything. To our own death, for example, or to the woman who rejects us. . . . The tango can be debated, and we have debates over it, but it still guards, as does all that is truthful, a secret. Dictionaries of music record its short, adequate definition, approved by all; this elementary definition promises no difficulties, but the French or Spanish composer who then follows it and correctly crafts a "tango" is shocked to discover he has constructed something that our ears do not recognize, that our memory does not harbor, and that our bodies reject. We might say that without the evenings and nights of Buenos Aires a tango cannot be made, and that in heaven there awaits us Argentines the Platonic idea of the tango, its universal form (barely spelled out by *"La tablada"* and *"El choclo"*) a valiant species which, however humble, has its place in the universe.

The Challenge

There is a legendary or historical account, perhaps both legend and history (which may be another way of saying legendary), that illustrates the cult of courage. Its best written versions can be found in Eduardo Gutierrez's novels, now unjustly forgotten, such as *Hormiga Negra* [Black Ant] or *Juan Moreira;* among its oral versions the first I heard came from a Buenos Aires neighborhood called Tierra del Fuego, bounded by a penitentiary, a river, and a cemetery. The hero of this version was Juan Muraña, wagon driver and knife fighter, in whom converged all the tales of courage circulating around the docks of the Northside. A man from Los Corrales or Las Barracas, knowing the fame of Juan Muraña, whom he has never seen, came up from his outlying slum in the Southside to pick a fight; he challenged him in a neighborhood bar, and the two moved out on the street to fight; each is wounded, but in the end Muraña slashes the man's face and says to him: "I'm letting you live so that you can come looking for me again."

   The detachment of that duel was engraved on my memory; it persisted in my conversations (as my friends knew too well); around 1927, I wrote it down and gave it the deliberately laconic title "Men Fought"; years later the anecdote helped me come up with a providential story—since it was hardly a good one—called "Streetcorner Man"; in 1950, Adolfo Bioy Casares and I took it up again to make a screenplay that film companies rejected enthusiastically and which would have been called *Los orilleros* [Riverbank Men]. I thought, after such extensive labors, that I had said good-bye to the story of the indifferent duel; then this year, in Chivilcoy, I picked up a much better version that I hope is the true one, although both could be, since destiny prefers to repeat forms, and what happened once happens often. Two mediocre stories and a film I believe to be good came out of the deficient version; nothing can come out of the second one, which is perfect and complete. Without adding metaphors or scenery, I shall tell it as it was told to me. The story, as they told me, took place in the district of Chivilcoy, sometime in the 1870s. Wenceslao Suárez—the hero's name—works as a rope braider and lives in an adobe hut. A man about forty or fifty years old, he has a reputation for bravery, and it is likely (given the facts of the story) that he once killed a man or two, but these deaths, committed in honor, do not trouble his conscience or sully his fame. One evening in this man's sedate life, something unexpected happens; in the general store, he is told that a letter for him has arrived. Don Wenceslao does not know how to read; the bartender haltingly deciphers the ceremonious missive, which also does not seem to be handwritten by the man who sent it. In the name of certain friends who value dexterity and true composure, the stranger greets Don Wenceslao, whose fame has crossed the Arroyo del Medio, and offers him the hospitality of his humble home in a town in the province of Santa Fe. Wenceslao Suárez dictates a reply to the bartender, thanking the stranger for his expression of friendship, and explains that he dare not leave his mother—who's well along in years—alone, but invites the other man to his simple abode in Chivilcoy, where he will be welcome to partake of a side of beef and a bottle of wine. Months pass, and a man on a horse harnessed and saddled in a manner unfamiliar to the area shows up at the general store and asks for Suárez's address. Suárez, who has come in to buy meat, overhears the question and tells him who he is; the stranger reminds him of the letters they wrote each other a while ago. Suárez is delighted that the other man has decided to come, and the two of them go off to a nearby field, where Suárez prepares the barbecue. They eat and drink and talk. About what? I suspect about bloodshed and barbarian matters, but with wary formality. They have eaten lunch, and the heavy afternoon heat hangs over the land when the stranger invites Don Wenceslao to join him in a bit of knife play. To say no would mean dishonor. The two men practice and play at fighting at first, but Wenceslao soon realizes that the stranger intends to kill him. He finally understands the meaning of the ceremonious letter and regrets having eaten and drunk so much. He knows that he will tire before the other man, who is still young. Out of scorn or courtesy, the stranger proposes a short rest. Don Wenceslao accepts, and when they resume the duel, he lets the other man wound him in the left hand, around which he has rolled his poncho.[3] The knife cuts through his wrist, the hand hangs loose, as if dead. Suárez leaps backward, lays his bloodied hand on the ground, steps on it with his boot, tears it off, fakes a blow to the stranger's chest, and with one thrust rips open his belly. Thus ends the story, save that in one version, the man from Santa Fe is left in the field, and in another (which steals from him the dignity of death) he returns to his province. In this last version, Suárez gives him first aid with the rum left over from lunch. . . .

In this feat of Manco [One Hand] Wenceslao—as Suárez is now known—certain mild or polite touches (his trade as rope maker, his scruples about leaving his mother alone, the two flowery letters, the conversation, the lunch) happily tone down or amplify the barbarous tale, giving it an epic or even chivalrous dimension that we do not find (unless we are determined to find it) in the drunken brawls of *Martín Fierro* or in the similar but paltry version about Juan Muraña and the Southside man. One feature common to both is, perhaps, significant. In both, the challenger is defeated. The reason may be the mere, deplorable necessity for the local champion to triumph, but also (and this is preferable) a tacit condemnation of provocation in these heroic fictions, or—this would be best of all—the dark and tragic conviction that man is always the maker of his own doom, like Ulysses in Canto XXVI of the *Inferno*. Emerson, who praised in Plutarch's biographies "a Stoicism not of the schools, but of the blood," would not have disdained this story.

We would seem to have, then, men who lived in utter poverty, gauchos and others from the banks of the River Plate and the Parana, creating, without realizing it, a religion that had its mythology and its martyrs—the hard and blind religion of courage, of being ready to kill and to die. A religion as old as the world, but rediscovered in the American republics and lived by herders, stockyard workers, drovers, outlaws, and hoodlums whose music was the *estilos,* the *milongas,* the first tangos. I have written that this religion is an age-old cult; in a twelfth-century saga we read:

> "Tell me thy faith," said the count.
> "I believe in my own strength," said Sigmund.

[3]Montaigne in his *Essays* (I, 49) speaks of this olden manner of combat with cape and sword, and cites a passage from Caesar: "*Sinistras sagis involvunt, gladiosque distringunt*" [They wrapped their cloaks around their left arms and drew their swords]. Lugones, in *El payador* [The Itinerant Singer], quotes an analogous motif in a sixteenth-century romance of Bernardo del Carpio: "*Revolviendo el manto al brazo,/La espada fuera a sacar*" [Wrapping the mantle round his arm/He would draw his sword].

Wenceslao Suárez and his anonymous contender, and others whom mythology has forgotten or has embodied in these two, doubtless professed such a manly faith, which in all likelihood was not vanity but an awareness that God may be found in any man.

[1955]   *[SJL]*

A History of the Echoes of a Name

Isolated in time and space, a god, a dream, and a man who is insane and aware of the fact repeat an obscure statement. Those words, and their two echoes, are the subject of these pages.

The first example is well known. It is recorded in the third chapter of the second book of Moses, called Exodus. We read there that Moses, pastor of sheep, author and protagonist of the book, asks God what His name is, and God replies: "I Am That I Am." Before examining these mysterious words, it is perhaps worth recalling that in primitive or magical thought, names are not arbitrary symbols but a vital part of what they define.[1] Thus, the Australian aborigines receive secret names that the members of the neighboring tribe are not allowed to hear. Among the ancient Egyptians, a similar custom prevailed: each person received two names, the "little" name that was known to all and the true or "great" name that was kept hidden. According to the funerary literature, the soul runs many risks after death, and forgetting one's name (losing one's personal identity) is perhaps the greatest. It is also important to know the true names of the gods, demons, and gates to the other world.[2] Jacques Vandier writes: "It is enough to know the name of a god or of a divine creature in order to have it in one's power" (*La Religion égyptienne*, 1949). Similarly, De Quincey reminds us that the true name of Rome was also secret: in the last days of the Republic, Quintus Valerius Sorano committed the sacrilege of revealing it, and was executed. . . .

The savage hides his name so that it will not be used in magical practices

---

[1] One of the Platonic dialogues, the *Cratylus*, discusses and seems to negate a necessary connection between words and things.

[2] The Gnostics inherited or rediscovered this unusual opinion, and they created a vast vocabulary of proper names, which Basilides (according to Irenaeus) reduced to a single cacophonous or cyclical word, "Kaulakau," a sort of universal key to all the heavens.

that may kill, drive insane, or enslave its owner. This superstition survives in the ideas of slander and insult; we cannot tolerate our names being tied to certain words. Mauthner has analyzed and censured this mental habit.

Moses asks God what His name is: this is not, as we have seen, a curiosity of a philological nature, but rather an attempt to ascertain who God is, or more precisely, what He is. (In the ninth century, John Scotus Erigena would write that God does not know who or what He is, because He is not a who or a what.)

What interpretations have been made of the tremendous answer Moses heard? According to Christian theology, "I Am That I Am" declares that only God truly exists, or, as the Maggid of Mesritch taught, that only God can say the word "I." The doctrine of Spinoza, which makes all thoughts and applications the mere attributes of an eternal substance which is God, could well be an amplification of this idea. "God exists; we are the ones who do not exist," a Mexican has similarly written.

According to this first interpretation, "I Am That I Am" is an ontological affirmation. Others have believed that the answer avoids the question: God does not say who He is because it would exceed the comprehension of his human interlocutor. Martin Buber points out that "*Ehyeh asher ehyeh*" may also be translated as "I Am What I Will Be" or "I Will Be Where I Will Be." Had Moses, in the manner of Egyptian magic, asked God His name in order to have Him in his power, God would have answered: "Today I am talking with you, but tomorrow I may take on another form, including the forms of oppression, injustice, and adversity." We read this in *Gog and Magog*.[3]

Multiplied into the human languages—*Ich Bin Der Ich Bin, Ego Sum Qui Sum, Soy El Que Soy*—the sententious name of God, the name that, in spite of having many words, is more solid and impenetrable than if it were only one word, grew and reverberated through the centuries, to 1602, when Shakespeare wrote a comedy. In this comedy we glimpse, almost sideways, a cowardly and swaggering soldier who has managed, because of some scheme, to be promoted to the rank of captain. The ruse is discovered, the man is publicly disgraced, and then Shakespeare intervenes and puts in his mouth some words that reflect, as though in a broken mirror, those that the god spoke on the mountain:

---

[3]Buber (in *What Is Man?*, 1938) writes that to live is to enter a strange house of the spirit, whose floor is the chessboard on which we play an unknown and unavoidable game against a changing and sometimes frightening opponent.

> Captain I'll be no more,
> But I will eat and drink and sleep as soft
> As captain shall. Simply the thing I am
> Shall make me live.

Thus Parolles speaks, and suddenly ceases to be a conventional character in a comic farce and becomes a man and all mankind.

The last version was produced in the 1740s, in one of the years when Swift was slowly dying, years that were perhaps for him a single unbearable moment, a form of the eternity of hell. With glacial intelligence and glacial hatred, Swift (like Flaubert) had always been fascinated by madness, perhaps because he knew that, at the end, insanity was waiting for him. In the third part of *Gulliver's Travels*, he imagined with meticulous loathing a race of decrepit and immoral men, given over to weak appetites they cannot satisfy; incapable of conversing with their kind, because the course of time had changed their language; or of reading, because their memories could not carry from one line to the next. One suspects that Swift imagined this horror because he feared it, or perhaps to magically exorcise it. In 1717, he said to Young, the author of *Night Thoughts*, "I am like that tree; I will begin to die at the top." Those years survive for us in a few terrifying sentences. His sententious and grim character sometimes extends to what was said about him, as if those who judged him did not want to become less than he. Thackeray wrote: "To think on him is to think on the ruin of a great empire." There was nothing, however, so touching as his application of God's mysterious words.

Deafness, dizziness, and the fear of madness leading to idiocy aggravated and deepened Swift's melancholy. He began to lose his memory. He didn't want to use glasses; he couldn't read, and he was incapable of writing. He prayed to God every day to send him death. And one evening, old and mad and wasted, he was heard repeating, we don't know whether in resignation or desperation or as one affirms or anchors oneself in one's own invulnerable personal essence: "I am that I am, I am that I am. . . ."

He may have felt, *I will be miserable, but I am,* and *I am a part of the universe, as inevitable and necessary as the others,* and *I am what God wants me to be, I am what the universal laws have made of me,* and perhaps *To be is to be all.*

Here ends the history of the sentence; I need only add, as a sort of epilogue, the words that Schopenhauer said, near death, to Eduard Grisebach:

> If at times I have thought myself misfortunate, it is because of a confusion, an error. I have mistaken myself for someone else; for example, a

deputy who cannot achieve a noble title, or the accused in a case of defamation, or a lover whom the girl disdains, or a sick man who cannot leave his house, or others who suffer similar miseries. I have not been those persons; it, in sum, has been the cloth of the clothes I have worn and thrown off. Who am I really? I am the author of *The World as Will and Representation*, I am the one who has given an answer to the mystery of Being that will occupy the thinkers of future centuries. That is what I am, and who can dispute it in the years of life that still remain for me?

Precisely because he had written *The World as Will and Representation*, Schopenhauer knew very well that to be a thinker is as illusory as being a sick man or a misfortunate man, and that he was profoundly something else. Something else: the will, the dark root of Parolles, the thing that Swift was.

[1955]   *[EW]*

L'Illusion Comique

For years of stupidity and shame, the methods of commercial advertising and of *littérature pour concierges* were applied to the governing of the Republic. Thus there were two histories: the criminal one, composed of jails, tortures, prostitutions, arsons, and deaths; and the theatrical one, tales and fables made for consumption by dolts. A preliminary examination of the second, perhaps no less despicable than the first, is the purpose of this page.

The dictatorship loathed (pretended to loathe) capitalism, yet, as in Russia, copied its methods, dictating names and slogans to the people with the same tenacity with which businesses impose their razor blades, cigarettes, or washing machines. That tenacity, as everyone knows, was counterproductive: the excess of effigies of the dictator led many to detest the dictator. From a world of individuals we have passed into an even more passionate world of symbols: the clash was not between parties or opponents of the dictator, but rather among parties and opponents of an effigy or a name. . . .

More curious was the manipulation of politics according to the rules of drama or melodrama. On October 17, 1945, it was pretended that a colonel had been seized and abducted and that the people had rescued him. No one bothered to explain who had kidnapped him, or how his whereabouts were known; nor were there ever legal charges pressed against the supposedly guilty parties; nor were their names ever revealed or even speculated on. Over the course of ten years, the acting grew considerably worse, with an increasing disdain for the prosaic scruples of realism. On the morning of August 31, the colonel, now dictator, pretended to resign from the presidency; his announcement was not made before the Congress, but rather to some sufficiently populist union functionaries. Everyone knew that the purpose of this maneuver was to provoke the people to beg him to withdraw his resignation. In case there was any doubt, bands of party hacks, aided by the police, plastered the city with portraits of the dictator and his wife. Crowds listlessly gathered in the Plaza de Mayo, where the state radio broadcast exhortations not to leave and musical compositions to alleviate the tedium. Just before night fell, the dictator came out on a balcony of the Pink House. He was, as expected, acclaimed, but he forgot to renounce his renunciation, or perhaps he didn't do so because everyone knew he was going to do so, and it would have been a bore to insist. He ordered, however, an indiscriminate massacre of his opponents, and the crowds cheered. Yet nothing happened that night: everyone (except, perhaps, the speaker) knew or sensed that it was all a fiction. The same, to a lesser degree, occurred with the burning of the flag. It was said that it was the work of Catholics; the defamed flag was photographed and exhibited, but as the flagpole itself wasn't enough of a show, they opted for a modest hole in the center of the symbol. It is useless to list the examples; one can only denounce the duplicity of the fictions of the former regime, which can't be believed and were believed.

It will be said that the public's lack of sophistication is enough to explain the contradiction; I believe that its cause is more profound. Coleridge spoke of the "willing suspension of disbelief" that is poetic faith; Samuel Johnson said, in defense of Shakespeare, that the spectators at a tragedy do not believe they are in Alexandria in the first act and Rome in the second, but submit to the pleasure of a fiction. Similarly, the lies of a dictatorship are neither believed nor disbelieved; they pertain to an intermediate plane, and their purpose is to conceal or justify sordid or atrocious realities.

They pertain to the pathetic or the clumsily sentimental. Happily, for the enlightenment and security of the Argentines, the current regime has understood that the function of government is not to inspire pathos.

[1955]   [EW]

PROLOGUES

Bret Harte, *The Luck of Roaring Camp and Other Sketches*

Dates are destined for oblivion, but they situate men in time and bear a multiplicity of connotations.

Like almost all his country's writers, Francis Bret Harte was born in the East. The event took place in Albany, capital city of the state of New York, on the 25th day of August, 1836. At the age of eighteen, he embarked on his journey to California, the place where he became famous, the place to which his name is now linked. He plied the trades of miner and journalist. He parodied poets who have now been forgotten and wrote the tales that make up this volume, which he would never surpass. He was mentor to Mark Twain, who would quickly forget his kindness. He was the United States consul in Crefeld, Prussia, and in Glasgow, Scotland. He died in London in 1902.

After 1870, he did little but plagiarize himself, to the indifference or indulgence of his readers.

Observation confirms this melancholy law: to do justice to a writer, one must be unjust to others. To exalt Poe, Baudelaire peremptorily rejected Emerson (whose skill is far superior to Poe's); to exalt Hernández, Lugones denies the other *gauchesco* writers any knowledge of the gaucho; to exalt Mark Twain, Bernard De Voto has written that Bret Harte was "a literary impostor" (*Mark Twain's America*, 1932). Lewisohn, too, in his *Story of American Literature*, treats Bret Harte with a certain disdain. The reason, I suspect, is a historical one: the North American literature of our time does not wish to be sentimental, and repudiates any writer who is susceptible to that description. It has discovered that brutality can be a literary virtue; it has verified that North Americans in the nineteenth century were incapable of that virtue. Fortunately or unfortunately incapable. (But not us: we could already point to Ascasubi's *La refalosa*, Esteban Echeverría's *El matadero*, the murder of the black man in *Martín Fierro*, and the monotonous scenes of atrocity that Eduardo Gutiérrez used to turn out in vast quantities. . . .) In 1912, John Macy observed: "Our literature is idealistic, sweet, delicate, nicely finished. . . . The Ulysses of great rivers and perilous seas is a connoisseur of Japanese prints. The warrior of 'Sixty-One rivals Miss Marie Corelli. He who is figured as gaunt, hardy and aggressive, conquering the desert with the steam locomotive, sings of a pretty little rose in a pretty little garden." The goal of avoiding mawkishness and being—God willing—brutal has had two consequences: the rise of the "hard-boiled" writers (Hemingway, Caldwell, Farrell, Steinbeck, James Cain) and the depreciation of many mediocre writers and a few good ones: Longfellow, William Dean Howells, Bret Harte.

Of course, we Americans of the South need not concern ourselves with this polemic. We suffer from onerous and perhaps irreparable defects, but not from that of being romantic. It is my sincere belief that we can frequent Bret Harte and the most unyielding and nebulous of the Germans without great risk of any permanent contagion. I also believe that Harte's romanticism does not require any distortion of that term. Unlike other doctrines, romanticism was much more than a pictorial or literary style; it was a style of life. Its history can do without the works of Byron but not without his tumultuous life and resplendent death. The fate of Victor Hugo's heroes errs on the side of implausibility; the fate of the lieutenant in Bonaparte's artillery errs on that same side. If Bret Harte was a romantic, so was the reality of the history recounted in his narratives; the deep continent that spanned so many mythologies, the continent of Sherman's march and Brigham Young's polygamous theocracy, of Western gold and bison beyond the sunsets, of Poe's anxious labyrinths and Walt Whitman's great voice.

Francis Bret Harte traveled the California gold fields around 1858. Those who accuse him of not having worked very hard at being a miner forget that if he had, he might not have been a writer, or he might have preferred a different subject; material that is too familiar often fails to stimulate.

The tales in this volume were originally published in the *Overland Monthly*. At the beginning of 1869, Dickens read one of them, the irresistible and perhaps timeless "Outcasts of Poker Flat." He discovered in the style of the writing a certain affinity with his own, but what he profusely applauded was "the subtle strokes of character, the matter fresh to a degree that had surprised him; the painting in all respects masterly; and the wild rude thing painted, a quite wonderful reality" (John Forster, *The Life of Charles Dickens* II, 7). There was no lack, both then and later, of admiring testimonials, such as that of the humanist Andrew Lang, who, in an examination of the sources of the early Kipling (*Essays in Little*, 1891) reduced them to Gyp and Bret Harte; and the very significant one of Chesterton, who nevertheless denies that there is anything peculiarly American in Harte's labor.

To debate this opinion would be less fruitful than to point out a faculty that Bret Harte shared with Chesterton and Stevenson: the invention (and energetic rendering) of memorable visual traits. Perhaps the strangest and most felicitous is the one I read at the age of twelve, and which will, I have no doubt, accompany me to the end of my road: the black and white deuce of clubs pinned by the bowie knife to the bark of the monumental pine, over the body of John Oakhurst, gambler.

[*1946*]   [*EA*]

Thomas Carlyle, *On Heroes, Hero-worship and the Heroic in History*
Ralph Waldo Emerson, *Representative Men*

The ways of God are inscrutable. Toward the end of 1839, Thomas Carlyle perused Edward William Lane's decorous version of *The Thousand and One Nights;* the narrations struck him as "obvious lies," but he approved of the many pious commentaries that adorn them. His reading led him to meditate on the bucolic tribes of Arabia who obscurely idolized wells and stars until a red-bearded man awoke them with the tremendous news that there is no god but God and drove them into a battle that has not yet ended and whose limits were the Pyrenees and the Ganges. What, Carlyle wondered, would have become of the Arabs if Mohammed had not existed? Such was the origin of the six lectures that make up this book.

Despite the impetuous tone and the reliance on hyperbole and metaphor, *On Heroes and Hero-worship* is a theory of history. Carlyle was in the habit of continually rethinking this issue; in 1830, he hinted that history is an impossible discipline, for there is no event that is not the offspring of all prior events, and the partial but indispensable cause of all future events, and therefore, "Narrative is *linear,* Action is *solid.*" In 1833, he declared that universal history is a Divine Scripture[1] which all men must decipher and write, and in which they are written. A year later, in *Sartor Resartus*, he re-

---

[1]Léon Bloy developed this conjecture in the Kabbalistic sense. See, for example, the second part of his autobiographical novel *Le Désespéré.*

peated that universal history is a gospel, and added, in the chapter entitled "Center of Indifference," that Great Men are the true sacred texts and that "your numerous talented men and your innumerable untalented men" are mere commentaries, glosses, annotations, Targums and sermons.

Although the form of this book is at times of an almost baroque complexity, the hypothesis it espouses is very simple. The first paragraph of the first lecture states it fully and vigorously. Here are the words:

> Universal History, the history of what man has accomplished in this world, is at bottom the History of the Great Men who have worked here. They were the leaders of men, these great ones; the modelers, patterns, and in a wide sense creators, of whatsoever the general mass of man contrived to do or to attain.

A subsequent paragraph abbreviates this to "The History of the World was the Biography of Great Men." For determinists, the hero is, above all, a consequence; for Carlyle, he is a cause.

Herbert Spencer observes that although Carlyle believed he had abjured the faith of his fathers, his concepts of the world, man, and ethics prove he never ceased to be a rigid Calvinist. His dark pessimism, his doctrine of the select few (the heroes) and the almost infinite multitudes of the damned (the rabble) are an obvious Presbyterian legacy, though he once declared during an argument that the immortality of the soul is "old Jewish rags" and, in an 1847 letter, that the faith of Christ has degenerated into a vile, cloying religion of cowards.

More important than Carlyle's religion is his political theory. His contemporaries did not understand it, but it can now be summed up in a single household word: Nazism. This was substantiated by Bertrand Russell in his study *The Ancestry of Fascism* (1935) and by Chesterton in *The End of the Armistice* (1940). Chesterton's lucid pages speak of the astonishment and even stupefaction produced in him by his first contact with Nazism, a new doctrine that brought back touching childhood memories. Writes G. K. C.:

> That in my normal journey towards the grave this sudden reappearance of all that was bad and barbarous and stupid and ignorant in Carlyle, without a touch of what was really quaint and humorous in him, should suddenly start up like a specter in my path strikes me as something quite incredible. It is as incredible as seeing Prince Albert come down from the Albert Memorial and walk across Kensington Gardens.

There is an ample supply of texts to prove it: Nazism (insofar as it is not merely the expression of certain racial vanities we all darkly possess, especially the blockheads and thugs among us) is a reedition of the wraths of the Scottish Carlyle, who, in 1843, wrote that democracy is the despair of not finding heroes to lead us. In 1870, he celebrated the victory of "noble, patient, deep, pious and solid Germany" over "vapouring, vainglorious, gesticulating, quarrelsome, restless and over-sensitive France." He praised the Middle Ages, denounced parliamentary windbags, and defended the memory of the god Thor, William the Bastard, Knox, Cromwell, Frederick II, the taciturn Dr. Francia, and Napoleon; he was pleased that every community had its barracks and its jail; he yearned for a world that was not "chaos equipped with ballot urns"; he thought about hatred; he thought about the death penalty; he abhorred the abolition of slavery; he proposed that statues— "horrendous bronze solecisms"—be converted into useful bronze bathtubs; he declared that a tortured Jew is preferable to a millionaire Jew; he said that any society that is neither dead nor rushing toward death is a hierarchy; he defended Bismarck, and venerated, and may have invented, the Germanic Race. Those who feel in need of further pronouncements by Carlyle—I have barely begun to glean them here—may examine *Past and Present* (1843) and the tumultuous *Latter-Day Pamphlets* of the year 1850. In the present book they abound, particularly in the final lecture, which, with arguments that are worthy of a South American dictator, defends the dissolution of the English Parliament by Cromwell's musketeers.

The concepts I have just detailed are not illogical. Once the hero's divine mission has been postulated, it is inevitable that we deem him (and that he deem himself) free of human obligation, like Dostoevsky's most famous protagonist, like Kierkegaard's Abraham. It is also inevitable that any political adventurer will consider himself a hero and will reason that his own excesses are reliable proof of that.

In the first book of the *Pharsalia*, Lucan has engraved this sharp line: *"Victrix causa diis placuit, sed victa Catoni"* [The victor's cause was pleasing to the gods, but that of the vanquished, to Cato], which posits that a man can be right against the universe. For Carlyle, on the contrary, history is conflated with justice. Those who deserve victory will triumph: a principle that reveals to students of history that Napoleon's cause was irreproachable until the morning of Waterloo, and unjust and hateful by ten o'clock that night.

Such corroborations do not invalidate Carlyle's sincerity. No one has felt as strongly as he did that this world is unreal (unreal as a nightmare, and as ghastly). From this general phantasmality, he salvages one thing: work. Not its result, which is mere vanity, mere image, but its execution. He writes that the works of mankind are transitory, small and insignificant in themselves; only the worker and the spirit that inhabits him have meaning.

A little over a hundred years ago, Carlyle believed he perceived the disintegration of an outmoded world taking place around him, and he saw no other remedy than the abolition of all parliaments and the unconditional surrender of power to strong, silent men.[2] Russia, Germany and Italy have drunk the benefits of this universal panacea to the dregs; the results are servility, fear, brutality, mental indigence, and treachery.

Much has been said of the influence of Jean-Paul Richter on Carlyle, who rendered Richter's *Das Leben des Quintus Fixlein* into English; no one, however distracted, could possibly confuse a single page with the translator's original work. Both are labyrinthine, but Richter is labyrinthine out of sentimentalism, languor, sensuality; Carlyle, because passion belabors him.

In August 1833, the youthful Emerson visited the Carlyles in the solitudes of Craigenputtock. (That same afternoon, Carlyle pondered Gibbon's history and called it the splendid bridge between the ancient world and the new.) In 1847, Emerson returned to England and gave the lectures that form *Representative Men*, whose outline is identical to that of Carlyle's series. I suspect that Emerson cultivated this formal likeness to make the essential differences stand out all the more.

Heroes, for Carlyle, are intractable demigods who—with some slight military frankness and foul language—rule a subaltern humanity; Emerson, on the contrary, venerates them as splendid examples of the possibilities that exist in every man. Pindar, for him, is proof of my poetic faculties; Swedenborg or Plotinus, of my capacity for ecstasy. "In every work of genius," he writes, "we recognize our own rejected thoughts: they come back to us with a certain alienated majesty." In another essay he observes: "It could be said that a single person has written all the books in the world; such central unity is in them that they are undeniably the work of a single, all-knowing master." And in another: "An everlasting Now reigns in Nature, which hangs the same roses on our bushes which charmed the Roman and the Chaldean in their hanging-gardens."

---

[2]Tennyson interspersed this yearning for a *Führer* in some of his poems; for example, in the fifth stanza of the tenth part of *Maud*: "One still strong man in a blatant land . . ."

The foregoing lines will suffice to establish the fantastic philosophy professed by Emerson: monism. Our destiny is tragic because we are, irreparably, individuals, restricted by time and by space; there is nothing, consequently, more favorable than a faith that eliminates circumstances and declares that every man is all men and that there is no one who is not the universe. Those who profess such a doctrine are generally unfortunate or mediocre, avid to annul themselves in the cosmos; despite a pulmonary disorder, Emerson was instinctively happy. He encouraged Whitman and Thoreau; he was a great intellectual poet, a skilled maker of aphorisms, a man who delighted in the varieties of being, a generous and sensitive reader of the Celts and the Greeks, the Alexandrians and the Persians.

The Latinists nicknamed Solinus "Pliny's monkey"; toward 1873, the poet Swinburne believed himself to have been injured by Emerson, and sent him a letter which includes these curious words, and others I do not wish to recall: "You, sir, are a gap-toothed and hoary-headed ape, carried at first into notice on the shoulder of Carlyle." In 1897, Groussac dispensed with the zoological simile but not with the imputation:

> As for the transcendental and symbolic Emerson, it is well known that he was a sort of American Carlyle, without the Scotchman's acute style or prodigious historic vision. Carlyle often becomes obscure by reason of his profundity, but I fear that at times Emerson appears profound by reason of his obscurity; in any case, he was never able to shake off the fascination that he who *was* exercised over he who *could have been;* and only the ingenuous vanity of his countrymen could place the modest disciple on the same level as the master, the disciple who to the end, in that master's regard, retained something of the respectful attitude of Eckermann before Goethe.

With or without the baboon, both accusations are mistaken; Emerson and Carlyle have almost no other trait in common than their enmity for the eighteenth century. Carlyle was a romantic writer, of plebeian vices and virtues; Emerson, a classical writer and a gentleman.

In an otherwise unsatisfactory article in the *Cambridge History of American Literature*, Paul Elmer More considers him "the outstanding figure in American letters"; previously, Nietzsche had written: "To no other book have I felt as close as to the books of Emerson; I do not have the right to praise them."

Through time, through history, Whitman and Poe, as inventors, as the founders of sects, have overshadowed Emerson's glory; line by line, they are greatly inferior to him.

[1949]   [EA]

Ray Bradbury, *The Martian Chronicles*

In the second century of our era, Lucian of Samosata composed a *True History* that includes, among other marvels, a description of the Selenites, who (according to the truthful historian) card and spin metals and glass, remove and replace their eyes, and drink air-juice or squeezed air; at the beginning of the sixteenth century, Ludovico Ariosto imagined a hero who discovers on the moon all that has been lost on earth, the tears and sighs of lovers, the time wasted on games, the fruitless attempts and the unfulfilled desires; in the seventeenth century, Kepler wrote a *Somnium Astronomicum* that purports to be a transcription of a book read in a dream, whose pages reveal at great length the appearance and habits of the lunar snakes, which take shelter in deep caves during the heat of the day and venture out at nightfall. Between the first and the second of these imaginary voyages there is one thousand three hundred years, and between the second and the third a hundred; the first two are, nevertheless, free and capricious inventions, and the third is dulled by an urge for verisimilitude. The reason is clear. For Lucian and Ariosto, a trip to the moon was a symbol or archetype of the impossible, as a black swan was for the former; for Kepler, it was a possibility, as it is for us. Did not John Wilkins, inventor of a universal language, publish at that time his *A Discovery of a New World; or, A Discourse Tending to Prove, that 'tis Probable There May Be Another Habitable World in the Moon: with a Discourse Concerning the Probability of a Passage Thither?* In Aulus Gellius' *Attic Nights* we read that Archytas the Pythagorean constructed a wooden dove that could fly through the air; Wilkins predicted that a vehicle with a similar mechanism or shape would one day take us to the moon.

In its character of anticipating a possible or probable future, the *Somnium Astronomicum* prefigures, if I am not mistaken, the new narrative genre which the Americans of the North call "science-fiction" or "scientifiction," of which a notable example is these *Chronicles*. Its subject is the conquest and colonization of the planet Mars. This arduous enterprise by the men of the future seems destined for its time, but Ray Bradbury has chosen to employ (without, perhaps, attempting to do so, and through the secret inspiration of his genius) an elegiac tone. The Martians, who at the beginning of the book are terrifying, become worthy of pity as they are annihilated. Mankind triumphs, and the author takes no delight in their victory. He announces with sadness and disappointment the future expansion of the human race to the red planet—which his prophecy reveals to us is a desert of shifting blue sands, with ruins of grid-patterned cities and yellow sunsets and ancient boats for traveling over the sand.

Other authors stamp a future date, and we don't believe them, for we know that it is merely a literary convention; Bradbury writes "2004," and we feel the gravitation, the fatigue, the vast and shifting accumulation of the past—Shakespeare's "dark backward and abysm of Time." As the Renaissance observed, through the words of Giordano Bruno and Bacon, we are the true ancients, not the people of Genesis or Homer.

What has this man from Illinois created—I ask myself, closing the pages of his book—that his episodes of the conquest of another planet fill me with such terror and solitude?

How can these fantasies move me, and in such an intimate manner? All literature (I would dare to answer) is symbolic; there are a few fundamental experiences, and it is unimportant whether a writer, in transmitting them, makes use of the "fantastic" or the "real," Macbeth or Raskolnikov, the invasion of Belgium in August 1914 or an invasion of Mars. What does it matter if it this is a novel, or novelty, of science fiction? In this outwardly fantastic book, Bradbury has set out the long empty Sundays, the American tedium, and his own solitude, as Sinclair Lewis did in *Main Street.*

Perhaps "The Third Expedition" is the most alarming story in this volume. Its horror (I suspect) is metaphysical; the uncertain identity of Captain John Black's guests disturbingly insinuates that we too do not know who we are, nor what we look like in the eyes of God. I would also like to note the episode entitled "The Martian," which includes a moving variation on the myth of Proteus.

Around 1909 I read, with fascination and distress, in the dim light of a huge house that no longer exists, Wells' *The First Men on the Moon.* Thanks to these *Chronicles,* though different in conception and execution, I was able, in the last days of the autumn of 1954, to relive that delicious terror.

[1955]   [EW]

LECTURES

The Argentine Writer and Tradition

I would like to express and justify certain skeptical propositions concerning the problem of the Argentine writer and tradition. My skepticism is not related to the difficulty or impossibility of resolving the problem, but to its very existence. I think we are faced with a rhetorical theme, suitable for pathetic elaboration, rather than a true cerebral difficulty; it is, to my mind, an appearance, a simulacrum, a pseudo-problem.

Before examining it, I would like to consider its standard expressions and solutions. I will start with a solution that has become almost instinctive and presents itself without benefit of any rationale: the one which affirms that the Argentine literary tradition already exists in *gauchesco* poetry. Consequently, the lexicon, techniques, and subject matter of *gauchesco* poetry should enlighten the contemporary writer, and are a point of departure and perhaps an archetype. This is the most common solution, and for that reason I intend to examine it at some length.

It was proposed by Lugones in *El payador;* there we read that we Argentines possess a classic poem, *Martín Fierro,* and that this poem should be for us what the Homeric poems were for the Greeks. It seems difficult to contradict this opinion without detriment to *Martín Fierro.* I believe that *Martín Fierro* is the most lasting work we Argentines have written; I also believe, with equal intensity, that we cannot take *Martín Fierro* to be, as has sometimes been said, our Bible, our canonical book.

Ricardo Rojas, who has also recommended the canonization of *Martín Fierro,* has written a page, in his *Historia de la literatura argentina,* that appears to be almost a platitude, but is quite shrewd.

Rojas studies the poetry of the *gauchescos*—the poetry of Hidalgo, Ascasubi, Estanislao del Campo, and José Hernández—and finds its origins in the poetry of the rural improvisational singers known as *payadores,* that is, the spontaneous poetry of the gauchos themselves. He points out that the meter of this popular poetry is octosyllabic, the same meter used by the authors of *gauchesco* poetry, and he concludes by considering the poetry of the *gauchescos* to be a continuation or magnification of the poetry of the *payadores.*

I suspect that this claim is based on a serious mistake; we might also call it a clever mistake, for it is clear that Rojas, in order to give popular roots to the poetry of the *gauchescos,* which begins with Hidalgo and culminates with Hernández, presents it as a continuation or derivation of the poetry of the gauchos; therefore Bartolomé Hidalgo is not the Homer of this poetry, as Mitre said, but only a link in the sequence.

Ricardo Rojas makes a *payador* of Hidalgo; nevertheless, according to the same *Historia de la literatura argentina,* this supposed *payador* began by composing lines of eleven syllables, a meter that is by its very nature barred to *payadores,* who do not perceive its harmony, just as Spanish readers did not perceive the harmony of the hendecasyllabic line when Garcilaso imported it from Italy.

There is, to my mind, a fundamental difference between the poetry of the gauchos and *gauchesco* poetry. One need only compare any collection of popular poetry with *Martín Fierro, Paulino Lucero,* or the *Fausto,* to become aware of this difference, which exists equally in the lexicon and in the intent of the poets. The popular poets of the countryside and the outskirts of the city versify general themes: the pain of love and absence, the sorrow of love, and they do so in a lexicon that is equally general; the *gauchesco* poets, on the contrary, cultivate a deliberately popular language that the popular poets do not even attempt. I do not mean that the idiom of the popular poets is a correct Spanish, I mean that whatever may be incorrect in it results from ignorance. In the *gauchesco* poets, on the contrary, there is a quest for native words, a profusion of local color. The proof is this: a Colombian, a Mexican, or a Spaniard can immediately understand the poems of the *payadores*—the gauchos—but needs a glossary in order to reach even an approximate understanding of Estanislao del Campo or Ascasubi.

All of this can be abbreviated as follows: *gauchesco* poetry, which has produced—I hasten to repeat—admirable works, is as artificial as any other literary genre. The first *gauchesco* compositions, the ballads of Bartolomé Hidalgo, attempt to present themselves in accordance with the gaucho, as if spoken by gauchos, so that the reader will read them with a gaucho intonation. Nothing could be further from popular poetry. When they versify, the people—and I have observed this not only among the *payadores* of the countryside, but also in the neighborhoods of Buenos Aires—do so in the conviction that they are engaging in something important; therefore they instinctively reject popular words and seek out high-sounding words and turns of phrase. In all likelihood, *gauchesco* poetry has influenced the *payadores* by now, so that they, too, abound in Argentinisms, but initially this was not the case, and we have evidence of that (evidence no one has noted) in *Martín Fierro*.

Martín Fierro is written in a *gauchesco*-accented Spanish, and for a long while the poem does not allow us to forget that the person singing it is a gaucho; it abounds in comparisons taken from life in the grasslands; and yet there is a famous passage in which the author forgets this concern with local color and writes in a general Spanish, speaking not of vernacular subjects but of great, abstract subjects: time, space, the sea, the night. I am referring to the *payada,* the improvised musical face-off between Martín Fierro and El Moreno that occupies the end of the second part. It is as if Hernández himself had wished to demonstrate the difference between his *gauchesco* poetry and the genuine poetry of the gauchos. When the two gauchos, Fierro and El Moreno, start singing, they forget all *gauchesco* affectation and address philosophical issues. I have been able to corroborate this by listening to *payadores* in the surroundings of Buenos Aires; they reject the idea of versifying in street slang, in *orillero* and *lunfardo,* and try to express themselves correctly. Of course they fail, but their aim is to make of poetry something high, something distinguished, we might say with a smile.

The idea that Argentine poetry must abound in Argentine differential traits and in Argentine local color seems to me to be a mistake. If we ask which book is more Argentine, *Martín Fierro* or the sonnets in *La urna* by Enrique Banchs, there is no reason to say that the former is more Argentine. It will be said that in Banchs' *La urna* there are neither Argentine landscapes nor Argentine topography nor Argentine botany nor Argentine zoology; nevertheless, there are other specifically Argentine conditions in *La urna*.

I can recall two lines of *La urna* that seem to have been written expressly to prevent anyone from saying that this is an Argentine book; the lines are:

> *El sol en los tejados*
> *y en las ventanas brilla. Ruiseñores*
> *quieren decir que están enamorados.*

[The sun glints on the tiled roofs/and on the windows. Nightingales/
mean to say they are in love.]

A denunciation of "the sun glints on the tiled roofs and on the windows" seems inevitable here. Enrique Banchs wrote these lines in a house
on the edge of Buenos Aires, and on the edges of Buenos Aires there are no
tiled roofs, there are flat, terrace roofs; "nightingales mean to say they are in
love"; the nightingale is not so much a real bird as a bird of literature, of the
Greek and Germanic tradition. Nevertheless, I would maintain that in the
use of these conventional images, in these incongruous tiled roofs and
nightingales, although neither the architecture nor the ornithology is Argentine, there is the Argentine reserve, the Argentine reticence; the fact that
Banchs, in speaking of a great sorrow that overwhelmed him, of a woman
who left him and left the world empty for him, makes use of conventional,
foreign imagery such as tiled roofs and nightingales, is significant: significant of a reserve, wariness, and reticence that are Argentine, significant of
the difficulty we have in confiding, in being intimate.

Furthermore, I do not know if it needs to be said that the idea that a literature must define itself by the differential traits of the country that produces it is a relatively new one, and the idea that writers must seek out
subjects local to their countries is also new and arbitrary. Without going
back any further, I think Racine would not have begun to understand anyone who would deny him his right to the title of French poet for having
sought out Greek and Latin subjects. I think Shakespeare would have been
astonished if anyone had tried to limit him to English subjects, and if anyone had told him that, as an Englishman, he had no right to write *Hamlet*,
with its Scandinavian subject matter, or *Macbeth*, on a Scottish theme. The
Argentine cult of local color is a recent European cult that nationalists
should reject as a foreign import.

A few days ago, I discovered a curious confirmation of the way in which
what is truly native can and often does dispense with local color; I found
this confirmation in Gibbon's *Decline and Fall of the Roman Empire*. Gibbon
observes that in the Arab book *par excellence*, the Koran, there are no
camels; I believe that if there were ever any doubt as to the authenticity of
the Koran, this lack of camels would suffice to prove that it is Arab. It was
written by Mohammed, and Mohammed, as an Arab, had no reason to
know that camels were particularly Arab; they were, for him, a part of
reality, and he had no reason to single them out, while the first thing a
forger, a tourist, or an Arab nationalist would do is bring on the camels,

whole caravans of camels on every page; but Mohammed, as an Arab, was unconcerned; he knew he could be Arab without camels. I believe that we Argentines can be like Mohammed; we can believe in the possibility of being Argentine without abounding in local color.

Permit me to confide something, just a small thing. For many years, in books now fortunately forgotten, I tried to compose the flavor, the essence, of the outskirts of Buenos Aires; naturally I abounded in local words such as *cuchilleros, milonga, tapia,* and others, and in such manner I wrote those forgettable and forgotten books; then, about a year ago, I wrote a story called "Death and the Compass," which is a kind of nightmare, a nightmare in which elements of Buenos Aires appear, deformed by the horror of the nightmare; and in that story, when I think of the Paseo Colón, I call it Rue de Toulon; when I think of the *quintas* of Adrogué, I call them Triste-le-Roy; after the story was published, my friends told me that at last they had found the flavor of the outskirts of Buenos Aires in my writing. Precisely because I had not abandoned myself to the dream, I was able to achieve, after so many years, what I once sought in vain.

Now I wish to speak of a justly illustrious work that the nationalists often invoke. I refer to *Don Segundo Sombra* by Güiraldes. The nationalists tell us that *Don Segundo Sombra* is the characteristic national book; but if we compare *Don Segundo Sombra* to the works of the *gauchesco* tradition, the first things we note are differences. *Don Segundo Sombra* abounds in a type of metaphor that has nothing to do with the speech of the countryside and everything to do with the metaphors of the Montmartre salons of that period. As for the plot, the story, it is easy to discern the influence of Kipling's *Kim*, which is set in India and was, in its turn, written under the influence of Mark Twain's *Huckleberry Finn*, the epic of the Mississippi. In making this observation, I do not wish to devalue *Don Segundo Sombra*; on the contrary, I wish to emphasize that in order for us to have this book it was necessary for Güiraldes to recall the poetic technique of the French salons of his time, and the work of Kipling, which he had read many years before; which is to say that Kipling and Mark Twain and the metaphors of the French poets were necessary to this Argentine book, to this book which is, I repeat, no less Argentine for having accepted those influences.

I wish to note another contradiction: the nationalists pretend to venerate the capacities of the Argentine mind but wish to limit the poetic exercise of that mind to a few humble local themes, as if we Argentines could only speak of neighborhoods and ranches and not of the universe.

Let us pass on to another solution. It is said that there is a tradition of which we Argentine writers must avail ourselves, and that tradition is the literature of Spain. This second piece of advice is, of course, a bit less narrow than the first, but it also tends to restrict us; many objections can be made to it, but two will suffice. The first is this: Argentine history can unequivocally be defined as a desire to move away from Spain, as a willed distancing from Spain. The second objection is that, among us, the pleasure of Spanish literature, a pleasure I personally share in, is usually an acquired taste; I have often loaned French and English works to people without any particular literary erudition, and those books were enjoyed immediately, without effort. However, when I have suggested that my friends read Spanish books, I have found that these books were difficult for them to enjoy in the absence of special training; I therefore believe that the fact that certain illustrious Argentine writers write like Spaniards is not so much a testimony to some inherited capacity as it is evidence of Argentine versatility.

I now arrive at a third opinion on Argentine writers and tradition, one that I read not long ago and that greatly astonished me. This is the opinion that we Argentines are cut off from the past; that there has been some sort of rupture between ourselves and Europe. According to this singular point of view, we Argentines are as if in the first days of creation; our search for European subject matters and techniques is an illusion, an error; we must understand that we are essentially alone, and cannot play at being European.

This opinion strikes me as unfounded. I understand why many people accept it: such a declaration of our solitude, our perdition, and our primitive character has, like existentialism, the charms of poignancy. Many people may accept this opinion because, having done so, they will feel themselves to be alone, disconsolate, and in some way, interesting. Nevertheless, I have observed that in our country, precisely because it is a new country, there is a strong feeling for time. Everything that has happened in Europe, the dramatic events there in recent years, has resonated deeply here. The fact that a given individual was on the side of Franco or the Republic during the Spanish Civil War, or was on the side of the Nazis or the Allies, was in many cases the cause of very serious disputes and estrangements. This would not happen if we were detached from Europe. As for Argentine history, I think we all feel it deeply; and it is only natural that we should, because that history is very close to us, in chronology and in the blood; the names, the battles of the civil wars, the war of independence, all of it is, in time and in family traditions, quite near.

What is Argentine tradition? I believe that this question poses no problem and can easily be answered. I believe that our tradition is the whole of Western culture, and I also believe that we have a right to this tradition, a greater right than that which the inhabitants of one Western nation or another may have. Here I remember an essay by Thorstein Veblen, the North American sociologist, on the intellectual preeminence of Jews in Western culture. He wonders if this preeminence authorizes us to posit an innate Jewish superiority and answers that it does not; he says that Jews are prominent in Western culture because they act within that culture and at the same time do not feel bound to it by any special devotion; therefore, he says, it will always be easier for a Jew than for a non-Jew to make innovations in Western culture. We can say the same of the Irish in English culture. Where the Irish are concerned, we have no reason to suppose that the profusion of Irish names in British literature and philosophy is due to any social preeminence, because many of these illustrious Irishmen (Shaw, Berkeley, Swift) were the descendants of Englishmen, men with no Celtic blood; nevertheless, the fact of feeling themselves to be Irish, to be different, was enough to enable them to make innovations in English culture. I believe that Argentines, and South Americans in general, are in an analogous situation; we can take on all the European subjects, take them on without superstition and with an irreverence that can have, and already has had, fortunate consequences.

This does not mean that all Argentine experiments are equally felicitous; I believe that this problem of the Argentine and tradition is simply a contemporary and fleeting version of the eternal problem of determinism. If I am going to touch this table with one of my hands, and I ask myself: "Will I touch it with the left hand or the right?" and I touch it with the right hand, the determinists will say that I could not have done otherwise and that the whole prior history of the universe forced me to touch the table with my right hand, and that touching it with my left hand would have been a miracle. Yet if I had touched it with my left hand, they would have told me the same thing: that I was forced to touch it with that hand. The same occurs with literary subjects and techniques. Everything we Argentine writers do felicitously will belong to Argentine tradition, in the same way that the use of Italian subjects belongs to the tradition of England through the work of Chaucer and Shakespeare.

I believe, moreover, that all the foregoing discussions of the aims of literary creation are based on the error of supposing that intentions and plans matter much. Take, for example, the case of Kipling: Kipling dedicated his life to writing in accordance with a given set of political ideals, he wanted to make his work a tool for propaganda, and nevertheless, at the end of his life he had to confess that the true essence of a writer's work is usually unknown by that writer; and he remembered the case of Swift, who while writing *Gulliver's Travels* wanted to raise an indictment against mankind and instead left behind a children's book. Plato said that poets are the amanuenses of a god who moves them against their will, against their intentions, as the magnet moves a series of iron rings.

Therefore I repeat that we must not be afraid; we must believe that the universe is our birthright and try out every subject; we cannot confine ourselves to what is Argentine in order to be Argentine because either it is our inevitable destiny to be Argentine, in which case we will be Argentine whatever we do, or being Argentine is a mere affectation, a mask.

I believe that if we lose ourselves in the voluntary dream called artistic creation, we will be Argentine and we will be, as well, good or adequate writers.

[1951] *[EA]*

German Literature in the Age of Bach

In De Quincey's famous essay on murder considered as one of the fine arts, there is a reference to a book about Iceland. That book, written by a Dutch traveler, has a chapter which has become famous in English literature and was mentioned by Chesterton. It is a chapter entitled "On the Snakes in Iceland," and it is brief and to the point, as it consists of a single sentence: "Snakes in Iceland; there aren't any."

The task that I will undertake today is a description of German literature in the age of Bach. After some investigation, I was tempted to imitate the author of that book on Iceland and say: "Literature in the age of Bach; there wasn't any." But such brevity strikes me as contemptuous, a lack of civility. Moreover, it would be unjust, as it concerns an era that produced so many didactic poems in imitation of Pope, so many fables in imitation of La Fontaine, so many epics in imitation of Milton. To this we may add the literary societies that flourished in a truly unusual manner, and all the polemics that were launched with a passion that is absent from the literature of our own time.

There are two distinct criteria for literature. There is the hedonistic, that of pleasure, which is the criterion of readers; from this point of view, the age of Bach was literarily quite poor. Then there is the other criterion, that of the history of literature, which is much more hospitable than literature itself; from that point of view, it was an important time, for it set the stage for the period to come: the Enlightenment and later the classical age of German literature, the richest it has had and one of the richest in all of literature: the age of Goethe, Hölderlin, Novalis, Heine, and so many others.

This phenomenon of a poor period in German literature is not unique. All the historians have noted that German literature is not successive, but rather periodic, intermittent. There have been ages of splendor and, between them, ages of almost nothing, of obscurity and inertia.

Explanations have been sought for this phenomenon. As far as I know, there are three. The first is political. It is said that Germany, which became a kind of campground for all the armies of Europe, was periodically invaded and destroyed. (As it was again not long ago.) And that the eclipses of German literature corresponded to these annihilations. This explanation is a good one, but I don't think it is sufficient.

There is a second explanation, the one preferred by the histories of German literature written by Germans. These say that the obscure periods are the ones in which the true German spirit has not been able to take flight, because the age was dedicated to the imitation of foreign models. This is true, yet one might make two observations against this explanation. First, when a country has a strong spirit, foreign and exotic influences do not debilitate that spirit, they strengthen it. This is the case in the Baroque period, the era before that of Bach. (In Germany they call the seventeenth the "Baroque century.") In that century, which was brilliant in that country, foreign influences predominated, but not in a way that oppressed the German spirit. They were assimilated and used by it.

In passing, I'd like to note—because it is especially interesting to us—that the influence that predominated German literature in the seventeenth century was Spanish. There is the influence of Quevedo's *Sueños* on Michael Moscherosch, the greatest German satirist of that period, who wrote a book called *Marvelous and True Visions*. The author says his book portrays all the acts of humankind, its true colors of hypocrisy, mendacity, and vanity. This was clearly influenced by Quevedo, who gave life to a German book.

Another, more famous case, is that of Grimmelshausen, who knew the Spanish picaresque novels, a fragmentary translation of the *Quixote*, Cervantes' *Rinconete y Cortadillo*, and a German version of Mateo Alemán's *Guzmán de Alfarache*, and attempted to apply their techniques to the story of a German soldier in the Thirty Years' War called Simplicissimus. That project was, of course, a success.

An observation that is quite easy to make about the Spanish picaresque novel is the limitation of its subjects. It does not attempt to embrace all the riches of the miserable and daily life of Spain. It deals, rather, with petty escapades, often among servants.

If we compare a book like Quevedo's *El Buscón* with the ballads by the same author, filled as they are with prostitutes, ruffians, murderers, and thieves, we see that there is a criminal world, a world of outlaws that is far richer in the ballads than in the picaresque novel.

Another difference between the Spanish model and the German imitation: the Spanish picaresque novel was written with a moral, satirical intent. In contrast, Grimmelshausen's *Simplicissimus*, particularly in the first books, seems to have no other aim than to reflect, like a vast mirror, all of the terrible life of Germany during the Thirty Years' War. Later, because the book was successful, Grimmelshausen kept adding chapters. In the final ones something occurs that is typical of the German mind: the work drifts away from concrete facts and turns into an allegory. The hero of so many bloody adventures becomes a hermit, first in the Black Forest and later on an island. That ending, of a hero on an island, is important in German literature, for it prefigures a genre of books that would become popular in the eighteenth century, in the age of Bach. They were called *Robinsonaden*, imitations of Defoe's *Robinson Crusoe*.

The Germans were very moved by Defoe's novel, and produced countless imitations. In the end, they were so enthusiastic about this idea of a solitary man on an island that they destroyed the pathos of the idea, and began writing novels in which there were thirty or fifty simultaneous Robinsons; novels that were not the stories of the solitude or patience of a single man, but rather of colonial empires or political utopias.

I now return to the problem I noted at the beginning: that of the eras of sterility and obscurity which may be seen periodically in German literature. I believe that, besides the political circumstances and the influence of foreign literatures (which, contrary to the opinion of patriotic critics, are not always maleficent), there is a third reason, which strikes me as the most likely of all, which does not exclude the others, and which is perhaps fundamental. I believe that the reason for those obscure periods in German literature is in the German character itself. Germans are incapable of acting spontaneously and always need a justification for what they are going to do.

They need to see themselves in the third person, and moreover to see themselves magnified before they act.

The proof of this is that the Germans for a long time were not, as they have recently become, a people of action but rather a nation of dreamers. I recall that famous epigram by Heine, where he says that God rewarded the French with dominion over the land, the English with dominion over the sea, and the Germans with dominion over the clouds. And I also recall a famous poem by Hölderlin, entitled "To the Germans." In it, Hölderlin tells his compatriots not to mock the boy who rides with spurs and a whip on a wooden horse, because they are like that boy: poor in deeds and rich in thoughts. Then he asks himself if lightning does not come from the clouds, or the golden fruit from the dark leaf, and if the silence of the German people is not the solemnity that precedes the festival and the tremor that announces the presence of the god.

Besides these literary examples, I believe we can all recall examples from German politics. I don't know if you will recall that, at the beginning of the 1914 war, a German chancellor, Bethmann Hollweg, had to justify their failure to honor their commitment to neutrality. Any other politician in any other part of the world would have invented some sophism to defend himself. In contrast, Bethmann Hollweg, to justify the German attack, which was clearly an act of disloyalty, constructed a theory of loyalty, and said in his speech that they did not have to obey a treaty because a treaty was nothing but a piece of paper. We have seen this even more exaggerated in Nazism. It was not enough for the Germans to be cruel; they thought it necessary to construct a theory prior to their cruelty, a justification of cruelty as a postulated ethic.

I believe this may explain the obscure periods in German literature. They are periods of preparation, in which the German spirit is making a decision.

I have often cited Valéry's project: to write a history of literature without proper names. A history that would present all the books of the world as though they were written by a single person, by the universal spirit. Let us accept Valéry's fiction and imagine that all of German literature was the work of the German spirit. We may then suppose that the era of the life of Bach—that is, from 1675 to 1750—corresponds to a period of meditation by the German spirit, which was preparing itself for the splendid age of Hölderlin, Lessing, Goethe, Novalis, and later Heine.

To speak of Germany in this era, however, may lead to an error. We think of Germany now as a great united country, but then it was a series of small independent kingdoms, principalities, and duchies. At the time, Germany was on the outskirts of Europe. To confirm this view, which was held by many Germans in this period, we need only consider the cases of two illustrious figures: Leibniz and Frederick II of Prussia.

Leibniz wrote a treatise in which he attempted to defend the German language. He urged his countrymen to cultivate their language, and told them that a cultivated German would no longer be a torpid and nebulous language, but would become like a crystal, like French. He added a few patriotic considerations, and then dedicated himself, for the rest of his life, to writing in French.

Leibniz's decision to abandon his language for a foreign one is proof of what he really thought. He was a man of universal curiosity. It was natural that he should be interested in the style of his own language, but at the same time, he felt that it was a provincial one.

We may take an even more explicit case: that of Frederick the Great. Frederick often said that no good literature could come from Germany. When he discovered the *Nibelungenlied*, he thought it childish and barbaric. It is well known that Frederick founded an Academy, and that the individuals who frequented that Academy all wrote in French. They were French literati, who were respected with provincial veneration.

There are other examples of the provincial nature of German at that time: Dr. Johnson, when he was quite old, decided to learn a new language to see if his mind was still functioning properly. He chose Dutch. It never occurred to him to study German, a language as obscure and as easily overlooked as Dutch is today.

I return to the polemics that were launched in that period. There was, among others, a celebrated one between Gottsched and two Swiss writers, Bodmer and Breitinger. Gottsched was a writer who wanted to be the literary dictator of his age, and he published many books in Leipzig, where he lived for a long time. The Swiss writers had translated Milton's *Paradise Lost*; one had written an epic poem on the Flood and the other an epic poem on Noah. They defended—in a way that was utterly without interest—the rights of the imagination in poetry, and aroused the ire of Gottsched, who represented French taste. He published a book called *The Poetic Art*, in which he defended the three Aristotelian unities. It is curious to compare Gottsched's defense with those that were being written in other parts of Europe. One clearly sees the provincial and bourgeois atmosphere of Germany, and this was also noted by his Swiss adversaries.

Gottsched said that plays must limit themselves to a unity of action (that is, they must have only one plot), a unity of place (they must be set in a single place), and a unity of time. Unity of time had always been interpreted to mean twenty-four hours. For Gottsched, twenty-four hours was excessive, for a very bourgeois reason. He said that, at the most, he could tolerate twelve hours, but that they must be twelve hours of the day and not the night. Then he added—without realizing his error—this extraordinary argument: the twenty-four hours of the play cannot contain the nighttime hours because, he explained, at night one must sleep. He was faithful to the bourgeois concept that it is inconvenient to stay up late.

There was also a poet, Günther, who is another interesting example of that period. He figures in all the histories of German literature. His poems are worthless, if we read them without knowing the era in which they were written; they are only good if we compare them to the other German poets of the time. I will read a few lines of his poem to Christ:

> From outside I am tormented
> by the strong tide of misfortune;
> from within, terrifying fears
> and the fury of all the sins.
> The only salvation, Christ,
> is my death and your pity.

This poet is important because he is the poet of Pietism, the religious form of the era in which Bach lived. It is a movement that arose within the Lutheran church, and may be explained in this way: Luther had begun by defending the freedom of the Christian individual, attacking the authority of the Church. In one of his treatises, *On the Freedom of a Christian Man*, he maintained this paradox: the Christian man is master of all men and of all things; and he is subject to all and to all things.

Luther translated the Bible into German. That translation founded modern German and is its first literary document. Luther maintained that the true strength of each man is in himself, in his own conscience, not in the authority of the Church. On this basis, he attacked the Papal sale of indulgences.

There is a curious Papal doctrine that defends the sale of indulgences. It was said and believed, in Luther's time, that Christ and the martyrs had accumulated an infinite number of merits, and that those merits were greater than the ones required to save themselves. It was imagined that those superfluous merits from the life of Christ, the Virgin Mary, and the martyrs had accumulated in heaven and had formed there the *thesaurus meritorum,* the "treasury of merits."

It was also believed that the *Sumo Pontifice,* the Pope, held the keys to this celestial treasury and could distribute it to the faithful. Those who bought indulgences were buying a part of those infinite merits hoarded in the sky.

Luther attacked this belief, which he said made no sense. He also said that to save oneself, deeds were not necessary, only faith. What was important was that every Christian should believe that he could be saved, and this would save him.

Later, when it triumphed, Lutheranism in turn became another church, and in Germany a second Papacy, as rigid as the first. Many religious people in Germany protested against that rigidity, against its exclusively dogmatic character. They wanted to return to a more personal religion, to a direct communication between man and God. These were the Pietists.

The most famous, the head of them all, was called Spener. He began by holding meetings in his house. They were called "gatherings of piety" or "gatherings of pious persons"; their enemies called them Pietists. What happened with the word *pietist* frequently occurs with such hostile nicknames: they are adopted by the people who are being attacked. This has happened many times in history: in England, with the "tories"; or in France, with the "cubists." The word *cubist* was a joke by a hostile critic, when he saw a number of cubes on a painting: *"Qu'est-ce que cela? C'est du cubisme?"* The word *cubist* was then adopted by the injured party.

Spener proposed various goals. One was to form gatherings for reading the Bible. Another—which must have seemed quite strange—was to practice Christianity. This meant that every Christian should give proof of what he was through the rectitude of his life, the simplicity of his dress, and in his irreproachable conduct. Spener said that every Christian should consider himself a priest and take part in the governing of the Church. He urged that heterodox opinions should be tolerated and that sermons should have a less rhetorical and more personal style.

The Pietist movement later disappeared, with the arrival of a second movement, the Enlightenment, which pretended to subject everything to reason. But it was founded, in part, on the earlier one.

Returning to our topic, we reach this conclusion, this fact: Bach created his music in an era that was poor in literature. Poor, that is—and we should not forget this distinction—if we look to it for enduring works, but not poor if we consider it from the point of view of intellectual activity, for it was a period of discussions, polemics, and uncertainties.

This conjunction of great music and a poor, almost worthless, literature leads us to suspect that every age has only one expression of itself, that those ages which have had their fullest expression in one art do not find it in another. We then understand that it is not a paradox but a normal fact that the great music of Johann Sebastian Bach was contemporary to the poor literature in Germany at that time.

[1953]   [EW]

VII
Dictations
1956-1986

PROLOGUES

Ryunosuke Akutagawa, *The Kappa*

Thales measured the shadow of a pyramid in order to determine its height; Pythagoras and Plato taught the transmigration of souls; seventy scribes, secluded on the island of Pharos, produced in seventy days seventy identical translations of the Pentateuch; Virgil, in the second *Georgic*, pondered the delicate silks embroidered by the Chinese; and in days past, horsemen in the outskirts of Buenos Aires would contest the outcome of a match in the Persian game of polo. Whether apocryphal or true, these stories (to which one should add, among many others, the presence of Attila in the cantos of the *Elder Edda*) mark successive stages in an intricate and secular process which still continues: the discovery of the East by the countries of the West. This process, as may be assumed, has its opposite: the West discovered by the East. To this other side belong the missionaries in saffron robes that a Buddhist emperor sent to Alexandria, the conquest of Christian Spain by Islam, and the enchanting and sometimes terrifying books of Akutagawa.

To strictly differentiate the Eastern and Western elements in Akutagawa's work is perhaps impossible; in any event, the terms are not opposites, inasmuch as Christianity, which is of Semitic origin, predominates in the West. Nevertheless, I would hazard to say that Akutagawa's subjects and sentiments are Eastern, but that some of his rhetorical structures are European. Thus, in *Kesa and Morito* and *Rashomon*, we hear different versions of the same tale, retold by the various protagonists, the same technique used by Robert Browning in *The Ring and the Book*. On the other hand, a certain restrained sorrow, a certain preference for the visual, a certain lightness of stroke, seem to me, despite the inevitable imperfections of any translation, essentially Japanese. Extravagance and horror are in his work, but never in his style, which is always crystal clear.

Akutagawa studied English, French, and German literature; the subject of his doctoral dissertation was William Morris; and it is evident that he knew Schopenhauer, Yeats, and Baudelaire well. The psychological reinterpretation of the traditions and legends of his country was one of the tasks he undertook.

Thackeray declared that to think about Swift is to think about the collapse of an empire. A similar process of vast disintegration and pain operates in Akutagawa's last works. In *The Kappa*, the novelist employs the familiar artifice of lambasting the human race under the guise of a fantastic species; perhaps he was inspired by Swift's Yahoos, or the penguins of Anatole France, or the strange kingdoms crossed by the stone monkey in the Buddhist allegory. Halfway through the story, Akutagawa forgets the satiric conventions: it hardly matters to him that the Kappa, who are water imps, turn into humans who talk about Marx, Darwin, or Nietzsche. According to the literary canons, this negligence is a flaw. In fact, the last pages of the story are infused with an indescribable melancholy; we sense that, in the author's imagination, everything has collapsed, even the dreams of his art. Shortly afterward, Akutagawa killed himself. For the author of these final pages, the world of the Kappa and the world of man, the everyday world and the aesthetic world, are equally fruitless and mutable.

A more literal document of the final twilight of his mind is *Cogwheels*. Like the *Inferno* of Strindberg, who appears toward the end, this story is the diary, atrocious and methodical, of a gradual hallucinatory process. One might say that the meeting of the two cultures is necessarily tragic. On account of forces that began in 1868, Japan has come to be one of the great powers of the world, defeating Russia and forging alliances with England and the Third Reich. This nearly miraculous rebirth exacted, as might be expected, a heart-rending and sorrowful spiritual crisis. One of the artists and martyrs of that metamorphosis was Akutagawa, who died on July 24, 1927.

[1959]   [EW]

Edward Gibbon, *Pages of History and Autobiography*

Edward Gibbon was born in the vicinity of London on the 27th of April, 1737. He was of ancient but not particularly illustrious lineage, though an ancestor of his was Marmorarius or architect to the king in the fourteenth century. His mother, Judith Porten, appears to have paid him little attention during the hazardous years of his childhood. The devotion of a spinster aunt, Catherine Porten, enabled him to overcome several lingering illnesses. Gibbon would later call her the true mother of his mind and his health; from her he learned to read and write, at so early an age that he was able to forget his apprenticeship and almost believe that those faculties were innate. At the age of seven he acquired, at the expense of many tears and some blood, a rudimentary acquaintance with Latin syntax. Aesop's fables, Homer's epic poems in the majestic version of Alexander Pope, and *The Thousand and One Nights* which Galland had just revealed to the European imagination were his preferred readings. To these Oriental sorceries must be added another from the classical sphere: Ovid's *Metamorphoses*, read in the original.

He first felt the call of history at the age of fourteen, in a library in Wiltshire: a supplementary volume of Echard's history of Rome revealed to him the vicissitudes of the Empire after Constantine's fall. "I was immersed in the passage of the Goths over the Danube, when the summons of the dinner bell reluctantly dragged me from my intellectual feast." Gibbon's other fascination, after Rome, was the Orient, and he studied the biography of Mohammed in French or Latin versions of the Arabic texts. From history he went on, by a natural gravitation, to geography and chronology, and at the age of fifteen he attempted to reconcile the systems of Scaliger and Petavius, Marsham and Newton. Around that time, he enrolled at Oxford University. Later he would write, "I have no reason to acknowledge an imaginary debt in order to assume the merit of a just or generous retribution." On the antiquity of Oxford, he observes,

> Perhaps in a separate annotation I may coolly examine the fabulous and real antiquities of our sister universities, a question which has kindled such fierce and foolish disputes among their fanatic sons. In the meanwhile it will be acknowledged that these venerable bodies are sufficiently old to partake of all the prejudices and infirmities of age.

The professors—he tells us—"had absolved their conscience from the toil of reading, or thinking, or writing"; their silence (class attendance was not obligatory) led the young Gibbon to undertake a course of theological study on his own. A reading of Bossuet converted him to Catholicism; he believed, or believed he believed—he tells us—in the real presence of Christ in the Eucharist. A Jesuit baptized him into the faith of Rome. Gibbon sent his father a long and polemical epistle, written with all the pomp, dignity, and complacency of a martyr. To be a student at Oxford and to be a Catholic were incompatible things; the fervent young apostate was expelled by the university authorities, and his father sent him to Lausanne, at that time a Calvinist stronghold. He took lodgings in the home of a Protestant minister, M. Pavilliard, who after two years of dialogue set him back on the straight path. Gibbon spent five years in Switzerland; the habit of the French language and an absorption in its literature were this period's most important results. These are also the years of the only sentimental episode recorded in Gibbon's biography: his love for Mlle. Curchod, who later became the mother of Mme. de Staël. Gibbon *père* registered an epistolary objection to the match: Edward "sighed as a lover, obeyed as a son."

In 1758 he returned to England; his first literary task was the gradual formation of a library. Neither ostentation nor vanity had any part in the purchase of its volumes, and over the years, he was able to confirm Pliny's tolerant maxim that there is no book so bad it does not contain something good.[1] In 1761, his first publication appeared, written in French, which remained the language of his innermost thoughts. Entitled *Essai sur l'étude de la littérature*, it defended classical letters, which then were somewhat scorned by the Encyclopedists. Gibbon tells us that his work was received with cold indifference in England, where it was scarcely read and quickly forgotten.

A trip to Italy that began in April 1765 required several years of preliminary readings. He visited Rome; his first night in the eternal city was sleepless, as if he had foreseen and was unsettled by the murmur of the millions of words that would make up its history. In his autobiography, he writes that he can neither forget nor express the strong feelings that shook him. Amid the ruins of the Capitol, as the barefoot friars sang vespers in the Temple of Jupiter, he glimpsed the possibility of writing the decline and fall of Rome. The vastness of the enterprise intimidated him at first, and he chose instead to write a history of the independence of Switzerland, a work he would not complete.

An unusual episode occurred during those years. In the mid-eighteenth century, the Deists argued that the Old Testament is not of divine origin, for its pages do not teach that the soul is immortal and do not mention a doctrine of future punishments and rewards. Despite the existence of certain

---

[1] Pliny the Younger retained this generous maxim from his uncle (*Letters* 3, 5). It is commonly attributed to Cervantes, who repeats it in the second part of the *Quixote*.

ambiguous passages, this observation is correct; Paul Deussen, in his *Philosophie der Bibel*, declares, "Initially, the Semites had no knowledge whatsoever of the immortality of the soul. This unconsciousness lasted until the Hebrews established relations with the Iranians." In 1737, the English theologian William Warburton published a lengthy treatise entitled *The Divine Legation of Moses*, which reasons, paradoxically, that the lack of any reference to immortality is an argument in favor of the divine authority of Moses, who knew himself to be sent by the Lord and therefore had no need to resort to supernatural rewards or punishments. The argument was very clever, but Warburton knew in advance that the Deists would counter it with the example of Greek paganism, also devoid of any teaching of future penalties and compensations, yet nevertheless not divine. To salvage his hypothesis, Warburton resolved to attribute a system of otherworldly pleasures and chastisements to the Greek religion, and maintained that these were revealed during the Eleusinian mysteries. Demeter lost her daughter Persephone, stolen away by Hades, and after years of wandering across the world, she came upon her in Eleusis. Such is the mythic origin of the rites which, though initially agrarian—Demeter is the goddess of wheat—later symbolized immortality, by a sort of metaphor analogous to one St. Paul would use. ("So also is the resurrection of the dead. It is sown in corruption; it is raised in incorruption.") Persephone is reborn from the underworld of Hades; the soul will be reborn after death. The legend of Demeter is recorded in one of the Homeric hymns, where we also read that the initiate will be happy after death. Warburton thus appears to have been right in the part of his hypothesis having to do with the meaning of the mysteries; but not in another part which he added as a sort of flourish and which was censured by the youthful Gibbon. The sixth book of the *Aeneid* relates the journey of the hero and the Sibyl to the infernal regions; Warburton speculated that this represented the initiation of Aeneas as an officiant in the mysteries of Eleusis. His descent to Avernus and the Elysian Fields completed, Aeneas goes out by the gate of ivory, which is reserved for vain dreams, not by the gate of polished horn, which is the gate of prophetic dreams; this could mean that Hell is fundamentally unreal, or that the world to which Aeneas returns is also unreal, or that Aeneas, the individual, is a dream, just as we ourselves may be. The entire episode, according to Warburton, is not illusory but mimetic. Virgil was describing the mechanism of the mysteries in this fiction; to erase or allay the betrayal he thus committed, he made the hero go out by the gate of ivory, which, as I said, corresponds to deluding lies. It is inexplicable, without this key, that Virgil would suggest that a vision prophesying the greatness of Rome is apocryphal. Gibbon, in an anonymous 1770 work, argued that if Virgil had not been initiated, he could not reveal what he had not seen, and if he had been initiated, he was equally prohibited, since such a revelation would (to the pagan sensibility) have constituted a profanation and an outrage. Those who betrayed the secret were sentenced to death and publicly crucified; divine justice could act in anticipation of this sentence, and it was fearsome to live beneath the same roof as a wretch accused of this crime. Gibbon's *Critical Observations* were his first exercise in English prose, Cotter Morrison notes, and perhaps his clearest and most direct. Warburton elected to remain silent.

After 1768, Gibbon devoted himself to the preliminary tasks of his enterprise; he knew the classics almost by heart, and now he read and reread, pen in hand, all the original sources of Roman history, from Trajan to the last Caesar in the West. Upon these texts he shed, in his own words, "the subsidiary rays of medals and inscriptions, of geography and chronology."

The composition of the first volume, which appeared in 1776 and sold out in a few days, took him seven years. The work inspired the congratulations of Robertson and Hume, and what Gibbon would call almost a library of polemics. "The first discharge of the ecclesiastic ordnance" (I transcribe his own words here) stunned him, but he soon found that "this empty noise was mischievous only in the intention," and he replied disdainfully to those who contradicted him. With regard to Davies and Chelsum, he says that a victory over such antagonists was a sufficient humiliation.

Two subsequent volumes of the *Decline and Fall* appeared in 1781; their subject was historical, not religious, and they did not give rise to controversies but were read, Rogers tells us, with silent avidity. The work was concluded in Lausanne in 1783. The three final volumes are dated 1788.

Gibbon was a member of the House of Commons; his political activities merit no further comment. He himself has confessed that his shyness rendered him useless for debates and that the success of his pen discouraged the efforts of his voice.

The composition of his autobiography took up the historian's final years. In April of 1793, the death of Lady Sheffield brought him back to England. Gibbon died without suffering on the 15th of January, 1794, after a brief illness. The circumstances of his death are provided in an essay by Lytton Strachey.

It is a perilous thing to attribute immortality to a literary work. The risk increases if the work is of a historic nature and was written centuries after the events it studies. Still, if we resolve to forget some moodiness on Coleridge's part, or certain incomprehensions by Sainte-Beuve, the critical consensus in England and the continent has for two hundred years lavished the title of classic on the history of the *Decline and Fall of the Roman Empire*, and this adjective is known to include the connotation of immortality. Gibbon's own deficiencies, or if you wish, forbearances, are favorable to the work. If it had been written in adherence to any theory, the reader's approval or disapproval would depend on his opinion of the hypothesis. This is certainly not the case with Gibbon. Except for the warning against religious feeling in general, and the Christian faith in particular, that he voices in certain famous chapters, Gibbon appears to abandon himself to the facts he narrates and reflects them with a divine unconsciousness that makes him resemble blind destiny or the course of history itself. Like a man who is dreaming and knows he is dreaming, like a man who lowers himself to the hazards and trivialities of a dream, Gibbon, in his eighteenth century, dreamed again what the men of earlier cycles had lived or dreamed, within the walls of Byzantium or in the deserts of Arabia. To construct his work, he had to consult and summarize hundreds of widely divergent texts, and it is indisputably more pleasurable to read his ironic synopses than to lose one's way in the original sources by obscure or inaccessible chroniclers. Good sense and irony are habits of Gibbon's. Tacitus praises the form of worship practiced by the Germans, who did not shut their gods inside walls and did not dare represent them in wood or marble; Gibbon confines himself to observing that a people who barely had huts were hardly in a position to have temples or statues. Rather than writing that there is no confirmation whatsoever of the miracles recounted in the Bible, Gibbon reproaches the inexcusable carelessness of the pagans, who in their long catalogs of wondrous occurrences tell us nothing of the sun and moon that stood still in their course for a whole day, or of the earthquake and eclipse that accompanied the death of Jesus.

De Quincey writes that history is an infinite discipline, or at least an indefinite one, as the same events may be combined or interpreted in many ways. This observation dates from the nineteenth century; since then, interpretations have expanded under the influence of the evolution of psychology, while previously unsuspected cultures and civilizations have been exhumed. Nevertheless, Gibbon's work remains undiminished and it may plausibly be conjectured that the vicissitudes of the future will not touch it. Two causes work together toward this longevity. The first and perhaps most important is of an aesthetic order; it arises from enchantment, which

according to Stevenson is the indispensable and essential virtue of literature. The other reason comes from the perhaps melancholy fact that with
the passage of time, the historian is transformed into history; what matters
to us is not only to know what Attila's camp was like but also how an English gentleman of the eighteenth century imagined it. There were periods
in which Pliny's pages were read in search of precise facts; today we read
them in search of marvels, and this change has not injured Pliny's fortunes.
For Gibbon, that day has not yet arrived, and we do not know if it will. We
suspect that Carlyle or any other Romantic historian is further from us than
Gibbon.

To think of Gibbon is to think of Voltaire, whom Gibbon read so often
and of whose aptitude for the theater he has left us an unenthusiastic estimation. They share the same disdain for human religions or superstitions,
but their literary conduct differs greatly. Voltaire employed his extraordinary style to show or suggest that the facts of history are contemptible; Gibbon has no better opinion of humanity, but man's actions attract him as a
spectacle, and he uses that attraction to entertain and fascinate the reader.
He never participates in the passions that moved the former ages, and he
views them with an incredulity that is not devoid of indulgence and, perhaps, compassion.

To read through the *Decline and Fall* is to enter and delightfully lose
oneself in a crowded novel, whose protagonists are the generations of
mankind, whose theater is the world, and whose enormous time span is
measured in dynasties, conquests, discoveries, and the mutations of languages and idols.

[1961]   [EA]

Catalog of the Exhibition *Books from Spain*

As the sunset contains both day and night, and the waves, foam and water,
two disparate elements of nature inseparably constitute a book. A book is a
thing among things, an object among the objects that coexist in three dimensions, but it is also a symbol like an algebra equation or an abstract
idea. We may compare it to a chess game: a checkered black and white
board with pieces and an almost infinite number of possible moves. The
analogy to musical instruments is also clear, such as the harp Bécquer
glimpsed in the corner of a drawing room and whose silent world of sound

he compared with a sleeping bird. Such images are mere approximations or shadows; a book is much more complex. Written symbols are mirrors of oral symbols, which in turn convey abstractions, dreams, or memories. Perhaps it will suffice to say that a book, like its writer, is made of body and soul. Hence the manifold delight it gives us, the joys of sight, touch, and intelligence. Each in his own way imagines Paradise; since childhood I have envisioned it as a library. Not as an infinite library, because anything infinite is somewhat uncomfortable and puzzling, but as a library fit for a man. A library in which there will always be books (and perhaps shelves) to discover, but not too many. In brief, a library that would allow for the pleasure of rereading, the serene and faithful pleasure of the classics, or the gratifying shock of revelation and of the unforeseen. The collection of Spanish books recorded in this gracious catalog seems to anticipate that vague and perfect library of my hopes.

The book is spirit and matter; the Spanish mind and Spanish craftsmanship come alive and conjoin in the pieces gathered here. The spectator will linger in his examination of these wise and delicate fruits of a secular tradition; it is worth remembering that traditions are not the mechanical repetition of an inflexible form but rather a joyful play of variations and rejuvenations. Here are the various literatures governed by the Spanish language on both sides of the sea; here, the inexhaustible yesterday and the changing today and the grave future we still cannot decipher, yet which we are writing.

[1962]   [SJL]

Walt Whitman, *Leaves of Grass*

Those who go from the bedazzlement and vertigo of *Leaves of Grass* to the laborious perusal of any of the pious biographies of its author always feel cheated. In the greyish, mediocre pages of those works, they hunt for the vagabond demigod revealed in the poetry and are astonished not to find him. Such, at least, has been my personal experience and that of all my friends. One of the aims of this prologue is to explain or attempt an explanation of this disconcerting discord.

Two memorable books appeared in New York in the year 1855, both of an experimental nature, though very different from one another. The first, instantly famous and today relegated to textbook anthologies or the curiosity of scholars and children, was Longfellow's *Hiawatha*. Longfellow wanted to give the Indians who once lived in New England a prophetic and mythical epic poem in English. In quest of a meter that would not bring the ordinary ones to mind and that might seem native, he turned to the Finnish *Kalevala* that had been forged—or reconstructed   by Elias Lonnrott. The other book, ignored at the time and now immortal, was *Leaves of Grass*.

I have written that the two were different. Their difference is undeniable. *Hiawatha* is the carefully thought-out work of a good poet who has explored libraries and is not devoid of imagination or ear; *Leaves of Grass*, the unprecedented revelation of a man of genius. The differences are so obvious that it seems incredible that the two volumes were contemporary. Yet one fact unites them: both are American epics.

America, at that time, was the famous symbol of an ideal, now a little worn down by an excessive dependence on the ballot box and by the eloquent excesses of rhetoric, though millions of men have given and continue to give it their blood. The eyes of the entire globe were on America and its "athletic democracy." Among the innumerable testimonials, I will remind the reader only of an epigram by Goethe: *"Amerika, du hast es besser"* [America, you have it better]. Under the influence of Emerson, who in some way was always his teacher, Whitman set himself the task of composing an epic of this new historical event: American democracy. We must not forget that the first of the revolutions of our time, the one that inspired the French revolution and our own revolutions, was America's, and that democracy was its doctrine.

How to sing of this, mankind's new faith, in a way that would be fitting? There was an obvious solution, the one almost any other writer would have chosen, tempted by the glibnesses of rhetoric or by simple inertia: the laborious plotting of an ode or perhaps an allegory, complete with its vocative interjections and capital letters. Happily, Whitman rejected it.

He believed that democracy was a new event and that its exaltation called for a technique that was no less new.

I have spoken of the epic. In each of the illustrious models the young Whitman was acquainted with, and which he called feudal, there is a central character—Achilles, Ulysses, Aeneas, Roland, El Cid, Siegfried, Christ—whose stature is superior to the rest, who are all subordinate to him. This primacy, Whitman told himself, corresponds to an abolished world, or one we aspire to abolish, the world of the aristocracy. My epic cannot be so; it must be plural, it must declare or take as its premise the incomparable and absolute equality of all mankind. Such a requirement would appear to lead inevitably to a mere hodgepodge of accumulation and chaos; Whitman, who was a man of genius, steered around this danger with prodigious skill. He carried out the most wide-ranging and audacious experiment that the history of literature records, and with happy results.

To speak of literary experiments is to speak of exercises that have failed in a more or less brilliant way, such as Góngora's *Soledades* or the work of Joyce. Whitman's experiment came out so well that we tend to forget it was an experiment.

In a line of his book, Whitman recalls medieval canvases peopled with many figures, some of them haloed and central, and declares that he proposes to paint an infinite canvas populated with infinite figures, each with its nimbus of gold-colored light. How to pull off such a feat? Whitman, unbelievably, did.

Like Byron, he needed a Hero, but his, symbol of manifold democracy, had of necessity to be innumerable and ubiquitous, like Spinoza's diffuse God. He came up with a strange creature we have not yet fully understood, and he gave this creature the name Walt Whitman. The creature has a biform nature; it is the modest journalist Walter Whitman, native of Long Island, whom some bustling friend might greet on the sidewalks of Manhattan, and it is, at the same time, the other man that Walt Whitman wanted to be and was not, a man of loves and adventures, the loafing, spirited, carefree traveler across America. Thus, on one page of the work, Whitman is born on Long Island; on others, in the South. Thus, in one of the most authentic sections of "Song of Myself," he relates a heroic episode of the Mexican War and says he heard the story told in Texas, a place he never went. Thus, he declares that he witnessed the execution of the abolitionist John Brown. The examples could be multiplied dizzyingly; there is almost no page on which the Whitman of his mere biography is not conflated with the Whitman he yearned to be and that, today, he is in the imagination and affections of the generations of humanity.

Whitman was already plural; the author resolved that he would be infinite. He made of the hero of *Leaves of Grass* a trinity; he added to him a third personage, the reader, the changing and successive reader. The reader has always tended to identify with the protagonist of the work; to read *Macbeth* is in some way to be Macbeth; a book by Hugo is entitled *Victor Hugo Narrated by a Witness to His Life*; Walt Whitman, as far as we know, was the first to exploit to its extreme, to its interminable and complex extreme, this momentary identification. Initially he relied on dialogue; the reader converses with the poet and asks him what he hears and what he sees, or

confides the sadness he feels at not having known and loved him. Whitman
answers his questions:

> I see the Wacho crossing the plains, I see the incomparable rider of horses
>   with his lasso on his arm.
> I see over the pampas the pursuit of wild cattle for their hides.

And also:

> These are the thoughts of all men in all ages and lands, they are not
>   original with me.
> If they are not yours as much as mine, they are nothing or next to nothing,
> If they do not enclose everything they are next to nothing,
> If they are not the riddle and the untying of riddle they are nothing,
> If they are not just as close as they are distant they are nothing.

> This is the grass that grows wherever the land is and the water is,
> This is the common air that bathes the globe.

Innumerable are those who, with varying success, have imitated Whitman's intonation: Sandburg, Edgar Lee Masters, Mayakovsky, Neruda. . . .
No one, except the author of the impenetrable and surely unreadable
Finnegans Wake, has ever again undertaken to create a multiple personage.
Whitman, I insist, is the modest man he was from 1819 to 1892, and is the
man he would have wanted to be but never fully was, and is also each one of
us and all those who will populate the earth.

My hypothesis of a triple Whitman, hero of his epic, is not senselessly
intended to nullify or in any way diminish the prodigious nature of his
pages. I seek rather to exalt them. To devise a double and triple and, over
time, infinite character could have been the ambition of a merely ingenious
man of letters; to carry this goal to a felicitous conclusion is Whitman's unparalleled feat. In a café argument over the genealogy of art and the diverse
influences of education, nationality, and milieu, the painter Whistler said
simply "Art happens," which is tantamount to admitting that the aesthetic
is, in essence, inexplicable. It was understood to be so by the Hebrews, who
spoke of the Spirit, and by the Greeks, who invoked the muse.

As for my translation . . . Paul Valéry has written that no one is as fully
aware of the deficiencies of a work as the person who carried it out; despite
the commercial superstition that the most recent translator has always left

his inept predecessors far behind, I shall not have the temerity to declare that my translation surpasses the others. Nor have I neglected them; I have consulted and profited from the version by Francisco Alexander (Quito, 1956), which still strikes me as the best, though it often falls into an excess of literalness which we may attribute to reverence or perhaps to an overre-liance on the Spanish-English dictionary.

Whitman's language is a contemporary one; hundreds of years will go by before it becomes a dead language. Then we will be able to translate and recreate him in all freedom, as Jáuregui did with the *Pharsalia*, or Chap-man, Pope, and Lawrence with the *Odyssey*. In the meantime, I see no other possibility but a version like mine, which wavers between personal interpre-tation and a resigned rigor.

One thing comforts me. I recall having attended, many years ago, a per-formance of *Macbeth*; the translation was every bit as shaky as the actors and the paint-caked set, but I went out onto the street shattered by tragic passion. Shakespeare had come through, and so will Whitman.

[1969]   [EA]

Emanuel Swedenborg, *Mystical Works*

Of another famous Scandinavian, Charles XII of Sweden, Voltaire wrote that he was the most extraordinary man who had ever lived on earth. The superlative mode is imprudent, as it tends less toward persuasion than a mere fruitless polemic, but I would like to apply Voltaire's definition, not to Charles XII, who was a military conqueror like many others, but rather to the most mysterious of his subjects, Emanuel Swedenborg.

Ralph Waldo Emerson, in his famous lecture of 1845, chose Swedenborg as the prototype of the mystic. The word, while accurate, runs the risk of suggesting a man apart, a man who instinctively removes himself from the circumstances and immediacies we call—I'll never know why—reality. No one is less like that image than Emanuel Swedenborg, who energetically and lucidly traveled through this world and the others. No one accepted life more fully, no one investigated it with such passion, with the same intellec-tual love, or with such impatience to understand it. No one was less like a monk than that sanguine Scandinavian who went farther than Erik the Red.

Like the Buddha, Swedenborg rejected asceticism, which impoverishes and can destroy men. Within the boundaries of Heaven, he saw a hermit who had sought to win admittance there and had spent his mortal life in solitude and the desert. Having reached his goal, this fortunate man discovered that he was unable to follow the conversation of the angels or fathom the complexities of paradise. Finally, he was allowed to project around himself a hallucinatory image of the wilderness. There he remains, as he was on earth, in self-mortification and prayer, but without the hope of ever reaching heaven.

Jesper Swedberg, his father, was an eminent Lutheran bishop, and a rare conjunction of fervor and tolerance. Emanuel was born in Stockholm at the beginning of the year 1688. From early childhood, he thought about God and eagerly talked with the clerics who frequented his father's house. It is significant that above salvation through faith, the cornerstone of the reform preached by Luther, he placed salvation through good works, as an irrefutable proof of the former.

This peerless, solitary man was many men. He loved craftsmanship: in London, as a young man, he worked as a bookbinder, cabinetmaker, optician, watchmaker, and maker of scientific instruments; he also made engravings for the maps on globes. All of this, as well as the study of the various natural sciences, algebra, and the new astronomy of Sir Isaac Newton, with whom he would have liked to have talked but never met. His applications were always inventive: he anticipated the nebular theory of Laplace and Kant, designed a ship that could travel through the air and another, for military purposes, that could travel beneath the sea. We are indebted to him for a personal method for determining longitude and a treatise on the diameter of the moon. In Uppsala around 1716, he founded a scientific journal with a beautiful title, *Daedalus Hyperboreus*, which lasted for two years. In 1717, his aversion to the purely speculative caused him to refuse a chair in astronomy offered him by the king. During the reckless and almost mythical wars waged by Charles XII—wars that turned Voltaire into an epic poet, author of the *Henriade*—he served as a military engineer. He invented and constructed a device to move boats over a stretch of land more than fourteen miles wide. In 1734, his three-volume *Opera Philosophica et Mineralia* appeared in Saxony. He wrote good Latin hexameters and was interested in English literature—Spenser, Shakespeare, Cowley, Milton, and Dryden—because of its imaginative power. Even if he had not devoted himself to mysticism, his name would be illustrious in science. Like Descartes, he was interested in the problem of the precise point where the soul is connected to the body. Anatomy, physics, algebra, and chemistry inspired many other detailed works which he wrote, as was usual at the time, in Latin.

In Holland, he was impressed by the faith and well-being of the inhabitants. He attributed this to the fact that the country was a republic: in kingdoms, the people, accustomed to adulating the king, also adulate God, a servile trait that could hardly please Him. We should also note, in passing, that in his travels Swedenborg visited schools, universities, poor neighborhoods, and factories; and he was fond of music, particularly opera. He served as an assessor to the Royal Board of Mines and sat in the House of Nobles. He preferred the study of the Holy Scriptures to that of dogmatic theology. The Latin translations did not satisfy him; he studied the original texts in Hebrew and Greek. In a private diary, he accused himself of monstrous pride: leafing through the volumes that lined the shelves of a bookstore, he thought that he could, without much effort, improve them, and then he realized that the Lord has a thousand ways of touching the human heart, and that there is no such thing as a worthless book. Pliny the Younger wrote that no book is so bad that there is nothing good in it, an opinion Cervantes would recall.

The cardinal event of his human life took place in London, on a night in April 1745. He himself called it the "discrete degree" or the "degree of separation." It was preceded by dreams, prayer, periods of doubt, fasting, and much more surprisingly, by diligent scientific and philosophical work. A stranger who had silently followed him through the streets of London, and about whose appearance nothing is known, suddenly appeared in his room and told him that he was the Lord. He then entrusted to Swedenborg the mission of revealing to mankind, then sunk in atheism, error, and sin, the true and lost faith of Jesus. The stranger told him that his spirit would travel through heavens and hells and that he would be able to talk with the dead, with demons, and with angels.

At the time, this chosen one was fifty-seven years old; for another thirty years more, he led a visionary life, which he recorded in dense treatises written in a clear and unequivocal prose. Unlike other mystics, he avoided metaphor, exaltation, and vague and passionate hyperbole.

The explanation is obvious. The use of any word presumes a shared experience, for which the word is the symbol. If someone speaks about the flavor of coffee, it is because we have already tasted it; if about the color yellow, because we have already seen lemons, gold, wheat, and sunsets. To suggest the ineffable union of a man's soul with the divinity, the Islamic Sufis found themselves obliged to resort to marvelous analogies, and to images of roses, intoxication, or carnal love. Swedenborg was able to refrain from this kind of rhetorical artifice because his subject matter was not the ecstasy of an enraptured and swooning soul but rather the detailed description of extraterrestrial, yet precise, worlds. To allow us to imagine, or begin to imagine, the lowest depth of Hell, Milton speaks of "no light, but rather darkness visible." Swedenborg prefers the exactitude and ultimately—why not say it?—the verbosity of the explorer or geographer describing unknown lands.

As I dictate these lines, I feel the reader's incredulity blocking me like an enormous wall of bronze. Two conjectures strengthen that wall: deliberate imposture on the part of the man who wrote such strange things, or the influence of a sudden or progressive madness. The first is inadmissible. Had Swedenborg intended to deceive, he would not have resorted to the anonymous publication of a good part of his work, as he did for the twelve volumes of his *Arcana Coelestia*, which did not avail themselves of the authority that might have been conferred by his illustrious name. We know that in conversation he did not attempt to proselytize. Like Emerson or Walt Whitman, he believed that "arguments convince no one," and that merely stating a truth is enough for those who hear it to accept it. He always avoided polemic. There is not a single syllogism in his entire work, only terse and tranquil statements. (I am referring, of course, to his mystical treatises.)

The hypothesis of madness is equally unavailing. If the writer of *Daedalus Hyperboreus* and *Prodromus Principiorum Rerum Naturalium* had gone mad, we would not have had from his tenacious pen the later publications of thousands of methodical pages, a labor of almost thirty years that have nothing in common with frenzy.

Let us consider his coherent and multiple visions, which certainly contain much that is miraculous. William White has acutely observed that we docilely surrender our faith to the visions of the ancients, while tending to reject or ridicule those of the moderns. We believe in Ezekiel because he is exalted by the remoteness of time and space; we believe in St. John of the Cross because he is an integral part of Spanish literature; but we do not believe in William Blake, Swedenborg's rebellious disciple, nor in his still-recent master. What was the exact date when true visions ended and were replaced by apocryphal ones? Gibbon said the same about miracles.

Swedenborg devoted two years to the study of Hebrew in order to examine the Scriptures directly. I happen to think—it must be understood that this is the no doubt unorthodox opinion of a mere man of letters and not of a scholar or theologian—that Swedenborg, like Spinoza or Francis Bacon, was a thinker in his own right who made an awkward mistake when he decided to adapt his ideas to the framework of the two Testaments. The same had occurred with the Hebrew Kabbalists, who were essentially Neo-platonists, when they invoked the authority of the verses, words, and even the letters and transpositions of the Bible in order to justify their system.

It is not my intent to expound the doctrine of the New Jerusalem—the name of the Swedenborgian church—but I would like to consider two points. The first is his extremely original concept of Heaven and Hell, which he explains at length in the best known and most beautiful of his treatises, *De coelo et inferno*, published in Amsterdam in 1758. Blake repeated it, and Bernard Shaw vividly summarized it in the third act of *Man and Superman* (1903), which tells John Tanner's dream. Shaw, as far as I know, never spoke of Swedenborg; it may be supposed that he was inspired by Blake, whom he mentions frequently and with respect; nor is it impossible to believe that he arrived at the same ideas on his own.

In a famous letter to Can Grande della Scala, Dante Alighieri notes that his *Commedia*, like the Holy Scriptures, may be read four different ways, of which the literal is only one. Overwhelmed by the beauty of the poetry, the reader nevertheless retains the indelible impression that the nine circles of Hell, the nine terraces of Purgatory, and the nine heavens of Paradise correspond to three establishments: one whose nature is penal; one, penitential; and another—if this archaism is bearable—premial. Passages such as *"Lasciate ogni speranza, voi ch'entrate"* [All hope abandon, ye who enter here] reinforce that topographical conviction made manifest through art. This is completely different from Swedenborg's extraterrestrial destinies. The Heaven and Hell in his doctrine are not places, although the souls of the dead who inhabit and, in a way, create them perceive them as being situated in space. They are conditions of the soul, determined by its former life. Heaven is forbidden to no one; Hell, imposed on no one. The doors, so to speak, are open. Those who have died do not know they are dead. For an indefinite period of time, they project an illusory image of their usual surroundings and friends.[2] At the end of that period, strangers approach. The wicked dead find the looks and manners of the demons agreeable and quickly join them; the righteous choose the angels. For the blessed, the diabolical sphere is a region of swamps, caves, burning huts, ruins, brothels,

---

[2] In England, there is a popular superstition that we do not know we are dead until we realize that we have no reflection in the mirror.

and taverns. The damned are faceless or have faces that are mutilated and atrocious, but they think of themselves as beautiful. The exercise of power and mutual hatred is their happiness. They devote their lives to politics, in the most South American sense of the word: that is, they live to scheme, to lie, and to impose their will on others. Swedenborg tells how a ray of celestial light once fell into the depths of Hell; the damned perceived it as a stench, an ulcerated wound, a darkness.

Hell is the other face of Heaven. This exact opposite is necessary for the balance of Creation. The Lord rules over it as he does over the heavens. The balance of the two spheres is necessary for free will, which must unceasingly choose between good, which emanates from Heaven, and evil, which emanates from Hell. Every day, every moment of every day, man is shaping his eternal damnation or his salvation. We will be what we are. The terrors or anxieties of dying, which usually appear when the dying person is frightened and confused, are of little importance.

Whether or not we believe in personal immortality, it is undeniable that the doctrine revealed by Swedenborg is more moral and reasonable than that of the mysterious gift obtained, almost by chance, at the final hour. For one thing, it leads to the practice of a virtuous life.

There are countless heavens in the Heaven Swedenborg saw, countless angels in each heaven, and each angel itself is a heaven. They are ruled by a burning love of God and neighbor. The general shape of Heaven (and of the heavens) is that of a man or, what amounts to the same thing, of an angel, for angels are not a separate species. Angels, like demons, are the dead who have passed into the angelic or demonic sphere. A curious trait, suggestive of the fourth dimension, and one which was prefigured by Henry More: the angels, wherever they are, always face the Lord. In the spiritual sphere, the sun is the visible image of God. Space and time only exist in an illusory manner; if one person thinks of another, the second is immediately at his side. The angels converse like people, with words that are spoken and heard, but the language they use is natural and need not be learned. It is common to all the angelic spheres. The art of writing is not unknown in heaven; more than once, Swedenborg received divine communications that seemed to be handwritten or printed, but he was unable to completely decipher them, for the Lord prefers direct, oral instruction. Regardless of baptism, regardless of the religion professed by their parents, all children go to heaven, where they are taught by the angels. Neither riches, nor happiness, nor hedonism, nor worldly life is a barrier to entering heaven. Poverty is not a virtue, nor is misfortune. Good will and the love of God are essential; external circumstances are not. We have already seen the case of the hermit who, through self-mortification and solitude, made himself unfit for heaven and was forced to give up its delights. In his *Treatise on Conjugal Love*, which appeared in 1768, Swedenborg said that marriage is never perfect on earth because the intellect predominates in men, and the will in women. In the celestial state, a man and a woman who loved each other will form a single angel.

In the Apocalypse, one of the canonical books of the New Testament, St. John of Patmos speaks of a heavenly Jerusalem; Swedenborg extended that idea to other great cities. Thus, in *Vera Christiana Religio* (1771), he writes that there are two extraterrestrial Londons. When men die, they do not lose their character. The English preserve their private intellectual manner and their respect for authority; the Dutch continue to engage in commerce; Germans are weighted down with books, and when someone asks them a question, they consult the appropriate volume before answering. Muslims are the most curious case of all. Because the concepts of Mohammed and religion are inextricably intertwined in their souls, God provides them with an angel who pretends to be Mohammed to teach them the faith. This is not always the same angel. Once, the real Mohammed appeared before the community of the faithful, said the words, "I am your Mohammed," and immediately turned black and sank back into the hells.

In the spiritual sphere there are no hypocrites; each person is what he is. An evil spirit ordered Swedenborg to write that the demons delight in lying and committing adultery, robbery, and fraud; they equally enjoy the smell of corpses and excrement. I am abridging this episode; the curious reader may consult the last page of the treatise *Sapientia Angelica de Divina Providentia* (1764).

Unlike those described by other visionaries, Swedenborg's Heaven is more precise than earth. Shapes, objects, structures, and colors are more complex and vivid.

In the Gospels, salvation is an ethical process. Righteousness is fundamental; humility, misery, and misfortune are also praised. To the requirement of righteousness, Swedenborg adds another, one that had never been mentioned by any theologian: intelligence. Let us again recall the ascetic who was forced to recognize that he was unworthy of the theological conversation of the angels. (The countless heavens of Swedenborg are full of love and theology.) When Blake writes, "The fool shall not enter into Glory, no matter how holy he may be," or "Strip yourselves of sanctity and clothe yourselves in intelligence," he is merely minting terse epigrams from Swedenborg's discursive thought. Blake also affirms that, besides intelligence and righteousness, the salvation of man has a third requirement: that he be an artist. Jesus Christ was an artist because he taught through parables and metaphor, and not through abstract reasoning.

It is not without some hesitation that I will now attempt to outline, in a partial and rudimentary fashion, the doctrine of correspondences, which for many is central to the subject we are studying. In the Middle Ages, it was thought that the Lord had written two books: one which we call the Bible and the other which we call the universe. To interpret them was our duty. I suspect that Swedenborg began with the exegesis of the first. He conjectured that each word of the Scriptures has a spiritual sense and came to elaborate a vast system of hidden meanings. Stones, for example, represent natural truths; precious stones, spiritual truths; stars, divine knowledge; the horse, the correct understanding of the Scriptures but also its distortion through sophistry; the Abomination of Desolation, the Trinity; the abyss, God or hell; etc. (Those who wish to pursue this study may examine the *Dictionary of Correspondences*, published in 1962, which examines more than 5,000 examples in the sacred texts.)

From a symbolic reading of the Bible, Swedenborg went on to a symbolic reading of the universe and of us. The sun in the sky is a reflection of the spiritual sun, which in turn is an image of God. There is not a single creature on earth that does not owe its continuing existence to the constant influence of the divinity. The smallest things, Thomas De Quincey—who was a reader of Swedenborg—would write, are secret mirrors of the greatest. Thomas Carlyle would state that universal history is a text we must continually read and write, and in which we, too, are written. The disturbing suspicion that we are ciphers and symbols in a divine cryptography, whose true meaning we do not know, is prevalent in the works of Léon Bloy, and was known to the Kabbalists.

The doctrine of correspondences has led me to mention the Kabbalah. As far as I know or remember, no one has investigated this intimate affinity. In the first chapter of the Scriptures, we read that God created man in his own image and likeness. This statement implies that God has the shape of a man. The Kabbalists who compiled the *Book of Creation* in the Middle Ages declared that the ten emanations, or *sefiroth*, whose source is the ineffable divinity, may be conceived of as a kind of tree or as a man, the Primordial Man, Adam Kadmon. If all things are in God, all things will be in man, who is His earthly reflection. Thus, Swedenborg and the Kabbalah both arrive at the concept of the microcosm: man as either the mirror or the compendium of the universe. According to Swedenborg, Hell and Heaven are in man, who equally contains plants, mountains, seas, continents, minerals, trees, herbs, flowers, thorns, animals, reptiles, birds, fish, tools, cities, and buildings.

In 1758, Swedenborg announced that, the year before, he had witnessed the Last Judgment, which had taken place in the world of the spirits on the exact date when faith was extinguished in all the churches. The decline began when the Roman Church was founded. The reform initiated by Luther and prefigured by Wycliffe was imperfect and in many ways heretical. Another Last Judgment also takes place at the moment of each man's death and is the consequence of his entire life.

On March 29, 1772, Emanuel Swedenborg died in London, the city he loved, the city in which, one night, God had entrusted to him the mission that would make him unique among men. Some accounts remain of his final days, of his old-fashioned black velvet suit, and of a sword with a strangely shaped hilt. His way of life was austere: coffee, milk, and bread were his only nourishment. At any hour of the night or day, the servants would hear him pacing in his room, talking with his angels.

Sometime around 1970, I wrote this sonnet:

Emanuel Swedenborg

Taller than the rest, that distant
Man would walk among men, faintly
Calling out to angels, speaking
Their secret names. What earthly eyes
Cannot see he saw: the burning
Geometries, the crystalline
Labyrinth of God, the sordid
Whirling of infernal delights.
He knew that Glory and Hades
And all their myths are in your soul;
He knew, like the Greeks, that each day's
The mirror of Eternity.
In flat Latin he catalogued
Whenless whyless ultimate things.

[1975]   [EW]

LECTURES

The Concept of an Academy and the Celts

In the second half of the nineteenth century, two justly famous writers, Ernst Rénan and Matthew Arnold, both wrote penetrating studies on both the concept of an academy and on Celtic literature. Neither noticed the curious affinity between those two subjects, and yet that affinity exists. Some friends of mine, when they read the title of this lecture, assumed I was merely being arbitrary, but I think that this affinity is profound and that I can justify it.

Let us begin with the concept of an academy. Of what does it consist? In the first place, we think of a language police, authorizing or prohibiting words. This is trivial, as we all know. Then we think of the original members of the French Academy who had periodic meetings. Here we have another theme—the theme of conversation, literary dialogue, and friendly discussion—and the other aspect of the Academy, which is perhaps the most essential: organization, legislation, the understanding of literature. I think that this is the most important part.

The thesis that I am going to expound today—or more exactly, the circumstances that I am going to recall—is the affinity of these two ideas: the Academy and the Celtic world. Let us think of the literary nation *par excellence*. That country is obviously France, and French literature is not only in French books but in the language itself. One need only leaf through a dictionary to feel the intense literary vocation of the French language. For example, in Spanish we say *"arco iris"*; in English, "rainbow"; in German, *"regenbogen,"* arch of rain. What are all these words next to the tremendous French one, as vast as a poem by Hugo and shorter than a poem by Hugo—*arc-en-ciel*—which seems to raise an architecture, an arch in the sky?

In France, a literary life exists—I don't know whether more intensely;

for that, one would have to enter into its mysteries—but certainly in a way that is more conscious than in other countries. One of its magazines, *La Vie Litteraire*, is read by everyone. Here, in contrast, writers are almost invisible; we write for our friends, which can be fine. When one thinks of the French Academy, one tends to forget that the literary life of France corresponds to a dialectical process, that literature functions within the history of literature. The Academy exists to represent tradition, and so does the Goncourt Academy, and the cenacles that are themselves academies in turn. It is curious that the revolutionaries have begun to enter into the Academy, that the tradition continues to enrich itself in all directions and through all the evolutions of its literature. At one time, there was an opposition between the Academy and the Romantics; then, between the Academy and the Parnassians and Symbolists; but ultimately they all formed part of the French tradition. Moreover, there is a kind of equilibrium: the rigors of the tradition are compensated by the audacities of the revolutionaries. For that reason, French literature has more extravagant exaggerations than any other, for each writer must deal with an adversary, much like a chess player. But in no other part of the world has literary life been organized in such a rigorous manner as among the Celtic nations, which I shall attempt to prove, or more exactly, recall.

I spoke of the literature of the Celts: the term is vague. They inhabited, in antiquity, the territories that a remote future would call Portugal, Spain, France, the British Isles, Holland, Belgium, Switzerland, Lombardy, Bohemia, Bulgaria, and Croatia, as well as Galicia on the coast of the Black Sea; the Germans and the Romans displaced or subjected them after arduous wars. Then a remarkable thing happened. The true culture of the Germans reached its maximum and final flowering in Iceland, in the Ultima Thule of Latin cosmography, where the nostalgia of a small group of fugitives rescued the ancient mythology and enriched the ancient rhetoric. Celtic culture took refuge on another lost island, Ireland. We know little about the arts and letters of the Celts in Iberia or in Wales; the tangible relics of their culture, particularly in language and literature, must be sought out in the libraries of Ireland or Wales. Rénan, applying Tertullian's famous sentence, writes that the Celtic soul is naturally Christian; what is extraordinary, almost incredible, is that Christianity, which was and is felt with such ardor by the Irish, did not erase their memory of the repudiated pagan myths and archaic legends. Thanks to Caesar, Pliny, Diogenes Laërtius, and Diodorus Siculus, we know that the Welsh were ruled by a theocracy, the Druids, who administered and executed the laws, declared war or proclaimed peace, had the power to depose the king, annually appointed magistrates, and were in charge of the education of the young and the ritual celebrations. They practiced astrology and taught that the soul is immortal. Caesar, in his *Commentaries*, attributes to them the Pythagorean and Platonic doctrine of the transmigration of souls. It has been said that the Welsh believed, as almost all people do, that magic could transform men into animals, and Caesar, misled by the memory of his readings in Greek, confused this superstitious belief with the doctrine of the purification of the soul through death and reincarnations. Later we will see a passage in Taliesin, whose indisputable subject is transmigration, not lycanthropy.

What I would like to note here is the fact that the Druids were divided into six classes, the first of which were the bards, and the third, the *vates*. Centuries later, this theocratic hierarchy would be the distant but not forgotten model for the academies of France.

In the Middle Ages, the conversion of the Celts to Christianity reduced the Druids to the category of sorcerers. One of their techniques was satire, to which was attributed magical powers, thanks to the lumps that would appear on the face of the person being satirized. Thus, protected by superstition and fear, the man of letters became predominant in Ireland. Each individual in feudal societies had a precise place; an incomparable example of this were the Irish literati. If the concept of an academy is based on the organization and direction of literature, then there was no more academic country, not even France or China.

A literary career required more than twelve years of strict studies, which included mythology, legendary history, topography, and law. To such disciplines we must obviously add grammar and the various branches of rhetoric. The teaching was oral, as it is with all esoteric material; there were no written texts, and the student had to commit to memory the entire *corpus* of the earlier literature. The annual examination lasted many hours; the student, kept in a dark cell and provided with food and water, had to versify certain set genealogical and mythological subjects in certain set meters and then memorize them. The lowest grade, that of *oblaire*, was given for poems on seven subjects; the highest grade, *ollam*, for 360, corresponding to the days in the lunar year. The poems were classified by themes: destructions of lineages or of castles, thefts of animals, loves, battles, sea voyages, violent deaths, expeditions, kidnappings, and fires. Other categories included visions, attacks, deceptions, and migrations. Each one of these corresponded to certain plots, certain meters, and a certain vocabulary, to which the poet was limited under the penalty of punishment. For the highest poets, versification was extremely complex, and included assonance, rhyme, and alliteration. Rather than direct reference, they preferred an intricate system of metaphors, based on myth or legend or personal invention. Something similar occurred with the Anglo-Saxon poets and, at a higher level, with the Scandinavians: the extraordinary and almost hallucinatory metaphor for battle, "weave of men," is common to the court poetry of both Ireland and Norway. Above the ninth level, the verses are indecipherable, due to their archaisms, periphrasis, and laborious images; tradition records the rage of a king who was incapable of understanding the panegyrics of his own learned poets. The inherent obscurity of all cultivated poetry hastened the decline and final dissolution of the literary colleges. It is also worth recalling that the poets constituted a heavy burden for the poor and minor kings of Ireland, who were required to maintain them in the luxury and pleasures appropriate for creativity.

It may be said that such vigilance and vigor can only stifle the poetic impulse; the unbelievable truth is that Irish poetry is rich in freshness and wonder. Such, at least, is the conviction formed by the fragments cited by Arnold and the English versions by the philologist Kuno Meyer.

All of you can recall poems in which the poet remembers his previous incarnations. For example, the splendid lines by Rubén Darío:

> *Yo fui un soldado que durmió en el lecho*
> *de Cleopatra, la reina. . . .*
> *¡Oh la rosa marmórea omnipotente!*

[I was a soldier who slept in the bed/of Cleopatra, the queen. . . ./Oh marble and omnipotent rose!]

And we have ancient examples, like that of Pythagoras, who declared that he recognized from another life the shield with which he fought at Troy.

Let us look at what Taliesin, the Welsh poet of the sixth century, did. Taliesin beautifully remembers having been many things: a wild boar, a chief in a battle, a sword in the hand of a chief, a bridge that crossed seventy rivers; he was in Carthage, he was on a wave in the sea; he has been a word in a book, he was, in the beginning, a book. Here we have a poet who is perfectly conscious of the privileges, of the merits that can arise from this kind of incoherent diversion. I think that Taliesin wanted to be all of these things, and I also believe that a list, in order to be beautiful, must consist of heterogenous elements. Thus he remembers having been a word in a book and a book itself. There are many other beautiful Celtic images, for example that of a tree that is green on one side and burning on the other, like the Burning Bush, with a flame that does not consume it, and whose two parts live in harmony.

Beyond the heroic centuries, the mythological centuries, there is an aspect of Celtic literature that particularly interests us, and that is the sea voyages. The Irish imagined voyages to the west, that is, to the sunset, to the unknown, or, as we now say, to America. I will refer to the story of Conn.

Conn is a king of Ireland; he is called Conn of the Five Battles. One afternoon, he is sitting with his son, watching the sunset from a hill, and he suddenly hears his son speaking with the invisible and the unknown. He asks him with whom he is speaking, and then a voice comes from the air, and that voice says: "I am a beautiful woman; I come from an island lost in the western seas; on that island there is no rain, no snow, no sickness, no death, no time. If your son, with whom I am in love, will come with me, he will never know death, and he will reign over happy people." The king summons his Druids—for this story is older than Christianity, although the Christians preserved it—and the Druids sing to silence the woman. She, invisibly, throws an apple at the prince and disappears. For a year, the prince eats nothing but this inexhaustible apple and is never hungry or thirsty, and he thinks only of the woman he has never seen. At the end of the year, she returns, he sees her, and together they board a glass ship and sail off to the west.

Here the legend branches off. One of the versions says that the prince never returned. Another, that he returned after many centuries and revealed who he was. The people looked at him with incredulity and said: "Yes, son of Conn of the Five Battles. A legend tells that you were lost in the seas, and that, if you ever return to land and touch the soil of Ireland, you will turn to ashes, for the time of gods is one thing and the time of man another."

Let us recall a similar story, the story of Abraham. Abraham is the son of a king, like all the protagonists of these stories. While walking on the beach, he suddenly hears a beautiful music coming from behind him. He turns around, but the music is still behind him. The music is very sweet, and he falls asleep; when he wakes, he finds in his hand a branch of silver with flowers that could be made of snow, except that they are living. (The silver branch is reminiscent of the golden bough in the *Aeneid*.) Returning to his house, he finds a woman who tells him, as in the other story of the prince, that she is in love with him. Abraham follows her, and then the story becomes the tale of his journeys. They say that he traveled over the sea and saw a man who seemed to walk on the water and was surrounded by fish, by salmon. That man was a Celtic god, and when he walks the sea, he is walking over the meadows of his island, surrounded by deer and sheep. That is, there is something like a double space, a double plane in space: for the prince, he is walking on water; for the king, over a meadow.

There is a curious fauna in those islands: gods, birds that are angels, laurels of silver and deer of gold, and there is also an island of gold, standing on four pillars, which stand, in turn, on a plain of silver. The most astonishing wonder is when Abraham crosses the western seas, looks up, and sees a river that flows through the air without falling, and in that river there are fish and boats, and all of it is religiously in the sky.

I should say something about the meaning of landscape in Celtic poetry. Matthew Arnold, in his remarkable study of Celtic literature, says that the sense of nature, which is one of the virtues of English poetry, is derived from the Celts. I would say that the Germans also felt nature. Their world is, of course, quite different, because in ancient Germanic poetry, what is felt above all is the horror of nature; the swamps and the forests and the twilights are populated by monsters. Dragons were called "the night horrors." In contrast, the Celts also understood nature as a living thing, but they felt that these supernatural presences could also be benign. The fantastic world of the Celts is a world of both angels and demons. We now speak of the "other world": the phrase, I think, appears for the first time in Lucan, referring to the Celts.

All of these facts I have noted lead to various observations. They explain, for example, the birth of the Academy in a country like France, a country with Celtic roots; they explain the absence of academies in a profoundly individualistic country like England. But you may draw better conclusions than I. For now, it is enough to merely note the curious phenomenon of the legislation of literature on the island of Ireland.

[1962]   [EW]

The Enigma of Shakespeare

The two final chapters of Paul Groussac's *Crítica literaria* are dedicated to the Shakespeare question, or as I have preferred to call it here, the enigma of Shakespeare. As you will have guessed, this is the theory that the individual William Shakespeare, who died in 1616, was not the father of the tragedies, comedies, history plays, and poems that are now admired throughout the world. In his two articles, Groussac defends the classic opinion, the opinion shared by all until the middle years of the nineteenth century, when Miss Delia Bacon, in a book with a prologue by Hawthorne—to a book Hawthorne had not read—elected to attribute the paternity of those works to the statesman and philosopher Francis Bacon, the founder and, in some sense, the martyr of modern science.

I, of course, believe that the William Shakespeare honored today in East and West was the author of the works we attribute to him, but I would like to add a few points to Groussac's argument. Moreover, in recent years a second candidacy has emerged, the most interesting of all from a psychological and, we might say, from a police detective point of view: that of the poet Christopher Marlowe, murdered in a tavern in Deptford, near London, in the year 1593.

Let us examine, first of all, the arguments against Shakespeare's paternity. They may be summarized as follows: Shakespeare received a fairly rudimentary education in the grammar school of his hometown, Stratford. Shakespeare, as attested by his friend and rival, the dramatic poet Ben Jonson, possessed "small Latin and less Greek." There are those who, in the nineteenth century, discovered or believed they had discovered an encyclopedic erudition in Shakespeare's work. It seems to me that while it is a fact that Shakespeare's vocabulary is gigantic, even within the gigantic English language, it is one thing to use terms from many disciplines and sciences and another thing altogether to have a profound or even superficial knowledge of those same disciplines and sciences. We can recall the analogous case of Cervantes. I believe a Mr. Barby, in the nineteenth century, published a book entitled *Cervantes, Expert in Geography*.

The truth is that the aesthetic is inaccessible to many people and they prefer to seek out the virtue of men of genius—which Cervantes and Shakespeare indisputably were—elsewhere: in their knowledge, for example. Miss Delia Bacon and the rest claimed that the profession of playwright was an insignificant one in the era of Elizabeth, the Virgin Queen, and James I, and that the erudition they believed they discovered in Shakespeare's work could not have belonged to poor William Shakespeare, for the author of those works had to be an encyclopedic man. Miss Delia Bacon discovered that man in her homonym, Francis Bacon.

The argument is as follows: Bacon was a man of vast political and scientific ambitions; Bacon wanted to renew science, to found what he called the *regnum hominis* or kingdom of man. It would have been out of keeping with his dignity as a statesman and philosopher to compose dramatic works. He therefore sought out the actor and theatrical impresario, William Shakespeare, to use his name as a pseudonym.

Those who endeavored to enrich Miss Bacon's thesis, or to carry it to an absurd extreme, had recourse—and now we are in the realm of the detective story, in the "Gold Bug" of the future Edgar Allan Poe—to cryptography. Incredible as it may seem, they pored over the complete works of William Shakespeare in search of a line that begins with a B, followed by a line beginning with an A, then by one beginning with a C, the penultimate with an O, and the last with an N. In other words, they were seeking a secret signature by Bacon in his work. They did not find it. Then one of them, even more absurd than his predecessors, which seems difficult, remembered that the English word "bacon" refers to the meat of the pig, and that Bacon, instead of signing his own name, even cryptographically or acrostically, might have preferred to sign "hog" or "pig" or "swine"—an extraordinarily improbable thing, since no one makes that kind of joke with his own name. This particular individual, I believe, had the good fortune to run across a line that began with a P, followed by one that began not with an I but with a Y, and a third beginning with a G. He believed his strange hypothesis was amply justified by this lone pig discovered in the works of Shakespeare.

There is also a long, meaningless Latinate word in which some have discovered the anagram *"Francis Bacon sic scriptit"* or *"Francis Bacon fecit"* or something like that. One of the partisans of the Baconian thesis was Mark Twain, who summarized all the arguments very wittily in a book entitled *Is Shakespeare Dead?*, which I recommend not for your convictions but for your amusement. All of this, as you can see, is purely speculative and hypothetical, and all of it was magisterially refuted by Groussac.

To those arguments, I would add others of diverse natures. Groussac speaks of the poor quality of the verse that has been attributed to Bacon; I would add that the minds of the two men are essentially and irreparably different. Bacon, of course, had a more modern mind than Shakespeare: Bacon had a sense of history; he felt that his era, the seventeenth century, was the beginning of a scientific age, and he wanted the veneration of the texts of Aristotle to be replaced by a direct investigation of nature.

Bacon was a precursor of what today we call science fiction; in his *New Atlantis*, he narrates the adventure of some travelers who arrive at a lost island in the Pacific on which many of the marvels of contemporary science have become realities. For example: there are ships that travel beneath the water, others that journey through the air; there are chambers in which rain, snow, storms, echoes, and rainbows are artificially created; there are fantastical zoos that exhaust the variety of all hybrids and current species of plants and animals.

Bacon's mind had no less of a propensity for metaphor than Shakespeare's, and here was a point of contact between the two, except that the metaphors differ greatly. Let us take, for example, a book of logic, such as John Stuart Mill's *System of Logic,* in which he points out the errors to which the human mind is prone. Mill, as many others have done, creates a classification of fallacies. Bacon, in doing the same thing, said that the human mind is not a perfectly flat mirror but a slightly concave or convex mirror, which distorts reality. He claimed that man is prone to error, and he called the errors to which we are prone "idols," and proceeded to list them.

First were the *"idola tribus,"* the idols of the tribe, the idols common to the entire human race. He declared that there are minds that note the affinities between things, and other minds that tend to notice or exaggerate the differences, and that the scientific observer must observe himself and correct this inclination to note differences or resemblances (differences or sympathies, Alfonso Reyes would say). Next, Bacon speaks of the idols of the cave, *"idola specus."* In other words, each man, without knowing it, is prone to a certain type of error. Let us imagine a man, an intelligent man, to whom, say, the poetry of Heine, the philosophy of Spinoza, and the doctrines of Einstein or Freud are explained. If this man is anti-Semitic, he will tend to reject these works, simply because they are by Jews; if he is Jewish or philo-Semitic he will tend to accept them, simply because he feels sympathy for Jews. In both cases he will not impartially examine these works, but will subordinate his estimation of them to his likes or dislikes.

Next, Bacon speaks of the *"idola forum,"* the idols of the forum or marketplace; that is, the errors caused by language. He observes that language is the work not of philosophers but of the people. Chesterton would later maintain that language was invented by hunters, fishermen, and nomads and therefore is essentially poetic. In other words, language was not created to be a description of truth, it was created by arbitrary and fanciful people; language is continually leading us into error. If you say that someone is deaf, for example, and someone else doubts your word, you will say "Yes, he's deaf as a post," simply because you have at hand the convenient phrase, "deaf as a post."

To these idols, Bacon adds a fourth type, the *"idola teatri,"* idols of the theater. Bacon notes that all scientific systems—without excluding his own system of philosophy, observation, and induction; of going not from the general to the particular, but from the particular to the general—replace the real world with a world that is more or less fantastical, or, in any case, simplified. Thus we have Marxism, which examines all historic events by economic criteria; or we have a historian like Bossuet, who sees the hand of Providence in the entire historic process; or the theories of Spengler; or the contemporary doctrines of Toynbee; and none of them, Bacon would say, is reality, but is a theater, a representation of reality.

Furthermore, Bacon had no faith in the English language. He believed the vernacular languages had no power, and therefore had all his works translated into Latin. Bacon, archenemy of the Middle Ages, believed, like the Middle Ages, that there is a single international language: Latin.

Shakespeare, on the contrary, had, as we know, a profound feeling for the English language, which is perhaps unique among Western languages in its possession of what might be called a double register. For common words, for the ideas, say, of a child, a rustic, a sailor, or a peasant, it has words of Saxon origin, and for intellectual matters it has words derived from Latin. These words are never precisely synonymous, there is a always a nuance of differentiation: it is one thing to say, Saxonly, "dark" and another to say "obscure"; one thing to say "brotherhood" and another to say "fraternity"; one thing—especially for poetry, which depends not only on atmosphere and on meaning but on the connotations of the atmosphere of words—to say, Latinly, "unique" and another to say "single."

Shakespeare felt all this; one might say that a good part of Shakespeare's charm depends on this reciprocal play of Latin and Germanic terms. For example, when Macbeth, gazing at his own bloody hand, thinks it could stain the vast seas with scarlet, making of their green a single red thing, he says:

> Will all great Neptune's ocean wash this blood
> Clean from my hand? No, this my hand will rather
> The multitudinous seas incarnadine,
> Making the green one red.

In the third line we have long, sonorous, erudite Latin words: "multitudinous," "incarnadine"; then, in the next, short Saxon words: "green one red."

There is, it seems to me, a psychological incompatibility between the minds of Bacon and Shakespeare, and this suffices to invalidate all of the Baconians' arguments and cryptographies, all the real or imaginary secret signatures they have discovered or think they have discovered in Shakespeare's work.

There are other candidates whom I choose to overlook, until I reach the least implausible of them all: the poet Christopher Marlowe, who is believed to have been murdered in the year 1593 at the age of twenty-nine, the age at which Keats died, the age at which Evaristo Carriego, our poet of the city's outskirts, died. Let us look briefly at Marlowe's life and work.

Marlowe was a "university wit," that is, he belonged to a group of young university students who condescended to the theater; moreover, Marlowe perfected the "blank verse" that would become Shakespeare's instrument of choice, and in Marlowe's work there are lines no less splendid than those in Shakespeare. For example, the line so greatly admired by Unamuno that he said this single line was superior to all of Goethe's *Faust*—perhaps forgetting that perfection is easier in a single line than in a vast work, where it may be impossible. Marlowe's *Doctor Faustus*, like Goethe's *Faust*, finds himself before the specter of Helen (the idea that Helen of Troy was a ghost or apparition is already present in the ancients) and says to her, "Sweet Helen, make me immortal with a kiss." And then, "O thou art fairer than the evening air clad in the beauty of a thousand stars." He does not say "evening sky," but "evening air." All of Copernican space is present in that word *air*, the infinite space that was one of the revelations of the Renaissance, the space in which we still believe, despite Einstein, the space that came to supplant the Ptolomaic system which presides over Dante's triple comedy.

But let us return to Marlowe's tragic fate. In the final decades of the sixteenth century, there were fears in England of a Catholic insurrection, incited by the power of Spain. At the same time, the city of London was agitated by riots. Many Flemish and French artisans had arrived in London and were being accused of eating "the bread of fatherless children." There was a kind of nationalist movement that attacked these foreigners and even threatened a general massacre. At that time, the State already had what we would call today a "secret service," and Marlowe was one of its men. It persecuted Catholics as well as Puritans; a playwright, Thomas Kyd, was arrested, and in his house certain papers were found. Among those papers was a manuscript with twenty or so heretical theses, some of them scandalous; one, for example, held that Jesus was a homosexual—there was, in addition, a defense of homosexuality—and another denied that a man, Christ, could be both man and God. There was also a panegyric to tobacco, which Ralegh had brought from America. Marlowe was part of the circle that surrounded Ralegh, the corsaire, the historian, who would later be executed, and in whose house were held the gatherings ominously called the School of Night.

Marlowe's characters, the characters with whom it is clear the author is in sympathy, are magnifications of Marlowe. They are atheists: Tamburlaine burns the Koran and finally, having conquered the world, wants, like Alexander, to conquer the heavens, and orders that his artillery be turned against the sky, and that black banners be hung from the sky to signify the hecatomb, the massacre of the gods: "And set black streamers in the firmament," etc. There is Doctor Faustus, who represents the Renaissance appetite to know everything, to read the book of nature, not in search of moral teachings, as in the Middle Ages, when the physiologies or bestiaries were compiled, but in search of the letters that compose the universe. There is *The Jew of Malta*, which is a magnification of greed.

Kyd's manuscript was examined by the police. He was tortured—torture is not an invention of our own time—and he confessed or declared, which was very natural, since his life was at stake, that this manuscript was not his but was written by the hand of Marlowe, with whom he had shared a room when the two of them worked together revising and correcting plays. A tribunal called the "Star Chamber" judged this type of crime; Marlowe was told that in one week he would have to appear before this tribunal to be accused of blasphemy and atheism, and to defend himself. Then, two days before the hearing, Marlowe's murdered body was found in a tavern in Deptford.

It seems that four men, all belonging to the secret service, went to the tavern, had lunch, took a nap, went out for a stroll in the small country garden around the tavern, played chess or backgammon, I don't know which, and then had an argument about the bill. Marlowe took out his knife (knives were then the weapon of choice), and was supposedly stabbed in the eye with it, with his own knife, and died. Now, according to Calvin Hoffman's hypothesis, the man who died was not Marlowe but another man, any one of the other three. In that day and age, there was no way of identifying people, fingerprints were unknown, it was very easy to pass one man off as another, and Marlowe had told his friends of his intention of fleeing to Scotland, then an independent kingdom. Hoffmann's theory has it that Marlowe passed the dead man off as himself, then fled to Scotland, and from there sent his friend, the actor and theatrical impresario William Shakespeare, the works today attributed to Shakespeare. From Scotland, he had the manuscripts of *Macbeth, Hamlet, Othello, Anthony and Cleopatra*, etc., delivered to Shakespeare. Then Marlowe died, according to this theory, about four or five years before Shakespeare's death. The latter, after selling his theater and retiring to his hometown of Stratford, forgot all about his literary work and devoted himself to being the richest man in town, giving himself over to the pleasures of litigation against his neighbors until the death that befell him after a drinking bout with some actors who came from London to see him in the year 1616.

The argument I will sketch out against this hypothesis is that although Marlowe was a great poet and has lines not unworthy of Shakespeare—and there are, as well, many lines by Marlowe interspersed, as though lost, in the works of Shakespeare—there exists, nevertheless, an essential difference between the two. Coleridge used Spinoza's vocabulary in praise of Shakespeare. He said that Shakespeare was what Spinoza calls *"natura naturans,"* creative nature: the force that takes all forms, that lies as if dead in rocks, that sleeps in plants, that dreams in the lives of animals, which are conscious only of the present moment, and that reaches its consciousness, or a certain consciousness in us, in mankind, the *"natura naturata."*

Hazlitt said that all the people who have existed in the universe are in Shakespeare; that is, Shakespeare had the power to multiply himself marvelously; to think of Shakespeare is to think of a crowd. However, in Marlowe's work we always have a central figure: the conqueror, Tamburlaine; the greedy man, Barabas; the man of science, Faust. The other characters are mere extras, they barely exist, whereas in Shakespeare's work all the characters exist, even incidental characters. The apothecary, for example, who sells poison to Romeo and says, "My poverty, but not my will consents," has already defined himself as a man by this single phrase. This appears to exceed Marlowe's possibilities.

In a letter to Frank Harris, Bernard Shaw wrote, "Like Shakespeare I understand everything and everybody; and like Shakespeare I am nobody and nothing." And here we arrive at the true enigma of Shakespeare: for us, he is one of the most visible men in the world, but he was certainly not that for his contemporaries. Here, the case of Cervantes is repeated. Lope de Vega wrote, "No one is so stupid as to admire Miguel de Cervantes." Gracián, in his *Agudeza y arte de ingenio* [Wit and the Art of Genius] does not find a single ingenious feature of the *Quixote* worth citing; Quevedo, in a romance, alludes offhandedly to Don Quixote's leanness. That is, Cervantes was almost invisible to his contemporaries; even his military action in the battle of Lepanto was so thoroughly forgotten that he himself had to remind people that he owed the loss of his arm to that battle.

As for Shakespeare, outside of an ambiguous accolade that speaks of his "sugar sonnets," his contemporaries do not seem to have had him much in view. The explanation for this, it seems to me, is that Shakespeare dedicated himself primarily to the genre of drama, except for the sonnets and the occasional poem such as "The Phoenix and the Turtle" or "The Passionate Pilgrim." Every era believes that there is a literary genre that has a kind of primacy. Today, for example, any writer who has not written a novel is asked when he is going to write one. (I myself am continually being asked.) In Shakespeare's time, the literary work *par excellence* was the vast epic poem, and that idea persisted into the eighteenth century, when we have the example of Voltaire, the least epic of men, who nevertheless writes an epic because without an epic he would not have been a true man of letters for his contemporaries.

As for our own time, consider the cinema. When we think of the cinema, most of us think of actors or actresses; I think, anachronistically, of Miriam Hopkins and Katharine Hepburn—you can undoubtedly fill in more current names—or we think of directors: I think of Josef von Sternberg, who seems to me to be the greatest of all film directors, or, more recently, of Orson Welles or Hitchcock; you can insert whatever names you like. But we do not think of the screenwriter. I remember the films *The Dragnet, Underworld, Specter of the Rose*—that last title from Sir Thomas Browne—but Ben Hecht had to die a few days ago in order for me to remember that he was the author of the screenplays of these films that I have so often watched and praised.

Something analogous happened with plays in Shakespeare's time. Plays belonged to the acting company, not to their authors. Each time they were staged, new scenes with up-to-date touches were added. People laughed at Ben Jonson when he published his plays in all solemnity and gave them the title *Works*. "What kind of 'works' are these?" they said. "These are just tragedies and comedies." "Works" would have to be lyric or epic or elegiac poems, for example, but not plays. So it is natural that his contemporaries did not admire Shakespeare. He wrote for actors.

One more mystery remains. Why does Shakespeare sell his theater, retire to his native town, and forget the works that are now one of the glories of humanity? An explanation has been formulated by the great writer De Quincey: it is that, for Shakespeare, publication was not the printed word. Shakespeare did not write to be read, but to be performed. The plays continued to be staged, and that was enough. Another explanation, this one psychological, is that Shakespeare needed the immediate stimulus of the theater. That is, when he wrote *Hamlet* or *Macbeth*, he adapted his words to one actor or another; as someone once said, when a character sings in Shakespeare's work it is because a certain actor knew how to play the lute or had a nice voice. Shakespeare needed this circumstantial stimulus. Goethe would say much later that all poetry is "*Gelegenheitsdichtung*," poetry of circumstances. And Shakespeare, no longer driven by the actors or by the demands of the stage, felt no need to write. This, to my mind, is the most probable explanation. Groussac says that there are many writers who have made a display of their disdain for literary art, who have extended the line "vanity of vanities, all is vanity" to literature; many literary people have disbelieved in literature. But, he says, all of them have given expression to their disdain, and all of those expressions are inexpressive if we compare them to Shakespeare's silence. Shakespeare, lord of all words, who arrives at the conviction that literature is insignificant, and does not even seek the words to express that conviction; this is almost superhuman.

I said earlier that Bacon had a vivid sense of history. For Shakespeare, on the contrary, all characters, whether they are Danish, like Hamlet, Scottish, like Macbeth, Greek, Roman, or Italian, all the characters in all the many works, are treated as if they were Shakespeare's contemporaries. Shakespeare felt the variety of men, but not the variety of historical eras. History did not exist for him; it did exist for Bacon.

What was Shakespeare's philosophy? Bernard Shaw has tried to find it in the maxims so widely dispersed throughout his work that say life is essentially oneiric, illusory: "We are such stuff as dreams are made of"; or when he says that life "is a tale/Told by an idiot, full of sound and fury/Signifying nothing" or before that when he compares every man to an actor, which is a double play on words, because the king who speaks these words, Macbeth, is also an actor, a poor actor, "that struts and frets his hour upon the stage/And then is heard no more." But we may also believe that this does not correspond to any conviction of Shakespeare's, but only to what his characters might have felt at that moment. In other words, life may not be a nightmare, a senseless nightmare, for Shakespeare, but life may have been felt to be a nightmare by Macbeth, when he saw that the fates and the witches had deceived him.

Here we arrive at the central enigma of Shakespeare, which is perhaps the enigma of all literary creation. I return to Bernard Shaw, who was asked if he truly believed that the Holy Spirit had written the Bible, and who answered that the Holy Spirit had written not only the Bible, but all the books in the world. We no longer speak of the Holy Spirit; we now have another mythology; we say that a writer writes with his subconscious mind, or with the collective unconscious. Homer and Milton preferred to believe in the Muse: "Sing, oh Muse, the wrath of Achilles," said Homer, or the poets who were called Homer. All of them believed in a force of which they were the amanuenses. Milton refers directly to the Holy Spirit, whose temple is the bosom of the just. All of them felt that there is something more in a work than the voluntary intentions of its author. On the final page of the *Quixote*, Cervantes says that his intention has been nothing other than to mock books of chivalry. We can interpret this in two ways: we can suppose that Cervantes said this to make us understand that he had something else in mind, but we can also take these words literally, and think that Cervantes had no other aim—that Cervantes, without knowing it, created a work that mankind will not forget. He did so because he wrote the *Quixote* with the whole of his being, unlike the *Persiles*, for example, which he wrote with merely literary aims, and into which he did not put all that was dark and secret within him. Shakespeare may also have been assisted by distraction; it may help to be a little distracted in order to write a masterpiece. It may be that the intention of writing a masterpiece inhibits the writer, makes him keep a close watch on himself. It may be that aesthetic creation should be more like a dream, a dream unchecked by our attention. And this may have happened in Shakespeare's case.

Furthermore, Shakespeare's work has been progressively enriched by the generations of its readers. Undoubtedly Coleridge, Hazlitt, Goethe, Heine, Bradley, and Hugo have all enriched Shakespeare's work, and it will undoubtedly be read in another way by readers to come. Perhaps this is one possible definition of the work of genius: a book of genius is a book that can be read in a slightly or very different way by each generation. This is what happened with the Bible. Someone has compared the Bible to a musical instrument that has been tuned infinitely. We can read Shakespeare's work, but we do not know how it will be read in a century, or in ten centuries, or even, if universal history continues, in a hundred centuries. We do know that for us the work of Shakespeare is virtually infinite, and the enigma of Shakespeare is only one part of that other enigma, artistic creation, which, in turn, is only a facet of another enigma: the universe.

[1964]   [EA]

Blindness

In the course of the many lectures—too many lectures—I have given, I've observed that people tend to prefer the personal to the general, the concrete to the abstract. I will begin, then, by referring to my own modest blindness.

Modest, because it is total blindness in one eye, but only partial in the other. I can still make out certain colors; I can still see blue and green. And yellow, in particular, has remained faithful to me. I remember when I was young I used to linger in front of certain cages in the Palermo zoo: the cages of the tigers and leopards. I lingered before the tigers' gold and black. Yellow is still with me, even now. I have written a poem, entitled "The Gold of the Tigers," in which I refer to this friendship.

People generally imagine the blind as enclosed in a black world. There is, for example, Shakespeare's line: "Looking on darkness which the blind do see." If we understand "darkness" as "blackness," then Shakespeare is wrong.

One of the colors that the blind—or at least this blind man—do not see is black; another is red. *Le rouge et le noir* are the colors denied us. I, who was accustomed to sleeping in total darkness, was bothered for a long time at having to sleep in this world of mist, in the greenish or bluish mist, vaguely luminous, which is the world of the blind. I wanted to lie down in darkness. The world of the blind is not the night that people imagine. (I should say that I am speaking for myself, and for my father and my grand-mother, who both died blind—blind, laughing, and brave, as I also hope to die. They inherited many things—blindness, for example—but one does not inherit courage. I know that they were brave.)

The blind live in a world that is inconvenient, an undefined world from which certain colors emerge: for me, yellow, blue (except that the blue may be green), and green (except that the green may be blue). White has disap-peared, or is confused with grey. As for red, it has vanished completely. But I hope some day—I am following a treatment—to improve and to be able to see that great color, that color which shines in poetry, and which has so many beautiful names in many languages. Think of *scharlach* in German, *scarlet* in English, *escarlata* in Spanish, *écarlate* in French. Words that are worthy of that great color. In contrast, *amarillo*, yellow, sounds weak in Spanish; in English it seems more like yellow. I think that in Old Spanish it was *amariello*.

I live in that world of colors, and if I speak of my own modest blind-ness, I do so, first, because it is not the total blindness that people imagine, and second, because it deals with me. My case is not especially dramatic. What is dramatic are those who suddenly lose their sight. In my case, that slow nightfall, that slow loss of sight, began when I began to see. It has con-tinued since 1899 without dramatic moments, a slow nightfall that has lasted more than three quarters of a century. In 1955, the pathetic moment came when I knew I had lost my sight, my reader's and writer's sight.

In my life I have received many unmerited honors, but there is one that has made me happier than all the others: the directorship of the National Library. For reasons more political than literary, I was appointed by the Aramburu government.

I was named director of the library, and I returned to that building of which I had so many memories, on the Calle México in Monserrat, in the south of the city. I had never dreamed of the possibility of being director of the library. I had memories of another kind. I would go there with my father, at night. My father, a professor of psychology, would ask for some book by Bergson or William James, who were his favorite writers, or perhaps by Gustav Spiller. I, too timid to ask for a book, would look through some volume of the *Encyclopedia Britannica* or the German encyclopedias of Brockhaus or of Meyer. I would take a volume at random from the shelf and read. I remember one night when I was particularly rewarded, for I read three articles: on the Druids, the Druses, and Dryden—a gift of the letters *DR*. Other nights I was less fortunate.

I knew that Paul Groussac was in the building. I could have met him personally, but I was then quite shy; almost as shy as I am now. At the time, I believed that shyness was very important, but now I know that shyness is one of the evils one must try to overcome, that in reality to be shy doesn't matter—it is like so many other things to which one gives an exaggerated importance.

I received the nomination at the end of 1955. I was in charge, I was told, of a million books. Later I found out it was nine hundred thousand—a number that's more than enough. (And perhaps nine hundred thousand seems more than a million.)

Little by little I came to realize the strange irony of events. I had always imagined Paradise as a kind of library. Others think of a garden or of a palace. There I was, the center, in a way, of nine hundred thousand books in various languages, but I found I could barely make out the title pages and the spines. I wrote the "Poem of the Gifts," which begins:

> No one should read self-pity or reproach
> into this statement of the majesty
> of God; who with such splendid irony
> granted me books and blindness at one touch.

Those two gifts contradicted each other: the countless books and the night, the inability to read them.

I imagined the author of that poem to be Groussac, for Groussac was also the director of the library and also blind. Groussac was more courageous than I: he kept his silence. But I knew that there had certainly been moments when our lives had coincided, as we both had become blind and we both loved books. He honored literature with books far superior to mine. But we were both men of letters, and we both passed through the library of forbidden books—one might say, for our darkened eyes, of blank books, books without letters. I wrote of the irony of God, and in the end I asked myself which of us had written that poem of a plural I and a single shadow.

At the time I did not know that there had been another director of the library who was blind, José Mármol. Here appears the number three, which seals everything. Two is a mere coincidence; three, a confirmation. A confirmation of a ternary order, a divine or theological confirmation.

Mármol was director of the library when it was on the Calle Venezuela. These days it is usual to speak badly of Mármol, or not to mention him at all. But we must remember that when we speak of the time of Rosas, we do not think of the admirable book by Ramos Mejía, *Rosas and His Time*, but of the era as it is described in Mármol's wonderfully gossipy novel, *La Amalia*. To bequeath the image of an age or of a country is no small glory.

We have, then, three people who shared the same fate. And, for me, the joy of returning to the Monserrat section, in the Southside. For everyone in Buenos Aires, the Southside is, in a mysterious way, the secret center of the city. Not the other, somewhat ostentatious center we show to tourists—in those days there was not that bit of public relations called the Barrio de San Telmo. But the Southside has come to be the modest secret center of Buenos Aires.

When I think of Buenos Aires, I think of the Buenos Aires I knew as a child: the low houses, the patios, the porches, the cisterns with turtles in them, the grated windows. That Buenos Aires was all of Buenos Aires. Now only the southern section has been preserved. I felt that I had returned to the neighborhood of my elders.

There were the books, but I had to ask my friends the titles of them. I remembered a sentence from Rudolf Steiner, in his books on anthroposophy, which was the name he gave to his theosophy. He said that when something ends, we must think that something begins. His advice is salutary, but the execution is difficult, for we only know what we have lost, not what we will gain. We have a very precise image—an image at times shameless—of what we have lost, but we are ignorant of what may follow or replace it.

I made a decision. I said to myself: since I have lost the beloved world of appearances, I must create something else. At the time I was a professor of English at the university. What could I do to teach that almost infinite literature, that literature which exceeds the life of a man, and even generations of men? What could I do in four Argentine months of national holidays and strikes? I did what I could to teach the love of that literature, and I refrained as much as possible from dates and names.

Some female students came to see me. They had taken the exam and passed. (All students pass with me!) To the girls—there were nine or ten—I said: "I have an idea. Now that you have passed and I have fulfilled my obligation as a professor, wouldn't it be interesting to embark on the study of a language or a literature we hardly know?" They asked which language and which literature. "Well, naturally the English language and English literature. Let us begin to study them, now that we are free from the frivolity of the exams; let us begin at the beginning."

I remembered that at home there were two books I could retrieve. I had placed them on the highest shelf, thinking I would never use them. They were Sweet's *Anglo-Saxon Reader* and *The Anglo-Saxon Chronicle*. Both had glossaries. And so we gathered one morning in the National Library.

I thought: I have lost the visible world, but now I am going to recover another, the world of my distant ancestors, those tribes of men who rowed across the stormy northern seas, from Germany, Denmark, and the Low Countries, who conquered England, and after whom we name England— since *Angle-land*, land of the Angles, had previously been called the land of the Britons, who were Celts.

It was a Saturday morning. We gathered in Groussac's office, and we began to read. There was a detail that pleased and mortified us, and at the same time filled us with a certain pride. It was the fact that the Saxons, like the Scandinavians, used two runic letters to signify the two sounds of *th*, as in "thing" and "the." This conferred an air of mystery to the page.

We were encountering a language that seemed different from English but similar to German. What always happens, when one studies a language, happened. Each one of the words stood out as though it had been carved, as though it were a talisman. For that reason poems in a foreign language have a prestige they do not enjoy in their own language, for one hears, one sees, each one of the words individually. We think of the beauty, of the power, or simply of the strangeness of them.

We had good luck that morning. We discovered the sentence, "Julius Caesar was the first Roman to discover England." Finding ourselves with the Romans in a text of the North, we were moved. You must remember we knew nothing of the language; each word was a kind of talisman we unearthed. We found two words. And with those two words we became almost drunk. (It's true that I was an old man, and they were young women—likely stages for inebriation.) I thought: "I am returning to the language my ancestors spoke fifty generations ago; I am returning to that language; I am reclaiming it. It is not the first time I speak it; when I had other names this was the language I spoke." Those two words were the name of London, "*Lundenburh,*" and the name of Rome, which moved us even more, thinking of the light that had fallen on those northern islands, "*Romeburh.*" I think we left crying, "Lundenburh, Romeburh . . ." in the streets.

So I began my study of Anglo-Saxon, which blindness brought me. And now I have a memory full of poetry that is elegiac, epic, Anglo-Saxon.

I had replaced the visible world with the aural world of the Anglo-Saxon language. Later I moved on to the richer world of Scandinavian literature: I went on to the *Eddas* and the sagas. I wrote *Ancient Germanic Literature* and many poems based on those themes, but most of all I enjoyed it. I am now preparing a book on Scandinavian literature.

I did not allow blindness to intimidate me. And besides, my publisher made me an excellent offer: he told me that if I produced thirty poems in a year, he would produce a book. Thirty poems means discipline, especially when one must dictate every line, but at the same time it allows for a sufficient freedom, as it is impossible that in one year there will not be thirty occasions for poetry. Blindness has not been for me a total misfortune; it should not be seen in a pathetic way. It should be seen as a way of life: one of the styles of living.

Being blind has its advantages. I owe to the darkness some gifts: the gift of Anglo-Saxon, my limited knowledge of Icelandic, the joy of so many lines of poetry, of so many poems, and of having written another book, entitled, with a certain falsehood, with a certain arrogance, *In Praise of Darkness.*

I would like to speak now of other cases, of illustrious cases. I will begin with that obvious example of the friendship of poetry and blindness, with the one who has been called the greatest of poets: Homer. (We know of another blind Greek poet, Tamiris, whose work has been lost. Tamiris was defeated in a battle with the Muses, who broke his lyre and took away his sight.)

Oscar Wilde had a curious hypothesis, one which I don't think is historically correct but which is intellectually agreeable. In general, writers try to make what they say seem profound; Wilde was a profound man who tried to seem frivolous. He wanted us to think of him as a conversationalist; he wanted us to consider him as Plato considered poetry, as "that winged, fickle, sacred thing." Well, that winged, fickle, sacred thing called Oscar Wilde said that Antiquity had deliberately represented Homer as blind.

We do not know if Homer existed. The fact that seven cities vie for his name is enough to make us doubt his historicity. Perhaps there was no single Homer; perhaps there were many Greeks whom we conceal under the name of Homer. The traditions are unanimous in showing us a blind poet, yet Homer's poetry is visual, often splendidly visual—as was, to a far lesser degree, that of Oscar Wilde.

Wilde realized that his own poetry was too visual, and he wanted to cure himself of that defect. He wanted to make poetry that was aural, musical—let us say like the poetry of Tennyson, or of Verlaine, whom he loved and admired so. Wilde said that the Greeks claimed that Homer was blind in order to emphasize that poetry must be aural, not visual. From that comes the *"de la musique avant toute chose"* of Verlaine and the symbolism contemporary to Wilde.

We may believe that Homer never existed, but that the Greeks imagined him as blind in order to insist on the fact that poetry is, above all, music; that poetry is, above all, the lyre; that the visual can or cannot exist in a poet. I know of great visual poets and great poets who are not visual—intellectual poets, mental ones—there's no need to mention names.

Let us go on to the example of Milton. Milton's blindness was voluntary. He knew from the beginning that he was going to be a great poet. This has occurred to other poets: Coleridge and De Quincey, before they wrote a single line, knew that their destiny was literary. I too, if I may mention myself, have always known that my destiny was, above all, a literary destiny— that bad things and some good things would happen to me, but that, in the long run, all of it would be converted into words. Particularly the bad things, since happiness does not need to be transformed: happiness is its own end.

Let us return to Milton. He destroyed his sight writing pamphlets in support of the execution of the king by Parliament. Milton said that he lost his sight voluntarily, defending freedom; he spoke of that noble task and never complained of being blind. He sacrificed his sight, and then he remembered his first desire, that of being a poet. They have discovered at Cambridge University a manuscript in which the young Milton proposes various subjects for a long poem.

"I might perhaps leave something so written to aftertimes, as they should not willingly let it die," he declared. He listed some ten or fifteen subjects, not knowing that one of them would prove prophetic: the subject of Samson. He did not know that his fate would, in a way, be that of Samson; that Samson, who had prophesied Christ in the Old Testament, also prophesied Milton, and with greater accuracy. Once he knew himself to be permanently blind, he embarked on two historical works, *A Brief History of Muscovia* and *A History of England*, both of which remained unfinished. And then the long poem *Paradise Lost*. He sought a theme that would interest all men, not merely the English. That subject was Adam, our common father.

He spent a good part of his time alone, composing verses, and his memory had grown. He would hold forty or fifty hendecasyllables of blank verse in his memory and then dictate them to whomever came to visit. The whole poem was written in this way. He thought of the fate of Samson, so close to his own, for now Cromwell was dead and the hour of the Restoration had come. Milton was persecuted and could have been condemned to death for having supported the execution of the king. But when they brought Charles II—son of Charles I, "The Executed"—the list of those condemned to death, he put down his pen and said, not without nobility, "There is something in my right hand which will not allow me to sign a sentence of death." Milton was saved, and many others with him.

He then wrote *Samson Agonistes*. He wanted to create a Greek tragedy. The action takes place in a single day, Samson's last. Milton thought on the similarity of destinies, since he, like Samson, had been a strong man who was ultimately defeated. He was blind. And he wrote those verses which, according to Landor, he punctuated badly, but which in fact had to be "Eyeless, in Gaza, at the mill, with the slaves"—as if the misfortunes were accumulating on Samson.

Milton has a sonnet in which he speaks of his blindness. There is a line one can tell was written by a blind man. When he has to describe the world, he says, "In this dark world and wide." It is precisely the world of the blind when they are alone, walking with hands outstretched, searching for props. Here we have an example—much more important than mine—of a man who overcomes blindness and does his work: *Paradise Lost, Paradise Regained, Samson Agonistes*, his best sonnets, part of *A History of England*, from the beginnings to the Norman Conquest. All of this was executed while he was blind; all of it had to be dictated to casual visitors.

The Boston aristocrat Prescott was helped by his wife. An accident, when he was a student at Harvard, had caused him to lose one eye and left him almost blind in the other. He decided that his life would be dedicated to literature. He studied, and learned, the literatures of England, France, Italy, and Spain. Imperial Spain offered him a world that was agreeable to his own rigid rejection of a democratic age. From an erudite he became a writer, and he dictated to his wife the histories of the conquest of Mexico and Peru, of the reign of the Catholic Kings and of Phillip II. It was a happy labor, almost impeccable, which took more than twenty years.

There are two examples that are closer to us. One I have already mentioned, Paul Groussac, who has been unjustly forgotten. People see him now as a French interloper in Argentina. It is said that his historical work has become dated, that today one makes use of greater documentation. But they forget that Groussac, like every writer, left two works: first, his subject, and second, the manner of its execution. Groussac revitalized Spanish prose. Alfonso Reyes, the greatest prose writer in Spanish in any era, once told me, "Groussac taught me how Spanish should be written." Groussac overcame his blindness and left some of the best pages in prose that have been written in our country. It will always please me to remember this.

Let us recall another example, one more famous than Groussac. In James Joyce we are also given a twofold work. We have those two vast and—why not say it?—unreadable novels, *Ulysses* and *Finnegans Wake*. But that is only half of his work (which also includes beautiful poems and the admirable *Portrait of an Artist as a Young Man*). The other half, and perhaps the most redeeming aspect (as they now say) is the fact that he took on the almost infinite English language. That language—which is statistically larger than all the others and offers so many possibilities for the writer, particularly in its concrete verbs—was not enough for him. Joyce, an Irishman, recalled that Dublin had been founded by Danish Vikings. He studied Norwegian—he wrote a letter to Ibsen in Norwegian—and then he studied Greek, Latin. . . . He knew all the languages, and he wrote in a language invented by himself, difficult to understand but marked by a strange music. Joyce brought a new music to English. And he said, valorously (and mendaciously) that "of all the things that have happened to me, I think the least important was having been blind." Part of his vast work was executed in darkness: polishing the sentences in his memory, working at times for a whole day on a single phrase, and then writing it and correcting it. All in the midst of blindness or periods of blindness. In comparison, the impotence of Boileau, Swift, Kant, Ruskin, and George Moore was a melancholic instrument for the successful execution of their work; one might say the same of perversion, whose beneficiaries today have ensured that no one will ignore their names. Democritus of Abdera tore his eyes out in a garden so that the spectacle of reality would not distract him; Origen castrated himself.

I have enumerated enough examples. Some are so illustrious that I am ashamed to have spoken of my own personal case—except for the fact that people always hope for confessions, and I have no reason to deny them mine. But, of course, it seems absurd to place my name next to those I have recalled.

I have said that blindness is a way of life, a way of life that is not entirely unfortunate. Let us recall those lines of the greatest Spanish poet, Fray Luis de León:

> *Vivir quiero conmigo,*
> *gozar quiero del bien que debo al cielo,*
> *a solas sin testigo,*
> *libre de amor, de celo,*
> *de odio, de esperanza, de recelo.*

[I want to live with myself,/I want to enjoy the good that I owe to heaven,/alone, without witnesses,/free of love, of jealousy,/of hate, of hope, of fear.]

Edgar Allan Poe knew this stanza by heart.

For me, to live without hate is easy, for I have never felt hate. To live without love I think is impossible, happily impossible for each one of us. But the first part—"I want to live with myself,/I want to enjoy the good that I owe to heaven"—if we accept that in the good of heaven there can also be darkness, then who lives more with themselves? Who can explore themselves more? Who can know more of themselves? According to the Socratic phrase, who can know himself more than the blind man?

A writer lives. The task of being a poet is not completed at a fixed schedule. No one is a poet from eight to twelve and from two to six. Whoever is a poet is always one, and continually assaulted by poetry. I suppose a painter feels that colors and shapes are besieging him. Or a musician feels that the strange world of sounds—the strangest world of art—is always seeking him out, that there are melodies and dissonances looking for him. For the task of an artist, blindness is not a total misfortune. It may be an instrument. Fray Luis de León dedicated one of his most beautiful odes to Francisco Salinas, a blind musician.

A writer, or any man, must believe that whatever happens to him is an instrument; everything has been given for an end. This is even stronger in the case of the artist. Everything that happens, including humiliations, embarrassments, misfortunes, all has been given like clay, like material for one's art. One must accept it. For this reason I speak in a poem of the ancient food of heroes: humiliation, unhappiness, discord. Those things are given to us to transform, so that we may make from the miserable circumstances of our lives things that are eternal, or aspire to be so.

If a blind man thinks this way, he is saved. Blindness is a gift. I have exhausted you with the gifts it has given me. It gave me Anglo-Saxon, it gave me some Scandinavian, it gave me a knowledge of a medieval literature I didn't know, it gave me the writing of various books, good or bad, but which justified the moment in which they were written. Moreover, blindness has made me feel surrounded by the kindness of others. People always feel good will toward the blind.

I want to end with a line of Goethe: *"Alles Nahe werde fern,"* everything near becomes far. Goethe was referring to the evening twilight. Everything near becomes far. It is true. At nightfall, the things closest to us seem to move away from our eyes. So the visible world has moved away from my eyes, perhaps forever.

Goethe could be referring not only to twilight but to life. All things go off, leaving us. Old age is probably the supreme solitude—except that the supreme solitude is death. And "everything near becomes far" also refers to the slow process of blindness, of which I hoped to show, speaking tonight, that it is not a complete misfortune. It is one more instrument among the many—all of them so strange—that fate or chance provide.

[1977]   *[EW]*

Immortality

In a book as fine as all of his books, *The Varieties of Religious Experience*, William James devotes only a single page to the question of personal immortality. He states that, for him, it is a minor problem, that the question of personal immortality is entwined with the problem of religion and that, for most of the world, for the commonality of people, "God is the producer of immortality."

Without understanding the joke, Don Miguel de Unamuno repeats it in

The Tragic Sense of Life, but he also says, quite often, that he wants to continue being Don Miguel de Unamuno. Here I do not understand Miguel de Unamuno. I don't want to continue being Jorge Luis Borges; I want to be someone else. I hope that my death will be total; I hope to die in body and soul.

I don't know if my attempt to speak of personal immortality—of the soul that preserves a memory of what it was on earth, and in the other world remembers its death—is ambitious or modest, or entirely justified. My sister Norah was at my house the other day, and she said, "I am going to paint a picture called 'Nostalgia for Earth,' whose subject will be what a fortunate person in heaven feels when thinking about the earth. It will have elements of Buenos Aires when I was a little girl." I have a poem that my sister doesn't know on a similar theme. In it, I think of Jesus, who remembers the rain in Galilee, the smell in the carpentry shop, and something he never sees in heaven and for which he is nostalgic: the vault of the stars.

This theme of nostalgia in heaven for the earth also appears in a poem by Dante Gabriel Rossetti. It deals with a girl who is in heaven and yet feels unfortunate because her lover is not with her; she hopes that he will arrive, but he will never arrive because he has sinned, and she will continue to keep hoping eternally.

William James says that, for him, it is a minor problem; that the great problems of philosophy are time, the reality of the external world, and understanding. Immortality occupies a minor place, a place that corresponds less to philosophy than to poetry and, of course, theology, although not all theologies.

There is another solution, that of the transmigration of souls, certainly a poetic solution, and one more interesting than the other, that of continuing to be who we are and remembering who we were—which, I'd say, is a poor subject.

I remember ten or twelve images from my childhood, and I try to forget them. When I think of my adolescence, I am not resigned to what I was; I would have preferred to be someone else. At the same time, all this may be transmuted by, may become a subject for, poetry.

The most poignant text in all of philosophy, without trying to be so, is Plato's *Phaedon*. That dialogue refers to Socrates' last day, when his friends know that the boat from Delos has arrived and that Socrates will drink the hemlock. Socrates receives them in jail, knowing that he will be executed. He sees all of them, except one. Here we find the most moving phrase that

Plato wrote in his entire life, as noted by Max Brod. He writes: "Plato, I think, was ill." According to Brod, this is the only time that Plato names himself in all of the dialogues. If Plato wrote the dialogue, undoubtedly he was there—or not there, it's the same—but he names himself in the third person. It shows us that he was troubled about witnessing that great moment.

It has been speculated that Plato added that phrase to allow himself to be freer, as if to say: "I don't know what Socrates said on that last day, but I would like to think he said these things." Or: "I can imagine him saying these things." I believe that Plato felt the unsurpassable literary beauty of saying "Plato, I think, was ill."

Then comes a marvelous statement, perhaps the finest in the dialogues. The friends enter; Socrates is seated on the bed; they have taken off the shackles. Rubbing his knees and feeling the pleasure of no longer having the weight of the chains, he says: "How strange. The chains weighed me down, it was a form of pain. Now I feel relieved because they have taken them away. Pleasure and pain go together, they are twins."

How wonderful it is that, in that moment, on the last day of his life, he doesn't say that he is going to die, but rather he reflects on the fact that pleasure and pain are inseparable. It shows us a valiant man, a man who is going to die and doesn't speak of his immediate death.

Then he says that he has to take the poison that day, and then comes the discussion that is marred for us by the fact that he speaks of two beings, of two substances, the body and the soul. Socrates says that the psychic substance (the soul) can live better without a body; that the body is an encumbrance. It echoes that doctrine, common in antiquity, that we are imprisoned in our bodies.

Here I would like to recall a few lines by the great English poet, Rupert Brooke, who says, with fine poetry but bad philosophy, that after death we will "feel, who have laid our groping hands away;/And see, no longer blinded by our eyes." Gustav Spiller, in an excellent treatise on psychology, says that if we think of other misfortunes of the body—a mutilation, a blow to the head—they are not beneficial to the soul. It is hard to imagine that a cataclysm of the body is good for the soul. Nevertheless Socrates, who believes in these two realities, the body and the soul, argues that the soul that is freed from the body can dedicate itself to thinking.

This recalls the myth of Democritus. It is said that he tore out his eyes in a garden in order to think and not be distracted by the outside world.

This is, of course, untrue, but beautiful. Here is a person who sees the visual world—that world of the seven colors I have lost—as an obstacle to pure thought and pulls out his eyes to continue thinking in tranquility.

For us, these ideas of the body and of the soul are suspicious. Let us briefly recall the history of philosophy. Locke said that the only thing that exists are perceptions and feelings, and the memories and perceptions of those feelings; that matter exists and that the five senses inform us about matter. Then Berkeley maintains that matter is a series of perceptions and that these perceptions are inconceivable without a consciousness that perceives them. What is red? Red depends on our eyes, and our eyes belong to a system of perceptions. Then comes Hume, who refutes both hypotheses, and destroys the soul and the body. What is the soul but that which perceives, and what is matter but that which is perceived? If nouns are suppressed in the world, they must be reduced to verbs. We ought not to say, "I think," because "I" is a subject; we should say, "It is thought," much as we say, "It is raining." In both verbs we have an action without a subject. When Descartes said, "I think, therefore I am," he should have said, "Something thinks," or "It is thought," because "I" assumes an entity, and I have no right to assume that. He would have to say, "It is thought, therefore something is."

As for personal immortality, we will see what arguments there are in favor of it. I will cite two. Fechner says that human consciousness is provided with a series of desires, appetites, hopes, and fears that do not correspond to the duration of our lives. When Dante says *"n'el mezzo del cammin de nostra vita,"* he reminds us that the Scriptures accord us seventy years of life. Thus, when he had that vision he had turned thirty-five. We, in the course of our seventy years of life—unfortunately, I have gone beyond the limit: I'm now seventy-eight—feel things that have no meaning in this life. Fechner thought of the embryo, of the body before it leaves the belly of the mother. In that body there are legs that do nothing, arms, hands—none of this has meaning; it can only have meaning in a later life. We ought to believe that the same happens with us, that we are full of hopes, fears, conjectures, and we can't say exactly what they mean for a purely mortal life. We can state exactly what animals have, and they can ignore all that which can be used in another, fuller life. It is an argument in favor of immortality.

Let us cite St. Thomas Aquinas, who left us this sentence: *"Intellectus naturaliter desiderat esse semper,"* the mind naturally desires to exist forever. To which we might respond that it also desires other things, and that it often desires to cease existing. We have the cases of suicides, and the common one of people who need to sleep, which is also a form of death. We can cite poetic texts based on the idea of death as a sensation. For example, this popular Spanish *copla: "Ven, muerte tan escondida / que no te sienta venir / porque el placer de morir / no me torne a dar la vida"* [Come, death so hidden/that I don't feel you come/for the pleasure of dying/doesn't make me want to go back to life]. Then there is a strophe from the French poet Leconte de Lisle: "Free him from time, from number, and from space, and return him to the repose that he has left."

We have many longings, among them the longing for life, to exist forever, but also the longing to cease existing, as well as fear and its opposite, hope. All of these things can exist without personal immortality, and do not require it. I myself do not desire it, and I fear it, for it would be frightening to know that I am going to continue, frightening to think that I am going to go on being Borges. I am tired of myself, of my name, and of my fame, and I want to free myself from all that.

There is a sort of compromise that I find in Tacitus, and which was taken up again by Goethe. Tacitus, in his *Life of Agrippa*, says, "*Non cum corpore periunt magnae animae*," the great souls do not die with the body. Tacitus believed that personal immortality was a gift reserved for some, not the common man, but that certain souls deserved to be immortal, that they were worth remembering who they were. Goethe takes up this thought again, and writes, when his friend Wieland has died: "It is horrible to think that Wieland has died inexorably." He cannot think that Wieland will not go on in some other place; he believes in the personal immortality of Wieland, but not of everyone. We have the idea that immortality is the privilege of a few. But everyone judges himself as great, everyone tends to believe his immortality is necessary. I don't believe in that.

Later, we have other immortalities that, I think, are the important ones. First, the idea of transmigration. This idea is in Pythagoras, and in Plato. Plato saw transmigration as a possibility. Transmigration helps to explain good and bad luck. If we are lucky or unlucky in this life we owe it to a previous life; we are receiving punishments or rewards. There is something that can be difficult: if our individual life, as Hinduism and Buddhism believe, depends on our previous life, that previous life in turn depends on a previous life, and thus continues infinitely toward the past. It has been said that if time is infinite, the infinite number of past lives is a contradiction. If the number is infinite, how can an infinite thing reach the present? We think that if time is infinite, and I believe it is, then that infinite time must include all the presents and, among all the presents, why not this present here, in the University of Belgrano, with you and I together? Why not that time also? If time is infinite, at any given moment we are in the center of time.

Pascal thought that if the universe is infinite, the universe is a sphere whose circumference is in all parts and its center in none. Why not say that this present moment has an infinite past behind it, an infinite yesterday, and that this past also passes through this present? At any given moment, we are at the center of an infinite line, in whatever place of the infinite center we are in the center of space, for time and space are infinite.

The Buddhists believe that we have lived an infinite number of lives, infinite in the sense of an unlimited number, in the strict sense of the word: a number without beginning or end, something like the transfinite number in Kantor's mathematics. We are now in the center—all moments are centers—of that infinite time. Now we are talking, you are thinking about what I am saying, you are agreeing or disagreeing.

Transmigration gives us the possibility of a soul that travels from body to body, in human bodies and in animals. We have that poem by Pietro di Agrigento where he tells how he recognized a shield that had been his in the Trojan war. We have John Donne's poem "The Progress of the Soul," which is slightly earlier than Shakespeare. Donne begins it by saying: "I sing the progress of the deathless soul," and that soul goes from one body to another. He declares that he is going to write a book that will be superior to all other books, except the Holy Scriptures. His project is ambitious, and although it was never realized, it includes many beautiful verses. He begins with a soul who inhabits the apple—that is, in Adam's fruit, the fruit of sin. Then it is in the belly of Eve and it engenders Cain; then it goes from body to body in each stanza (one of them being Queen Elizabeth). The poem remains unfinished. Donne believed in the transmigration of souls, and in one of his prologues, he invokes the illustrious origins of the concept and names two sources: Pythagoras and Socrates in the last dialogue.

It is interesting to note that Socrates, that afternoon, talking with his friends, does not want to say good-bye pathetically. He expels his wife and children, he wants to expel a friend who is weeping, he wants to talk calmly, to simply keep on talking and thinking. The fact of personal death does not affect him. His role, his custom, is something else: to discuss, to discuss in a certain way.

Why does he drink the hemlock? There was no reason.

He says curious things: "Orpheus wanted to transform himself into a nightingale; Agamemnon, shepherd of men, into an eagle; Ulysses, strangely, into the most humble and unknown of men." Socrates is talking, death interrupts him. The blue death is seen climbing his legs. He has taken the hemlock. He tells a friend that he remembers the vow he had made to Aesculapius, and to offer him a cock. He means by this that Aesculapius, the god of medicine, has cured him of the essential evil, life itself. "I owe a cock to Aesculapius, he has cured me of life, I am going to die." That is, he doesn't believe what he has said before: he thinks that he is going to personally die.

We have another classical text, Lucretius' *De rerum natura*, where personal immortality is denied. The most memorable of the arguments given by Lucretius is this: A person complains that he is going to die. He thinks that the future will forget him. As Victor Hugo said: "He will go alone in the middle of the feast/nothing will be missing in the radiant and happy world." In that great poem, as ambitious as Donne's, Lucretius uses the following argument: "You are pained because you will lack the future. Yet you believe that before you there was an infinite time, that, when you were born, the moment had already passed when Carthage and Troy battled to rule the world. It doesn't matter to you. So why should it matter what shall come? You have lost the infinite past, what matter if you lose the infinite future?" This is what Lucretius says. It's a pity that I don't know enough Latin to remember his beautiful lines, which I have been reading lately with the help of a dictionary.

Schopenhauer answered—and I think Schopenhauer is the greatest authority—that the doctrine of transmigration is nothing but the popular form of another doctrine, which would later be expressed by Shaw and Bergson, the doctrine of the will to live. There is something that wants to live, something that opens a passage across matter, or in spite of matter. That something is what Schopenhauer called *wille*, which he conceived of as the will to resurrection.

Later, Shaw speaks of the "life force," and finally Bergson will talk about the "*élan vital*," the vital impetus that is manifested in all things, that created the universe, and that is in every one of us. It is dead in minerals, dormant in plants, like a dream in animals, but in us it is conscious of itself. Here we have the explanation of that line of Aquinas: "*Intellectus naturaliter desiderat esse semper*," the mind naturally desires to be exist forever. But in what way does it desire it? It does not desire it in a personal way; it does not desire it in Unamuno's sense, that it wants to keep on being Unamuno; it desires it in a general way.

Our "I" is the least important thing for us. What does it mean for us to feel ourselves as an I? In what way can it differ that I feel myself Borges than that you feel yourselves A, B, or C? Absolutely not at all. That I is what we share, it is what is present, in one form or another, in all creatures. We could say that immortality is necessary—not the personal, but this other immortality. For example, each time that someone loves an enemy, the immortality of Christ appears. In that moment he is Christ. Each time we repeat a line by Dante or Shakespeare, we are, in some way, that instant when Dante or Shakespeare created that line. Immortality is in the memory of others and in the work we leave behind. What does it matter if that work is forgotten?

I have devoted the last twenty years to Anglo-Saxon poetry, and I know many Anglo-Saxon poems by heart. The only thing I don't know is the names of the poets. What does it matter, as long as I, reciting the poems from the ninth century, am feeling something that someone felt back then? He is living in me in that moment, I am that dead man. Every one of us is, in some way, all the people who have died before us. And not only those of our blood.

Of course, we inherit things in our blood. I know—my mother told me—that every time I recite English poems, I say them in the voice of my father, who died in 1938. When I recite Shakespeare, my father is living in me. The people who have heard me will live in my voice, which is a reflection of a voice that was, perhaps, a reflection of the voice of its elders. The same may be said of music and of language. Language is a creation, it becomes a kind of immortality. I am using the Castilian language. How many dead Castilians are living within me?

Every one of us collaborates, in one form or another, in this world. Every one of us wants this world to be better, and if the world truly became better—that eternal hope—if the country saved itself—and why can't the country save itself?—we would become immortal in that salvation, whether they know our names or not. That is the least important; what matters is that immortality is obtained in works, in the memory that one leaves in others.

My opinions do not matter, nor my judgment; the names of the past do not matter as long as we are continually helping the future of the world, our immortality. That immortality has no reason to be personal, it can do without the accident of names, it can ignore our memory. For why should we suppose that we are going to continue in another life with our memory, as though I were to keep thinking my whole life about my childhood in Palermo, in Adrogué, or in Montevideo? Why should I always return to that? It is a literary recourse; I could forget all that and keep on being, and all that would live within me although I do not name it. Perhaps the most important things are those we don't remember in a precise way, that we remember unconsciously.

To conclude, I would say that I believe in immortality, not in the personal but in the cosmic sense. We will keep on being immortal; beyond our physical death our memory will remain, and beyond our memory will remain our actions, our circumstances, our attitudes, all that marvelous part of universal history, although we won't know, and it is better that we won't know it.

[1978]   *[EW]*

The Detective Story

A book by Van Wyck Brooks called *The Flowering of New England* deals with an extraordinary fact, explainable only by astrology: the flowering of genius in a small part of the United States during the first half of the nineteenth century. (I, obviously, am partial to this New England, which has so much in common with Old England.) It would be easy to compile an infinite list of names: Emily Dickinson, Herman Melville, Thoreau, Emerson, William James, Henry James, and of course Edgar Allan Poe, who was born in Boston in the year 1809, I believe. I am known to be weak on dates. To speak of the detective story is to speak of Edgar Allan Poe, who invented the genre, but before speaking of the genre, there is a small prior question that should be discussed: Do literary genres exist?

It is well known that Croce, on some page of his formidable *Aesthetics*, says: "To claim that a book is a novel, an allegory, or a treatise on aesthetics has more or less the same value as saying that it has a yellow cover and can be found on the third shelf to the left." Genres, in other words, are negated, and individuals are affirmed. A fitting reply to this would be that although all individuals are real, to specify them is to generalize them. Of course, this statement of mine is a generalization, and should not be allowed.

To think is to generalize, and we need these useful Platonic archetypes in order to say anything. So why not say that there are such things as literary genres? I would add a personal observation: literary genres may depend less on texts than on the way texts are read. The aesthetic event requires the conjunction of reader and text; only then does it exist. It is absurd to suppose that a book is much more than a book. It begins to exist when a reader opens it. Then the aesthetic phenomenon exists, which can be similar to the moment when the book was created.

There exists a certain species of contemporary reader: the reader of detective fiction. This reader—who may be found in every country in the world and who numbers in the millions—was invented by Edgar Allan Poe. Let us imagine that this reader doesn't exist, or rather, let us imagine something that might be even more interesting: that this reader is someone far removed from us. He may be Persian, a Malaysian, a peasant, a child. In any case, this reader is told that *Don Quixote* is a detective novel; we will suppose that this hypothetical figure is familiar with detective novels, and he begins to read: "In a place in La Mancha whose name I do not wish to recall, there lived, not long ago, a gentleman . . ." Already this reader is full of doubt, for the reader of detective novels reads with incredulity and suspicions, or rather with one particular suspicion.

For example, if he reads: "In a place in La Mancha . . . ," he naturally assumes that none of it really happened in La Mancha. Then: "whose name I do not wish to recall"—and why didn't Cervantes want to remember? Undoubtedly because Cervantes was the murderer, the guilty party. Then: "not long ago"—quite possibly the future holds even more terrifying things in store.

The detective novel has created a special type of reader. This tends to be forgotten when Poe's work is evaluated, for if Poe created the detective story, he subsequently created the reader of detective fiction.

In order to understand the detective story, we must keep in mind the general context of Poe's life. I believe that Poe was an extraordinary romantic poet, more extraordinary in the whole of his work, in our memory of his work, than on any given page of his work. He is better in prose than in poetry. In Poe's poetry, we have ample justification for what Emerson said when he called Poe "the jingle man." He was a lesser Tennyson, although a few memorable lines remain.

Poe was a projector of multiple shadows. How many things come out of Poe? It could be said that there are two men without whom contemporary literature would not be what it is, both of them Americans, and both of the past century: Walt Whitman—from whom derives what we can call civic-minded poetry, from whom Neruda derives, along with so many other things, good or bad—and Edgar Allan Poe, from whom derives the symbolism of Baudelaire, who was Poe's disciple and prayed to him every night, and two other things, which appear to be separate but are actually related: the idea of literature as an intellectual activity, and the detective story. The first of these contributions—literature considered as an operation of the mind, not the spirit—is very important. The other is minimal, despite having inspired great writers (Stevenson, Dickens, Chesterton—Poe's most illustrious heir). Detective literature may seem subaltern, and indeed is currently in decline; at present it has been surpassed or replaced by science fiction, which also has Poe as one of its possible forefathers.

Let us return to the idea that poetry is a creation of the mind. This goes against the whole of prior tradition, for which poetry was an operation of the spirit. We have the extraordinary case of the Bible, a series of texts by different authors, dating from different periods and dealing with very different subjects, but all attributed to a single invisible figure: the Holy Spirit. The Holy Spirit, the divinity or an infinite intelligence, has supposedly dictated these different works to different amanuenses in different countries and times. These works include, for example, a metaphysical dialogue (the Book of Job), a history (the Book of Kings), a theogony (Genesis), and the declarations of the prophets. All of these works are different, and we read them as if a single person had written them.

Perhaps, if we are pantheists, there is no need to take the fact that we are now different individuals too seriously: we are different organs of the continual divinity. That is, the Holy Spirit has written all books and also reads all books, since it is, to varying degrees, in each one of us.

Now, Poe was a man who, as we know, lived an unhappy life. He died at the age of forty, given over to alcohol, melancholy, and neurosis. We have no reason to enter into the details of the neurosis; we need only know that Poe was a very unfortunate man who lived predestined for misfortune. To free himself from it, he took to ostentatiously displaying and perhaps exaggerating his intellectual virtues. Poe considered himself a great romantic poet, a romantic poet of genius, especially when he wasn't writing in verse—for example, when he wrote the story of Arthur Gordon Pym. There we have the first name, the Saxon Arthur (Edgar); the second, the Scottish Gordon (Allan); and, finally, Pym, which is similar to Poe. Poe saw himself as an intellectual, and Pym boasted of being a man capable of evaluating and thinking everything.

At that point, Poe had written the famous poem that everyone knows, and perhaps too well, for it is not one of his good poems: "The Raven." Then he gave a lecture in Boston in which he explained how he came up with this topic. He began by considering the virtues of the refrain, and then thought about English phonetics. He decided that the two most memorable and effective letters in the English language were *o* and *r*, and immediately came up with the expression "nevermore." Then another problem arose: he had to justify the reiteration of the word, since it would be very odd for a human being to repeat "nevermore" regularly at the end of each stanza. Then he realized it did not have to be a rational being, and that led him to the idea of a talking bird. He thought about making it a parrot, but a parrot is unworthy of the dignity of poetry; then he thought of a raven. Or rather, he was reading Charles Dickens' novel *Barnaby Rudge* at the time, in which a raven figures. So he had a raven which is named Nevermore and which continually repeats its name. That is all Poe started out with.

Then he thought, what is the saddest and most melancholy event that can be recorded? It must be the death of a beautiful woman. Who best to lament such an event? The woman's lover, of course. Then he thought about the lover who has just lost his beloved, who is named Lenore to rhyme with "nevermore." Where to place the lover? The raven is black, he thought, where does blackness stand out most starkly? It must stand out against something white, the whiteness of a bust. And this bust, of whom might it be? It is a bust of Pallas Athena; and where could it be? In a library. For, says Poe, the unity of his poem requires an enclosed space.

So he placed the bust of Minerva in a library, and there too is the lover, alone, surrounded by his books, and lamenting the death of his beloved, so lovesick more. Enter the raven. Why does the raven enter? Well, the library is a quiet place and must be contrasted with something turbulent; he imagines a storm, he imagines the stormy night that makes the raven come inside.

The man asks who he is, and the raven answers, "Nevermore," and then the man, to torture himself masochistically, asks more questions so that the bird will answer all of them with "Nevermore," "Nevermore," "Nevermore." Finally the man says to the raven, in what can be understood as the poem's first metaphor: "Take thy beak from out my heart, and take thy form from off my door!"; and the raven (who is now simply an emblem of memory, accursedly immortal memory) answers, "Nevermore." The lover realizes he is doomed to spend the rest of his life, his fantastical life, conversing with the raven, which will always tell him "Nevermore," and asking questions whose answer he already knows.

All of which is to say that Poe seeks to make us believe he wrote this poem in an intellectual fashion, but we need only look a little closer at its plot to understand the fallacy of that. Poe could have reached the idea of an irrational being by using not a raven but an idiot, a drunkard; we would have then had a completely different and less explicable poem.

Poe, I believe had great pride in his own intelligence; when he duplicated himself in a character, he chose a distant character—the character we
all know and who is undoubtedly our friend, though he does not seek our
friendship: a gentleman, Auguste Dupin, the first detective in the history of
literature. He is a French gentleman, an impoverished French aristocrat,
who lives in an isolated neighborhood of Paris with a friend.

Here we have another tradition of the detective story: the fact of a mystery that is solved by the intellect, by an intellectual operation. This feat is
carried out by a very intelligent man named Dupin, who will later be
named Sherlock Holmes, who will later be named Father Brown, and who
will someday have other famous names as well, no doubt. The first of them
all, the model, the archetype, we might say, is the gentleman Charles Auguste Dupin, who lives with a friend, and it is the friend who tells the story.
This is also part of the tradition, and it was taken up long after Poe's death
by the Irish writer Conan Doyle, who picks up the theme, an attractive
theme in itself, of the friendship between two quite different people, which
becomes in some way the theme of the friendship between Don Quixote
and Sancho, except that those two never reach a perfect friendship. Later it
will be the theme of *Kim*, the friendship between the young boy and the
Hindu priest, and of *Don Segundo Sombra*, the trooper and the boy. This
theme of friendship, which is multiplied in Argentine literature, can also be
found in many books by Gutiérrez.

Conan Doyle imagines a rather dull-witted character he calls Dr. Watson, whose intelligence is somewhat inferior to the reader's; the other character is somewhat comical and somewhat awe-inspiring: Sherlock Holmes.
Conan Doyle has Watson recount the intellectual feats of his friend Sherlock Holmes, while never ceasing to marvel at them; Watson is always
guided by appearances and enjoys allowing himself to be dominated by
Sherlock Holmes.

All of this is already present in the first detective story that Poe wrote
without knowing that he was inaugurating a genre, "The Murders in the
Rue Morgue." Poe did not want the detective genre to be a realist genre; he
wanted it to be an intellectual genre, a fantastic genre, if you wish, but a fantastic genre of the intellect and not only of the imagination; a genre of both
things, no doubt, but primarily of the intellect.

He could have placed his crimes and his detectives in New York, but
then the reader would have been wondering whether the events really took
place in that way, whether the New York City police force is like that or is different. As it turned out, it was easier and more fruitful to Poe's imagination

to set it all in Paris, in a desolate portion of the Faubourg St.-Germain. Thus the first detective recorded in literature is a foreigner, a Frenchman. Why a Frenchman? Because the person writing the work is an American and needs a character who is distant. To make these characters stranger, he has them live quite differently from the way men generally do. At dawn they close the shutters and light candles; at nightfall they go out walking through the deserted streets of Paris in search of that infinite blue which, says Poe, only occurs in a great city that is asleep, feeling at the same time multitudinousness and solitude, which must be a stimulus to thought.

I imagine the two friends crossing the deserted streets of Paris at night and talking—about what? They speak of philosophy, intellectual matters. Then we have the crime, the first crime in detective literature: the murder of two women. I would call it "The Crimes in the Rue Morgue"; "crime" is stronger than "murder." Here is the situation: two women have been murdered in a room that appears inaccessible. With this, Poe inaugurates the mystery of the locked room. One of the women was strangled, the other one's throat was slashed with a razor. A great deal of money, four thousand francs, is scattered across the floor, everything is scattered, everything suggests madness. That is, we have a brutal, terrible beginning and then, at the end, the solution.

But that solution is not a solution for us, because we all know the plot before reading Poe's story, and of course that strips it of much of its strength. (The same thing happens with the analogous case of Dr. Jekyll and Mr. Hyde: we know the two are a single person, but that can only be known by readers of Stevenson, who was another of Poe's disciples. When he speaks of "the strange case of Dr. Jekyll and Mr. Hyde," he is proposing from the start a duality of personae.) Who would ever have guessed, moreover, that the murderer would turn out to be an orangutan, a monkey?

The solution is reached by an artifice: the testimony of those who entered the room before the discovery of the crime. All of them recognized a gruff voice, the voice of a Frenchman, as well as a few of the words that it spoke, and they also recognized a shrill voice that spoke without syllables, the voice of a foreigner. The Spaniard believes it was the voice of a German; the German, a Dutchman; the Dutchman, an Italian, etc. That voice is the inhuman voice of the monkey, and then the crime is solved: it is solved, but we already knew the solution.

For that reason we might think poorly of Poe, we might think that his plots are so weak they are almost transparent. They are for those of us who already know them, but not for the first readers of detective fiction; they were not trained as we are, they were not an invention of Poe's, as we are. Those who first read this tale were wonderstruck; the rest came later.

Poe has left five examples, one of which, called "Thou Art the Man," is the weakest of all. There we have a figure, the detective who turns out to be the murderer, who was later imitated in Gaston Leroux's *The Mystery of the Yellow Room.* Then there is another tale that has become exemplary, "The Purloined Letter." The plot is very simple. A letter has been stolen by a government minister; the police know he has it. Twice they have him waylaid in the street. Then they examine the house; to keep anything from escaping them, the entire house has been divided and subdivided; the police use microscopes, magnifying glasses. They take each book down from the library shelves, look to see if it has been re-bound, look for traces of dust on the spine. Then Dupin intervenes. He says the police are mistaken; they have the idea a schoolboy might have, the idea that something is hidden in a hiding place, but that is not the case. Dupin goes to visit the minister, who is a friend of his, and sees lying on a table, in plain sight, a torn envelope. He realizes that this is the letter everyone has been looking for. It is the idea of hiding something in a visible way, making something so visible that no one finds it. Moreover, at the beginning of each tale, to make us aware that Poe understood the detective story in an intellectual way, there are disquisitions on analysis, or a discussion of chess, to which whist or draughts is deemed superior.

Poe leaves us these five tales, and we also have another one, "The Mystery of Marie Rogêt," which is the strangest of all and the least interesting to read. It concerns a crime committed in New York: a girl, Mary Rogers, was murdered. She was a florist, I believe—Poe simply takes the information from the newspapers. He moves the crime to Paris and renames the girl Marie Rogêt, then suggests how the crime may have been committed. And indeed, years later the murderer was found and confirmed what Poe had written.

We have, then, the detective story as an intellectual genre, a genre based on something entirely fictitious: the idea that a crime is solved by abstract reasoning and not by informants or by carelessness on the part of the criminals. Poe knew that what he was doing was not realistic, which was why he chose Paris as the setting and made his reasoner an aristocrat, not a policeman, an aristocrat who makes the police look ridiculous. In other words, Poe created a genius of all that is intellectual.

What happens after Poe's death? He dies, I believe, in 1849; Walt Whitman, his other great contemporary, writes an obituary for him saying that

Poe was a performer who only knew how to play the low notes of the piano, who did not represent American democracy—something Poe had never sought to do. Whitman was unfair to him, and so was Emerson. Even today there are critics who underestimate him. But I believe that Poe, if we look at his work as a whole, produced the work of a genius, though his stories, except for the *Narrative of Arthur Gordon Pym*, are flawed. Nevertheless, they construct a character, a character who outlives all the characters Poe created, who outlives Charles Auguste Dupin, and who outlives the crimes and the mysteries that no longer frighten us.

In England, where this genre is approached from a psychological point of view, we have the best detective novels that have ever been written: Wilkie Collins' *The Woman in White* and *The Moonstone*. Then we have Chesterton, Poe's great successor. Chesterton said that he never wrote any detective stories that were better than Poe's, but Chesterton, it seems to me, is better than Poe. Poe wrote stories that are purely fantastic; for example, "The Masque of the Red Death" or "The Cask of Amontillado." In addition, he wrote stories based on reason, like the five detective stories. But Chesterton did something different; he wrote stories that are at once fantastic and, in the end, have a detective solution. I will tell one of them, "The Invisible Man," published in 1905 or 1908.

The plot amounts, in brief, to this. The story concerns a maker of mechanical dolls—cooks, porters, chambermaids, and mechanics—who lives in a house at the top of a snowy hill in London. He receives death threats—it is a very short story, that is important to know. He lives alone with his mechanical servants, which already has something horrible about it: a man who lives alone, surrounded by machines that vaguely resemble the forms of men. Finally, he receives a letter telling him he will die that afternoon. He calls his friends; his friends go for the police and leave him alone among his dolls, but first they ask the porter to pay close attention if anyone goes into the house. They ask a nearby patrolman and a vendor of roasted chestnuts to do the same. The three promise that they will. When the friends come back with the police, they notice tracks in the snow. The tracks approaching the house are shallow, while the tracks that leave it are deeper, as if something heavy were being carried. They enter the house and find that the maker of dolls has disappeared. Then they see ashes in the fireplace. This is the strongest moment in the story: the suspicion of a man devoured by his mechanical dolls; that is what makes the greatest impression on us, a greater impression than the eventual solution. The murderer went into the house and was seen by the chestnut vendor, the guard, and the porter, but they did not see him because he was the mailman who comes at the same time every afternoon. He killed his victim and stuffed him into the mail sack. Then he burned the mail and left. Father Brown sees him, chats, hears his confession, and absolves him, because in Chesterton's stories there are no arrests, nothing violent.

Currently, the detective genre has greatly declined in the United States, where it has become realistic and about violence—sexual violence, as well. In any event, it has disappeared. The intellectual origins of the detective story have been forgotten. They have, however, been maintained in England, where very calm novels are still written. They take place in an English town; everything is intellectual, everything is calm, there is no violence, and not too much bloodshed.

I have on occasion attempted the detective genre, and I'm not very proud of what I have done. I have taken it to a symbolic level, which I am not sure is appropriate. I wrote "Death and the Compass," as well as certain detective stories with Bioy Casares, whose stories are much better than mine—for example, the stories about Isidro Parodi, a prisoner who solves crimes from jail.

What might we say as an apologia for the detective genre? One thing is quite obvious and certain: our literature tends toward the chaotic. It tends toward free verse because free verse appears easier than regular verse, though the truth is that free verse is very difficult. It tends to eliminate character, plot; everything is very vague. In this chaotic era of ours, one thing has humbly maintained the classic virtues: the detective story. For a detective story cannot be understood without a beginning, middle, and end. Some have been written by inferior writers, while a few were written by excellent writers: Dickens, Stevenson and, above all, Wilkie Collins. I would say in defense of the detective novel that it needs no defense; though now read with a certain disdain, it is safeguarding order in an era of disorder. That is a feat for which we should be grateful.

[1978]   [EA]

PROLOGUES TO
THE LIBRARY OF BABEL

The Library of Babel

1. Jack London, *The Concentric Deaths.*
2. Jorge Luis Borges, *August 25, 1983.*
3. Gustav Meyrink, *Cardinal Napellus.*
4. Léon Bloy, *Discourteous Tales.*
5. Giovanni Papini, *The Escaping Mirror.*
6. Oscar Wilde, *The Crime of Lord Arthur Savile.*
7. Villiers de l'Isle-Adam, *The Guest at the Last Banquets.*
8. Pedro de Alarcón, *The Friend of Death.*
9. Herman Melville, *Bartleby the Scrivener.*
10. William Beckford, *Vathek.*
11. H. G. Wells, *The Door in the Wall.*
12. P'u Sung-Ling, *The Tiger Guest.*
13. Arthur Machen, *The Shining Pyramid.*
14. Robert Louis Stevenson, *The Island of the Voices.*
15. G. K. Chesterton, *The Eye of Apollo.*
16. Jacques Cazotte, *The Devil in Love.*
17. Franz Kafka, *The Vulture.*
18. Edgar Allan Poe, *The Purloined Letter.*
19. Leopoldo Lugones, *The Statue of Salt.*
20. Rudyard Kipling, *The House of Desires.*
21. *The Thousand and One Nights* according to Galland.
22. *The Thousand and One Nights* according to Burton.
23. Henry James, *The Friends of Friends.*
24. Voltaire, *Micromegas.*
25. Charles H. Hinton, *Scientific Romances.*
26. Nathaniel Hawthorne, *The Great Stone Face.*

Franz Kafka, *The Vulture*

It is well known that Virgil, dying, asked his friends to reduce to ashes the unfinished manuscript of the *Aeneid,* to which he had dedicated eleven years of noble and delicate labor; Shakespeare never considered gathering his plays into a book; Kafka entrusted Max Brod to destroy the novels and stories that would ensure his fame. The affinity of these illustrious episodes is, if I am not mistaken, illusory. Virgil knew he could depend on the pious disobedience of his friends, as Kafka did with Max Brod. Shakespeare's case is entirely different. De Quincey speculates that, for Shakespeare, public corresponded to performance, not publication; the staging was what was important to him. In any event, the man who truly desires the disappearance of his books does not assign this task to others. Kafka and Virgil did not seek the destruction of their work; they only wanted to free themselves from the responsibility that a book imposes. Virgil, I think, acted for aesthetic reasons: he wanted to revise certain cadences or epithets. The case of Kafka is more complex. One could define his work as a parable or a series of parables whose theme is the moral relation of the individual with God and with His incomprehensible universe. Despite this contemporary ambiance, Kafka is closer to the Book of Job than to what has been called "modern literature." His work is based on a religious, and particularly Jewish, consciousness; its imitation in other contexts becomes meaningless. Kafka saw his work as an act of faith, and he did not want to be discouraging to mankind. For that reason, he asked his friend to destroy the work. But we may suspect other motives. Kafka could only dream nightmares, which he knew that reality endlessly supplies. At the same time, he realized the possibly pathetic results of procrastination, realized them in almost all his books. Both things, sadness and procrastination, no doubt exhausted him. He would have preferred to write a few happy pages, but his honor would not let him fabricate them.

I will never forget my first reading of Kafka in a certain professionally modern publication in 1917. Its editors—who didn't always lack talent—were dedicated to the abolition of punctuation, the abolition of capital letters, the abolition of rhyme, the alarming simulation of metaphor, the abuse of compound words, and other tasks appropriate to youth at the time and perhaps to youth in any time. Amidst this clatter of type, an apologue signed by one Franz Kafka seemed to my young reader's docility inexplicably insipid. After all these years, I dare to confess my unpardonable literary insensibility: I saw a revelation and didn't notice it.

Everyone knows that Kafka always felt mysteriously guilty toward his father, in the manner of Israel with its God; his Judaism, which separated him from the rest of mankind, affected him in a complex way. The consciousness of approaching death and the feverish exaltation of tuberculosis must have sharpened those faculties. These observations are besides the point; in reality, as Whistler said, "Art happens."

Two ideas—or more exactly, two obsessions—rule Kafka's work: subordination and the infinite. In almost all his fictions there are hierarchies, and those hierarchies are infinite. Karl Rossmann, the hero of his first novel, is a poor German boy making his way through an impenetrable continent; in the end he is admitted into the Great Nature Theater of Oklahoma; that infinite theater is no less populous than the world and prefigures Paradise. (A very personal characteristic: not even in that image of heaven do men become happy, and there are various brief delays.) The hero of his second novel, Josef K., progressively overwhelmed by a meaningless trial, never ascertains the crime for which he has been charged, nor does he ever face the invisible tribunal that is judging him and, without a trial, sentences him to the guillotine. K., hero of the third and last novel, is a surveyor called to a castle that he can never enter, and he dies without being recognized by its governing authorities. The motif of infinite procrastination also rules his stories. One of them deals with an imperial messenger who can never arrive, due to various people who slow the trajectory of his message; another, with a man who dies without having been able to visit the next village; another, with two neighbors who are never able to meet. In the most memorable of them all—"The Great Wall of China" (1919)—the infinite is manifold: to halt the progress of infinitely distant armies, an emperor who is infinitely remote in time and space orders that infinite generations infinitely erect an infinite wall around his infinite empire.

The most unquestionable virtue of Kafka is the invention of intolerable situations. A few lines are enough to indelibly demonstrate. For example:

"The animal seizes the whip from the hands of its master and beats him in order to become the master and doesn't realize that this is nothing but an illusion produced by a new knot in the whip." Or: "Leopards invade the temples and drink the wine from the chalices; this happens suddenly; in the end it was foreseen that this would happen and it is incorporated into the liturgy." The elaboration, in Kafka, is less admirable than the invocation. There is only a single man in his work: the *homo domesticus,* so German and so Jewish, desirous of a place, no matter how humble, in some Order—in the universe, in a ministry, in an insane asylum, in jail. The plot and the atmosphere are what is essential, not the evolution of the fable or the psychological depth. Thus the superiority of his stories to his novels; thus the right to maintain that this present compilation of stories fully allows us to take the measure of such an extraordinary writer.

[1979]   [EW]

Jack London, *The Concentric Deaths*

Jack London was born in 1876 in San Francisco, California. His true name was John Griffith; that Welsh surname will suffice to refute H. L. Mencken's claim that he was Jewish, on the grounds that all surnames that are the names of cities betray a Hebrew origin. It has been said that he was the illegitimate son of an itinerant astrologer, a trace prophetic of his vagabond fate. His school was the lower depths of San Francisco, the so-called "Barbary Coast," where he gained a well-earned reputation for violence. Then he became a gold prospector in Alaska, as Stevenson had been in California. As a young man he was a soldier and then a pearl fisherman, events he would recall when he plotted the vicissitudes of "The House of Mapuhi." He crossed the Pacific on a boat that took him to Japan, where he was a seal hunter, an illegal occupation; one of Kipling's ballads reveals that the most fearless hunters, rivals of the English and of the Russians, were the North Americans. On his return, he studied for a semester at the university in his native city, and there he converted to socialism, which at the time meant the brotherhood of all men and the abolition of personal wealth. He became well known as a journalist, and was sent to cover the Russo-Japanese War. Dressed as a beggar, he learned the misery and hardness of the most sordid slums of London. From this voluntary adventure came the book *The People of the Pit.* His books, which are of various kinds, were translated into every

language, and earned him a huge fortune that compensated for the depriva-
tions of his childhood. He outfitted a boat called "The Snark," a splendid
yacht that cost him $1,930,000.

Among his many works, we cannot forget *Before Adam*, a novel about a
man who recovers in fragmentary dreams the lost vicissitudes of one of his
prehistoric lives. Of an autobiographical character, and doubtless magnificent, are *Martin Eden* and *Burning Daylight*, set in Alaska. The protagonist
of his most famous novel, *The Call of the Wild*, is a dog, Buck, who in the
Arctic wastes has become a wolf.

For this volume we have chosen five stories that are further proofs of
his effectiveness and variety. Only toward the end of "The House of Mapuhi" does the reader realize who the true protagonist is; "The Law of Life"
presents us with an atrocious destiny, accepted by all with naturalness and
almost with innocence; "Lost Face" is the salvation of a man under torture
by a terrible artifice; "The Minions of Midas" details the pitiless methods of
a group of anarchists; "The Shadow and the Flash" renews and enriches an
old motif in literature: the possibility of being invisible.

In Jack London two opposing ideologies join together and become
brothers: the Darwinian doctrine of the survival of the fittest in the struggle
for life and the infinite love of mankind.

Over the multifaceted work of Jack London—like that of Hemingway,
who in a certain sense, continues and raises it to another level—two tall
shadows are cast: Kipling and Nietzsche. Yet there was a fundamental difference. Kipling saw war as an obligation, but he never sang of victory, only of
the peace that victory brings, and of the hardships of battle. Nietzsche, who
had witnessed the proclamation of the German Empire in the Palace of Versailles, wrote that all empires are a stupidity and that Bismarck was merely
adding another number to that stupid series. Kipling and Nietzsche, sedentary men, longed for the action and dangers that their fates denied them;
London and Hemingway, men of adventure, were attached to it. They un-
forgivably celebrated the gratuitous cult of violence and even of brutality.
Kipling and Nietzsche, in their times, were accused of belonging to that
cult; we may recall the diatribes of Belloc and the fact that Bernard Shaw
had to defend Nietzsche from the charge of "having composed a Gospel for
hoodlums." Both London and Hemingway repented of their infatuation
with mere violence; it is no coincidence that both, sick of fame and danger
and money, took refuge in suicide.

London's effectiveness was that of an able journalist adept at his job;
Hemingway's that of a man of letters who professed certain theories and

discussed them at length; but both were quite alike, although we will never know what opinion the author of *The Old Man and the Sea* pronounced on *The Sea-Wolf* in the cenacles of France. It may well be that the vacillations of taste have obscured the affinities between the two and emphasized their differences.

Jack London died at forty, having drained the life of the body and of the spirit. He was never satisfied with anything, and he sought in death the sullen splendor of nothingness.

[1979] *[EW]*

Villiers de l'Isle-Adam, *The Guest at the Last Banquets*

Jean Marie Matthias Philippe Augustus, Count of Villiers de l'Isle-Adam, was born in Brittany on the 7th of November in 1838, and died in Paris, in the hospital of the Frères de Saint Jean de Dieu, on the 19th of August in 1889. The unrestrained and generous imagination of the Celts was one of the gifts that chance or fate bestowed upon him, as well as an illustrious lineage—he was descended from the first Grand Master of the Knights of Malta—and a sonorous disdain for mediocrity, science, progress, his times, money, and serious people. His *Future Eve* (1886) is one of the first examples of science fiction. His play *Axel* recreates the theme of the philosopher's stone. *Rebellion*, staged in Paris in 1870, anticipates Ibsen's *The Doll House*.

Romantic in the rhetorical manner of the French, he declared that the human race is divided into romantics and imbeciles. The customs of his time demanded that a writer abound not only in memorable phrases but also in impertinent epigrams. Anatole France relates that one morning he went to Villiers' house to get information about his ancestors. Villiers replied: "At ten in the morning, in broad daylight, you expect me to speak of the Grand Master and the celebrated Mariscal?" Seated at the table of Henri V, aspirant to the throne of France, and hearing him criticize someone who had sacrificed everything for him, he said: "Lord, I drink to the health of Your Majesty. Your qualifications are decidedly unquestionable. You have the ingratitude of a king." He was a great friend of Wagner's and was once asked if the composer's conversation was agreeable. "Do you think conversation with Mt. Etna would be agreeable?" he replied.

There is something histrionic in his life and in his work; although it is true that the circumstances of being both an aristocrat and extremely poor favor such postures. It is also worth recalling that Villiers, because of the image that he was always trying to project in Paris, was essentially defending himself. A meager standing would have mortified him as much as his meager straits, which at times verged on miserable poverty.

Where can a poet go, through the excess that is his imagination, to escape his own time and place? It is obvious that the Verona of Romeo and Juliet is not exactly situated in Italy, that the magical sea of the "Rime of the Ancient Mariner" is the magnificent dream of an English poet at the end of the eighteenth century, and not the sea of Conrad or the sea of Homer. Will I someday perhaps write a poem that does not take place in Buenos Aires? The same occurred in Villiers with Spain and the Orient: they are as French as Flaubert's laborious *Salammbô*.

The best tale in our series and one of the masterpieces of the short story is "Hope." The action takes place in a very personal Spain, and the time is vague. Villiers knew little about Spain, nor did he know much about Edgar Allan Poe. Nevertheless, both "Hope" and "The Pit and the Pendulum" are similarly unforgettable, because both understand the cruelty that can come to the human soul. In Poe, the horror is of a physical order; Villiers, more subtly, reveals a hell of a moral order. After the incredible Spain of "Hope," we have the incredible China of "The Adventure of Tse-i-la." The story bears the epigraph "Guess or I shall devour you," which Villiers ingenuously attributes to the Sphinx. It deals with an artifice whose object is to trick the reader. The whole story is based on the pride of the two characters and the atrocious cruelty of one of them; the end reveals an unsuspected generosity that includes a humiliation. "The Secret of the Church" conceals an affirmation of all Protestant sects; its strength is in the fact that the believer implicitly confesses that his soul is lost. The theme of "Queen Ysabeau" is, again, the cruelty of the powerful, enriched in this case by the passion of jealousy. The unexpected ending is no less atrocious. "The Guest at the Last Banquets" deliberately begins in a frivolous mode; there is nothing more banal than some carefree and happy revelers deciding how to amuse themselves until dawn. The appearance of a new participant darkens the story and brings it to a horror in which, incredibly, justice and madness converge. In the same way that the parodic *Don Quixote* is a book about knights, "Somber Tale, More Somber Narrator" is both a cruel story and a parody of a cruel story. Of all of his works, "Vera" is, without a doubt, the most fantastic and the closest to the oneiric world of Poe. To console his sadness, the protagonist creates a hallucinatory world; this magic is rewarded with a tiny and forgettable object which contains one last promise.

Villiers in Paris wanted to play with the concept of cruelty in the same way that Baudelaire played with evil and sin. Now, unfortunately, we know too much to play with any of them. *Cruel Stories* is now a naive title; it was not when Villiers de l'Isle-Adam, between grandiloquence and emotion, proposed it to the cenacles of Paris. This almost indigent great lord, who saw himself as the luxuriously outfitted protagonist of imaginary duels and imaginary fictions, has impressed his image on the history of French litera-ture. Less than Vera or the Aragonese Jew or Tse-i-la, we think and will think of Villiers de l'Isle-Adam.

[1984]   [EW]

P'u Sung-ling, *The Tiger Guest*

The *Analects* of the very rational Confucius advise us that we must respect supernatural beings, but immediately adds that we must keep them at a dis-tance. The myths of Taoism and Buddhism have not mitigated that ancient advice; there is no country more superstitious than China. The vast realist novels it has produced—*The Dream of the Red Chamber* is the one to which I most often return—abounds in wonders precisely because it is realist, and marvels are not considered impossible or even unlikely.

Most of the stories chosen for this book come from the *Liao-chai* of P'u Sung-ling, whose pen name was the Last Immortal or Willow Springs. They date from the seventeenth century. We have chosen the English version, *Strange Stories from a Chinese Studio*, by Herbert Allen Giles, published in 1880. Of P'u Sung-ling, very little is known, except that he failed his exami-nation for a doctorate in letters in 1651. Thanks to that lucky disaster, he dedicated himself entirely to literature, and we have the book that would make him famous. In China, the *Liao-chai* occupies the place held by *The Thousand and One Nights* in the West.

Unlike Poe or Hoffmann, P'u Sung-ling does not marvel at the marvels he presents. He is closer to Swift, not only in the fantasy of his fables but in the laconic and impersonal, intentionally satirical tone with which he tells them. P'u Sung-ling's hells remind us of those of Quevedo; they are admin-istrative and opaque. His tribunals, lictors, judges, and scribes are no less venal and bureaucratic than the terrestrial prototypes in any place in any century. The reader should not forget that the Chinese, given their supersti-tious nature, tend to read these stories as if they were real events, for in their

imagination the higher order is a mirror of the lower order, as the Kabbalists said.

At first, the text may seem naive; then we realize the obvious humor
and satire and the powerful imagination which, from ordinary elements—a
student preparing for an exam, a picnic on a hill, a foolish man getting
drunk—manages to invisibly weave a world as unstable as water and as
changing and marvelous as the clouds. A kingdom of dreams, and even
more, the corridors and labyrinths of nightmares. The dead return to life, a
stranger who visits turns into a tiger, the apparently beautiful girl is merely
a piece of skin on a green-faced demon. A ladder climbs into the sky, another down a well that is inhabited by infernal executioners, magistrates,
and masters.

To the stories of P'u Sung-ling we have added two that are as unexpected as they are astonishing from the almost infinite novel, *The Dream of
the Red Chamber*. Of the author or authors, little is known with any certainty, for in China fiction and drama are subaltern genres. *The Dream of
the Chamber* or *Hung Lou Meng* is the most illustrious and perhaps the
most populated Chinese novel. It has 421 characters—189 women and 232
men—numbers that surpass the Russian novel or the Icelandic saga, and
which, at first sight, could overwhelm a reader. A complete translation,
which is yet to be done, would require three thousand pages and a million
words. Dating from the eighteenth century, its most probable author was
Tsao Hsueh-chin. "The Dream of Pao-yu" prefigures that chapter in Lewis
Carroll where Alice dreams of the Red King who is dreaming her, except
that Carroll's dream is a metaphysical fantasy, and Pao-yu's is charged with
sadness, despair, and a deep irreality. "The Wind-Moon Mirror," whose title
is an erotic metaphor, is perhaps the one moment in literature that, with
melancholy and a certain dignity, deals with solitary pleasure.

There is nothing more characteristic of a country than its imaginations.
In its few pages, this book offers a glimpse of one of the oldest cultures on
the planet and, at the same time, one of the most unusual approaches to
fantastic literature.

[1985]   *[EW]*

Charles Howard Hinton, *Scientific Romances*

If I am not mistaken, Edith Sitwell is the author of a book entitled *The English Eccentrics*. No one has more right to appear in its hypothetical pages

than Charles Howard Hinton. Others seek and achieve notoriety; Hinton has achieved almost total obscurity. He is no less mysterious than his work. The biographical dictionaries ignore him; we have only been able to find a few passing references in Ouspensky's *Tertium Organum* (1920) and Henry Parker Manning's *Four Dimensions* (1928). Wells does not mention him, but the first chapter of his admirable *The Time Machine* (1895) unquestionably suggests that he not only knew his work, but studied it to his delight and subsequently ours.

Hinton's *A New Era of Thought* (1888) includes a note from the editors which says: "The manuscript that is the basis for this book was sent to us by its author, shortly before his departure from England for an unknown and remote destination. He gave us complete liberty to amplify or modify the text, but we have used that privilege sparingly." This suggests a probable suicide or, more likely, that our fugitive friend had escaped to the fourth dimension which he had glimpsed, as he himself told us, thanks to a steadfast discipline. Hinton believed that this discipline did not require any supernatural faculties. He gave an address in London where one could acquire, for a laughable sum, certain toys consisting of small wooden polyhedrons. With these pieces, one could construct pyramids, cylinders, prisms, cubes, etc., by adhering to rigid and predetermined correspondences of edges, planes, and colors that bore strange names. Having memorized each heterogenous structure, one then had to exercise mentally by imagining the movements of its various pieces. For example, moving the red-black cube upward and to the left set off a complex series of movements in the whole. Through such exercises, the devotee would slowly intuit the fourth dimension.

We tend to forget that the elements of geometry that are learned in elementary school pertain to abstract concepts and correspond to nothing in so-called reality. These concepts are the point, which occupies no space; the line, which, no matter how long, consists of an infinite number of lines, one on top of the other; and volume, made from an infinite number of planes like an infinite deck of cards. To these concepts, Hinton—anticipated by the so-called Cambridge Platonists in the seventeenth century, and especially Henry More—added another: that of the hypervolume formed by an infinite number of volumes, and limited by volumes, not by planes. He believed in the objective reality of hypercubes, hyperprisms, hyperpyramids, hypercones, truncated hypercones, hyperspheres, etc. He did not consider that, of all the geometric concepts, the only real one is volume, as there is nothing in the universe that lacks size. In a magnifying glass and even in a microscope, the tiniest particle has three dimensions. Hinton believed that there are universes of two, four, five, six dimensions, and so infinitely until one has exhausted all of the natural numbers. Algebra calls 3 multiplied by 3 "three squared" and 3 x 3 x 3 "three cubed"; this progression brings us to an infinite number of exponents and, according to the hypothesis of multidimensional geometry, to an infinite number of dimensions. As is well known, that geometry exists; what we don't know is whether there are bodies in reality that correspond to it.

To illustrate his curious thesis—which was refuted by, among others, Gustav Spiller (*The Mind of Man*, London, 1902)—Hinton published various books, including one of fantastic tales, of which we offer three in this volume.

In order to help our imagination accept a world of four dimensions, Hinton, in the first story here, proposes a no less fictitious, but possibly more accessible idea: a world of two. He does so with an integrity that is so tireless in its details that to follow it can be arduous, despite the scrupulous diagrams that complement the exposition. Hinton is not a storyteller; he is a solitary thinker who instinctively took shelter in a speculative world that will not betray him, because he is its source and inventor. He would like, naturally, to share it with us; he had already attempted it, in an abstract form, in *A New Era of Thought* and in *The Fourth Dimension*; in *Scientific Romances* (1888), he sought a narrative form. In the book, his secret geometry unites with a grave moral sense. This illuminates "The Persian King," the third story here, which at first seems to be a game in the manner of *The Thousand and One Nights* but by the end is a parable of the universe, not without an inevitable incursion into mathematics.

Hinton has an assured place in the history of literature. His *Scientific Romances* are earlier than the gloomy imaginations of Wells. The very title of the series unequivocally prefigures the seemingly inexhaustible wave of the works of "science fiction" that have invaded our century.

Why not suppose Hinton's book to be perhaps an artifice to evade an unfortunate fate? Why not suppose the same of all creators?

[1986]   [EW]

PROLOGUES TO
A PERSONAL LIBRARY

A Personal Library

1. Julio Cortázar, *Stories.*
2 & 3. The Apocryphal Gospels.
4. Franz Kafka, *Amerika; Short Stories.*
5. G. K. Chesterton, *The Blue Cross and Other Stories.*
6 & 7. Wilkie Collins, *The Moonstone.*
8. Maurice Maeterlink, *The Intelligence of Flowers.*
9. Dino Buzzati, *The Desert of the Tartars.*
10. Henrik Ibsen, *Peer Gynt; Hedda Gabler.*
11. J. M. Eça de Queiroz, *The Mandarin.*
12. Leopoldo Lugones, *The Jesuit Empire.*
13. André Gide, *The Counterfeiters.*
14. H. G. Wells, *The Time Machine; The Invisible Man.*
15. Robert Graves, *The Greek Myths.*
16 & 17. Fyodor Dostoevsky, *Demons.*
18. E. Kasner & J. Newman, *Mathematics and the Imagination.*
19. Eugene O'Neill, *The Great God Brown; Strange Interlude;*
    Mourning Becomes Electra.
20. Ariwara no Narihara, *Tales of Ise.*
21. Herman Melville, *Benito Cereno; Billy Budd; Bartleby the Scrivener.*
22. Giovanni Papini, *The Tragic Everyday; The Blind Pilot; Words and Blood.*
23. Arthur Machen, *The Three Imposters.*
24. Fray Luis de León, tr., *The Song of Songs.*
25. Fray Luis de León, *An Explanation of the Book of Job.*
26. Joseph Conrad, *The End of the Tether; Heart of Darkness.*
27. Edward Gibbon, *Decline and Fall of the Roman Empire.*
28. Oscar Wilde, *Essays and Dialogues.*

29. Henri Michaux, *A Barbarian in Asia.*

30. Hermann Hesse, *The Bead Game.*

31. Arnold Bennett, *Buried Alive.*

32. Claudius Elianus, *On the Nature of Animals.*

33. Thorstein Veblen, *The Theory of the Leisure Class.*

34. Gustave Flaubert, *The Temptation of St. Anthony.*

35. Marco Polo, *Travels.*

36. Marcel Schwob, *Imaginary Lives.*

37. George Bernard Shaw, *Caesar and Cleopatra; Major Barbara; Candide.*

38. Francisco de Quevedo, *Marcus Brutus; The Hour of All.*

39. Eden Phillpots, *The Red Redmaynes.*

40. Søren Kierkegaard, *Fear and Trembling.*

41. Gustav Meyrink, *The Golem.*

42. Henry James, *The Lesson of the Master; The Figure in the Carpet; The Private Life.*

43 & 44. Herodotus, *The Nine Books of History.*

45. Juan Rulfo, *Pedro Páramo.*

46. Rudyard Kipling, *Tales.*

47. William Beckford, *Vathek.*

48. Daniel Defoe, *Moll Flanders.*

49. Jean Cocteau, *The Professional Secret and Other Texts.*

50. Thomas De Quincey, *The Last Days of Emmanuel Kant and Other Stories.*

51. Ramón Gómez de la Serna, *Prologue to the Work of Silverio Lanza.*

52. *The Thousand and One Nights.*

53. Robert Louis Stevenson, *New Arabian Nights; Markheim.*

54. Léon Bloy, *Salvation for the Jews; The Blood of the Poor; In the Darkness.*

55. *The Bhagavad-Gita; The Epic of Gilgamesh.*

56. Juan José Arreola, *Fantastic Stories.*

57. David Garnett, *Lady into Fox; A Man in the Zoo; The Sailor's Return.*

58. Jonathan Swift, *Gulliver's Travels.*

59. Paul Groussac, *Literary Criticism.*

60. Manuel Mujica Láinez, *The Idols.*

61. Juan Ruíz, *The Book of Good Love.*

62. William Blake, *Complete Poetry.*

63. Hugh Walpole, *Above the Dark Circus.*

64. Ezequiel Martínez Estrada, *Poetical Works.*

65. Edgar Allan Poe, *Tales.*

66. Virgil, *The Aeneid.*

67. Voltaire, *Stories.*

68. J. W. Dunne, *An Experiment with Time.*

69. Atilio Momigliano, *An Essay on Orlando Furioso.*

70 & 71. William James, *The Varieties of Religious Experience; The Study of Human Nature.*

72. Snorri Sturluson, *Egil's Saga.*

73. *The Book of the Dead.*

74 & 75. J. Alexander Gunn, *The Problem of Time.*

Prologue to the Collection

Over time, one's memory forms a disparate library, made of books or pages whose reading was a pleasure and which one would like to share. The texts of that personal library are not necessarily famous. The reason is clear. The professors, who are the ones who dispense fame, are interested less in beauty than in literature's dates and changes, and in the prolix analysis of books that have been written for that analysis, not for the joy of the reader.

This series is intended to bring such pleasure. I will not select titles according to my literary habits, or a certain tradition, or a certain school or nation or era. I once said, "Others brag of the books they've managed to write; I brag of the books I've managed to read." I don't know if I am a good writer, but I think I am an excellent reader, or in any case, a sensitive and grateful one. I would like this library to be as diverse as the unsatisfied curiosity that has led me, and continues to lead me, in my exploration of so many languages and literatures. I know that the novel is no less artificial than the allegory or the opera, but I will include novels because they too have entered into my life. This series of heterogenous books is, I repeat, a library of preferences.

María Kodama and I have wandered the globe of land and sea. We have visited Texas and Japan, Geneva, Thebes, and now, to gather the texts that are essential to us, we have traveled through the corridors and palaces of memory, as St. Augustine wrote.

A book is a thing among things, a volume lost among the volumes that populate the indifferent universe, until it meets its reader, the person destined for its symbols. What then occurs is that singular emotion called beauty, that lovely mystery which neither psychology nor criticism can describe. "The rose has no why," said Angelus Silesius; centuries later, Whistler declared, "Art happens."

I hope that you will be the reader these books await.

[1985]   [EW]

Julio Cortázar, *Stories*

In the 1940s I was an editor of a literary magazine that was more or less a secret. One afternoon, an afternoon like others, a very tall boy whose features I cannot recall brought me the manuscript of a short story. I told him to come back in ten days and I would let him know what I thought. He came the next week. I told him that I liked his story very much and that it had already been sent to the printer. Soon after, Julio Cortázar read the printed letters of "House Taken Over," accompanied by two pencil drawings by Norah Borges. The years went by, and one night in Paris he mentioned that this was his first publication. I am honored to have been instrumental.

The subject of that story is the gradual occupation of a house by an invisible presence. In later pieces, Cortázar took up this theme in a manner that was more indirect and even more effective.

When Dante Gabriel Rossetti read the novel *Wuthering Heights*, he wrote to a friend: "The action takes place in Hell, but the places, I don't know why, have English names." Something similar occurs in Cortázar. The characters of the fable are deliberately trivial. They are ruled by a routine of casual love affairs and casual discords. They move among trivial things: brands of cigarettes, shop windows, display cases, whiskey, drugstores, airports, and railway platforms. They are immersed in the radio and newspapers. The topography corresponds to Buenos Aires or Paris, and at first we may think that this is mere reportage. Little by little we realize that it is not. The narrator has very subtly drawn us into his terrible world, where happiness is impossible. It is a porous world in which beings intermingle; a man's consciousness may enter that of an animal, or an animal's into a man. He also plays with the matter of which we are made, time. In some of these stories two different temporal series flow and mingle.

The style does not seem careful, but each word has been chosen. No one can retell the plot of a Cortázar story; each one consists of determined words in a determined order. If we try to summarize them, we realize that something precious has been lost.

[1985] *[EW]*

The Apocryphal Gospels

To read this book is to return in an almost magical way to the first centuries of our era, when religion was a passion. The dogmas of the Church and the arguments of the theologians came much later; what mattered at the beginning was the new idea that the Son of God had been, for thirty-three years, a man, a tortured and sacrificed man whose death would redeem all the generations of Adam. Among the books that announced this truth were the Apocryphal Gospels. The word "apocryphal" now means "false" or "falsified"; its original meaning was "hidden." The apocryphal texts were those forbidden to the masses, those which only a few were allowed to read.

Quite beyond our lack of faith, Christ is the most vivid figure in human memory. It was his lot to preach his doctrine, which spread throughout the planet, in an obscure province. His twelve disciples were illiterate and poor. Except for some words that he drew in the sand and quickly erased, he wrote nothing. (Pythagoras and the Buddha were also oral teachers.) He used no logical arguments; the natural form of his thinking was the metaphor. To condemn the pompous vanity of funerals, he said that the dead will bury the dead. To condemn the hypocrisy of the Pharisees, he said that they were whited sepulchres. Still young, he died obscurely on the cross that was then a gallows and is now a symbol. Without suspecting his vast future, Tacitus mentioned him in passing, calling him Chrestus. No one else has so governed, and continued to govern, the course of history.

This book does not contradict the canonical Gospels. It tells the same biography with strange variations. It reveals unexpected miracles. It says that, at the age of five, Jesus modeled some sparrows out of clay that, to the amazement of the children playing with him, took flight and were lost in the air singing. It also attributes cruel miracles to him, those of an all-powerful boy who has not yet achieved the power of reason. For the Old Testament, Hell (*Sheol*) is the grave; for the tercets of the *Divine Comedy*, a system of subterranean jail cells and a precise typography; in this book it is a somber character who converses with Satan, Prince of Death, and who glorifies the Lord.

Along with the canonical books of the New Testament, these Apocryphal Gospels, forgotten for so many centuries and now rediscovered, were the most ancient instruments of the doctrine of Jesus.

[1985]   *[EW]*

H. G. Wells, *The Time Machine; The Invisible Man*

The opposite of Beckford or of Poe, the narratives gathered in this book are nightmares that deliberately refuse to employ a fantastic style. They were dreamed in the last years of the nineteenth century and the first of the twentieth. Wells had observed that that era, which is ours, did not believe in magic and talismans, in rhetorical pomp and exaggeration. Then, as now, the imagination accepted the fabulous if it had a scientific, not a supernatural, origin. In each of these texts there is a single wonder; the circumstances that frame it are minuscule, grey, and ordinary. Consider *The Invisible Man* (1897). For Gyges to become invisible, the Greeks had to resort to a bronze ring found in a bronze horse; Wells, for greater verisimilitude, gives us an albino man who bathes in a strange liquid and who must go barefoot and naked, for his clothes and shoes are not equally invisible. In Wells, the poignant is as important as the fabulous. His invisible man is a symbol—one that will last a long time—of our solitude. Wells said that the inventions of Jules Verne were merely prophetic and that his own were impossible to realize. Both believed that man would never reach the moon; our century, duly astonished, has witnessed that feat.

The fact that Wells was a genius is no less remarkable than the fact that he always wrote with a modesty that was sometimes ironic.

He was born not far from London in 1866. Of humble origins, he knew misfortune and poverty. He was a republican and a socialist. In the last decades of his life, he moved from the writing of dreams to the laborious production of huge books that could help mankind become citizens of the world. In 1922 he published a universal history. The best biography of Wells is the one he gave us in two volumes, *Experiment in Autobiography* (1932). He died in 1946. Wells' fictions were the first books that I read; perhaps they will be the last.

[1985]   *[EW]*

Fyodor Dostoevsky, *Demons*

Like the discovery of love, like the discovery of the sea, the discovery of Dostoevsky marks an important date in one's life. This usually occurs in adolescence; maturity seeks out more serene writers. In 1915, in Geneva, I avidly read *Crime and Punishment* in the very readable English version by Constance Garnett. That novel, whose heroes are a murderer and a prostitute, seemed to me no less terrible than the war that surrounded us. I looked for a biography of the author. The son of a military doctor who was murdered, Dostoevsky (1821–1881) knew poverty, sickness, prison, exile; the assiduous exercise of writing, traveling, and gambling; and, at the end of his days, fame. He professed the cult of Balzac. Involved in an indeterminate conspiracy, he was sentenced to death. Practically at the foot of the gallows where his comrades had been executed, Dostoevsky's sentence was commuted, but he spent four years in forced labor in Siberia, which he would never forget.

He studied and expounded the utopias of Fourier, Owen, and Saint-Simon. He was a socialist and a pan-Slavicist. I imagined at the time that Dostoevsky was a kind of great unfathomable God, capable of understanding and justifying all beings. I was astonished that he had occasionally descended to mere politics, that he discriminated and condemned.

To read a book by Dostoevsky is to penetrate a great city unknown to us, or the shadow of a battle. *Crime and Punishment* revealed to me, among other things, a world different from my own. When I read *Demons*, something very strange occurred. I felt that I had returned home. The steppes were a magnification of the pampas. Varvara Petrovna and Stepan Trofimovich Verkhovensky were, despite their unwieldy names, old irresponsible Argentines. The book began with joy, as if the narrator did not know its tragic end.

In the preface to an anthology of Russian literature, Vladimir Nabokov stated that he had not found a single page of Dostoevsky worthy of inclusion. This ought to mean that Dostoevsky should not be judged by each page but rather by the total of all the pages that comprise the book.

[1985]   *[EW]*

Thorstein Veblen, *The Theory of the Leisure Class*

When, many years ago, I happened to read this book, I thought it was a satire. I later learned it was the first work of an illustrious sociologist. In any event, one need only look closely at a society to realize that it is not a utopia, and that its description runs the risk of bordering on satire. In this book from 1899, Veblen discovers and defines the leisure class, whose strange obligation is the ostentatious spending of money. Thus they live in a certain neighborhood because that neighborhood is famous for being the most expensive. Liebermann or Picasso charge huge sums, not because they are greedy, but rather so as not to disappoint the buyers, whose intention is to demonstrate that they are able to pay for a canvas that bears the painter's signature. According to Veblen, the success of golf is due to the circumstance that it requires a great deal of land. He mistakenly claims that the study of Latin and Greek has its origin in the fact that both languages are useless. If an executive does not have time for ostentatious spending, his wife or children will do it for him, with the periodic changes in fashion that requires its uniforms.

Veblen created and wrote this book in the United States. Here the phenomenon of the leisure class is even more grave. Except for the penniless, every Argentine pretends to belong to that class. As a boy, I knew families who, during the hot months, hid in their houses so that people would think they were summering on some ranch or in the city of Montevideo. A lady confessed to me her intention of adorning her "hall" with a signed painting, certainly not by virtue of its calligraphy.

The son of Norwegian immigrants, Thorstein Veblen was born in Wisconsin in 1857 and died in California in 1929. (America owes much to the Scandinavians; recall Whitman's best successor, Carl Sandburg.) His work is vast. He austerely professed the socialist doctrine. In his last books he prophesied a fateful end of history.

[1985]   [EW]

Søren Kierkegaard, *Fear and Trembling*

Søren Kierkegaard, whose prophetic surname means cemetery (Churchyard) was born in 1813 in Copenhagen and died in that same city in 1855. He is considered to be the founder, or more exactly the father, of existentialism.

Less desirous of publicity than his sons, he lived a quiet and obscure life. Like that other celebrated Dane, Prince Hamlet, he was wracked with doubt and with anguish, a word of Latin origin which he endowed with a new shiver of fear. He was less a philosopher than a theologian, and less a theologian than an eloquent and sensitive man. A Lutheran evangelist, he denied the arguments that prove the existence of God and the incarnation of Jesus, considering them absurd from a rational point of view, and he proposed an act of individual faith for every believer. He did not accept the authority of the Church, and he wrote that each person has the right to choose. He rejected the dialectics and the dialect of Hegel. His sedentary biography is far less rich in outward facts than it is in reflections and prayers. Religion was the strongest of his passions. He was unusually preoccupied with Abraham's sacrifice.

A newspaper published a caricature that ridiculed him; Kierkegaard said that having provoked such a drawing was perhaps the true end of his life. He famously credited Pascal with the salvation of his soul. He wrote: "If, after the Final Judgment, there remains only one sinner in Hell and I happen to be that sinner, I will celebrate from the abyss the Justice of God."

Unamuno undertook the study of Danish in order to read Kierkegaard and declared that his arduous apprenticeship was worth the effort.

In a page that the anthologists prefer, Kierkegaard modestly praised his maternal language, which some have judged inappropriate for philosophical debate.

[1985]   [EW]

Virgil, *The Aeneid*

Leibniz has a parable about two libraries: one of a hundred different books of different worth, the other of a hundred books that are all equally perfect. It is significant that the latter consists of a hundred Aeneids. Voltaire wrote that Virgil may be the work of Homer, but he is the greatest of Homer's works. Virgil's preeminence lasted for sixteen hundred years in Europe; the Romantic movement denied and almost erased him. Today he is threatened by our custom of reading books as a function of history, not of aesthetics.

The Aeneid is the highest example of what has been called, without discredit, the artificial epic; that is to say, the deliberate work of a single man, not that which human generations, without knowing it, have created. Virgil set out to write a masterpiece; curiously, he succeeded.

I say "curiously" because masterpieces tend to be the daughters of chance or of negligence.

As though it were a short poem, this epic was polished, line by line, with the felicitous care that Petronius praised—I'll never know why—in Horace. Let us examine, almost at random, a few examples.

Virgil does not tell us that the Achaeans waited for darkness to enter Troy; he speaks of the friendly silence of the moon. He does not write that Troy was destroyed, but rather, "Troy was." He does not write that a life was unfortunate, but rather "The gods understood him in another way." To express what is now called pantheism, he says, "All things are full of Jupiter." He does not condemn the aggressive madness of men; he calls it "the love of iron." He does not tell us that Aeneas and the Sybil wandered alone among the shadows in the dark night; he writes, *"Ibant obscuri sola sub nocte per umbram."* This is not a mere rhetorical figure, a hyperbaton: "alone" and "dark" have not changed places in the phrase; both forms, the usual and the Virgilian, correspond with equal precision to the scene they represent.

The selection of each word and each turn of phrase also makes Virgil the classic of the classics, in some serene way, a Baroque poet. The carefulness of his writing did not impede the fluidity of his narration of Aeneas' deeds and adventures. There are events that are almost magical: Aeneas, exiled from Troy, disembarks in Carthage and sees on the walls of a temple images of the Trojan War, images of Priam, Achilles, Hector, and even himself. There are tragic events: the Queen of Carthage who watches the Greek boats leaving and knows that her lover has abandoned her. There is a predictable abundance of heroism, such as these words spoken by a warrior: "My son, learn from me strength and genuine valor; and from others, luck."

Virgil. Of all the poets of the earth, there is none other who has been listened to with such love. Even beyond Augustus, Rome, and the empire that, across other nations and languages, is still the Empire. Virgil is our friend. When Dante made Virgil his guide and the most continual character in the *Commedia*, he gave an enduring aesthetic form to that which all men feel with gratitude.

[1986]   [EW]

William James, *Varieties of Religious Experience;*
The Study of Human Nature

Like David Hume, like Schopenhauer, William James was a thinker and a writer. He wrote with the clarity that is the product of a good education; he did not fabricate awkward dialects, in the manner of Spinoza, Kant, or the Scholastics.

He was born in New York in 1842. His father, the theologian Henry James, did not want his two sons to be mere provincial Americans. William and Henry were educated in England, France, and Italy. William undertook the study of painting. After his return to the United States, he accompanied the Swiss naturalist Agassiz on an expedition to the source of the Amazon. From medicine he went to physiology, from there to psychology, and from there to metaphysical speculation. In 1876 he founded a psychological laboratory. His health was poor. He once attempted suicide; he repeated, like nearly all men, Hamlet's monologue. An act of faith saved him from that darkness. "My first act of free will," he wrote, "was to believe in free will." He thus freed himself from the overwhelming faith of his parents, Calvinism.

Pragmatism, which he founded with Charles Sanders Peirce, was an extension of that act of faith. The doctrine propounded by that word would make him famous. He urged us to interpret every conception in the light of its consequences in human behavior. The name of one his books, *The Will to Believe* (1897), may be considered a summary of his doctrine.

James stated that experience is the elemental substance of that which we call the universe, and that it is prior to the categories of subject and object, knower and known, spirit and matter. This curious solution to the problem of being is, of course, closer to idealism than materialism, to Berkeley's divinity than to Lucretius' atoms.

James was opposed to war. He proposed that military conscription be replaced by a conscription of manual labor, which would impose discipline and liberate men from their aggressive impulses.

In this book, James accepts the plurality of religions, and he considers it natural that each individual should profess the faith of his own tradition. He declares that all of them can be beneficial, as long as their origins are in conviction, not in authority. He believes that the visible world is part of a wider and more varied spiritual world which can be revealed by the senses. He studies specific cases of conversion, saintliness, and mystical experience. He promotes the efficacy of prayer without a destination.

The year 1910 marks the death of two men of genius, William James and Mark Twain, and the appearance of the comet we now await.

[1986]   [EW]

Notes

A complete annotation of this volume would require a book of equal or greater length. Here, only some of the passing allusions, otherwise not explained in the text and not available in general reference books, are glossed. In the notes to the individual selections, the original Spanish title is given, followed by first periodical publication and date, and reprinting in book form, if any. Unless otherwise noted, all periodicals were published in Argentina.

Sources

Early (Suppressed) Writings:

Inquisiciones [Inquisitions], 1925. Reprinted in 1994.
El tamaño de mi esperanza [The Extent of My Hope], 1926. Reprinted in 1994.
El idioma de los argentinos [The Language of the Argentines], 1928. Reprinted in 1994.

Contemporary Collections:

Evaristo Carriego, 1930. (In English: *Evaristo Carriego*, tr. Norman Thomas di Giovanni, 1984.)
Discusión [Discussion], 1932.
Historia de la eternidad [History of Eternity], 1936.
Otras inquisiciones, 1952. (In English: *Other Inquisitions*, tr. Ruth L. C. Simms, 1964.)

Lectures:

Borges, oral [Borges, Speaking], 1979.
Siete noches, 1980. (In English: *Seven Nights*, tr. Eliot Weinberger, 1984.)

Late and Posthumous Collections:

Antología personal, 1961. (In English: *A Personal Anthology*, ed. Anthony Kerrigan, 1967.) Borges' favorite Borges; also includes poetry and fiction.
Nueva antología personal [A New Personal Anthology], 1968. A second selection of favorites; also includes poetry and fiction.
Prólogos con un prólogo de prologos [Prologues with a Prologue to the Prologues], 1975.

Borges en/y/sobre cine, ed. Edgardo Cozarinsky, 1980. (In English: *Borges in/and/on Film*, tr. Gloria Waldman & Ronald Christ, 1988.) Film criticism.

Páginas de Jorge Luis Borges [Pages from JLB], 1982. Also includes poetry and fiction.

Nueve ensayos dantescos [Nine Dantesque Essays], 1982.

Ficcionario, ed. Emir Rodríguez Monegal, 1985. (In English: *Borges: A Reader*, 1981.) Also includes poetry and fiction.

Textos cautivos [Captive Texts], ed. Emir Rodríguez Monegal & Enrique Sacerio-Garí, 1986. Articles from *El Hogar* [Home].

Biblioteca personal, prólogos [A Personal Library, Prologues], 1988.

Textos recobrados 1919–1929 [Recovered Texts, 1919–1929], 1998. Also includes poetry and fiction.

Complete Works:

Obras completas I: 1923–1949, 1989. (*Evaristo Carriego; Discusión; Historia de la eternidad*; plus poetry and fiction.)

Obras completas II: 1952–1972, 1989. (*Otras inquisiciones*; plus poetry and fiction.)

Obras completas III: 1975–1985, 1989. (*Siete noches; Nueve ensayos dantescos*; plus poetry and fiction.)

Obras completas IV: 1975–1988, 1996. (*Prólogos con un prólogo de prólogos; Borges, oral; Textos cautivos; Biblioteca personal, prólogos.*)

Obras completas en colaboración, 1997. (Collaborative works of fiction and non-fiction.)

The best biography and bibliography to date are, respectively: Emir Rodríguez Monegal, *Jorge Luis Borges: A Literary Biography* (1978), and Nicolás Helft, *Jorge Luis Borges: Bibliografía completa* (1998). A useful dictionary of references is Daniel Balderston's *The Literary Universe of Jorge Luis Borges* (1986).

Some Recurring References

Almafuerte: "Strong Soul," pseudonym of Pedro Bonifacio Palacios (1854–1917), the self-styled Whitman of Argentina. A standard reference book states that Palacios "produced a sequence of misanthropic, megalomaniac poems of titanic defiance"—a description that can only lead to the reader's disappointment—but Borges claimed that Almafuerte taught all Argentines the aesthetic function of language.

Black Ant: "*Hormiga Negra*," the legendary gaucho outlaw Guillermo Hoyo, subject of a popular book by Eduardo Gutiérrez (see below).

Bloy, Léon (1846–1917): French writer whose work, according to Borges, is "full of lamentation and invective." Borges was particularly attracted to Bloy's notion that everything in the universe, including ourselves, is a symbol that we cannot decipher.

Bossuet, Jacques-Bénigne (1627–1704): French theologian, Bishop of Condom, tutor to the Dauphin, and important defender of traditional Catholicism against Protestantism, theaters, new readings of the Bible, Quietism, intellectual curiosity, Spinoza, etc. (Not to be confused with Wilhelm Bousset, the Gnostic scholar whom Borges occasionally cites.)

Carriego, Evaristo (1883–1912): Popular poet in the Palermo section of Buenos Aires where Borges spent his childhood. A friend of Borges' father, Carriego used to visit every Sunday, and the child would listen to their literary discussions. Borges' 1930 book on Carriego uses the poet as the central figure for his evocation of "old-time" Buenos Aires.

Don Segundo Sombra: The 1926 novel by Ricardo Güiraldes and an idealized portrait of gaucho life.

El criticón: See *Baltasar Gracián*, below.

Fernández, Macedonio (1874–1952): Argentine poet, philosopher, short-story writer, friend and mentor to Borges. His insistence on the dreamlike quality of the material world and the blurred boundaries between fiction and reality were enormously influential on Borges.

Gracián, Baltasar (1601–1658): Spanish writer and Jesuit. His *El criticón* [The Criticizer], one of Schopenhauer's favorite books, is an allegory about an Innocent and a Man of the World who visit such Borgesian places as the Source of Illusion, the palace of Queen Artemia (who turns beasts into men), the Inn of the World (with a separate room for every vice), the House of Madmen (home to all humanity), the Wheel of Time, and the Castle of Adventurers, where the travelers become invisible until disillusion returns them to their human form. Gracián's *Agudeza y el arte del ingenio* [Wit and the Art of Genius] is the major *ars poetica* of the Spanish Baroque.

Groussac, Paul (1848–1929): Historian, playwright, literary critic, and one of Borges' predecessors as director of the National Library. Born in France, Groussac arrived in Argentina at age eighteen, and began to write in Spanish. Borges considered Groussac second only to the Mexican Alfonso Reyes as the greatest modern prose stylist in the language.

Gutiérrez, Eduardo (1853–1890): Argentine writer of gaucho adventure novels published in serial form, the most famous of which is *Juan Moreira*. Borges said he was infinitely superior to James Fenimore Cooper.

Jáuregui, Juan de (1583–1641): Spanish poet and translator who introduced *terza rima* into Spanish and is also known for having painted Cervantes' portrait.

Lugones, Leopoldo (1874–1938): Major Argentine symbolist poet, journalist, and short-story writer. Borges violently attacked him in his early, Ultraist years, but later wrote a monograph and various essays on Lugones, calling him "Argentina's greatest writer."

Martín Fierro: The eponymous gaucho hero of José Hernández's narrative poem, published in 1872 and 1879, and generally considered the Argentine national epic. Fierro, the nostalgic symbol of gaucho values, is also a deserter, a murderer, and a coward, as Borges frequently likes to point out.

Mauthner, Fritz (1849–1923): German poet turned philosopher, and one of Borges' favorite writers. Mauthner was the first philosopher to devote himself to the problems raised by ordinary language. Among his Borgesian beliefs were: the self cannot be found and therefore self-knowledge is impossible; psychology does not exist because language can only describe exterior sense impressions; today's religion is yesterday's science; morals are not a possible subject matter of knowledge; truth is historically relative; ordinary philosophy is afflicted by "word superstition," the belief that reality can be known through language; and language is most suitable for poetry or the expression of religious feelings for there the question of truth or falsity does not arise.

Paulino Lucero: 1872 book of *gauchesco* poems by Hilario Ascasubi (1807–1875). Its full, and more engrossing, title is: *Paulino Lucero; or The Gauchos of the Río de la Plata Singing and Fighting against the Tyrannies of the Republics of Argentina and Uruguay.*

Rosas, Juan Manuel de (1793–1877): The ruler of Argentina from 1835 to 1852. The archetype—for both Borges and Argentina—of the cruel and ruthless dictator, Rosas, oddly, was a distant relative of Borges.

Sarmiento, Domingo Faustino (1811–1888): The most important Argentine intellectual of the nineteenth century: writer, historian, educator, and president of the country from 1868 to 1874. His 1845 book *Facundo* is an exploration of Argentine identity and a condemnation of the Rosas dictatorship through the figure of a historical gaucho warlord. Borges wrote that Argentine history would have changed for the better if Facundo Quiroga, rather than Martín Fierro, were its national hero.

Torres Villarroel, Diego de (1693–1770): Spanish poet and satirist, and the leading disciple of Quevedo. His picaresque and corrosive autobiography is considered a masterpiece in Spanish. A favorite of Borges in his early, "baroque" years.

I. Early Writings, 1922–1928

Borges, born in 1899, spent a cloistered childhood in Buenos Aires; English was the first language he learned to read. In 1914, the family moved to Europe, settling in Geneva and later Lugano, where he learned French, Latin, and German. In 1919, the family relocated to Spain, where Borges became associated with the Ultraist group of young poets, and began to publish poems and articles, largely championing the new movement.

It is worth noting that, by age twenty, Borges had discovered most of the writers and books that would become his lifelong companions: Berkeley, Hume, William James, Spencer, the English Romantic poets, and *The Thousand and One Nights* (all of which he inherited from his father, who also taught him Zeno's paradoxes); *Don Quixote* (which he first read in English), Quevedo, Torres Villarroel, Schopenhauer, De Quincey, Kipling, Carlyle, Swinburne, Browning, Chesterton, Wells, Shakespeare, Stevenson, Poe, Twain, Whitman (whom he first read in German), Jack London, Bret Harte, the *Encyclopedia Britannica*, Virgil, Dante, Flaubert, Baudelaire, Rimbaud, Mallarmé, Apollinaire, de Gourmont, *The Golem*, Heine, Nietzsche, Rilke, the German Expressionist poets, and the Kabbalah, among many others.

In 1921, the family returned to Buenos Aires, and Borges developed the habit of long daily walks and explorations of the city that would continue until his blindness. He founded an Ultraist magazine, *Prisma* [Prism], which lasted for two issues, and began

the regular publication of essays and poems in Argentine and some Spanish magazines. In 1923, his first book of poetry: *Fervor de Buenos Aires* [Fervor for Buenos Aires]. Shortly after, the family spent a year in Europe attending to Borges' father's health. It was to be Borges' last trip abroad until late in his life.

For the rest of the decade, Borges was, in the words of Rodríguez Monegal, "the acknowledged leader of the young and one of the most public writers in Argentina's literary history." He founded an important little magazine, *Proa* [Prow], regularly contributed to many others, edited an anthology of the new Latin American poetry, and was included in various others, and published two more books of poetry and three books of essays: *Inquisiciones* [Inquisitions, 1925]; *El tamaño de mi esperanza* [The Extent of My Hope, 1926]; and *El idioma de los argentinos* [The Language of the Argentines, 1928].

Borges rejected the complex styles of the early books of essays, which for him, veered between a baroque "Latin in Spanish" and an over-reliance on obscure Argentine words, idioms, and spellings. He never allowed them to be reprinted—except in French translation—and they did not appear again until 1994. Nearly all scholars and critics, however, take the major essays of this period to be essential to an understanding of the work as a whole, and Borges himself used to joke that posterity would probably consider these first books to be his best.

None of the essays in this section are in the *Complete Works*.

The Nothingness of Personality
"La nadería de la personalidad," *Proa* no. 1, Aug. 1922. Included in *Inquisiciones*.

Despite his later rejection of all the prose of this period, Borges felt, at the time, that this was his first fully realized essay.

After Images
"Después de las imágenes," *Proa* no. 5, Dec. 1924. Included in *Inquisiciones*.

> *p. 10: Luis Carlos López:* Colombian poet (1883–1950) of folkloric simplicity, deliberately pitched against modernism.

> *p. 11: mirrors are like water:* A reference to the 1916 book of Creationist poetry *El espejo de agua* [*The Mirror of Water*], by the Chilean poet Vicente Huidobro (1893–1948).

Joyce's *Ulysses*
"El *Ulises* de Joyce," *Proa* no. 6, Jan. 1925. Included in *Inquisiciones*.

Borges may or may not have been, as he claims, the first Spanish-speaker to read *Ulysses*, but a Spanish translation of the novel did not appear until 1948.

A History of Angels
"Historia de los ángeles," *La Prensa*, 7 Mar. 1926. Included in *Tamaño*.

Verbiage for Poems
"Palabrería para versos." An earlier version, under the title "Acerca del vocabulario" [An Approach to Vocabulary] was published in *La Prensa*, 2 May 1926. Included in *Tamaño*.

> *p. 22: Esteban Manuel de Villegas:* Spanish poet (1589–1669) and translator of Horace and Anacreon.

p. 22: Juan de Mena: Spanish poet (1411–1456) and the first to write in a "purified," non-colloquial, literary form of the language.

A Profession of Literary Faith
"Profesión de fe literaria." Originally published under the title "A manera de profesión de fe literaria" [By Way of a Profession of Literary Faith] in *La Prensa*, 27 June 1926. Included in *Tamaño*.

> *p. 24: [Julio] Herrera y Reissig:* Important turn-of-the-century Uruguayan poet (1875–1910); bohemian, Symbolist, and ultimately, Ultraist.

> *p. 24: Fernán Silva Valdés:* Uruguayan poet (1887–1975) who proposed a national "nativism" to replace local "criollism."

> *p. 25: commited by a famous poet:* Herrera y Reissig, in the poem *"Sepelio"* [Interment] in his 1909 book *Los peregrinos de piedra* [The Pilgrims of Stone]. On the previous page, Borges had identified another citation from the same book, but here does not.

> *p. 26: Manuel Gálvez:* Argentine realist novelist (1882–1962).

Literary Pleasure
"La fruición literaria," *La Prensa*, 23 Jan. 1927. Included in *Idioma*.

> *p. 28: The Student of Salamanca:* The 1836–37 Romantic narrative poem of the Don Juan story, by José de Espronceda.

> *p. 28: Don Juan Tenorio:* The 1844 popular play, also of the Don Juan story, by José Zorrilla.

An Investigation of the Word
"Indigación de la palabra," published in two parts, *Sintesis* no. 1, June 1927, and no. 3, August 1927. Included in *Idioma*.

> Rodríguez Monegal compares this essay to I. A. Richards' nearly contemporary book, *Practical Criticism* (1929): "Both start from the same experience: the discussion of a text whose author is unknown to the reader and which, therefore, can only be deciphered by itself. Yet, contrary to Dr. Richards, [Borges] postulates the utter impossibility of scientific criticism . . . for him, every critic (every reader) places himself, willingly or not, in a conditioned perspective; before judging, every reader prejudges. Criticism, or reading, creates the text anew." The opening sentence of *Don Quixote* will be placed in another context, decades later, in Borges' lecture on detective stories (p. 491).

> *p. 37: [Joseph] Joubert:* The great French writer of epigrammatic *pensées* (1754–1824).

II. 1929–1936

Throughout the 1930s, Borges wrote almost no poetry. The first of his "canonical" non-fiction prose books was *Evaristo Carriego* (1930)—see note on Carriego above. (The book, considered unsuccessful by both Borges and readers, was greatly improved in its second edition, twenty-five years later, which added "A History of the Tango" [p. 394] and other essays.) A few weeks after its publication, the democratically elected government of Hipólito Irigoyen was overthrown by the military, and Argentina's "infamous decade" began; Borges would respond with increasing passion to the rising fascism and anti-Semitism of the Argentine bourgeoisie and intelligentsia.

In 1931, Borges' friend Victoria Ocampo—whom André Malraux called the "Empress of the Pampas"—founded *Sur*, the most important South American literary magazine of the century, and to which Borges would be, in her words, the "chief contributor and adviser" for decades. The 1932 book *Discusión* [Discussion] marks the beginning of Borges' most fertile and enduring non-fiction writing, a period that would end with his blindness in 1956. The following year, he took a job as literary editor of the "Saturday Color Magazine" of the tabloid newspaper *Crítica*, to which he contributed articles, translations of authors ranging from Chesterton to Novalis, and, under a pseudonym, his first short stories, including "Hombre de la esquina rosada" (known in English as "Streetcorner Man" or "Man on Pink Corner"), and the fictionalized biographies that would be collected in *Historia universal de la infamia* [Universal History of Infamy, 1935]. His next book of essays, *Historia de la eternidad* [History of Eternity, 1936], played a metaphysical joke on its readers by including "The Approach to al-Mu'tasim," a review of a fictional book (it would later be moved to *Ficciones*). By 1936, Borges was the best-known young poet and essayist in Argentina; literary magazines had devoted special supplements to his work. Yet his reputation did not extend beyond a small circle in Buenos Aires: *Eternidad*, for example, sold exactly thirty-seven copies in its first year.

The Perpetual Race of Achilles and the Tortoise

"La perpetua carrera de Aquiles y la tortuga," *La Prensa*, 1 Jan. 1929. Included in *Discusión*.

Another, better known version of this essay is the 1939 "Avatares de la tortuga" [Avatars of the Tortoise], which is included in *Otras inquisiciones*.

The Duration of Hell

"La duración del infierno," *Sintesis* no. 25, June 1929. Included in *Discusión*.

The Superstitious Ethics of the Reader

"La supersticiosa ética del lector," *Azul* no. 8, Jan. 1931. Included in *Discusión*.

p. 53: Guzmán de Alfarache: The 1599 novel by Mateo Alemán that started the craze for the picaresque novel.

Our Inabilities

"Nuestras imposibilidades," *Sur* no. 4, Spring 1931. Included in the first edition of *Discusión*, where it was the first essay, but omitted from later editions. Not in the *Complete Works*.

p. 56: a Russian: In Argentina, *ruso* [Russian] was a derogatory word for an Ashkenazi Jew. (Sephardic Jews, with similar exactitude, were *turcos*, Turks.) Borges continues to play with this confusion later in the essay when he refers to "Russian gold."

p. 56: the pseudo-serious: Borges uses the word *seriola* and puts it in quotation marks. The word is found in no dictionary, and only one Spanish speaker I consulted knew what it meant. According to the Argentine painter César Paternosto, "*ola*" was a slang suffix indicating disbelief in Buenos Aires in the 1920s and 1930s.

p. 57: the Italian immigrant: Borges uses the word *gringo,* which in Argentina once referred to Italians, not North Americans.

p. 57: Hallelujah: The 1929 King Vidor film, featuring an all-African-American cast.

p. 57: one of von Sternberg's heroic films: Underworld (1927).

The Postulation of Reality
"La postulación de la realidad," *Azul* no. 10, June 1931. Included in *Discusión.*

p. 59: Hume noted . . . : The first half of this sentence reappears in the 1940 story "Tlön, Uqbar, Orbis Tertius," where Borges notes that it is entirely true on earth and entirely false on Tlön.

p. 60: Don Quixote: The translation cited is Tobias Smollett's 1755 version.

p. 61: Lehrjahre: Goethe's 1796 novel, *The Apprenticeship of Wilhelm Meister.*

p. 63: Enrique Larreta: Argentine novelist (1875–1961). His 1908 historical neo-Walter Scott novel, *La gloria de Don Ramiro* [The Glory of Don Ramiro], mixes narration in contemporary Spanish with dialogue in the archaic.

p. 63: [George] Moore: The Anglo-Irish novelist (1852–1933) and co-founder of the Abbey Theatre, who wrote some French poems in his youth.

A Defense of Basilides the False
"Una vindicación del falso Basílides." Published under the title "Una vindicación de los gnósticos" [A Defense of the Gnostics] in *La Prensa,* 1 Jan. 1932. Included in *Discusión.*

The Homeric Versions
"Las versiones homéricas," *La Prensa,* 8 May 1932. Included in *Discusión,* and revised for later editions.

p. 70: the Quixote is to me an unchanging monument: But Borges, curiously, first read the book in English translation.

p. 71: Augustín Moreto: Spanish cleric and extremely popular comic playwright (1618–1669).

p. 71: Browning's most famous book: The Ring and the Book (1869).

Narrative Art and Magic
"El arte narrativo y la magia," *Sur* no. 5, Summer 1932. Included in *Discusión.*

p. 80: Kenelm Digby's ointment: Sir Kenelm Digby (1603–1665) was a naval commander who defeated the French and Venetian fleets in the Battle of Scanderoon, an author of theological tracts and a memoir of his courtship and secret marriage to the celebrated beauty Venetia Stanley, a scientist who discovered the necessity of oxygen for plant life, and the inventor of a "powder of sympathy"— here transformed into an ointment—which could cure a wound by treating the object that inflicted it.

p. 81: Estanislao del Campo: Argentine gaucho poet (1834–1880). His 1866 *Fausto* is a poetic dialogue of naive gauchos attending a performance of Gounod's opera *Faust.*

p. 81: The Showdown: 1928 film by Victor Schertzinger; *Underworld:* 1927 film by Josef von Sternberg; *Dishonored:* 1931 film by von Sternberg.

A Defense of the Kabbalah

"Una vindicación de la cábala." First published in *Discusión*, 1932.

>   *p. 85: St. Paulinus:* Italian theologian and Bishop of York (d. 644).

>   *p. 85: [St.] Athanasius:* Theologian and Bishop of Alexandria (293–373).

>   *p. 85: Macedonius:* Heterodox theologian and Bishop of Constantinople from 342 to 360.

>   *p. 85: Socinians:* Followers of Lelio Sozzini (1525–1562), known as Socin, a theologian, exiled in Switzerland, who rejected the Trinity, original sin, predestination, eternal suffering, and other cornerstones of Christianity.

The Art of Verbal Abuse

"Arte de injuriar," *Sur* no. 8, Sept. 1933. Included in *Eternidad*.

>   *p. 87: truco:* Popular Argentine card game, and the subject of an essay in *Evaristo Carriego*.

>   *p. 91: [José] Santos Chocano:* Peruvian poet (1875–1934) who consciously sought to become the Latin American Whitman.

>   *p. 91: José María Monner Sans:* Argentine academic critic, author of *History Considered as a Genre of Poetry*.

>   *p. 91: Miguel Servet:* Also known as Michael Servetus (1511–1533), a Spanish theologian burned at the stake as a heretic.

The Translators of *The Thousand and One Nights*

>   "Los traductores de las 1001 Noches." Sections first appeared in *Crítica*, 10 Mar. 1934. First published in its entirety in *Eternidad*, 1936.

>   *p. 97: [Paul] Morand:* Popular French novelist and travel writer (1888–1976), translated by, among others, Ezra Pound.

>   *p. 98: al-Mutanabbi's Diwan:* Abu-t-Tayyib al-Mutanabbi, Arabic poet (916–965).

>   *p. 100: Toulet's Contrerimes*: Posthumously published book of poems by Paul-Jean Toulet (1867–1920), known for its technical perfection. Borges said he preferred Toulet to Baudelaire.

>   *p. 103: Marchand's withdrawal:* The 1898 diplomatic crisis, known as the "Fashoda incident," when the British and Lord Kitchener forced the French and Major Marchand out of a small settlement in the Sudan, almost precipitating a European war.

>   *p. 108: Mannequin d'osier* [The Wicker Dummy]: The second in Anatole France's four-volume series *Histoire contemporaine* (1896–1901).

I, a Jew

"Yo, judío," *Megáfono* no. 12, April 1934. First reprinted in *Ficcionario*, 1985. Not in the *Complete Works*.

Rodríguez Monegal notes that in Borges' "mock search" for a Jewish ancestor, the most likely suspects turn out to be the Acevedos, "the very Catholic and bigoted maternal branch of his family."

>   *p. 110: Crisol* [Crucible]: An Argentine Fascist magazine.

The Labyrinths of the Detective Story and Chesterton

>   "Los laberintos policiales y Chesterton," *Sur* no. 10, May 1935. First reprinted in *Ficcionario*, 1985. Not in the *Complete Works*.

The Doctrine of Cycles
"La doctrina de los ciclos," *Sur* no. 20, May 1936. Included in *Eternidad.*
> *p. 115: [Ernest] Rutherford:* Baron Rutherford, English physicist (1871–1937), dis-
> coverer of the atomic nucleus.

A History of Eternity
"Historia de la eternidad." First published in *Eternidad,* 1936.
> The citations from the *Enneads* are adapted from the Stephen MacKenna translation.
> *p. 126: Pedro Malón de Chaide:* Spanish Augustinian monk and writer (1530–1589),
> and disciple of Fray Luis de León; against the Dominicans, he defended the posi-
> tion that the Scriptures should be translated into Spanish.
> *p. 127: Abubeker Abentofail:* Better known as Ibn Tufail (c. 1105–1185), the Andalusian
> Arabic writer whose revision of Avicenna's philosophical romance of a man's
> spiritual development on a desert island, *Alive, Son of Awake,* was one of Ramón
> Llull's favorite books.
> *p. 132: Hans Lassen Martensen:* Danish theologian (1808–1884), author of a life of
> Jakob Boehme and works on Christian ethics.

Film Reviews and Criticism
Borges was a lifelong movie fan. In the years of his blindness, he would go to the
movies simply to listen to the dialogue.

The Cinematograph, the Biograph
"El cinematógrafo El biógrafo," *La Prensa,* 28 Apr. 1929. First reprinted in *Textos recobrados,* 1998. Not in the *Complete Works.*
> *Biógrafo*—undoubtedly derived from D. W. Griffith's Biograph Studios—was the
word preferred by the lower-middle and working classes in Buenos Aires; the Fran-
cophilic upper classes called a movie a *cinematógrafo,* the Lumière Brothers' name for
their invention.

Films
> "Films," *Sur* no. 3, Winter 1931. Included in *Discusión.*

Street Scene
> *Sur* no. 5, Summer 1932. Included in *Discusión.*

King Kong
> One of "Cinco breve noticias" [Five Brief Notices], *Selección* no. 3, July 1933. Never
> reprinted. Not in the *Complete Works.*

The Informer
> "El delator, film," *Sur* no. 11, Aug. 1935. First reprinted in *Cine,* 1980. Not in the *Com-
> plete Works.*

Two Films
> "Dos films," *Sur* no. 19, April 1936. First reprinted in *Cine,* 1980. Not in the *Complete
> Works.*

The Petrified Forest
"El bosque petrificado, film de Archie Mayo," *Sur* no. 24, Sept. 1936. First reprinted in *Cine*, 1980. Not in the *Complete Works*.

> *p. 150: The Passing of the Third Floor Back:* 1935 British film, directed by Berthold Viertel.

Wells, the Visionary
> "Wells, previsor," *Sur* no. 26, Nov. 1936. First reprinted in *Cine*, 1980. Not in the *Complete Works*.

III. Writings for *El Hogar* [*Home*] Magazine, 1936–1939

By 1936, Borges' father's health had worsened, and Borges, living at home, decided to supplement the family income by taking a job with *El Hogar* [Home], a weekly magazine for the Argentine middle- and upper-class housewife. Borges was in charge of writing the "Foreign Books and Authors" page, which alternated with one devoted to Spanish-language writers. The "Books" page had a strict format which Borges continued: a "capsule biography" of a living writer, one longer review or essay, a few short reviews, and an occasional short note on "the literary life." Although Borges was at his lightest and perhaps wittiest in *El Hogar*, he by no means limited the range of his subject matter, nor curtailed his habit of citing texts in various languages without a translation. It is remarkable that Borges' page lasted for three years.

All of these texts were first reprinted in *Textos cautivos*, 1986.

Ramón Llull's Thinking Machine
"La máquina de pensar de Raimundo Lulio," 15 Oct. 1937.

When Fiction Lives in Fiction
"Cuando la ficción vive en la ficción," 2 June 1939.

Capsule Biographies
Besides the texts included here, Borges wrote "capsule biographies" of Richard Aldington, Henri Barbusse, Sir James Barrie, Hillaire Belloc, Van Wyck Brooks, Karel Capek, Countee Cullen, e. e. cummings, Alfred Döblin, Lord Dunsany, Edna Ferber, Lion Feuchtwanger, E. M. Forster, Leonhard Frank, David Garnett, Julien Green, Gerhart Hauptmann, Langston Hughes, James Joyce, Franz Kafka, H. R. Lenormand, Arthur Machen, Edgar Lee Masters, Gustav Meyrink, Harold Nicolson, Eden Phillpotts, T. F. Powys, Elmer Rice, Romain Rolland, Carl Sandburg, George Santayana, Olaf Stapledon, Lytton Strachey, Hermann Sudermann, Fritz von Unruh, Evelyn Waugh, and Franz Werfel.

First publication dates for the included texts: Isaac Babel, 4 Feb. 1938; Ernest Bramah, 18 Feb. 1938; Benedetto Croce, 27 Nov. 1936; Theodore Dreiser, 19 Aug. 1938; T. S. Eliot, 25 June 1937; Will James, 7 Jan. 1938; Liam O'Flaherty, 9 July 1937; Oswald Spengler, 25 Dec. 1936; Paul Valéry, 22 Jan. 1937; S. S. Van Dine, 11 June 1937; Virginia Woolf, 30 Oct. 1936.

> *p. 172: the most dexterous:* The translation Borges is referring to is by Borges himself.

p. 174: Orlando: Borges published a translation of Woolf's novel in 1937, and, the previous year, a translation of *A Room of One's Own.*

Book Reviews and Notes

Borges wrote 141 book reviews and 15 notes on "The Literary Life" for *El Hogar.* First publication dates for the included texts:

Gustav Meyrink, *Der Engel vom Westlichen Fenster,* 16 Oct. 1936.

Alan Pryce-Jones, *Private Opinion,* 13 Nov. 1936.

Louis Golding, *The Pursuer,* 11 Dec. 1936.

Lord Halifax's Ghost Book, 25 Dec. 1936.

William Faulkner, *Absalom! Absalom!,* 22 Jan. 1937.

Gustaf Janson, *Gubben Kommer,* 16 Apr. 1937.

Aldous Huxley, *Stories, Essays, and Poems,* 16 Apr. 1937.

Rabindranath Tagore, *Collected Poems and Plays,* 11 June 1937.

Ellery Queen, *The Door Between,* 25 June 1937.

William Barrett, *Personality Survives Death,* 21 Jan. 1938.

Wolfram Eberhard, tr., *Chinese Fairy Tales and Folk Tales,* 4 Feb. 1938.

"The Literary Life: Marinetti," 4 Mar. 1938

> *p. 184: [Julio] Cejador [y Frauca]:* Spanish literary historian (1864–1927) and martinet of the Spanish language.

Richard Hull, *Excellent Intentions,* 15 Apr. 1938.

> *p. 184: One of the projects . . . :* The hypothetical novel that Borges conceives would later be ascribed to an imaginary author in his story "A Survey of the Works of Herbert Quain" (1941).

Meadows Taylor, *The Confessions of a Thug,* 27 May 1938.

William Faulkner, *The Unvanquished,* 24 June 1938.

Lady Murasaki, *The Tale of Genji,* 19 Aug. 1938.

Lord Dunsany, *Patches of Sunlight,* 2 Sept. 1938.

"Two Fantasy Novels," 14 Oct. 1938.

"The Literary Life: Oliver Gogarty," 14 Oct. 1938.

"An English Version of the Oldest Songs in the World," 28 Oct. 1938.

Alan Griffiths, *Of Course, Vitelli!,* 18 Nov. 1938.

"A Grandiose Manifesto from Breton," 2 Dec. 1938.

> *p. 192: André Breton:* It was not known until many years later that the actual author of the Breton/Rivera manifesto was Leon Trotsky.

"H. G. Wells' Latest Novel," 2 Dec. 1938.

E. S. Pankhurst, *Delphos, or the Future of International Language,* 10 Mar. 1939.

"Joyce's Latest Novel," 16 June 1939.

"The Literary Life: The Dionne Quints," 7 July 1939.

> This was Borges' last contribution to the foreign books page.

IV. 1937–1945

As his income from *El Hogar* was paltry, in 1937 Borges took a job as a low-level bureaucrat in an unimportant municipal library; he would finish his work in an hour and then disappear into the basement for the rest of the day to read and write. Not surprisingly, he discovered and began translating Kafka. In 1938, the death of his father left Borges as head of a household that included his mother, sister Norah, and her husband. Some months later, he developed blood poisoning from a freak accident and nearly died; for reasons too complex to summarize here, the experience both tied him closer to his mother and prompted him to devote himself more seriously to fiction. The result was his greatest book of stories: the 1941 *El jardín de los senderos que se bifurcan* [The Garden of Forking Paths], which was expanded in 1944 as *Ficciones* [Fictions]. Those stories, and his contemporary theoretical essays, set into motion a process that would later combine with folkloric and indigenous elements to produce Latin American "magical realism."

During this period, Borges also began writing books of stories with his best friend, Adolfo Bioy Casares, under the pseudonym H. Bustos Domecq. He collaborated with Bioy and Bioy's wife, the fiction writer Silvina Ocampo, editing anthologies of fantastic literature (1940), Argentine poetry (1941), and detective stories (1943). Besides Kafka, Borges translated Virginia Woolf's *Orlando*, Henri Michaux's *A Barbarian in Asia* (which was translated into German by Walter Benjamin), Herman Melville's *Bartleby the Scrivener*, and William Faulkner's *The Wild Palms* (a translation that was enormously influential on young Latin American novelists, such as Gabriel García Márquez), as well as many shorter texts. He put together a slim retrospective collection of his poetry, *Poemas (1922–1943)*, with only six new poems from the last fourteen years. Despite the hundreds of essays he wrote during this period, he published no books of non-fictions.

Notes on Germany and the War

Argentina, ruled by the army and with a large Italian population, generally supported the Spanish, Italian, and German Fascists at all levels of society. The exceptions, among the intellectuals, were, on the one hand, the Marxists, and on the other, the Anglophiles and Francophiles centered around *Sur* and a few other small literary magazines. Borges was not only unwaveringly anti-Fascist; he was ardently Semitophile in a period when anti-Semitism was fashionable, and a Germanophile dedicated to salvaging German culture from the Nazis and their Argentine supporters. Borges' courageous wartime articles remain little known, even in Spanish.

A Pedagogy of Hatred

"Una pedagogía del odio," *Sur* no. 32, May 1937. First reprinted in *Páginas*, 1982. Not in the *Complete Works*.

A Disturbing Exposition

"Una exposición afligente," *Sur* no. 49, Oct. 1938. Never reprinted. Not in the *Complete Works*.

An Essay on Neutrality

"Ensayo de imparcialidad," *Sur* no. 61, Oct. 1939. First reprinted in *Páginas*, 1982. Not in the *Complete Works*.

Definition of a Germanophile

"Definición de germanófilo," *El Hogar*, 13 Dec. 1940. First reprinted in *Textos cautivos*, 1986.

After an absence of a year and a half, Borges returned to *El Hogar* to contribute this note, which, remarkably, was published on the first page of the magazine.

1941
"1941," *Sur* no. 87, Dec. 1941. Never reprinted. Not in the *Complete Works.*

> *p. 206: Maurice Leblanc:* French writer (1864–1941), creator of the Arsène Lupin mystery series.

> *p. 206: [E.] Phillips Oppenheim:* British writer (1866–1946) and author of immensely popular espionage novels in the 1910s and 1920s.

> *p. 206: Baldur von Schirach:* German head of the Hitler Youth (1907–1974), who was later tried and convicted at Nuremberg.

Two Books
"Dos libros." Originally published under the title "Dos libros de este tiempo" [Two Books of this Era], *La Nación,* 10 Dec. 1941. Included in *Otras inquisiciones.*

> *p. 208: Gauleiter:* A Nazi community organizer.

> *p. 209: Hitler . . . is a pleonasm of Carlyle:* In the guarded diary Robert Musil kept in Vienna in 1938, his code word for Hitler was "Carlyle."

A Comment on August 23, 1944
"Anotación al 23 agosto 1944," *Sur* no. 120, Oct. 1944. Included in *Otras inquisiciones.*

> *p. 210: [José] San Martín:* Argentina's revered military leader (1778–1850), hero of the Wars of Independence and liberator of Chile and Peru.

A Note on the Peace
"Nota sobre la paz," *Sur* no. 129, July 1945. Never reprinted. Not in the *Complete Works.*

The Total Library
"La biblioteca total," *Sur* no. 59, Aug. 1939. First reprinted in *Ficcionario,* 1985. Not in the *Complete Works.*

This essay, inspired by his dreary job at the municipal library, soon turned into the famous story "The Library of Babel" (1941).

> *p. 214: Gustav Theodor Fechner:* German philosopher and physicist (1801–1887), inventor of psychophysics and investigator of the exact relationships among psychology, physiology, and aesthetics.

> *p. 214: Kurd Lasswitz:* German science fiction writer (1848–1910), best known for his Wellsian 1897 novel, *To Two Planets.*

Time and J. W. Dunne
"El tiempo y J. W. Dunne," *Sur* no. 72, Sept. 1940. Included in *Otras inquisiciones.*

> *p. 217: number 63 of Sur:* The essay Borges refers to is "The Avatars of the Tortoise," another version of "The Perpetual Race of Achilles and the Tortoise," which is included here.

> *p. 217: [Johann Friedrich] Herbart:* German philosopher and educator (1776–1841).

A Fragment on Joyce
"Fragmento sobre Joyce," *Sur* no. 77, Feb. 1941. First reprinted in *Páginas,* 1982. Not in the *Complete Works.*

p. 220: *Among the works I have not written:* A Borgesian joke: the story, "Funes the Memorious," had indeed been written, but would not be published until the following year.

p. 220: *compadrito:* Young tough of the slums.

p. 221: *M. Victor Bérard:* A French translator of the *Odyssey,* who, following the archeologist Heinrich Schliemann, insisted on the factual basis of Homer's epics.

The Creation and P. H. Gosse

"La creación y P. H. Gosse," *Sur* no. 81, June 1941. Included in *Otras inquisiciones.*

p. 222: *Legenda Aurea: The Golden Legend,* the collection of ecclesiastical lore by Jacobus de Voragine (1230–1298); after the Bible, the most popular book of the late Middle Ages.

p. 224: *Chateaubriand:* The translation is by Charles I. White (1856).

Circular Time

"El tiempo circular." First published under the title "Tres formas del eterno regreso" [Three Forms of Eternal Return], *La Nación,* 14 Dec. 1941. Included in later editions of *Eternidad,* from 1953 on.

p. 227: *Chrysippus:* Greek Stoic philosopher (c. 280–207 B.C.).

p. 227: *Condorcet's decimal history:* The mathemetician Marie Jean Antoine Nicolas Caritat, Marquis de Condorcet (1743–1794), wrote a *Sketch for a Historical Picture of the Progress of the Human Mind*—published after his death in prison—dividing human history into nine stages that ended with the French Revolution, which had imprisoned him. In the tenth stage, humanity would achieve perfection.

p. 227: *Gerald Heard:* English writer (1889–1971) and author of the encompassing *Pain, Sex, and Time.* In the 1930s, he moved with his friend Aldous Huxley to California in search of spiritual enlightenment.

John Wilkins' Analytical Language

"El idioma analítico de John Wilkins," *La Nación,* 8 Feb. 1942. Included in *Otras inquisiciones.*

On Literary Description

"Sobre la descripción literaria," *Sur* no. 97, Oct. 1942. First reprinted in *Páginas,* 1982. Not in the *Complete Works.*

p. 233: *[Calixto] Oyuela:* Classical, Catholic, and conservative Argentine poet and essayist (1857–1935).

p. 234: *[Gabriel] Miró:* Impressionistic Spanish fiction writer (1879–1930).

On William Beckford's *Vathek*

"Sobre el *Vathek* de William Beckford," *La Nación,* 4 Apr. 1943. Included in *Otras inquisiciones.*

Coleridge's Flower

"La flor de Coleridge," *La Nación,* 23 Sept. 1945. Included in *Otras inquisiciones.* Selected for the *New Personal Anthology,* 1968.

p. 242: Wells . . . not acquainted with Coleridge's text: This is either an error or a joke: Coleridge's lines are the epigraph to *The Time Machine*.

Prologues
Adolfo Bioy Casares, *The Invention of Morel*
La invención de Morel (Losada, 1940). First reprinted in *Prólogos*, 1975.

> *p. 244: Le Voyageur sur la terre* [The Wanderer on the Earth]: 1930 novel by Julien Green.
>
> *p. 245: Las fuerzas extrañas* [The Strange Forces]: 1906 short story collection by Leopoldo Lugones.
>
> *p. 245: Santiago Dabove:* Argentine fiction writer (1889–1949) whom Borges and Bioy included in their anthology of fantastic fiction.
>
> *p. 245: Moreau:* Wells' 1896 novel, *The Island of Dr. Moreau.*

Herman Melville, *Bartleby the Scrivener*
Bartleby (Emecé, 1944). First reprinted in *Prólogos*, 1975.

> Borges was the translator of the Melville story.

Henry James, *The Abasement of the Northmores*
> *La humiliación de los Northmore*, Emecé, 1945. First reprinted in *Prólogos*, 1975.

Book Reviews
Edward Kasner & James Newman, *Mathematics and the Imagination*
Sur no. 73, Oct. 1940. Included in later editions of *Discusión*, from 1957 on.

Edward Shanks, *Rudyard Kipling: A Study in Literature and Political Ideas*
Sur no. 78, Mar. 1941. Never reprinted. Not in the *Complete Works*.

Arthur Waley, *Monkey*
Published under the title "Sobre una alegoria china" [On a Chinese Allegory], *La Nación*, 25 Nov. 1942. Never reprinted. Not in the *Complete Works*.

Leslie Weatherhead, *After Death*
Sur no. 105, July 1943. Included in later editions of *Discusión*, from 1957 on.

Film Reviews and Criticism
Two Films (*Sabotage; Los muchachos de antes*)
"Dos films," *Sur* no. 31, Apr. 1937. First reprinted in *Cine*, 1980. Not in the *Complete Works*.

An Overwhelming Film (*Citizen Kane*)
"Un film abrumador," *Sur* no. 83, Aug. 1941. First reprinted in *Cine*, 1980. Not in the *Complete Works*.

It is now forgotten that *Citizen Kane* opened to generally dismissive reviews; Borges, despite his reservations, must be seen as one of its first champions. He was also the first, by decades, to note a connection with the 1933 *The Power and the Glory* (screenplay by Preston Sturges), a film now generally considered to be the ur-*Kane*.

(No relation, by the way, to the Graham Greene novel, which was written years later.)
    p. 259: Koheleth: The Hebrew name for the Book of Ecclesiastes.

Dr. Jekyll and Mr. Hyde, Transformed
"El doctor Jekyll y Edward Hyde, transformados," *Sur* no. 87, Dec. 1941. Included in later editions of *Discusión*, from 1957 on.

Two Films (*Now Voyager; Nightmare*)
"Dos films," *Sur* no. 103, Apr. 1943. First reprinted in *Cine*, 1980. Not in the *Complete Works*.

On Dubbing
"Sobre el doblaje," *Sur* no. 128, June 1945. Included in later editions of *Discusión*, from 1957 on.

V. *Nine Dantesque Essays* 1945–1951

Although some sections form part of the "Estudio preliminar" [Preliminary Study] to a 1949 edition of Dante, these essays were first collected in the book *Nueve ensayos dantescos*, 1982. Their order here follows that of the book, which is presented in its entirety. The Dante citations are based on the Charles Singleton translation.

Prologue
"Prologo," first published in *Nueve ensayos dantescos*. The date of composition is unknown.
    p. 268: [*Henry Francis*] *Cary:* English translator of Dante (1772–1844), whose edition
        was the first publication of the Italian text in England, and the one that the En-
        glish Romantics read.

The Noble Castle of the Fourth Canto
"El noble castillo del canto cuarto," *La Nación*, 22 Apr. 1951.

The False Problem of Ugolino
"El falso problema de Ugolino." Published under the title "El seudo problema de Ugolino" [The Pseudo-problem of Ugolino] in *La Nación*, 30 May 1948.
    p. 278: Malvezzi's pen: Virgilio Malvezzi (1595–1654), a Bolognese nobleman who
        lived at the Spanish court and whose sententious style was widely imitated.

The Last Voyage of Ulysses
"El último viaje de Ulises," *La Nación*, 22 Aug. 1948.

The Pitying Torturer
"El verdugo piadoso," *Sur* no. 163, May 1948.
    p. 286: [*Pierre Simon*] *Marquis de Laplace:* French astronomer and mathematician
        (1749–1827), who proved Newton's theory of gravitation and expounded a nebu-
        lar origin of the universe.

Dante and the Anglo-Saxon Visionaries
"Dante y los visionarios anglosajones," *Ars* no. 78, 1957.
>   The citations from Bede are taken from the J. A. Giles 1847 adaptation of the 1723 John Stevens translation.

Purgatorio I, 13
"*Purgatorio* I, 13," first published in *Nueve ensayos dantescos*.

The Simurgh and the Eagle
"El Simurgh y el águila," *La Nación*, 14 Mar. 1948.
>   *p. 294: Visio Tundali:* Medieval Latin poem of the visions of heaven and hell seen by the legendary Irish knight, Tundalus.

The Meeting in a Dream
"El encuentro en un sueño," *La Nación*, 3 Oct. 1948. Included in the first edition of *Otras inquisiciones*, but omitted from later ones.

Beatrice's Last Smile
"La última sonrisa de Beatriz," first published in *Nueve ensayos dantescos*.

VI. 1946–1955

In October 1945, in a complicated piece of political theater, Colonel Juan Domingo Perón—the power behind the scenes in Argentina in the 1940s—fell into disgrace, was exiled, and returned triumphantly eight days later. Borges made a public statement that began: "The situation in Argentina is very serious, so serious that a great number of Argentines are becoming Nazis without being aware of it." A few months after Perón's official election as president in early 1946, he "promoted" Borges from his job as third assistant at the library to Inspector of Poultry and Rabbits in the Córdoba municipal market. Borges, needless to say, declined.

Borges reluctantly became a lecturer. (Previously, he had been so shy that on the few occasions when he spoke in public, a friend was asked to read the speech while Borges sat silently behind him.) Often accompanied by his mother, Borges traveled to provincial towns and universities throughout Argentina and Uruguay. He was increasingly recognized as Argentina's greatest writer and a symbol of resistance to Perón. In 1948, Perón escalated his campaign against Borges by imprisoning his sister and placing his mother under house arrest.

In 1946, Borges took over the editorship of an academic magazine, *Los Anales de Buenos Aires*, and was the first publisher of two major fiction writers, Felisberto Hernández and Julio Cortázar. In 1949, he published *El Aleph* [The Aleph]—with *Ficciones*, his greatest fiction work. In 1952, he collected some of the essays from the 1930s and 1940s in *Otras inquisiciones* [Other Inquisitions]. That book, he later said, had two tendencies: "The first [was] to evaluate religious or philosophical ideas on the basis of their aesthetic worth. . . . The other [was] to presuppose (and to verify) that the number of fables or metaphors of which men's imaginations is capable is limited, but that these few inventions can be all things for all men."

Borges continued his collaboration on anthologies, stories, and some unproduced film scripts with Bioy Casares. New editions of his old books began to appear, as well as critical articles on his work. Thanks to Roger Callois, who had spent the war years in Argentina, *Ficciones* was translated into French in 1951.

Perón was overthrown by another faction of the military in 1955. Borges was made the Director of the National Library, a lifelong dream. With that appointment, however, came the news that his blindness had progressed to the point where the doctors forbade him to read or write.

Our Poor Individualism

"Nuestro pobre individualismo," *Sur* no. 141, July 1946. Included in *Otras inquisiciones.*

> *p. 310: the Lamed Wufniks:* In *The Book of Imaginary Beings,* Borges writes: "There are on earth, and always were, thirty-six righteous men whose mission is to justify the world before God. They are the Lamed Wufniks. They do not know each other and are very poor. If a man comes to the knowledge that he is a Lamed Wufnik, he immediately dies and somebody else, perhaps in another part of the world, takes his place. Lamed Wufniks are, without knowing it, the secret pillars of the universe. Were it not for them, God would annihilate the whole of mankind. Unawares, they are our saviors." (trans. Norman Thomas di Giovanni)

The Paradox of Apollinaire

"La paradoja de Apollinaire," *Los Anales de Buenos Aires* no. 8, Aug. 1946. First reprinted in *Ficcionario,* 1985. Not in the *Complete Works.*

> *p. 312: [Fritz von] Unruh:* German expressionist poet and playwright, and antimilitarist (1885-1970).
>
> *p. 312: [Henri] Barbusse:* French antiwar novelist (1873–1935), author of the World War I novel *Under Fire.*
>
> *p. 312: [Wilhelm] Klemm:* German expressionist poet (1881–1968) who also wrote under the name Felix Brazil, and published little after 1922.
>
> *p. 312: Guillermo de Torre:* Spanish critic and poet (1900–1971) who was married to Borges' sister, Norah.

On Oscar Wilde

"Sobre Oscar Wilde," *Los Anales de Buenos Aires* no. 11, Dec. 1946. Included in *Otras inquisiciones.* Selected for the *New Personal Anthology,* 1968.

> *p. 314: Hugh Vereker:* The protagonist of Henry James' story "The Figure in the Carpet."
>
> *p. 314: Les Palais nomades* [The Wandering Palaces]: 1887 book of poetry by Gustave Kahn (1859–1936), a theorist of the new *vers libre.*
>
> *p. 314: Los crepúsculos del jardín* [Twilights in the Garden]: 1905 book of poetry by Leopoldo Lugones.
>
> *p. 315: [Jean] Moréas:* French symbolist poet (1856–1910).

A New Refutation of Time

"Nueva refutación del tiempo." First published in its entirety as a pamphlet by "Oportet y Haereses" (a nonexistent publisher) in 1947. The first part appeared in *Sur* no. 115, May 1944, under the title "Una de las posibles metafísicas" [One of the Possible

Metaphysics]. The whole essay was included in the first edition of *Otras inquisiciones*; dropped from later editions; selected for the *Personal Anthology*, 1961; and reinstated as part of *Otras inquisiciones* for the *Complete Works*.

> *pp. 322–23: buried there, as I shall be:* In fact, Borges is buried in Geneva.

> *p. 323: Guide to Socialism:* Borges, for whatever reason, does not cite the full title of Shaw's 1928 book: *The Intelligent Woman's Guide to Socialism, Capitalism, Sovietism and Fascism.*

> *p. 324: "Feeling in Death":* Borges also reprints this 1928 prose piece in the 1936 "A History of Eternity" (p. 123). As both that essay and the present one are "canonical" (included in the *Complete Works*), it must be assumed that Borges is using the repetition—like the passages from Berkeley in parts A and B—as an example of the cyclical (or nonexistent) nature of time. Equally Borgesian, perhaps, is the fact that in this book the two texts are in somewhat different translations.

> *p. 332: Time is a river . . . :* These words would later be spoken by the computer that rules the world in Jean-Luc Godard's 1965 film *Alphaville.*

Biathanatos
"El *Biathanatos.*" First published under the title "John Donne, *Biathanatos*," *Sur* no. 159, Jan. 1948. Included in *Otras inquisiciones.*

From Allegories to Novels
"De las alegorías a las novelas," *La Nación*, 7 Aug. 1949. Included in *Otras inquisiciones.* Selected for the *New Personal Anthology*, 1968.

From Someone to Nobody
"De alguien a nadie," *Sur* no. 186, Mar. 1950. Included in *Otras inquisiciones.* Selected for the *Personal Anthology*, 1961.

A footnote to the penultimate paragraph, on Buddhism, is included in the *Complete Works* but omitted here, as it appears embedded in the essay "Personality and the Buddha" (p. 347, the passage beginning "The first books of the canon . . .").

> *p. 342: Shankara:* Indian philosopher and saint (788–820) and the main representative of Advaita-Vedanta. He wrote: "May this one sentence proclaim the essence of a thousand books: *Brahman* [the Eternal Absolute] alone is real; the world is appearance; the Self is nothing but *Brahman.*"

The Wall and the Books
"La muralla y los libros," *La Nación*, 22 Oct. 1950. Included in *Otras inquisiciones.* Selected for the *Personal Anthology*, 1961, and the *New Personal Anthology*, 1968.

Personality and the Buddha
"La personalidad y el Buddha," *Sur* nos. 192–194, Oct.–Dec. 1950. Never reprinted. Not in the *Complete Works.*

Pascal's Sphere
"La esfera de Pascal," *La Nación*, 14 Jan. 1951. Included in *Otras inquisiciones.* Selected for the *New Personal Anthology*, 1968.

The Innocence of Layamon
"La inocencia de Layamón," *Sur* no. 197, Mar 1951. Included in early editions of *Otras inquisiciones*, but omitted from later ones. Not in the *Complete Works*.

> p. 354: [*Emile*] *Legouis:* French literary historian (1861–1937), co-author of a *History of English Literature*.

On the Cult of Books
"Del culto de los libros," *La Nación*, 8 July 1951. Included in *Otras inquisiciones*.
The passage from St. Augustine is taken from the Henry Chadwick translation.

Kafka and His Precursors
"Kafka y sus precursores," *La Nación*, 19 Aug. 1951. Included in *Otras inquisiciones*.

The Enigma of Edward FitzGerald
"El enigma de Edward FitzGerald," *La Nación*, 7 Oct. 1951. Included in *Otras inquisiciones*. Selected for the *Personal Anthology*, 1961.

Borges does not mention a third incarnation of Omar-FitzGerald: his own father, whose translation of the *Rubáiyát* Borges published in his magazine *Proa* in the 1920s. According to Rodríguez Monegal, Borges' description of the sensitive, sad, and bookish FitzGerald is equally applicable to Borges Sr.

Coleridge's Dream
"El sueño de Coleridge," *La Nación*, 18 Nov. 1951. Included in *Otras inquisiciones*. Selected for the *New Personal Anthology*, 1968.

The quotation from Bede is taken from the J. A. Giles 1847 revision of the 1723 John Stevens translation.

Forms of a Legend
"Formas de una leyenda," *La Nación*, 8 June 1952. Included in *Otras inquisiciones*. Selected for the *Personal Anthology*, 1961.

The Scandinavian Destiny
"Destino escandinavo," *Sur* nos. 219–220, Jan.-Feb. 1953. First reprinted in *Páginas*, 1982. Not in the *Complete Works*.

The Dialogues of Ascetic and King
"Diálogos del asceta y del rey," *La Nación*, 20 Sept. 1953. First reprinted in *Páginas*, 1982. Not in the *Complete Works*.

A Defense of *Bouvard and Pécuchet*
"Vindicación de *Bouvard y Pecuchet*," *La Nación*, 14 Nov. 1954. Included in later editions of *Discusión*, from 1957 on.

Flaubert and His Exemplary Destiny
"Flaubert y su destino ejemplar," *La Nación*, 12 Dec. 1954. Included in later editions of *Discusión*, from 1957 on.

p. 393: O primo Basilio [Cousin Basilio]: 1878 novel by the Portuguese novelist Eça de Queiroz.

A History of the Tango
"Historia del tango." First printed in its entirety in the 1955 edition of *Evaristo Carriego.* One section, "El desafío" [The Challenge], appeared in *La Nación,* 28 Dec. 1952.

    p. 400: [Friedrich August] Wolf: German philologist and critic (1759–1824).

    p. 400: Andrew Fletcher: Scottish writer and politician (1655–1716).

A History of the Echoes of a Name
"Historia de los ecos de un nombre," *Cuadernos del Congreso por la Libertad de la Cultura* [Papers of the Congress for Cultural Freedom], Paris, Nov. 1955. Included in the 1960 edition of *Otras inquisiciones;* omitted from later editions. Not in the *Complete Works.*

    p. 406: Shakespeare wrote a comedy: All's Well That Ends Well.

L'Illusion Comique
"L'illusion comique," *Sur* no. 237, Nov.–Dec. 1955. Never reprinted. Not in the *Complete Works.*

    The title comes from the Corneille play that Borges discusses in "When Fiction Lives in Fiction" (p. 160).

Prologues
Bret Harte, *The Luck of Roaring Camp and Other Sketches*
Bocetos californianos (Emecé, 1946). First reprinted in *Prólogos,* 1975.

Thomas Carlyle, *On Heroes, Hero-worship and the Heroic in History,* and Ralph Waldo Emerson, *Representative Men*
    De los héroes; Hombres representativos (Jackson, 1949). First reprinted in *Prólogos,* 1975. The translation was by Borges.

Ray Bradbury, *The Martian Chronicles*
    Crónicas marcianas (Minotauro, 1955). First reprinted in *Prólogos,* 1975.

Lectures
The Argentine Writer and Tradition
"El escritor argentino y la tradición." Lecture given at the Colegio Libre de Estudios Superiores, Buenos Aires, 1951. Published in *Cursos y conferencias* nos. 250–252, Jan.–Mar. 1953; reprinted in *Sur* no. 232, Jan.–Feb. 1955; and included in later editions of *Discusión,* from 1957 on.

German Literature in the Age of Bach
"La literatura alemana en la epoca de Bach." No date given for the lecture. Published in *Cursos y conferencias* nos. 250–252, Jan.–Mar. 1953; never reprinted. Not in the *Complete Works.*

    Unlike the previous lecture, which was written, this text is based on a transcript.

VII. Dictations, 1956–1986

The onset of blindness ironically coincided with fame: in 1956 and 1957 alone, Borges became the Director of the National Library and a professor of English and American literature at the University of Buenos Aires; he received his first important prize; and the first of a flood of book-length critical studies on his work appeared. In 1961, he suddenly became internationally famous when a group of European and American publishers awarded the first Formentor Prize jointly to Borges and Samuel Beckett. *Ficciones* was simultaneously published in translation in six countries, which led to countless other translations. Borges, accompanied by his mother, began to travel abroad—for the first time since 1924—to deliver lectures throughout the United States, Latin America, Europe, and Israel, and to receive a cascade of some fifty prizes and honorary doctorates. He became a pop icon: in the 1972 film *Performance*, for example, Mick Jagger reads *Ficciones* in the bathtub, and when he is shot in the head, a photo of Borges flies out.

Blindness also brought a radical change in Borges' work. He could no longer write complex pieces of prose, and he returned, after a twenty-year absence, to poetry, which he could compose in his head. He published a dozen books of poems and prose poems in this period. There were two further books of Bustos Domecq stories written with Bioy Casares, and in 1970, after another twenty-year gap, he returned to his own short stories with *El informe de Brodie* [Brodie's Report, 1970] and *El libro de arena* [The Book of Sand, 1975]. Apart from some important prologues and short notes for newspapers, he wrote no essays as such; he did, however, collaborate with assistants on books about English, American, and medieval Germanic literature; Buddhism; and imaginary creatures. Besides poetry, his major genres in the last thirty years of his life were spoken: the "lecture," a spontaneous monologue on a given subject, and the interview. There are countless magazine articles and dozens of books of "conversations with Borges."

Borges married an old friend in 1967; the marriage lasted three years. With the return of Perón in 1973, Borges resigned his post at the National Library; for much of his last years—the period of the Argentine military dictatorship—he was out of the country. His mother died in 1975 at the age of ninety-nine. Beginning in 1971, Borges was accompanied in his travels and life by María Kodama, whom he married shortly before his death in Geneva in 1986.

Prologues

Ryunosuke Akutagawa, *The Kappa*

Kappa. Los Engranadajes (Mundonuevo, 1959). Never reprinted. Not in the *Complete Works.*

Edward Gibbon, *Pages of History and Autobiography*

Páginas de historia y autobiografía (Universidad de Buenos Aires, 1961). First reprinted in *Prólogos,* 1977.

Catalog of the Exhibition *Books from Spain*

Catálogo de la Exposición de Libros Españoles (Buenos Aires, no publisher, 1962). Never reprinted. Not in the *Complete Works.*

    p. 444: [*Gustavo Adolfo*] *Bécquer:* The leading Spanish Romantic poet (1836–1870).

Walt Whitman, *Leaves of Grass*
Hojas de hierba (Júarez, 1969). First reprinted in *Prólogos*, 1977.
  The translation was by Borges.
  p. 448: Wacho: Whitman's spelling of "gaucho."

Emanuel Swedenborg: *Mystical Works*
There are two versions of this text. One, dated by Borges "April 1972," was first published as the prologue to Sig Synnenstvedt, *Swedenborg: Testigo de lo invisible* (Marymar, 1982). The other—and the basis for the translation here—was the prologue to an undated American edition of the *Mystical Works*, published by the New Jerusalem Church in New York. According to the bibliographer Nicolás Helft, this book was published in 1977, but the prologue had already been "reprinted" in the 1975 *Prólogos*.
    p. 454: Henry More: English theologian (1614–1687) and one of the "Cambridge Platonists" who attempted to evolve a more rational form of Christianity.
    p. 457: "Emanuel Swedenborg": The poem was first published in Borges' book *El
    otro, el mismo* [The Self and the Other] in 1966. A phrase in the original poem, *"el
    cristalino/Edificio de Dios"* [the crystalline/Edifice of God] was changed here to
    "el cristalino/Laberinto de Dios" [the crystalline/Labyrinth of God], perhaps consciously, perhaps unconsciously in Borges' dictation.

Lectures
Borges' lectures from this period were, of course, spoken extemporaneously; there was no written text. The publications in Spanish tend to be exact transcriptions of every word Borges said on the occasion. For the translations here, some false starts and minor repetitions have been silently edited out.

The Concept of an Academy and the Celts
Published under the title "Discurso de don Jorge Luis Borges en su recepción académica" [Lecture by *Don* JLB at his Academic Reception], *Boletín de la Academia Argentina de Letras* XXVII, nos. 105–106 (July–Dec. 1962); but Borges refers to the title as "El concepto de una Academia y los celtas." First reprinted in *Páginas*, 1982, under the title "Recepción académica." Not in the *Complete Works*.

The Enigma of Shakespeare
"El enigma de Shakespeare," *Revista de Estudios de Teatro* no. 8, 1964. Never reprinted in book form. Not in the *Complete Works*.

Blindness
"La ceguera," *La Opinión*, 31 Aug. 1977. Reprinted in *Siete noches*, 1980.
  The lecture was delivered on 3 Aug. 1977 in the Teatro Coliseo in Buenos Aires, and was one of seven given that summer. The other six were on the *Divine Comedy*, nightmares, *The Thousand and One Nights*, Buddhism, poetry, and the Kabbalah.
    p. 475: "Poem of the Gifts": The translation is by Alastair Reid.

Immortality
"La inmortalidad." First published in *Borges, oral* (1979).

One of a series of five lectures given in June 1978 at the University of Belgrano in Buenos Aires. The others were on the detective story (below), Swedenborg, the book, and time.

The Detective Story
"El cuento policial." First published in *Borges, oral* (1979).
See note on "Immortality" above.

Prologues to The Library of Babel
The Library of Babel was a series of short volumes of fantastic tales, each selected and introduced by Borges, and published by Ediciones Siruela in Spain from 1978 to 1986. None of these prologues has been reprinted. They are not in the *Complete Works*.

Spanish titles and year of publication of the prologues included here: Franz Kafka, *The Vulture* (*El buitre*, 1979); Jack London, *The Concentric Deaths* (*Las muertes concéntricas*, 1979); Villiers de l'Isle-Adam, *The Guest at the Last Banquets* (*El convidado de las últimas fiestas*, 1984); P'u Sung-ling, *The Tiger Guest* (*El invitado tigre*, 1985); Charles Howard Hinton, *Scientific Romances* (*Relatos científicos*, 1986).

Prologues to A Personal Library
A Personal Library was Borges' last project, published in 1985 and 1986 by Emecé in Spain and Argentina, and in Italian translation by Franco Mario Ricci. Borges was unable to write the prologues for the last three of the seventy-five volumes. The prologues were collected and reprinted in 1988.

Other books proposed by Borges for the series were: Malcolm Grant, *A New Argument for God and Survival and a Solution to the Problem of Supernatural Events;* Hans Leisegang, *Gnosis;* R. B. Cunninghame Graham, *A Brazilian Mystic;* Novalis, *Fragments;* Kobo Abe, *Woman in the Dunes;* Jack London, *Valley of the Moon;* Aeschylus, *Tragedies;* Francis Bacon and Thomas More, *Utopias;* Miguel Asín Palacios, *Dante and Islam;* Infante Don Juan Manuel, *Count Lucanor;* Cicero, *On Divination* and *On the Nature of the Gods;* Pliny, *Selections;* Vicente Rossi, *Negro Things: The Origins of the Tango;* Hillaire Belloc, *Milton;* Stephen Vincent Bénet, *Tales before Midnight;* Horacio Quiroga, *Selections;* Arnold Silcock, *Introduction to Chinese Art and History;* Hans Jacob von Grimmelshausen, *The Adventures of Simplicissimus;* Martin Buber, *Hassidic Tales;* Dame Bertha Surtees Phillpots, *Edda and Saga; The Tibetan Book of the Dead;* Alfred Kubin, *The Other Side;* Arthur Waley, *Chinese Poetry;* Bertrand Russell, *Why I Am Not a Christian;* Olaf Stapledon, *Starmaker;* Alfonso Alvarez Villasandino, *Selections;* Leo Frobenius, *The Culture of Africa;* G. S. Kirk & J. Raven, *The Pre-Socratic Philosophers; An Anthology of the Spanish Sonnet;* Marguerite Yourcenar, *Stories;* Enrique Banchs, *The Urn;* Sappho, *Poems;* and Manuel Peyrou, *The Sleeping Sword.*

Spanish titles of the prologues included here: Julio Cortázar, *Stories* (*Cuentos*)*;* The Apocryphal Gospels (*Evangelios apócrifos*)*;* H. G. Wells, *The Time Machine; The Invisible Man* (*La máquina del tiempo; El hombre invisible*)*;* Fyodor Dostoevsky, *Demons* (*Los demonios*)*;* Thorstein Veblen, *The Theory of the Leisure Class* (*Teoría de la clase ociosa*)*;* Søren Kierkegaard, *Fear and Trembling* (*Temor y temblor*)*;* Virgil, *The Aeneid* (*La Eneida*)*;* William James, *Varieties of Religious Experience; The Study of Human Nature* (*Las variedades de la experiencia religiosa; Estudio sobre la naturaleza humana*)*.*

p. 518: [*Max*] *Liebermann:* German naturalist and impressionist painter (1847–1935), now largely forgotten, who dominated the German art market from the 1890s until the 1930s, when he was banned by the Nazis.

Acknowledgments

Endless thanks to my co-workers, Esther Allen and Suzanne Jill Levine; thanks to María Kodama and Irma Zangara of the Fundación Borges in Buenos Aires for sending me some obscure texts; thanks to Odile Cisneros for help in tracking down quotes and further texts. During the making of this book, I continually missed the presence of my long-gone friend and ur-Borgesian, Emir Rodríguez Monegal, the man who could have answered all my questions.

—EW

Index